W9-AQK-929

NOTES

ON THE

NEW TESTAMENT

EXPLANATORY AND PRACTICAL

BY

ALBERT BARNES

ENLARGED TYPE EDITION

EDITED BY

ROBERT FREW, D.D.

LUKE AND JOHN

BAKER BOOK HOUSE
GRAND RAPIDS, MICHIGAN

Library of Congress Catalog Card Number: 50-7190

ISBN: 0-8010-0530-2

First Printing, February 1949
Second Printing, February 1950
Third Printing, May 1953
Fourth Printing, October 1954
Fifth Printing, December 1954
Sixth Printing, March 1956
Seventh Printing, November 1956
Eighth Printing, December 1957
Ninth Printing, August 1958
Tenth Printing, August 1960
Eleventh Printing, September 1962
Twelfth Printing, June 1965
Thirteenth Printing, February 1967
Fourteenth Printing, April 1971
Fifteenth Printing, September 1972

PRINTED IN THE UNITED STATES OF AMERICA

PREFACE

TO THE GOSPEL ACCORDING TO LUKE.

LITTLE is *certainly* known concerning the time and place of writing this Gospel, or concerning the author. The first time we have any mention of the author is in his own history, Ac. xvi. 10, 11. He was then the companion of Paul in his travels, and it is evident that he often attended Paul in his journeys, comp. Ac. xvi. 11–17; xxi. 1–6. In each of these places the author of "the Acts" speaks of *his* being in company with Paul. That the same person was the writer of this Gospel is also clear from Ac. i. 1.

From this circumstance the ancients regarded this Gospel as in fact the Gospel which Paul had preached. They affirm that Luke recorded what the apostle preached. Thus Irenæus says, "Luke, the companion of Paul, put down in a book the gospel preached by him." He also says, "Luke was not only a companion, but also a fellow-labourer of the apostles, especially of Paul." Origen, speaking of the Gospels, says, "The third is that according to Luke, the gospel commended by Paul, published for the sake of the Gentile converts." The testimony of the fathers is uniform that it was written by Luke, the companion of Paul, and was therefore regarded by them as really the gospel which Paul preached.

It is not known *where* it was written. Jerome says it was composed in Achaia. There seems to be some probability that it was written to persons that were well acquainted with Jewish manners, as the author does not stop to explain the peculiar customs of the Jews, as some of the other evangelists have done. Respecting the *time* when it was written nothing very definite is known. All that can with certainty be ascertained is that it was written before the death of Paul (A.D. 65), for it was written before the Acts (Ac. i. 1), and that book only brings down the life of Paul to his imprisonment at Rome, and previous to his going into Spain.

It has been made a matter of inquiry whether Luke was a Gentile or a Jew. On this subject there is no positive testimony. Jerome and others of the fathers say that he was a Syrian, and born at Antioch. The most probable opinion seems to be that he was a proselyte to the Jewish religion, though descended from Gentile parents. For this opinion two reasons may be assigned of some weight. 1st. He was intimately acquainted, as appears by the Gospel and the Acts, with the Jewish rites, customs, opinions, and prejudices; and he wrote in their *dialect*, that is, with much of the Hebrew phraseology, in a style similar to the other evangelists, from which it appears that he was accustomed to the Jewish religion, and was, therefore, probably a proselyte. Yet the *preface* to his Gospel, as critics have remarked, is pure classic Greek, unlike the Greek that was used by native Jews; from which it seems not improbable that he was by birth and education a Gentile. 2d. In Acts xxi. 27, it is said that the Asiatic Jews excited the multitude against Paul because he had introduced *Gentiles* into the temple, thus defiling it. In ver. 28 it is said that the Gentile to whom they had reference was *Trophimus*, an Ephesian. Yet *Luke* was also at that time with Paul. If *he* had been regarded as *a Gentile* it is probable that they would have made complaint respecting *him* as well as *Trophimus;* from which it is supposed that he was a Jewish proselyte.

But again, in the Epistle to the Colossians, ch. iv. 9–11, we find Paul saying that Aristarchus, and Marcus, and Barnabas, and Justus saluted them, "who are," he adds, "*of the circumcision*," that is, Jews by birth. In ver. 14 he says that *Luke*, the beloved physician, and Demas also saluted them; from which it is inferred that they were *not of the circumcision*, but were by birth Gentiles.

Most writers suppose that Luke, the writer of this Gospel, was intended in the above place in Colossians. If so, his profession was that of *a physician;* and it has been remarked that his descriptions of diseases are more accurate and circumstantial, and have more of *technical* correctness than those of the other evangelists.

Luke does not profess to have been an eye-witness of what he recorded. See ch. i. 2, 3. It is clear, therefore, that he was not one of the seventy disciples, nor one of the two who went to Emmaus, as has been sometimes supposed. Nor was he an apostle. By the fathers he is uniformly called the *companion* of the apostles, and especially of Paul.

If he was not one of the apostles, and if he was not one of those expressly commissioned by our Lord to whom the promise of the infallible teaching of the Holy Ghost was given, the question arises by what authority his Gospel and the Acts have a place in the sacred canon, or what evidence is there that he was divinely inspired?

In regard to this question the following considerations may give satisfaction: 1st. They were received by all the churches on the same footing as the first three Gospels. There is not a dissenting voice in regard to their authenticity and authority. The value of this argument is this—that if they had been spurious, or without authority, the fathers were the proper persons to know it. 2d. They were published during the lives of the apostles Peter, Paul, and John, and were received *during* their lives as books of sacred authority. If the writings of Luke were not inspired, and had no authority, those apostles could easily have destroyed their credit, and we have reason to think it would have been done. 3d. It is the united testimony of the fathers that this Gospel was submitted to Paul, and received his express approbation. It was regarded as the substance of his preaching, and if it received his approbation it comes to *us* on the authority of his name. Indeed, if this be the case, it rests on the same authority as the epistles of Paul himself. 4th. It bears the same marks of inspiration as the other books. It is simple, pure, yet sublime; there is nothing unworthy of God; and it is elevated far above the writings of any uninspired man. 5th. If he was *not* inspired—if, as we suppose, he was a Gentile by birth—and if, as is most clear, he was not an eye-witness of what he records, it is inconceivable that he did not contradict the other evangelists. That he did not *borrow* from them is clear. Nor is it possible to conceive that he could write a book varying in the order of its *arrangement* so much, and adding so many new facts, and repeating so many recorded also by the others, without *often* having contradicted what was written by them. Let any man compare this Gospel with the spurious gospels of the following centuries, and he will be struck with the force of this remark. 6th. If it be objected that, not being an apostle, he did not come within the *promise* of inspiration (Jn. xiv. 26; xvi. 13, 14) made to the apostles, it may be replied that this was also the case with Paul; yet no small part of the New Testament is composed of his writings. The evidence of the inspiration of the writings of Luke and Paul is to be judged, not only by that *promise*, but by the early reception of the churches; by the testimony of the fathers as to the judgment of *inspired men* when living, and by the internal character of the works. Luke has all these equally with the other evangelists.

THE GOSPEL ACCORDING TO LUKE.

CHAPTER I.

FORASMUCH as many have taken in hand to set forth in order a declaration of those things which are most surely believed among us,

2 Even as they delivered them unto us, which [a]from the beginning were eye-witnesses and [b]ministers of the word;

3 It seemed good to me also, having had perfect understanding

[a] Jn.15.27; He.2.3; 1 Pe.5.1; 2 Pe.1.16; 1 Jn.1.1.
[b] Ro.15.16; Ep.3.7; 4.11,12.

---

1. *Forasmuch as many.* It has been doubted who are referred to here by the word *many.* It seems clear that it could not be the other evangelists, for the gospel by *John* was not yet written, and the word *many* denotes clearly more than *two.* Besides, it is said that they undertook to record what the *eye-witnesses* had delivered to them, so that the writers did not pretend to be eye-witnesses themselves. It is clear, therefore, that other writings are meant than the gospels which we now have, but what they were is a matter of conjecture. What are now known as spurious gospels were written long after Luke wrote his. It is probable that Luke refers to *fragments* of history, or to narratives of *detached* sayings, acts, or parables of our Lord, which had been made and circulated among the disciples and others. His doctrines were original, bold, pure, and authoritative. His miracles had been extraordinary, clear, and awful. His life and death had been peculiar; and it is not improbable—indeed it is highly probable—that such broken accounts and narratives of detached facts would be preserved. That this is what Luke means appears farther from ver. 3, where *he* professes to give a regular, full, and systematic account from the very beginning—"having had perfect understanding of *all things from the very first.*" The records of the others—the "many"—were broken and incomplete. His were to be regular and full. ¶ *Taken in hand.* Undertaken, attempted. ¶ *To set forth in order.* To compose a narrative. It does not refer to the *order* or *arrangement,* but means simply to give a narrative. The word rendered here *in order* is different from that in the third verse, which *has* reference *to order,* or to a full and fair *arrangement* of the principal facts, &c., in the history of our Lord. ¶ *A declaration.* A narrative—an account of. ¶ *Which are most surely believed among us.* Among Christians—among *all* the Christians then living. Here we may remark—1st. That Christians of *that* day had the best of all opportunities for knowing whether those things were true. Many had seen them, and all others had had the account from those who had witnessed them. 2d. That infidels now cannot *possibly* be as good judges in the matter as those who lived at the time, and who were thus competent to determine whether these things were true or false. 3d. That all Christians do *most surely believe* the truth of the gospel. It is their life, their hope, their all. Nor can they doubt that their Saviour lived, bled, died, rose, and still lives; that he was their atoning sacrifice, and that he is God over all, blessed for ever.

2. *As they delivered them.* As they *narrated* them. As they gave an account of them. ¶ *From the beginning.* From the commencement of these things—that is, from the birth of John, or perhaps from the beginning of the ministry of Jesus. ¶ *Eye-witnesses.* Who had seen those things themselves, and who were therefore proper witnesses. ¶ *Ministers of the word.* The term *word* here means the *gospel.* Luke never uses it, as *John* does, to denote the second person of the Trinity. These eye-witnesses and ministers refer, doubtless, to the seventy disciples, to the apostles, and perhaps to other preachers who had gone forth to proclaim the same things.

of all things from the very first, to
write unto thee [c]in order, most excellent [d]Theophilus,
4 That thou mightest [e]know the
certainty of those things wherein
thou hast been instructed.

c Ac.11.4. d Ac.1.1. e Jn.20.31.

5 THERE was, [f]in the days of
Herod the king of Judea,
a certain priest named Zacharias,
of the course of [g]Abia: and his wife
was of the daughters of Aaron, and
her name *was* Elisabeth.

f Mat.2.1. g 1 Ch.24.10; Ne.12.4,17.

---

3. *It seemed good.* I thought it best; or, I have also determined. It seemed *to be called for* that there should be a full, authentic, and accurate account of these matters. ¶ *Having had perfect understanding*, &c. The literal translation of the original here would be, "having exactly traced everything from the first;" or, "having, by diligent and careful investigation, *followed up* everything to the *source*, to obtain an accurate account of the matter." This much better expresses the idea. Luke did not profess to have *seen* these things, and this expression is designed to show how he acquired his information. It was by *tracing up* every account till he became satisfied of its truth. Here observe, 1st. That in religion God does not set aside our natural faculties. He calls us to look at evidence; to examine accounts; to make up our own minds. Nor will any man be convinced of the truth of religion who does *not* make investigation and set himself seriously to the task. 2d. We see the nature of Luke's inspiration. It was consistent with his using his natural faculties or his own powers of mind in investigating the truth. God, by his Holy Spirit, presided *over* his faculties, directed them, and kept him from error. ¶ *In order.* This word does not indicate that the exact order of *time* would be observed, for that is *not* the way in which he writes; but it means *distinctly*, *particularly*, in opposition to the confused and broken accounts to which he had referred before. ¶ *Most excellent Theophilus.* The word Theophilus means *a friend of God*, or a pious man; and it has been supposed by some that Luke did not refer to any particular *individual*, but to any man that loved God; but there is no reason for this opinion. Significant names were very common, and there is no good reason to doubt that this was some individual known to Luke. The application of the title "*most excellent*" farther proves it. It would not be given to an unknown man. The title *most excellent* has by some been supposed to be given to express his *character*, but it is rather to be considered as denoting *rank* or *office*. It occurs only in three other places in the New Testament, and is there given to men *in office*—to Felix and Festus, Ac. xxiii. 26; xxiv. 3; xxvi. 25. These titles express no quality of the *men*, but belong to the *office;* and we may hence learn that it is not improper for Christians, in giving honour to whom honour is due, to address men in office by their customary titles, even if their moral character be altogether unworthy of it. Who *Theophilus* was is unknown. It is probable that he was some distinguished Roman or Greek who had been converted, who was a friend of Luke, and who had requested an account of these things. It is possible that this *preface* might have been sent to him as a *private* letter *with* the gospel, and Theophilus chose to have them published together.

4. *The certainty.* Have full evidence or proof of. ¶ *Been instructed.* By the preachers of the gospel. The original word is the one from which is derived our word *catechism—been catechised;* but it does not here denote the *manner* in which the instruction was imparted, as it does with us, but simply the *fact* that he had been *taught* those things.

5. *In the days of Herod.* See Notes on Mat. ii. 1. ¶ *Of the course of Abia.* When the priests became so numerous that they could not at once minister at the altar, David divided them into twenty-four classes or *courses*, each one of which officiated for a week, 1 Ch. xxiv. The class or course of Abia was the *eighth* in order, 1 Ch. xxiv. 10. Comp. 2 Ch. viii. 14. The word *course* means the same as *class*, or order. The *Greek* word *Abia* is the same as the *Hebrew* word *Abijah.* ¶ *His wife* was *of the daughters of Aaron.* A descendant of Aaron, the first high-priest of the Jews; so that *John the Baptist* was descended, on the father's and the mother's side, from priests. Our Saviour was not on either side. John would have been *legally* entitled to a place among the

6 And they were both [h]righteous before God, walking in all the commandments and [i]ordinances of the Lord blameless.

7 And they had no child, because that Elisabeth was barren, and they both were *now* well stricken in years.

8 And it came to pass, that while he executed the priest's office before God in the order of his course,

9 According to the custom of the priest's office, his lot was to [k]burn incense when he went into the temple of the Lord.

10 And the whole multitude of the people were praying [l]without, at the time of incense.

11 And there appeared unto him an angel of the Lord standing on the right side of the [m]altar of incense.

h Ge.7.1; 1 Ki.9.4; 2 Ki.20.3. *i* 1 Co.11.2; Phi.3.6. *k* Ex.30.7,8. *l* Le.16.17. *m* Ex.30.1; Re.8.3,4.

priests; our Saviour, being of the tribe of *Judah*, would not.

6. *Both righteous.* Both *just* or holy. This means here more than external conformity to the law. It is an honourable testimonial of their *piety* toward God. ¶ *Walking in*, &c. *Keeping* the commandments. To *walk* in the way that God commands is *to obey.* ¶ *Ordinances.* Rites and customs which God had *ordained* or appointed. These words refer to all the duties of religion which were made known to them. ¶ *Blameless.* That is, no fault or deficiency could be found in them. They were strict, exact, punctual. Yet this, if it had been mere *external* observance, might have been no proof of piety. Paul, before his conversion, also kept the law *externally* blameless, Phi. iii. 6. But in the case of Zachariah and Elisabeth it was real love to God and sincere regard for his law.

7. *Well stricken in years.* Old or advanced in life, so as to render the prospect of having children hopeless.

8. *Before God.* In the temple, where God dwelt by the symbols of his presence. The temple was regarded by the Jews as the *house* or dwelling of God; and in the *first* temple there was, in the most holy place, a *cloud* called the Shechinah, or a visible sign of the presence of God. It was thus *before God* that Zachariah offered incense.

9. *According to the custom of the priest's office, his lot was.* The Jewish writers inform us that it was customary for the priests to divide their daily task by *lot.* ¶ *To burn incense.* Incense is an aromatic or white rosin procured from trees, chiefly in Arabia. It is obtained by making incisions in the tree, and the gum flows out. It is distinguished for a peculiarly pleasant *smell* when burned, and was therefore used in ancient worship. It was burned by the priest twice a day (Ex. xxx. 7), and it seems to have been emblematic of prayer and praise, or of the grateful offerings of the heart wafted toward heaven. The incense used in the temple was made of stacte, onycha, and galbanum (Ex. xxx. 34), with pure frankincense, and it was not lawful for this compound to be used elsewhere than in the house of God. ¶ *Into the temple.* See Notes on Mat. xxi. 12. The *part* of the temple where incense was burned was the *holy place.*

10. *The whole multitude.* This was the regular time of evening prayer, and multitudes came up to the temple to worship. ¶ *Praying without.* That is, in the *courts* around the temple, particularly in the court of the women.

11. *An angel.* An *angel* is a messenger sent from God. See Notes on Mat. i. 20. It had now been about four hundred years since the time of *Malachi*, and since there had been any divine revelation. During that time the nation was looking for the Messiah, but still with nothing more than the ancient prophecies to direct them. Now that he was about to appear, God sent his messenger to announce his coming, to encourage the hearts of his people, and to prepare them to receive him. ¶ *On the right side*, &c. The altar of incense stood close by the veil which divided the holy place from the most holy. On the north stood the table of shew-bread; on the south the golden candlestick. As Zacharias entered, therefore, with his face to the west, the angel would stand on the north, or near the table of shew-bread. That table was 18 inches square and 3 feet high. The top, as well as the sides and horns, was overlaid with pure gold, and it was finished around the upper surface with a crown

12 And when Zacharias saw *him*,
he was [n]troubled, and fear fell
upon him.
13 But the angel said unto him,
Fear not, Zacharias; for thy prayer
is heard; and thy wife Elisabeth
shall bear thee a son, and thou
shalt call his name [o]John.
14 And thou shalt have joy and
gladness; and many shall [p]rejoice
at his birth.
15 For he shall be [q]great in the
sight of the Lord, and shall [r]drink
neither wine nor strong drink; and
he shall be filled with the Holy
Ghost, even [s]from his mother's
womb.

n Ju.13.22; ver.29. o ver.60,63.

p ver.58. q ch.7.28. r Nu.6.3. s Je.1.5.

or border of gold. Just below this border, four golden rings were attached to each side of the altar, one near each corner. The staves or rods for bearing the altar passed through these rings, and were made of the same wood with the altar itself, and richly overlaid with the same precious metal. Upon this altar incense was burned every morning and every evening, so that it was literally perpetual, Ex. xxx. 8. Neither burnt-sacrifice, nor meat-offering, nor drink-offering was permitted upon this altar; nor was it ever stained with blood except once annually, when the priest made atonement, Le. xvi. 18, 19.

12. *He was troubled.* He was alone, in the presence of God. The appearance of the angel was sudden, unexpected, and therefore fearful.

13. *Thy prayer is heard.* That is, thy prayer for offspring. This, among the Jews, was an object of intense desire. No prospect was more gloomy to them than that of dying childless, so that their *name should perish.* Special pains, therefore, had been taken in the law to keep up the names of families by requiring a man to marry his brother's wife, De. xxv. 5.

14. *Many shall rejoice at his birth.* This does not refer so much to the *time* of his birth as to the subsequent rejoicing. Such will be his *character*, that he will be an honour to the family, and many will rejoice that he lived; or, in other words, he will be a blessing to mankind.

15. *Shall be great.* Shall be eminent, or distinguished as a preacher. ¶ *In the sight of the Lord.* Greek, *before the Lord.* That is, shall be *really* or *truly* great. God shall regard him as such. ¶ *Shall drink neither wine.* The kind of wine commonly used in Judea was a light wine, often not stronger than cider in this country. It was the common drink of all classes of the people. See Notes on Jn. ii. 11. The use of wine was forbidden only to the Nazarite, Nu. vi. 3. It was because John sustained this character that he abstained from the use of wine. ¶ *Strong drink.* It is not easy to ascertain precisely what is meant by this word, but we are certain that it does not mean strong drink in *our* sense of the term. Distilled spirits were not then known. The art of distilling was discovered by an Arabian chemist in the ninth or tenth century; but distilled liquors are not used by Arabians. They banished them at once, as if sensible of their pernicious influence; nor are they used in Eastern nations at all. Europe and America have been the places where this poison has been most extensively used, and there it has beggared and ruined millions, and is yearly sweeping thousands unprepared into a wretched eternity. The *strong drink* among the Jews was probably nothing more than fermented liquors, or a drink obtained from fermented dates, figs, and the juice of the palm, or the lees of wine, mingled with sugar, and having the property of producing intoxication. Many of the Jewish writers say that by the word here translated *strong drink* was meant nothing more than *old wine*, which probably had the power of producing intoxication. See Notes on Is. v. 11. ¶ *Shall be filled with the Holy Ghost*, &c. Shall be divinely designated or appointed to this office, and qualified for it by all needful communications of the Holy Spirit. To be *filled* with the Holy Spirit is to be illuminated, sanctified, and guided by his influence. In this place it refers—1st. To the divine *intention* that he should be set apart to this work, as God designed that Paul should be an apostle from his mother's womb, Ga. i. 15. 2d. It refers to an actual fitting for the work from the birth by the influence of the Holy Spirit, as was the case with Jeremiah (Je. i. 5), and with the Messiah himself, Ps. xxii. 9, 10.

16 And many of the children of
Israel shall he turn to the Lord
their God.
17 And[t] he shall go before him
in the spirit and power of Elias, to
turn the hearts of the fathers to the
children, and the disobedient [1]to
the [u]wisdom of the just; to make
ready a [v]people prepared for the
Lord.
18 And Zacharias said unto the
angel, Whereby shall I know this?
for [w]I am an old man, and my wife
well stricken in years.
19 And the angel answering, said
unto him, I am [x]Gabriel, that stand

t Mal.4.5,6; Mat.11.14; Mar.9.12,13. 1 or, *by*. u Ps.111.10. v 1 Pe.2.9. w Ge.17.17. x Da.8.16; ver.26.

16. *Children of Israel.* Jews. Descendants of Israel or Jacob. ¶ *Shall he turn.* By repentance. He shall call them from their sins, and persuade them to forsake them, and to seek the Lord their God.

17. *Shall go before him.* Before the Messiah. The connection here leads us to suppose that the word *him* refers to the "Lord their God" in the previous verse. If so, then it will follow that the Messiah was the Lord God of Israel—a character abundantly given him in other parts of the New Testament. ¶ *In the spirit and power of Elias.* See Notes on Mat. xi. 14. ¶ *To turn the hearts of the fathers to the children.* In the time of John the Jews were divided into a number of different sects. See Notes on Mat. iii. 7. They were opposed violently to each other, and pursued their opposition with great animosity. It was impossible but that this opposition should find its way into *families*, and divide parents and children from each other. John came that he might allay these animosities and produce better feeling. By directing them *all* to *one Master*, the Messiah, he would divert their attention from the causes of their difference and bring them to union. He would restore peace to their families, and reconcile those parents and children who had chosen different sects, and who had suffered their attachment *to sect* to interrupt the harmony of their households. The effect of true religion on a family will always be to produce harmony. It attaches all the family to *one* great Master, and by attachment to *him* all minor causes of difference are forgotten. ¶ *And the disobedient to the wisdom of the just.* The *disobedient* here are the unbelieving, and hence the impious, the wicked. These he would turn to the wisdom of the just, or to such wisdom as the *just* or pious manifest—that is, to true wisdom. ¶ *To make ready a people,* &c. To prepare them for his coming by announcing that the Messiah was about to appear, and by calling them to repentance. God has always required men to be pure in a special manner when he was about to appear among them. Thus the Israelites were required to purify themselves for three days when he was about to come down on Mount Sinai, Ex. xix. 14, 15. And so, when God the Son was about to appear as the Redeemer, he required that men should *prepare* themselves for his coming. So in view of the future judgment—the second coming of the Son of man—he requires that men should repent, believe, and be pure, 1 Pe. iv. 7; 2 Pe. iii. 11, 12.

18. *Whereby shall I know this?* The thing was improbable, and he desired *evidence* that it would take place. The testimony of an *angel*, and in such *a place*, should have been proof enough; but men are slow to believe the testimony of heavenly messengers. As a consequence of not believing, he was struck dumb.

19. *I am Gabriel.* The word *Gabriel* is made up of two Hebrew words, and signifies *man of God.* This angel is mentioned as having been deputed to inform *Daniel* that his prayers were heard. See Notes on Da. viii. 16; ix. 21. ¶ *That stand in the presence of God.* To stand in the presence of one is a phrase denoting *honour* or *favour.* To be admitted to the presence of a king, or to be with him, was a token of favour. So to stand before God signifies merely that he was honoured or favoured by God. He was permitted to come near him, and to see much of his glory. Comp. 1 Ki. x. 8; xii. 6; xvii. 1; Pr. xxii. 29. ¶ *And am sent,* &c. The angels are "*ministering spirits* sent forth to minister for them who shall be heirs of salvation," He. i. 7, 14. They delight to do the will of God, and one way of doing that will is by aiding his children here, by succouring the afflicted, and by defending those who are in danger.

in the presence of God; and am
[y]sent to speak unto thee, and to
show thee these glad tidings.
20 And, behold, thou [z]shalt be
dumb, and not able to speak, until
the day that these things shall be
performed, because thou believest
not my words, which shall be fulfilled in their season.
21 And the people waited for
Zacharias, and marvelled that he
tarried so long in the temple.
22 And when he came out he
could not speak unto them; and
they perceived that he had seen a
vision in the temple; for he beckoned unto them, and remained
speechless.
23 And it came to pass that, as
soon as the days of his ministration were accomplished, he departed to his own house.
24 And after those days his wife
Elisabeth conceived, and hid herself five months, saying,
25 Thus hath the Lord dealt

y He.1.14. *z* Eze.3.26.

There is no more absurdity or impropriety in supposing that *angels* may render such aid, than there is in supposing that good men may assist one another; and there can be no doubt that it affords high pleasure to the angels of God to be *permitted* to aid those who are treading the dangerous and trying path which leads to eternity. Holiness is the same as benevolence, and holy beings seek and love opportunities to do good to their fellow-creatures. In the eye of holy beings all God's creatures are parts of one great family, and whenever they can do them good they rejoice in the opportunity, at any sacrifice. ¶ *These glad tidings.* This good news respecting the birth of a son.

20. *Because thou believest not,* &c. This was both a sign and a judgment—a sign that he had come from God, and that the thing would be fulfilled; and a judgment for not giving credit to what he had said. There is no sin in the sight of God more aggravated than unbelief. When GOD speaks, man should believe; nor can he that *will not* believe escape punishment. God speaks only truth, and we should believe him. God speaks only what is for our good, and it is right that we should suffer if we do not credit what he says.

21. *The people waited.* That is, beyond the usual time. ¶ *Marvelled.* Wondered. The priest, it is said, was not accustomed to remain in the temple more than half an hour commonly. Having remained on this occasion a longer time, the people became apprehensive of his safety, and wondered what had happened to him.

22. *Had seen a vision.* The word *vision* means *sight, appearance,* or *spectre,* and is commonly applied to spirits, or to beings from another world. When he came out of the temple, it is probable that they *suspected* that something of this nature had detained him there, and that, on inquiry of him, he signified by a nod that this was the case. He was unable to speak, and they had no way of "*perceiving*" it but by such a sign. On the word *vision,* see Notes on Is. i. 1. ¶ *For he beckoned unto them.* That is, by beckoning unto them, or by a sign, he informed them of what he had seen.

23. *As soon as the days of his ministration,* &c. As soon as he had fulfilled the duties of the week. It might have been supposed that the extraordinary occurrence in the temple, together with his own calamity, would have induced him at once to leave this place and return home; but his duty was in the temple. His piety prompted him to remain there in the service of God. He was not unfitted for burning incense by his dumbness, and it was not proper for him to leave his post. It is the duty of ministers of religion to remain at their work until they are unfitted for it, and unable to serve God in their profession. Then they *must* retire. But until that time, he that for trifling causes forsakes his post is guilty of unfaithfulness to his Master.

24. *Hid herself.* Did not go forth into public, and concealed her condition. This might have been done that she might spend her time more entirely in giving praise to God for his mercies, and that she might have the fullest proof of the accomplishment of the promise before she appeared in public or spoke of the mercies of God.

25. *Thus.* In this merciful manner. ¶ *To take away my reproach.* Among

with me in the days wherein he looked on *me*, to [a]take away my reproach among men.

26 And in the sixth month the angel Gabriel was sent from God unto a city of Galilee named Nazareth,

27 To a [b]virgin espoused to a man whose name was Joseph, of the house of David; and the virgin's name *was* Mary.

28 And the angel came in unto her, and said, Hail, [c]*thou that art* highly[2] favoured, [d]the Lord *is* with thee: blessed *art* thou among women.

a Ge.30.23; 1 Sa.1.6; Is.54.1,4.
b Mat.1.18. *c* Da.9.23.
2 or, *graciously accepted;* or, *much graced.*
d Ju.6.12.

29 And when she saw *him*, she was troubled at his saying, and cast in her mind what manner of salutation this should be.

30 And the angel said unto her, Fear not, Mary; for thou hast found favour with God.

31 And, behold, [e]thou shalt conceive in thy womb, and bring forth a son, and shalt call his name JESUS.

32 He shall be [f]great, and shall be called the [g]Son of the Highest: and the Lord God shall give unto him the [h]throne of his father David:

e Is.7.14; Mat.1.21. *f* Mat.12.42. *g* He.1.2-8.
h 2 Sa.7.11,12; Is.9.6,7.

---

the Jews, a family of children was counted a signal blessing, an evidence of the favour of God, Ps. cxiii. 9; cxxviii. 3; Is. iv. 1; xliv. 3, 4; Le. xxvi. 9. To be *barren*, therefore, or to be destitute of children, was considered a *reproach* or a *disgrace*, 1 Sa. i. 6.

26. *In the sixth month.* The sixth month after Elisabeth's conception. ¶ *A city of Galilee, named Nazareth.* See Notes on Mat. ii. 22, 23.

27. *To a virgin espoused,* &c. See Notes on Mat. i. 18, 19. Comp. Notes on Is. vii. 14. ¶ *House of David.* Family of David, or descendants of David.

28. *Hail.* This word of salutation is equivalent to *Peace be with thee*, or *Joy be with thee;* a form of speech implying that she was signally favoured, and expressing joy at meeting her. ¶ *Highly favoured.* By being the mother of the long-expected Messiah—the mother of the Redeemer of mankind. Long had he been predicted; long had the eyes of the nation been turned to him, and long had his coming been an object of intense desire. To be reckoned among his *ancestors* was accounted sufficient honour for even Abraham and David. But now the happy *individual* was designated who was to be his mother; and on Mary, a poor virgin of Nazareth, was to come this honour, which would have rendered infinitely illustrious any of the daughters of Adam—the honour of giving birth to the world's Redeemer and the Son of God. ¶ *The Lord is with thee.* The word *is* is not in the original, and the passage may be rendered either "the Lord *is* with thee," or "the Lord *be* with thee," implying the prayer of the angel that all blessings from God might descend and rest upon her. ¶ *Blessed art thou among women.* This passage is equivalent to saying "thou art the most happy of women."

29. *Troubled at his saying.* Disturbed or perplexed at what he said. It was so unexpected, so sudden, so extraordinary, and was so high an honour, that she was filled with anxious thoughts, and did not know what to make of it. ¶ *Cast in her mind.* Thought, or revolved in her mind. ¶ *What manner of salutation.* What this salutation could mean.

30. *Fear not, Mary.* Do not be alarmed at this appearance of an angel. He only comes to announce to you good tidings. Similar language was addressed by an angel to Joseph. See Notes on Mat. i. 20. ¶ *Thou hast found favour with God.* Eminent favour or mercy in being selected to be the mother of the Messiah.

31. *And, behold, thou shalt conceive in thy womb.* See Notes on Is. vii. 14. ¶ *And shalt call his name Jesus.* A Saviour. See Notes on Mat. i. 21. All this was announced, also, by an angel to Joseph, *after* this visitation to Mary. See Notes on Mat. i. 20, 21.

32. *He shall be great.* There is undoubted reference in this passage to Is. ix. 6, 7. By his being *great* is meant he shall be distinguished or illustrious; great in power, in wisdom, in dominion, on earth and in heaven. ¶ *Shall be*

33 And he shall reign over the
house of Jacob for ever; and [i]of
his kingdom there shall be no end.
34 Then said Mary unto the
angel, How shall this be, seeing I
know not a man?
35 And the angel answered and
said unto her, The Holy Ghost
shall come upon thee, and the
power of the Highest shall over-
shadow thee; therefore also that
holy thing which shall be born of
thee shall be called [k]the Son of
God.

i Da.7.14,27; Mi.4.7. *k* Mar.1.1; Jn.1.34.

36 And, behold, thy cousin Elisabeth, she hath also conceived a
son in her old age: and this is the
sixth month with her who was
called barren.
37 For[l] with God nothing shall
be impossible.
38 And Mary said, Behold the
[m]handmaid of the Lord; be it unto
me [n]according to thy word. And
the angel departed from her.
39 And Mary arose in those days,
and went into the hill country with
haste, into a [o]city of Juda;

l Mat.19.26; Ro.4.21. *m* Ps.116.16. *n* Ps.119.38. *o* Jos.21.9-11.

called. This is the same as to say he *shall be* the Son, &c. The Hebrews often used this form of speech. See Mat. xxi. 13. ¶ *The Highest.* God, who is infinitely exalted; called *the* Highest, because he is exalted over all his creatures on earth and in heaven. See Mar. v. 7. ¶ *The throne.* The kingdom; or shall appoint him as the lineal successor of David in the kingdom. ¶ *His father David.* David is called his *father* because Jesus was lineally descended from him. See Mat. i. 1. The promise to David was, that there should *not fail a man to sit on his throne*, or that his throne should be perpetual (1 Ki. ii. 4; viii. 25; ix. 5; 2 Ch. vi. 16), and the promise was fulfilled by exalting Jesus to be a Prince and a Saviour, and the perpetual King of his people.

33. *Over the house of Jacob.* The *house* of Jacob means the same thing as the *family* of Jacob, or the descendants of Jacob—that is, the children of Israel. This was the name by which the ancient people of God were known, and it is the same as saying that he would reign over his own church and people for ever. This he does by giving them laws, by defending them, and by guiding them; and this he will do for ever in the kingdom of his glory. ¶ *Of his kingdom there shall be no end.* He shall reign among his people on earth until the end of time, and be their king for ever in heaven. *His* is the only kingdom that shall never have an end; *He* the only King that shall never lay aside his diadem and robes, and that shall never die. *He* the only King that can defend us from all our enemies, sustain us in death, and reward us in eternity. O how important, then, to have an interest in his kingdom! and how unimportant, compared with *his* favour, is the favour of all earthly monarchs!

35. *The Holy Ghost shall come upon thee.* See Mat. i. 20. ¶ *The power of the Highest*, &c. This evidently means that the body of Jesus would be created by the direct power of God. It was not by ordinary generation; but, as the Messiah came to redeem sinners—to make atonement for *others*, and not for himself—it was necessary that his human nature should be pure, and free from the corruption of the fall. God therefore prepared him a body by direct creation that should be pure and holy. See He. x. 5. ¶ *That holy thing*, &c. That holy progeny or child. ¶ *Shall be called the Son of God.* This is spoken in reference to the human nature of Christ, and this passage proves, beyond controversy, that *one* reason why Jesus was called the Son of God was because he was begotten in a supernatural manner. He is also called the *Son of God* on account of his resurrection, Ro. i. 4; Ac. xiii. 33, compared with Ps. ii. 7.

36, 37. *Thy cousin Elisabeth*, &c. The case of Elisabeth is mentioned to inspire Mary with confidence, and to assure her that what was now promised would be fulfilled. It was almost as improbable that Elisabeth should have a child at her time of life, as it was that Mary should under the circumstances promised.

38. *And Mary said, Behold the handmaid*, &c. This was an expression of resignation to the will of God, and of faith in the promise. To be the *handmaid of the Lord* is to be submissive and obedient, and is the same as saying, "I fully credit all that is said, and am per-

40 And entered into the house of
Zacharias, and saluted Elisabeth.
41 And it came to pass, that,
when Elisabeth heard the salutation of Mary, the babe leaped in
her womb; and Elisabeth was
filled with the Holy Ghost:
42 And she spake out with a
loud voice; and said, [p]Blessed *art*
thou among women; and blessed
is the fruit of thy womb.
43 And whence *is* this to me,
that the mother of my [q]Lord
should come to me?
44 For lo, as soon as the voice
of thy salutation sounded in mine
ears, the babe leaped in my womb
for joy.
45 And blessed *is* she [3]that
believed: for there shall be a per-
formance of those things which
were told her from the Lord.
46 And Mary said, [r]My soul
doth magnify the Lord,

p Ju.5.24; ver.28.

q Jn.13.13.
3 or, *which believed that there shall be.*
r 1 Sa.2.1; Ps.34.2,3.

---

fectly ready to obey all the commands of the Lord."

39. *And Mary arose.* The word *arose* here is equivalent to *setting out*, or starting on a journey. ¶ *The hill country.* The region in the vicinity of Jerusalem, commonly called the hill country of Judea. ¶ *City of Juda.* What city is meant is not known. Some have supposed it to be Jerusalem, others Hebron; but all is conjecture. It was probably a Levitical city, and the residence of Zacharias when he was not employed in the temple.

40. *Saluted Elisabeth.* Expressed great joy and gratification at seeing her, and used the customary tokens of affectionate salutation.

41. *Elisabeth was filled with the Holy Ghost.* The meaning of this seems to be that she was filled with joy; with a disposition to praise God; with a prophetic spirit, or a knowledge of the character of the child that should be born of her. All these were produced by the Holy Ghost.

42. *Blessed* art *thou among women.* She here repeated nearly the words of the angel to Mary, esteeming it to be the highest honour among mothers to be the mother of the Messiah. See Notes on ver. 28.

43. *And whence is this to me?* An expression of humility. Why is it that the mother of my Lord should come to *me*, as if to honour me? ¶ *Mother of my Lord.* The word *Lord* sometimes denotes *divinity*, and sometimes superior, master, teacher, or governor. It was given by the Jews to their expected Messiah; but whether they understood it as denoting divinity cannot now be ascertained. It is clear only that Elisabeth used it as denoting great dignity and honour.

45. *Blessed* is *she that believed.* That is, *Mary*, who believed what the angel spoke to her. She was blessed not only in the *act* of believing, but because the thing promised would certainly be fulfilled.

From these expressions of Elisabeth we may learn—1st. That the spirit of prophecy had not entirely ceased among the Jews. 2d. That the Holy Ghost is the source of light, comfort, and joy. 3d. That everything about the birth of Jesus was remarkable, and that he must have been more than a mere man. 4th. That the prospect of the coming of the Messiah was one of great joy and rejoicing to ancient saints; and, 5th. That it was a high honour to be *the mother* of him that should redeem mankind. It is from *that honour* that the Roman Catholics have determined that it is right to worship the Virgin Mary and to offer prayers to her—an act of worship as idolatrous as any that could be offered to a creature. For—1st. It is not anywhere commanded in the Bible. 2d. It is expressly forbidden to worship any being but God, Ex. xxxiv. 14; xx. 4, 5; De. vi. 13, 14; Is. xlv. 20. 3d. It is idolatry to worship or pray to a creature. 4th. It is absurd to suppose that the Virgin Mary can be in all places at the same time to hear the prayers of thousands at once, or to aid them. There is no idolatry more gross, and of course more wicked, than to worship *the creature* more than *the Creator*, Ro. i. 25.

46. *My soul doth magnify the Lord.* To *magnify* means to *make great*, and then to *extol*, to *praise*, to *celebrate.* It does not mean here strictly to *make great*, but to increase *in our estimation*

47 And my spirit hath [s]rejoiced
in God my Saviour.
48 For he hath regarded the
low[t] estate of his handmaiden;
for, behold, from henceforth all
generations shall [u]call me blessed.
49 For he that is [v]mighty hath
done to me [w]great things; and
[x]holy is his name.
50 And[y] his mercy *is* on them
that fear him, from generation to
generation.
51 He[z] hath showed strength
with his arm; he hath [a]scattered

s Ps.35.9; Hab.3.18. t Ps.136.23. u Mal.3.12; ch.11.27. v Ge.17.1.
w Ps.71.21; 126.2,3; Ep.3.20. x Ps.111.9. y Ge.17.17; Ex.20.6; Ps.103.17. z Ps.98.1; Is.51.9; 52.10; 63.5. a 1 Sa.2.9; Da.4.37.

—that is, to praise or extol. See Ps. xxxiv. 3; 2 Sa. vii. 26.

47. *In God my Saviour.* God is called *Saviour*, as he saves people from sin and death. He was *Mary's* Saviour, as he had redeemed her soul and given her a title to eternal life; and she rejoiced for that, and especially for his mercy in honouring her by her being made the mother of the Messiah.

48. *He hath regarded the low estate of his handmaid.* Literally, he has looked upon the low or humble condition of his handmaid. That is, notwithstanding her humble rank and poverty, he has shown her favour. And this example abundantly teaches what is elsewhere fully taught in the Bible, that God is not a respecter of persons; that he is not influenced, in conferring favours, by wealth, honour, or office, Ro. ii. 11; x. 11, 12. He seeks the humble and the contrite; he imparts his rich blessings to those who feel that they need them, and who will bless him for them, Ps. cxxxviii. 6; Is. lvii. 15. ¶ *From henceforth.* Hereafter, or in consequence of this. ¶ *All generations.* All men. All posterity. ¶ *Call me blessed.* Pronounce me highly favoured or happy in being the mother of the Messiah. It is therefore right to consider her as highly favoured or happy; but this certainly does not warrant us to worship her or to pray to her. Abraham was blessed in being the father of the faithful; Paul in being the apostle to the Gentiles; Peter in first preaching the gospel to them; but who would think of worshipping or praying to Abraham, Paul, or Peter?

49. *He that is mighty.* God. ¶ *Hath done to me great things.* Hath conferred on me great favours and distinguished mercies. ¶ *And holy is his name.* This is an expression of Mary's feelings, desiring to bestow on God all honour and praise. As the highest honour, she declared that his *name* was *holy*—that is, that God was free from sin, injustice, and impurity. The "*name*" of God is often put for God himself. The proper name of God is *Jehovah*, a word expressive of his *essential being*, derived from the word *to be*, Ex. iii. 14; vi. 3; Ps. lxxxiii. 18. That name is holy; is to be regarded as holy; and to make a common or profane use of it is solemnly forbidden, Ex. xx. 7.

50. *His mercy.* Favour shown to the miserable and the guilty. ¶ Is *on them.* Is *shown* or manifested to them. ¶ *That fear him.* That *reverence* or honour him. One kind of fear is that which a servant has of a cruel master, or which a man has of a precipice, the plague, or death. This is not the *fear* which we ought to have toward God. It is the fear which a dutiful child has of a kind and virtuous father—a fear of injuring his feelings; of dishonouring him by our life; of doing anything which he would disapprove. It is on those who have *such* fear of God that his mercy descends. This is the fear of the Lord which is the beginning of wisdom, Ps. cxi. 10; Job xxviii. 28. ¶ *From generation to generation.* From one age to another —that is, it is unceasing; it continues and abounds. But it means also more than this. It means that God's mercy will descend on the children and children's children of those that fear him and keep his commandments, Ex. xx. 6. In this respect it is an unspeakable privilege to be descended from pious parents; to have been the subject of their prayers, and to have received their blessing. It is also a matter of vast guilt *not* to copy their example and to walk in their steps. If God is *disposed* to show mercy to thousands of generations, how heavy will be the condemnation if the children of pious parents do not avail themselves of it and early seek his favour!

51. *Hath showed strength with his arm.* The *arm* is the symbol of strength. The expression in this and the subsequent verses has no particular reference to his

the proud in the imagination of
their hearts.
52 He[b] hath put down the
mighty from *their* seats, and exalted them of low degree.
53 He[c] hath filled the hungry

b Job 5.11; ch.18.14. c 1 Sa.2.5.

with good things, and the rich he
hath sent empty away.
54 He hath holpen his servant
Israel, [d]in remembrance of *his*
mercy;
55 As he [e]spake to our fathers,

d Ps.98.3. e Ge.17.19; Ps.132.11.

---

mercy to *Mary*. From a contemplation of his goodness to *her*, she enlarges her views to a contemplation of his goodness and power *in general*, and to a celebration of the praises of God for *all* that he has done to all men. This is the nature of true piety. It does not terminate in thinking of God's mercy toward *ourselves*. It thinks of *others*, and praises God that *others* also are made partakers of his mercy, and that his goodness is manifested to all his works. ¶ *He scattereth the proud.* He hath often done it in time of battle and war. When the proud Assyrian, Egyptian, or Babylonian had come against the people of God, he had often scattered them and driven away their armies. ¶ *In the imagination of their hearts.* Those who were lifted up or exalted in their own view. Those who *thought themselves* to be superior to other men.

52. *Hath put down the mighty.* The *mighty* here denotes princes, kings, or conquerors. See Is. xiv. 12–14. ¶ Their *seats.* Their *thrones*, or the places where they sat in pomp and power. ¶ *Exalted them.* Raised them up, or placed them in the seats of those who had been removed. ¶ *Low degree.* Low or humble birth and condition in life. This probably has reference to the case of her ancestor David. Mary was celebrating the mercies of God to *herself*, to her *family*, and of course to her ancestors. It was natural to allude to that great event in their history when Saul was overcome in battle, and when *David* was taken from the sheepfold and placed on the throne. The origin of illustrious families is often obscure. Men are often raised by industry, talent, and the favour of God, from very humble stations —from the farm or mechanic's shop—to places of great trust in the church and state. They who are thus elevated, if imbued with right feelings, will not despise their former employments nor their former companions, nor will they esteem their parents or friends the less *because* they still remain in the same rank in life. No conduct is more odious and unchristian than to be ashamed of our birth or the humble circumstances of our friends.

53. *He hath filled the hungry with good things.* This is a celebration of the general mercy of God. He hath daily fed the poor, the needy, and those who came to him with humble hearts. ¶ *The rich he hath sent*, &c. While the poor come to him for a supply of their daily wants, the rich come not that their necessities should be supplied, but come with lofty hearts, and insatiable desires that their riches may be increased. When this is the case, God not unfrequently not only *withholds* what they ask, but he takes their riches away by fire, or flood, or disappointments, and sends them away empty, Pr. xxiii. 5. It is better to be poor and go to God for our daily bread, than to be rich and forget our dependence on him, and to seek only a great increase of our property.

54. *Hath holpen.* Hath *helped* or assisted. The word rendered "holpen" denotes properly, *to take hold of one, to help him up when he is in danger of falling*, and here means that God had succoured his people when they were feeble, and were in danger of falling or being overthrown. ¶ *His servant Israel.* His people the Israelites, or those who truly feared him and kept his commandments. See Is. xli. 8, 9; Ho. xi. 1. ¶ *In remembrance of* his *mercy.* Or that his mercy *may* be remembered.

55. *As he spake to our fathers*, &c. That is, he has dealt mercifully with the children of Israel, according as he promised Abraham, Isaac, and Jacob. The promise *particularly* here referred to is that respecting the *Messiah* which was now about to be fulfilled; but there is no doubt that there was also included the promises respecting all the other mercies which had been conferred on the children of Israel. See Ge. xxii. 17, 18. ¶ *For ever.* These words are to be referred to the preceding verse—"in remembrance of his mercy *for ever*,

to Abraham, and to his seed for
ever.
56 And Mary abode with her
about three months, and returned
to her own house.
57 Now Elisabeth's full time came
that she should be delivered; and
she brought forth a son.
58 And her neighbours and her
cousins heard how the Lord had
showed great mercy upon her; and
they[f] rejoiced with her.
59 And it came to pass, that on the
eighth day they came to circumcise
the child; and they called him
Zacharias, after the name of his
father.
60. And his mother answered
and said, Not *so;* but he shall be
called John.

[f] ver.14.

61 And they said unto her,
There is none of thy kindred that
is called by this name.
62 And they made signs to his
father how he would have him
called.
63 And he asked for a writing
table, and wrote, saying, His
name is [g]John. And they marvelled all.
64 And his [h]mouth was opened
immediately, and his tongue *loosed,*
and he spake, and praised God.
65 And fear came on all that
dwelt round about them: and all
these [4]sayings were noised abroad
throughout all the hill country of
Judea;
66 And all they that heard *them*
[i]laid *them* up in their hearts, saying,

[g] ver.13. [h] ver.20. [4] or, *things.* [i] ch.2.19,51.

as he spake," &c. They denote that the *mercy of God* manifested to his people should be had in everlasting remembrance.

There is a striking similarity between this song of praise by Mary and that spoken by *Hannah,* 1 Sa. ii. 2–10. There are few pieces of *poetry*—for this is poetry, and almost the only poetry in the New Testament—more beautiful than this. It is the language of a humble, thankful, pious, female heart praising God—1st. For his mercy to her, ver. 46–49; 2d. For his mercy to all men—his *general* goodness, ver. 50–53; and, 3d. His special goodness to his people, ver. 54, 55.

59. *On the eighth day.* This was the day on which it was required to circumcise children, Ge. xxi. 4. ¶ *And they called him Zacharias.* The *name* of the child was commonly given at the time of the circumcision, Ge. xxi. 3, 4. The name *commonly* given to the eldest son was that of the father.

60. *Shall be called John.* This was the name which the angel had said should be given to him, of which Zacharias had probably informed Elisabeth by writing.

61. *There is none of thy kindred,* &c. The Jewish tribes and families were kept distinct. To do this, and to avoid confusion in their genealogical tables, they probably gave only those names which were found among their ancestors. Another reason for this, common to all people, is the respect which is felt for honoured parents and ancestors.

63. *He asked.* That is, by signs. ¶ *A writing table.* The table denoted by this word was usually made of wood and covered with wax. The ancients used to write on such tables, as they had not the use of paper. The instrument used for writing was an iron pen or *style,* by which they *marked* on the wax which covered the table. Sometimes the writing-table was made entirely of lead.

64. *His mouth was opened,* &c. That is, he was enabled to speak. For nine months he had been dumb, and it is probable that they supposed that he had been afflicted with a paralytic affection, and that he would not recover. Hence their amazement when he spoke. For one act of disbelief all this calamity had come upon him, and it had not come without effect. With true gratitude he offered praise to God for the birth of a son, and for his restoration to the blessings of speech.

65. *And fear came,* &c. The word fear often denotes *religious reverence.* The remarkable circumstances attending the birth of John, and the fact that Zacharias was suddenly restored to speech, convinced them that *God* was there, and filled their minds with awe and veneration.

What manner of child shall this be?
And the [k]hand of the Lord was
with him.
67 And his father Zacharias was
filled with the Holy Ghost, and prophesied, saying,

k Ps.80.17.

68 Blessed[l] *be* the Lord God of
Israel; for he hath visited and
redeemed his people,
69 And hath raised up an horn
of [m]salvation for us in the house
of his servant David;

l Ps.72.18. *m* Ps.111.9.

---

66. *What manner of child*, &c. Such were the remarkable circumstances of his birth that they apprehended that he would be distinguished as a prophet, or that great events would result from his life. ¶ *The hand of the Lord was with him.* The word *hand* is used to denote *aid, protection, favour.* We stretch out the hand to aid those whom we wish to help. The expression here means that God *aided* him, *protected* him, or showed him favour. Some think that these words are a part of the speech of the neighbours—"What manner of child shall this be? God is so evidently with him!"

67. *Filled with the Holy Ghost.* See ver. 15. ¶ *And prophesied.* The word *prophesy* means—1st. To foretell future events. 2d. To celebrate the praises of God (see 1 Sa. x. 5, 6; 1 Ki. xviii. 29); then to, 3d. Teach or preach the gospel, &c. See Notes on Ro. xii. 6. This song of Zacharias partakes of all. It is principally employed in the praises of God, but it also predicts the future character and preaching of John.

68. *Blessed.* See Notes on Mat. v. 3. ¶ *Hath visited.* The word here rendered *visited* means properly *to look upon;* then to look upon in order *to know the state of anyone;* then to visit for the purpose of *aiding those who need aid*, or alleviating misery. Comp. Mat. xxv. 43. In this sense it is used here. God *looked upon* the world—he saw it miserable—he came to relieve it, and brought salvation. ¶ *And redeemed.* That is, was *about to redeem*, or had given the pledge that he *would redeem.* This was spoken under the belief that the Messiah, *the Redeemer*, was about to appear, and would certainly accomplish his work. The literal translation of this passage is, "He hath made a *ransom* for his people. A *ransom* was the *price* paid to deliver a captive taken in war. A is a prisoner taken in war by B. B has a right to detain him as a prisoner by the laws of war, but C offers B a *price* if he will release A and suffer him to go at liberty. The price which he pays, and which must be *satisfactory* to B—that is, be a *reason* to B why he should release him—is called *a price or ransom.* Men are sinners. They are bound over to just punishment by the law. The law is holy, and God, as a just governor, must see that the law is honoured and the wicked punished; but if anything can be done which will have the same *good effect* as the punishment of the sinner, or which will be an *equivalent* for it—that is, be of equal value to the universe—God may consistently release him. If he can show the same hatred of sin, and deter others from sinning, and secure the purity of the sinner, the sinner may be released. Whatever will accomplish *this* is called a *ransom,* because it is, in the eye of God, a sufficient *reason* why the sinner should not be punished; it is an *equivalent* for his sufferings, and God is satisfied. The *blood of Jesus*—that is, his *death* in the place of sinners—constitutes such a ransom. It is in their stead. It is for them. It is equivalent to their punishment. It is not itself a *punishment*, for that always supposes *personal crime*, but it is what God is pleased *to accept* in the place of the eternal sufferings of the sinner. The king of the *Locrians* made a law that an adulterer should be punished with the loss of his eyes. His *son* was the first offender, and the father decreed that his son should lose *one* eye, and *he himself* one also. This was the *ransom.* He showed his *love*, his regard for the honour of his law, and the determination that the guilty should not escape. So God gave his Son *a ransom* to show his love, his regard to justice, and his willingness to save men; and his Son, in his death, was a ransom. He is often so called in the New Testament, Mat. xx. 28; Mar. x. 45; Tit. ii. 14; He. ix. 12. For a fuller view of the nature of a *ransom*, see Notes on Ro. iii. 24, 25.

69. *And hath raised up a horn.* A *horn* is a symbol of *strength.* The figure is taken from the fact that in horned animals the strength lies in the *horn.*

70 As he [n]spake by the mouth of his holy prophets, which have been since the world began:

71 That we should be [o]saved from our enemies, and from the hand of all that hate us;

72 To perform the mercy *promised* to our fathers, and to [p]remember his holy covenant,

73 The [q]oath which he sware to our father Abraham,

74 That he would grant unto us, that we, being delivered out of the hand of our enemies, might [r]serve him without fear,

75 In[s] holiness and righteousness before him, [t]all the days of our life.

76 And thou, child, shalt be called

n Je.23.5,6; Da.9.24. *o* Is.54.7–17; Je.30.10,11. *p* Le.26.42; Ps.105.8–10; Eze.16.60.

q Ge.22.16,17. *r* Ro.6.22. *s* Tit.2.11,12; 1 Pe.1.14,15. *t* Re.2.10.

Particularly, the great power of the rhinoceros or unicorn is manifested by the use of a single horn of great strength, placed on the head near the end of the nose. When the sacred writers, therefore, speak of great *strength* they often use the word *horn*, Ps. cxlviii. 14; De. xxxiii. 17; Da. vii. 7, 8; viii. 21. The word *salvation*, connected here with the word *horn*, means that this *strength*, or this mighty Redeemer, was able to save. It is possible that this whole figure may be taken from the Jewish *altar*. On each of the four corners of the altar there was an eminence or small projection called a *horn*. To this persons might flee for safety when in danger, and be safe, 1 Ki. i. 50; ii. 28. Comp. Notes on ch. i. 11. So the Redeemer *may be* called the "horn of salvation," because those who flee to him are safe. ¶ *In the house.* In the *family*, or among the *descendants* of David.

70. *His holy prophets*, &c. All the prophets are said to have referred to the Messiah, from the beginning of the world. The most striking of these were Jacob (Ge. xlix. 10); Moses (De. xviii. 15); Isaiah (ix. 6, 7; liii.). ¶ *Since the world began.* This is not to be taken *literally*, for there were no prophets *immediately* after the creation. It is merely a *general* expression, designed to denote that *all* the prophets had predicted the coming of the Messiah. Comp. Notes on Lu. xxiv. 27; Re. xix. 10.

71. *Saved from our enemies.* The enemies of *man* are his sins, his carnal propensities, his lusts, and the great adversary Satan and his angels, who continually seek to destroy him. From *these* the Messiah came to save us. Comp. Ge. iii. 15; Mat. i. 21. ¶ *The hand.* The power; or to save us from *them*.

72. *To perform the mercy.* To show the mercy promised. The expression in the *original* is, "To make mercy with our fathers"—that is, to show kindness to our fathers; and the propriety of it is founded on the fact that mercy to *children* is regarded as kindness to the *parent*. Blessing the *children* was blessing the *nation;* was fulfilling the promises made to the fathers, and *showing* that he regarded them in mercy. ¶ *His holy covenant.* The word *covenant* means compact or agreement. This is in use among men. It implies equality in the parties; freedom from constraint; freedom from previous obligation to do the thing now covenanted; and freedom from obligation to enter into a compact, unless a man chooses so to do. Such a transaction evidently can never take place between man and God, for they are not equal. Man is not at liberty to *decline* what God proposes, and he is under obligation to do *all* that God commands. When the word *covenant*, therefore, is used in the Bible, it means sometimes a *command;* sometimes a *promise;* sometimes a *regular law*—as *the covenant of the day and night;* and sometimes the way in which God dispenses mercy—that is, by the old and new covenants. In the place before us it means *the promise* made to Abraham, as the following verses clearly show.

73. *The oath.* This oath is recorded in Ge. xxii. 16, 17. It was an oath in which God swore by himself (because he could swear by no greater, He. vi. 13, 14) that he would surely bless Abraham and his posterity. That promise was now to be entirely fulfilled by the coming of the Messiah.

74. *Might serve him.* Might obey, honour, and worship him. This was regarded as a *favour*. This was what was promised, and for this Zacharias praised God. ¶ *Without fear.* Fear of death, of spiritual enemies, or of ex-

the Prophet of the Highest, for thou shalt [u]go before the face of the Lord, to prepare his ways;

77 To give knowledge of salvation unto his people [5]by the [v]remission of their sins,

78 Through the [6]tender mercy of our God; whereby the [7]dayspring from on high hath visited us.

79 To[w] give light to them that sit in darkness and *in* the shadow of death, to guide our feet into the way of peace.

80 And the child grew, and waxed strong in spirit, and was in the deserts till the day of his showing unto Israel.

u Mal.3.1. 5 or, *for.* v Ac.5.31. 6 or, *bowels of the mercy.* 7 or, *sunrising;* or, *branch,* Is.11.1; Zec.3.8; 6.12.

w Is.9.2; 49.9.

ternal foes. In the sure hope of God's *eternal* favour beyond the grave.

75. *In holiness,* &c. In piety and strict justice. ¶ *Before him.* In the presence of God. Performed as in his presence, and with the full consciousness that he sees the heart. The *holiness* was not to be merely *external,* but spiritual, internal, pure, such as *God* would see and approve. ¶ *All the days of our life.* To death. True religion increases and expands till death.

76. *And thou, child,* &c. Zacharias predicts in this and the following verses the dignity, the employment, and the success of John. He declares what would be the subject of his preaching, and what his success. ¶ *Prophet of the Highest.* Prophet of God; a prophet *appointed by God* to declare his will, and to prepare the way for the coming of the Messiah. ¶ *The face of the Lord.* The Lord Jesus, the Messiah, that was about to appear. To go before *the face of one* is the same as to go *immediately* before one, or to be *immediately* followed by another. ¶ *To prepare his ways.* This is taken from Is. xl. 3. See Notes on Mat. iii. 3, and on Is. xl. 3.

77. *To give knowledge of salvation.* Knowledge of the *way* of salvation; that it was provided, and that the author of salvation was about to appear. ¶ *By the remission of their sins.* The word remission means pardon or forgiveness. It implies that God will treat the sinner *as if* he had not committed the sin. The idea here is, that the *salvation* about to be offered was that which was connected with the pardon of sin. There can be no other. God cannot treat men as his friends unless they come to him by repentance and obtain forgiveness. When that is obtained, which he is always disposed to grant, they can be treated with kindness and mercy.

78. *Whereby the dayspring,* &c. The word *dayspring* means the morning light, the aurora, the rising of the sun. It is called the dayspring *from on high* because the light of the gospel shines forth from heaven. God is its author, and through his mercy it shines on men. There is here, doubtless, a reference to Is. lx. 1, 2; indeed, almost the very words of that place are quoted. Comp. also Re. xxii. 16.

79. *To give light,* &c. See Notes on Mat. iv. 16. ¶ *To guide our feet,* &c. The figure in these verses is taken from travellers, who, being overtaken by night, know not what to do, and who wait patiently for the morning light, that they may know which way to go. So man wandered. So he became benighted. So he sat in the shadow of death. So he knew not which way to go until the Sun of righteousness arose, and *then* the light shone brightly on his way, and the road was open to the promised land of rest—to heaven.

This song of Zacharias is exceedingly beautiful. It expresses with elegance the great points of the plan of redemption, and the mercy of God in providing that plan. That mercy *is great.* It is worthy of praise—of our highest, loftiest songs of thanksgiving; for we were in the shadow of death—sinful, wretched, wandering—and the light arose, the gospel came, and men may rejoice in hope of eternal life.

80. *Waxed strong in spirit.* That is, in courage, understanding, and purposes of good, fitting him for his future work. The word *wax* means to *increase, to grow,* from an old Saxon word. ¶ *In the deserts.* In Hebron, and in the hill country where his father resided. He dwelt in obscurity, and was not known publicly by the people. ¶ *Until the day of his showing.* Until he entered on his public ministry, as recorded in Mat. iii.—that is, probably, until he was about thirty years of age. See Lu. iii.

CHAPTER II.

AND it came to pass in those days that there went out a decree from Cæsar Augustus that all the world should be [1]taxed.

2 (*And* this taxing was first made when Cyrenius was governor of Syria.)

3 And all went to be taxed, every one into his own city.

[1] or, *inrolled.*

CHAPTER II.

1. *In those days.* About the time of the birth of John and of Christ. ¶ *A decree.* A law commanding a thing to be done. ¶ *Cæsar Augustus.* This was the Roman emperor. His first name was Octavianus. He was the nephew of Julius Cæsar, and obtained the empire after his death. He took the name *Augustus—i.e. august*, or honourable—as a compliment to his own greatness; and from him the month *August*, which was before called *Sextilis*, received its name. ¶ *That all the world.* There has been much difficulty respecting this passage, from the fact that no such taxing *of all the world* is mentioned by ancient writers. It should have been rendered *the whole land*—that is, the whole land of Palestine. The *whole land* is mentioned to show that it was not *Judea* only, but that it included also *Galilee*, the place where Joseph and Mary dwelt. That the passage refers only to the land of Palestine, and not to the whole world, or to all the Roman empire, is clear from the following considerations: 1st. The fact that no such taxing is mentioned as pertaining to any other country. 2d. The account of Luke demands only that it should be understood of Palestine, or the country where the Saviour was born. 3d. The words *world* and *whole world* are not unfrequently used in this limited sense as confined to a single country. See Mat. iv. 8, where Satan is said to have shown to Christ all the kingdoms *of the world*, that is, of the land of Judea. See also Jos. ii. 3; Lu. iv. 25 (Greek); Lu. xxi. 26; Ac. xi. 28. ¶ *Should be taxed.* Our word *tax* means to levy and raise money for the use of the government. This is not the meaning of the original word here. It means rather to *enroll*, or take a *list* of the citizens, with their employments, the amount of their property, &c., equivalent to what was meant by *census.* Judea was at that time tributary to Rome. It paid taxes to the Roman emperor; and, though Herod was *king*, yet he held his appointment under the Roman emperor, and was subject in most matters to him. Farther, as this *enrolment* was merely to ascertain the numbers and property of the Jews, it is probable that they were very willing to be enrolled in this manner; and hence we hear that they went willingly, without tumult—contrary to the common way when they were *to be taxed.*

2. And *this taxing was first made*, &c. This verse has given as much perplexity, perhaps, as any one in the New Testament. The difficulty consists in the fact that *Cyrenius*, or *Quirinius*, was not governor of Syria until twelve or fifteen years after the birth of Jesus. Jesus was born during the reign of Herod. At that time *Varus* was president of Syria. Herod was succeeded by *Archelaus*, who reigned eight or nine years; and *after* he was removed, Judea was annexed to the province of Syria, and Cyrenius was sent as the governor (Josephus, *Ant.*, b. xvii. § 5). The difficulty has been to reconcile this account with that in Luke. Various attempts have been made to do this. The one that seems most satisfactory is that proposed by Dr. Lardner. According to his view, the passage here means, "This was the *first* census of Cyrenius, governor of Syria." It is called the *first* to distinguish it from one *afterward* taken by Cyrenius, Ac. v. 37. It is said to be the census taken by *Cyrenius, governor of Syria;* not that he was *then* governor, but that it was taken by him who was *afterward* familiarly known as governor. *Cyrenius, governor of Syria*, was the name by which the man was known when Luke wrote his gospel, and it was not improper to say that the taxing was made by *Cyrenius, the governor of Syria*, though he might not have been actually governor for many years afterward. Thus Herodian says that "to Marcus *the emperor* were born several daughters and two sons," though several of those children were born to him *before* he was emperor. Thus it is not improper to say that General Washington saved Braddock's army, or was engaged in the old French war, though he was not actually made *general* till

4 And Joseph also went up from Galilee, out of the city of Nazareth, into Judea, unto the city of David, which is called Bethlehem, (because he was of the house and lineage of David,)

5 To be taxed with Mary, his espoused wife, being great with child.

6 And so it was that while they were there the days were accomplished that she should be delivered.

---

many years afterward. According to this Augustus sent Cyrenius, an active, enterprising man, to take the census. At that time he was a Roman senator. Afterward he was made governor of the same country, and received the title which Luke gives him. ¶ *Syria.* The region of country north of Palestine, and lying between the Mediterranean and the Euphrates. *Syria*, called in the Hebrew *Aram*, from a son of Shem (Ge. x. 22), in its largest acceptation extended from the Mediterranean and the river Cydnus to the Euphrates, and from Mount Taurus on the north to Arabia and the border of Egypt on the south. It was divided into *Syria Palestina*, including Canaan and Phœnicia; *Cœle-Syria*, the tract of country lying between two ridges of Mount Lebanon and *Upper Syria.* The last was known as *Syria* in the restricted sense, or as the term was commonly used.

The leading features in the physical aspect of Syria consist of the great mountainous chains of Lebanon, or Libanus and Anti-Libanus, extending from north to south, and the great desert lying on the south-east and east. The valleys are of great fertility, and yield abundance of grain, vines, mulberries, tobacco, olives, excellent fruits, as oranges, figs, pistachios, &c. The climate in the inhabited parts is exceedingly fine. Syria is inhabited by various descriptions of people, but Turks and Greeks form the basis of the population in the cities. The only tribes that can be considered as peculiar to Syria are the tenants of the heights of Lebanon. The most remarkable of these are the Druses and Maronites. The general language is Arabic; the soldiers and officers of government speak Turkish. Of the old Syriac language no traces now exist.

4. *The city of David.* Bethlehem, called the city of David because it was the place of his birth. See Notes on Mat. ii. 1. ¶ *Because he was of the house.* Of the family. ¶ *And lineage.* The *lineage* denotes that he was descended from David as his father or ancestor. In taking a Jewish census, families were kept distinct; hence all went to the *place* where their family had resided. Joseph was of the *family* of David, and hence he went up to the city of David. It is not improbable that he might also have had a small paternal estate in Bethlehem that rendered his presence there more desirable.

7. *Her first-born son.* Whether Mary had any other children or not has been a matter of controversy. The obvious meaning of the Bible is that she had; and if this be the case, the word *first-born* is here to be taken in its common signification. ¶ *Swaddling clothes.* When a child among the Hebrews was born, it was washed in water, rubbed in salt, and then wrapped in swaddling clothes; that is, not garments regularly made, as with us, but bands or blankets that confined the limbs closely, Eze. xvi. 4. There was nothing peculiar in the manner in which the infant Jesus was treated. ¶ *Laid him in a manger.* The word rendered "inn" in this verse means simply a place of halting, a lodging-place; in modern terms, a khan or caravanserai (Robinson's *Bib. Res. in Palest.*, iii. 431). The word rendered "manger" means simply a crib or place where cattle were fed. "Inns," in our sense of the term, were anciently unknown in the East, and now they are not common. Hospitality was generally practised, so that a traveller had little difficulty in obtaining shelter and food when necessary. As travelling became more frequent, however, khans or caravanserais were erected for public use—large structures where the traveller might freely repair and find lodging for himself and his beast, he himself providing food and forage. Many such khans were placed at regular intervals in Persia. To such a place it was, though already crowded, that Joseph and Mary resorted at Bethlehem. Instead of finding a place in the "inn," or the part of the caravanserai where the travellers themselves found a place of repose, they were obliged to be contented in one of the stalls or re-

7 And she [a]brought forth her first-born son, and wrapped him in swaddling clothes, and laid him in a manger; because there was no room for them in the inn.
8 And there were in the same

a Mat.1.25.

cesses appropriated to the beasts on which they rode.

The following description of an Eastern inn or caravanserai, by Dr. Kitto, will well illustrate this passage: "It presents an external appearance which suggests to a European traveller the idea of a fortress, being an extensive square pile of strong and lofty walls, mostly of brick upon a basement of stone, with a grand archway entrance. This leads . . . to a large open area, with a well in the middle, and surrounded on three or four sides with a kind of piazza raised upon a platform 3 or 4 feet high, in the wall behind which are small doors leading to the cells or oblong chambers which form the lodgings. The cell, with the space on the platform in front of it, forms the domain of each individual traveller, where he is completely secluded, as the apparent piazza is not open, but is composed of the front arches of each compartment. There is, however, in the centre of one or more of the sides a large arched hall quite open in front. . . . The cells are completely unfurnished, and have generally no light but from the door, and the traveller is generally seen in the recess in front of his apartment except during the heat of the day. . . . Many of these caravanserais have no stables, the cattle of the travellers being accommodated in the open area; but in the more complete establishments . . . there are . . . spacious stables, formed of covered avenues extending between the back wall of the lodging apartments and the outer wall of the whole building, the entrance being at one or more of the corners of the inner quadrangle. The stable is on the same level with the court, and thus below the level of the tenements which stand on the raised platform. Nevertheless, this platform is allowed to project behind into the stable, so as to form a bench. . . . It also often happens that not only this bench exists in the stable, forming a more or less narrow platform along its extent, but also recesses corresponding to these *in front* of the cells toward the open area, and formed, in fact, by the side-walls of these cells being allowed to project behind to the boundary of the platform. These, though small and shallow, form convenient retreats for servants and muleteers in bad weather. . . . Such a recess we conceive that Joseph and Mary occupied, with their ass or mule—if they had one, as they perhaps had—tethered in front. . . . It might be rendered quite private by a cloth being stretched across the lower part."

It may be remarked that the fact that Joseph and Mary were in that place, and under a necessity of taking up their lodgings there, was in itself no proof of poverty; it was a simple matter of necessity—there was *no room* at the inn. Yet it is worthy of our consideration that Jesus was born *poor*. He did not inherit a princely estate. He was not cradled, as many are, in a palace. He had no rich friends. He had virtuous, pious parents, of more value to a child than many riches. And in this we are shown that it is no dishonour to be poor. Happy is that child who, whether his parents be rich or poor, has a *pious* father and mother. It is no matter if he has not as much wealth, as fine clothes, or as splendid a house as another. It is enough for him to be as *Jesus* was, and God will bless him. ¶ *No room at the inn.* Many people assembled to be *enrolled*, and the tavern was filled before Joseph and Mary arrived.

8. *The same country.* Round about Bethlehem. ¶ *Shepherds.* Men who tended flocks of sheep. ¶ *Abiding in the field.* Remaining out of doors, under the open sky, with their flocks. This was commonly done. The climate was mild, and, to keep their flocks from straying, they spent the night with them. It is also a fact that the Jews sent out their flocks into the mountainous and desert regions during the summer months, and took them up in the latter part of October or the first of November, when the cold weather commenced. While away in these deserts and mountainous regions, it was proper that there should be some one to attend them to keep them from straying, and from the ravages of wolves and other wild beasts. It is probable from this that our Saviour was born before the 25th of December, or before

country shepherds abiding in the
field, keeping [2]watch over their
flock by night.
9 And, lo, the angel of the Lord
came upon them, and the glory of
the Lord shone round about them;
and they were sore afraid.
10 And the angel said unto them,
Fear not: for, behold, I bring you
good tidings of great joy, which
shall be to all people.
11 For [b]unto you is born this
day, in the city of David, a
Saviour, which is Christ the Lord.
12 And this *shall be* a sign
unto you: Ye shall find the babe
wrapped in swaddling clothes,
lying in a manger.
13 And suddenly there was
[c]with the angel a multitude of
the heavenly host, praising God,
and saying,
14 Glory to God in the highest,
and on earth [d]peace, good will
toward men.
15 And it came to pass, as the
angels were gone away from them
into heaven, [3]the shepherds said
one to another, Let us now go even
unto Bethlehem, and see this thing

2 or, *the night-watches*. b Is.9.6.

c Ps.103.20,21; 1 Pe.1.12. d Is.57.19.
3 *the men, the shepherds*.

what we call *Christmas*. At that time it is cold, and especially in the high and mountainous regions about Bethlehem. But the exact time of his birth is unknown; there is no way to ascertain it. By different learned men it has been fixed at each month in the year. Nor is it of consequence to *know* the time; if it were, God would have preserved the record of it. Matters of moment are clearly revealed; those which *he* regards as of no importance are concealed. ¶ *Keeping watch*, &c. More literally, "tending their flocks *by turns* through the night watches."

9. *The glory of the Lord.* This is the same as a *great* glory—that is, a splendid appearance or *light*. The word *glory* is often the same as light, 1 Co. xv. 41; Lu. ix. 31; Ac. xxii. 11. The words *Lord* and *God* are often used to denote *greatness* or *intensity*. Thus, *trees of God* mean great trees; *hills of God*, high or lofty hills, &c. So *the glory of the Lord* here means an exceedingly great or bright luminous appearance—perhaps not unlike what Paul saw on the way to Damascus.

12. *This* shall be *a sign*, &c. The evidence by which you shall know the child is that you will find him wrapped in swaddling clothes and lying in a manger.

14. *Glory to God.* Praise be to God, or honour be to God. That is, the praise of redeeming man is due to God. The plan of redemption will bring glory to God, and is designed to express his glory. This it does by evincing his love to men, his mercy, his condescension, and his regard to the honour of his law and the stability of his own government. It is the highest expression of his love and mercy. Nowhere, so far as *we* can see, could his glory be more strikingly exhibited than in giving his only-begotten Son to die for men. ¶ *In the highest.* This is capable of several meanings: 1st. In the highest *strains*, or in the highest possible manner. 2d. *Among* the highest—that is, among the angels of God; indicating that *they* felt a deep interest in this work, and were called on to praise God for the redemption of man. 3d. In the highest *heavens*—indicating that the praise of redemption should not be confined to the *earth*, but should spread throughout the universe. 4th. The words "God in the highest" may be equivalent to *the most high God*, and be the same as saying, "Let the most high God be praised for his love and mercy to men." Which of these meanings is the true one it is difficult to determine; but in this they all agree, that high praise is to be given to God for his love in redeeming men. O that not only *angels*, but *men*, would join universally in this song of praise! ¶ *On earth peace.* That is, the gospel will bring peace. The Saviour was predicted as the Prince of peace, Is. ix. 6. The world is at war with God; sinners are at enmity against their Maker and against each other. There is no peace to the wicked. But Jesus came to make peace; and this he did, 1st. By reconciling the world to God by his atonement. 2d. By bringing the sinner to a state of peace with his Maker; inducing him to lay down the weapons of rebellion and to submit his soul to God, thus giving him the peace which passeth all

which is to come to pass, which the Lord hath made known unto us.

16 And they came with haste, and found Mary and Joseph, and the babe lying in a manger.

17 And when they had seen *it*, they made known abroad the saying which was told them concerning this child.

18 And all they that heard *it* wondered at those things which were told them by the shepherds.

19 But Mary kept all these things, and pondered *them* in her heart.

---

understanding. 3d. By diffusing in the heart universal good-will to men—*disposing* men to lay aside their differences, to love one another, to seek each other's welfare, and to banish envy, malice, pride, lust, passion, and covetousness—in all ages the most fruitful causes of difference among men. And, 4th. By diffusing the principles of universal peace among nations. If the gospel of Jesus should universally prevail, there would be an end of war. In the days of the millennium there will be universal peace; all the causes of war will have ceased; men will love each other and do justly; all nations will be brought under the influence of the gospel. O how should each one toil and pray that the great object of the gospel should be universally accomplished, and the world be filled with peace! ¶ *Good will toward men.* The gift of the Saviour is an expression of good-will or *love* to men, and therefore God is to be praised. The work of redemption is uniformly represented as the fruit of the *love of God*, Jn. iii. 16; Ep. v. 2; 1 Jn. iv. 10; Re. i. 5. No words can express the greatness of that love. It can only be measured by the *misery*, *helplessness*, and *danger* of man; by the extent of his sufferings here and in the world of woe if he had not been saved; by the condescension, sufferings, and death of Jesus; and by the eternal honour and happiness to which he will raise his people. All these are beyond our full comprehension. Yet how little does man feel it! and how many turn away from the highest love of God, and treat the expression of that love with contempt! Surely, if God so loved us *first*, we ought also to love him, 1 Jn. iv. 19.

16. *Unto Bethlehem.* The city of David, where the angel had told them they would find the Saviour. These shepherds appear to have been pious men. They were waiting for the coming of the Messiah. On the first intimation that he had actually appeared they went with haste to find him. So all men should without delay seek the Saviour. When told of him by the servants of God, they should, like these shepherds, forsake all, and give no rest to their eyes until they have found him. We may *always* find him. We need not travel to Bethlehem. We have only to cast our eyes to heaven; to look to him and to believe on him, and we shall find him ever near to us, and for ever *our* Saviour and friend.

17. *When they had seen* it. When they had satisfied themselves of the truth of the coming of the Messiah, and had ascertained that they could not have been mistaken in the appearance of the angels. There was evidence enough to satisfy *them* that what the angels said was true, or they would not have gone to Bethlehem. Having seen the child themselves, they had now evidence that would satisfy others; and accordingly they became the first preachers of the *gospel*, and went and proclaimed to others that the Messiah had come. One of the first duties of those who are newly converted to God, and a duty in which they delight, is to proclaim to others what they have seen and felt. It should be done in a proper way and at the proper time; but nothing can or should prevent a Christian recently converted from telling his feelings and views to others—to his friends, to his parents, to his brothers, and to his old companions. And it may be remarked that often more good may be done then than during any other period of their life. Entreaties then make an impression; nor can a sinner well resist the appeals made to him by one who was just now with him in the way to ruin, but who now treads the way to heaven.

19. *Mary kept all these things.* All that happened, and all that was said respecting her child. She *remembered* what the angel had said to *her;* what had happened to Elisabeth and to the shepherds—all the extraordinary circumstances which had attended the birth of her son. Here is a delicate and beautiful expression of the feelings

20 And the shepherds returned, glorifying and praising God for all the things that they had heard and seen, as it was told unto them.

21 And when [e]eight days were accomplished for the circumcising of the child, his name was called JESUS, which was so named of the angel[f] before he was conceived in the womb.

22 And when [g]the days of her purification, according to the law of Moses, were accomplished, they brought him to Jerusalem, to present *him* to the Lord;

23 (As it is written in the law of the Lord, [h]Every male that openeth the womb shall be called holy to the Lord;)

24 And to offer a sacrifice accord-

e Le.12.3. *f* Mat.1.21; ch.1.31. *g* Le.12.2,&c. *h* Ex.13.12; 22.29; Nu.8.17.

---

of a mother. A *mother* forgets none of those things which occur respecting her children. Everything they do or suffer — everything that is said of them, is treasured up in her mind; and often, often, she thinks of those things, and anxiously seeks what they may indicate respecting the future character and welfare of her child. ¶ *Pondered.* Weighed. This is the original meaning of the word *weighed.* She kept them; she revolved them; she *weighed* them in her mind, giving to each circumstance its just importance, and anxiously seeking what it might indicate respecting her child. ¶ *In her heart.* In her mind. She *thought* of these things often and anxiously.

20. *The shepherds returned.* To their flocks. ¶ *Glorifying,* &c. Giving honour to God, and celebrating his praises.

21. *Eight days,* &c. This was the regular time for performing the rite of circumcision, Ge. xvii. 12. ¶ *Called Jesus.* See Notes on Mat. i. 21.

22. *Days of her purification.* Among the Hebrews a mother was required to remain at home for about forty days after the birth of a male child and about eighty for a female, and during that time she was reckoned as *impure* —that is, she was not permitted to go to the temple or to engage in religious services with the congregation, Le. xii. 3, 4. ¶ *To Jerusalem.* The place where the temple was, and where the ordinances of religion were celebrated. ¶ *To present* him *to the Lord.* Every first-born male child among the Jews was regarded as *holy* to the Lord, Ex. xiii. 2. By their being *holy unto the Lord* was meant that unto them belonged the office of *priests.* It was theirs to be set apart to the service of God—to offer sacrifice, and to perform the duties of religion. It is probable that at first the duties of religion devolved on the *father*, and that, when he became infirm or died, that duty devolved on the eldest son.; and it is still manifestly proper that where the father is infirm or has deceased, the duty of conducting family worship should be performed by the eldest son. Afterward God chose *the tribe of Levi in the place* of the eldest sons, to serve him in the sanctuary, Nu. viii. 13–18. Yet still it was proper to present the child to God, and it was required that it should be done with an offering.

23. *As it is written*, &c., Ex. xiii. 2.

24. *And to offer a sacrifice*, &c. Those who were able on such an occasion were required to offer a lamb for a burnt-offering, and a pigeon or a turtle-dove for a sin-offering. If not able to bring a *lamb*, then they were permitted to bring two turtle-doves or two young pigeons, Le. xii. 6, 8. ¶ *Turtle-doves.* Doves distinguished for having a plaintive and tender voice. By Mary's making this offering she showed her poverty; and our Saviour, by coming in a state of poverty, has shown that it is not dishonourable to be poor. No station is dishonourable where *God* places us. He knows what is best for us, and he often makes a state of poverty an occasion of the highest blessings. If *with* poverty he grants us, as is often the case, peace, contentment, and religion, it is worth far more than all the jewels of Golconda or the gold of Mexico. If it be asked why, since the Saviour was pure from any moral defilement in his conception and birth, it was necessary to offer such a sacrifice; why was it necessary that he should be circumcised, since he had no sin, it may be answered—1st. That it was proper to fulfil all righteousness, and to show obedience to the law, Mat. iii. 15. 2d. It was necessary for the future usefulness of Christ. Unless he had been circumcised, he could not

ing to that which is said in the law
of the Lord, A pair of turtle-doves,
or two young pigeons.
25 And, behold, there was a
man in Jerusalem whose name
was Simeon; and the same man
was just and [i]devout, waiting for
the [k]consolation of Israel: and the
Holy Ghost was upon him.
26 And it was revealed unto him
by the Holy Ghost that he should
not [l]see death before he had seen
the Lord's Christ.
27 And he came by the Spirit into
the temple: and when the parents
brought in the child Jesus, to do for
him after the custom of the law,
28 Then took he him up in his
arms, and blessed God, and said,
29 Lord, [m]now lettest thou thy

i Mar.15.43; ver.38. *k* Is.40.1. *l* Ps.89.48; He.11.5. *m* Ge.46.30.

---

have been admitted to any synagogue or to the temple. He would have had no access to the people, and *could* not have been regarded as the Messiah. Both he and Mary, therefore, yielded obedience to the laws of the land, and thus set us an example that we should walk in their steps. Comp. Notes on on Mat. iii. 15.

25. *Whose name* was *Simeon.* Some have supposed that this Simeon was a son of the famous *Hillel*, a distinguished teacher in Jerusalem, and president of the Sanhedrim; but nothing is certainly known of him but what is here related. He was an aged man, of distinguished piety and reputation, and was anxiously expecting the coming of the Messiah. Such an *old age* is peculiarly honourable. No spectacle is more sublime than an old man of piety and high character looking for the appearing of the Lord, and patiently waiting for the time to come when he may be blessed with the sight of his Redeemer. ¶ *Just.* Righteous before God and man; approved by God as a righteous man, and discharging faithfully his duty to man. ¶ *Devout.* This word means *a religious man*, or a *pious* man. The original expresses the idea of *good reputation, well received*, or of high standing among the people. ¶ *Waiting for the consolation of Israel.* That is, waiting for the *Messiah*, who is called *the consolation of Israel* because he would give comfort to them by his appearing. This term was often applied to the Messiah before he actually appeared. It was common to swear, also, by "the consolation of Israel"—that is, by the Messiah about to come. See Lightfoot on this place. ¶ *The Holy Ghost*, &c. He was a holy man, and was *divinely inspired* respecting the Messiah about to appear.

26. *And it was revealed unto him.* In what way this was done we are not informed. Sometimes a revelation was made by a dream, at others by a voice, and at others by silent suggestion. All we know of this is that it was by the Holy Ghost. ¶ *Not see death.* Should not die. To *see* death and to *taste* of death, was a common way among the Hebrews of expressing death itself. Comp. Ps. lxxxix. 48. ¶ *The Lord's Christ.* Rather *the Lord's Anointed.* The word *Christ* means *anointed*, and it would have been better to use that word here. To an aged man who had been long waiting for the Messiah, how grateful must have been this revelation—this solemn assurance that the Messiah was near! But this revelation is now given to every man, that he need not taste of death till, by the eye of faith, he may see the Christ of God. He is offered freely. He has come. He waits to manifest himself to the world, and he is not willing that any should die for ever. To us also it will be as great a privilege in our dying hours to have seen Christ by faith as it was to Simeon. It will be the only thing that can support us then—the only thing that will enable us to depart in peace.

27. *By the Spirit.* By the *direction* of the Spirit. ¶ *Into the temple.* Into that part of the temple where the public worship was chiefly performed—into the court of the women. See Notes on Mat. xxi. 12. ¶ *The custom of the law.* That is, to make an offering for purification, and to present him to God.

28. *Blessed God.* Thanked or praised God.

29. *Now lettest.* Now thou *dost* let or permit. This word is in the indicative mood, and signifies that God *was permitting* him to die in peace, by having relieved his anxieties, allayed his

servant depart in [n]peace, according to thy word;
30 For mine eyes have [o]seen thy salvation,
31 Which thou hast prepared before the face of all people:

n Is.57.2; Re.14.13. *o* Is.52.10; ch.3.6; Ac.4.12.

32 A light to lighten the [p]Gentiles, and the glory of thy people Israel.
33 And Joseph and his mother marvelled at those things which were spoken of him.

p Is.42.6; 49.6; 60.3; Ac.13.47,48.

---

fears, fulfilled the promises, and having, by the appearing of the Messiah, removed every reason why he should live any longer, and every wish to live. ¶ *Depart.* Die. ¶ *According to thy word.* Thy promise made by revelation. God never disappoints. To many it might have appeared improbable, when such a promise was made to an old man, that it should be fulfilled. But God fulfils all his word, keeps all his promises, and NEVER disappoints those who trust in him.

30. *Thy salvation.* Him who is to procure salvation for his people; or, the Saviour.

31. *Before the face of all people.* Whom thou hast provided *for* all people, or whom thou dost design *to reveal to* all people.

32. *A light to lighten the Gentiles.* This is in accordance with the prophecies in the Old Testament, Is. xlix.; ix. 6, 7; Ps. xcviii. 3; Mal. iv. 2. The Gentiles are represented as sitting in darkness—that is, in ignorance and sin. Christ is *a light* to them, as by him they will be made acquainted with the character of the true God, his law, and the plan of redemption. As the darkness rolls away when the sun arises, so ignorance and error flee away when Jesus gives light to the mind. Nations shall come to his light, and kings to the brightness of his rising, Is. lx. 3. ¶ *And the glory,* &c. The first offer of salvation was made to the Jews, Jn. iv. 22; Lu. xxiv. 47. Jesus was born among the Jews; to them had been given the prophecies respecting him, and his first ministry was among them. Hence he was their glory, their honour, their light. But it is a subject of special gratitude to us that the Saviour was given also for the Gentiles; for, 1. We are Gentiles, and if *he* had not come we should have been shut out from the blessings of redemption. 2. It is he only that now

"Can make our dying bed
Feel soft as downy pillows are,
While on his breast we lean our head,
And breathe our life out sweetly there."

Thus our departure may be like that of Simeon. Thus we may die in peace. Thus it will be a blessing to die. But, 3. In order to do this, our life must be like that of Simeon. We must *wait* for the consolation of Israel. We must look for his coming. We must be holy, harmless, undefiled, *loving* the Saviour. Then death to us, like death to Simeon, will have no terror; we shall depart in peace, and in heaven see the salvation of God, 2 Pe. iii. 11, 12. But, 4. Children, as well as the hoary-headed Simeon, may look for the coming of Christ. They too must die; and *their* death will be happy only as they depend on the Lord Jesus, and are prepared to meet him.

34. *Simeon blessed them.* Joseph and Mary. On them he sought the blessing of God. ¶ *Is set.* Is appointed or constituted for that, or such will be the effect of his coming. ¶ *The fall.* The word *fall* here denotes *misery, suffering, disappointment,* or *ruin.* There is a plain reference to the passage where it is said that he should be *a stone of stumbling and a rock of offence,* Is. viii. 14, 15. Many expected a *temporal* prince, and in this they were disappointed. They loved darkness rather than light, and rejected him, and *fell* unto destruction. Many that were proud were brought low by his preaching. They *fell* from the vain and giddy height of their own self-righteousness, and were humbled before God, and then, through him, rose again to a better righteousness and to better hopes. The nation also rejected him and put him to death, and, as a judgment, *fell* into the hands of the Romans. Thousands were led into captivity, and thousands perished. The nation rushed into ruin, the temple was destroyed, and the people were scattered into all the nations. See Ro. ix. 32, 33; 1 Pe. ii. 8; 1 Co. i. 23, 24. ¶ *And rising again.* The word "again" is not expressed in the Greek. It seems to be supposed, in our translation, that the *same persons* would fall and rise again; but this is not the meaning of the passage. It denotes that many would be

34 And Simeon blessed them,
and said unto Mary his mother,
Behold, this *child* is set for the
fall[q] and rising again of many in
Israel; and for a sign which shall
be [r]spoken against;
35 (Yea, a [s]sword shall pierce
through thy own soul also;) that
the[t] thoughts of many hearts may
be revealed.
36 And there was one Anna,
a prophetess, the daughter of
Phanuel, of the tribe of Aser;
she was of a great age, and had
lived with an husband seven years
from her virginity;
37 And she *was* a widow of
about fourscore and four years,
which departed not from the
temple, but served *God* with fastings and [u]prayers night and day.
38 And she, coming in that
instant, gave thanks likewise unto
the Lord, and spake of him to all
them that [v]looked for redemption
in [4]Jerusalem.
39 And when they had per-
formed all things according to the

q Is.8.14; Ro.9.32,33; 1 Co.1.23,24; 2 Co.2.16; 1 Pe. 2.7,8. *r* Ac.28.22. *s* Jn.19.25. *t* Ju.5.15,16; 1 Co.11.19.

u Ac.26.7; 1 Ti.5.5. *v* ver.25. 4 or, *Israel.*

ruined by his coming, and that many *others* would be made happy or be saved. Many of the poor and humble, that were *willing* to receive him, would obtain pardon of sin and peace—would *rise* from their sins and sorrows here, and finally ascend to eternal life. ¶ *And for a sign*, &c. The word *sign* here denotes a conspicuous or distinguished object, and the Lord Jesus was such an object of contempt and rejection by all the people. He was despised, and his religion has been the common *mark* or *sign* for all the wicked, the profligate, and the profane, to curse, and ridicule, and oppose. Comp. Is. viii. 18, and Ac. xxviii. 22. Never was a prophecy more exactly fulfilled than this. Thousands have rejected the gospel and fallen into ruin; thousands are still falling of those who are ashamed of Jesus; thousands blaspheme him, deny him, speak all manner of evil against him, and would crucify him again if he were in their hands; but thousands also *by* him are renewed, justified, and raised up to life and peace.

35. *Yea, a sword*, &c. The sufferings and death of thy Son shall deeply afflict thy soul. And if Mary had not been thus forewarned and sustained by strong faith, she could not have borne the trials which came upon her Son; but God prepared her for it, and the holy mother of the dying Saviour was sustained. ¶ *That the thoughts*, &c. This is connected with the preceding verse: "He shall be a sign, a conspicuous object to be spoken against, that the thoughts of many hearts may be made manifest"—that is, that they *might show* how much they hated holiness. Nothing so *brings out* the feelings of sinners as to tell them of Jesus Christ. Many treat him with silent contempt; many are ready to gnash their teeth; many curse him; all show how much by nature the heart is opposed to religion, and thus are really, in spite of themselves, fulfilling the Scriptures and the prophecies. So true is it that "none can say that Jesus is Lord but by the Holy Ghost," 1 Co. xii. 3.

36. *Of the tribe of Aser.* The tribe of Aser, or Asher, dwelt in the northern part of the land of Canaan. Why Anna was called a prophetess is not known. It might be because she had been the wife of a prophet, or because she was employed in celebrating the praises of God (comp. 1 Ch. xxv. 1, 2, 4; 1 Sa. x. 5), or because she herself had foretold future events, being inspired.

37. *And she* was *a widow of about fourscore and four years.* That is, she was about eighty-four years *of age*. It does not mean that she had been a *widow* for that long time. ¶ *Fastings and prayers.* Constant religious service. Spending her time in prayer, and in all the ordinances of religion. ¶ *Night and day.* Continually—that is, at the usual times of public worship and in private. When it is said that she departed not from the temple, it is meant that she was *constant* and *regular* in all the public services at the temple, or was never absent from those services. God blesses those who wait at his temple gates.

39. *They returned into Galilee.* Not immediately, but after a time. Luke has omitted the flight into Egypt recorded by Matthew; but he has not denied it, nor are his words to be pressed

law of the Lord, they returned
into Galilee, to their own city
Nazareth.
40 And the child grew, and
waxed strong in spirit, [w] filled
with wisdom; and the grace of
God was upon him.
41 Now his parents went to
Jerusalem [x] every year at the feast
of the passover.
42 And when he was twelve
years old, they went up to Jerusalem, after the custom of the feast.
43 And when they had fulfilled
the days, as they returned, the child
Jesus tarried behind in Jerusalem;
and Joseph and his mother knew
not *of it*.
44 But they, supposing him to
have been in the company, went

w Is.11.2,3; ver.52. *x* Ex.23.15; De.16.1.

---

as if he meant to affirm that they went *immediately* to Nazareth. A parallel case we have in the life of Paul. When he was converted it is said that he came to Jerusalem, as if he had gone there immediately after his conversion (Ac. ix. 26); yet we learn in another place that this was after an interval of three years, Ga. i. 17, 18. In the case before us there is no improbability in supposing that they returned to Bethlehem, then went to Egypt, and then to Galilee.

40. *Strong in spirit.* In mind, intellect, understanding. Jesus had a human soul, and *that* soul was subject to all the proper laws of a human spirit. It therefore increased in knowledge, strength, and character. Nor is it any more inconsistent with his being God to say that his soul expanded, than to say that his body grew. ¶ *Filled with wisdom.* Eminent for wisdom when a child—that is, exhibiting an extraordinary understanding, and *wise* to flee from everything sinful and evil. ¶ *And the grace of God*, &c. The word *grace* in the New Testament commonly means unmerited favour shown *to sinners.* Here it means no more than *favour*. God showed him *favour*, or was pleased with him and blessed him.

It is remarkable that this is all that is recorded of the infancy of Jesus; and this, with the short account that follows of his going to Jerusalem, is all that we know of him for thirty years of his life. The design of the evangelists was to give an account of his *public ministry*, and not his private life. Hence they say little of him in regard to his first years. What they *do* say, however, corresponds entirely with what we might expect. He was wise, pure, pleasing God, and deeply skilled in the knowledge of the divine law. He set a lovely example for all children; was subject to his parents, and increased in favour with God and man.

42. *Twelve years old.* All males among the Hebrews were required to appear three times a year before God, to attend on the ordinances of religion in the temple, and it is probable that this was the age at which they first went up to Jerusalem, Ex. xxiii. 14–17; De. xvi. 16. ¶ *To Jerusalem.* Where the feasts of the Jews were all held. This was a journey from Nazareth of about 70 miles. ¶ *After the custom of the feast.* According to the usual manner of the feast.

43. *Had fulfilled the days.* The days of the Passover. These were eight days in all—one day for killing the paschal lamb, and seven days for the observance of the feast of unleavened bread, Ex. xii. 15; Le. xxiii. 5, 6.

44. *Supposing him to have been in the company.* It may seem very remarkable that parents should not have been more attentive to their only son, and that they should not have been assured of his presence with them when they left Jerusalem; but the difficulty may be explained by the following considerations: 1. In going to these great feasts, families and neighbours would join together, and form a large collection. 2. It is not improbable that Jesus was *with* them when they were about to start from Jerusalem and were making preparations. Seeing him then, they might have been certain as to his presence. 3. A part of the company might have left before the others, and Joseph and Mary may have supposed that he was with them, until they overtook them at night and ascertained their mistake. ¶ *Kinsfolk.* Relatives. ¶ *Acquaintances.* Neighbours who had gone up with them in the same company to Jerusalem.

46. *After three days.* This means, probably, *on the third day* after they had left Jerusalem—that is, the first day they went toward Galilee, on the second

a day's journey; and they sought
him among *their* kinsfolk and
among their acquaintance.
45 And when they found him
not, they turned back again to
Jerusalem, seeking him.
46 And it came to pass, that
after three days they found him in
the temple, sitting in the midst of
the doctors, both hearing them and
asking them questions.
47 And all that heard him were
astonished at his [y]understanding
and answers.
48 And when they saw him,
they were amazed: and his mother
said unto him, Son, why hast thou
thus dealt with us? behold, thy
father and I have sought thee
sorrowing.
49 And he said unto them,
How is it that ye sought me?
wist ye not that [z]I must be about
my Father's business?
50 And they understood not the
saying which he spake unto them.
51 And he went down with
them and came to Nazareth, and

y Ps.119.99; Mat.7.28; Mar.1.22; ch.4.22,32; Jn.7.15,46.

z Jn.5.17; 9.4.

---

they returned to Jerusalem, and on the third they found him. Comp. Mat. xxvii. 63; Mar. viii. 31. ¶ *In the temple.* In the *court* of the temple, for Jesus, not being a Levitical priest, could not enter into the temple itself. See Mat. xxi. 12. ¶ *In the midst of the doctors.* The *teachers*, the *Rabbins*, who were the instructors of the people in matters of religion. ¶ *Asking them questions.* Proposing questions to them respecting the law and the prophets. There is no reason to suppose that this was for the purpose of perplexing or confounding them. The questions were doubtless proposed in a respectful manner, and the answers listened to with proper deference to their age and rank. Jesus was a child, and religion does not teach a child to be rude or uncivil, even though he may really know much more than more aged persons. Religion teaches all, and especially the young, to treat others with respect, to show them the honour that is due, to venerate age, and to speak kindly to all, 1 Pe. ii. 17; iii. 8, 9; Ex. xx. 12; Mat. xxiii. 3; Ro. xiii. 7.

48. *Why hast thou thus dealt with us?* Why hast thou given us all this trouble and anxiety, in going so far and returning with so much solicitude? ¶ *Thy father.* Joseph was not the *real* father of Jesus, but he was *legally* so; and as the secret of his birth was not commonly known, he was called his father. Mary, in accordance with that usage, also called him so. ¶ *Sorrowing.* Anxious, lest in the multitude he might not be found, or lest some accident might have happened to him.

49. *How is it*, &c. *Why* have ye sought me with so much anxiety? *Mary* should have known that the Son of God was safe; that his heavenly Father would take care of him, and that he *could* do nothing amiss. ¶ *Wist ye not. Know* ye not. You had reason to know. You knew my design in coming into the world, and that design was *superior* to the duty of obeying earthly parents, and *they* should be willing always to give me up to the proper business for which I live. ¶ *My Father's business.* Some think that this should be translated "in my Father's house"—that is, in the temple. Jesus reminded them here that he came down from heaven; that he had a higher Father than an earthly parent; and that, even in early life, it was proper that he should be engaged in the work for which he came. He did not enter, indeed, upon his *public* work for eighteen years after this; yet still the work of God was *his* work, and always, even in childhood, it was proper for him to be engaged in the great business for which he came down from heaven.

50. *They understood not*, &c. It is remarkable that they did not understand Jesus in this, but it shows how slow persons are to believe. Even his parents, after all that had taken place, did not seem to comprehend that *he* was to be the Saviour of men, or if they did, they understood it in a very imperfect manner.

51. *Went down with them.* Down from Jerusalem, which was in a high, mountainous region. ¶ *Was subject unto them.* Performed the duty of a faithful and obedient child, and not improbably was engaged in the trade of Joseph—that of a carpenter. Every Jew was required

was subject unto them: but his
mother [a]kept all these sayings in
her heart.
52 And Jesus [b]increased in
wisdom and [5]stature, and in favour
with God and man.

a Da.7.28; ver.19. *b* 1 Sa.2.26; ver.40. [5] or, *age*.

CHAPTER III.

NOW in the fifteenth year of
the reign of Tiberius Cæsar,
Pontius Pilate being governor of
Judea, and Herod being tetrarch
of Galilee, and his brother Philip

---

to learn some trade, and there is every reason to think that our Saviour followed that of his reputed father. And from this we learn—1. That obedience to parents is a duty. Jesus has set an example in this that all children should follow. Though he was the Son of God, and on proper occasions was engaged in the great work of redemption, yet he was also the *son of Mary*, and he loved and obeyed his mother, and was *subject* to her. 2. It is no dishonour to be a mechanic, or to be brought up in an obscure employment. Jesus has conferred honour on virtuous industry, and no man should be ashamed of industrious parents, though poor, or of a condition of life that is far from ease and affluence. Industry is honourable, and virtuous poverty should not be regarded as a matter of reproach. The only thing to be ashamed of, in regard to this matter, is when men are idle, or when children are too proud to hear or speak of the occupation of their parents, or to *follow* the same occupation.

52. *In favour with God.* That is, in proportion to his advance in wisdom. This does not imply that he ever *lacked* the favour of God, but that God regarded him with favour *in proportion* as he showed an understanding and spirit like his own. Happy are those children who imitate the example of Jesus—who are obedient to parents—who increase in wisdom—who are sober, temperate, and industrious, and who thus increase in favour with God and men.

CHAPTER III.

1. *Now in the fifteenth year.* This was the *thirteenth* year of his being sole emperor. He was *two* years joint emperor with Augustus, and Luke reckons from the time when he was admitted to share the empire with Augustus Cæsar. See Lardner's *Credibility*, vol. i. ¶ *Tiberius Cæsar.* Tiberius succeeded Augustus in the empire, and began his *sole* reign Aug. 19, A.D. 14. He was a most infamous character—a scourge to the Roman people. He reigned twenty-three years, and was succeeded by *Caius Caligula*, whom he appointed his successor on account of his notorious wickedness, and that he might be, as he expressed it, a *serpent* to the Romans. ¶ *Pontius Pilate.* Herod the Great left his kingdom to three sons. See Notes on Mat. ii. 22. To *Archelaus* he left *Judea.* Archelaus reigned *nine* years, when, on account of his crimes, he was banished into Vienne, and Judea was made a Roman province, and placed entirely under Roman governors or *procurators*, and became completely tributary to Rome. Pontius Pilate was the *fifth* governor that had been sent, and of course had been in Judea but a short time. See the chronological table at the end of the volume. ¶ *Herod being tetrarch of Galilee.* This was *Herod Antipas*, son of Herod the Great, to whom Galilee had been left as his part of his father's kingdom. The word *tetrarch* properly denotes one who presides over a *fourth part* of a country or province; but it also came to be a general title, denoting one who reigned over any part—a third, a half, &c. In this case Herod had a *third* of the dominions of his father, but he was called tetrarch. It was this Herod who imprisoned John the Baptist, and to whom our Saviour, when arraigned, was sent by Pilate. ¶ *And his brother Philip tetrarch of Iturea. Iturea* was so called from *Jetur*, one of the sons of Ishmael, Ge. xxv. 15; 1 Ch. i. 31. It was situated on the east side of the Jordan, and was taken from the descendants of Jetur by the tribes of Reuben and Gad and the half tribe of Manasseh, 1 Ch. v. 19. ¶ *Region of Trachonitis.* This region was also on the east of the Jordan, and extended northward to the district of Damascus and eastward to the deserts of Arabia. It was bounded on the west by Gaulonitis and south by the city of Bostra. Philip had obtained this region from the Romans on condition that he would extirpate the robbers. ¶ *Lysanias the tetrarch of Abilene.* Abilene was so called from *Abila*, its chief city. It was situated in Syria, north-west of

tetrarch of Iturea, and of the
region of Trachonitis, and Lysanias
the tetrarch of Abilene,
2 Annas[a] and Caiaphas being
the high-priests, the word of God
came unto John, the son of Zacharias, in the wilderness.
3 And[b] he came into all the
country about Jordan, preaching
the[c] baptism of repentance for the
remission of sins;
4 As it is written in the book of
the words of Esaias the prophet,
saying, [d]The voice of one crying
in the wilderness, Prepare ye the
way of the Lord, make his paths
straight.
5 Every valley shall be filled,
and every mountain and hill shall
be brought low; and the crooked
shall be made straight, and the
rough ways *shall be* made smooth;
6 And[e] all flesh shall see the
salvation of God.
7 Then said he to the multitude
that came forth to be baptized of
him, [f]O generation of vipers! who
hath warned you to flee from the
wrath to come?
8 Bring forth, therefore, fruits
[1]worthy of repentance; and begin
not to say within yourselves, We
have Abraham to *our* father: for I
say unto you, that God is able of
these stones to raise up children
unto Abraham.
9 And now also the axe is laid
unto the root of the trees: [g]every
tree, therefore, which bringeth not
forth good fruit is hewn down and
cast into the fire.
10 And the people asked him,
saying, What shall we do, then?
11 He answereth and saith unto

a Jn.11.49,51; 18.13; Ac.4.6. *b* Mat.3.1; Mar.1.4. *c* ch.1.77. *d* Is.40.3.

e Ps.98.2; Is.40.5; 49.6; 52.10; Ro.10.12,18. *f* Mat.3.7. 1 or, *meet for*. *g* Mat.7.19; ch.13.7,9.

Damascus and south-east of Mount Lebanon, and was adjacent to Galilee.

2. *Annas and Caiaphas being high-priests.* There was, properly speaking, but *one* high-priest of the Jews; yet the *name* of high-priest continued to be given to those who had been in that office, and especially when they still possessed some civil office after they had left the high-priesthood. In this case it appears that *Caiaphas* was high-priest, and Annas *had been*, but had been dismissed from the office. It is highly probable that he still held an office under the Romans, and was perhaps president of the Sanhedrim. He is mentioned *before* Caiaphas because he was father-in-law to Caiaphas, and probably was the eldest, and had been longest in office. Instances similar to this may be found in Josephus.

There is one remark to be made here about the manner in which the gospels are written. They have every mark of openness and honesty. An impostor does not mention names, and times, and places particularly. If he did, it would be easy to ascertain that he *was* an impostor. But the sacred writers describe objects and men as if they were perfectly familiar with them. They never appear to be *guarding* themselves. They speak of things most minutely. If, therefore, they had been impostors, it would have been easy to detect them. If, for example, John did *not* begin to preach in the fifteenth year of Tiberius—if Philip was *not* tetrarch of Iturea—if Pontius Pilate was *not* governor of Judea, how easy would it have been to detect them in falsehood! Yet it was never done. Nay, we have evidence of that age, in Josephus, that these descriptions are strictly true; and, consequently, the gospels must have been written by men who were personally acquainted with what they wrote, who were not impostors, and who were *honest* men. If they were *honest*, then the Christian religion is true.

3–9. On the baptism of John, see Notes on Mat. iii.

10. *What shall we do, then?* John had told them to bring forth fruits appropriate to repentance, or to lead a life which showed that their repentance was genuine. They very properly, therefore, asked how it should be done, or what *would be* such a life.

11. *He that hath two coats,* &c. Or, in other words, aid the poor according to your ability; be benevolent, and you will thus show that your repentance is

them, [h]He that hath two coats, let him impart to him that hath none; and he that hath meat, let him do likewise.

12 Then came also [i]publicans to be baptized, and said unto him, Master, what shall we do?

13 And he said unto them, [k]Exact no more than that which is appointed you.

14 And the soldiers likewise demanded of him, saying, And what shall we do? And he said unto them, [2]Do violence to no man,

h ch.11.41; 2 Co.8.14; 1 Jn.3.17. *i* Mat.21.32; ch.7.29.

k ch.19.8; 1 Co.6.10. [2] or, *Put no man in fear.*

genuine. It is remarkable that one of the *first* demands of religion is to do good, and it is in *this* way that it may be shown that the repentance is not feigned. For 1st. The *nature* of religion is to do good. 2d. This requires self-denial, and none will deny themselves who are not attached to God. And 3d. This is to imitate Jesus Christ, who, though he was rich, yet for our sakes became poor. ¶ *Coats.* See Notes on Mat. v. 40. ¶ *Meat.* Provision of any kind.

12. *The publicans.* See Notes on Mat. v. 47. There is reason to think that the *publicans* or *tax-gatherers* were peculiarly oppressive and hard in their dealings with the people; and that, as they had every opportunity of exacting more than they ought, so they often did it, and thus enriched themselves. The evidence of repentance in them would be to break off their sins in this respect, and to deal justly.

13. *Exact.* Demand, or take, no more. ¶ *Than that which is appointed.* That is, by the government. John does not condemn the office, or say that the employment should be forsaken. Though it was hated by the people—though often abused and therefore unpopular—yet *the office itself* was not dishonourable. If there is a government, it must be supported; and of course there must be men whose duty it is to collect taxes, as the means of the proper support of the government; and as such a support of the government is necessary, so the people should pay cheerfully the just apportionment of their rulers, and regard favourably those who are authorized to collect it. See Ro. xiii. 1–6.

14. *The soldiers likewise.* It seems that *they* also came to his baptism. Whether these were Jews or Romans cannot be ascertained. It is not improbable that, as Judea was a Roman province, they were Jews or Jewish proselytes in the service of Herod Antipas or Philip, and so were really in the Roman service. ¶ *Do violence,* &c. Do not take the property of any by unlawful force, or do not use unjust force against the person or property of any individual. It is probable that many of them were oppressive, or prone to violence, rapine, or theft, and burdensome even in times of peace to the inhabitants. ¶ *Neither accuse* any *falsely.* It is probable that when they wished the property of others and could not obtain it by violence, or when there was no pretext for violence, they often attempted the same thing in another way, and falsely accused the persons of crime. The word rendered *falsely accused* is the one from which our word *sycophant* is derived. The proper meaning of the word *sycophant* was this: There was a law in Athens which prohibited the importation of *figs.* The *sycophant* (literally *the man who made figs to appear,* or who showed them) was one who made complaint to the magistrate of persons who had imported figs contrary to law, or who was an *informer;* and then the word came to be used in a general sense to denote *any* complainer—a calumniator—an accuser—an informer. As such persons were usually cringing and fawning, and looked for a reward, the word came to be used also to denote a fawner or flatterer. It is always used in a bad sense. It is correctly rendered here, "do not accuse any falsely." ¶ *Be content,* &c. Do not murmur or complain, or take unlawful means to increase your wages. ¶ *Wages.* This word means not only the *money* which was paid them, but also their *rations* or daily allowance of food. By this they were to show that their repentance was genuine; that it had a practical influence; that it produced a *real* reformation of life; and it is clear that *no other* repentance would be genuine. Every profession of repentance which is not attended with a change of life is mere hypocrisy. It may farther be remarked that John

neither [l]accuse *any* falsely; and be
content[m] with your [3]wages.
15 And as the people were [4]in
expectation, and all men [5]mused
in their hearts of John, whether
he were the Christ or not;
16 John answered, saying unto
them all, I indeed baptize you with
water; but one mightier than I
cometh, the latchet of whose shoes
I am not worthy to unloose: he
shall baptize you with the Holy
Ghost, and with fire:
17 Whose [n]fan *is* in his hand,
and he will thoroughly purge his
floor, and [o]will gather the wheat
into his garner; but the [p]chaff he
will [q]burn with fire unquenchable.
18 And many other things, in his
exhortation, preached he unto the
people.
19 But[r] Herod the tetrarch, being reproved by him for Herodias
his brother Philip's wife, and for
all the evils which Herod had
done,
20 Added yet this above all, that
he shut up John in prison.
21 Now when all the people were
baptized, [s]it came to pass, that Jesus also being baptized, and praying, the heaven was opened,
22 And the Holy Ghost de-
scended in a bodily shape like a
dove upon him; and a voice came
from heaven, which said, Thou art
my beloved Son; in thee I am well
pleased.

l Ex.23.1; Le.19.11. *m* 1 Ti.6.8. [3] or, *allowance.* [4] or, *in suspense.* [5] or, *reasoned;* or, *debated.* *n* Je.15.7. *o* Mi.4.12; Mat.13.30. *p* Ps.1.4. *q* Ps.21.9; Mar.9.44,48.

r Mat.14.3; Mar.6.17. *s* Mat.3.13,&c.; Jn.1.32,&c.

did not condemn their profession, or say that it was unlawful to be a soldier, or that they must abandon the business in order to be true penitents. It was possible to be a good man and yet a soldier. What was required was that in their profession they should show that they were really upright, and did not commit the crimes which were often practised in that calling. It is lawful to defend one's self, one's family, or one's country, and hence it is lawful to be a soldier. Man everywhere, in all professions, should be a Christian, and then he will do honour to his profession, and his profession, if it is not a direct violation of the law of God, will be honourable.

15. *In expectation.* Expecting the Messiah. Marg. *suspense.* That is, they were not certain whether John was not himself the Messiah. They confidently *expected* his appearing, and there minds were in *suspense,* or they were in a state of doubt whether he had not already come, and whether John was not the Messiah. ¶ *Mused in their hearts of John.* Thought of his character, his preaching, and his success, and anxiously inquired whether he did not do the things which were expected of the Messiah.

16–18. See Notes on Mat. iii. 11, 12.

19, 20. See Notes on Mat. xiv. 1–13. *Added this above all.* To all his former crimes he added this; not implying that this was the *worst* of his acts, but that this was *one* of his deeds, of like character as the others. The event here mentioned did not take place until some time after this, but it is mentioned here to show what was the end of John's preaching, or to *fill out* the account concerning him.

21, 22. See Notes on Mat. iii. 13–17. *Jesus being baptized;* or, Jesus *having been* baptized. This took place *after* the baptism, and not *during* its administration, Mat. iii. 16. ¶ *Praying.* This circumstance is omitted by the other evangelists; and it shows, 1st. That Jesus was in the habit of prayer. 2d. That it is proper to offer up special prayer at the administration of the ordinances of religion. 3d. That it is possible to pray in the midst of a great multitude, yet in secret. The prayer consisted, doubtless, in lifting up the heart silently to God. So *we* may do it anywhere—about our daily toil—in the midst of multitudes, and thus may pray *always.*

22. *In a bodily shape.* This was a real visible appearance, and was doubtless seen by the people. The dove is an emblem of purity and harmlessness, and the form of the dove was assumed on this occasion to signify, probably, that the spirit with which Jesus would be endowed would be one of purity and innocence. The *Holy Spirit,* when he assumes a visible form, assumes that

23 And Jesus himself began to
be about thirty years of age, being
(as was supposed) the [t]son of Joseph, which was *the son* of Heli,
24 Which was *the son* of Matthat,
which was *the son* of Levi, which
was *the son* of Melchi, which was
the son of Janna, which was *the son*
of Joseph,
25 Which was *the son* of Mattathias, which was *the son* of Amos,
which was *the son* of Naum, which
was *the son* of Esli, which was *the*
son of Nagge,
26 Which was *the son* of Maath,
which was *the son* of Mattathias,
which was *the son* of Semei, which
was *the son* of Joseph, which was
the son of Juda,
27 Which was *the son* of Joanna,
which was *the son* of Rhesa, which
was *the son* of Zorobabel, which
was *the son* of Salathiel, which was
the son of Neri,
28 Which was *the son* of Melchi,
which was *the son* of Addi, which
was *the son* of Cosam, which was
the son of Elmodam, which was *the*
son of Er,
29 Which was *the son* of Jose,
which was *the son* of Eliezer, which
was *the son* of Jorim, which was
the son of Matthat, which was *the*
son of Levi,
30 Which was *the son* of Simeon,
which was *the son* of Juda, which
was *the son* of Joseph, which was
the son of Jonan, which was *the son*
of Eliakim,
31 Which was *the son* of Melea,
which was *the son* of Menan, which
was *the son* of Mattatha, which was
the son of [u]Nathan, which was *the*
son of David,
32 Which was *the son* of [v]Jesse,
which was *the son* of Obed, which
was *the son* of Booz, which was *the*
son of Salmon, which was *the son*
of Naasson,
33 Which was *the son* of Amina-
dab, which was *the son* of Aram,
which was *the son* of Esrom, which
was *the son* of Phares, which was
the son of Juda,
34 Which was *the son* of Jacob,
which was *the son* of Isaac, which
was *the son* of [w]Abraham, which
was *the son* of Thara, which was
the son of Nachor,
35 Which was *the son* of Saruch,
which was *the son* of Ragau, which
was *the son* of Phalec, which was
the son of Heber, which was *the son*
of Sala,
36 Which was *the son* of Cainan,
which was *the son* of [x]Arphaxad,
which was *the son* of Sem, which
was *the son* of Noe, which was *the*
son of [y]Lamech,
37 Which was *the son* of Mathu-
sala, which was *the son* of Enoch,
which was *the son* of Jared, which
was *the son* of Maleleel, which was
the son of Cainan,
38 Which was *the son* of Enos,
which was *the son* of Seth, which
was *the son* of Adam, which was
the [z]*son* of God.

t Mat.13.55; Jn.6.42.
u Zec.12.12; 2 Sa.5.14. *v* Ru.4.18,22. *w* Ge.11.24-26. *x* Ge.11.12. *y* Ge.5.25. *z* Ge.1.26; 2.7; Is.64.8; 1 Co.15.45,47.

---

which will be emblematic of the thing to be represented. Thus he assumed the form of *tongues*, to signify the miraculous powers of language with which the apostles would be endowed; the appearance of *fire*, to denote their power, &c., Ac. ii. 3.

23. *Jesus began to be*, &c. This was the age at which the priests entered on their office, Nu. iv. 3, 47; but it is not evident that Jesus had any reference to that in delaying his work to his thirtieth year. He was not subjected to the Levitical law in regard to the priesthood, and it does not appear that prophets and teachers did not commence their work before that age. ¶ *As was supposed.* As was commonly thought, or perhaps being *legally* reckoned as his son.

24–38. See, on this genealogy, the Notes on Mat. i. 1–16.

CHAPTER IV.

1–14. On the temptation of Jesus see Notes on Mat. iv. 1–11.

CHAPTER IV.

AND[a] Jesus, being full of the
Holy Ghost, returned from
Jordan, and was led by the Spirit
into the wilderness,
2 Being forty days tempted of
the devil. And [b]in those days he
did eat nothing: and when they
were ended he afterward hungered.
3 And the devil said unto him,
If thou be the Son of God, command
this stone that it be made
bread.
4 And Jesus answered him, saying,
[c]It is written, that man shall
not live by bread alone, but by
every word of God.
5 And the devil, taking him up
into a high mountain, showed unto
him all the kingdoms of the world
in a moment of time.
6 And the devil said unto him,
All this power will I give thee, and
the glory of them: [d]for that is delivered
unto me; and to whomsoever
I will I give it.
7 If thou, therefore, wilt [1]worship
me, all shall be thine.
8 And Jesus answered and said
unto him, Get thee behind me, Satan:
for it is written, [e]Thou shalt
worship the Lord thy God, and
him only shalt thou serve.
9 And he brought him to Jerusalem,
and set him on a pinnacle
of the temple, and said unto him,
If thou be the Son of God, cast
thyself down from hence:
10 For it is written, [f]He shall
give his angels charge over thee,
to keep thee;
11 And in *their* hands they shall
bear thee up, lest at any time thou
dash thy foot against a stone.
12 And Jesus, answering, said
unto him, It is said, [g]Thou shalt
not tempt the Lord thy God.
13 And when the devil had ended
[h]all the temptation, he departed
from him for a season.
14 And Jesus [i]returned in the
power of the Spirit into Galilee:
and there went out a fame of
him through all the region round
about.
15 And he taught in their synagogues,
being glorified of all.
16 And he came to [k]Nazareth,
where he had been brought up:

a Mat.4.1,&c.; Mar.1.12,&c.; ver.14.
b Ex.34.28; 1 Ki.19.8.
c De.8.3. *d* Jn.12.31; 14.30; Ep.2.2; Re.13.2,7.
1 or, *fall down before me.*
e De.6.13; 10.20. *f* Ps.91.11. *g* De.6.16.
h He.4.15. *i* Jn.4.43; Ac.10.37. *k* Mat.2.23.

2. *Being forty days tempted.* That is, through forty days he was *tried* in various ways by the devil. The temptations, however, which are recorded by Matthew and Luke did not take place until the forty days were *finished.* See Mat. iv. 2, 3. ¶ *He did eat nothing.* He was sustained by the power of God during this season of extraordinary fasting.

13. *Departed for a season.* For a time. From this it appears that our Saviour was *afterward* subjected to temptations by Satan, but no *particular* temptations are recorded after this. From Jn. xiv. 30, it seems that the devil tried or tempted him in the agony in Gethsemane. Comp. Notes on He. xii. 4. It is more than probable, also, that Satan did much to excite the Pharisees and Sadducees to endeavour to *entangle him,* and the priests and rulers to oppose him; yet out of all his temptations God delivered him; and so he will make a way to escape for *all* that are tempted, and will not suffer them to be tempted above that which they are able to bear, 1 Co. x. 13.

14. *In the power of the Spirit.* By the *influence* or direction of the Spirit. ¶ *A fame.* A report. See Matthew iv. 24.

15. *Glorified of all.* Praised by all; or, all were pleased with his instructions, and admired his wisdom.

16. *And, as his custom was, he went,* &c. From this it appears that the Saviour regularly attended the service of the synagogue. In that service the Scriptures of the Old Testament were read, prayers were offered, and the Word of God was explained. See Notes on Mat. iv. 23. There was great corruption in doctrine and practice at that time, but Christ did not on that account

and, as his custom was, [l]he went into the synagogue on the sabbath-day, and stood up for to read.
17 And there was delivered unto him the book of the prophet Esaias. And when he had opened the book, he found the place where it was written,
18 The[m] Spirit of the Lord *is* upon me, because he hath anointed

l Mat.13.54; Jn.18.20; Ac.13.14; 17.2.

m Is.61.1.

---

keep away from the place of public worship. From this we may learn—1st. That it is our duty *regularly* to attend public worship. 2d. That it is better to attend a place of worship which is not entirely pure, or where just such doctrines are not delivered as we would wish, than not attend at all. It is of vast importance that the public worship of God should be maintained; and it is *our* duty to assist in maintaining it, to show by our example that we love it, and to win others also to love it. See He. x. 25. At the same time, this remark should not be construed as enjoining it as our duty to attend where the *true* God is not worshipped, or where he is worshipped by pagan rites and pagan prayers. If, therefore, the Unitarian does not worship the true God, and if the Roman Catholic worships God in a manner forbidden, and offers homage to the *creatures* of God, thus being guilty of idolatry, it cannot be a duty to attend on such a place of worship. ¶ *The synagogue.* See Mat. iv. 23. ¶ *Stood up for to read.* The books of Moses were so divided that they could be read through in the synagogues once in a year. To these were added portions out of the prophets, so that no small part of them was read also once a year. It is not known whether our Saviour read the lesson which was the regular one for that day, though it might seem *probable* that he would not depart from the usual custom. Yet, as the eyes of all were fixed on him; as he deliberately looked out a place; and as the people were evidently surprised at what he did, it seems to be intimated that he selected a lesson which was *not* the regular one for that day. The same ceremonies in regard to conducting public worship which are here described are observed at Jerusalem by the Jews at the present time. Professor Hackett (*Illustrations of Scripture*, p. 232) says: "I attended the Jewish worship at Jerusalem, and was struck with the accordance of the ceremonies with those mentioned in the New Testament. The sacred roll was brought from the chest or closet where it was kept; it was handed by an attendant to the reader; a portion of it was rehearsed; the congregation rose and stood while it was read, whereas the speaker, as well as the others present, sat during the delivery of the address which formed a part of the service."

17. *There was delivered unto him.* By the minister of the synagogue, or the keeper of the sacred books. They were kept in an *ark* or chest, not far from the pulpit, and the minister gave them to whomsoever he chose, to read them publicly. ¶ *The book.* The volume contained the prophecy of Isaiah. It would seem, from this, that the books were kept separate, and not united into one as with us. ¶ *When he had opened the book.* Literally, when he had *unrolled* the book. Books, among the ancients, were written on parchments or vellum that is, skins of beasts, and were *rolled* together on two rollers, beginning at each end, so that while reading they rolled *off* from one to the other. Different forms of books were indeed used, but this was the most common. When used the reader unrolled the MS. as far as the place which he wished to find, and kept before him just so much as he would read. When the roller was done with, it was carefully deposited in a case. ¶ *The place where it was written.* Is. lxi. 1, 2.

18. *The Spirit of the Lord* is *upon me.* Or, I speak by divine appointment. I am divinely inspired to speak. There can be no doubt that the passage in Isaiah had a principal reference to the Messiah. Our Saviour directly applies it to himself, and it is not easily applicable to any other prophet. Its *first* application might have been to the restoration of the Jews from Babylon; but the language of prophecy is often applicable to two similar events, and the secondary event is often the most important. In this case the prophet uses most striking poetic images to depict the return from Babylon, but the same images also describe the appro-

me to preach the gospel to the poor; he hath sent me to [n]heal the broken-hearted, to preach deliverance to the captives, and [o]recovering of sight to the blind, to set at liberty [p]them that are bruised,

19 To preach the [q]acceptable year of the Lord.

n 2 Ch.34.27; Ps.34.18; 51.17; 147.3; Is.57.15. *o* Ps.146.8; Is.29.18. *p* Is.42.3; Mat.12.20. *q* Is.61.2; 63.4.

priate work of the Son of God. ¶ *Hath anointed me.* Anciently kings and prophets and the high-priest were set apart to their work by anointing with oil, 1 Ki. xix. 15, 16; Ex. xxix. 7; 1 Sa. ix. 16, &c. This oil or ointment was made of various substances, and it was forbidden to imitate it, Ex. xxx. 34–38. Hence those who were set apart to the work of God as king, prophet, or priest, were called the Lord's anointed, 1 Sa. xvi. 6; Ps. lxxxiv. 9; Is. xlv. 1. Hence the Son of God is called the *Messiah*, a Hebrew word signifying the *Anointed*, or the *Christ*, a Greek word signifying the same thing. And by his being *anointed* is not meant that he was *literally* anointed, for he was never set apart in that manner, but that *God had set him apart* for this work; that *he* had constituted or appointed him to be the prophet, priest, and king of his people. See Notes on Mat. i. 1. ¶ *To preach the gospel to the poor.* The English word *gospel* is derived from two words—*God* or *good*, and *spell*, an old Saxon word meaning *history*, *relation*, *narration*, *word*, or *speech*, and the word therefore means *a good communication* or *message*. This corresponds exactly with the meaning of the Greek word—*a good* or *joyful message*—*glad tidings*. By the *poor* are meant all those who are destitute of the comforts of this life, and who therefore may be more readily disposed to seek treasures in heaven; all those who are sensible of their sins, or are poor in spirit (Mat. v. 3); and all the *miserable* and the afflicted, Is. lviii. 7. Our Saviour gave it as one proof that he was the Messiah, or was from God, that he preached to *the poor*, Mat. xi. 5. The Pharisees and Sadducees despised the poor; ancient philosophers neglected them; but the gospel seeks to bless them—to give comfort where it is felt to be needed, and where it will be received with gratitude. Riches fill the mind with pride, with self-complacency, and with a feeling that the gospel is not needed. The poor *feel* their need of some sources of comfort that the world cannot give, and accordingly our Saviour met with his greatest success among the poor; and there also, *since*, the gospel has shed its richest blessings and its purest joys. It is also one proof that the gospel is true. If it had been of *men*, it would have sought the rich and mighty; but it pours contempt on all human greatness, and seeks, like God, to do good to those whom the world overlooks or despises. See Notes on 1 Co. i. 26. ¶ *To heal the broken-hearted.* To console those who are deeply afflicted, or whose hearts are *broken* by external calamities or by a sense of their sinfulness. ¶ *Deliverance to the captives.* This is a figure originally applicable to those who were in captivity in Babylon. They were miserable. To grant deliverance to *them* and restore them to their country—to grant deliverance to those who are in prison and restore them to their families—to give liberty to the slave and restore him to freedom, was to confer the highest benefit and impart the richest favour. In this manner the gospel imparts favour. It does not, indeed, *literally* open the doors of prisons, but it releases the *mind* captive under sin; it gives comfort to the prisoner, and it will finally open all prison doors and break off all the chains of slavery, and, by preventing *crime*, prevent also the sufferings that are the consequence of crime. ¶ *Sight to the blind.* This was often literally fulfilled, Mat. xi. 5; Jn. ix. 11; Mat. ix. 30, &c. ¶ *To set at liberty them that are bruised.* The word *bruised*, here, evidently has the same *general* signification as *broken-hearted* or the contrite. It means those who are *pressed down* by great calamity, or whose hearts are *pressed* or *bruised* by the consciousness of sin. To set them *at liberty* is the same as to free them from this pressure, or to give them consolation.

19. *To preach the acceptable year of the Lord.* The time when God is willing to accept of men, or to receive sinners coming to him. The gospel assures us that the guilty *may* return, and that God will graciously receive them. There is, perhaps, here, an allusion to the year of jubilee—the fiftieth year, when the trumpet was blown, and through the whole land proclama-

20 And he closed the book, and he gave *it* again to the minister, and sat down. And the eyes of all them that were in the synagogue were fastened on him.

21 And he began to say unto them, This day is this scripture fulfilled in your ears.

22 And all bare him witness, and wondered at the [r]gracious words which proceeded out of his mouth. And they said, [s]Is not this Joseph's son?

23 And he said unto them, Ye will surely say unto me this proverb, Physician, heal thyself: what-

r Ps.45.2; Is.50.4; Mat.13.54; Mar.6.2; ch.2.47.
s Jn.6.42.

---

tion was made of the liberty of Hebrew slaves, of the remission of debts, and of the restoration of possessions to their original families, Le. xxv. 8–13. The phrase "the acceptable year" means the time when it would be acceptable to God to proclaim such a message, or *agreeable* to him—to wit, under the gospel.

20. *And he closed the book.* That is, he rolled it up again. See Notes on ver. 17. ¶ *And he gave* it *again to the minister.* That is, to the one in the synagogue who had charge of the books. The word means *servant*, and the office was not much unlike that of a sexton now. It was his duty, among other things, to take charge of the books, to hand them to the reader of the law, and then return them to their place. ¶ *And sat down.* This was usual in speaking in their synagogues. See Notes on Mat. v. 1. ¶ *Were fastened on him.* Were intently fixed on him, waiting to see what explanation he would give of the words.

21. *This scripture.* This *writing*, or this *part* of the Scriptures. ¶ *Fulfilled.* It is coming to pass; the thing originally intended by it is about to be accomplished. ¶ *In your ears.* In your *hearing;* or you *hear*, in my preaching, the fulfilment of this prophecy. It is probable that he said much *more* than is here recorded, but Luke has preserved only the *substance* of his discourse. This was the *amount* or *sum* of his sermon, or his explanation of the passage, that it was now receiving its accomplishment.

22. *All bare him witness.* All were witnesses of the power and truth of what he said. Their reason and conscience approved of it, and they were constrained to admit the force and propriety of it, and on this account they wondered. ¶ *They wondered.* They were struck with the truth and force of his words; and especially when they remembered that he was a native of their own place, and that they had been long acquainted with him, and that he should *now* claim to be the Messiah, and give so much evidence that he *was* the Christ. ¶ *The gracious words.* The words of grace or favour; the kind, affectionate, and tender exposition of the words, and explanation of the design of his coming, and the nature of the plan of redemption. It was so different from the harsh and unfeeling mode of the Pharisees; so different from all their expectations respecting the Messiah, who they supposed to be a prince and a bloody conqueror, that they were filled with astonishment and awe.

23. *Physician, heal thyself.* This proverb was probably in common use at that time. The meaning is this: Suppose that a man should attempt to heal another when he was himself diseased in the same manner; it would be natural to ask him *first* to cure himself, and thus to render it manifest that he was worthy of confidence. The connection of this proverb, here, is this: "You profess to be the Messiah. You have wrought miracles at Capernaum. You profess to be able to deliver us from our maladies, our sins, our afflictions. Show that you have the power, that you are worthy of our confidence, by working miracles *here*, as you profess to have done at Capernaum." It does not refer, therefore, to any purification of his own, or imply any reflection on him for setting up to teach them. It was only a demand that he would show the proper evidence *by miracles* why they should trust in him, and he proceeds to show them why he would not give them this evidence. ¶ *Whatsoever we have heard done.* Whatsoever we have heard that thou hast done. It would seem, from this, that Christ had *before* this wrought miracles in Capernaum, though the evangelist has not recorded them. ¶ *In Capernaum.* Capernaum was on the north-west corner of the Sea of Tiberias, and was not far from Nazareth.

soever we have heard [t]done in Capernaum, do also here in thy country.
24 And he said, Verily I say unto you, [u]No prophet is accepted in his own country.
25 But I tell you of a truth, Many[v] widows were in Israel in the days of Elias, when [w]the heaven was shut up three years and six months, when great famine was throughout all the land;
26 But unto none of them was Elias sent, save unto Sarepta, *a city* of Sidon, unto a woman *that was* a widow.
27 And[x] many lepers were in Israel in the time of Eliseus the prophet, and none of them was cleansed saving Naaman the Syrian.
28 And all they in the synagogue, when they heard these things, were filled with wrath,

t Mat.4.13; 11.23,&c. *u* Mat.13.57; Jn.4.44. *v* 1 Ki.17.9. *w* Ja.5.17. *x* 2 Ki.5.14.

It is not improbable that some of those who then heard him might have been present and witnessed some of his miracles at Capernaum. See Notes on Mat. iv. 13.

24. *No prophet is accepted.* Has honour, or is acknowledged as a prophet. See Notes on Mat. xiii. 57.

25. *Of a truth.* Truly, and therefore worthy of your credit. He calls attention to two cases where *acknowledged* prophets had so little honour in their own nation that they bestowed their favours on foreigners. So, says he, such is the want of faith in my own country, that I shall work no miracles here, but shall give the evidence of my divine mission to others. ¶ *In Israel.* In the land of Israel, or Judea. It was therefore the more remarkable, since there were so many in his own country whom he *might* have helped, that the prophet should have gone to a heathen city and aided a poor widow there. ¶ *The days of Elias.* The days of Elijah. See the account of this in 1 Ki. xvii. 8–24. ¶ *Three years and six months.* From 1 Ki. xviii. 1, 45, it would seem that the rain fell on the *third year*—that is, at the *end* of the third year after the rain had ceased to fall at the usual time. There were two seasons of the year when rains fell in Judea—in October and April, called the *early* and *latter* rain; consequently there was an interval between them of six months. To the three years, therefore, when rain was withheld *at the usual times*, are to be added the previous six months, when no rain fell as a matter of course, and consequently three years *and six months* elapsed without rain. ¶ *A great famine.* A great want of food, from long-continued and distressing drought.

26. *Save unto Sarepta.* Sarepta was a town between Tyre and Sidon, near the Mediterranean Sea. It was not a *Jewish* city, but a Sidonian, and therefore a *Gentile* town. The word "save" in this verse does not express the meaning of the original. It would seem to imply that the city was Jewish. The meaning of the verse is this: "He was sent to none of the widows in Israel. He was not sent except to Sarepta, to a woman that was a *Sidonian.*" Dr. Thomson (*The Land and the Book*, vol. i. p. 232–236) regards Sarepta as the modern Sarafend. He says that the ruins have been frequently dug over for stone to build the barracks at Beirout, and that the broken columns, marble slabs, sarcophagi, and other ruins indicate that it was once a flourishing city. A large town was built there in the time of the Crusades.

27. *Many lepers.* For an account of the leprosy see Notes on Mat. viii. 1. ¶ *Time of Eliseus.* Time of *Elisha.* The word *Eliseus* is the Greek way of writing the word Elisha, as Elias is of Elijah. ¶ *Saving Naaman the Syrian.* The account of his cure is contained in 2 Ki. v.

28. *Filled with wrath.* They were enraged, probably, for the following reasons: 1st. They saw that the cases applied to themselves, because they would not receive the miraculous evidences of his mission. 2d. That he would direct his attention to others, and not to them. 3d. That the *Gentiles* were objects of compassion with God, and that God often showed more favour to a *single* Gentile than to multitudes of Jews in the same circumstances. 4th. That they might be *worse* than the Gentiles. And, 5th. That it was a part of his design to preach the gospel to the

29 And rose up, and thrust him
out of the city, and led him unto
the [2]brow of the hill whereon their
city was built,[y]that they might cast
him down headlong.
30 But he, [z]passing through the
midst of them, went his way,
31 And came down to Capernaum, a city of Galilee, and taught
them on the sabbath-days.
32 And they were astonished at
his doctrine; [a]for his word was
with power.
33 And[b] in the synagogue there
was a man which had a spirit of
an unclean devil, and cried out
with a loud voice,
34 Saying, [3]Let *us* alone; [c]what
have we to do with thee, *thou* Jesus
of Nazareth? art thou come to destroy us? [d]I know thee who thou
art; [e]the Holy One of God.
35 And Jesus rebuked him, saying, Hold thy peace, and come out
of him. And when the devil had
thrown him in the midst, he came
out of him, and hurt him not.
36 And they were all amazed,
and spake among themselves, saying, What a word *is* this! for with
authority and power he commandeth the unclean spirits, [f]and
they come out.
37 And the fame of him went
out into every place of the country
round about.
38 And he arose out of the
synagogue, and entered into Simon's house. And[g] Simon's wife's
mother was taken with a great
fever; and they besought him for
her.
39 And he stood over her, and
rebuked the fever, and it left her;
and immediately she arose and
ministered unto them.
40 Now when the sun was setting, all they that had any sick
with divers diseases brought them
unto him; and he laid his hands
on every one of them, and healed
them.
41 And devils also came out of
many, crying out, and saying, Thou
art Christ the Son of God. And
he, rebuking *them*, suffered them
not [4]to speak; for they knew that
he was Christ.

2 or, *edge*. *y* Ps.37.14,32,33. *z* Jn.8.59; 10.39. *a* Je.23.29; Mat.7.28,29; Tit.2.15; He.4.12. *b* Mar.1.23. 3 or, *Away*. *c* Ja.2.19. *d* ver.41. *e* Ps.16.10; Da.9.24; ch.1.35; Ac.3.14.

f 1 Pe.3.22. *g* Mat.8.14,&c.; Mar.1.29,&c. 4 or, *to say that they knew him to be Christ.*

Gentiles, and not confine his labours to them only. On these accounts their favour was soon turned to wrath, and the whole transaction shows us—1st. That popular applause is of little value. 2d. That the slightest circumstances may soon turn the warmest professed friendship to hatred. And, 3d. That men are exceedingly unreasonable in being unwilling to hear the truth and profit by it.

29. *The brow of the hill whereon*, &c. The region in which Nazareth was is hilly, though Nazareth was situated *between* two hills, or in a vale among mountains. The place to which they led the Saviour is still shown, and is called the *Mount of Precipitation*. It is at a short distance to the *south* of Nazareth. See Notes on Mat. ii. 23. ¶ *Cast him down.* This was the effect of a popular tumult. They had no legal right to take life on any occasion, and least of all in this furious and irregular manner. The whole transaction shows—1st. That the character given of the Galileans elsewhere as being peculiarly wicked was a just one. 2d. To what extremities the wickedness of the heart will lead men when it is acted out. And, 3d. That men are opposed to the truth, and that they would do *anything*, if not restrained, to manifest their opposition.

30. *Passing through the midst of them, went his way.* This escape was very remarkable. It is remarkable that he should escape out of their hands when their very object was to destroy him, and that he should escape in so peaceful a manner, without violence or conflict. A similar case is recorded in Jn. viii. 59. There are but two ways of accounting for this: 1st. That *other Nazarenes*, who had not been present in the synagogue, heard what was doing and came to rescue him, and in the contest that rose between the two par-

42 And when it was day, he departed, and went into a desert place: and the people sought him, and came unto him, and stayed him, that he should not depart from them.

43 And he said unto them, I must preach the kingdom of God to other cities also; for [h]therefore am I sent.

44 And he preached in the synagogues of Galilee.

h Mar.1.38.

CHAPTER V.

AND[a] it came to pass, that, as the people pressed upon him to hear the word of God, he stood by the lake of Gennesaret,

2 And saw two ships standing by the lake; but the fishermen

a Mat.4.18,&c.; Mar.1.16,&c.

ties Jesus silently escaped. 2d. More probably that Jesus by divine power, by the force of a word or look, stilled their passions, arrested their purposes, and passed silently through them. That he *had* such a power over the spirits of men we learn from the occurrence in Gethsemane, when he said, "I am he; and they went backward and fell to the ground," Jn. xviii. 6.

31–44. See this explained in the Notes on Mar. i. 21–39.

CHAPTER V.

1. *The people pressed upon him.* Multitudes came to hear. There were times in the life of our Saviour when thousands were anxious to hear him, and when many, as we have no reason to doubt, became his true followers. Indeed, it is not possible to tell what *might* have been his success, had not the Pharisees and scribes, and those who were in office, opposed him, and taken measures to draw the people away from his ministry; *for the common people heard him gladly*, Mar. xii. 37. ¶ *The Lake of Gennesaret.* Called also the Sea of Galilee and the Sea of Tiberias. "Gennesaret was the more ancient name of the lake, taken from a small territory or plain of that name on its western borders. See Nu. xxxiv. 11; Jos. xix. 35, where, after the Hebrew orthography, it is called Chinnereth" (Owen). The plain lying between Capernaum and Tiberias is said by Dr. Thomson (*The Land and the Book*, vol. i. p. 536) to be a little longer than thirty, and not quite twenty furlongs in breadth. It is described by Josephus as being, in his time, universally fertile. "Its nature is wonderful as well as its beauty. Its soil is so fruitful that all sorts of trees can grow upon it, and the inhabitants accordingly plant all sorts of trees there; for the temperature of the air is so well mixed that it agrees very well with those several sorts; particularly walnuts, which require the coldest air, flourish there in vast plenty. One may call this the ambition of Nature, where it forces those plants which are naturally enemies to one another to agree together. It is a happy conjunction of the seasons, as if every one laid claim to this country; for it not only nourishes different sorts of autumnal fruits beyond men's expectations, but preserves them a great while. It supplies men with the principal fruits; with grapes and figs continually during ten months of the year, and the rest of the fruits, as they become ripe, through the whole year; for, besides the good temperature of the air, it is also watered from a most fertile fountain." Dr. Thomson describes it now as "preeminently fruitful in thorns." This was the region of the early toils of our Redeemer. Here he performed some of his first and most amazing miracles; here he selected his disciples; and here, on the shores of this little and retired lake, among people of poverty and inured to the privations of fishermen, he laid the foundation of a religion which is yet to spread through all the world, and which *has* already blessed millions of guilty and miserable men, and translated them to heaven.

2. *Two ships.* The *ships* used on so small a lake were probably no more than fishing-boats without decks, and easily drawn up on the beach. Josephus says there were 230 of them on the lake, attended by four or five men each. That they were small is also clear from the account commonly given of them. A single large draught of fishes endangered them and came near sinking them. ¶ *Standing by the lake.* Anchored by the lake, or drawn up upon the beach.

3. *Which was Simon's.* Simon Peter's. ¶ *Prayed him.* Asked him. ¶ *He sat*

were gone out of them, and were washing *their* nets.

3 And he entered into one of the ships, which was Simon's, and prayed him that he would thrust out a little from the land. And he sat down, and taught the people out of the ship.

4 Now when he had left speaking, he said unto Simon, [b]Launch out into the deep, and let down your nets for a draught.

5 And Simon, answering, said unto him, [c]Master, we have toiled all the night and have taken nothing: nevertheless, at thy word I will let down the net.

6 And[d] when they had this done, they inclosed a great multitude of fishes: and their net brake.

7 And they beckoned unto *their* partners, which were in the other ship, that they should come and [e]help them. And they came, and

b Jh.21.6.

c Ps.127.1,2; Eze.37.11,12. d Ec.11.6; Ga.6.9. e Ex.23.5; Ga.6.2; Pr.18.24.

down. This was the common posture of Jewish teachers. They seldom or never spoke to the people *standing*. Comp. Mat. v. 1. It may be somewhat difficult to conceive why Jesus should go into a boat and put off from the shore in order to speak to the multitude; but it is probable that this was a small bay or cove, and that when he was *in* the boat, the people on the shore stood round him in the form of an amphitheatre. It is not improbable that the lake was still; that scarcely a breeze passed over it; that all was silence on the shore, and that there was nothing to disturb his voice. In such a situation he could be heard by multitudes; and no spectacle could be more sublime than that of the Son of God—the Redeemer of the world—thus speaking from the bosom of a placid lake—the emblem of the peaceful influence of his own doctrines—to the poor, the ignorant, and the attentive multitudes assembled on the shore. Oh how much *more* effect may we suppose the gospel would have in such circumstances, than when proclaimed among the proud, the gay, the honoured, even when assembled in the most splendid edifice that wealth and art could finish!

4. *Launch out.* Go out with your vessels. ¶ *Into the deep.* Into the sea; at a distance from the shore. ¶ *For a draught.* A draught of fish; or let down your nets for the *taking* of fish.

5. *Master.* This is the first time that the word here translated *Master* occurs in the New Testament, and it is used only by Luke. The other evangelists call him Rabbi, or Lord. The word here used means a *prefect*, or one placed *over* others, and hence it comes to mean *teacher* or *guide.* ¶ *At thy word.* At thy command. Though it seemed so improbable that they would take anything after having in vain toiled all night, yet he was willing to trust the *word* of Jesus and make the trial. This was a remarkable instance of *faith.* Peter, as it appears, knew little then of Jesus. He was not then a chosen apostle. Jesus came to these fishermen almost a stranger and unknown, and yet at his command Peter resolved to make another trial, and go once more out into the deep. Oh, if *all* would as readily obey him, all would be in like manner blessed. If sinners would thus obey him, they would find *all* his promises sure. He never disappoints. He asks only that we have *confidence* in him, and he will give to us every needful blessing.

6. *Their net brake.* Or their net *began* to break, or was *about* to break. This is all that is implied in the Greek word. If their nets had actually *broken*, as our English word seems to suppose, the fish would have escaped; but no more is meant than that there was such a multitude of fishes that their net was *on the point* of being rent asunder.

7. *They beckoned.* They gave signs. Perhaps they were at a considerable distance, so that they could not be easily heard. ¶ Their *partners.* James and John. See ver. 10. The following remarks of Dr. Thomson (*The Land and the Book*, vol. ii. p. 80, 81) will furnish a good illustration of this passage. After describing the mode of fishing with the "hand-net" and the "drag-net," he adds: "Again, there is the bag-net and basket-net, of various kinds, which are so constructed and worked as to inclose the fish out in deep water. I have seen them of almost every conceivable size and pattern. It was with some one of this sort,

filled both the ships, so that they
began to sink.
8 When Simon Peter saw *it*, [f]he
fell down at Jesus' knees, saying,
Depart from me; for I am a sinful
man, O Lord.
9 For he was astonished, and
all that were with him, at the
draught of the [g]fishes which they
had taken;
10 And so *was* also James and
John, the sons of Zebedee, which
were partners with Simon. And
Jesus said unto Simon, Fear not;
from henceforth thou shalt catch
men.
11 And when they had brought
their ships to land, they [h]forsook
all and followed him.
12 And[i] it came to pass, when

f Ju.13.22; 2 Sa.6.9; 1 Ki.17.18; Is.6.5. *g* Ps.8.6,8.
h Mat.4.20; 19.27; Phi.3.7,8.
i Mat.8.2,&c.; Mar.1.40,&c.

I suppose, that Simon had toiled all night without catching anything, but which, when let down at the command of Jesus, inclosed so great a multitude that the net brake, and they filled two ships with the fish until they began to sink. Peter here speaks of toiling all night; and there are certain kinds of fishing always carried on at night. It is a beautiful sight. With blazing torch the boat glides over the flashing sea, and the men stand gazing keenly into it until their prey is sighted, when, quick as lightning, they fling their net or fly their spear; and often you see the tired fishermen come sullenly into harbour in the morning, having toiled all night in vain. Indeed, every kind of fishing is uncertain. A dozen times the angler jerks out a naked hook; the hand-net closes down on nothing; the drag-net brings in only weeds; the bag comes up empty. And then again, every throw is successful—every net is full; and frequently without any other apparent reason than that of throwing it on the right side of the ship instead of the left, as it happened to the disciples here at Tiberias."

8. *When Simon Peter saw* it. Saw the great amount of fishes; the remarkable success of letting down the net. ¶ *He fell down at Jesus' knees.* This was a common posture of *supplication.* He had no doubt now of the power and knowledge of Jesus. In amazement, wonder, and gratitude, and not doubting that he was in the presence of some divine being, he prostrated himself to the earth, trembling and afraid. So should sinful men *always* throw themselves at the feet of Jesus at the proofs of his power; so should they humble themselves before him at the manifestations of his goodness. ¶ *Depart from me.* This is an expression of Peter's humility, and of his consciousness of his unworthiness. It was not from want of love to Jesus; it did not show that he would not be pleased with his favour and presence; but it was the result of being convinced that Jesus was a messenger from God—a high and holy being; and he felt that *he* was unworthy to be in his presence. In his deep consciousness of sin, therefore, he requested that Jesus would depart from him and his little vessel. Peter's feeling was not unnatural, though it was not proper to request Jesus to leave him. It was an involuntary, sudden request, and arose from ignorance of the character of Jesus. We *are* not worthy to be with him, to be reckoned among his friends, or to dwell in heaven with him; but he came to seek the lost and to save the impure. He graciously condescends to dwell with those who are humble and contrite, though they are conscious that they are not worthy of his presence; and we may therefore come boldly to him, and ask him to receive us to his home—to an eternal dwelling with him in the heavens.

10. *Fear not.* He calmed their fears. With mildness and tenderness he stilled all their troubled feelings, and to their surprise announced that henceforward they should be appointed as heralds of salvation. ¶ *From henceforth.* Hereafter. ¶ *Shalt catch men.* Thou shalt be a minister of the gospel, and thy business shall be to win men to the truth that they may be saved.

11. *Forsook all.* It was not *much* that they left—a couple of small boats and their nets; but it was all they had, even all their living. But this showed their love of Jesus, and their willingness to deny themselves, as *really* as if they had forsaken palaces and gold. All that Jesus asks is that we should leave *all* we have for him; that we should love him *more* than we do whatever friends

he was in a certain city, behold, a
man full of leprosy; who, seeing
Jesus, fell on *his* face, and besought
him, saying, Lord, if thou wilt, thou
canst make me clean.
13 And he put forth *his* hand,
and touched him, saying, [k]I will;
be thou clean. And immediately
the leprosy departed from him.
14 And he charged him to tell
no man; but go and show thyself
to the priest, and offer for thy
cleansing, according as [l]Moses commanded,
for a testimony unto
them.
15 But so much the more went
there a fame abroad of him: [m]and
great multitudes came together, to
hear, and to be healed by him of
their infirmities.
16 And[n] he withdrew himself
into the wilderness and prayed.
17 And it came to pass on a certain
day, as he was teaching, [o]that
there were Pharisees and doctors
of the law sitting by, which were
come out of every town of Galilee,
and Judea, and Jerusalem; and
the power of the Lord was *present*
to heal them.
18 And,[p] behold, men brought in
a bed a man which was taken with
a palsy; and they sought *means* to
bring him in, and to lay *him* before
him.
19 And when they could not find
by what *way* they might bring him
in because of the multitude, they
went upon the house-top, and let
him down through the tiling, with
his couch, into the midst before
Jesus.
20 And when he saw their faith,
he said unto him, Man, thy sins
are forgiven thee.
21 And the scribes and the Pharisees
began to reason, saying, Who
is this which speaketh blasphemies?
Who can [q]forgive sins but
God alone?
22 But when Jesus perceived
their thoughts, he, answering, said
unto them, What reason ye in your
hearts?
23 Whether is easier to say, Thy
sins be forgiven thee, or to say,
Rise up and walk?
24 But that ye may know that
the Son of man hath power upon
earth to forgive sins, (he said unto
the sick of the palsy,) I say unto
thee, Arise, and [r]take up thy couch,
and go unto thine house.
25 And immediately he rose up
before them, and took up that
whereon he lay, and departed to
his own house, glorifying God.
26 And they were all amazed,
and [s]they glorified God, and [t]were
filled with fear, saying, We have
seen strange things to-day.
27 And[u] after these things he
went forth, and saw a publican,
named Levi, sitting at the receipt
of custom: and he said unto him,
Follow me.
28 And he left all, rose up, and
followed him.
29 And Levi made him a great
feast in his own house: and [v]there

k 2 Ki.5.10,14. *l* Le.14.4,&c. *m* Mat.4.25; Mar.3.7; Jn.6.2. *n* Mat.14.23; Mar.6.46. *o* Jn.3.21. *p* Mat.9.2,&c.; Mar.2.3,&c.

q Ps.32.5; 103.3; 130.4; Is.1.18; 43.25. *r* Jn.5.8,12. *s* Ac.4.21; Ga.1.24. *t* ver.8. *u* Mat.9.9,&c.; Mar.2.13. *v* ch.15.1,&c.

---

or property we may possess, and be willing to give them all up when he requires it.

12–16. See Notes on Mat. viii. 2–4.

17–26. See this passage explained in the Notes on Mat. ix. 1–7.

17. *On a certain day.* The time and place are not particularly mentioned here, but from Mat. ix. 1 it seems it was at Capernaum.

19. *The tiling.* See Notes on Mat. ix. 1–7.

27–32. See Notes on Mat. ix. 9–13.

29. *Made him a great feast.* This circumstance *Matthew,* or *Levi* as he is here called, has omitted in his own gospel. This fact shows how little inclined the evangelists are to say anything in favour of themselves or to praise themselves. True religion does

was a great company of publicans and of others that sat down with them.

30 But their scribes and Pharisees murmured against his disciples, saying, Why do ye eat and drink with publicans and sinners?

31 And Jesus, answering, said unto them, They that are whole need not a [w]physician; but they that are sick.

32 I came not to call the righteous but [x]sinners to repentance.

33 And they said unto him, Why do the disciples of John fast often, and make prayers, and likewise *the disciples* of the Pharisees; [y]but thine eat and drink?

34 And he said unto them, Can ye make the children of the bridechamber fast while the bridegroom is with them?

35 But the days will come when the bridegroom shall be taken away from them, and then shall they [z]fast in those days.

36 And[a] he spake also a parable unto them: No man putteth a piece of a new garment upon an old; if otherwise, then both the new maketh a rent, and the piece that was *taken* out of the new [b]agreeth not with the old.

37 And no man putteth new wine into old bottles; else the new wine will burst the bottles and be spilled, and the bottles shall perish.

38 But new wine must be put into new bottles, and both are preserved.

w Je.8.22.
x Lu.15.7,10; 1 Co.6.9–11; 1 Ti.1.15; 2 Pe.3.9.
y ch.7.34,35.
z Is.22.12. *a* Mat.9.16,17; Mar.2.21,22.
b Le.19.19; De.22.11; 2 Co.6.16.

---

not seek to commend itself, or to speak of what it does, even when it is done for the Son of God. It seeks retirement; it delights rather in the *consciousness* of doing well than in its being known; and it leaves its good deeds to be spoken of, if spoken of at all, by others. This is agreeable to the direction of Solomon (Pr. xxvii. 2): "Let another man praise thee, and not thine own mouth." This feast was made expressly for our Lord, and was attended by many publicans, probably men of wicked character; and it is not improbable that Matthew got them together for the purpose of bringing them into contact with our Lord to do them good. Our Saviour did not refuse to go, and to go, too, at the risk of being accused of being a gluttonous man and a winebibber, a friend of publicans and sinners, Mat. xi. 19. But his motives were pure. In the thing itself there was no harm. It afforded an opportunity of doing good, and we have no reason to doubt that the opportunity was improved by the Lord Jesus. Happy would it be if all the *great feasts* that are made were made in honour of our Lord; happy if *he* would be a welcome guest there; and happy if ministers and pious people who attend them demeaned themselves as the Lord Jesus did, and they were always made the means of advancing his kingdom. But, alas! there are few places where our Lord would be *so unwelcome* as at great feasts, and few places that serve so much to render the mind gross, dissipated, and irreligious.

33–39. See this passage illustrated in the Notes on Mat. ix. 14–17.

39. *Having drunk old* wine, &c. Wine increases its strength and flavour, and its mildness and mellowness, by age, and the old is therefore preferable. They who had tasted such mild and mellow wine would not readily drink the comparatively sour and astringent juice of the grape as it came from the press. The meaning of this proverb in this place seems to be this: You Pharisees wish to draw my disciples to the *austere* and *rigid* duties of the ceremonial law—to fasting and painful rites; but they have come under a milder system. They have tasted the gentle and tender blessings of the gospel; they have no *relish* for your stern and harsh requirements. To insist *now* on their observing them would be like telling a man who had tasted of good, ripe, and mild wine to partake of that which is sour and unpalatable. At the proper time all the sterner duties of religion will be properly regarded; but *at present*, to teach them to fast when they see *no occasion* for it—when they are full of joy at the presence of their

39 No man, also, having drunk
old *wine*, straightway desireth new;
for he saith, [z]The old is better.

CHAPTER VI.

AND[a] it came to pass on the
second sabbath after the first,
that he went through the corn-
fields, and his disciples plucked
the ears of corn, and did eat, rubbing *them* in *their* hands.
2 And certain of the Pharisees
said unto them, Why do ye [b]that
which is not lawful to do on the
sabbath-days?
3 And Jesus answering them,
said, Have ye not read so much as
this, [c]what David did when himself was an hungered, and they
which were with him;
4 How he went into the house
of God, and did take and eat the
shew-bread, and gave also to them
that were with him; [d]which it is
not lawful to eat, but for the
priests alone?
5 And he said unto them, That
the Son of man is Lord also of the
sabbath.
6 And[e] it came to pass also on
another sabbath, that he entered
into the synagogue and taught;
and there was a man whose right
hand was withered.
7 And the scribes and Pharisees
watched him, whether he would

z Je.6.16. a Mat.12.1,&c.; Mar.2.23,&c. b Ex.20.10; Is.58.13. c 1 Sa.21.6. d Le.24.9. e Mat.12.10,&c.; Mar.3.1,&c.; ch.13.14; 14.3.

Master—would be like putting a piece of new cloth on an old garment, or new wine into old bottles, or drinking unpleasant wine after one had tasted that which was pleasanter. It would be ill-timed, inappropriate, and incongruous.

CHAPTER VI.

1–11. See this passage explained in the Notes on Mat. xii. 1–13.

1. *Second sabbath after the first.* See Notes on Mat. xii. 1. This phrase has given great perplexity to commentators. A *literal* translation would be, "on the Sabbath called *second first*," or second first Sabbath. The word occurs nowhere else. It is therefore exceedingly difficult of interpretation. The most natural and easy explanation is that proposed by Scaliger. The *second* day of the Passover was a great festival, on which the wave-sheaf was offered, Le. xxiii. 11. From *that day* they reckoned *seven weeks*, or seven *Sabbaths*, to the day of Pentecost. The *first* Sabbath after that *second day* was called the *second first*, or the *first* from the second day of the feast. The *second* Sabbath was called the *second second*, or the second Sabbath from the second day of the feast; the third the *third second*, &c. *This* day, therefore, on which the Saviour went through the fields, was the first Sabbath that occurred after the second day of the feast. ¶ *Rubbing* them *in* their *hands*. The word *corn* here means wheat or barley, and not maize, as in America. They *rubbed* it in their hands to separate the grain from the chaff. This was common and allowable. Dr. Thomson (*The Land and the Book*, vol. ii. p. 510, 511) says: "I have often seen my muleteers, as we passed along the wheat-fields, pluck off ears, rub them in their hands, and eat the grains, unroasted, just as the apostles are said to have done. This also is allowable. The Pharisees did not object to the thing itself, only to the time when it was done. They said it was not lawful to do this on the Sabbath-day. It was work forbidden by those who, through their traditions, had made man for the Sabbath, not the Sabbath for man." So Professor Hackett (*Illustrations of Scripture*, p. 176, 177) says: "The incident of plucking the ears of wheat, rubbing out the kernels in their hands, and eating them (Lu. vi. 1), is one which the traveller sees often at present who is in Palestine at the time of the gathering of the harvest. Dr. Robinson relates the following case: 'Our Arabs were an hungered, and, going into the fields, they plucked the ears of corn and did eat, rubbing them in their hands. On being questioned, they said this was an old custom, and no one would speak against it; they were supposed to be hungry, and it was allowed as a charity.'* The Pharisees complained of the disciples for violat-

* *Biblical Researches*, vol. ii. p. 192.

heal [f]on the sabbath-day, that they
might find an accusation against
him.
8 But he [g]knew their thoughts,
and said to the man which had
the withered hand, Rise up, and
stand forth in the midst. And he
arose, and stood forth.
9 Then Jesus said unto them, I
will ask you one thing: [h]Is it lawful on the sabbath-days to do
good, or to do evil? to save life,
or to destroy *it?*

f Jn.9.16. *g* Job 42.2. *h* Ex.20.10; ch.14.3.

10 And[i] looking round about
upon them all, he said unto the
man, Stretch forth thy hand. And
he did so; and his hand was restored whole as the other.
11 And they were filled with
madness; and [k]communed one
with another what they might do
to Jesus.
12 And[l] it came to pass in those
days, that he went out [m]into a
mountain to pray, and continued
all night in prayer to God.

i Mar.3.5. *k* Ps.2.1,2. *l* Mat.14.23. *m* Mat.6.6.

---

ing the Sabbath, and not any rights of property."

8. *But he knew their thoughts.* He knew their thoughts—their dark, malicious designs—by the *question* which they proposed to him, whether it was lawful to heal on the Sabbath-days (Matthew). In *reply* to their question, Jesus asked them whether they would not release a *sheep* on the Sabbath-day if it was fallen into a pit, and also asked *them* whether it was better to do good than to do evil on that day, implying that to *omit* to do *good* was, in fact, doing *evil.*

11. *Were filled with madness.* Probably—1st. Because he had shown his *power* to work a miracle. 2d. Because he had shown his power to do it *contrary* to what *they* thought was right. 3d. Because by doing it he had shown that he was from *God,* and that *they* were therefore *wrong* in their views of the Sabbath. And, 4th. Because he had shown no respect to *their views* of what the law of God demanded. Pride, obstinacy, malice, and disappointed self-confidence were *all* combined, therefore, in producing madness. Nor were they alone. Men are often enraged because others do good in a way which *they* do not approve of. God gives success to others; and because he has not accommodated himself to *their* views of what is right, and done it in the way which *they* would have prescribed, they are enraged, and filled with envy at men more successful than themselves. ¶ *Communed one with another.* Spoke together, or laid a plan.

12. *And it came to pass in those days.* The designation of the time here is very general. It means *about* the time when the events occurred which had been just narrated. ¶ *He went out into a mountain.* Jesus was accustomed to resort to such places to hold communion with God, Mar. vi. 46. He did it because it was retired, free from interruption, and fitted by impressiveness and grandeur to raise the thoughts to the God that had formed the high hills and the deep-shaded groves. ¶ *And continued all night in prayer to God.* There has been a difference of opinion about this passage, whether it means that he spent the night in the act of *praying* to God, or in a *place of* prayer. The Jews had places of prayer, called *oratories,* built *out* of their cities or towns, where they could retire from the bustle of a city and hold communion with God. They were built on the banks of rivers (comp. Ac. xvi. 13), in groves, or on hills. They were rude inclosures, made by building a rough wall of stone around a level piece of ground, and capable of accommodating a small number who might resort thither to pray. But the more probable opinion is that he spent the whole night in supplication; for—1st. This is the obvious meaning of the passage. 2d. The object for which he went out was *to pray.* 3d. It was an occasion of great importance. He was about to send out his apostles—to lay the foundation of his religion—and he therefore set apart this time specially to seek the divine blessing. 4th. It was no unusual thing for Jesus to spend much time in prayer, and we are not to wonder that he passed an entire night in supplication. If it be asked why Jesus should pray *at all* if he was divine, it may be replied that he was also *a man*—a man subject to the same sufferings as others, and, *as a man,*

13 And when it was day, he called *unto him* his disciples; and of them he [n]chose twelve, whom also he named apostles;

14 Simon, (whom he [o]also named Peter,) and Andrew his brother, James and John, Philip and Bartholomew,

15 Matthew and Thomas, James the *son* of Alpheus, and Simon called Zelotes,

16 And [p]Judas *the brother* of James, and Judas Iscariot, which also was the traitor.

17 And he came down with them, and stood in the plain, and the company of his disciples, and a [q]great multitude of people out of all Judea and Jerusalem, and from the sea-coast of Tyre and Sidon, which came to hear him, and [r]to be healed of their diseases;

18 And they that were vexed with unclean spirits, and they were healed.

19 And the whole multitude sought to [s]touch him; for [t]there went virtue out of him, and healed *them* all.

20 And[u] he lifted up his eyes on

n Mat.10.1,&c.; Mar.3.13; 6.7. o Jn.1.42. p Jude 1.

q Mat.4.25,&c.; Mar.3.7,&c. r Ps.103.3; 107.17-20. s Nu.21.8,9; Mat.14.36; Jn.3.14,15. t Mar.5.30; ch.8.46. u Mat.5.2,&c.

needing the divine blessing. There was no more inconsistency in his *praying* than there was in his *eating*. Both were *means* employed for an end, and both were equally consistent with his being divine. But Jesus was also *Mediator*, and as such it was proper to seek the divine direction and blessing. In *this* case he has set us an example that we should follow. In great emergencies, when we have important duties, or are about to encounter special difficulties, we should seek the divine blessing and direction by *prayer*. We should set apart an unusual portion of time for supplication. Nay, if we pass the *whole night* in prayer, it should not be charged as enthusiasm. Our Saviour did it. Men of the world often pass whole nights in plans of gain or in dissipation, and shall it be esteemed strange that Christians should spend an equal portion of time in the far more important business of religion?

13–16. See Notes on Mat. x. 1–4.

17. *And stood in the plain.* It is not affirmed, however, that he stood in the plain when he delivered the following discourse. There has been some doubt whether the following discourse is the same as that recorded in the 5th, 6th, and 7th chapters of Matthew, or whether the Saviour *repeated* the substance of that discourse, and that Luke recorded it as he repeated it. The reasons which have led many to suppose that they refer to the same are—1st. That the beginning and the close are alike. 2d. That the *substance* of each is the same. And, 3d. That *after* the discourse was delivered, both affirm that Jesus went to Capernaum and healed the servant of the centurion, Mat. viii. 5-13; Lu. vii. 1–10. On the other hand, *Matthew* says that the sermon was delivered on the *mountain* (Mat. v. 1); it is thought to be implied that *Luke* affirms that it was in the *plain*. Matthew says that he *sat;* Luke, that he *stood.* Yet there is no reason to suppose that there is a difference in the evangelists. Jesus spent the night on the mountain in prayer. In the morning he descended into the open plain and healed many. While there, as Luke says, he "*stood*" and received those who came to him, and healed their diseases. There is no impropriety in supposing that, being pressed by multitudes, he retired into the mountain again, or to an eminence in the plain, or to the side of the mountain, where the people might be more conveniently arranged and seated to hear him. There he *sat*, as recorded by Matthew, and delivered the discourse; for it is to be observed that Luke does *not* say that he delivered the sermon *on the plain*, but only that he *healed the sick there.* ¶ *Tyre and Sidon.* See Notes on Mat. xi. 21.

18. *Vexed.* The word *vex* with us means to provoke, or irritate by petty provocations. Here it means, however, to *afflict*, to *torment*—denoting deep and heavy trials. ¶ *Unclean spirits.* Demons that were impure and unholy, having a delight in tormenting, and in inflicting painful and loathsome diseases.

19. *Virtue.* Healing power. See Notes on Mar. v. 30.

his disciples, and said, Blessed *be ye* [v]poor; for yours is the kingdom of God.

21 Blessed *are ye* [w]that hunger now; for ye [x]shall be filled. Blessed *are ye* [y]that weep now; for ye shall laugh.

22 Blessed are ye when men shall [z]hate you, and when they shall [a]separate you *from their company*, and shall reproach *you*, and cast out your name as evil, for the Son of man's sake.

23 Rejoice[b] ye in that day, and leap for joy; for, behold, your reward *is* great in heaven; [c]for in the like manner did their fathers unto the prophets.

24 But woe unto [d]you that are rich! for ye [e]have received your consolation.

25 Woe unto [f]you that are full! for ye shall hunger. Woe unto you that [g]laugh now! for ye shall mourn and weep.

26 Woe unto you when all men

v Ja.2.5. *w* Is.55.1. *x* Ps.107.9. *y* Is.61.3; Re.21.4. *z* Jn.17.14. *a* 1 Pe.2.19,20; 3.14; 4.14.

b Ac.5.41; Col.1.24; Ja.1.2. *c* Ac.7.52; He.11.32-39. *d* Hab.2.9; Ja.5.1. *e* ch.16.25. *f* Is.28.7; 65.13. *g* Pr.14.13; Ep.5.4.

20-49. See this passage fully illustrated in the sermon on the mount, in the 5th, 6th, and 7th chapters of Matthew.

21. *That hunger now.* Matthew has it, "that hunger and thirst after righteousness." Matthew has expressed *more fully* what Luke has briefly, but there is no contradiction.

24-26. These verses have been omitted by Matthew. They seem to have been spoken to the Pharisees. ¶ *Who are rich.* In this world's goods. They loved them; they had sought for them; they found their consolation in them. It implies, farther, that they would not seek or receive consolation from the gospel. They were proud, and would not seek it; satisfied, and did not desire it; filled with cares, and had no time or disposition to attend to it. All the consolation which they had reason to expect they *had received.* Alas! how poor and worthless is *such* consolation, compared with that which the gospel would give! ¶ *Woe unto you that are full!* Not hungry. Satisfied with their wealth, and not feeling their need of anything better than earthly wealth can give. Many, alas! are thus *full.* They profess to be satisfied. They desire nothing but wealth, and a sufficiency to satisfy the wants of the body. They have no anxiety for the riches that shall endure for ever. ¶ *Ye shall hunger.* Your property shall be taken away, or you shall see that it is of little value; and then you shall see the need of something better. You shall feel your want and wretchedness, and shall *hunger* for something to satisfy the desires of a dying, sinful soul. ¶ *That laugh now.* Are happy, or thoughtless, or gay, or filled with levity. ¶ *Shall mourn and weep.* The time is coming when you shall sorrow deeply. In sickness, in calamity, in the prospect of death, in the fear of eternity, your laughter shall be turned into sorrow. *There is* a place where you cannot laugh, and there you will see the folly of having passed the *proper time* of preparing for such scenes in levity and folly. Alas! how many thus spend their youth! and how many weep when it is too late! God gives them over, and *laughs at* THEIR *calamity*, and mocks when their fear comes, Pr. i. 26. To be happy in *such scenes*, it is necessary to be sober, humble, pious in early life. *Then* we need not weep in the day of calamity; then there will be no terror in death; then there will be nothing to fear in the grave.

26. *When all men shall speak well of you.* When they shall praise or applaud you. The men of the world will not praise or applaud *my* doctrine; they are *opposed* to it, and therefore, if they speak well of *you* and of *your teaching*, it is proof that you do not teach the true doctrine. If you do *not* do this, then there will be woe upon you. If men teach false doctrines for true; if they declare that God has spoken that which he has not spoken, and if they oppose what he *has* delivered, then heavy punishments will await them. ¶ *For so did their fathers.* The *fathers* or *ancestors* of this people; the ancient Jews. ¶ *To the false prophets.* Men who pretended to be of God—who delivered their *own* doctrines as the truth of God, and who accommodated themselves to the desires of the people. Of

shall [h]speak well of you! for so did their fathers to the false prophets.

27 But I say unto you which hear, [i]Love your enemies, do good to them which hate you;

28 Bless them that curse you, and [k]pray for them which despitefully use you.

29 And[l] unto him that smiteth thee on the *one* cheek, offer also the other; [m]and him that taketh away thy cloak, forbid not *to take thy* coat also.

30 Give[n] to every man that asketh of thee; and of him that taketh away thy goods, ask *them* not again.

31 And[o] as ye would that men should do to you, do ye also to them likewise.

32 For if ye love them which love you, what thank have ye? for sinners also love those that love them.

33 And if ye do good to them which do good to you, what thank have ye? for sinners also do even the same.

34 And if ye lend *to them* of whom ye hope to receive, what thank have ye? for sinners also lend to sinners, to receive as much again.

35 But[p] love ye your enemies, and do good, and [q]lend, hoping for nothing again; and your reward shall be great, and [r]ye shall be the children of the Highest; for he is kind unto the unthankful, and *to* the evil.

36 Be ye therefore merciful, as your Father also is merciful.

37 Judge[s] not, and ye shall not be judged; condemn not, and ye shall not be condemned; forgive, and ye shall be forgiven:

38 Give, and it [t]shall be given unto you; good measure, pressed down, and shaken together, and running over, shall men give [u]into your bosom. For[v] with the same measure that ye mete withal, it shall be measured to you again.

39 And he spake a parable unto them: [w]Can the blind lead the blind? shall they not both fall into the ditch?

h Jn.15.19; 1 Jn.4.5.
i Ex.23.4,5; Pr.25.21; Mat.5.44; ver.35; Ro.12.20.
k ch.23.24; Ac.7.60. *l* Mat.5.39. *m* 1 Co.6.7.
n De.15.7,8,10; Pr.19.17; 21.26; Mat.5.42,&c.
o Mat.7.12.

p ver.27. *q* Ps.37.26; 112.5. *r* Mat.5.45.
s Mat.7.1. *t* Pr.19.17; Mat.10.42. *u* Ps.79.12.
v Mat.7.2; Mar.4.24; Ja.2.13. *w* Mat.15.14.

---

this number were the prophets of Baal, the false prophets who appeared in the time of Jeremiah, &c.

27, 28. See Mat. v. 44, 45.

29. See Mat. v. 39, 40.

30. See Mat. v. 42.

31. See Mat. vii. 12.

32–36. See Mat. v. 46–48.

37–42. See Mat. vii. 1–9.

38. *Good measure.* They shall give you good measure, or *full* measure. ¶ *Pressed down.* As figs or grapes might be, and thus many more might be put into the measure. ¶ *Shaken together.* To make it more compact, and thus to give more. ¶ *Running over.* So full that the measure would overflow. ¶ *Shall men give.* This is said to be the reward of *giving* to the poor and needy; and the meaning is that the man who is liberal will find others liberal to him in dealing with them, and when he is also in circumstances of want. A man who is himself kind to the poor—who has that *character* established—will find many who are ready to help *him* abundantly when he is in want. He that is parsimonious, close, niggardly, will find few or none who will aid him. ¶ *Into your bosom.* That is, to you. The word *bosom* here has reference to a custom among Oriental nations of making the bosom or front part of their garments *large*, so that articles could be carried in them, answering the purpose of our pockets. Comp. Ex. iv. 6, 7; Pr. vi. 27; Ru. iii. 15.

39. *A parable.* A proverb or similitude. ¶ *Can the blind lead the blind?* See Notes on Mat. xv. 14.

40. *The disciple is not,* &c. The learner is not above his teacher, does not know more, and must expect to fare no better. This seems to have been spoken to show them that they

40 The[x] disciple is not above his
master; but every one [1]that is perfect shall be as his master.

41 And why beholdest thou the
mote that is in thy brother's eye,
but perceivest not the beam that
is in thine own eye?

42 Either how canst thou say to
thy brother, Brother, let me pull
out the mote that is in thine eye,
when thou thyself beholdest not
the beam that is in thine own eye?
Thou hypocrite! [y]cast out first the
beam out of thine own eye, and
then shalt thou see clearly to pull
out the mote that is in thy brother's
eye.

43 For[z] a good tree bringeth not
forth corrupt fruit; neither doth a
corrupt tree bring forth good fruit.

44 For[a] every tree is known by
his own fruit: for of thorns men
do not gather figs, nor of a bramble-
bush gather they [2]grapes.

45 A[b] good man, out of the good
treasure of his heart, bringeth forth
that which is good; and an evil
man, out of the evil treasure of his
heart, bringeth forth that which is
evil; for of the abundance of the
heart his mouth speaketh.

46 And why [c]call ye me, Lord,
Lord, and do not the things which
I say?

47 Whosoever cometh to me,
and heareth my sayings, and doeth
them, I will show you to whom he
is like:

48 He[d] is like a man which built
a house, and digged deep, and laid
the foundation on a rock; and
when the flood arose, the stream
beat vehemently upon that house,
and [e]could not shake it; for it was
[f]founded upon a rock.

49 But he that [g]heareth, and
doeth not, is like a man that without a foundation built an house
upon the earth; against which the
stream did beat vehemently, and
immediately [h]it fell; and the ruin
of that house was great.

CHAPTER VII.

NOW[a] when he had ended all
his sayings in the audience
of the people, he entered into Capernaum.

2 And a certain centurion's servant, who was [b]dear unto him, was
sick, and ready to die.

3 And when he heard of Jesus,

x Mat.10.24; Jn.13.16; 15.20.
1 or, *shall be perfected as his master.*
y Pr.18.17; Ro.2.1,21,&c. z Mat.7.16,17.
a Mat.12.33. 2 *a grape.* b Mat.12.35.

c Mal.1.6; Mat.7.21; 25.11; ch.13.25; Ga.6.7.
d Mat.7.25,26. e 2 Pe.1.10; Jude 24.
f Ps.46.1-3; 62.2. g Ja.1.24-26.
h Pr.28.18; Ho.4.14.
a Mat.8.5,&c. b Job 31.15; Pr.29.21.

were not to expect that their disciples would go *beyond them* in attainments; that if *they* were blind, their followers would be also; and that therefore it was important for *them* to understand fully the doctrines of the gospel, and not to be blind leaders of the blind. ¶ *Every one that is perfect.* The word rendered *is perfect* means sometimes to *repair* or *mend*, and is thus applied to mending *nets*, Mat. iv. 21; Mar. i. 19. Hence it means to repair or amend in a moral sense, or to make whole or complete. Here it means, evidently, *thoroughly instructed* or *informed.* The Christian should be *like his Master*—holy, harmless, and undefiled, and separate from sinners. He should copy his example, and grow into the likeness of his Redeemer. Nor can any other be a Christian.

41, 42. See Notes on Mat. vii. 3-5.

43, 44. See Notes on Mat. vii. 16-18.

45. This verse is not found in the sermon on the mount as recorded by Matthew, but is recorded by him in ch. xii. 35. See Notes on that passage.

46-49. See Notes on Mat. vii. 21-27.

CHAPTER VII.

1-10. See Notes on Mat. viii. 5-13.

1. *In the audience of the people.* In the hearing of the people.

2. *Who was dear unto him.* That is, he was valuable, trusty, and honoured.

4. *They besought him instantly.* Urgently or earnestly. ¶ *He was worthy.* The centurion. He had showed favour to the Jews, and it was not improper to show him a kindness.

11. *A city called Nain.* This city was

he sent unto him the elders of the
Jews, beseeching him that he
would come and heal his servant.
4 And when they came to Jesus,
they besought him instantly, saying, That he was worthy for whom
he should do this:
5 For he [c]loveth our nation, and
he hath built us a synagogue.
6 Then Jesus went with them.
And when he was now not far
from the house, the centurion sent
friends to him, saying unto him,
Lord, [d]trouble not thyself; for I
am not worthy that thou shouldest
enter under my roof:
7 Wherefore neither thought I
myself worthy to come unto thee;
but [e]say in a word, and my servant
shall be healed.
8 For I also am a man set under
authority, having under me soldiers; and I say unto [1]one, Go,
and he goeth; and to another,
Come, and he cometh; and to my
servant, Do this, and he doeth *it*.
9 When Jesus heard these things,
he marvelled at him, and turned

c 1 Ki.5.1; Ga.5.6; 1 Jn.3.14; 5.1,2. *d* ch.8.49. *e* Ps.107.20. 1 *this man*.

him about, and said unto the people that followed him, I say unto
you, I have not found so great
faith, no, not in Israel.
10 And they that were sent, returning to the house, found the
servant whole that had been sick.
11 And it came to pass the day
after that he went into a city called
Nain; and many of his disciples
went with him, and much people.
12 Now when he came nigh to
the gate of the city, behold, there
was a dead man carried out, the
only son of his mother, and she
was a widow; and much people
of the city was with her.
13 And when the Lord saw her,
he had compassion on her, and
said unto her, Weep not.
14 And he came and touched
the [2]bier; and they that bare *him*
stood still. And he said, Young
man, I say unto thee, [f]Arise.
15 And he that was dead [g]sat
up, and began to speak. And he
delivered him to his mother.
16 And there came a fear on

2 or, *coffin*. *f* ch.8.54; Ac.9.40; Ro.4.17. *g* 2 Ki.4.32-37; 13.21; Jn.11.44.

---

in Galilee, in the boundaries of the tribe of Issachar. It was about two miles south of Mount Tabor, and not far from Capernaum. It is now a small village inhabited by Jews, Mohammedans, and Christians. Dr. Thomson (*The Land and the Book*, vol. ii. p. 158) locates it on the north-west corner of a mount now called Jebel ed Dûhy, one hour's ride from the foot of Mount Tabor. Of this place he says: "This mount is now called Jebel ed Dûhy, and that small hamlet on the north-west corner of it is Nain, famous for the restoration of the widow's son to life. It was once a place of considerable extent, but is now little more than a cluster of ruins, among which dwell a few families of fanatical Moslems. It is in keeping with the one historic incident that renders it dear to the Christian, that its only antiquities are tombs. These are situated mainly on the east of the village, and it was in that direction, I presume, that the widow's son was being carried on that memorable occasion. It took me just an hour to ride from the foot of Tabor to Nain."

12. *The gate of the city.* Cities were surrounded by walls, to defend them from their enemies. They were entered through *gates* placed at convenient distances from each other. In most cities it was not allowed to bury the dead within the walls; hence they were borne to some convenient burial-place in the vicinity of the city. ¶ *A dead man carried out.* A funeral procession. Anciently no Jews were buried within the walls of the city, except the kings and distinguished persons, 1 Sa. xxviii. 3; 2 Ki. xxi. 18. The custom of burying within cities, and especially within the walls of churches or in their vicinity, had its origin among Christians very early; yet perhaps few customs are more deleterious to health than burials within large cities, especially within the walls of frequented buildings. The effluvia from dead bodies is excessively unwhole-

all; and they glorified God, saying, That a [h]great prophet is risen up among us; and, That [i]God hath visited his people.
17 And this rumour of him went forth throughout all Judea, and throughout all the region round about.
18 And the disciples of John showed him of all these things.
19 And[k] John, calling *unto him* two of his disciples, sent *them* to Jesus, saying, Art thou [l]he that should come, or look we for another?
20 When the men were come unto him, they said, John Baptist hath sent us unto thee, saying, Art thou he that should come, or look we for another?
21 And in the same hour he cured many of *their* infirmities and plagues, and of evil spirits; and unto many *that were* blind he gave sight.
22 Then Jesus, answering, said unto them, Go your way, and [m]tell John what things ye have seen and heard; how that [n]the blind see, the lame walk, the lepers are cleansed, the deaf hear, the dead are raised, [o]to the poor the gospel is preached.
23 And blessed is *he* whosoever shall not be [p]offended in me.
24 And when the messengers of John were departed, he began to speak unto the people concerning John, What went ye out into the wilderness for to see? A reed shaken with the wind?
25 But what went ye out for to

h ch.24.19. *i* ch.1.68. *k* Mat.11.2. *l* Zec.9.9.

m Jn.1.46. *n* Is.35.5,6. *o* ch.4.18; Ja.2.5. *p* Is.8.14,15; Mat.11.6; 13.57; ch.2.34; Jn.6.66; 1 Co.1.21-28.

some. Burial-places should be in situations of retirement, far from the tread of the gay and busy world, where all the feelings may be still and calm, and where there can be no injury to health from the mouldering bodies of the dead.

16. *Came a fear on all.* An *awe* or solemnity at the presence of one who had power to raise the dead, and at the miracle which had been performed. ¶ *Glorified God.* Praised or honoured God that he had sent such a prophet. ¶ *And, That God hath visited his people.* Some said one thing and some another, but all expressing their belief that God had showed peculiar favour to the people. ¶ *Hath visited.* See Lu. i. 68.

The raising of this young man was one of the most decisive and instructive of our Lord's miracles. There was no doubt that he was dead. There could be no delusion, and no agreement to impose on the people. He came near to the city with no reference to this young man; he met the funeral procession, as it were, by accident, and by a word he restored him to life. All those who had the best opportunity of judging—the mother, the friends—believed him to be dead, and were about to bury him. The evidence that he came to life was decisive. He sat up, he spake, and *all* were impressed with the full assurance that God had raised him to life. Many witnesses were present, and none doubted that Jesus *by a word* had restored him to his weeping mother.

The whole scene was affecting. Here was a widowed mother who was following her only son, her stay and hope, to the grave. He was borne along—one in the prime of life and the only comfort of his parent—impressive proof that the young, the useful, the vigorous, and the lovely may die. Jesus met them, apparently a stranger. He approached the procession as if he had something important to say; he touched the bier, and the procession stood still. He was full of compassion for the weeping parent, and by a word restored the youth, stretched upon the bier, to life. He sat up, and spake. Jesus therefore had power over the dead. He also has power to raise sinners, dead in trespasses and sins, to life. He can speak the word, and, though in their death of sin they are borne along toward ruin, he can open their eyes, and raise them up, and restore them revived to *real* life or to their friends. Often he raises up children in this manner, and gives them, converted to God, to their friends, imparting as *real* joy as he gave to the widow of Nain by raising her son from the dead. And

see? A man clothed in soft raiment? Behold, they which are
gorgeously apparelled, and live
delicately, are [q]in kings' courts.
26 But what went ye out for to
see? A [r]prophet? Yea, I say unto
you, and much more than a prophet.
27 This is *he* of whom it is written, [s]Behold, I send my messenger before thy face, which shall
prepare thy way before thee.
28 For I say unto you, Among
those that are born of women,
there is not a greater prophet
than John the Baptist: but he
that is least in the kingdom of
God is greater than he.
29 And all the people that heard
him, and the publicans, [t]justified
God, being [u]baptized with the
baptism of John.
30 But the Pharisees and law-

q 2 Sa.19.35; Es.1.3,11. r ch.1.76.
s Mal.3.1; ch.1.15-17.
t Ps.51.4; Ro.3.4. u Mat.3.5,6; ch.3.12.

yers [3]rejected the [v]counsel of God
[4]against themselves, being not baptized of him.
31 And the Lord said, [w]Where-
unto then shall I liken the men
of this generation? and to what
are they like?
32 They are like unto children
sitting in the market-place, and
calling one to another, and saying,
We have piped unto you, and ye
have not danced; we have mourned
to you, and ye have not wept.
33 For John the Baptist [x]came
neither eating bread nor drinking
wine; and ye say, He hath a devil.
34 The[y] Son of man is come eating and drinking; and ye say, Behold, a gluttonous man, and a winebibber, a friend of publicans and
sinners!
35 But[z] Wisdom is justified of
all her children.

3 or, *frustrated*. v Ac.20.27.
4 or, *within themselves*. w Mat.11.16,&c.
x Mat.3.4; Mar.1.6; ch.1.15.
y Jn.2.2; 12.2; ver.36. z Pr.8.32-36; 17.16.

---

every child should remember, if he has pious parents, that there is *no way* in which he can give so much joy to them as by embracing Him who is the resurrection and the life, and resolving to live to his glory.

19-35. See this passage explained in Mat. xi. 2-19.

29. *The people*. The common people. ¶ *That heard* him. That heard *John*. ¶ *The publicans*. The tax-gatherers, the worst kind of people, who had, however, been converted. ¶ *Justified God*. Considered God as *just* or *right* in the counsel which he gave by John—to wit, in calling men to repentance, and in denouncing future wrath on the impenitent. Comp. Mat. xi. 19. ¶ *Being baptized*, &c. They *showed* that they approved of the message of God by submitting to the ordinance which he commanded—the ordinance of baptism. This verse and the following are not to be considered as the words of *Luke*, but the continuation of the discourse of our Lord. He is saying what took place in regard to John. Among the common people he was approved and obeyed; among the rich and learned he was despised.

30. *But the Pharisees and lawyers rejected*, &c. It appears from Mat. iii. 7 that some of the Pharisees came to John to be baptized; but still this is entirely consistent with the supposition that the great mass of Pharisees and lawyers rejected him. ¶ *The counsel of God*. The *counsel of God* toward them was the solemn admonition by John to *repent* and be baptized, and be prepared to receive the Messiah. This was the command or revealed will of God in relation to them. When it is said that they *rejected* the counsel of God, it does not mean that they could frustrate his purposes, but merely that they violated his commands. Men cannot frustrate the *real* purposes of God, but they can contemn his messages, they can violate his commands, and thus they can reject the counsel which he gives them, and treat with contempt the desire which he manifests for their welfare. ¶ *Against themselves*. To their own hurt or detriment. God is wise and good. He knows what is best for us. He, therefore, that rejects what God commands, rejects it to his own injury. It *cannot* be well for any mortal to despise what God commands him to do.

31-35. See this passage explained in

36 And[a] one of the Pharisees desired him that he would eat with
him. And he went into the Pharisee's house, and sat down to meat.

37 And, behold, a woman in the
city, which was a [b]sinner, when
she knew that *Jesus* sat at meat in
the Pharisee's house, brought an
alabaster-box of ointment,

38 And stood at his feet behind
him weeping, and began to wash
his feet with tears, and did wipe
them with the hairs of her head,
and kissed his feet, and anointed
them with the ointment.

39 Now when the Pharisee which
had bidden him saw *it*, he spake
within himself, saying, [c]This man,
if he were a prophet, would have
known who and what manner of
woman *this is* that toucheth him;
for [d]she is a sinner.

a Mat.26.6,&c.; Mar.14.3,&c.; Jn.11.2,&c. *b* ch.5.32; ver.34; 1 Ti.1.15.

c Jn.9.24. *d* ch.15.2.

the Notes on Mat. xi. 16–19. *And the Lord said.* This clause is wanting in almost all the manuscripts, and is omitted by the best critics.

36. *One of the Pharisees.* His name was Simon, ver. 10. Nothing more is known of him. It is not improbable, however, from what follows (ver. 40–47), that he had been healed by the Saviour of some afflictive disease, and made this feast to show his gratitude. ¶ *Sat down to meat.* The original word here means only that he placed himself or reclined at the table. The notion of *sitting* at meals is taken from modern customs, and was not practised by the Jews. See Notes on Mat. xxiii. 6. ¶ *Meat.* Supper. Food of any kind. Sat down to eat.

37. *In the city.* What city is meant is unknown. Some have supposed it was Nain; some Capernaum; some Magdala; and some Jerusalem. ¶ *Which was a sinner.* Who was depraved or wicked. This woman, it seems, was known to be a sinner—perhaps an abandoned woman or a prostitute. It is certain that she had much to be forgiven, and she had probably passed her life in crime. There is no evidence that this was the woman commonly called Mary Magdalene. ¶ *An alabaster-box,* &c. See Notes on Mar. xiv. 3.

38. *Stood at his feet behind* him. They reclined, at their meals, on their left side, and their feet, therefore, were extended *from* the table, so that persons could easily approach them. See Notes on Mat. xxiii. 6. ¶ *Began to wash his feet.* The Jews wore sandals. These were taken off when they entered a house. It was an act of hospitality and kindness to wash the feet of a guest. *She* therefore began to show her love for the Saviour, and at the same time her humility and penitence, by pouring forth a flood of tears, and washing his feet in the manner of a servant. ¶ *Kissed his feet.* The kiss was an emblem of love and affection. In this manner she testified her love for the Lord Jesus, and at the same time her humility and sense of sin by kissing his feet. There could be few expressions of penitence more deep and tender than were these. A sense of all her sins rushed over her mind; her heart burst at the remembrance of them, and at the presence of the pure Redeemer; with deep sorrow she humbled herself and sought forgiveness. She showed her love for him by a kiss of affection; her humility, by bathing his feet; her veneration, by breaking a costly box—perhaps procured by a guilty life—and anointing his feet. In this way we should all come, embracing him as the loved Redeemer, humbled at his feet, and offering *all* we have—all that we have gained in lives of sin, in our professions, by merchandise and toil, while we were sinners—offering *all* to his service. Thus shall we show the sincerity of our repentance, and thus shall we hear his gracious voice pronounce our sins forgiven.

39. *He spake within himself.* Thought. ¶ *If he were a prophet.* The word *prophet* here means, not one who predicts future events, but one who knows the hearts of men. If Jesus had been sent from God as a prophet, he supposed that he would have known the character of the woman and would have rebuked her. ¶ *Would have known,* &c. Because Jesus did not rebuke her and drive her from his presence, he inferred that he could not be acquainted with her character. The Pharisees considered it improper to hold communion with those who were notorious sinners.

40 And Jesus, answering, said unto him, Simon, I have somewhat to say unto thee. And he saith, Master, say on.

41 There was a certain creditor which had two debtors: the one owed five hundred [5]pence, and the other fifty:

42 And when they had [e]nothing to pay, he frankly forgave them both. Tell me, therefore, which of them will love him most?

43 Simon answered and said, I suppose that *he* to whom he forgave most. And he said unto him, Thou hast [f]rightly judged.

44 And he turned to the woman, and said unto Simon, Seest thou this woman? I entered into thine house, thou gavest me no water for my feet; but she hath washed my feet with tears, and wiped *them* with the hairs of her head.

45 Thou gavest me no kiss; but

[5] See Mat.18.28. *e* Ps.49.7,8; Ro.5.6. *f* Ps.116.16–18; 1 Co.15.9; 2 Co.5.14; 1 Ti.1.13–16.

They judged our Saviour by their own rules, and supposed that *he* would act in the same way; and Simon therefore concluded that he did not know her character and could not be a prophet. Jesus did not refuse the society of the guilty. He came to save the lost; and no person ever came to him so sure of finding a *friend*, as those who came conscious that they were deeply depraved, and mourning on account of their crimes. ¶ *That toucheth him.* The *touch* of a Gentile, or a person singularly wicked, they supposed to be polluting, and the Pharisees avoided it. See Mat. ix. 11.

41. *A certain creditor.* A man who had lent money or sold property, the payment for which was yet due. ¶ *Five hundred pence.* About 69 dollars 26 cents, or £14, 11*s.* 8*d.* See Notes on Mat. xviii. 28. ¶ *Fifty.* About 7 dollars, or £1, 9*s.* 2*d.*

42. *Frankly forgave.* Freely forgave, or forgave entirely without any compensation. This is not designed to express anything about the way in which God forgives sinners. He forgives—forgives freely, but it is in connection with the *atonement* made by the Lord Jesus. If it was a mere *debt* which we owed to God, he might forgive, as this creditor did, without *any* equivalent. But it is *crime* which he forgives. He pardons as a moral governor. A parent might forgive a *debt* without any equivalent; but he cannot pardon an offending child without regarding his own *character* as a parent, the *truth* of his threatenings, the good order of his house, and the maintenance of his authority. So our sins against God, though they are called *debts*, are called so *figuratively*. It is not an affair of *money*, and God cannot forgive us without maintaining his word, the honour of his government, and law—in other words, without an *atonement*. It is clear that by the *creditor* here our Saviour meant to designate GOD, and by the *debtors*, sinners and the woman present. Simon, whose life had been comparatively upright, was denoted by the one that owed *fifty* pence; the woman, who had been an open and shameless sinner, was represented by the one that owed *five hundred*. Yet *neither* could pay. Both must be forgiven or perish. So, however much difference there is among men, *all* need the pardoning mercy of God, and *all*, without that, must perish.

43. *I suppose*, &c. He saw not *the point* of our Lord's parable. By thus saying, therefore, he condemned himself, and prepared the way for our Lord's reproof.

44. *Seest thou this woman?* You see what this woman has done to me, compared with what you have done. *She* has shown me expressions of regard which you, in your own house, have not shown. ¶ *I entered into thine house.* I came at your invitation, where I might expect all the usual rites of hospitality. ¶ *Thou gavest me no water for my feet.* Among Eastern people it was customary, before eating, to wash the feet; and to do this, or to bring water for it, was one of the rites of hospitality. See Ge. xviii. 4; Ju. xix. 21. The reasons for this were, that they wore *sandals*, which covered only the bottom of the feet, and that when they ate they reclined on couches or sofas. It became therefore necessary that the feet should be often washed.

45. *Thou gavest me no kiss.* The kiss was a token of affection or a common mode of salutation, and Simon had even neglected this mark of welcoming

this woman, since the time I came in, hath not ceased to kiss my feet.

46 My[g] head with oil thou didst not anoint; but this woman hath anointed my feet with ointment.

47 Wherefore I say unto thee, Her sins, which are many, are for-

g Ps.23.5.

him to his house. It was often used among *men* as a sign of salutation. Comp. Ge. xxxiii. 4; Ex. xviii. 7; Mat. xxvi. 49. ¶ *Hath not ceased to kiss my feet.* How striking the difference between the conduct of Simon and this woman! *He*, with all the richness of a splendid preparation, had omitted the common marks of regard and affection. *She*, in humility, had bowed at his feet, had watered them with tears, and had not ceased to kiss them. The most splendid entertainments do not always express the greatest welcome. There may be in such entertainments much insincerity—much seeking of popularity or some other motive; but no such motive could have operated in inducing a broken-hearted sinner to wash the Saviour's *feet* with tears.

46. *My head with oil.* The custom of pouring *oil* upon the head was universal among the Jews. The oil used was sweet oil or oil of olives, prepared in such a way as to give an agreeable smell. It was also used to render the hair more smooth and elegant. See Ru. iii. 3; 2 Sa. xii. 20; xiv. 2; Ps. xxiii. 5. ¶ *With ointment.* This *ointment* was a mixture of various aromatics, and was therefore far more costly and precious than the *oil* commonly used for anointing the head. Her conduct, compared with that of Simon, was therefore more striking. *He* did not give even the common oil *for his head* used on such occasions. *She* had applied to *his feet* a far more precious and valuable *unguent.* *He*, therefore, showed comparatively *little* love. *She* showed *much.*

47. *Wherefore I say unto thee.* As the result of this, or because she has done this; meaning by this that she had given *evidence* that her sins had been forgiven. The inquiry with Simon was whether it was proper for Jesus to *touch her* or to allow her to touch him, because she was such a sinner, ver. 39. Jesus said, in substance, to Simon, "Grant that she has been as great a sinner as you affirm, and even grant that if she had *continued so* it might be improper to suffer her to touch me, yet *her conduct* shows that her sins have been forgiven. She has evinced so much love for me as to show that she is no longer *such a sinner* as you suppose, and it is not, therefore, *improper* that she should be suffered to come near me." ¶ *For she loved much.* In our translation this would seem to be given as a reason why her sins had been forgiven—that she had loved much *before* they were pardoned; but this is clearly not the meaning. This would be contrary to the whole New Testament, which supposes that love *succeeds*, not *precedes* forgiveness; and which nowhere supposes that sins are forgiven *because* we love God. It would be also contrary to the design of the Saviour here. It was not to show *why* her sins had been forgiven, but to show that she had given evidence that they actually *had* been, and that it was proper, therefore, that she should come near to him and manifest this love. The meaning may be thus expressed: "That her sins, so many and aggravated, have been forgiven—that she is no longer such a sinner as you suppose, is manifest from her conduct. She shows deep gratitude, penitence, love. Her conduct is the *proper expression* of that love. While you have shown comparatively little evidence that you felt that *your sins* were great, and comparatively little love at their being forgiven, *she* has shown that she *felt* hers to be great, and has loved much." ¶ *To whom little is forgiven.* He who feels that little has been forgiven—that his sins were not as great as those of others. A man's love to God will be in proportion to the obligation he *feels* to him for forgiveness. God is to be *loved* for his perfections, apart from what he has *done* for us. But still it is proper that our love should be increased by a consideration of his goodness; and they who feel—as Christians do—that they are *the chief of sinners*, will feel under infinite obligation to love God and their Redeemer, and that no *expression* of attachment to him can be *beyond* what is due.

48. *Thy sins are forgiven.* What a gracious assurance to the weeping, loving penitent! How that voice, spoken to the troubled sinner, stills his anguish, allays his troubled feelings, and produces peace to the soul! And how manifest is it that he that could say

given, for she loved much; but to
whom little is forgiven, *the same*
loveth little.
48 And he said unto her, Thy
sins are forgiven.
49 And they that sat at meat
with him began to say within
themselves, [h]Who is this that for-
giveth sins also?
50 And he said to the woman,
Thy[i] faith hath saved thee; go in
peace.

CHAPTER VIII.

AND it came to pass afterward
that he went throughout every
city and village, preaching and
showing the glad tidings of the
kingdom of God; and the twelve
were with him;
2 And[a] certain women which had
been healed of evil spirits and infirmities, Mary called Magdalene,
[b]out of whom went seven devils,
3 And Joanna the wife of Chuza,
Herod's steward, and Susanna, and
many others, which [c]ministered
unto him of their substance.
4 And when much people were
gathered together, and were come
to him out of every city, he spake
by a parable:
5 A[d] sower went out to sow
his seed: and as he sowed, some

h Mat.9.2,3; Mar.2.7.
i Hab.2.4; Mat.9.22; Mar.5.34; 10.52; ch.8.48; 18.42; Ep.2.8.

a Mat.27.55. b Mar.16.9; ver.30.
c 2 Co.8.9. d Mat.13.3,&c.; Mar.4.3,&c.

---

thus *must* be God! No man has a *right* to forgive sin. No man *can* speak peace to the soul, and give assurance that its transgressions are pardoned. Here, then, Jesus gave indubitable proof that he was God as well as man; that he was Lord of the conscience as well as the pitying friend; and that he was as able to read the heart and give peace there, as he was to witness the external expression of sorrow for sin.

49. *Who is this*, &c. A very pertinent question. Who *could* he be but God? Man could not do it, and there is no wonder that they were amazed.

50. *Thy faith hath saved thee; go in peace.* See Notes on Mar. v. 34.

CHAPTER VIII.

1. *Every city and village.* Of Galilee. ¶ *Preaching and showing the glad tidings of the kingdom of God.* That the kingdom of God was about to come, or that his reign in the gospel was about to be set up over men. See Notes on Mat. iii. 2. ¶ *The twelve.* The twelve apostles.

2. *Infirmities.* Sickness. ¶ *Mary called Magdalene.* So called from *Magdala*, the place of her residence. It was situated on the Sea of Galilee, south of Capernaum. To this place Jesus retired after feeding the four thousand. See Notes on Mat. xv. 39. ¶ *Out of whom went.* By the power of Jesus. ¶ *Seven devils.* The word *seven* is often used for an indefinite number, and *may* signify merely *many* devils. The expression is used to signify that she was grievously tormented, and rendered, doubtless, insane by the power of evil spirits. See Notes on Mat. iv. 24. It has been commonly supposed that Mary Magdalene was a woman of abandoned character, but of this there is not the least evidence. All that we know of her is that she was formerly grievously afflicted by the presence of those evil spirits, that she was perfectly cured by Jesus, and that afterward she became one of his most faithful and humble followers. She was at his crucifixion (Jn. xix. 25) and burial (Mar. xv. 47), and she was among those who had prepared the materials to embalm him (Mar. xvi. 1), and who first went to the sepulchre after the resurrection; and what is particularly interesting in her history, she was the first to whom the risen Redeemer appeared (Mar. xvi. 9), and his conversation with her is exceeded in interest and pathos by no passage of history, sacred or profane, Jn. xx. 11–18.

3. *Herod's steward.* Herod Antipas, who reigned in Galilee. He was a son of Herod the Great. The word *steward* means one who has charge of the domestic affairs of a family, to provide for it. This office was generally held by a *slave* who was esteemed the most faithful, and was often conferred as a reward of fidelity. ¶ *Ministered.* Gave for his support. ¶ *Of their substance.* Their property; their possessions. Christians then believed, when they professed to

fell by the way-side; and it was
trodden[e] down, and fowls of the
air devoured it.
6 And some fell upon a [f]rock:
and as soon as it was sprung up it
withered away, because it lacked
moisture.
7 And some fell [g]among thorns:
and the thorns sprang up with it,
and choked it.
8 And other fell on good ground,
and sprang up, and bare fruit [h]an
hundred-fold. And when he had
said these things, he cried, [i]He
that hath ears to hear, let him
hear.
9 And his disciples asked him, saying, What might this parable be?
10 And he said, Unto you it is
given to know the mysteries of the
kingdom of God, but to others in
parables; [k]that seeing they might
not see, and hearing they might
not understand.
11 Now[l] the parable is this:
The [m]seed is the word of God.
12 Those by the way-side are
they that hear; then cometh the
devil, and [n]taketh away the word
out of their hearts, lest they should
believe and be saved.
13 They on the rock *are they*
which, when they hear, [o]receive
the word with joy; and these
have[p] no root, which for a while
believe, and in time of temptation
fall away.
14 And that which fell among
thorns are they which, when they
have heard, go forth, and [q]are
choked with cares, and riches, and
pleasures of *this* life, and [r]bring
no fruit to perfection.
15 But that on the good ground
are they which, in an [s]honest and
good heart, having heard the word,
keep *it*, and bring forth fruit with
[t]patience.
16 No[u] man, when he hath
lighted a candle, covereth it with
a vessel, or putteth *it* under a bed;
but setteth *it* on a candlestick, that
they which enter in may see the
light.
17 For[v] nothing is secret that
shall not be made manifest, neither
any thing hid that shall not be
known and come abroad.
18 Take[w] heed, therefore, how ye
hear; for [x]whosoever hath, to him
shall be given; and whosoever hath
not, from him shall be taken even
that which he [1]seemeth to have.
19 Then[y] came to him *his*
mother and his brethren, and
could not come at him for the
press.
20 And it was told him *by certain*,
which said, Thy mother and thy
brethren stand without, desiring
to see thee.
21 And he answered and said
unto them, My mother and my
brethren are these which hear the
word of God, and do it.
22 Now[z] it came to pass on a
certain day that he went into a
ship with his disciples; and he
said unto them, Let us go over
unto the other side of the lake.
And they launched forth.
23 But as they sailed, he fell

e Ps.119.118; Mat.5.13. *f* Je.5.3. *g* Je.4.3.
h Ge.26.12. *i* Pr.20.12; Je.13.15; 25.4. *k* Is.6.9.
l Mat.13.18; Mar.4.14,&c. *m* 1 Pe.1.23.
n Pr.4.5; Is.65.11; Ja.1.23,24.
o Ps.106.12,13; Is.58.2; Ga.3.1,4; 4.15.
p Pr.12.3; Ho.6.4.
q 1 Ti.6.9,10; 2 Ti.4.10; 1 Jn.2.15-17.
r Jn.15.6. *s* Je.32.39. *t* He.10.36; Ja.1.4.
u Mat.5.15; Mar.4.21; ch.11.33.
v Ec.12.14; Mat.10.26; ch.12.2; 1 Co.4.5.
w Ja.1.21-25. *x* Mat.13.12; 25.29; ch.19.26.
1 or, *thinketh that he hath.*
y Mat.12.46,&c.; Mar.3.32,&c.
z Mat.8.23,&c.; Mar.4.35,&c.

follow Christ, that it was proper to give *all* up to him—their property as well as their hearts; and the same thing is still required—that is, to commit all that we have to his disposal; to be willing to part with it for the promotion of his glory, and to leave it when he calls us away from it.

4–15. See the parable of the sower explained in the Notes on Mat. xiii. 1–23.

16–18. See Notes on Mar. iv. 21–25.

asleep; and there came down a storm of wind on the lake; and they were filled *with water*, and were in jeopardy.

24 And they came to him [a]and awoke him, saying, Master, master, we perish! Then he arose, and rebuked the wind and the raging of the water; and they ceased, and there was a calm.

25 And he said unto them, Where is your faith? And they, being afraid, wondered, saying one to another, What manner of man is this? for he commandeth even the winds and water, and they obey him.

26 And[b] they arrived at the country of the Gadarenes, which is over against Galilee.

27 And when he went forth to land, there met him out of the city a certain man which had devils long time, and ware no clothes, neither abode in *any* house, but in the tombs.

28 When he saw Jesus, he cried out, and fell down before him, and with a loud voice said, What have I to do with thee, Jesus, *thou* Son of God most high? I beseech thee, torment[c] me not.

29 (For he had commanded the unclean spirit to come out of the man. For oftentimes it had caught him: and he was kept bound with chains and in fetters; and he brake the bands, and was driven of the devil into the wilderness.)

30 And Jesus asked him, saying, What is thy name? And he said, Legion; because many devils were entered into him.

31 And they besought him that he would not command them to go out into the [d]deep.

32 And there was there an herd of many swine feeding on the mountain; and they besought him that he would suffer them to enter into them; and he suffered them.

33 Then went the devils out of the man, and entered into the swine; and the herd ran violently down a steep place into the lake, and were choked.

34 When they that fed *them* saw what was done, [e]they fled, and went and told *it* in the city and in the country.

35 Then they went out to see what was done; and came to Jesus, and found the man out of whom the devils were departed, sitting at the feet of Jesus, clothed and in his [f]right mind; and they were afraid.

36 They also which saw *it* told them by what means he that was possessed of the devils was healed.

37 Then the whole multitude of the country of the Gadarenes round about [g]besought him to depart from them, for they were taken with great fear; and he went up into the ship, and returned back again.

38 Now the man out of whom the devils were departed [h]besought him that he might be with him: but Jesus sent him away, saying,

39 Return to [i]thine own house, and show how [k]great things God hath done unto thee. And he went his way, and published throughout the whole city how great things Jesus had done unto him.

40 And it came to pass, that, when Jesus was returned, the people *gladly* received him; for they were all waiting for him.

41 And behold, [l]there came a man named Jairus, and he was a ruler of the synagogue; and he fell

a Ps.44.23; Is.51.9,10. *b* Mat.8.28,&c.; Mar.5.1,&c. *c* Is.27.1; Ja.2.19; Re.20.10. *d* Re.20.3.

e Ac.19.16,17. *f* Ps.51.10. *g* Ac.16.39. *h* De.10.20,21; Ps.116.12,16. *i* 1 Ti.5.8. *k* Ps.126.2,3. *l* Mat.9.18,&c.; Mar.5.22,&c.

19-21. See Notes on Mat. xii. 46-50.

22-39. See this passage explained in the Notes on Mat. viii. 23-34, and Mar. v. 1-20.

down at Jesus' feet, and besought him that he would come into his house;

42 For he had one only daughter, about twelve years of age, and she lay a dying. But as he went the people thronged him.

43 And a woman having an issue of blood twelve years, which [m]had spent all her living upon [n]physicians, neither could be healed of any,

44 Came behind *him*, and touched the border of his garment; and immediately[o] her issue of blood stanched.

45 And Jesus said, Who touched me? When all denied, Peter, and they that were with him, said, Master, the multitude throng thee and press *thee*, and sayest thou, Who touched me?

46 And Jesus said, Somebody hath touched me; for I perceive that [p]virtue is gone out of me.

47 And when the woman saw that [q]she was not hid, she [r]came trembling, and falling down before him, she declared unto him, before all the people, for what cause she had touched him, and how she was healed immediately.

48 And he said unto her, Daughter, be of good comfort; thy faith hath made thee whole: go in peace.

49 While[s] he yet spake, there cometh one from the [t]ruler of the synagogue's *house*, saying to him, Thy daughter is dead; trouble not the Master.

50 But when Jesus heard *it*, he answered him, saying, [u]Fear not: believe only, and she shall be made whole.

51 And when he came into the house, he suffered no man to go in, save Peter, and James, and John, and the father and the mother of the maiden.

52 And all wept, and bewailed her: but he said, Weep not; she is not dead, but [v]sleepeth.

53 And they [w]laughed him to scorn, knowing that she was dead.

54 And he put them all out, and took her by the hand, and called, saying, Maid, [x]arise.

55 And her spirit came again, and she arose straightway; and he commanded to give her meat.

56 And her parents were astonished; but he [y]charged them that they should tell no man what was done.

CHAPTER IX.

THEN[a] he called his twelve disciples together, and gave them power and authority over all devils, and to cure diseases.

2 And he sent them to preach the kingdom of God, and to heal the sick.

3 And he said unto them, [b]Take nothing for *your* journey, neither staves, nor scrip, neither bread, neither money; neither have two coats apiece.

4 And whatsoever house ye enter into, there abide, and thence depart.

5 And whosoever will not receive you, when ye go out of that city [c]shake off the very dust from your feet for a testimony against them.

6 And they departed, and went through the towns, preaching the gospel, and healing everywhere.

7 Now[d] Herod the tetrarch heard of all that was done by him; and

m 2 Ch.16.12; Is.55.2. *n* Job 13.4. *o* Mat.8.3; 20.34; ch.13.13. *p* ch.6.19; 1 Pe.2.9. *q* Ps.38.9; Ho.5.3. *r* Is.66.2; Ho.13.1; Ac.16.29. *s* Mat.9.23,&c.; Mar.5.35,&c. *t* ver.41,42. *u* Jn.11.25; Ro.4.17.

v Jn.11.11,13. *w* Ps.22.7; ch.16.14. *x* ch.7.14; Jn.11.43. *y* Mat.8.4; 9.30; Mar.5.43. *a* Mat.10.1,&c.; Mar.3.13,&c.; 6.7,&c. *b* ch.10.4,&c.; 12.22. *c* Ne.5.13; Ac.13.51; 18.6. *d* Mat.14.1,&c.; Mar.6.14,&c.

40–56. See this passage explained in the Notes on Mat. ix. 18–26, and Mar. v. 21–43.

CHAPTER IX.

1–6. See Notes on Mat. x. 1–14.

7–9. See Notes on Mat. xiv. 1, 2. Comp. Mar. vi. 14–16.

he was perplexed, because that it was said of some that John was risen from the dead;

8 And of some, That Elias had appeared; and of others, That one of the old prophets was risen again.

9 And Herod said, John have I beheaded; but who is this of whom I hear such things? And he [e]desired to see him.

10 And the apostles, when they were returned, told him all that they had done. And he took them, and went aside privately into a desert place, belonging to the city called Bethsaida.

11 And the people, [f]when they knew *it*, followed him; and [g]he received them, and spake unto them of the [h]kingdom of God, and healed them that [i]had need of healing.

12 And[k] when the day began to wear away, then came the twelve, and said unto him, Send the multitude away, that they may go into the towns and country round about, and lodge, and get victuals; for we are here in a [l]desert place.

13 But he said unto them, Give ye them to eat. And they said, We have no more but five loaves and two fishes; except we should go and buy meat for all this people.

14 (For they were about five thousand men.) And he said to his disciples, [m]Make them sit down by fifties in a company.

15 And they did so, and made them all sit down.

16 Then he took the five loaves and the two fishes; and looking up to heaven, he blessed them, and brake, and gave to the disciples to set before the multitude.

17 And they did eat, and [n]were all filled; and there was taken up of fragments that remained to them, twelve baskets.

18 And[o] it came to pass, as he was alone praying, his disciples were with him; and he asked them, saying, Whom say the people that I am?

19 They answering, said, [p]John the Baptist; but some *say*, Elias; and others *say*, That one of the old prophets is risen again.

20 He said unto them, But whom say ye that I am? Peter [q]answering said, The Christ of God.

21 And he straitly charged them, and commanded *them* to tell no man that thing;

22 Saying, [r]The Son of man must suffer many things, and be rejected of the elders, and chief priests, and scribes, and be slain, and be raised the third day.

23 And he said to *them* all, [s]If any *man* will come after me, let him deny himself, and take up his cross daily, and follow me.

24 For whosoever will save his life shall lose it; but whosoever will lose his life for my sake, the same shall save it.

25 For what is a man advantaged if he gain the whole world and lose himself, or be cast away?

26 For[t] whosoever shall be ashamed of me and of my words, of him shall the Son of man be

e ch.23.8. *f* Ro.10.14,17. *g* Jn.6.37. *h* Ac.28.31. *i* ch.1.53; 5.31; He.4.16. *k* Mat.14.15,&c.; Mar.6.35,&c.; Jn.6.5,&c. *l* Ps.78.19,20; Eze.34.25; Ho.13.5. *m* 1 Co.14.40.

n Ps.107.9. *o* Mat.16.13,&c.; Mar.8.27,&c. *p* Mat.14.2; ver.7,8. *q* Jn.6.69. *r* Mat.16.21; 17.22. *s* Mat.10.38; 16.24; Mar.8.34; ch.14.27; Ro.8.13; Col.3.5. *t* Mat.10.33; Mar.8.38; 2 Ti.2.12.

10–17. See Notes on Mat. xiv. 13–21, and Mar. vi. 30–44.

10. *Bethsaida.* A city on the east bank of the river Jordan, near where the river enters into the Sea of Tiberias. In the neighbourhood of that city were extensive wastes or deserts.

12. *Day began to wear away.* To decline, or as it drew near toward evening.

18–26. See Notes on Mat. xvi. 13–27; Mar. viii. 27–38.

20. *The Christ of God.* The *Anointed* of God. The *Messiah* appointed by God,

ashamed when he shall come in
his own glory, and *in his* Father's,
and of the holy angels.
27 But[u] I tell you of a truth,
there be some standing here which
shall not [v]taste of death till they
see the kingdom of God.
28 And[w] it came to pass about
an eight days after these [1]sayings,
he took Peter, and John, and
James, and went up into a mountain to pray.
29 And as he prayed, the fashion
of his countenance was altered, and
his raiment *was* white *and* glistering.
30 And, behold, there talked with
him two men, which were Moses
and Elias,
31 Who appeared in glory, and
spake of his decease which he
should accomplish at Jerusalem.
32 But Peter and they that were
with him were [x]heavy with sleep;
and when they were awake, [y]they
saw his glory, and the two men
that stood with him.
33 And it came to pass, as they
departed from him, Peter said unto
Jesus, Master, [z]It is good for us to
be here: and let us make three
tabernacles; one for thee, and one
for Moses, and one for Elias; [a]not
knowing what he said.
34 While he thus spake, there
came a cloud and overshadowed
them; and they feared as they entered into the cloud.
35 And there came a voice out
of the cloud, saying, [b]This is my
beloved Son: [c]hear him.
36 And when the voice was past,
Jesus was found alone. And they
kept *it* close, and [d]told no man in
those days any of those things
which they had seen.
37 And[e] it came to pass, that on
the next day, when they were come
down from the hill, much people
met him.
38 And, behold, a man of the
company cried out, saying, Master, I beseech thee look upon my
son; for he is mine [f]only child:
39 And, lo, a spirit taketh him,
and he suddenly crieth out; and

u Mat.16.28; Mar.9.1. *v* Jn.8.52; He.2.9. *w* Mat.17.1,&c.; Mar.9.2,&c. 1 or, *things*. *x* Da.8.18; 10.9. *y* Jn.1.14.

z Ps.27.4; 73.28. *a* Mar.10.38. *b* Mat.3.17; 2 Pe.1.17,18. *c* De.18.15; Ac.3.22. *d* Ec.3.7. *e* Mat.17.14,&c.; Mar.9.17,&c. *f* Zec.12.10.

---

and who had been long promised by him. See Notes on Mat. i. 1.

28–36. See an account of the transfiguration in Mat. xvii. 1–13, and Mar. ix. 2–13.

29. *The fashion.* The *appearance.* ¶ *Glistering.* Shining like lightning—of a bright, dazzling whiteness. As Mark says, "more white than any fuller could make it."

31. *In glory.* Of a glorious appearance. Of an appearance like that which the saints have in heaven. ¶ *His decease.* Literally his *exit* or *departure.* The word translated here *decease*—that is, *exit*, or *going out*—is elsewhere used to denote death. See 2 Pe. i. 15. Death is a departure or going out from this life. In *this* word there may be an allusion to the *departure* of the children of Israel from Egypt. As that was going out from *bondage*, pain, and humiliation, so death, to a saint, is but going forth from a land of captivity and thraldom to one of plenty and freedom; to the land of promise, the Canaan in the skies. ¶ *He should accomplish.* Which was about to take place.

32. *Heavy with sleep.* Borne down with sleep—oppressed, overcome with sleep. It may seem remarkable that they should fall asleep on such an occasion; but we are to bear in mind that this may have been in the night, and that they were weary with the toils of the day. Besides, they did not *fall asleep* while the transfiguration lasted. While Jesus was praying, or perhaps after he closed, they fell asleep. *While* they were sleeping his countenance was changed, and Moses and Elias appeared. The first that *they* saw of it was after they awoke, having been probably awakened by the shining of the light around them.

36. *Jesus was found alone.* That is, the two men had left him. In respect to *them* he was alone.

it teareth him that he foameth
again; and, bruising him, hardly
departeth from him.
40 And I besought thy disciples
to cast him out, and [g]they could
not.
41 And Jesus answering said, O
faithless[h] and [i]perverse generation!
how long shall I be with you, and
suffer you? Bring thy son hither.
42 And as he was yet a coming,
the devil threw him down and tare
him. And Jesus [k]rebuked the unclean spirit, and healed the child,
and delivered him again to his
father.
43 And they were all [l]amazed
at the mighty power of God. But
while they wondered every one at
all things which Jesus did, he said
unto his disciples,
44 Let these sayings sink down
into your ears; [m]for the Son of man
shall be delivered [n]into the hands
of men.
45 But[o] they understood not this
saying, and it was hid from them,
that they perceived it not; and they
feared to ask him of that saying.
46 Then[p] there arose a reasoning
among them, which of them should
be greatest.
47 And Jesus, perceiving the
thought of their heart, took a
child, and set him by him,
48 And said unto them, [q]Who-
soever shall receive this child in
my name, receiveth me; and whosoever shall receive me, receiveth
him that sent me: [r]for he that is
least among you all, the same shall
be great.
49 And John answered and said,
Master, [s]we saw one casting out
devils in thy name; and we forbad
him, because he followeth not
with us.
50 And Jesus said unto him,
Forbid *him* not; [t]for he that is
not against us is for us.
51 And it came to pass, when
the time was come that he should

g Ac.19.13-16. *h* Jn.20.27; He.4.2. *i* De.32.5; Ps.78.8. *k* Mar.1.27. *l* Ps.139.14; Zec.8.6. *m* Mat.17.22. *n* 2 Sa.24.14. *o* Mar.9.32; ch.2.50; 18.34.

p Mat.18.1,&c.; Mar.9.34,&c. *q* Mat.10.40; Jn.12.44; 13.20. *r* Mat.23.11,12; ch.14.11. *s* Nu.11.27-29. *t* Mat.12.30; ch.16.13.

37–43. See this passage explained in the Notes on Mat. xvii. 14–21, and Mar. ix. 14–29.

44. *Let these sayings.* Probably this refers to the *sayings of the people*, who had seen his miracles, and who on that account had praised and glorified God. On that ground they had acknowledged him to be the Christ. As if he had said, "I am about to die. *You* will then be disconsolate, and perhaps doubtful about my being the Christ. *Then* do you remember these miracles, and the confessions of the people—the evidence which I gave you that I was from God." Or it may mean, "Remember that I am about to die, and let my sayings in regard to that sink down into your hearts, for it is a most important event; and you will have need of remembering, when it takes place, that I told you of it." This last interpretation, however, does not agree as well with the Greek as the former.

45. *It was hid from them.* They had imbibed the common notions of the Jews that he was to be a prince and a conqueror, to deliver the nation. They could not understand how that could be, if he was soon to be delivered into the hands of his enemies to die. In this way it was hid from them—not by God, but by their previous false belief. And from this we may learn that the plainest truths of the Bible are unintelligible to many because they have embraced some belief or opinion before which is erroneous, and which they are unwilling to abandon. The proper way of reading the Bible is to lay aside all previous opinions and submit entirely to God. The apostles should have supposed that their previous notions of the Messiah were wrong, and should have renounced them. They should have believed that what Jesus *then* said was consistent with his being the Christ. So *we* should believe that *all* that God says is consistent with truth, and should forsake all other opinions.

46–50. See Notes on Mat. xviii. 1–5. Comp. Mar. ix. 33–38.

be [u]received up, he stedfastly set
his face to go to Jerusalem,
52 And sent messengers before
his face; and they went, and entered
into a village of the [v]Samaritans, to
make ready for him.
53 And they did not receive him,
because his face was as though he
would go to Jerusalem.
54 And when his disciples, James
and John, saw *this*, they said, Lord,
wilt thou that we command fire to
come down from heaven and consume them, even as [w]Elias did?

u Mar.16.19; Ac.1.2. v Jn.4.4. w 2 Ki.1.10,12.

---

51. *Should be received up.* The word here translated "received up" means literally a removal from a lower to a higher place, and here it refers evidently to the solemn ascension of Jesus to heaven. It is often used to describe that great event. See Ac. i. 11, 22; Mar. xvi. 19; 1 Ti. iii. 16. The time appointed for him to remain on the earth was about expiring, and he resolved to go to Jerusalem and die. And from this we learn that Jesus made a *voluntary* sacrifice; that he *chose* to give his life for the sins of men. Humanly speaking, had he remained in Galilee he would have been safe; but that it might appear that he did not shun danger, and that he was really a *voluntary* sacrifice — that no man had power over his life except as he was *permitted* (Jn. xix. 11)—he chose to put himself in the way of danger, and even to go into scenes which he knew would end in his death. ¶ *He stedfastly set his face.* He determined to go to Jerusalem, or he set out resolutely. When a man goes toward an object, he may be said to set his face toward it. The expression here means only that he *resolved* to go, and it implies that he was not appalled by the dangers—that he was determined to brave all, and go up into the midst of his enemies — to die.

52. *Sent messengers.* In the original the word is *angels;* and the use of that word here shows that the word *angel* in the Bible does not always mean heavenly beings. ¶ *To make ready.* To prepare a place, lodgings, refreshments. He had no reason to expect that he would experience any kind treatment from the Samaritans if he came suddenly among them, and if they saw that he was going to Jerusalem. He therefore made provision beforehand, and thus has shown us that it is not *improper* to look out beforehand for the supply of our wants, and to guard against want and poverty. ¶ *Samaritans.* See Notes on Mat. x. 5. They had no dealings with the Jews, Jn. iv. 9.

53. *They did not receive him.* Did not entertain him hospitably, or receive him with kindness. ¶ *Because his face was,* &c. Because they ascertained that he was going to Jerusalem. One of the subjects of dispute between the Jews and Samaritans pertained to the proper situation of the temple. The Jews contended that it should be at Jerusalem; the Samaritans, on Mount Gerizim, and accordingly they had built one there. They had probably heard of the miracles of Jesus, and that he claimed to be the Messiah. Perhaps they had hoped that he would decide that *they* were right in regard to the building of the temple. Had he decided the question in that way, they would have received him as the Messiah gladly; but when they saw that he was going among the Jews—that *by going* he would decide in their favour, they resolved to have nothing to do with him, and they rejected him. And from this we may learn—1st. That men wish all the teachers of religion to fall in with their own views. 2d. That if a doctrine does not accord with their selfish desires, they are very apt to reject it. 3d. That if a religious teacher or a doctrine favours a rival sect, it is commonly rejected without examination. And, 4th. That men, from a regard to their own views and selfishness, often reject the true religion, as the Samaritans did the Son of God, and bring upon themselves swift destruction.

54. *James and John.* They were called *Boanerges*—sons of thunder—probably on account of their energy and power in preaching the gospel, or of their vehement and rash zeal—a remarkable example of which we have in this instance, Mar. iii. 17. ¶ *Wilt thou,* &c. The insult had been offered to Jesus, their friend, and they felt it; but their zeal was rash and their spirit bad. Vengeance belongs to God: it was not theirs to attempt it. ¶ *Fire from*

55 But he turned and rebuked them, and said, Ye know not what manner of spirit ye are of.
56 For[x] the Son of man is not come to destroy men's lives, but to save *them*. And they went to another village.
57 And[y] it came to pass, that, as they went in the way, a certain *man* said unto him, Lord, I will follow thee whithersoever thou goest.
58 And Jesus said unto him, Foxes have holes, and birds of the air *have* nests; but the Son of man hath not where to lay *his* head.
59 And he said unto another, Follow me. But he said, [z]Lord, suffer me first to go and bury my father.
60 Jesus said unto him, Let the dead bury their dead; but go thou and preach the kingdom of God.
61 And another also said, Lord, I will follow thee; but let me first go bid them farewell which are at home at my house.
62 And Jesus said unto him, No man, having put his hand to the plough, and looking back, is fit for the kingdom of God.

x Jn.3.17; 12.47. *y* Mat.8.19,&c. *z* 1 Ki.19.20.

---

heaven. Lightning, to consume them. ¶ *As Elias did*. By this they wished to justify their zeal. Perhaps, while they were speaking, they saw Jesus look at them with disapprobation, and to vindicate themselves they referred to the case of Elijah. The case is recorded in 2 Ki. i. 10–12.

55. *Ye know not what manner of spirit ye are of*. You suppose that you are actuated by a proper love for me; but you know not yourselves. It is rather a love of revenge; rather revengeful feelings toward the *Samaritans* than proper feelings toward *me*. We learn here—1st. That *apparent* zeal for God may be only improper opposition toward our fellow-men. 2d. That men, when they wish to honour God, should examine their spirit, and see if there is not lying at the bottom of their professed zeal for God some bad feeling toward their fellow-men. 3d. That the highest opposition which Jesus met with was not inconsistent with *his* loving those who opposed him, and with his seeking to do them good.

56. *For the Son of man*, &c. You should imitate, in your spirit, the Son of man. *He* came not to destroy. If he had come for that purpose, he would have destroyed these Samaritans; but he came to save. He is not soon angry. *He* bears patiently opposition to himself, and *you* should bear opposition to *him*. You should catch his spirit; temper your zeal like his; seek to do good to those who injure you and him; be mild, kind, patient, and forgiving.

57–60. See Notes on Mat. viii. 19–22.

61. *Bid them farewell*. To take leave, inform them of the design, and set things at home in order. Jesus did not suffer this, because he probably saw that he would be influenced by a love of his friends, or by their persuasions, not to return to him. The purpose to be a Christian requires *decision*. Men should not tamper with the world. They should not consult earthly friends about it. They should not even allow worldly friends to give them *advice* whether to be Christians or not. God is to be obeyed rather than man, and they should come forth boldly, and resolve at once to give themselves to his service.

62. *No man, having put his hand*, &c. To put one's hand to a plough is a proverbial expression to signify undertaking any business. In order that a ploughman may accomplish his work, it is necessary to look onward—to be intent on his employment—not to be looking back with regret that he undertook it. So in religion. He that enters on it must do it with his whole heart. He that comes still loving the world—still looking with regret on its pleasures, its wealth, and its honours—that has not *wholly* forsaken them as his portion, cannot be a Christian, and is not fit for the kingdom of God. How searching is this test to those who profess to be Christians! And how solemn the duty of all men to renounce all earthly objects, and to be not only *almost*, but *altogether*, followers of the Son of God! It is perilous to tamper with the world—to look at its pleasures or to seek its society. He that would enter heaven

CHAPTER X.

AFTER[a] these things the Lord appointed other seventy also, and sent them two and two before his face into every city and place, whither he himself would come.

2 Therefore said he unto them, [b]The harvest truly *is* great, but [c]the labourers *are* few: pray ye therefore the Lord of the harvest, that he would send forth labourers into his harvest.

3 Go your ways: behold, I send you forth as lambs among wolves.

a Mat.10.1,&c.; Mar.6.7,&c.

b Mat.9.37; Jn.4.35. c 1 Co.3.9; 1 Ti.5.17.

must come with a heart full of love to God; giving *all* into his hands, and prepared always to give up all his property, his health, his friends, his body, his soul to God, when he demands them, or he cannot be a Christian. Religion is everything or nothing. He that is not willing to sacrifice *everything* for the cause of God, is really willing to sacrifice nothing.

CHAPTER X.

1. *After these things.* After the appointment of the twelve apostles, and the transactions recorded in the previous chapters. ¶ *Other seventy.* Seventy others besides the apostles. They were appointed for a different purpose from the apostles. The apostles were to be with him; to hear his instructions; to be witnesses of his miracles, his sufferings, his death, his resurrection and ascension, that they might *then* go and proclaim all these things to the world. The seventy were sent out to preach immediately, and chiefly where he himself was about to come. They were appointed for a temporary object. They were to go into the villages and towns, and prepare the way for his coming. The number *seventy* was a favourite number among the Jews. Thus the family of Jacob that came into Egypt consisted of seventy, Ge. xlvi. 27. The number of elders that Moses appointed to aid him was the same, Nu. xi. 16, 25. The number which composed the great Sanhedrim, or council of the nation, was the same. It is not improbable that our Saviour appointed this *number* with reference to the fact that it so often occurred among the Jews, or after the example of Moses, who appointed seventy to aid him in his work; but it is evident that the office was *temporary*—that it had a specific design—and of course that it would be improper to attempt to find now a *continuation* of it, or a parallel to it, in the Christian ministry. ¶ *Two and two.* There was much wisdom in sending them in this manner. It was done, doubtless, that they might aid one another by mutual counsel, and that they might sustain and comfort one another in their persecutions and trials. Our Lord in this showed the propriety of having *a religious friend*, who would be a confidant and help. Every Christian, and especially every Christian minister, needs such a friend, and should seek some one to whom he can unbosom himself, and with whom he can mingle his feelings and prayers.

2. See Notes on Mat. ix. 36, 37.

3. See Notes on Mat. x. 16.

4. *Purse—scrip—shoes.* See Notes on Mat. x. 10. ¶ *Salute no man by the way. Salutations* among the Orientals did not consist, as among us, of a slight bow or an extension of the hand, but was performed by many embraces and inclinations, and even prostrations of the body on the ground. All this required much *time;* and as the business on which the seventy were sent was urgent, they were required not to *delay* their journey by long and formal salutations of the persons whom they met. "If two Arabs of equal rank meet each other, they extend to each other the right hand, and having clasped, they elevate them as if to kiss them. Each one then draws back his hand and kisses it instead of his friend's, and then places it upon his forehead. The parties then continue the salutation by kissing each other's beard. They give thanks to God that they are once more permitted to see their friend—they pray to the Almighty in his behalf. Sometimes they repeat not less than ten times the ceremony of grasping hands and kissing." It may also be added, in the language of Dr. Thomson (*The Land and the Book*, vol. i. p. 534), that "there is such an amount of insincerity, flattery, and falsehood in the terms of salutation prescribed by etiquette, that our Lord, who is truth itself, desired his representatives to dispense with them as far as possible, perhaps tacitly

4 Carry[d] neither purse, nor scrip,
nor shoes; and [e]salute no man by
the way.
5 And into whatsoever house ye
enter, first say, Peace *be* to this
house.
6 And if the [f]son of peace be
there, [g]your peace shall rest upon
it; if not, it shall turn to you again.
7 And in the same house remain,
eating and drinking such things
as they give; for [h]the labourer is
worthy of his hire. Go[i] not from
house to house.
8 And into whatsoever city ye
enter, and they receive you, [k]eat
such things as are set before you;
9 And heal the sick that are
therein, and say unto them, [l]The
kingdom of God is come nigh
unto you.
10 But into whatsoever city ye
enter, and they receive you not,
go your ways out into the streets
of the same, and say,
11 Even[m] the very dust of your
city, which cleaveth on us, we do
wipe off against you: notwithstanding, be ye sure of this, that
the kingdom of God is come nigh
unto you.
12 But I say unto you, that it
shall be more tolerable in that day
for Sodom than for that city.
13 Woe[n] unto thee, Chorazin!
woe unto thee, Bethsaida! for [o]if
the mighty works had been done in
Tyre and Sidon which have been
done in you, they had a great while
ago repented, sitting in sackcloth
and ashes.
14 But it shall be more tolerable
for Tyre and Sidon at the judgment than for you.
15 And thou, Capernaum, [p]which
art exalted to heaven, [q]shalt be
thrust down to hell.
16 He[r] that heareth you, heareth
me; and [s]he that despiseth you,
despiseth me; and [t]he that de-

d ch.9.3,&c. *e* Ge.24.33,56; 2 Ki.4.29; Pr.4.25. *f* Is.9.6. *g* 2 Th.3.16; Ja.3.18. *h* 1 Co.9.4-14; 1 Ti.5.18. *i* 1 Ti.5.13. *k* 1 Co.10.27. *l* Mat.3.2.

m ch.9.5. *n* Mat.11.21,&c. *o* Eze.3.6. *p* Is.14.13-15; Je.51.53; Am.9.2,3. *q* Eze.26.20; 31.18. *r* Jn.13.20. *s* Ac.5.4. *t* Jn.5.23.

---

to rebuke them. These 'instructions' were also intended to reprove another propensity which an Oriental can scarcely resist, no matter how urgent his business. If he meets an acquaintance, he must stop and make an endless number of inquiries and answer as many. If they come upon men making a bargain or discussing any other matter, they must pause and intrude their own ideas, and enter keenly into the business, though it in no wise concerns them; and more especially, an Oriental can never resist the temptation to assist *where accounts are being settled* or *money counted out*. The clink of coin has a positive fascination to them. Now the command of our Saviour strictly forbade all such loiterings. They would waste time, distract attention, and in many ways hinder the prompt and faithful discharge of their important mission." The salutation of friends, therefore, was a ceremony which consumed much time; and it was on this account that our Lord on this occasion forbade them to delay their journey to greet others. A similar direction is found in 2 Ki. iv. 29.

5. See Notes on Mat. x. 13.

6. *The son of peace.* That is, if the *house* or *family* be *worthy*, or be disposed to receive you in *peace* and kindness. See Mat. x. 13. *The son of peace* means one *disposed* to peace, or peaceful and kind in his disposition. Comp. Mat. i. 1.

7. See Notes on Mat. x. 11. On this passage Dr. Thomson (*The Land and the Book*, vol. i. p. 534) remarks: "The reason [for the command, 'Go not from house to house'] is very obvious to one acquainted with Oriental customs. When a stranger arrives in a village or an encampment, the neighbours, one after another, must invite him to eat with them. There is a strict etiquette about it, involving much ostentation and hypocrisy, and a failure in the due observance of this system of hospitality is violently resented, and often leads to alienations and feuds among neighbours; it also consumes much time, causes unusual distraction of mind, leads to levity, and every way counteracts the success of a spiritual mission."

spiseth me, despiseth him that sent me.

17 And the seventy returned again with joy, saying, Lord, even the devils are subject unto us through thy name.

18 And he said unto them, I beheld [u] Satan as lightning fall from heaven.

19 Behold, I give unto you power to [v] tread on serpents and scorpions, and over all the power of the enemy; and nothing shall by any means hurt you.

20 Notwithstanding, in this rejoice not, that the spirits are subject unto you; but rather rejoice because [w] your names are written in heaven.

21 In that hour Jesus rejoiced in spirit, and said, I thank thee, O Father, Lord of heaven and earth, that thou hast hid these things from the wise and prudent, and hast revealed them unto babes: even so, Father; for so it seemed good in thy sight.

22 [1] All [x] things are delivered to

u Re.12.8,9. *v* Mar.16.18; Ac.28.5.

w Ex.32.32; Ps.69.28; Is.4.3; Da.12.1; Phi.4.3; He. 12.23; Re.13.8; 20.12; 21.27.

1 Many ancient copies add, *And turning to his disciples, he said.* *x* Mat.28.18; Jn.3.35.

8–12. See Notes on Mat. x. 14, 15.

13–15. See Notes on Mat. xi. 21–24.

16. See Notes on Mat. x. 40.

17. *The devils are subject unto us.* The devils obey us. We have been able to cast them out. ¶ *Through thy name.* When commanded in thy name to come out of those who are possessed.

18. *I beheld Satan*, &c. *Satan* here denotes evidently the prince of the devils who had been cast out by the seventy disciples, for the discourse was respecting their power over evil spirits. *Lightning* is an image of *rapidity* or *quickness.* I saw Satan fall *quickly* or rapidly—as quick as lightning. The phrase "from heaven" is to be referred to the lightning, and does not mean that he saw *Satan* fall *from heaven*, but that he fell as quick as lightning from heaven or from the clouds. The whole expression then may mean, "I saw at your command devils immediately depart, as quick as the flash of lightning. I gave you this power—I saw it put forth—and I give also now, in addition to this, the power to tread on serpents," &c.

19. *To tread on serpents.* Preservation from danger. If you tread on a poisonous reptile that would otherwise injure you, *I* will keep you from danger. If you go among bitter and malignant enemies that would seek your life, *I* will preserve you. See Notes on Mar. xvi. 18. ¶ *Scorpions.* The scorpion is an animal with eight feet, eight eyes, and a long jointed tail, ending in a pointed weapon or sting. It is found in tropical climates, and seldom exceeds 4 inches in length. Its sting is extremely poisonous, and it is sometimes fatal to life. It is in Scripture the emblem of malicious and crafty men. When rolled up it has some resemblance to an egg, Lu. xi. 12; Eze. ii. 6. The

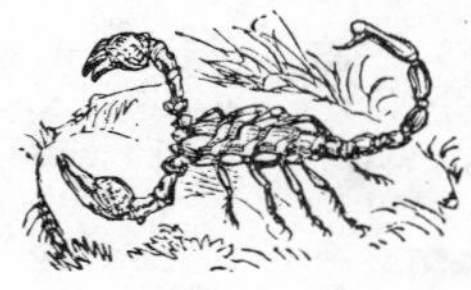

Scorpion.

annexed cut will give an idea of its usual form and appearance. ¶ *The enemy.* Satan. The meaning of this verse is, that Jesus would preserve them from the power of Satan and all his emissaries—from all wicked and crafty men; and this shows that he had divine power. He that can control Satan and his hosts—that can be present to guard from all their machinations, see all their plans, and destroy all their designs, must be clothed with no less than almighty power.

20. *Rather rejoice*, &c. Though it was an honour to work miracles, though it is an honour to be endowed with talents, and influence, and learning, yet it is a subject of *chief* joy that we are numbered among the people of God, and have a title to everlasting life. ¶ *Names are written in heaven.* The names of citizens of a city or state were accustomed to be written in a book or register, from which they were blotted out when they became unworthy, or forfeited the favour of their country. Comp. Ps. lxix. 28; Ex. xxxii. 32; De. ix. 14; Re. iii. 5. That their *names were written in heaven* means that

me of my Father; and [y]no man
knoweth who the Son is, but the
Father; and who the Father is,
but the Son, and *he* to whom the
Son will reveal *him*.
23 And he turned him unto *his*
disciples, and said privately, Blessed
are the eyes which see the things
that ye see:
24 For I tell you that [z]many
prophets and kings have desired
to see those things which ye see,
and have not seen *them;* and to
hear those things which ye hear,
and have not heard *them*.
25 And, behold, a certain lawyer
stood up, and tempted him, saying,
Master, [a]what shall I do to
[b]inherit eternal life?
26 He said unto him, What is
written in the law? how readest
thou?
27 And he answering said, [c]Thou
shalt love the Lord thy God with
all thy heart, and with all thy soul,
and with all thy strength, and with
all thy mind; and [d]thy neighbour
as thyself.
28 And he said unto him, Thou
hast answered right; [e]this do, and
thou shalt live.
29 But he, willing to [f]justify
himself, said unto Jesus, And who
is my [g]neighbour?

y Jn.6.44,46. *z* 1 Pe.1.10.

a Ac.16.30,31. *b* Ga.3.18. *c* De.6.5. *d* Le.19.18. *e* Le.18.5; Ne.9.29; Eze.20.11,21; Ro.10.5; Ga.3.12. *f* Job 32.2; ch.16.15; Ro.4.2; Ga.3.11; Ja.2.24. *g* Mat.5.43,44.

they were *citizens* of heaven; that they were friends of God and *approved* by him, and would be permitted to dwell with him. This was of far more value than all *earthly* honour, power, or wealth, and *in* this men should rejoice more than in eminent endowments of influence, learning, talents, or possessions.

21, 22. See Notes on Mat. xi. 25–27.

23, 24. See Notes on Mat. xiii. 16, 17.

25. *A certain lawyer*. One who professed to be well skilled in the laws of Moses, and whose business it was to explain them. ¶ *Stood up*. Rose—came forward to address him. ¶ *Tempted him*. Feigned a desire to be instructed, but did it to perplex him, or to lead him, if possible, to contradict some of the maxims of the law. ¶ *Inherit eternal life*. Be saved. This was the common inquiry among the Jews. *They* had said that man must keep the commandments—the written and oral law.

26. *What is written*, &c. Jesus referred him to the *law* as a safe rule, and asked him what was said there. The lawyer was doubtless endeavouring to justify himself by obeying the law. He trusted to his own works. To bring him off from that ground—to make him feel that it was an unsafe foundation, Jesus showed him what the law *required*, and thus showed him that he needed a better righteousness than his own. This is the proper use of the law. By comparing ourselves with *that* we see our own defects, and are thus prepared to welcome a better righteousness than our own—that of the Lord Jesus Christ. Thus the law becomes a schoolmaster to lead us to him, Ga. iii. 24.

27, 28. See this subject explained in the Notes on Mat. xxii. 37–40.

29. *To justify himself*. Desirous to appear blameless, or to vindicate himself, and show that he had kept the law. Jesus wished to lead him to a proper view of his own sinfulness, and his real departure from the law. The man was desirous of showing that he had kept the law; or perhaps he was desirous of justifying himself for asking the question; of showing that it could not be so easily settled; that a mere reference to the *words* of the law did not determine it. It was still a question what was meant by *neighbour*. The Pharisees held that the *Jews* only were to be regarded as such, and that the obligation did not extend at all to the Gentiles. The lawyer was probably ready to affirm that he had discharged faithfully his duty to his countrymen, and had thus kept the law, and could justify himself. Every sinner is desirous of *justifying himself*. He seeks to do it by his own works. For this purpose he perverts the meaning of the law, destroys its spirituality, and brings *down* the law to *his* standard, rather than attempt to frame his life by *its* requirements.

30. *Jesus answering*. Jesus answered him in a very different manner from

30 And Jesus answering said, A certain *man* went down from Jerusalem to Jericho, and fell among thieves, which stripped him of his raiment, and wounded *him*, and departed, leaving *him* half dead.
31 And by chance there came down a certain priest that way;

---

what he expected. By one of the most tender and affecting narratives to be found anywhere, he made the lawyer his own judge in the case, and constrained him to admit what at first he would probably have denied. He compelled him to acknowledge that a *Samaritan*—of a race most hated of all people by the Jews—had shown the kindness of a neighbour, while a *priest* and a *Levite* had denied it *to their own countrymen.* ¶ *From Jerusalem to Jericho.* Jericho was situated about 15 miles to the north-east of Jerusalem, and about 8 west of the river Jordan. See Notes on Mat. xx. 29. ¶ *Fell among thieves.* Fell among *robbers.* The word *thieves* means those who merely take *property.* These were highwaymen, and not merely took the property, but endangered the life. They were *robbers.* From Jerusalem to Jericho the country was rocky and mountainous, and in some parts scarcely inhabited. It afforded, therefore, among the rocks and fastnesses, a convenient place for highwaymen. This was also a very frequented road. Jericho was a large place, and there was much travelling to Jerusalem. At this time, also, Judea abounded with robbers. Josephus says that at one time Herod the Great dismissed forty thousand men who had been employed in building the temple, a large part of whom became highwaymen (Josephus' *Antiquities*, xv. 7). The following remarks of Professor Hackett, who visited Palestine in 1852, will furnish a good illustration of the scene of this parable. It is remarkable that a parable uttered more than eighteen hundred years ago might still be appropriately *located* in this region. Professor Hackett (*Illustrations of Scripture*, p. 215, 216) says of this region: "It is famous at the present day as the haunt of thieves and robbers. No part of the traveller's journey is so dangerous as the expedition to Jericho and the Dead Sea. The Oriental pilgrims who repair to the Jordan have the protection of an escort of Turkish soldiers; and others who would make the same journey must either go in company with them, or provide for their safety by procuring a special guard. I was so fortunate as to be able to accompany the great caravan at the time of the annual pilgrimage. Yet, in spite of every precaution, hardly a season passes in which some luckless wayfarer is not killed or robbed in 'going down from Jerusalem to Jericho.' The place derives its hostile character from its terrible wildness and desolation. If we might conceive of the ocean as being suddenly congealed and petrified when its waves are tossed mountain high, and dashing in wild confusion against each other, we should then have some idea of the aspect of the desert in which the Saviour has placed so truthfully the parable of the good Samaritan. The ravines, the almost inaccessible cliffs, the caverns, furnish admirable lurking-places for robbers. They can rush forth unexpectedly upon their victims, and escape as soon almost beyond the possibility of pursuit.

"Every circumstance in this parable, therefore, was full of significance to those who heard it. The Saviour delivered it near Bethany, on the border of the frightful desert, Lu. x. 25, 38. Jericho was a sacerdotal city. The passing of priests and Levites between that place and Jerusalem was an everyday occurrence. The idea of a caravanserai or 'inn' on the way was not invented, probably, for the sake of the allegory, but borrowed from the landscape. There are the ruins now of such a shelter for the benighted or unfortunate on one of the heights which overlook the infested road. Thus it is that the instructions of our Lord derive often the form and much of their pertinence from the accidental connections of time and place."

31. *By chance.* Accidentally, or as it happened. It means that he did not do it with a *design* to aid the man that was wounded. ¶ *A certain priest.* It is said that not less than twelve thousand priests and Levites dwelt at Jericho; and as their business was at Jerusalem, of course there would be many of them constantly travelling on that road. ¶ *When he saw him.* He saw him lie, but came not near him. ¶ *Passed by on the other side.* On the farther side of the way. Did not turn out of his course even to come and see him.

and when he saw him, he [h]passed
by on the other side.
32 And likewise a Levite, when
he was at the place, [i]came and
looked *on him*, and passed by on
the other side.
33 But a certain [k]Samaritan, as
he journeyed, came where he was;
and when he saw him he had [l]compassion
on him,
34 And went to *him*, and [m]bound
up his wounds, pouring in oil and
wine, and set him on his own beast,
and brought him to an inn, and
took care of him.
35 And on the morrow, when he
departed, he took out two [2]pence,
and gave *them* to the host, and
said unto him, Take care of him;
and whatsoever thou spendest
more, when I come again [n]I will
repay thee.

h Ps.38.11. *i* Ps.109.25; Pr.27.10. *k* Jn.4.9. *l* Ex.2.6. *m* Ps.147.3; Is.1.6.

2 See Mat.20.2. *n* Pr.19.17; ch.14.14.

---

32. *A Levite.* The Levites, as well as the priests, were of the tribe of Levi, and were set apart to the duties of religion. The peculiar duty of the priest was *to offer sacrifice* at the temple; to present incense; to conduct the morning and evening services of the temple, &c. The office or duty of the *Levites* was to render assistance to the priests in their services. In the journey of the Israelites through the wilderness, it was their duty to transport the various parts of the tabernacle and the sacred utensils. It was their duty to see that the tabernacle and the temple were kept clean; to prepare supplies for the sanctuary, such as oil, incense, wine, &c: They had also the care of the sacred revenues, and after the time of David they conducted the sacred *music* of the temple service, Nu. viii. 5–22; 1 Ch. xxiii. 3–5, 24–32; xxiv. 27–31. ¶ *Came and looked on him.* It is remarked by critics, here, that the expression used does not denote, as in the case of the priest, that he accidentally saw him and took no farther notice of him, but that he *came and looked on him more attentively*, but still did nothing to relieve him.

33. *A certain Samaritan.* The Samaritans were the most inveterate foes of the Jews. They had no dealings with each other. See Notes on Mat. x. 5. It was this fact which rendered the conduct of this good man so striking, and which was thus set in strong contrast with the conduct of the priest and the Levite. *They* would not help their own afflicted and wounded countryman. *He*, who could not be expected to aid a Jew, overcame all the usual hostility between the people; saw in the wounded man a neighbour, a brother, one who needed aid; and kindly denied himself to show kindness to the stranger.

34. *Pouring in oil and wine.* These were often used in medicine to heal wounds. Probably they were mingled together, and had a highly sanative quality. How strikingly is his conduct contrasted with the priest and Levite! and how particularly as well as beautifully by this does our Saviour show what *we* ought to do to those who are in circumstances of need! He does not merely say *in general* that he showed him kindness, but he *told how* it was done. He stopped—came where he was—pitied him—bound up his wounds—set him on his own beast—conducted him to a tavern—passed the night with him, and then secured the kind attendances of the landlord, promising him to pay him for his trouble—and all this without desiring or expecting any reward. If this had been by a *Jew*, it would have been signal kindness; if it had been by a *Gentile*, it would also have been great kindness; but it was by a *Samaritan*—a man of a nation most hateful to the Jews, and therefore it most strikingly shows what *we* are to do to friends and foes when they are in distress.

35. *Two pence.* About 27 cents, or 1*s.* 2*d.* This may seem a small sum, but we are to remember that that sum was probably ten times as valuable then as now—that is, that it would purchase ten times as much food and the common necessaries of life as the same sum would now. Besides, it is probable that all the man wanted was *attention* and kindness, and for all these it was the purpose of the Samaritan to *pay* when he returned. ¶ *The host.* The innkeeper.

36. *Was neighbour.* Showed the kindness of a neighbour, or evinced the proper feelings of a neighbour. The lawyer had asked him who was his neighbour? Jesus in this beautiful nar-

36 Which now of these three, thinkest thou, was neighbour unto him that fell among the thieves?
37 And he said, [o]He that showed mercy on him. Then said Jesus unto him, Go, and do thou likewise.
38 Now it came to pass, as they went, that he entered into a certain village; and a certain woman, named [p]Martha, received him into her house.
39 And she had a sister called

o Pr.14.21; Ho.6.6; Mi.6.8; Mat.23.23.

p Jn.11.1; 12.2,3.

rative showed him who and what a neighbour was, and he did this in a way that disarmed his prejudice, deeply affected him in regard to his own duty, and evinced the beauty of religion. Had he *at first* told him that a Samaritan might be a neighbour to a Jew and deserve his kindness, he would have been at once revolted at it; but when, by a beautiful and affecting narrative, he brought the *man himself* to see that it might be, he was constrained to admit it. Here we see the beauty of a parable and its use. It disarmed prejudice, fixed the attention, took the mind gently yet irresistibly, and prevented the possibility of cavil or objection. Compare, also, the address of Nathan to David, 2 Sa. xii. 1–7.

37. *He that showed mercy.* His *Jewish* prejudice would not permit him *to name* the Samaritan, but there was no impropriety, even in his view, in saying that the man who showed so much mercy was really the neighbour to the afflicted, and not he who *professed* to be his neighbour, but who would *do nothing* for his welfare. ¶ *Go, and do thou likewise.* Show the same kindness to *all*—to friend and foe—and *then* you will have evidence that you keep the law, and not *till* then. Of this man we know nothing farther; but from this inimitably beautiful parable we may learn—1. That the knowledge of the law is useful to make us acquainted with our own sinfulness and need of a Saviour. 2. That it is not he who *professes* most kindness that really loves us most, but he who will most deny himself that he may do us good in times of want. 3. That religion requires us to do good to *all* men, however *accidentally* we may become acquainted with their calamities. 4. That we should do good to our enemies. Real love to them will lead us to deny ourselves, and to sacrifice our own welfare, that we may help them in times of distress and alleviate their wants. 5. That he is really our neighbour who does us the most good—who helps us in our necessities, and especially if he does this when there has been *a controversy or difference* between us and him. 6. We hence see the beauty of religion. Nothing else will induce men to surmount their prejudices, to overcome opposition, and to do good to those who are at enmity with them. True religion teaches us to regard every man as our neighbour; prompts us to do good to all, to forget all national or sectional distinctions, and to aid all those who are in circumstances of poverty and want. If religion were valuable for nothing *but this*, it would be the most lovely and desirable principle on earth, and all, especially in their early years, should seek it. Nothing that a young person can gain will be so valuable as the feeling that regards all the world as one great family, and to learn early to do good TO ALL. 7. The difference between the Jew and the Samaritan was a difference in *religion* and *religious opinion;* and from the example of the latter we may learn that, while men differ in *opinions* on subjects of religion, and while they are zealous for what they hold to be the truth, still they should treat each other kindly; that they should aid each other in necessity; and that they should thus show that religion is a principle superior to the love of sect, and that the cord which binds man to man is one that is to be sundered by no difference of opinion, that Christian kindness is to be marred by no forms of worship, and by no bigoted attachment for what we esteem the doctrines of the gospel.

38. *A certain village.* Bethany. See Jn. xi. 1. It was on the eastern declivity of the Mount of Olives. See Notes on Mat. xxi. 1. ¶ *Received him.* Received him kindly and hospitably. From this it would seem that *Martha* was properly the mistress of the house. Possibly she was a widow, and her brother Lazarus and younger sister Mary lived with her; and as *she* had the care of the household, this will also show why she was so diligently employed about domestic affairs.

Mary, which also [q]sat at Jesus' feet, and heard his word.

40 But Martha was cumbered about much serving, and came to him and said, Lord, dost thou not care that my sister hath left me to serve alone? Bid her, therefore, that she help me.

q ch.8.35; Ac.22.3.

41 And Jesus answered and said unto her, Martha, Martha, [r]thou art careful and troubled about many things:

42 But [s]one thing is needful; and Mary hath chosen that good part, which shall not be taken away from her.

r Mar.4.19; ch.21.34; 1 Co.7.32,35.
s Ps.27.4; 73.25; Ec.12.13; Mar.8.36; ch.18.22; 1 Co. 13.3.

---

39. *Sat at Jesus' feet.* This was the ancient posture of disciples or learners. They sat at the *feet* of their teachers—that is, beneath them, in a humble place. Hence Paul is represented as having been brought up at the *feet* of Gamaliel, Ac. xxii. 3. When it is said that Mary sat at Jesus' feet, it means that she was *a disciple* of his; that she listened attentively to his instructions, and was anxious to learn his doctrine.

40. *Martha was cumbered about much serving.* Was much distracted with the cares of the family, and providing suitably to entertain the Saviour. It should be said here that there is no evidence that Martha had a worldly or covetous disposition. Her anxiety was to provide suitable entertainment for the Lord Jesus. As mistress of the family, this care properly devolved on her; and the only fault which can be charged on her was too earnest a desire to make such entertainment, when she might have sat with Mary at his feet, and, perhaps, too much haste and fretfulness in speaking to Jesus about Mary. ¶ *Dost thou not care*, &c. This was an improper reproof of our Lord, as if *he* encouraged Mary in neglecting her duty. Or perhaps Martha supposed that Mary was sitting there to show him the proper expressions of courtesy and kindness, and that she would not think it proper to leave him without his direction and permission. She therefore *hinted* to Jesus her busy employments, her need of the aid of her sister, and requested that he would signify his wish that Mary should assist her.

41. *Thou art careful.* Thou art *anxious.* ¶ *Troubled.* Disturbed, distracted, very solicitous. ¶ *Many things.* The many objects which excite your attention in the family. This was probably designed as a slight reproof, or a tender hint that she was improperly anxious about those things, and that she should, with Mary, rather choose to hear the discourses of heavenly wisdom.

42. *But one thing is needful.* That is, religion, or piety. This is eminently and peculiarly needful. Other things are of little importance. This should be secured *first*, and then all other things will be added. See 1 Ti. iv. 8; Mat. vi. 33. ¶ *That good part.* The portion of the gospel; the love of God, and an interest in his kingdom. She had chosen to be a Christian, and to give up her time and affections to God. ¶ *Which shall not be taken away. God* will not take away his grace from his people, neither shall any man pluck them out of his hand, Jn. x. 28, 29.

From this interesting narrative we learn—1st. That the cares of this life are dangerous, even when they seem to be most lawful and commendable. Nothing of a worldly nature could have been more proper than to provide for the Lord Jesus and supply his wants. Yet even *for this*, because it too much engrossed her mind, the Lord Jesus gently reproved Martha. So a care for our families may be the means of our neglecting religion and losing our souls. 2d. It is of more importance to attend to the instructions of the Lord Jesus than to be engaged in the affairs of the world. The one will abide for ever; the other will be but for a little time. 3d. There *are* times when it is proper to suspend worldly employments, and to attend to the affairs of the soul. It *was* proper for Mary to do it. It would have been proper for Martha to have done it. It *is* proper for all—on the Sabbath and at other occasional seasons—seasons of prayer and for searching the word of God—to suspend worldly concerns and to attend to religion. 4th. If attention to religion be omitted at *the proper time*, it will always be omitted. If Mary had neglected to hear Jesus *then*, she might never have heard him. 5th. Piety is the chief thing needed. Other things will perish. We shall soon die. All that we can

CHAPTER XI.

AND it came to pass, that as
he was praying in a certain
place, when he ceased, one of his
disciples said unto him, Lord,
teach us to pray, as John also
taught his disciples.
2 And he said unto them, When
ye pray, say, [a]Our Father which
art in heaven, Hallowed be thy
name. Thy kingdom come. Thy
will be done, as in heaven, so in
earth.
3 Give us [1]day by day our daily
bread.

a Mat.6.9,&c. 1 or, *for the day.*

4 And forgive us our sins; [b]for
we also forgive every one that is
indebted to us. And lead us not
into temptation; but deliver us
from evil.
5 And he said unto them, Which
of you shall have a friend, and
shall go unto him at midnight,
and say unto him, Friend, lend
me three loaves;
6 For a friend of mine [2]in his
journey is come to me, and I have
nothing to set before him:
7 And he from within shall answer and say, Trouble me not: the

b Mar.11.25,26. 2 or, *out of his way.*

gain we must leave. But the *soul* will live. There is a judgment-seat; there is a heaven; there is a hell; and *all* that is needful to prepare us to die, and to make us happy for ever, is to be a friend of Jesus, and to listen to his teaching. 6th. Piety is the chief ornament in a female. It sweetens every other virtue; adorns every other grace; gives new loveliness to the tenderness, mildness, and grace of the female character. Nothing is more lovely than a female sitting at the feet of the meek and lowly Jesus, like Mary; nothing more unlovely than entire absorption in the affairs of the world, like Martha. The most lovely female is she who has most of the spirit of Jesus; the least amiable, she who neglects her soul—who is proud, gay, thoughtless, envious, and unlike the meek and lowly Redeemer. At his feet are peace, purity, joy. Everywhere else an alluring and wicked world steals the affections and renders us vain, gay, wicked, proud, and unwilling to die.

CHAPTER XI.

1. *As he was praying.* Luke has taken notice of our Saviour's praying often. Thus, at his baptism (ch. iii. 21); in the wilderness (ch. v. 16); before the appointment of the apostles, he continued all night in prayer (ch. vi. 12); he was alone praying (ch. ix. 18); his transfiguration also took place when he went up to pray (ch. ix. 28, 29). ¶ *Teach us to pray.* Probably they had been struck with the excellency and fervour of his prayers, and, recollecting that *John* had taught his disciples to pray, they asked him also to teach *them.* We learn, therefore—1st. That the gifts and graces of others should lead us to desire the same. 2d. That the true method of praying can be learned only by our being properly taught. Indeed, we cannot pray acceptably at all unless God shall teach us how to pray. 3d. That it is proper for us to meditate beforehand what we are to ask of God, and to arrange our thoughts, that we may not come thoughtlessly into his presence.

2–4. See this passage explained in the Notes on Mat. vi. 9–13.

4. *For we also forgive,* &c. This is somewhat different from the expression in Matthew, though the sense is the same. The idea is, that unless we forgive others, God will not forgive us; and unless we come to him *really* forgiving all others, we cannot expect pardon. It does not mean that by forgiving others we *deserve* forgiveness ourselves, or *merit it,* but that this is a disposition or state of mind without which God cannot consistently pardon us. ¶ *Every one that is indebted to us.* Every one that has *injured* us. This does not refer to pecuniary transactions, but to offences similar to those which *we* have committed against God, and for which we ask forgiveness. Besides the variations in the *expressions* in this prayer, Luke has omitted the doxology, or close, altogether; and this shows that Jesus did not intend that we should always use just this *form,* but that it was a general direction how to pray; or, rather, that we were to pray for these *things,* though not always using the same words.

door is now shut, and my children are with me in bed; I cannot rise and give thee.
8 I say unto you, Though he will not rise and give him because he is his friend, yet [c]because of his importunity he will rise and give him as many as he needeth.

c ch.18.1-8.

9 And I say unto you, [d]Ask, and it shall be given you; seek, and ye shall find; knock, and it shall be opened unto you.
10 For every one that asketh, receiveth; and he that seeketh, findeth; and to him that knocketh, it shall be opened.

d Mat.7.7; 21.22; Jn.15.7; Ja.1.5; 1 Jn.3.22.

5-7. *And he said unto them*, &c. Jesus proceeds to show that, in order to obtain the blessing, it was necessary to *persevere* in asking for it. For this purpose he introduces the case of a friend's asking bread of another for one who had come to him unexpectedly. His design is solely to show the necessity of being *importunate* or persevering in prayer to God. ¶ *At midnight.* A time when it would be most inconvenient for his friend to help him; an hour when he would naturally be in bed and his house shut. ¶ *Three loaves.* There is nothing particularly denoted by the number *three* in this place. Jesus often threw in such particulars merely to fill up the story, or to preserve the consistency of it. ¶ *My children are with me in bed.* This does not necessarily mean that they were in the *same bed* with him, but that they were *all* in bed, the house was still, the door was shut, and it was troublesome for him to rise at that time of night to accommodate him. It should be observed, however, that the customs of Orientals differ in this respect from our own. Among them it is not uncommon—indeed it is the common practice—for a whole family—parents, children, and servants—to sleep in the same room. See *The Land and the Book*, vol. i. p. 180. This is *not* to be applied to God, as if it were troublesome to him to be sought unto, or as if *he* would ever reply to a sinner in that manner. All that is to be applied to God in this parable is simply that it is proper to *persevere* in prayer. As a *man* often gives because the request is *repeated*, and as one is not discouraged because the favour that he asks of his neighbour is *delayed*, so God often answers us after long and importunate requests.

8. *I tell you.* The Latin Vulgate here adds, "if he shall continue knocking." Though this is not in the Greek, yet it is indispensable that it should be understood in order to the sense. Knocking *once* would not denote *importunity*, but it was because he *continued* knocking. ¶ *His importunity.* His troublesome perseverance; his continuing to disturb the man, and refusing to take any denial. The word *importunity* denotes perseverance in an object, without any regard to time, place, or circumstances—an improper perseverance. By this the man was influenced. Rather than be disturbed, he would rise and give what was asked. This is to be applied to God in no other sense than that he often hears prayers and grants blessings even *long after* they appear to be unanswered or withheld. He does not promise to give blessings *at once.* He promises only that he will do it, or *will answer* prayer. But he often causes his people long to wait. He tries their faith. He leaves them to persevere for months or years, until they feel *entirely* their dependence on him, until they see that they can obtain the blessing in no other way, and until they are *prepared* to receive it. Often they are not *prepared* to receive it when they ask it at first. They may be proud, or have no just sense of their dependence, or they would not value the blessing, or it may *at that time* not be best for them to obtain it. But let no one despair. If the thing is for *our* good, and if it is proper that it *should* be granted, God will give it. Let us first ask aright; let us see that our minds are in a proper state; let us feel our need of the blessing; let us inquire whether God has *promised such* a blessing, and *then* let us persevere until God gives it. Again. men, when they ask anything of God, often give over seeking. They go *once*, and if it is not granted they are discouraged. It is not so when we ask anything of men. *Then* we persevere; we take no denial; we go again, and *press* the matter till we obtain it. So we should of God. We should go again and again, until the prayer is heard, and God grants what we ask of him.

11 If a son shall ask bread of any of you that is a father, will he give him a stone? or if *he ask* a fish, will he for a fish give him a serpent?

12 Or if he shall ask an egg, will he [3]offer him a scorpion?

13 If ye then, being evil, know how to give good gifts unto your children, how much more shall *your* heavenly Father give the Holy Spirit to them that ask him!

14 And[e] he was casting out a devil, and it was dumb. And it came to pass, when the devil was gone out, the dumb spake; and the people wondered.

15 But some of them said, He casteth out devils through [4]Beelzebub, the chief of the devils.

16 And others, [f]tempting *him*, sought of him a sign from heaven.

17 But he, [g]knowing their thoughts, said unto them, [h]Every kingdom divided against itself is brought to desolation; and a house *divided* against a house falleth.

18 If Satan also be divided against himself, how shall his kingdom stand? because ye say that I cast out devils through Beelzebub.

19 And if I by Beelzebub cast out devils, by whom do your sons cast *them* out? therefore shall they be your judges.

[3] *give.*
[4] *Beelzebul*, so ver.18,19.
g Jn.2.25.
e Mat.9.32; 12.22,&c.
f Mat.12.38; 16.1.
h Mat.12.25; Mar.3.24.

20 But if I with the [i]finger of God cast out devils, no doubt the kingdom of God is come upon you.

21 When a strong man armed keepeth his palace, his goods are in peace;

22 But when a [k]stronger than he shall come upon him, and overcome him, he taketh from him all his armour wherein he trusted, and divideth his spoils.

23 He that is not with me is against me; and he that gathereth not with me scattereth.

24 When the unclean spirit is gone out of a man, he walketh through dry places, seeking rest; and finding none, he saith, I will return unto my house whence I came out.

25 And when he cometh, he findeth *it* swept and garnished.

26 Then goeth he, and taketh *to him* seven other spirits more wicked than himself; and they enter in, and dwell there: and the last *state* of that man is [l]worse than the first.

27 And it came to pass, as he spake these things, a certain woman of the company lifted up her voice and said unto him, [m]Blessed *is* the womb that bare thee, and the paps which thou hast sucked.

28 But he said, [n]Yea, rather

i Ex.8.19.
k Is.53.12; Col.2.15.
l Jn.5.14; He.6.4; 10.26,27; 2 Pe.2.20,21.
m ch.1.28,48.
n Ps.119.1,2; Mat.7.21; ch.8.21; Ja.1.25.

9–12. See this explained in the Notes on Mat. vii. 7–11.

12. *A scorpion.* See Notes on Lu. x. 19. Dr. Thomson (*The Land and the Book*, vol. i. p. 379) says: "There is no imaginable likeness between an egg and the ordinary black scorpion of this country, neither in colour nor size, nor, when the tail is extended, in shape; but old writers speak of a *white* scorpion, and such a one, with the tail folded up, as in specimens of fossil trilobites, would not look unlike a small egg. Perhaps the contrast, however, refers only to the different properties of the egg and the scorpion, which is sufficiently emphatic."

Pliny (*N. H.*, xi. 25) says that in Judea the scorpions are about the size of an egg, and not unlike one in shape.

14–23. See this passage explained in the Notes on Mat. xii. 22–30.

24–26. See Notes on Mat. xii. 43–45.

27, 28. *A certain woman.* One of the crowd. ¶ *Blessed is the womb*, &c. She thought that the *mother* of such a person must be peculiarly happy in having such a son. ¶ *Yea, rather blessed*, &c. Jesus admits that she was happy—that

blessed *are* they that hear the
word of God, and keep it.
29 And when the people were
gathered thick together, he began
to say, This is an evil generation:
they seek a sign, and [o]there shall
no sign be given it but the sign of
Jonas the prophet.
30 For as [p]Jonas was a sign unto
the Ninevites, so shall also the Son
of man be to this generation.
31 The [q]queen of the south shall
rise up in the judgment with the
men of this generation, and condemn
them; for she came from
the utmost parts of the earth to
hear the wisdom of Solomon; and,
behold, a greater than Solomon *is*
here.
32 The men of Nineveh shall
rise up in the judgment with this
generation, and shall condemn it;
for[r] they repented at the preaching
of Jonas; and, behold, a greater
than Jonas *is* here.
33 No[s] man, when he hath
lighted a candle, putteth *it* in a
secret place, neither under a bushel,
but on a candlestick, that they
which come in may see the light.
34 The [t]light of the body is the
eye: therefore, when thine eye is
single, thy whole body also is full
of light; but when [u]*thine eye* is
evil, thy body also *is* full of darkness.
35 Take heed, therefore, that
the light which is in thee be not
darkness.
36 If thy whole body, therefore,
be [v]full of light, having no part
dark, the whole shall be full of
light, as when [5]the [w]bright shining
of a candle doth give thee light.
37 And as he spake, a certain
Pharisee besought him to dine

o Mat.12.40,&c.; Mar.8.12. p Jonah 1.17; 2.10. q 1 Ki.10.1,&c. r Jonah 3.5,10.

s Mat.5.15,&c.; Mar.4.21; ch.8.16. t Mat.6.22,&c. u Pr.28.22; Mar.7.22. v Ps.119.105; Pr.6.23; Is.8.20; 2 Co.4.6. 5 *a candle by its bright shining.* w Pr.4.18; 20.27.

it was an honour to be his mother, but he says that the chief happiness, the highest honour, was to obey the word of God. Compared with this, all earthly distinctions and honours are as nothing. Man's greatest dignity is in keeping the holy commandments of God, and in being prepared for heaven. See Notes on ch. x. 20.

29–32. See Notes on Mat. xii. 38–42.

33–36. These verses are found in Matthew, but in a different connection. See Notes on Mat. v. 15; vi. 22, 23.

37. *And as he spake.* While he was addressing the people, and particularly while he was reproving that generation and declaring its crimes. ¶ *A certain Pharisee.* The Pharisees had been particularly referred to in the discourse of the Saviour recorded in the previous verses. This one, perhaps, having felt particularly the force of the remarks of Jesus, and being desirous of being alone with him, invited him to go home with him. There is little doubt that this was for the purpose of drawing him away from the people; that he did it with a malignant intention, perhaps with a design to confute Jesus in private, or to reprove him for thus condemning the whole nation as he did. He might have seen that those who attacked Jesus *publicly* were commonly unsuccessful, and he desired, probably, to encounter him more privately. ¶ *Besought him.* Asked him. ¶ *To dine with him.* The Jews, as well as the Greeks and Romans, had but two principal meals. The first was a slight repast, and was taken about ten or eleven o'clock of our time, and consisted chiefly of fruit, milk, cheese, &c. The second meal was partaken of about three o'clock P.M., and was their principal meal. The *first* is the one here intended. ¶ *He went in.* Though he knew the evil design of the Pharisee, yet he did not decline the invitation. He knew that it might afford him an opportunity to do good. These two things are to be observed in regard to our Saviour's conduct in such matters: 1st. That he did not decline an invitation to dine with a man simply because he was a Pharisee, or because he was a wicked man. Hence he was charged with being gluttonous, and a friend of publicans and sinners, Mat. xi. 19. 2d. He seized upon all occasions to do good. He never shrank from declaring the truth, and making such

with him; and he went in and
sat down to meat.

38 And[x] when the Pharisee saw
it, he marvelled that he had not
first washed before dinner.

39 And the Lord said unto him,
Now[y] do ye Pharisees make clean
the outside of the cup and the
platter, but [z]your inward part is
full of ravening and wickedness.

40 *Ye* fools, did not he that made
that which is without make that
which is within also?

41 But[a] rather give alms [6]of
such things as ye have; and, behold,
all things are clean unto you.

x Mar.7.3. y Mat.23.25. z Tit.1.15. a Is.58.7; ch.12.33. 6 or, *as you are able.*

---

occasions the means of spreading the gospel. If Christians and Christian ministers would follow the example of the Saviour always, they would avoid all scandal, and might do even in such places a vast amount of good. ¶ *Sat down.* Reclined at the table. See Notes on Mat. xxiii. 6.

38. *Saw* it. Saw that he sat immediately down without washing. ¶ *Marvelled.* Wondered. Was amazed. It was so unusual, and in his view so improper. ¶ *Had not first washed.* He wondered particularly, as he had been among a mixed multitude, and they esteemed the *touch* of such persons polluting. They never ate, therefore, without such washing. The origin of the custom of washing with so much formality *before* they partook of their meals was that they did not use, as we do, knives and forks, but used their hands only. Hence, as their hands would be often in a dish on the table, it was esteemed proper that they should be washed clean before eating. Nor was their impropriety in the thing itself, but the Pharisees made it a matter of ceremony; they placed no small part of their religion in such ceremonies; and it was right, therefore, that our Lord should take occasion to reprove them for it. Comp. Mar. vii. 4.

39. See Mat. xxiii. 25. *Ravening.* Robbery, plunder. Here the sense is that the cup and platter were filled with what had been unjustly taken from others. That is, they lived by their wickedness; their food was procured by dishonesty and extortion. This was a most terrible charge; and as it was applied, among others, to the man who had invited the Saviour to dine with him, it shows that nothing would prevent his dealing faithfully with the souls of men. Even in the Pharisee's own house, and when expressly invited to partake of his hospitality, he loved his soul so much that he faithfully warned him of his crimes.

40. Ye *fools.* How unwise and wicked is your conduct! The word denotes not only *want of wisdom*, but also *wickedness.* Comp. Ps. xiv. 1; Pr. xiii. 19; xiv. 9. Your conduct is not merely *foolish*, but it is a cloak for sin—designed to countenance wickedness. ¶ *Did not he*, &c. Did not God, who made the *body*, make also the *soul?* You Pharisees take great pains to cleanse the *body*, under a pretence of pleasing *God.* Did *he* not also make the *mind?* and is it not of as much importance that *that* should be pure, as that the body should?

41. *Alms.* Charity. Benefactions to the poor. ¶ *Such things as ye have.* Your property; though it has been gained unjustly: though you have lived by rapine, and have amassed wealth in an improper manner, yet, *since you have it*, it is your duty to make the best of it and do good. By giving to the poor, you may show your repentance for your crimes in amassing money in this manner. You may show that you disapprove of your former course of life, and are disposed henceforward to live honestly. If this be the meaning of this passage, then it shows what is the duty of those who have by unjust gains become wealthy, and who are *then* converted to God. It may not be possible for them in every case to make exact restitution to those whom they have injured; thousands of instances of wrong they may have forgotten; many persons whom they have injured may have died; but still they may show, by giving to others, that they do not think their gains acquired honestly, and that they truly repent. They may devote their property to God; distribute it to the poor; or give it to send the gospel to the heathen world. Thus may they show that they disapprove of their former conduct; and thus may be seen one great principle of God's government —*that good finally comes out of evil.* ¶ *And behold*, &c. Doing this will show that you are a true penitent, and the

42 But [b]woe unto you, Pharisees! for ye tithe mint, and rue,
and all manner of herbs, and pass
over judgment and the love of
God. These ought ye to have done,
and not to leave the other undone.
43 Woe unto you, Pharisees! [c]for
ye love the uppermost seats in the
synagogues, and greetings in the
markets.
44 Woe unto you, scribes and
Pharisees, hypocrites! for ye are
as [d]graves which appear not, and
the men that walk over *them* are
not aware *of them*.
45 Then answered one of the
lawyers, and said unto him, Master, thus saying, thou reproachest
us also.

b Mat.23.23,27. *c* Mat.23.6; Mar.12.38. *d* Ps.5.9.

46 And he said, Woe unto you
also, *ye* lawyers! for ye lade men
with burdens grievous to be borne,
and ye yourselves [e]touch not the
burdens with one of your fingers.
47 Woe unto you! for ye build
the sepulchres of the prophets, and
your fathers killed them.
48 Truly ye bear witness that [f]ye
allow the deeds of your fathers: for
[g]they indeed killed them, and ye
build their sepulchres.
49 Therefore also said the wisdom of God, I will send them
prophets and apostles, and *some*
of them they shall slay and persecute;
50 That the blood of all the
prophets, which was shed from

e Is.58.6. *f* Eze.18.19. *g* He.11.35,37.

remainder of your property you will enjoy with a feeling that you have done your duty, and no longer be smitten with the consciousness of hoarding unjust gains. The object of the Saviour here seems to have been to bring the Pharisee to repentance. Repentance consists in sorrow for sin, and in forsaking it. This he endeavoured to produce by showing him—1st, the *evil* and hypocrisy of his conduct; and, 2d, by exhorting him to *forsake* his sins, and to *show* this by doing good. Thus doing, he would evince that the *mind* was clean as well the *body;* the *inside* as well as the *outside*.

42. See Mat. xxiii. 23. ¶ *Rue.* This is a small garden plant, and is used as a medicine. It has a rosy flower, a bitter, penetrating taste, and a strong smell.

43, 44. See Mat. xxiii. 6, 27.

45. *Lawyers.* Men learned in the law; but it is not known in what way the lawyers differed from the *scribes*, or whether they were Pharisees or Sadducees. ¶ *Thus saying, thou*, &c. He felt that the remarks of Jesus about loving the chief seats, &c., applied to them as well as to the Pharisees. His conscience told him that if *they* were to blame, *he* was also, and he therefore applied the discourse to himself. ¶ *Reproachest.* Accusest. Dost calumniate or blame *us*, for we do the same things. Sinners often consider *faithfulness* as *reproach*—they know not how to separate them. Jesus did *not* reproach or abuse them. He dealt faithfully with them; reproved them; told them the unvarnished truth. Such faithfulness is rare; but when it *is* used, we must expect that men will flinch, perhaps be enraged. Though their consciences tell them they are *guilty*, still they will consider it as abuse.

46. See Notes on Mat. xxiii. 4.

47–51. See Notes on Mat. xxiii. 29–36.

49. *The wisdom of God.* By the *wisdom of God*, here, is undoubtedly meant the Saviour himself. What he immediately says is not written in the Old Testament. Jesus is called *the word of God* (Jn. i. 1), because he is the medium by which God *speaks* or makes his will known. He is called *the wisdom of God*, because by him God makes his wisdom known in creation (Col. i. 13–18) and in redemption (1 Co. i. 30). Many have also thought that the Messiah was referred to in the 8th chapter of Proverbs, under the name of Wisdom. ¶ *I will send*, &c. See Lu. x. 3; Mat. x. 16. ¶ *Shall slay*, &c. Comp. Jn. xvi. 2; Ac. vii. 52, 59; Ja. v. 10; Ac. xii. 2; xxii. 19; 2 Co. xi. 24, 25; 2 Ch. xxxvi. 15, 16.

52. *Woe unto you, lawyers!* See Notes on Mat. xxiii. 13. ¶ *The key of knowledge.* A key is made to open a lock or door. By their false interpretation of the Old Testament they had taken away the true key or method of understanding it. They had hindered the people

the foundation of the world, may
be [h]required of this generation;
51 From the blood of [i]Abel unto
the blood of [k]Zacharias, which
perished between the altar and
the temple: verily I say unto you,
It shall be [l]required of this generation.
52 Woe unto you, lawyers! for
ye have taken away the [m]key of
knowledge: ye entered not in
yourselves, and them that were
entering in ye [7]hindered.
53 And as he said these things
unto them, the scribes and Pharisees
began to urge *him* vehemently,
and to [n]provoke him to speak of
many things;
54 Laying wait for him, [o]and
seeking to catch something out of
his mouth, that they might accuse
him.

h Ex.20.5; Je.51.56. *i* Ge.4.8. *k* 2 Ch.24.20. *l* Je.7.28,29. *m* Mal.2.7.

7 or, *forbad*. *n* 1 Co.13.5. *o* Mar.12.13.

from understanding it aright. "You endeavour to prevent the people also from understanding the Scriptures respecting the Messiah, and those who were coming to *me* ye hindered." If there is any sin of peculiar magnitude, it is that of keeping the people in ignorance; and few men are so guilty as they who by false instructions prevent them from coming to a knowledge of the truth, and embracing it as it is in Jesus.

53. *To urge* him *vehemently*. To press upon him *violently*. They were enraged against him. They therefore pressed upon him; asked him many questions; sought to entrap him, that they might accuse him. ¶ *Provoke him*, &c. This means that they put many questions to him about various matters, without giving him proper time to answer. They proposed questions as fast as possible, and about as many things as possible, that they might get him, in the hurry, to say something that would be wrong, that they might thus accuse him. This was a remarkable instance of their cunning, malignity, and unfairness.

54. *Laying wait for him*. Or, rather, laying *snares* for him. It means that they endeavoured to entangle him in his talk; that they did as men do who catch birds—who lay snares, and deceive them, and take them unawares. ¶ *That they might accuse him*. Before the Sanhedrim, or great council of the nation, and thus secure his being put to death.

From this we may learn—1st. That faithful reproofs must be expected to excite opposition and hatred. Though the *conscience* may be roused, and may testify against the man that is reproved, yet that does not prevent his hating the reproof and the reprover. 2d. We see here the manner in which wicked men endeavour to escape the reproofs of conscience. Instead of repenting, they seek vengeance, and resolve to put the reprover to shame or to death. 3d. We see the exceeding malignity which men have against the Lord Jesus. Well was it said that he was set for the fall of many in Israel, that thereby the thoughts of many hearts might be revealed! Lu. ii. 34, 35. Men, *now*, are not by nature less opposed to Jesus than they were then. 4th. We see the wisdom, purity, and firmness of the Saviour. To their souls he had been faithful. He had boldly reproved them for their sins. They sought his life. Multitudes of the artful and learned gathered around him, to endeavour to draw out something of which they might accuse him, yet in vain. Not a word fell from his lips of which they could accuse him. Everything that he said was calm, mild, peaceful, wise, and lovely. Even his cunning and bitter adversaries were always confounded, and retired in shame and confusion. Here, surely, must have been something more than man. None but *God manifest in the flesh* could have known all their designs, seen all their wickedness and their wiles, and escaped the cunning stratagems that were laid to confound and entangle him in his conversation. 5th. The same infinitely wise Saviour can still meet and confound all his own enemies and those of his people, and deliver all his followers, as he did himself, from all the snares laid by a wicked world to lead them to sin and death.

CHAPTER XII.

1. *In the mean time*. While he was discoursing with the scribes and Pharisees, as recorded in the last chapter.

CHAPTER XII.

IN[a] the mean time, when there were gathered together an innumerable multitude of people, insomuch that they trode one upon another, he began to say unto his disciples first of all, Beware ye of the leaven of the Pharisees, which is hypocrisy.

2 For[b] there is nothing covered that shall not be revealed, neither hid that shall not be known.

3 Therefore whatsoever ye have spoken in darkness shall be heard in the light; and that which ye have spoken in the ear, in closets, shall be proclaimed upon the housetops.

4 And I say unto you, [c]my friends, [d]Be not afraid of them that kill the body, and after that have no more that they can do.

a Mat.16.6,&c.; Mar.8.15,&c.
b Mat.10.26; Mar.4.22; ch.8.17.
c Jn.15.14. *d* Is.51.7-13; Mat.10.28,&c.

5 But I will forewarn you whom ye shall fear: Fear him which, after he hath killed, hath power to cast into hell; yea, I say unto you, Fear him.

6 Are not five sparrows sold for two [1]farthings? and not one of them is forgotten before God;

7 But even the very hairs of your head are all numbered. Fear not, therefore; ye are of more value than many sparrows.

8 Also I say unto you, [e]Whosoever shall confess me before men, him shall the Son of man also [f]confess before the angels of God;

9 But he that [g]denieth me before men, shall be [h]denied before the angels of God.

10 And whosoever shall speak a word against the Son of man, it shall be forgiven him; but unto

1 See Mat.10.29.
e 1 Sa.2.30; Ps.119.46; 2 Ti.2.12; Re.2.10.
f Jude 24. *g* Ac.3.13,14; Re.3.8. *h* Mat.25.31.

¶ *An innumerable multitude.* The original word is *myriads*, or ten thousands. It is used here to signify that there was a great crowd or collection of people, who were anxious to hear him. Multitudes were attracted to the Saviour's ministry, and it is worthy of remark that he never had more to hear him than when he was most faithful and severe in his reproofs of sinners. Men's consciences are on the side of the faithful reprover of their sins; and though they deeply feel the reproof, yet they will still respect and hear him that reproves. ¶ *To his disciples first of all.* This does not mean that his disciples were, before all others, to avoid hypocrisy, but that this was the *first* or chief thing of which they were to beware. The meaning is this: "He said to his disciples, *Above all things beware,*" &c. ¶ *The leaven.* See Notes on Mat. xvi. 6. ¶ *Which is hypocrisy.* See Notes on Mat. vii. 5. Hypocrisy is like leaven or yeast, because—1st. It may exist without being immediately detected. Leaven mixed in flour is not known until it produces its effects. 2d. It is insinuating. Leaven will soon pervade the whole mass. So hypocrisy will, if undetected and unremoved, soon pervade all our exercises and feelings. 3d. It is swelling. It puffs us up, and fills us with pride and vanity. No man is more proud than the hypocrite, and none is more odious to God. When Jesus cautions them to beware of *the leaven of the Pharisees,* he means that they should be cautious about imbibing their spirit and becoming like them. The religion of Jesus is one of sincerity, of humility, of an entire want of disguise. The humblest man is the best Christian, and he who has the least disguise is most like his Master.

2–9. *Nothing covered.* See Notes on Mat. x. 26–32.

3. *Shall be proclaimed upon the housetops.* See Notes on Mat. x. 27. The custom of making proclamation from the tops or roofs of houses still prevails in the East. Dr. Thomson (*The Land and the Book*, vol. i. p. 51, 52) says: "At the present day, local governors in country districts cause their commands thus to be published. Their proclamations are generally made in the evening, after the people have returned from their labours in the field. The public crier ascends the highest roof at hand, and lifts up his voice in a long-drawn call upon all faithful subjects to give ear and obey. He then proceeds to announce, in a set form,

him that blasphemeth against the Holy Ghost, [i]it shall not be forgiven.

11 And when they bring you unto the synagogues, and *unto* magistrates and powers, [k]take ye no thought how or what thing ye shall answer, or what ye shall say;

12 For the [l]Holy Ghost shall teach you in the same hour what ye ought to say.

13 And one of the company said unto him, [m]Master, speak to my brother, that he divide the inheritance with me.

14 And he said unto him, [n]Man, who made me a judge or a divider over you?

15 And he said unto them, [o]Take heed and beware of covetousness; for a man's [p]life consisteth not in the abundance of the things which he possesseth.

16 And he spake a parable unto

i Mat.12.31; 1 Jn.5.16. *k* Mat.10.19; Mar.13.11; ch.21.14. *l* Ac.6.10; 26.1,&c.
m Eze.33.31. *n* Jn.18.35. *o* 1 Ti.6.7-10. *p* Job 2.4; Mat.6.25.

---

the will of their master, and demand obedience thereto."

10. See Notes on Mat. xii. 32.

11, 12. See Notes on Mat. x. 17-20.

13. *One of the company.* One of the multitude. This man had probably had a dispute with his brother, supposing that his brother had refused to do him justice. Conceiving that Jesus had power over the people—that what he said must be performed—he endeavoured to secure him on his side of the dispute and gain his point. From the parable which follows, it would appear that he had no *just* claim on the inheritance, but was influenced by covetousness. Besides, if he *had* any just claim, it might have been secured by the laws of the land. ¶ *Speak to my brother.* Command my brother. ¶ *Divide the inheritance.* An inheritance is the property which is left by a father to his children. Among the Jews the older brother had two shares, or twice as much as any other child, De. xxi. 17. The remainder was then equally divided among all the children.

14. *Who made me a judge?* It is not my business to settle controversies of this kind. They are to be settled by the magistrate. Jesus came for another purpose—to preach the gospel, and so to bring men to a *willingness to do* right. Civil affairs are to be left to the magistrate. There is no doubt that Jesus *could* have told him what was right in this case, but then it would have been interfering with the proper office of the magistrates; it might have led him into controversy with the Jews; and it was, besides, evidently apart from the proper business of his life. We may remark, also, that the appropriate business of ministers of the gospel is to attend to spiritual concerns. They should have little to do with the temporal matters of the people. If they can *persuade men* who are at variance to be reconciled, it is right; but they have no power to take the place of a magistrate, and to settle contentions in a legal way.

15. *Beware of covetousness.* One of these brothers, no doubt, was guilty of this sin; and our Saviour, as was his custom, took occasion to warn his disciples of its danger. ¶ *Covetousness.* An unlawful desire of the property of another; also a desire of gain or riches beyond what is necessary for our wants. It is a violation of the tenth commandment (Ex. xx. 17), and is expressly called idolatry (Col. iii. 5). Compare, also, Ep. v. 3, and He. xiii. 5. ¶ *A man's life.* The word *life* is sometimes taken in the sense of happiness or felicity, and some have supposed this to be the meaning here, and that Jesus meant to say that a man's comfort does not depend on affluence—that is, on more than is necessary for his daily wants; but this meaning does not suit the parable following, which is designed to show that property will not lengthen out a man's life, and therefore is not too ardently to be sought, and is of little value. The word *life*, therefore, is to be taken *literally.* ¶ *Consisteth not.* Rather, *dependeth* not on his possessions. His possessions will not prolong it. The passage, then, means: Be not anxious about obtaining wealth, for, however much you may obtain, it will not prolong your life. *That* depends on the will of God, and it requires something besides wealth to make us ready to meet him. This sentiment he proceeds to illustrate by a beautiful parable.

them, saying, The ground of a certain rich man brought forth plentifully;
17 And he thought within himself, saying, What shall I do, because I have no room where to bestow my fruits?
18 And he said, [q]This will I do:
I will pull down my barns and
build greater, and there will I bestow all my fruits and my goods.
19 And I will say to my soul,
[r]Soul, thou hast much goods laid
up for many years; [s]take thine ease,
eat, drink, *and* be merry.
20 But God said unto him, *Thou*
fool! [t]this night [2]thy soul shall be
required of thee: then [u]whose shall
those things be which thou hast
provided?
21 So *is* he that [v]layeth up treasure for himself, and [w]is not rich
toward God.
22 And he said unto his disci-

q Ja.4.15,16.

r Ps.49.18. *s* Ec.11.9; 1 Co.15.32; Ja.5.5. *t* Job 20.20-23; 27.8; Ps.52.7; Ja.4.14. [2] or, *do they require thy soul.* *u* Ps.39.6; 49.16,17; Je.17.11. *v* Hab.2.9. *w* 1 Ti.6.18; Ja.2.5; ver.33.

16. *A parable.* See Notes on Mat. xiii. 3. ¶ *Plentifully.* His land was fertile, and produced even beyond his expectations, and beyond what he had provided for.

17. *He thought within himself.* He reasoned or inquired. He was anxious and perplexed. Riches inorease thought and perplexity. Indeed, this is almost their only effect — to engross the thoughts and steal the heart away from better things, in order to take care of the useless wealth. ¶ *No room.* Everything was full. ¶ *To bestow.* To place, to hoard, to collect. ¶ *My fruits.* Our word *fruits* is not applied to *grain;* but the Greek word is applied to all the produce of the earth—not only *fruit,* but also grain. This is likewise the old meaning of the English word, especially in the plural number.

18. *I will pull down my barns.* The word *barns,* here, properly means, *granaries,* or places exclusively designed to put wheat, barley, &c. They were commonly made, by the ancients, *underground,* where grain could be kept a long time more safe from thieves and from vermin. If it be asked why he did not let the old ones remain and build new ones, it may be answered that it would be easier to *enlarge* those already excavated in the earth than to dig new ones.

19. *Much goods.* Much property. Enough to last a long while, so that there is no need of anxiety or labour. ¶ *Take thine ease.* Be free from care about the future. Have no anxiety about coming to want. ¶ *Eat, drink,* and *be merry.* This was just the doctrine of the ancient Epicureans and atheists, and it is, alas! too often the doctrine of those who are rich. They think that all that is valuable in life is to eat, and drink, and be cheerful or merry. Hence their chief anxiety is to obtain the "delicacies of the season"—the luxuries of the world; to secure the productions of every clime at any expense, and to be distinguished for splendid repasts and a magnificent style of living. What a portion is this for an immortal soul! What folly to think that *all* that a man lives for is to satisfy his sensual appetites; to forget that he has an intellect to be cultivated, a heart to be purified, a soul to be saved!

20. Thou *fool.* If there is any supreme folly, it is this. As though riches could prolong life, or avert for a moment the approach of pain and death. ¶ *This night,* &c. What an awful sentence to a man who, as he thought, had got just ready to live and enjoy himself! In a single moment all his hopes were blasted, and his soul summoned to the bar of his long-forgotten God. So, many are surprised as suddenly and as unprepared. They are snatched from their pleasures, and hurried to a world where there is no pleasure, and where all their wealth cannot purchase one moment's ease from the gnawings of the worm that never dies. ¶ *Shall be required of thee.* Thou shalt be required to die, to go to God, and to give up your account. ¶ *Then whose,* &c. Whose they may be is of little consequence to the man that lost his soul to gain them; but they are often left to heirs that dissipate them much sooner than the father procured them, and thus they secure *their* ruin as well as his own. See Ps. xxxix. 6; Ec. ii. 18, 19.

21. *So* is *he.* This is the portion or the doom. ¶ *Layeth up treasure for*

ples, Therefore I say unto you,
Take[x] no thought for your life,
what ye shall eat; neither for the
body, what ye shall put on.
23 The life is more than meat,
and the body *is more* than raiment.
24 Consider the [y]ravens; for
they neither sow nor reap; which
neither have store-house nor barn;
and God feedeth them. How much
more are ye better than the fowls?
25 And which of you, with taking thought, can add to his stature
one cubit?
26 If ye, then, be not able to do
that thing which is least, why take
ye thought for the rest?
27 Consider the lilies, how they
grow; they toil not, they spin not;
and yet I say unto you, that Solomon in all his glory was not arrayed like one of these.
28 If, then, God so clothe the
grass, which is to-day in the field,
and to-morrow is cast into the
oven, how much more *will he clothe*
you, O ye of little faith!
29 And seek not ye what ye shall
eat, or what ye shall drink, [3]nei-
ther be ye of doubtful mind.
30 For all these things do the
nations of the world seek after;
and your Father knoweth that ye
have need of these things.
31 But[z] rather seek ye the kingdom of God, and [a]all these things
shall be added unto you.
32 Fear not, [b]little flock; for [c]it
is your Father's good pleasure to
give you the kingdom.

x Mat.6.25,&c. *y* Job 38.41; Ps.147.9.

3 or, *live not in careful suspense.* *z* Mat.6.33.
a Ps.34.10; Is.33.16; Ro.8.31,32.
b Is.40.11; Jn.10.27,28.
c Mat.25.34; Jn.18.36; He.12.28; Ja.2.5; 2 Pe.1.11; Re.1.6; 22.5.

himself. Acquires riches for his own use—for *himself.* This is the characteristic of the covetous man. It is all for *himself.* His plans terminate there. He lives only for himself, and acts only with regard to his own interest. ¶ *Rich toward God.* Has no inheritance in the kingdom of God—no riches laid up in heaven. His affections are all fixed on this world, and he has none for God.

From this instructive parable we learn—1st. That wicked men are often signally prospered—their ground brings forth plentifully. God gives them their desire, but sends leanness into their souls. 2d. That riches bring with them always an increasing load of cares and anxieties. 3d. That they steal away the affections from God—are sly, insinuating, and dangerous to the soul. 4th. That the anxiety of a covetous man is not what *good* he may do with his wealth, but where he may hoard it, and keep it secure from doing any good. 5th. That riches cannot secure their haughty owners from the grave. Death will come upon them suddenly, unexpectedly, awfully. In the very midst of the brightest anticipations —in a moment—in the twinkling of an eye—it may come, and all the wealth that has been accumulated cannot alleviate one pang, or drive away one fear, or prolong life for one moment. 6th. That the man who is trusting to his riches in this manner is a fool in the sight of God. Soon, also, he will be a fool in his *own* sight, and will go to hell with the consciousness that his life has been one of eminent folly. 7th. That the path of true wisdom is to seek first the kingdom of God, and to be ready to die; and *then* it matters little what is our portion here, or how suddenly or soon we are called away to meet our Judge. If our affections are not fixed on our riches, we shall leave them without regret. If our treasures are laid up in heaven, death will be but *going home*, and happy will be that moment when we are called to our rest.

22–31. See this passage explained in the Notes on Mat. vi. 25–33.

32. *Little flock.* Our Saviour often represents himself as a shepherd, and his followers as a flock or as sheep. The figure was beautiful. In Judea it was a common employment to attend flocks. The shepherd was with them, defended them, provided for them, led them to green pastures and beside still waters. In all these things Jesus was and is eminently the Good Shepherd. His flock was small. Few *really* followed him, compared with the multitude who professed to love him. But, though small in number, they were not to fear. God was their Friend. He

33 Sell[d] that ye have, and
give alms: provide yourselves bags
which wax not old, a [e]treasure in
the heavens that faileth not, where
no thief approacheth, neither moth
corrupteth.
34 For where your treasure is,
there will your heart be also.
35 Let[f] your loins be girded
about, and [g]*your* lights burning;
36 And ye yourselves like unto
men that wait for their lord, when
he will return from the wedding;
that, when he cometh and knocketh, they may open unto him immediately.
37 Blessed[h] *are* those servants
whom the lord, when he cometh,
shall find watching: verily I say
unto you, that he shall gird himself, and make them to sit down
to meat, and will come forth and
serve them.
38 And if he shall come in the

d Mat.19.21; Ac.2.45; 4.34.
e Mat.6.20; 1 Ti.6.19. f Ep.6.14; 1 Pe.1.13.
g Mat.25.1,13.
h Mat.24.46,&c.

---

would provide for them. It was his *purpose* to give them the kingdom, and they had nothing to fear. See Mat. vi. 19–21.

33. *Sell that ye have.* Sell your property. Exchange it for that which you can use in distributing charity. This was the condition of their being disciples. Their property they gave up; they forsook it, or they put it into common stock, for the sake of giving alms to the poor, Ac. ii. 44; iv. 32; Jn. xii. 6; Ac. v. 2. ¶ *Bags which wax not old.* The word *bags*, here, means *purses*, or the bags attached to their girdles, in which they carried their money. See Notes on Mat. v. 38. By bags which wax not old Jesus means that we should lay up treasure in heaven; that our aim should be to be prepared to enter there, where all our wants will be for ever provided for. Purses, here, grow old and useless. Wealth takes to itself wings. Riches are easily scattered, or *we* must soon leave them; but that wealth which is in heaven abides for ever. It never is corrupted; never flies away; never is to be left. ¶ *Wax.* This word is from an old Saxon word, and in the Bible means *to grow.*

35, 36. *Let your loins,* &c. This alludes to the ancient manner of dress. They wore a long flowing robe as their outer garment. See Notes on Mat. v. 38-41. When they laboured, or walked, or ran, it was necessary to *gird* or tie this up by a *sash* or girdle about the body, that it might not impede their progress. Hence, to gird up the loins means to be *ready*, to be active, to be diligent. Comp. 2 Ki. iv. 29; ix. 1; Je. i. 17; Ac. xii. 8. ¶ Your *lights burning.* This expresses the same meaning. Be ready at all times to leave the world and enter into rest, when your Lord shall call you. Let every obstacle be out of the way; let every earthly care be removed, and be prepared to follow him into his rest. Servants were expected to be ready for the coming of their lord. If in the night, they were expected to keep their lights trimmed and burning. When their master was away in attendance on a wedding, as they knew not the hour when he would return, they were to be continually ready. So we, as we know not the hour when God shall call us, should be *always* ready to die. Comp. Notes on Mat. xxv. 1–13.

37. *Shall gird himself.* Shall take the place of the servant himself. Servants who waited on the table were girded in the manner described above. ¶ *Shall make them sit,* &c. Shall place them at his table and feast them. This evidently means that if we are faithful to Christ, and are ready to meet him when he returns, he will receive us into heaven—will admit us to all its blessings, and make us happy there—as if *he* should serve us and minister to our wants. It will be as if a master, instead of sitting down at the table *himself*, should place his faithful *servants* there, and be himself the servant. This shows the exceeding kindness and condescension of our Lord. For *us*, poor and guilty sinners, he denied himself, took the form of a servant (Phi. ii. 7), and ministered to our wants. In our nature he has wrought out salvation, and he has done it in one of the humblest conditions of the children of men. How should our bosoms burn with gratitude to him, and how should *we* be willing to serve one another! See Notes on Jn. xiii. 1–17.

38–46. See Notes on Mat. xxiv. 42–51. ¶ *Second watch.* See Notes on Mat. xiv. 25.

second watch, or come in the third
watch, and find *them* so, blessed
are those servants.
39 And this know, that if the
goodman of the house had known
what hour [i]the thief would come,
he would have watched, and not
have suffered his house to be
broken through.
40 Be[k] ye therefore ready also;
for the Son of man cometh at an
hour when ye think not.
41 Then Peter said unto him,
Lord, speakest thou this parable
unto us, or even to all?
42 And the Lord said, Who, then,
is that [l]faithful and wise steward,
whom *his* lord shall make ruler
over his household, to give *them*
their portion of meat in due season?
43 Blessed[m] is that servant whom
his lord, when he cometh, shall find
so doing.
44 Of a truth I say unto you,
that he will make him ruler over
all that he hath.

i 1 Th.5.2; 2 Pe.3.10; Re.3.3; 16.15.
k ch.21.34,36. *l* 1 Co.4.2. *m* ver.37.

45 But and if that servant say
in his heart, My lord delayeth his
coming; and shall begin to [n]beat
the men-servants and maidens,
and to eat and drink, and to be
drunken;
46 The lord of that servant will
come in a day when he looketh
not for *him*, and at an hour when
he is not aware, and [o]will [4]cut
him in sunder, and will appoint
him his portion with the unbe-
lievers.
47 And that servant [p]which
knew his lord's will, and prepared
not *himself*, neither did according
to his will, [q]shall be beaten with
many *stripes*.
48 But he [r]that knew not, and
did commit things worthy of
stripes, shall be beaten with few
stripes. For[s] unto whomsoever
much is given, of him shall be
much required; and to whom men
have [t]committed much, of him
they will ask the more.
49 I am come to send fire on

n Mat.22.6. *o* Ps.37.9; 94.14. 4 or, *cut him off*.
p Ja.4.17. *q* De.25.2. *r* Ac.17.30.
s Le.5.17; Jn.15.22; 1 Ti.1.13. *t* 1 Ti.6.20.

---

47. *Which knew his lord's will.* Who knew what his master wished him to do. He that knows what God commands and requires. ¶ *Many stripes.* Shall be severely and justly punished. They who have many privileges, who are often warned, who have the gospel, and do not repent and believe, shall be far more severely punished than others. They who are early taught in Sunday-schools, or by pious parents, or in other ways, and who grow up in sin and impenitence, will have much more to answer for than those who have no such privileges.

48. *Few* stripes. The Jews never inflicted more than forty stripes for one offence, De. xxv. 3. For smaller offences they inflicted only four, five, six, &c., according to the nature of the crime. In allusion to this, our Lord says that he *that knew not*—that is, he who had comparatively little knowledge—would suffer a punishment proportionally light. He refers, doubtless, to those who have fewer opportunities, smaller gifts, or fewer teachers. ¶ *Much is given.* They who have much committed to their disposal, as stewards, &c. See the parable of the talents in Mat. xxv. 14–30.

49. *I am come*, &c. The result of my coming will be that there will be divisions and contentions. He does not mean that he came *for* that purpose, or that he *sought* and *desired* it; but that such was the state of the human heart, and such the opposition of men to the truth, that that would be the *effect* of his coming. See Notes on Mat. x. 34. ¶ *Fire.* Fire, here, is the emblem of discord and contention, and consequently of calamities. Thus it is used in Ps. lxvi. 12; Is. xliii. 2. ¶ *And what will I*, &c. This passage might be better expressed in this manner: "And what would I, but that it were kindled. Since it is *necessary* for the advancement of religion that such divisions should take place; since the gospel cannot be established without conflicts, and strifes, and hatreds, I am even desirous that they should come. Since the greatest bless-

the earth; and what will I if it be already kindled?

50 But I have a baptism to be baptized with; and how am I straitened[5] till it be accomplished!

51 Suppose [u]ye that I am come to give peace on earth? I tell you, Nay; but rather division:

52 For from henceforth there shall be five in one house divided, three against two, and two against three.

53 The [v]father shall be divided against the son, and the son against the father; the mother against the daughter, and the daughter against the mother; the mother-in-law against her daughter-in-law, and the daughter-in-law against her mother-in-law.

54 And he said also to the people, When[w] ye see a cloud rise out of the west, straightway ye say, There cometh a shower; and so it is.

55 And when *ye see* the south wind blow, ye say, There will be heat; and it cometh to pass.

56 *Ye* hypocrites! ye can discern the face of the sky, and of the earth; but how is it that ye do not discern this time?

57 Yea, and why even [x]of yourselves judge ye not what is right?

58 When[y] thou goest with thine adversary to the magistrate, [z]*as thou art* in the way, give diligence that thou mayest be delivered from him; lest he hale thee to the judge, and the judge deliver thee to the officer, and the officer cast thee into prison.

59 I tell thee, thou shalt not depart thence till thou hast paid the very last [6]mite.

5 or, *pained.* u Mat.10.34. v Mi.7.6. w Mat.16.2,&c.

x 1 Co.11.14. y Mat.5.25. z Is.55.6. 6 See Mar.12.42.

ing which mankind can receive must be attended with such unhappy divisions, I am willing, nay, desirous that they should come." He did not wish evil in itself; but, as it was the occasion of good, he was desirous, if it *must* take place, that it should take place soon. From this we learn—1st. That the promotion of religion may be expected to produce many contests and bitter feelings. 2d. That the heart of man must be exceedingly wicked, or it would not oppose a work like the Christian religion. 3d. That though God cannot look on evil with approbation, yet, for the sake of the benefit which may grow out of it, he is willing to permit it, and suffer it to come into the world.

50. *A baptism.* See Notes on Mat. xx. 22. ¶ *Am I straitened.* How do I earnestly desire that it were passed! Since these sufferings *must* be endured, how anxious am I that the time should come! Such were the feelings of the Redeemer in view of his approaching dying hour. We may learn from this—1st. That it is not improper to *feel deeply* at the prospect of dying. It is a sad, awful, terrible event; and it is impossible that we should look at it aright *without* feeling—scarcely without trembling. 2d. It is not improper to desire that the time should come, and that the day of our release should draw nigh, Phi. i. 23. To the Christian, death is but the entrance to life; and since the pains of death *must* be endured, and since they lead to heaven, it matters little how soon he passes through these sorrows, and rises to his eternal rest.

51–53. See Notes on Mat. x. 34–36.

54–57. See Notes on Mat. xvi. 2, 3. ¶ *South wind.* To the south and southwest of Judea were situated Arabia, Egypt, and Ethiopia, all warm or hot regions, and consequently the air that came from those quarters was greatly heated. ¶ *How is it that ye do not discern this time?* You see a cloud rise, and predict a shower; a south wind, and expect heat. These are regular events. So you see my miracles; you hear my preaching; you have the predictions of me in the prophets; why do you not, in like manner, infer that *this is the time* when the Messiah should appear?

58, 59. See Notes on Mat. v. 25, 26.

CHAPTER XIII.

1. *There were present.* That is, some persons who were present, and who had heard his discourse recorded in the previous chapter. There was probably a pause in his discourse, when they mentioned what had been done by Pilate to the Galileans. ¶ *At that sea-*

CHAPTER XIII.

THERE were present at that season some that told him of the [a]Galileans, whose blood Pilate had [b]mingled with their sacrifices.
2 And Jesus, answering, said unto them, Suppose ye that these Galileans were sinners above all the Galileans, because they suffered such things?
3 I tell you, Nay; but [c]except ye repent, ye shall all likewise perish.
4 Or those eighteen, upon whom

a Ac.5.37. b La.2.20. c Ac.3.19; Re.2.21,22.

son. At that time—that is the time mentioned in the last chapter. At what period of our Lord's ministry this was, it is not easy to determine. ¶ *Some that told him.* This was doubtless an event of recent occurrence. Jesus, it is probable, had not before heard of it. Why they told him of it can only be a matter of conjecture. It might be from the desire to get him to express an opinion respecting the conduct of Pilate, and thus to involve him in difficulty with the reigning powers of Judea. It might be as a mere matter of news. But, from the answer of Jesus, it would appear that *they* supposed that the Galileans *deserved* it, and that they meant to pass a judgment on the character of those men, a thing of which they were exceedingly fond. The answer of Jesus is a reproof of their habit of hastily judging the character of others. ¶ *Galileans.* People who lived in Galilee. See Notes on Mat. ii. 22. They were not under the jurisdiction of Pilate, but of Herod. The Galileans, in the time of Christ, were very wicked. ¶ *Whose blood Pilate had mingled,* &c. That is, while they were sacrificing at Jerusalem, Pilate came suddenly upon them and slew them, and *their* blood was mingled with the blood of the animals that they were slaying for sacrifice. It does not mean that Pilate *offered* their blood in sacrifice, but only that as they were sacrificing he slew them. The fact is not mentioned by Josephus, and nothing more is known of it than what is here recorded. We learn, however, from Josephus that the Galileans were very wicked, and that they were much disposed to broils and seditions. It appears, also, that Pilate and Herod had a quarrel with each other (Lu. xxiii. 12), and it is not improbable that Pilate might feel a particular enmity to the subjects of Herod. It is likely that the Galileans excited a tumult in the temple, and that Pilate took occasion to come suddenly upon them, and show his opposition to them and Herod by slaying them. ¶ *Pilate.* The Roman governor of Judea. See Notes on Mat. xxvii. 2.

2, 3. *Suppose ye,* &c. From this answer it would appear that they supposed that the fact that these men had been slain in this manner proved that they were very great sinners. ¶ *I tell you, Nay.* Jesus assured them that it was not right to draw such a conclusion respecting these men. The fact that men come to a sudden and violent death is not proof that they are peculiarly wicked. ¶ *Except ye repent.* Except you forsake your sins and turn to God. Jesus took occasion, contrary to their expectation, to make a practical use of that fact, and to warn them of their own danger. He never suffered a suitable occasion to pass without warning the wicked, and entreating them to forsake their evil ways. The subject of religion was always present to his mind. He introduced it easily, freely, fully. In this he showed his love for the souls of men, and in this he set us an example that we should walk in his steps. ¶ *Ye shall all likewise perish.* You shall all be destroyed in a similar manner. Here he had reference, no doubt, to the calamities that were coming upon them, when thousands of the people perished. Perhaps there was never any reproof more delicate and yet more severe than this. They came to him believing that these men who had perished were peculiarly wicked. He did not tell them that *they* were as bad as the Galileans, but left them to *infer* it, for if they did not repent, they must soon likewise be destroyed. This was remarkably fulfilled. Many of the Jews were slain in the temple; many while offering sacrifice; thousands perished in a way very similar to the Galileans. Comp. Notes on Mat. xxiv. From this account of the Galileans we may learn—(1.) That men are very prone to infer, when any great calamity happens to others, that they are peculiarly guilty.

the tower in Siloam fell, and slew them, think ye that they were sinners[1] above all men that dwelt in Jerusalem?

5 I tell you, Nay; but except ye repent, ye shall all likewise perish.

[1] or, *debtors.*

See the Book of Job, and the reasonings of his three "*friends.*" (2.) That that conclusion, in the way in which it is usually drawn, is erroneous. If we see a man bloated, and haggard, and poor, who is in the habit of intoxication, we may infer properly that he is guilty, and that God hates his sin and punishes it. So we may infer of the effects of licentiousness. But we should not thus infer when a man's house is burned down, or when his children die, or when he is visited with a loss of health; nor should we infer it of the nations that are afflicted with famine, or the plague, or with the ravages of war; nor should we infer it when a man is killed by lightning, or when he perishes by the blowing up of a steamboat. Those who thus perish may be far more virtuous than many that live. (3.) This is not a world of retribution. Good and evil are mingled; the good and the bad suffer, and all are exposed here to calamity. (4.) There is another world—a future state—a world where the good will be happy and the wicked punished. There all that is irregular on earth will be regulated; all that appears unequal will be made equal; all that is chaotic will be reduced to order. (5.) When men are disposed to speak about the great guilt of others, and the calamities that come upon them, they should inquire about *themselves.* What is *their* character? what is *their* condition? It *may be* that they are in quite as much danger of perishing as those are whom they regard as so wicked. (6.) WE MUST REPENT. We must ALL repent or we shall perish. No matter what befalls others, *we* are sinners; *we* are to die; *we* shall be lost unless we repent. Let us, then, think of *ourselves* rather than of *others;* and when we hear of any signal calamity happening to others, let us remember that there is calamity in another world as well as here; and that while our fellow-sinners are exposed to trials *here,* we may be exposed to more awful woes *there.* Woe *there* is eternal; here, a calamity like that produced by a falling tower is soon over.

4. *Or those eighteen.* Jesus himself adds another similar case, to warn them —a case which had probably occurred not long before, and which it is likely they judged in the same manner. ¶ *Upon whom the tower in Siloam fell.* The name Siloah or Siloam is found only three times in the Bible as applied to water—once in Is. viii. 6, who speaks of it as running water; once as a pool near to the king's garden, in Ne. iii. 15; and once as a pool, in the account of the Saviour's healing the man born blind, in Jn. ix. 7–11. Josephus mentions the fountain of Siloam frequently as situated at the mouth of the Valley of Tyropœon, or the Valley of Cheesemongers, where the fountain long indicated as that fountain is still found. It is on the south side of Mount Moriah, and between that and the Valley of Jehoshaphat. The water at present flows out of a small artificial basin under the cliff, and is received into a large reservoir 53 feet in length by 18 in breadth. The small upper basin or fountain excavated in the rock is merely the entrance, or rather the termination of a long and narrow subterranean passage beyond, by which the water comes from the Fountain of the Virgin. For what purpose the *tower* here referred to was erected is not known; nor is it known at what time the event here referred to occurred. It is probable that it was not far from the time when the Saviour made use of the illustration, for the manner in which he refers to it implies that it was fresh in the recollection of those to whom he spoke.

5. *I tell you, Nay.* It is improper to suppose that those on whom heavy judgments fall in this world are the worst of men. This is not a world of retribution. Often the most wicked are suffered to prosper here, and their punishment is reserved for another world; while the righteous are called to suffer much, and *appear* to be under the sore displeasure of God, Ps. lxxiii. This only we know, that the wicked will not *always* escape; that God is just; and that none who *do* suffer here or hereafter, suffer more than they deserve. In the future world, all that seems to be unequal here will be made equal and plain.

6 He spake also this parable:
A[d] certain *man* had a fig-tree
planted in his vineyard; and he
came and [e]sought fruit thereon,
and found none.
7 Then said he unto the dresser
of his vineyard, Behold, these
three years I come seeking fruit
on this fig-tree and find none: [f]cut
it down; why cumbereth it the
ground?

8 And he, answering, said unto
him, Lord, [g]let it alone this year
also, till I shall dig about it and
dung *it:*
9 And if it bear fruit, *well;* and
if not, *then* [h]after that thou shalt
cut it down.
10 And he was teaching in one
of the synagogues on the sabbath.
11 And, behold, there was a woman which had a [i]spirit of infirmity

d Is.5.1,&c.; Mat.21.19.
e Jn.15.16; Ga.5.22; Phi.4.17. f Ex.32.10.
g Ps.106.23; 2 Pe.3.9. h Jn.15.2; He.6.8. i Ps.6.2.

6. *This parable.* See Notes on Mat. xiii. 3. ¶ *Vineyard.* A place where vines were planted. It was not common to plant fig-trees in them, but our Lord represents it as having been sometimes done.

7. *The dresser of his vineyard.* The man whose duty it was to trim the vines and take care of his vineyard. ¶ *These three years.* These words are not to be referred to the time which Christ had been preaching the gospel, as if he meant to specify the exact period. They mean, as applicable to the vineyard, that the owner had been *a long time* expecting fruit on the tree. For three successive years he had been disappointed. In his view it was long enough to show that the tree was barren and would yield no fruit, and that therefore it should be cut down. ¶ *Why cumbereth it the ground?* The word *cumber* here means to render *barren* or *sterile.* By taking up the juices of the earth, this useless tree rendered the ground sterile, and prevented the growth of the neighbouring vines. It was not merely *useless*, but was doing mischief, which may be said of all sinners and all hypocritical professors of religion. Dr. Thomson (*The Land and the Book*, vol. i. p. 539) says of the barren fig-tree: "There are many such trees now; and if the ground is not properly cultivated, especially when the trees are young—as the one of the parable was, for only *three* years are mentioned—they do not bear at all; and even when full grown they quickly fail, and wither away if neglected. Those who expect to gather good crops of well-flavoured figs are particularly attentive to their culture — not only plough and dig about them frequently, and manure them plentifully, but they carefully gather out the stones from the orchards, contrary to their general slovenly habits."

This parable is to be taken in connection with what goes before, and with our Saviour's calling the Jewish nation to repentance. It was spoken to illustrate the dealings of God with them, and their own wickedness under all his kindness, and we may understand the different parts of the parable as designed to represent—1st. God, by the man who owned the vineyard. 2d. The vineyard as the Jewish people. 3d. The coming of the owner for fruit, the desire of God that they should produce good works. 4th. The barrenness of the tree, the wickedness of the people. 5th. The dresser was perhaps intended to denote the Saviour and the other messengers of God, pleading that God would spare the Jews, and save them from their enemies that stood ready to destroy them, as soon as God should permit. 6th. His waiting denotes the delay of vengeance, to give them an opportunity of repentance. And, 7th. The remark of the dresser that he might *then* cut it down, denotes the acquiescence of all in the belief that such a judgment would be just.

We may also remark that God treats sinners in this manner now; that he spares them long; that he gives them opportunities of repentance; that many live but to cumber the ground; that they are not only useless to the church, but pernicious to the world; that in due time, when they are fairly tried, they shall be cut down; and that the universe will bow to the awful decree of God, and say that their damnation is just.

11. *There was a woman which had a spirit of infirmity.* Was infirm, or was weak and afflicted. This was produced by Satan, ver. 16. ¶ *Eighteen years.* This affliction had continued a long time.

eighteen years, and was bowed together, and could in no wise lift up *herself*.

12 And when Jesus saw her, he called *her to him*, and said unto her, Woman, [k]thou art loosed from thine infirmity.

13 And [l]he laid *his* hands on her; and immediately she was made straight, and glorified God.

14 And the ruler of the synagogue answered with indignation, because that Jesus had [m]healed on the sabbath-day, and said unto the people, [n]There are six days in which men ought to work: in them, therefore, come and be healed, and not on the sabbath-day.

15 The Lord then answered him, and said, [o]*Thou* hypocrite! doth not each one of you [p]on the sabbath loose his ox or *his* ass from the stall, and lead *him* away to watering?

16 And ought not this woman,

k Joel 3.10. *l* Mar.16.18; Ac.9.17. *m* Mat.12.10; Mar.3.2; ch.6.7; 14.3; Jn.5.16. *n* Ex.20.9. *o* Pr.11.9; Mat.7.5; 23.13,28; ch.12.1. *p* ch.14.5.

This shows that the miracle was *real;* that the disease was not feigned. Though thus afflicted, yet it seems she was regular in attending the worship of God in the synagogue. There in the sanctuary, is the place where the afflicted find consolation; and there it was that the Saviour met her and restored her to health. It is in the sanctuary and on the Sabbath, also, that he commonly meets his people, and gives them the joys of his salvation.

12. *Thou art loosed from thine infirmity.* This was a remarkable declaration. It does not appear that the woman *applied* to him for a cure; yet Jesus addressed her, and the disease departed. How clear would be the proofs from such a case that he was the Messiah! And how mighty the power of him that by a word could restore her to health!

13. *Glorified God.* Praised God. Gave thanks to him for healing her. They who are restored to health from sickness owe it to God; and they should devote their lives to his service, as expressive of their sense of gratitude to him who has spared them.

14. *Answered with indignation, because,* &c. He considered this a violation of the Sabbath, doing work contrary to the fourth commandment. If he had reasoned aright, he would have seen that he who could perform such a miracle could not be a violator of the law of God. From this conduct of the ruler we learn—1st. That men are often opposed to good being done, because it is not done *in their own way* and *according to their own views.* 2d. That they are more apt to look at what they consider a violation of the law in others, than at the good which others may do. 3d. That this opposition is manifested not only against those who *do good,* but also against those who are *benefited.* The ruler of the synagogue seemed particularly indignant that *the people* would come to Christ to be healed. 4th. That this conduct is often the result of envy. In this case it was rather hatred that the people should follow Christ instead of the Jewish rulers, and therefore envy at the popularity of Jesus, than any real regard for religion. 5th. That opposition to the work of Jesus may put on the appearance of great professed regard for religion. Many men oppose revivals, missions, Bible societies, and Sunday-schools—strange as it may seem—*from professed regard to the purity of religion.* They, like the ruler here, have formed their notions of religion as consisting in something *very different from doing good,* and they oppose those who are attempting to spread the gospel throughout the world.

15. Thou *hypocrite!* You condemn *me* for an action, and yet you perform one exactly similar. You condemn *me* for doing to a woman what you do to a beast. To her I have done good on the Sabbath; you provide for your cattle, and yet blame me for working a miracle to relieve a sufferer on that day. ¶ *Stall.* A place where cattle are kept to be fed, and sheltered from the weather.

16. *A daughter of Abraham.* A descendant of Abraham. See Notes on Mat. i. 1. She was therefore a Jewess; and the ruler of the synagogue, professing a peculiar regard for the Jewish people, considering them as peculiarly favoured of God, should have rejoiced that she was loosed from this infirmity. ¶ *Whom Satan hath bound.* Satan is

being a [q]daughter of Abraham, whom Satan hath bound, lo, these eighteen years, be loosed from this bond on the sabbath-day?

17 And when he had said these things, [r]all his adversaries were ashamed: and all the people rejoiced for all the [s]glorious things that were done by him.

18 Then said he, [t]Unto what is the kingdom of God like? and whereunto shall I resemble it?

19 It is like a grain of mustard-seed, which a man took and cast into his garden; and it grew, and waxed a great tree; and the fowls of the air lodged in the branches of it.

20 And again he said, Whereunto shall I liken the kingdom of God?

21 It is like leaven, which a woman took and hid in three [2]measures of meal, till the whole was leavened.

22 And he went through the cities and villages, teaching, and journeying toward Jerusalem.

23 Then said one unto him, Lord, are there few that be saved? And he said unto them,

24 Strive[u] to enter in at the

q ch.19.9. r Is.45.24; 1 Pe.3.16. s Ex.15.11; Ps.111.3; Is.4.2. t Mat.13.31; Mar.4.30,&c.

2 See Mat.13.33. u Mat.7.13.

the name given to the prince or leader of evil spirits, called also the devil, Beelzebub, and the old serpent, Mat. xii. 24; Re. xii. 9; xx. 2. By his *binding* her is meant that he had inflicted this disease upon her. It was not properly a *possession* of the devil, for that commonly produced derangement; but God had suffered him to afflict her in this manner, similar to the way in which he was permitted to try Job. See Notes on Job i. 12; ii. 6, 7. It is no more *improbable* that God would suffer *Satan* to inflict pain, than that he would suffer a wicked *man* to do it; yet nothing is more common than for one *man* to be the occasion of bringing on a disease in another which may terminate only with the life. He that seduces a virtuous man and leads him to intemperance, or he that wounds him or strikes him, may disable him as much as Satan did this woman. If God permits it in one case, he may, for the same reason, in another.

17. *Adversaries.* The ruler of the synagogue, and those who felt as he did. ¶ *All the people.* The persons who attended the synagogue, and who had witnessed the miracle. It is to be remarked—1st. That those who opposed Christ were chiefly the *rulers.* They had an *interest* in doing it. Their popularity was at stake. They were afraid that he would draw off the people from them. 2d. The common people heard him gladly. Many of them believed in him. The condition of the poor, and of those in humble life, is by far the most favourable for religion, and most of the disciples of Jesus have been found there.

18–21. See these parables explained in the Notes on Mat. xiii. 31, 32.

22. *Cities and villages.* Chiefly of Galilee, and those which were between Galilee and Jerusalem. ¶ *Teaching and journeying.* This evinces the diligence of our Lord. Though on a journey, yet he remembered his work. He did not excuse himself on the plea that he was in haste. Christians and Christian ministers should remember that when their Master travelled he did not *conceal* his character, or think that he was then freed from obligation to do good.

23. *Then said one.* Who this was does not appear. It is probable that he was not one of the disciples, but one of the Jews, who came either to perplex him, or to involve him in a controversy with the Pharisees. ¶ *Are there few that be saved?* It was the prevalent opinion among the Jews that few would enter heaven. As but two of all the hosts that came out of Egypt entered into the land of Canaan, so some of them maintained that a proportionally small number would enter into heaven (Lightfoot). On this subject the man wished the opinion of Jesus. It was a question of idle curiosity. The answer to it would have done little good. It was far more important for the man to secure his own salvation, than to indulge in such idle inquiries and vain speculations. Our Lord therefore advised *him,* as he does *all, to strive* to enter into heaven.

24. *Strive.* Literally, *agonize.* The word is taken from the Grecian games.

strait gate; [v]for many, I say unto
you, will seek to enter in, and shall
not be able.

25 When[w] once the master of
the house is risen up, and [x]hath
shut to the door, and ye begin to
stand without, and to knock at
the door, saying, [y]Lord, Lord, open
unto us; and he shall answer and
say unto you, I know you not
whence ye are;

26 Then shall ye begin to say,
We have eaten and drunk in thy
presence, and thou hast taught in
our streets.

27 But[z] he shall say, I tell you,

v Jn.7.34; 8.21; Ro.9.31. w Ps.32.6; Is.55.6. x Mat.25.10. y ch.6.46.

z Mat.7.22,23; 25.12,41.

In their races, and wrestlings, and various athletic exercises, they *strove* or *agonized*, or put forth all their powers to gain the victory. Thousands witnessed them. They were long trained for the conflict, and the honour of victory was one of the highest honours among the people. So Jesus says that we should strive to enter in; and he means by it that we should be diligent, be active, be earnest; that we should make it our first and chief business to overcome our sinful propensities, and to endeavour to enter into heaven. This same figure or allusion to the Grecian games is often used in the New Testament, 1 Co. ix. 24–26; Phi. ii. 16; He. xii. 1. ¶ *Strait gate.* See Notes on Mat. vii. 13, 14. Dr. Thomson (*The Land and the Book*, vol. i. p. 32) says: "I have seen these strait gates and narrow ways, 'with here and there a traveller.' They are in retired corners, and must be sought for, and are opened only to those who knock; and when the sun goes down and the night comes on, they are shut and locked. It is then too late." ¶ *Will seek to enter in.* Many in various ways manifest some desire to be saved. They seek it, but do not agonize for it, and hence they are shut out. But a more probable meaning of this passage is that which refers this *seeking* to a time that shall be *too late;* to the time when the master has risen up, &c. In this life they neglect religion, and are engaged about other things. At death, or at the judgment, they will seek to enter in; but it will be too late—the door will be shut; and because they did not make religion the chief business of their life, they cannot *then* enter in. ¶ *Shall not be able.* This is not designed to affirm anything respecting the inability of the sinner, provided he seeks salvation in a proper time and manner. It means that at the time when many *will* seek—when the door is shut—they will not be able *then* to enter in, agreeable to Mat. vii. 22. In the proper time, when the day of grace was lengthened out, they *might* have entered in; but there *will be* a time when it will be too late. The day of mercy will be ended, and death will come, and the doors of heaven barred against them. How important, then, to strive to enter in while we have opportunity, and before it shall be too late!

25. *When once the master*, &c. The figure here used is taken from the conduct of a housekeeper, who is willing to see his friends, and who at the proper time keeps his doors open. But there is a proper time for closing them, when he will not see his guests. At night it would be improper and vain to seek an entrance—the house would be shut. So there is a proper time to seek an entrance into heaven; but there will be a time when it will be too late. At death the time will have passed by, and God will be no longer gracious to the sinner's soul.

26. *We have eaten*, &c. Comp. Mat. vii. 22, 23. To have eaten with one is evidence of acquaintanceship or friendship. So the sinner may allege that he was a professed follower of Jesus, and had some evidence that Jesus was his friend. There is no allusion here, however, to the sacrament. The figure is taken from the customs of men, and means simply that they had professed attachment, and perhaps supposed that Jesus was their friend. ¶ *In thy presence.* With thee—as one friend does with another. ¶ *Thou hast taught.* Thou didst favour us, as though thou didst love us. Thou didst not turn away from us, and we did not drive thee away. All this is alleged as proof of friendship. It shows us—1st. On how slight evidence men will suppose themselves ready to die. How slender is the preparation which even many professed friends of Jesus have for death! How easily they are satisfied about their

I know you not whence ye are;
depart from me, all [a]*ye* workers
of iniquity.

28 There[b] shall be weeping and
gnashing of teeth, when ye shall
see Abraham, and Isaac, and Jacob, and all the prophets, in the
kingdom of God, and you *yourselves* thrust out.

29 And[c] they shall come from
the east, and *from* the west, and
from the north, and *from* the
south, and shall sit down in the
kingdom of God.

30 And, behold, [d]there are last
which shall be first, and there are
first which shall be last.

31 The same day there came
certain of the Pharisees, saying
unto him, Get thee out and depart
hence; for Herod will kill thee.

32 And he said unto them, Go,
ye and tell [e]that fox, Behold, I cast
out devils, and I do cures to-day

a Ps.6.8; 101.8.
b Mat.8.12; 13.42; 24.51.
c Re.7.9,10.
d Mat.19.30.
e Zep.3.3.

own piety! A profession of religion, attendance on the preaching of the word or at the sacraments, or a decent external life, is all they have and all they seek. With this they go quietly on to eternity—go to disappointment, wretchedness, and woe! 2d. None of these things will avail in the day of judgment. It will be only true love to God, a real change of heart, and a life of piety, that can save the soul from death. And oh! how important it is that all should search themselves and see what is the real foundation of their hope that they shall enter into heaven!

27. See Notes on Mat. vii. 23.

28–30. See Notes on Mat. viii. 11, 12.

31. *Came certain of the Pharisees.* Their coming to him in this manner would have the appearance of friendship, as if they had conjectured or secretly learned that it was Herod's intention to kill him. Their suggestion had much appearance of probability. Herod had killed John. He knew that Jesus made many disciples, and was drawing away many of the people. He was a wicked man, and he might be supposed to fear the presence of one who had so strong a resemblance to John, whom he had slain. It might seem probable, therefore, that he intended to take the life of Jesus, and this might appear as a friendly hint to escape him. Yet it is more than possible that Herod might have sent these Pharisees to Jesus. Jesus was eminently popular, and Herod might not dare openly to put him to death; yet he desired his removal, and for this purpose he sent these men, as if in a friendly way, to advise him to retire. This was probably the reason why Jesus called him a fox. ¶ *Herod.* Herod Antipas, a son of Herod the Great. He ruled over Galilee and Perea, and wished Jesus to retire beyond these regions. See Notes on ch. iii. 1.

32. *Tell that fox.* A fox is an emblem of slyness, of cunning, and of artful mischief. The word is also used to denote a dissembler. Herod was a wicked man, but the *particular thing* to which Jesus here alludes is not his *vices*, but his *cunning*, his *artifice*, in endeavouring to remove him out of his territory. He had endeavoured to do it by stratagem—by sending these men who pretended great friendship for his life. ¶ *Behold, I cast out devils*, &c. Announce to him the fact that I am working miracles in his territory, and that I shall continue to do it. I am not afraid of his art or his enmity. I am engaged in my appropriate work, and shall continue to be as long as is proper, in spite of his arts and his threats. ¶ *To-day and to-morrow.* A little time. The words seem here to be used not strictly, but proverbially—to denote a short space of time. Let not Herod be uneasy. I am doing no evil; I am not violating the laws. I only cure the sick, &c. In a little time this part of my work will be done, and I shall retire from his dominions. ¶ *The third* day. After a little time. Perhaps, however, he meant *literally* that he would depart on that day for Jerusalem; that for two or three days more he would remain in the villages of Galilee, and then go on his way to Jerusalem. ¶ *I shall be perfected.* Rather, I shall have ended my course *here;* I shall have *perfected* what I purpose to do in Galilee. It does not refer to his *personal* perfection, for he was always perfect, but it means that he would have *finished* or *completed* what he purposed to do in the regions of

and to-morrow, and the third *day*
I shall be [f]perfected.
33 Nevertheless, I must walk
to-day, and to-morrow, and the *day*
following; for it cannot be that a
prophet perish out of Jerusalem.
34 O[g] Jerusalem, Jerusalem,
which killest the prophets, and
stonest them that are sent unto
thee; how often would I have
gathered thy children together, as
a hen *doth gather* her brood under
her wings, and ye would not!
35 Behold, [h]your house is left
unto you desolate; and verily I
say unto you, Ye shall not see me,
until *the time* come when ye shall
say, [i]Blessed *is* he that cometh in
the name of the Lord.

CHAPTER XIV.

AND it came to pass, as he went into the house of one of the chief Pharisees, to eat bread on the sabbath-day, that [a]they watched him.

f He.2.10. g Mat.23.37.

h Le.26.31,32; Ps.69.25; Is.1.7; 5.5,6; Da.9.27; Mi. 3.12. i ch.19.38; Jn.12.13.
a Ps.37.32; Is.29.20,21; Je.20.10,11.

Herod. He would have completed his work, and would be ready then to go.

33. *I must walk*, &c. I must remain here this short time. These three days I must do cures here, and then I shall depart, though not for fear of Herod. It will be because my time will have come, and I shall go up to Jerusalem to die. ¶ *For it cannot be that a prophet should perish out of Jerusalem.* I have no fear that *Herod* will put me to death in Galilee. I shall not depart on that account. *Jerusalem* is the place where the prophets die, and where *I* am to die. I am not at all alarmed, therefore, at any threats of *Herod*, for my life is safe until I arrive at Jerusalem. Go and tell him, therefore, that I fear him not. I shall work here as long as it is proper, and shall then go up to Jerusalem to die. The reason why he said that a prophet could not perish elsewhere than in Jerusalem might be—1st. That he knew that he would be tried on a charge of blasphemy, and no other court could have cognizance of that crime but the great council or Sanhedrim, and so he was not afraid of any threats of Herod. 2d. It *had been* the fact that the prophets had been chiefly slain there. The meaning is, "It cannot easily be done elsewhere; it is not usually done. Prophets have generally perished there, and there *I* am to die. I am safe, therefore, from the fear of Herod, and shall not take the advice given and leave his territory."

34, 35. See Notes on Mat. xxiii. 37–39.

From the message which Jesus sent to Herod we may learn—1st. That our lives are safe in the hands of God, and that wicked men can do no more to injure us than he shall permit. Compare Jn. xix. 11. 2d. That we should go on fearlessly in doing our duty, and especially if we are doing good. We should not regard the threats of men. God is to be obeyed; and even if obedience *should* involve us in difficulty and trials, still we should not hesitate to commit our cause to God and go forward. 3d. We should be on our guard against crafty and unprincipled men. They often *profess* to seek our good when they are only plotting our ruin. Even those professedly coming from our enemies to caution us are often also our enemies, and are secretly plotting our ruin or endeavouring to prevent our doing good. 4th. We see here the nature of religion. It shrinks at nothing which is duty. It goes forward trusting in God. It comes out boldly and faces the world. And, 5th. How beautiful and consistent is the example of Christ! How *wise* was he to detect the arts of his foes! how *fearless* in going forward, in spite of all their machinations, to do what God had appointed for him to do!

CHAPTER XIV.

1. *It came to pass.* It so happened or occurred. ¶ *As he went*, &c. It is probable that he was invited to go, being in the neighbourhood (ver. 12); and it is also probable that the Pharisee invited him for the purpose of getting him to say something that would involve him in difficulty. ¶ *One of the chief Pharisees.* One of the Pharisees who were *rulers*, or members of the great council or the Sanhedrim. See Notes on Mat. v. 22. It does not mean that he was the head of the *sect* of the Pharisees, but one of those who hap-

2 And, behold, there was a certain man before him which had the dropsy.

3 And Jesus, answering, spake unto the lawyers and Pharisees, saying, [b]Is it lawful to heal on the sabbath-day?

4 And they held their peace. And he took *him*, and healed him, and let him go;

5 And answered them, saying, [c]Which of you shall have an ass or an ox fallen into a pit, and will not straightway pull him out on the sabbath-day?

6 And they could not answer him again to these things.

7 And he put forth a parable to those which were bidden, when he marked how they chose out the chief rooms; saying unto them,

8 When[d] thou art bidden of any

b ch.13.14. *c* ch.13.15. *d* Pr.25.6,7.

---

pened to be a member of the Sanhedrim. He was therefore a man of influence and reputation. ¶ *To eat bread.* To dine. To partake of the hospitalities of his house. ¶ *On the sabbath-day.* It may seem strange that our Saviour should have gone to dine with a man who was a stranger on the Sabbath; but we are to remember—1st. That he was travelling, having no home of his own, and that it was no more improper to go there than to any other place. 2d. That he did not go there for the purpose of feasting and amusement, but to do good. 3d. That as several of that class of persons were together, it gave him an opportunity to address them on the subject of religion, and to reprove their vices. If, therefore, the example of Jesus should be pled to authorize accepting an invitation to dine on the Sabbath, it should be pled JUST AS IT WAS. If we can go *just as he did*, it is right. If when away from home; if we go to do good; if we make it an occasion to discourse on the subject of religion and to persuade men to repent, then it is not improper. Farther than this we cannot plead the example of Christ. And surely this should be the last instance in the world to be adduced to justify dinner-parties, and scenes of riot and gluttony on the Sabbath. ¶ *They watched him.* They malignantly fixed their eyes on him, to see if he did anything on which they could lay hold to accuse him.

2. *A certain man before him.* In what way he came there we know not. He might have been one of the Pharisee's family, or might have been placed there by the Pharisees to see whether he would heal him. This last supposition is not improbable, since it is said in ver. 1 that they watched him. ¶ *The dropsy.* A disease produced by the accumulation of water in various parts of the body; very distressing, and commonly incurable.

3. *Jesus, answering.* To *answer*, in the Scriptures, does not always imply, as among us, that anything had been said before. It means often merely to *begin* or to take up a subject, or, as here, to remark on the case that was present. ¶ *Is it lawful*, &c. He knew that they were watching him. If he healed the man at once, they would accuse him. He therefore proposed the question to them, and when it was asked, they could not say that it was not lawful.

4. *They held their peace.* They were silent. They *could* not say it was not lawful, for the law did not forbid it. If it had they would have said it. Here was the time for them to make objections if they had any, and not after the man was healed; and as they *made* no objection *then*, they could not with consistency afterward. They were therefore effectually silenced and confounded by the Saviour. ¶ *He took* him. Took hold of the man, or perhaps took him apart into another room. By taking hold of him, or touching him, he showed that the power of healing went forth from himself.

5, 6. See Notes on Mat. xii. 11. ¶ *Which of you*, &c. In this way Jesus refuted the notion of the Pharisees. If it was lawful to save an ox on the Sabbath, it was also to save the life of a man. To this the Jews had nothing to answer.

7. *A parable.* The word parable, here, means rather a *precept*, an *injunction*. He gave a *rule* or *precept* about the proper manner of attending a feast, or about the humility which ought to be manifested on such occasions. ¶ *That were bidden.* That were invited by the Pharisee. It seems that he had invited

man to a wedding, sit not down
in the highest room; lest a more
honourable man than thou be bidden of him;
9 And he that bade thee and
him come and say to thee, Give
this man place; and thou begin
with shame to take the lowest
room.
10 But when thou art bidden, go
and sit down in the lowest room;
that when he that bade thee cometh, he may say unto thee, Friend,
go up higher; then shalt thou have
worship in the presence of them
that sit at meat with thee.
11 For[e] whosoever exalteth himself shall be abased; and he that
humbleth himself shall be exalted.
12 Then said he also to him that
bade him, When thou makest a
dinner or a supper, call not thy

e 1 Sa.15.17; Job 22.29; Ps.18.27; Pr.15.33; 29.23; Mat.23.12; ch.18.14; Ja.4.6; 1 Pe.5.5.

---

his friends to dine with him on that day. ¶ *When he marked.* When he observed or saw. ¶ *Chief rooms.* The word *rooms* here does not express the meaning of the original. It does not mean *apartments*, but *the higher places* at the table; those which were nearest the head of the table and to him who had invited them. See Notes on Mat. xxiii. 6. That this was the common character of the Pharisees appears from Mat. xxiii. 6.

8, 9. *Art bidden.* Art invited. ¶ *To a wedding.* A wedding was commonly attended with a feast or banquet. ¶ *The highest room.* The seat at the table nearest the head. ¶ *A more honourable man.* A more aged man, or a man of higher rank. It is to be remarked that our Saviour did not consider the courtesies of life to be beneath his notice. His chief design here was, no doubt, to reprove the pride and ambition of the Pharisees; but, in doing it, he teaches us that religion does not violate the courtesies of life. It does not teach us to be rude, forward, pert, assuming, and despising the proprieties of refined intercourse. It teaches humility and kindness, and a desire to make all happy, and a willingness to occupy our appropriate situation and rank in life; and this is true *politeness*, for true politeness is a desire to make all others happy, and a readiness to do whatever is necessary to make them so. They have utterly mistaken the nature of religion who suppose that because they are professed Christians, they must be rude and uncivil, and violate all the distinctions in society. The example and precepts of Jesus Christ were utterly unlike such conduct. He teaches us to be kind, and to treat men according to their rank and character. Comp. Mat. xxii. 21; Ro. xiii. 7; 1 Pe. ii. 17.

10. *The lowest room.* The lowest seat at the table; showing that you are not desirous of distinctions, or greedy of that honour which may properly belong to you. ¶ *Shalt have worship.* The word *worship* here means *honour.* They who are sitting with you shall treat you with respect. They will learn your rank by your being invited nearer to the head of the table, and it will be better to learn it thus than by putting yourself forward. They will do you honour because you have shown a humble spirit.

11. *Whosoever exalteth,* &c. This is universal among men, and it is also the way in which God will deal with men. *Men* will perpetually endeavour to bring down those who endeavour to exalt themselves; and it is a part of God's regular plan to abase the proud, to bring down the lofty, to raise up those that be bowed down, and show *his* favours to those who are poor and needy.

12. *Call not thy friends,* &c. This is not to be understood as commanding us not to entertain *at all* our relatives and friends; but we are to remember the *design* with which our Lord spoke. He intended, doubtless, to reprove those who sought the society of the wealthy, and particularly rich relatives, and those who claimed to be intimate with the great and honourable, and who, to show their intimacy, were in the habit of *seeking* their society, and making for them expensive entertainments. He meant, also, to commend charity shown to the poor. The passage means, therefore, call *not only* your friends, but call also the poor, &c. Comp. Ex. xvi. 8; 1 Sa. xv. 22; Jer. vii. 22, 23; Mat. ix. 13. ¶ *Thy kinsmen.* Thy relations. ¶ *A recompense.* Lest they feel themselves bound to treat you with the same kindness, and, in so doing, neither you nor they will show

friends, nor thy brethren, neither thy kinsmen, [f]nor *thy* rich neighbours; lest they also bid thee again, and a recompense be made thee.

13 But when thou makest a feast, [g]call the poor, the maimed, the lame, the blind:

14 And thou shalt be blessed, for they cannot recompense thee; for thou shalt be recompensed at the resurrection of the just.

15 And when one of them that sat at meat with him heard these things, he said unto him, [h]Blessed *is* he that shall eat bread in the kingdom of God.

16 Then said he unto him, [i]A certain man made a [k]great supper, and bade many;

17 And sent his servant at supper-time to say unto them that were bidden, [l]Come, for all things are now ready.

f Pr.22.16. g Ne.8.10,12.

h Re.19.9. i Mat.22.2,&c. k Is.25.6,7. l Pr.9.2,5; Ca.5.1; Is.55.1,2.

any kind spirit, or any disposition to do good beyond what is repaid.

13. *The poor.* Those who are destitute of comfortable food. ¶ *The maimed.* Those who are deprived of any member of their body, as an arm or a leg, or who have not the use of them so that they can labour for their own support.

14. *Shalt be blessed.* Blessed in the *act* of doing good, which furnishes more *happiness* than riches can give, and blessed or rewarded *by God* in the day of judgment. ¶ *They cannot recompense thee.* They cannot invite you again, and thus pay you; and by inviting *them* you show that you have a *disposition* to do good. ¶ *The resurrection of the just.* When the just or holy shall be raised from the dead. Then *God* shall reward those who have done good to the poor and needy from love to the Lord Jesus Christ, Mat. x. 42; xxv. 34–36.

15. *Blessed* is *he that shall eat bread in the kingdom of God.* The kingdom of God here means the kingdom which the Messiah was to set up. See Notes on Mat. iii. 2. The Jews supposed that he would be a temporal prince, and that his reign would be one of great magnificence and splendour. They supposed that the *Jews* then would be delivered from all their oppressions, and that, from being a degraded people, they would become the most distinguished and happy nation of the earth. To that period they looked forward as one of great happiness. There is some reason to think that they supposed that the ancient just men would then be raised up to enjoy the blessings of the reign of the Messiah. Our Saviour having mentioned the *resurrection of the just,* this man understood it in the common way of the Jews, and spoke of the peculiar happiness which they expected at that time. The Jews *only,* he expected, would partake of those blessings. Those notions the Saviour corrects in the parable which follows.

16. *A great supper.* Or great feast. It is said to be *great* on account of the number who were invited. ¶ *Bade many.* Invited many beforehand. There is little difficulty in understanding this parable. The man who made the supper is, without doubt, designed to represent God; the supper, the provisions which he has made for the salvation of men; and the invitation, the offers which he made to men, particularly to the Jews, of salvation. See a similar parable explained in the Notes on Mat. xxii. 1–14.

17. *Sent his servant.* An invitation had been sent before, but this servant was sent at the time that the supper was ready. From this it would seem that it was the custom to announce to those invited just the time when the feast was prepared. The custom here referred to still prevails in Palestine. Dr. Thomson (*The Land and the Book,* vol. i. p. 178) says: "If a sheikh, beg, or emeer invites, he always sends a servant to call you at the proper time. This servant often repeats the very formula mentioned in Lu. xiv. 17: Tefŭddŭlû, el 'asha hâder—Come, for the supper is ready. The fact that this custom is mainly confined to the wealthy and to the nobility is in strict agreement with the parable, where the certain man who made the great supper and bade many is supposed to be of this class. It is true now, as then, that to refuse is a high insult to the maker of the feast, nor would such excuses as those in the parable be more acceptable to a Druse emeer than they were to the lord of this 'great supper.'"

18 And they all with one *consent*
began to make excuse. The[m] first
said unto him, I have bought a
piece of ground, and I must needs
go and see it: I pray thee have
me excused.
19 And another said, I have
bought five yoke of oxen, and I
go to prove them: I pray thee
have me excused.
20 And another said, [n]I have
married a wife, and therefore I
cannot come.
21 So that servant came and
showed his lord these things.
Then the master of the house, [o]being angry, said to his servant,
Go out quickly [p]into the streets
and lanes of the city, and bring in
hither the [q]poor, and the maimed,
and the [r]halt, and the blind.
22 And the servant said, Lord, it

m ch.8.14. *n* ver.26; 1 Co.7.33.

o Ps.2.12. *p* Re.22.17. *q* 1 Sa.2.8; Ps.113.7,8. *r* Ps.38.7; Is.33.23; 35.6.

---

18. *I have bought a piece of ground.* Perhaps he had purchased it on condition that he found it as good as it had been represented to him. ¶ *I must needs go.* I have necessity, or am obliged to go and see it; possibly pleading a contract or an agreement that he would go soon and examine it. However, we may learn from this that sinners sometimes plead that they are under a *necessity* to neglect the affairs of religion. The affairs of the world, they pretend, are so pressing that they cannot find time to attend to their souls. They have no time to pray, or read the Scriptures, or keep up the worship of God. In this way many lose their souls. God cannot regard such an excuse for neglecting religion with approbation. He commands us to seek *first* the kingdom of God and his righteousness, nor can he approve any excuse that men may make for not doing it.

19. *I go to prove them.* To try them, to see if he had made a good bargain. It is worthy of remark that this excuse was very trifling. He could as easily have tried them at any other time as then, and his whole conduct shows that he was more disposed to gratify *himself* than to accept the invitation of his friend. He was selfish; just as all sinners are, who, to gratify their own worldliness and sins, refuse to accept the offers of the gospel.

20. *I have married a wife,* &c. Our Saviour here doubtless intends to teach us that the love of earthly relatives and friends often takes off the affections from God, and prevents our accepting the blessings which he would bestow on us. This was the most trifling excuse of all; and we cannot but be amazed that *such* excuses are suffered to interfere with our salvation, and that men can be satisfied for *such* reasons to exclude themselves from the kingdom of God.

21. *Showed his lord.* Told his master of the excuses of those who had been invited. Their conduct was remarkable, and it was his duty to acquaint him with the manner in which his invitation had been received. ¶ *Being angry.* Being angry at the men who had slighted his invitation; who had so insulted him by neglecting his feast, and preferring *for such reasons* their own gratification to his friendship and hospitality. So it is no wonder that God is angry with the wicked every day. So foolish as well as wicked is the conduct of the sinner, so trifling is his excuse for not repenting and turning to God, that it is no wonder if God cannot look upon their conduct but with abhorrence. ¶ *Go out quickly.* The feast is ready. There is no time to lose. They who partake of it must do it soon. So the gospel is ready; time flies; and they who partake of the gospel must do it soon, and they who preach it must give diligence to proclaim it to their fellow-men. ¶ *The streets and lanes of the city.* The places where the poor, &c., would be found. Those first invited were the rich, who dwelt at ease in their own houses. By these the Jews were intended; by those who were in the streets, the Gentiles. Our Lord delivered this parable to show the Jews that the Gentiles would be called into the kingdom of God. They despised the Gentiles, and considered them cast out and worthless, as they did those who were in the lanes of the city. ¶ *The maimed,* &c. See Notes on ver. 13.

22. *Yet there is room.* He went out and invited all he found in the lanes, and yet the table was not full. This

is done as thou hast commanded,
and [s]yet there is room.
23 And the lord said unto the
servant, Go out into the highways
and hedges, and [t]compel *them* to
come in, that my house may be
filled.
24 For I say unto you, [u]that
none of those men which were
bidden shall taste of my supper.

s Ps.103.6; 130.7. *t* Ps.110.3. *u* Pr.1.24; Mat.21.43; He.12.25.

he also reported to his master. *There is room!* What a glorious declaration is this in regard to the gospel! There yet is room. Millions have been saved, but there yet is room. Millions have been invited, and have come, and have gone to heaven, but heaven is not yet full. There is a banquet there which no number can exhaust; there are fountains which no number can drink dry; there are harps there which other hands may strike; and there are seats there which others may occupy. Heaven is not full, and there yet is room. The Sabbath-school teacher may say to his class, there yet is room; the parent may say to his children, there yet is room; the minister of the gospel may go and say to the wide world, there yet is room. The mercy of God is not exhausted; the blood of the atonement has not lost its efficacy; heaven is not full. What a sad message it *would* be if we were compelled to go and say, "There is no more room—heaven is full —not another one can be saved. No matter what their prayers, or tears, or sighs, they cannot be saved. Every place is filled; every seat is occupied." But, thanks be to God, this is not the message which we are to bear; and if there yet is room, come, sinners, young and old, and enter into heaven. Fill up that room, that heaven may be full of the happy and the blessed. If any part of the universe is to be vacant, O let it be the dark world of woe!

23. *Go out into the highways.* Since enough had not been found in the lanes and streets, he commands the servant to go into the roads—the public highways *out* of the city, as well as to the streets *in* it—and invite them also. ¶ *Hedges.* A hedge is the inclosure around a field or vineyard. It was commonly made of thorns, which were planted thick, and which kept the cattle out of the vineyard. "A common plant for this purpose is the prickly pear, a species of cactus, which grows several feet high, and as thick as a man's body, armed with sharp thorns, and thus forming an almost impervious defence" (Professor Hackett, *Scripture Illustrations*, p. 174). Those in the hedges were poor labourers employed in planting them or trimming them—men of the lowest class and of great poverty. By his directing them to go first into the streets of the city and then into the highways, we are not to understand our Saviour as referring to different classes of men, but only as denoting the *earnestness* with which God offers salvation to men, and his willingness that the most despised should come and live. Some parts of parables are thrown in for the sake of *keeping*, and they should not be pressed or forced to obtain any obscure or fanciful signification. The great point in this parable was, that God would call in the Gentiles after the Jews had rejected the gospel. This should be kept always in view in interpreting all the parts of the parable. ¶ *Compel* them. That is, urge them, press them earnestly, one and all. Do not hear their excuses on account of their poverty and low rank of life, but urge them so as to overcome their objections and lead them to the feast. This expresses the *earnestness* of the man; his anxiety that his table should be filled, and his purpose not to reject any on account of their poverty, or ignorance, or want of apparel. So God is earnest in regard to the most polluted and vile. He commands his servants, his ministers, to *urge* them to come, to *press* on them the salvation of the gospel, and to use ALL the means in their power to bring into heaven poor and needy sinners.

24. *For I say unto you.* These may be considered as the words of Jesus, making an application of the parable to the Pharisees before him. ¶ *None of those men.* This cannot be understood as meaning that no *Jews* would be saved, but that none of those who had *treated him in that manner*—none who had so decidedly rejected the offer of the gospel—would be saved. We may here see how dangerous it is *once* to reject the gospel; how dangerous to grieve away the Holy Spirit. How often God

25 And there went great multitudes with him; and he turned and said unto them,
26 If any *man* come to me, [v]and hate not his father, and mother, and wife, and children, and brethren, and sisters, yea, and [w]his own life also, he cannot be my disciple.
27 And[x] whosoever doth not bear his cross, and come after me, cannot be my disciple.
28 For which of you, [y]intending to build a tower, sitteth not down first and counteth the cost, whether ye have *sufficient* to finish *it?*
29 Lest haply, after he hath laid the foundation, and is not able to finish *it*, all that behold *it* begin to mock him,
30 Saying, This man began to build, and [z]was not able to finish.
31 Or what king, going to make war against another king, sitteth not down first, and [a]consulteth whether he be able with ten thousand to meet him that cometh against him with twenty thousand?
32 Or else, while the other is yet a great way off, he sendeth an

v De.33.9; Mat.10.37. *w* Ac.20.24; Re.12.11. *x* Mat.16.24; Mar.8.34; ch.9.23; 2 Ti.3.12. *y* Pr.24.27. *z* He.7.11. *a* Pr.20.18.

forsakes for ever the sinner who has been once awakened, and who grieves the Holy Spirit. The invitation is full and free; but when it is rejected, and men turn wilfully away from it, God leaves them to their chosen way, and they are drowned in destruction and perdition. How important, then, is it to embrace the gospel *at once;* to accept the gracious invitation, and enter without delay the path that conducts to heaven!

25, 26, 27. See Notes on Mat. x. 37, 38.

26. *And hate not.* The word *hate*, here, means simply to *love less.* See the meaning of the verse in Mat. x. 37. It may be thus expressed: "He that comes after me, and does not love his father *less* than he loves me, &c., cannot be my disciple." We are not at liberty literally to *hate* our parents. This would be expressly contrary to the fifth commandment. See also Ep. vi. 1–3; Col. iii. 20. But we are to love them *less* than we love Christ; we are to obey Christ rather than them; we are to be willing to forsake them if he calls us to go and preach his gospel; and we are to submit, without a murmur, to him when he takes them away from us. This is not an uncommon meaning of the word *hate* in the Scriptures. Comp. Mal. i. 2, 3; Ge. xxix. 30, 31; De. xxi. 15–17.

28. *Intending to build a tower.* See Mat. xxi. 33. A tower was a place of defence or observation, erected on high places or in vineyards, to guard against enemies. It was made *high*, so as to enable one to see an enemy when he approached; and *strong*, so that it could not be easily taken. ¶ *Counteth the cost.* Makes a calculation how much it will cost to build it.

29. *Haply.* Perhaps. ¶ *To mock him.* To ridicule him. To laugh at him.

31. *With ten thousand to meet,* &c. Whether he will be able, with the forces which he *has*, to meet his enemy. Christ here perhaps intends to denote that the enemies which we have to encounter in following him are many and strong, and that *our* strength is comparatively feeble. ¶ *To meet him.* To contend with him. To gain a victory over him.

32. *Or else.* If he is not able. If he is satisfied that he would be defeated. ¶ *An ambassage.* Persons to treat with an enemy and propose terms of peace. These expressions are not to be improperly pressed in order to obtain from them a spiritual signification. The general scope of the parable is to be learned from the connection, and may be thus expressed: 1st. Every man who becomes a follower of Jesus should calmly and deliberately look at all the consequences of such an act and be prepared to meet them. 2d. Men in other things act with prudence and forethought. They do not begin to build without a reasonable prospect of being able to finish. They do not go to war when there is every prospect that they will be defeated. 3d. Religion is a work of soberness, of thought, of calm and fixed purpose, and no man can properly enter on it who does not resolve by the grace of God to fulfil all its requirements and make it the business of his life. 4th. We are to expect diffi-

ambassage, and desireth conditions
of peace.
33 So likewise, whosoever he be
of you that [b]forsaketh not all that
he hath, he cannot be my disciple.
34 Salt[c] *is* good; but if the salt
have lost its savour, wherewith
shall it be seasoned?
35 It is neither fit for the land,
nor yet for the dunghill; [d]*but* men
cast it out. He that hath ears to
hear, let him hear.

b Phi.3.7,8. *c* Mat.5.13; Mar.9.50. *d* Jn.15.6.

CHAPTER XV.

THEN[a] drew near unto him all the publicans and sinners, for to hear him.
2 And the Pharisees and scribes
murmured, saying, This man receiveth sinners, and [b]eateth with
them.
3 And he spake this parable
unto them, saying,
4 What[c] man of you, having an
hundred sheep, if he lose one of

a Mat.9.10,&c. *b* Ac.11.3; 1 Co.5.9-11; Ga.2.12. *c* Mat.18.12.

culties in religion. It will cost us the mortification of our sins, and a life of self-denial, and a conflict with our lusts, and the enmity and ridicule of the world. Perhaps it may cost us our reputation, or possibly our lives and liberties, and all that is dear to us; but we must cheerfully undertake all this, and be prepared for it all. 5th. If we do not deliberately resolve to leave all things, to suffer all things that may be laid on us, and to persevere to the end of our days in the service of Christ, we cannot be his disciples. No man can be a Christian who, when he makes a profession, is resolved after a while to turn back to the world; nor can he be a true Christian if he *expects* that he *will* turn back. If he comes not with a *full* purpose *always* to be a Christian; if he means not to persevere, by the grace of God, through all hazards, and trials, and temptations; if he is not willing to bear his cross, and meet contempt, and poverty, and pain, and death, without turning back, he *cannot* be a disciple of the Lord Jesus.

34, 35. See Notes on Mat. v. 13; Mar. ix. 49, 50. ¶ *Salt* is *good.* It is useful. It is good to preserve life and health, and to keep from putrefaction. ¶ *His savour.* Its saltness. It becomes tasteless or insipid. ¶ *Be seasoned.* Be salted again. ¶ *Fit for the land.* Rather, it is not fit *for land*—that is, it will not bear fruit of itself. You cannot sow or plant on it. ¶ *Nor for the dunghill.* It is not good for manure. It will not enrich the land. ¶ *Cast it out.* They throw it away as useless. ¶ *He that hath ears*, &c. See Mat. xi. 15. You are to understand that he that has not grace in his heart; who merely makes a profession of religion, and who sustains the same relation to true piety that this insipid and useless mass does to good salt, is useless in the church, and will be rejected. *Real* piety, true religion, is of vast value in the world. It keeps it pure, and saves it from corruption, as salt does meat; but a mere *profession* of religion is fit for nothing. It does no good. It is a mere encumbrance, and all such professors are fit only to be cast out and rejected. All such *must* be rejected by the Son of God, and cast into a world of wretchedness and despair. Comp. Mat. vii. 22, 23; viii. 12; xxiii. 30; xxv. 30; Re. iii. 16; Job viii. 13; xxxvi. 13.

CHAPTER XV.

1. *Publicans and sinners.* See Notes on Mat. ix. 10.

2. *Murmured.* They affected to suppose that if Jesus treated sinners kindly he must be fond of their society, and be a man of similar character. *They* considered it disgraceful to be with them or to eat with them, and they therefore brought a charge against him for it. They *would* not suppose that he admitted them to his society for the purpose of doing them good; nor did they remember that the very object of his coming was to call the wicked from their ways and to save them from death. ¶ *Receiveth sinners.* Receives them in a tender manner; treats them with kindness; does not drive them from his presence. ¶ *And eateth with them.* Contrary to the received maxims of the scribes. By eating with them he showed that he did not despise or overlook them.

3. *This parable.* See Notes on Mat. xiii. 3.

4–6. See Notes on Mat. xviii. 12, 13.

7. *Likewise joy*, &c. It is a principle of human nature that the *recovery* of an

them, doth not leave the ninety
and nine in the wilderness, and go
after that which is lost, until he
find it?
5 And when he hath found *it*, he
layeth *it* on his shoulders, rejoicing.
6 And when he cometh home,
he calleth together *his* friends and
neighbours, saying unto them, Rejoice with me; [d]for I have found
my sheep which was lost.
7 I say unto you, that likewise
joy shall be in heaven over one
sinner that repenteth, more than
over ninety and nine just persons
which [e]need no repentance.
8 Either what woman having ten
[1]pieces of silver, if she lose one
piece, doth not light a candle, and
sweep the house, and seek diligently
till she find *it?*
9 And when she hath found *it*,
she calleth *her* friends and *her*
neighbours together, saying, Rejoice with me; for I have found
the piece which I had lost.
10 Likewise, I say unto you,

d Ps.119.176; 1 Pe.2.25.

e ch.5.32.

[1] *Drachma*, here translated *a piece of silver*, is the eighth part of an ounce, which cometh to sevenpence halfpenny, and is equal to the Roman penny. See Mat.18.28.

object in danger of being lost, affords much more intense joy than the quiet *possession* of many that are safe. This our Saviour illustrated by the case of the lost sheep and of the piece of silver. It might also be illustrated by many other things. Thus we rejoice most in our health when we recover from a dangerous disease; we rejoice over a child rescued from danger or disease more than over those who are in health or safety. We rejoice that property is saved from conflagration or the tempest more than over much more that has not been in danger. This feeling our Lord represents as existing in heaven. *Likewise*, in like manner, or on the same principle, there is joy. ¶ *In heaven.* Among the angels of God. Comp. ver. 10. Heavenly beings are thus represented as rejoicing over those who repent on earth. They see the guilt and danger of men; they know what God has done for the race, and they rejoice at the recovery of any from the guilt and ruins of sin. ¶ *One sinner.* One rebel against God, however great may be his sins or however small. If a sinner, he must perish unless he repents; and they rejoice at his repentance because it recovers him back to the love of God, and because it will save him from eternal death. ¶ *That repenteth.* See Notes on Mat. ix. 13. ¶ *Just persons.* The word *persons* is not in the original. It means simply *just ones*, or those who have not sinned. The word may refer to angels as well as to men. There are no *just* men on earth who need no repentance, Ec. vii. 20; Ps. xiv. 2, 3; Ro. iii. 10–18. Our Saviour did not mean to imply that there were any such. He was speaking of what took place *in heaven*, or among *angels*, and of *their* emotions when they contemplate the creatures of God; and he says that *they* rejoiced in the repentance of one *sinner* more than in the holiness of many who had not fallen. We are not to suppose that he meant to teach that there were just ninety-nine holy angels to one sinner. He means merely that they rejoice more over the *repentance* of one sinner than they do over many who have not fallen. By this he vindicated his own conduct. The Jews did not deny the existence of angels. They would not deny that their feelings were proper. If *they* rejoiced in this manner, it was not improper for *him* to show similar joy, and especially to seek their conversion and salvation. If they rejoice also, it shows how desirable is the repentance of a sinner. They know of how much value is an immortal soul. They see what is meant by eternal death; and they do not feel *too much*, or have *too much anxiety* about the soul that can never die. Oh that men saw it as *they* see it! and oh that they would make an effort, such as angels see to be proper, to save their own souls and the souls of others from eternal death!

8–10. *Ten pieces of silver.* In the original, ten *drachmas*. The drachma was about the value of fifteen cents, and consequently the whole sum was about a dollar and a half, or six shillings. The sum was small, but it was all she had. The loss of one piece, therefore, was severely felt. ¶ *There is joy in the presence*, &c. Jesus in this parable expresses the same sentiment which he

there[f] is joy in the presence of the angels of God over one sinner that repenteth.

11 And he said, A certain man had two sons;

12 And the younger of them said to *his* father, Father, give me the portion of goods that falleth *to me.* And[g] he divided unto them *his* living.

13 And not many days after, the younger son gathered all together and took his journey into a far country, and there wasted his substance with riotous living.

14 And when he had spent all, there arose a mighty [h]famine in that land; and he began to be in want.

15 And he went and joined him-

f Eze.18.23,32; 33.11; Ac.11.18; Phile.15,16. *g* Mar.12.44.

h Am.8.11,12.

---

did in the preceding. A woman would have more immediate, present joy at finding a lost piece, than she would in the possession of those which had not been lost. *So*, says Christ, there is joy among the angels at the recovery of a single sinner.

11. *And he said.* Jesus, to illustrate still farther the sentiment which he had uttered, and to show that it was proper to rejoice over repenting sinners, proceeds to show it by a most beautiful and instructive parable. We shall see its beauty and propriety by remembering that the *design* of it was simply to *justify his conduct in receiving sinners*, and to show that to rejoice over their return was proper. This he shows by the feelings of a *father* rejoicing over the *return* of an ungrateful and dissipated son.

12. *And the younger of them said.* By this younger son we are to understand the publicans and sinners to be represented. By the elder, the Pharisees and scribes. ¶ *Give me the portion.* The part. ¶ *Of goods.* Of property. ¶ *That falleth* to me. That is properly my share. There is no impropriety in supposing that he was of age; and, as he chose to leave his father's house, it was proper that his father should, if he chose, give him the part of the estate which would be his. ¶ *He divided unto them his living.* His property, or *means* of living. The division of property among the Jews gave the elder son twice as much as the younger. In this case it seems the younger son received only money or movable property, and the elder chose to remain with his father and dwell on the paternal estate. The lands and fixed property remained in their possession. Among the ancient Romans and Syrophœnicians, it was customary, when a son came to the years of maturity, if he demanded his part of the inheritance, for the father to give it to him. This the son might claim by law. It is possible that such a custom may have prevailed among the Jews, and that our Saviour refers to some such demand made by the young man.

13. *Gathered all together.* Collected his property. If he had received flocks or grain, he sold them and converted them into money. As soon as this arrangement had been made he left his father's house. ¶ *Took his journey.* Went, or travelled. ¶ *Into a far country.* A country far off from his father's house. He went probably to trade or to seek his fortune, and in his wanderings came at last to this dissipated place, where his property was soon expended. ¶ *Wasted his substance.* Spent his property. ¶ *In riotous living.* Literally, "Living without saving anything." He lived extravagantly, and in the most dissolute company. See ver. 30. By his wandering away we may understand that sinners wander far away from God; that they fall into dissolute and wicked company; and that their wandering so far off is the reason why they fall into such company, and are so soon and so easily destroyed.

14. *A mighty famine.* Famines were common in Eastern nations. They were caused by the failure of the crops—by a want of timely rains, a genial sun, or sometimes by the prevalence of the plague or of the pestilence, which swept off numbers of the inhabitants. In this case it is very naturally connected with the luxury, the indolence, and the dissipation of the people in that land.

15. *Joined himself.* Entered the service of that citizen. Hired himself out to him. It would seem that he engaged to do any kind of work, even of the lowest kind. ¶ *A citizen.* One of the inhabitants of one of the cities or towns

self to a citizen of that country; and he sent him into his fields to feed swine.

16 And he would fain have [i]filled his belly with the husks that [k]the swine did eat; and no man gave unto him.

17 And when he came to himself, he said, How many hired servants of my father's have bread enough

[i] Is.44.20; Ho.12.1. [k] Ps.73.22.

of that region, probably a man of property. ¶ *Into the fields.* Out of the city where the owner lived. ¶ *To feed swine.* This was a very low employment, and particularly so to a *Jew.* It was forbidden to the Jews to eat swine, and of course it was unlawful to keep them. To be compelled, therefore, to engage in such an employment was the deepest conceivable degradation. The *object* of this image, as used by the Saviour in the parable, is to show the loathsome employments and the deep degradation to which sin leads men, and no circumstance could possibly illustrate it in a more striking manner than he has done here. Sin and its results everywhere have the same relation to that which is noble and great, which the feeding of swine had, in the estimation of a Jew, to an honourable and dignified employment.

16. *He would fain.* He would gladly. He desired to do it. ¶ *The husks.* The word *husks* with us denotes the outward covering of corn. In this there is little nourishment, and it is evident that this is not intended here; but the word used here denotes not only *husks*, but also leguminous plants, as beans, &c. It is also used to denote the fruit of a tree called the *carob* or *kharub-tree*, which is common in Ionia, Syria, and Rhodes. The tree is more bushy and thick-set than the apple-tree, and the leaves are larger and of a much darker green. The following is Dr. Thomson's description of the fruit of this tree (*The Land and the Book*, vol. i. p. 22): "The 'husks'—a mistranslation—are fleshy pods, somewhat like those of the locust-tree, from six to ten inches long and one broad, laid inside with a gelatinous substance, not wholly unpleasant to the taste when thoroughly ripe. I have seen large orchards of this kharub in Cyprus, where it is still the food which the swine do eat. The kharub is often called St. John's Bread, and also Locust-tree, from a mistaken idea about the food of the Baptist in the wilderness." The cut will give an idea of these *pods*, or "*husks*," as they are called in our translation. ¶ *No man gave unto him.* Some have understood this as meaning "no one gave him anything—

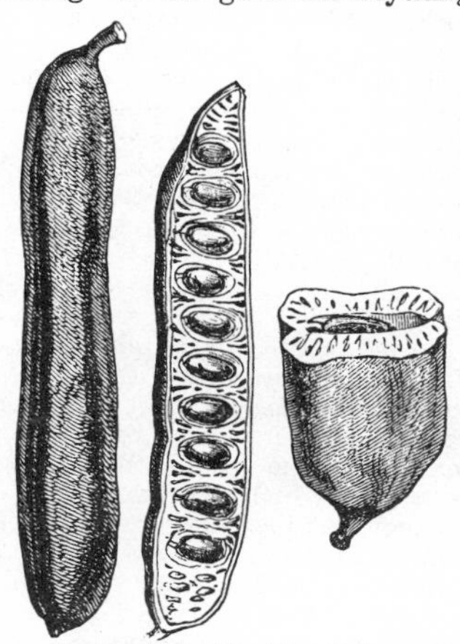

Husks—Pods of the Kharub-tree.

any bread or provisions;" but the connection requires us to understand it of the "husks." He did not go a begging—his master was bound to provide for his wants; but the provision which he made for him was so poor that he would have preferred the food of the swine. He desired a portion of *their* food, but that was not given him. A certain quantity was measured out for *them*, and *he* was not at liberty to eat it himself. Nothing could more strikingly show the evil of his condition, or the deep degradation, and pollution, and wretchedness of sin.

17. *He came to himself.* This is a very expressive phrase. It is commonly applied to one who has been *deranged*, and when he recovers we say he has *come to himself.* In this place it denotes that the folly of the young man was a kind of derangement—that he was insane. So it is of every sinner. Madness is in their hearts (Ec. ix. 3); they are estranged from God, and led, by the influence of evil passions, contrary to their better judgment and the decisions of a sound mind. ¶ *Hired servants.*

and to spare, and I perish with hunger!

18 I[l] will arise, and go to my father, and will say unto him, Father, I have sinned against heaven and before thee,

19 And am no more worthy to be called thy son: make me as one of thy hired servants.

20 And he arose, and came to his father. But when he was yet a [m]great way off, his father saw

l Ps.32.5.

m Ac.2.39; Ep.2.13,17.

Those in a low condition of life—those who were not born to wealth, and who had no friends to provide for them. ¶ *I perish.* I, who had property and a kind father, and who might have been provided for and happy.

18. *I will arise.* This is a common expression among the Hebrews to denote *entering on a piece of business.* It does not imply that he was *sitting*, but that he meant immediately to return. This should be the feeling of every sinner who is conscious of his guilt and danger. ¶ *To my father.* To his father, although he had offended him, and treated him unkindly, and had provoked him, and dishonoured him by his course of conduct. So the sinner. He has nowhere else to go but to *God.* He has offended him, but he may trust in his kindness. If *God* does not save him he cannot be saved. There is no other being that has an arm strong enough to deliver from sin; and though it is painful for a man to go to one whom he has offended—though he cannot go but with shame and confusion of face—yet, unless the sinner is willing to go to *God* and confess his faults, he can never be saved. ¶ *I have sinned.* I have been wicked, dissipated, ungrateful, and rebellious. ¶ *Against heaven.* The word *heaven* here, as it is often elsewhere, is put for God. I have sinned against *God.* See Mat. xxi. 25. It is also to be observed that one evidence of the genuineness of repentance is the feeling that our sins have been committed chiefly against *God.* Commonly we think most of our offences as committed against *man;* but when the sinner sees the true character of his sins, he sees that they have been aimed chiefly against *God*, and that the sins against *man* are of little consequence compared with those against God. So David, even after committing the crimes of adultery and murder—after having inflicted the deepest injury on *man*—yet felt that the sin as committed against *God* shut every other consideration out of view: *Against thee, thee* ONLY, *have I sinned*, &c., Ps. li. 4. ¶ *Before thee.* This means the same as *against* thee. The offences had been committed mainly against God, but they were to be regarded, also, as sins against his *father*, in wasting property which he had given him, in neglecting his counsels, and in plunging himself into ruin. He felt that he had *disgraced* such a father. A sinner will be sensible of his sins against his relatives and friends as well as against God. A true penitent will be as ready to *acknowledge* his offences against his fellow-men as those against his Maker.

19. *No more worthy*, &c. "Such has been my conduct that I have been a disgrace to my father. I am not fit to be honoured by being called the son of a man so kind and virtuous." ¶ *Make me as one*, &c. "Treat me as a servant. Let me come again into your family, but I do not ask to be treated *as a son.* I am willing to come in if you will give me only the support that you give to a servant." This evinced, 1st. Deep humility—such as a sinner should have. 2d. Love for his father's house—such as all penitents should have toward God's dwelling-place in heaven. 3d. Confidence in his father that he would treat him kindly, even if he treated him as a servant. Such confidence all returning penitents feel in God. They are assured that God will treat them kindly—that *whatever* he gives them will be more than they deserve, and they are therefore willing to be in his hands. Yet, 4th. He had no adequate sense of his father's kindness. He did not fully appreciate his character. He was far more kind than he had dared to hope he would be; just as all sinners undervalue the character of God, and find him always more kind than they had supposed. No sinner comes to God with a just and adequate view of his character, but *always* finds him more merciful than he had dared to hope.

20. *He arose, and came.* Was coming. But here is no indication of *haste.* He did not *run*, but came driven by his wants, and, as we may suppose, filled

him, and had compassion, and ran
and fell on his neck, and kissed
him.
21 And the son said unto him,
Father, [n]I have sinned against
heaven, and in thy sight, and am
no more worthy to be called thy
son.
22 But the father said to his
servants, [o]Bring forth the best
robe and put *it* on him; and put
a ring on his hand, and shoes on
his feet;
23 And bring hither the fatted
calf, and kill *it;* and let us eat and
be merry:
24 For[p] this my son [q]was dead,
and [r]is alive again; he [s]was lost,

n Ps.51.4.

o Zec.3.3-5. p ver.32. q Ep.2.1; 5.14; Re.3.1. r Ro.6.11,13. s Eze.34.4,16; ch.19.10.

with shame, and even with some doubts whether his father would receive him. ¶ *A great way off.* This is a beautiful description—the image of his father's happening to see him clad in rags, poor, and emaciated, and yet he recognized *his son*, and all the feelings of a father prompted him to go and embrace him. ¶ *Had compassion.* Pitied him. Saw his condition—his poverty and his wretched appearance—and was moved with compassion and love. ¶ *And ran.* This is opposed to the manner in which the son came. The beauty of the picture is greatly heightened by these circumstances. The son came slowly—the father *ran.* The love and joy of the old man were so great that he hastened to meet him and welcome him to his home. ¶ *Fell on his neck.* Threw his arms around his neck and embraced him. ¶ *And kissed him.* This was a sign at once of affection and reconciliation. This must at once have dissipated every doubt of the son about the willingness of his father to forgive and receive him. A kiss is a sign of affection, 1 Sa. x. 1; Ge. xxix. 13. This is evidently designed to denote the *readiness of God* to pity and pardon returning sinners. In this verse of inimitable beauty is contained the point of the parable, which was uttered by the Saviour to vindicate *his own conduct* in receiving sinners kindly. Who could *blame* this father for thus receiving his repenting son? Not even a Pharisee could blame him; and our Saviour thus showed them, so that *they* could not resist it, that *God* received returning sinners, and that it was right for *him* also to receive them and treat them with attention.

22. *The best robe.* The son was probably in rags. The joy of the father is expressed by clothing him in the best raiment, that he might appear well. The *robe* here mentioned is probably the outer garment; and the father told them to put on him the best one that was in the house—one reserved for festival occasions. See Ge. xxvii. 15. ¶ *A ring on his hand.* To wear a ring on the hand was one mark of wealth and dignity. The rich and those in office commonly wore them. Comp. Ja. ii. 2. To *give* a ring was a mark of favour, or of affection, or of conferring office. Comp. Ge. xli. 42; Es. viii. 2. Here it was expressive of the *favour* and affection of the father. ¶ *Shoes on* his *feet.* Servants, probably, did not usually wear shoes. The son returned, doubtless, without shoes—a condition very unlike that in which he was when he left home. When, therefore, the father commanded them to put shoes on him, it expressed his wish that he should not be treated *as a servant*, but *as a son.* The word *shoes* here, however, means no more than *sandals*, such as were commonly worn. And the meaning of all these images is the same—*that God will treat those who return to him with kindness and affection.* These images should not be attempted to be *spiritualized.* They are beautifully thrown in to fill up the narrative, and to express with more force the *general* truth that *God* will treat returning penitents with mercy and with love. To dress up the son in this manner was a proof of the father's affection. So God will bestow on sinners the marks of his confidence and regard.

23. *Be merry.* Literally, "eating, let us rejoice." The word *merry* does not quite express the meaning of the Greek. *Merriment* denotes a light, playful, jovial mirth. The Greek denotes simply *joy*—let us be *happy*, or *joyful.*

24. *Was dead.* This is capable of two significations: 1st. *I supposed* that he was dead, but I know now that he is alive. 2d. He was *dead* to *virtue*—he was sunk in pleasure and vice. The word is not unfrequently thus used. See 1 Ti. v. 6; Mat. viii. 22; Ro. vi. 13.

and is found. And they began to
be merry.
25 Now his elder son was in the
field: and as he came and drew
nigh to the house, he heard [t]music
and dancing.
26 And he called one of the
servants, and asked what these
things meant.
27 And he said unto him, Thy
brother is come; and thy father
hath killed the fatted calf, because
he hath received him safe and
sound.
28 And he was [u]angry, and
would not go in: therefore came
his father out and entreated him.
29 And he, answering, said to *his*
father, Lo, these many years do [v]I
serve thee, [w]neither transgressed
I at any time thy commandment;
and yet thou never gavest me a
kid, that I might make merry with
my friends;
30 But as soon as this thy son
was come, which hath devoured
thy living with harlots, thou hast
killed for him the fatted calf.
31 And he said unto him, [x]Son,

t Ps.30.11; 126.1,2. *u* Jonah 4.1-3; Ro.10.19.
v Is.65.5; ch.18.11. *w* Phi.3.6. *x* Ro.9.4; 11.1.

Hence to be restored to *virtue* is said to be restored again to life, Ro. vi. 13; Re. iii. 1; Ep. ii. 1. It is probable that this latter is the meaning here. See ver. 32. ¶ *Was lost.* Had wandered away from home, and we knew not where he was.

25. *In the field.* At work. This eldest son is designed to represent the Pharisees who had found fault with the Saviour. Their conduct is likened to that of this envious and unnatural brother. ¶ *Music and dancing.* Dancing was not uncommon among the Hebrews, and was used on various occasions. Thus Miriam celebrated the deliverance of the children of Israel from Egypt in dances as well as songs, Ex. xv. 20. David danced before the ark, 2 Sa. vi. 14. It was common at Jewish feasts (Ju. xxi. 19–21) and in public triumphs (Ju. xi. 34), and at all seasons of mirth and rejoicings, Ps. xxx. 11; Je. xxxi. 4, 13. It was also used in religious services by the idolaters (Ex. xxxii. 19), and also by the Jews, at times, in their religious services, Ps. cxlix. 3; cl. 4. In this case it was an expression of rejoicing. Our Lord expresses no opinion about its *propriety.* He simply states *the fact,* nor was there occasion for comment on it. His *mentioning it* cannot be pleaded for its lawfulness or propriety, any more than his mentioning the vice of the younger son, or the wickedness of the Pharisees, can be pleaded to justify their conduct. It is an expressive image, used in accordance with the known customs of the country, to express joy. It is farther to be remarked, that if the example of persons in Scripture be pleaded for dancing, it can be *only for just such dances as they practised*—for sacred or triumphal occasions.

26–28. *Safe and sound.* In health.

29. *A kid.* A young goat. This was of less value than the calf; and he complains that while his father had never given *him* a thing of so little value as *a kid,* he had now given his other son *the fatted calf.* ¶ *Make merry with.* Entertain them—give them a feast. This complaint was unreasonable, for his father had divided his property, and he *might* have had his portion, and his father had uniformly treated him with kindness. But it serves to illustrate the conduct of the scribes and Pharisees, and the folly of their complaint.

30. *This thy son.* This son of *thine.* This is an expression of great contempt. He did not call him *his brother,* but *his father's son,* to show at once his contempt for his younger brother, and for his father for having received him as he did. Never was there a more striking instance of petty malice, or more unjustifiable disregard of a father's conduct and will. ¶ *Thy living.* Thy property. This is still designed to irritate the father, and set him against his younger son. It was true that the younger son had been guilty, and foolish, and ungrateful; but he was penitent, and *that* was of more consequence to the father than all his property; and in the joy that he was penitent and was safe, he forgot his ingratitude and folly. So should the elder son have done.

31. *All I have is thine.* The property was divided. What remained was in reality the elder son's. He was heir to it all, and had a right, if he chose, to

thou art ever with me, and all that I have is thine.

32 It was [y]meet that we should [z]make merry and be glad; [a]for

y Jonah 4.10,11. z Ps.51.8; Is.35.10. a ver.24.

use it. He had therefore no right to complain.

This instructive and beautiful parable was designed to vindicate the conduct of Jesus—to show that it was right to receive sinners, and that the conduct of the Pharisees was unreasonable. The elder son represents the Pharisees; the younger, the returning sinner, whether Jew or Gentile; and the father, God, who is willing to receive them. The parable had the designed effect. It silenced the adversaries of Jesus and vindicated his own conduct. There is not, perhaps, anywhere to be found a more beautiful and touching narrative than this. Every circumstance is tender and happily chosen; every word has a meaning; every image is beautiful; and the narrative closes just where it is fitted to make the deepest impression. In addition to what has been suggested, we may learn from this parable the following lessons:—

1st. That the disposition of a sinner is selfish. He desires to get all that he can, and is impatient of delay, ver. 12.

2d. Sinners waste their blessings, and reduce themselves to a state of want and wretchedness, ver. 13. A life of sin brings on spiritual want and misery. It destroys the faculties, benumbs the mind, hardens the heart, abuses the beneficence of God, and makes us careless of him who gave us all that we have, and indifferent to the consequences of our own conduct.

3d. Sinners disregard the future woes that will come upon them. The young man cared not for any calamities that might be the result of his conduct. He went on heedlessly—like every sinner—to enjoy himself, and to squander what the toils of his father had procured for him.

4th. Afflictions are often the means of bringing sinners to reflection, ver. 14. While his property lasted the prodigal cared little about his father. When that was gone, and he was in the midst of a famine, he thought of his ways. When sinners are in prosperity they think little about God. When he takes away their mercies, and they are called to pass through afflictions, then they think of their ways, and remember that God can give them comfort.

5th. We have here an impressive exhibition of the wants and woes of a sinner. 1st. He had spent all. He had nothing. So the sinner. He has no righteousness, no comfort. 2d. He was far from God, away from his father, and in a land of strangers. The sinner has wandered, and has no friend. His miseries came upon him *because* he was so far away from God. 3d. His condition was wretched. He was needy, in famine, and without a friend. So the sinner. His condition is aptly denoted by that of the prodigal, who would gladly have partaken of the food of the swine. The sinner has taken the world for his portion, and it neither supplies the wants of his soul, nor gives him comfort when he is far away from his Father's home and from God.

6th. The sinner in this situation often applies to the wrong source for comfort, ver. 15. The prodigal should at once have returned to his father, but he rather chose to become a servant of a citizen of that region. The sinner, when sensible of his sins, should return at once to God; but he often continues still to wander. He tries new objects. He seeks new pleasures and new friends, and finds them equally unsatisfactory. He engages in new pursuits, but all in vain. He is still comfortless, and in a strange, a famished land.

7th. The repentance required in the gospel is a return to a right mind, ver. 17. Before his conversion the sinner was alienated from God. He was spiritually deranged. He saw not things as they are. Now he looks on the world as vain and unsatisfactory, and comes to himself. He thinks *aright* of God, of heaven, of eternity, and resolves to seek his happiness there. No man regards things as they are but he who sees the world to be vain, and eternity to be near and awful; and none acts with a *sane mind* but he who acts on the belief that he must soon die; that there is a God and a Saviour—a heaven and a hell.

8th. When the sinner returns he becomes sensible of the following things: 1st. That he is in danger of perishing, and must soon die but for relief—"I perish with hunger." 2d. That God is willing and able to save him—"How

this thy brother was dead, and is alive again; and was lost, and is found.

CHAPTER XVI.

AND he said also unto his disciples, There was a certain

many hired servants have bread enough *and to spare*." There is abundance of mercy for all, and all may come. 3d. He begins to cherish a hope that this may be his. God is willing, and he feels that all that is needful is for him to go to him. 4th. He resolves to go to God—"I will arise and go." 5th. He comes to him willing to confess all his sins, and desirous of concealing none—"I will say, Father, I have sinned."

9th. True repentance is a voluntary act. It is not forced. It is the resolution of the sinner to go, and he cheerfully and cordially arises and goes, ver. 18.

10th. A real penitent feels that his sins have been committed against GOD, ver. 18.

11th. A true penitent also is willing to acknowledge his offences against his parents, brothers, friends, and all men, ver. 18.

12th. A real penitent is humble, ver. 18. He has no wish to conceal anything, or to be thought more highly of than he *ought* to be.

13th. God is willing to receive the true penitent, and has made the richest provision for his return and for his comfort. None need to hesitate to go. All who go, feeling that they are poor, and miserable, and blind, and naked, will find God willing to receive them, and none will be sent empty away.

14th. The joy at the return of sinners is great. Angels rejoice over it, and all holy beings are glad.

15th. We should not be envious at any favours that God may be pleased to bestow on others, ver. 32. He has given *us* more than we deserve; and if, by the sovereignty of his grace, he is pleased to endow others with more grace, or to give them greater talents, or to make them more useful, *we* have no cause to complain. We should rather rejoice that he is pleased to give such mercies to any of our race, and should praise him for the manifestation of his goodness, whether made to us or to other men.

16th. The sensible joy when the sinner returns to God is often greater than that which may be felt *after* the return, and yet the real *cause* of rejoicing be no greater. In times of revival, the sensible joy of Christians may be greater than in ordinary seasons. Their graces are quickened, their zeal kindled, and their hopes strengthened.

17th. If God is willing to receive sinners, if all holy beings rejoice, then how should Christians strive for their conversion, and seek for their return!

18th. If God is willing to receive sinners *now*, then all should at once return. There *will* be a time when he will not be willing to receive them. The day of mercy will be ended; and from the misery and want of this wretched world, they will go down to the deeper miseries and wants of a world of despair—where hope never comes; from whence the sinner can never return; and where the cheering thought can never enter the mind that in his Father's house there is bread enough and to spare, or where he must feel that if there *is*, it will be for ever untasted by the wretched prodigal in the land of eternal famine and death.

CHAPTER XVI.

1. *His disciples.* The word *disciples*, here, is not to be restricted to the twelve apostles or to the seventy. The parable appears to have been addressed to all the professed followers of the Saviour who were present when it was delivered. It is connected with that in the preceding chapter. Jesus had there been discoursing with the scribes and Pharisees, and vindicating his conduct in receiving kindly publicans and sinners. These *publicans and sinners* are here particularly referred to by the word *disciples*. It was with reference to *them* that the whole discourse had arisen. After Jesus had shown the Pharisees, in the preceding chapter, the propriety of his conduct, it was natural that he should turn and address his disciples. Among them there might have been some who were wealthy. The *publicans* were engaged in receiving taxes, in collecting money, and their chief danger arose from that quarter—from covetousness or dishonesty. Jesus always adapted his instructions to the circumstances of his hearers, and it was proper, therefore, that he should give *these disciples* instructions about their *peculiar* duties and dangers. He related this parable,

rich man which had a steward; and the same was accused unto him that he had wasted his goods.
2 And he called him, and said unto him, How is it that I hear this of thee? [a]give an account of thy stewardship; for thou mayest be no longer steward.
3 Then the steward said within himself, What shall I do, for my

a ch.12.42; 1 Co.4.2; 1 Ti.4.14; 1 Pe.4.10.

therefore, to show them *the danger of the love of money;* the guilt it would lead to (ver. 1); the perplexities and shifts to which it would drive a man when once he had been dishonest (ver. 3–7); the necessity of using money aright, since it was their chief business (ver. 9); and the fact that if they would serve God aright they must give up supreme attachment to money (ver. 13); and that the first duty of religion demanded that they should resolve to serve God, and be honest in the use of the wealth intrusted to them. This parable has given great perplexity, and many ways have been devised to explain it. The above solution is the most simple of any; and if these plain principles are kept in view, it will not be difficult to give a consistent explanation of its particular parts. It should be borne in mind, however, that in this, as well as in other parables, we are not to endeavour to spiritualize every circumstance or allusion. We are to keep in view the great moral truth taught in it, that we cannot serve God and mammon, and that all attempts to do this will involve us in difficulty and sin. ¶ *A steward.* One who has charge of the affairs of a family or household; whose duty it is to provide for the family, to purchase provisions, &c. This is, of course, an office of trust and confidence. It affords great opportunity for dishonesty and waste, and for embezzling property. The master's eye cannot always be on the steward, and he may therefore squander the property, or hoard it up for his own use. It was an office commonly conferred on a slave as a reward for fidelity, and of course was given to him that, in long service, had shown himself most trustworthy. By the *rich man,* here, is doubtless represented God. By the *steward,* those who are his professed followers, particularly the *publicans* who were with the Saviour, and whose chief danger arose from the temptations to the improper use of the money intrusted to them. ¶ *Was accused.* Complaint was made. ¶ *Had wasted.* Had squandered or scattered it; had not been prudent and saving.

2. *Give an account.* Give a statement of your expenses and of your conduct while you have been steward. This is not to be referred to the day of judgment. It is a circumstance thrown into the parable to prepare the way for what follows. It is true that all will be called to give an account at the day of judgment, but we are not to derive that doctrine from such passages as this, nor are we to interpret this as teaching that our conscience, or the law, or any beings will *accuse us* in the day of judgment. All that will be indeed true, but it is not the truth that is taught in this passage.

3. *Said within himself.* Thought, or considered. ¶ *My lord.* My master, my employer. ¶ *I cannot dig.* This may mean either that his employment had been such that he could not engage in agriculture, not having been acquainted with the business, or that he was *unwilling* to stoop to so low an employment as to work daily for his support. *To dig,* here, is the same as to till the earth, to work at daily labour. ¶ *To beg.* These were the only two ways that presented themselves for a living—either to work for it, or to beg. ¶ *I am ashamed.* He was too proud for that. Besides, he was in good health and strength, and there was no good reason *why* he should beg—nothing which he could give as a cause for it. It is proper for the sick, the lame, and the feeble to beg; but it is *not* well for the able-bodied to do it, nor is it well to aid them, except by giving them employment, and compelling them to work for a living. He does a beggar who is able to work the most real kindness who sets him to work, and, as a general rule, we should not aid an able-bodied man or woman in any other way. Set them to work, and pay them a fair compensation, and you do them good in two ways, for the habit of labour may be of more value to them than the price you pay them.

4. *I am resolved.* He thought of his condition. He looked at the plans which occurred to him. He had been

lord taketh away from me the stewardship? I cannot dig; to beg I am ashamed.
4 I am resolved what to do, that when I am put out of the stewardship they may receive me into their houses.
5 So he called every one of his lord's debtors *unto him*, and said unto the first, How much owest thou unto my lord?
6 And he said, An hundred [1]measures of oil. And he said unto him, Take thy bill, and sit down quickly, and write fifty.
7 Then said he to another, And

[1] The measure *Batos*, in the original, contained nine gallons three quarts. See Eze.45.10-14.

dishonest, and knew that he must lose his place. It would have been better to have *considered before this*, and resolved on a proper course of life, and to be faithful to his trust; and his perplexity here teaches us that dishonesty will sooner or later lead us into difficulty, and that the path of honesty is not only the *right* path, but is the path that is filled with most comfort and peace. ¶ *When I am put out*, &c. When I lose my place, and have no home and means of support. ¶ *They may receive me*, &c. Those who are now under me, and whom I am resolved now to favour. He had been dishonest to his master, and, having *commenced* a course of dishonesty, he did not shrink from pursuing it. Having injured his master, and being now detected, he was willing still farther to injure him, to take revenge on him for removing him from his place, and to secure his own interest still at his expense. He was resolved to lay these persons under such obligations, and to show them so much kindness, that they could not well refuse to return the kindness to him and give him a support. We may learn here, 1st. That one sin leads on to another, and that one act of dishonesty will be followed by many more, if there is opportunity. 2d. Men who commit one sin cannot get along *consistently* without committing many more. One lie will demand many more to make it *appear* like the truth, and one act of cheating will demand many more to avoid detection. The beginning of sin is like the letting out of waters, and no man knows, if he indulges in one sin, where it will end. 3d. Sinners are selfish. They care more about *themselves* than they do either about God or truth. If they seek salvation, it is only for selfish ends, and because they desire a comfortable *abode* in the future world rather than because they have any regard to God or his cause.

5. *Called every one.* As he was *steward*, he had the management of all the affairs, and, of course, debts were to be paid to him. ¶ *Debtors.* Those who *owed* his master, or perhaps *tenants;* those who rented land of his master.

6. *An hundred measures.* The measure here mentioned is the *bath*, which contained, according to Dr. Arbuthnot's tables, $7\frac{1}{2}$ gallons, or, according to the marginal note, about 9 gallons and 3 quarts. ¶ *Oil.* Oil of olives, or sweet oil. It was much used for lamps, as an article of food (Ex. xxix. 2), and also for anointing, and, of course, as an article of commerce, 1 Ki. v. 11. These were persons, doubtless, who had *rented* land of the rich man, and who were to give him a certain proportion of the produce. ¶ *Thy bill.* The contract, obligation, or *lease*. It was probably written as a *promise* by the debtor and signed by the steward, and thus became binding. Thus he had power to alter it, without supposing that his master would detect it. The bill or contract was in the hands of the steward, and he gave it back to him to write a new one. ¶ *Quickly.* He supposed that his master would soon remove him, and he was therefore in haste to have all things secure beforehand. It is worthy of remark, also, that *all* this was wrong. His master had called for the account; but, instead of rendering it, he engaged in other business, disobeyed his lord still, and, in contempt of his commands, sought his own interest. All sinners would be slow to give in their account to God if they could do it; and it is only because, when God calls them by death, they *cannot but go*, that they do not engage still in their own business and disobey him.

7. *Measures of wheat.* The measure here mentioned—the *kor*, or homer—contained, according to the tables of Dr. Arbuthnot, about 32 pecks, or 8 bushels; or, according to the marginal note, about 14 bushels and a *pottle*. A *pottle* is 4 pints. The Hebrew *kor*,

how much owest thou? And he
said, An hundred [2]measures of
wheat. And he said unto him,
Take thy bill, and write fourscore.
8 And the lord commended the
unjust steward because he had
done wisely: for the children of
this world are in their generation
wiser than [b]the children of light.
9 And I say unto you, [c]Make

[2] The measure here indicated contained about fourteen bushels and a pottle.

b Jn.12.36; Ep.5.8. c Ec.11.1; 1 Ti.6.18,19.

כֹּר—or *homer*, חֹמֶר—was equal to 10 baths or 70 gallons, and the actual amount of the measure, according to this, was not far from 8 gallons. Robinson (*Lex.*), however, supposes that the bath was 11½ gallons, and the kor or homer 14·45 bushels. The amount is not material to the proper understanding of the parable. ¶ *Fourscore.* Eighty.

8. *The lord commended.* Praised, or expressed admiration at his wisdom. These are not the words of Jesus, as commending him, but a part of the narrative or parable. His *master* commended him—saw that he was wise and considerate, though he was dishonest. ¶ *The unjust steward.* It is not said that his master commended him because he was *unjust*, but because he was *wise.* This is the only thing in his conduct of which there is any approbation expressed, and this approbation was expressed by *his master.* This passage cannot be brought, therefore, to prove that Jesus meant to commend his dishonesty. It was a commendation of his *shrewdness* or *forethought;* but the master could no more *approve* of his conduct as a moral act than he could the first act of cheating him. ¶ *The children of this world.* Those who are *devoted* to this world; who live for this world only; who are careful only to obtain property, and to provide for their temporal necessities. It does not mean that they are peculiarly wicked and profligate, but only that they are *worldly*, and anxious about earthly things. See Mat. xiii. 22; 2 Ti. iv. 10. ¶ *Are wiser.* More prudent, cunning, and anxious about their particular business. They show more skill, study more plans, contrive more ways to provide for themselves, than the children of light do to promote the interests of religion. ¶ *In their generation.* Some have thought that this means *in their manner of living*, or *in managing their affairs.* The word *generation* sometimes denotes the manner of life, Ge. vi. 9; xxxvii. 2. Others suppose that it means *toward* or *among the men of their own age.* They are more prudent and wise than Christians in regard to the people of their own time; they turn their connection with them to good account, and make it subserve their worldly interests, while Christians fail much more to use the world in such a manner as to subserve their spiritual interests. ¶ *Children of light.* Those who have been enlightened from above — who are Christians. This may be considered as the application of the parable. It does not mean that it is more wise to be a worldly man than to be a child of light, but that those who *are* worldly show much prudence in providing for themselves; seize occasions for making good bargains; are active and industrious; try to turn everything to the best account, and thus exert themselves to the utmost to advance their interests; while Christians often suffer opportunities of doing good to pass unimproved; are less steady, firm, and anxious about eternal things, and thus show less wisdom. Alas! this is too true; and we cannot but reflect here how different the world would be if all Christians were as anxious, and diligent, and prudent in religious matters as others are in worldly things.

9. *I say unto you.* I, Jesus, say to you, my disciples. ¶ *Make to yourselves friends.* Some have understood the word *friends*, here, as referring to the poor; others, to holy angels; and others, to God. Perhaps, however, the word should not be considered as referring to any particular *persons*, but is used in accordance with the preceding parable; for in the application our Saviour uses the *language* appropriated to the conduct of the steward to express the *general* truth that we are to make a proper use of riches. The steward had so managed his pecuniary affairs as to secure future comfort for himself, or so as to find friends that would take care of him *beyond* the time when he was put out of the office. That is, he would not be destitute, or cast off, or without comfort, when he was removed from his office. So, says our Saviour to the

to yourselves friends of the [3]mammon of unrighteousness; that, when ye fail, they may receive you into everlasting habitations.

10 He[d] that is faithful in that which is least, is faithful also in much; and he that is unjust in the least, is unjust also in much.

11 If, therefore, ye have not been faithful in the unrighteous [4]mam-

[3] or, *riches.* *d* Mat.25.21,23.

[4] or, *riches.*

publicans and those who had property, so use your property as *to secure* happiness and comfort beyond the time when you shall be removed from the present life. *Have reference*, in the use of your money, to the future. Do not use it so that it shall not avail you anything hereafter; but so employ it that, as the steward found friends, comfort, and a home by *his* wisdom in the use of it, so *you* may, after you are removed to another world, find friends, comfort, and a home—that is, may be happy in heaven. Jesus, here, does not say that we should do it *in the same way* that the steward did, for that was unjust; but only that we should *secure the result.* This may be done by using our riches as we *should do;* that is, by not suffering them to entangle us in cares and perplexities dangerous to the soul, engrossing the time, and stealing away the affections; by employing them in works of mercy and benevolence, aiding the poor, contributing to the advance of the gospel, bestowing them where they will do good, and in such a manner that God will *approve* the deed, and will bless us for it. Commonly riches are a *hindrance* to piety. To many they are snares; and, instead of positively *benefiting* the possessor, they are an injury, as they engross the time and the affections, and do not contribute at all to the eternal welfare of the soul. Everything may, by a proper use, be made to contribute to our welfare in heaven. Health, wealth, talents, and influence may be so employed; and this is what our Saviour doubtless means here. ¶ *Of the mammon. By means* of the mammon. ¶ *Mammon.* A Syriac word meaning riches. It is used, also, as an idol—the god of riches. ¶ *Of unrighteousness.* These words are an Hebrew expression for *unrighteous mammon*, the noun being used for an adjective, as is common in the New Testament. The word *unrighteous*, here, stands opposed to "*the true riches*" in verse 11, and means *deceitful, false, not to be trusted.* It has this meaning often. See 1 Ti. vi. 17; Lu. xii. 33; Mat. vi. 19; xix. 21. It does not signify, therefore, that they had acquired the property *unjustly*, but that property was *deceitful* and not to be trusted. The wealth of the steward was deceitful; he could not rely on its continuance; it was liable to be taken away at any moment. So the wealth of the world is deceitful. We cannot *calculate* on its continuance. It may give us support or comfort now, but it may be soon removed, or we taken from *it*, and we should therefore so use it as to derive benefit from it hereafter. ¶ *When ye fail.* When ye *are left*, or when ye *die.* The expression is derived from the parable as referring to the *discharge* of the steward; but it refers to *death*, as if God then *discharged* his people, or took them from their stewardship and called them to account. ¶ *They may receive you.* This is a form of expression denoting merely *that you may be received.* The plural form is used because it was used in the corresponding place in the parable, ver. 4. The direction is, so to use our worldly goods that *we may be received* into heaven when we die. *God* will receive us there, and we are to employ our property so that he will not cast us off for abusing it. ¶ *Everlasting habitations.* Heaven, the eternal *home* of the righteous, where all our wants will be supplied, and where there can be no more anxiety, and no more removal from enjoyments, 2 Co. v. 1.

10. *He that is faithful*, &c. This is a maxim which will almost universally hold true. A man that shows fidelity in small matters will also in large; and he that will cheat and defraud in little things will also in those involving more trust and responsibility. Fidelity is required in small matters as well as in those of more importance.

11. *Who will commit*, &c. If you are not faithful in the small matters pertaining to this world, if you do not use aright your property and influence, you cannot expect that God will commit to you the true riches of his grace. Men who are dishonest and worldly, and who do not employ the deceitful mam-

mon, who will commit to your trust
the true *riches?*
12 And if ye have not been
faithful in that which is another
man's, who shall give you that
which is your own?
13 No[e] servant can serve two
masters: for either he will hate
the one, and love the other; or
else he will hold to the one, and
despise the other. Ye cannot serve
God and mammon.
14 And the Pharisees also, [f]who
were covetous, heard all these
things; and they derided him.
15 And he said unto them, Ye
are they which [g]justify yourselves
before men; but [h]God knoweth
your hearts: for that which is
highly [i]esteemed among men is
abomination in the sight of God.
16 The[k] law and the prophets
were until John: since that time
the kingdom of God is preached,
and every man presseth into it.
17 And[l] it is easier for heaven

e Jos.24.15; Mat.6.24. f Mat.23.14.

g ch.10.29. h Ps.7.9; Je.17.10. i Pr.16.5; Mal.3.15. k Mat.11.12,13. l Ps.102.26; Is.40.8; 51.6.

mon as they ought, cannot expect to grow in grace. God does not confer grace upon them, and their being unfaithful in earthly matters is evidence that they *would be* also in much greater affairs, and would likewise *misimprove* the true riches. ¶ *True* riches. The graces of the gospel; the influences of the Spirit; eternal life, or religion. The riches of this world are false, deceitful, not to be trusted (ver. 9); the treasures of heaven are *true*, faithful, never-failing, Mat. vi. 19, 20.

12. *Another man's.* The word *man's* is not in the original. It is, "If ye have been unfaithful managers *for another.*" It refers, doubtless, to *God.* The wealth of the world is *his.* It is committed to us as his stewards. It is uncertain and deceitful, and at any moment he can take it away from us. It is still *his;* and if, while intrusted with *this*, we are unfaithful, we cannot expect that he will confer on us the rewards of heaven. ¶ *That which is your own.* The riches of heaven, which, if once given to us, may be considered as *ours*—that is, it will be permanent and fixed, and will not be taken away *as if* at the pleasure of another. We may *calculate* on it, and look forward with the assurance that it will *continue* to be *ours* for ever, and will not be taken away like the riches of this world, *as if* they were not ours. The meaning of the whole parable is therefore thus expressed: If we do not use the things of this world as we ought—with honesty, truth, wisdom, and integrity, we cannot have evidence of piety, and shall not be received into heaven. If we are true to that which is least, it is an evidence that we are the children of God, and he will commit to our trust that which is of infinite importance, even the eternal riches and glory of heaven.

13. See Notes on Mat. vi. 24.

14, 15. *They derided him.* The fact that they were "covetous" is here stated as the reason why they derided him, or, as it is literally, "they turned up the nose at him." They contemned or despised the doctrine which he had laid down, probably because it showed them that with their love of money they could not be the true friends of God, or that their profession of religion was really false and hollow. They were *attempting* to serve God and mammon, and they therefore looked upon his doctrine with contempt and scorn. ¶ *Justify yourselves. Attempt* to appear just; or, you aim to appear righteous in the sight of men, and do not regard the *heart.* ¶ *That which is highly esteemed.* That is, mere external works, or actions performed merely to *appear* to be righteous. ¶ *Is abomination.* Is abominable, or hateful. The word used here is the one that in the Old Testament is commonly given to *idols,* and denotes God's *abhorrence* of such conduct. These words are to be applied *chiefly* to what Jesus was discoursing about. There are many things esteemed among men which are *not* abomination in the sight of God; as, for example, truth, parental and filial affection, industry, &c. But many things, much sought and admired, *are* hateful in his sight. The love of wealth and show, ambition and pride, gay and splendid vices, and all the wickedness that men contrive to *gild* and to make appear like virtue—external acts that *appear* well while the heart is evil—are abominable in the sight of God, and

and earth to pass, than one tittle of the law to fail.

18 Whosoever [m]putteth away his wife, and marrieth another, committeth adultery; and whosoever marrieth her that is put away from *her* husband, committeth adultery.

19 There was a certain rich man, which was clothed in purple and fine linen, and fared sumptuously every day:

20 And there was a certain beggar named Lazarus, which was laid at his gate, full of sores,

m Mat.5.32; 1 Co.7.10,11.

---

should be in the sight of men. Comp. Lu. xviii. 11-14; 1 Sa. xvi. 7.

16. See Notes on Mat. xi. 12-14. ¶ *Every man.* Many men, or multitudes. This is an expression that is very common, as when we say everybody is engaged in a piece of business, meaning that it occupies general attention.

17. See Notes on Mat. v. 18.

18. See Notes on Mat. v. 32. These verses occur in Matthew in a different order, and it is not improbable that they were spoken by our Saviour at different times. The design, here, seems to be to reprove the Pharisees for not observing the law of Moses, notwithstanding their great pretensions to external righteousness, and to show them that they had *really* departed from the law.

19. *There was a certain rich man.* Many have supposed that our Lord here refers to a *real history*, and gives an account of some man who had lived in this manner; but of this there is no evidence. The probability is that this narrative is to be considered as a parable, referring not to any particular case which *had* actually happened, but teaching that such cases *might* happen. The *design* of the narrative is to be collected from the previous conversation. He had taught the danger of the love of money (ver. 1 and 2); the deceitful and treacherous nature of riches (ver. 9-11); that what was in high esteem on earth was hateful to God (ver. 15); that men who did not use their property aright could not be received into heaven (ver. 11, 12); that they ought to listen to Moses and the prophets (ver. 16, 17); and that it was the duty of men to show kindness to the poor. The design of the parable was to impress all these truths more vividly on the mind, and to show the Pharisees that, with all their boasted righteousness and their external correctness of character, they might be lost. Accordingly he speaks of no great fault in the rich man—no external, degrading vice—no open breach of the law; and leaves us to infer that *the mere possession of wealth* may be dangerous to the soul, and that a man surrounded with every temporal blessing may perish for ever. It is remarkable that he gave no *name* to this rich man, though the poor man is mentioned by name. If this was a parable, it shows us how unwilling he was to fix suspicion on anyone. If it was not a parable, it shows also that he would not drag out wicked men before the public, but would conceal as much as possible all that had any connection with them. The *good* he would speak well of by name; the evil he would not *injure* by exposing them to public view. ¶ *Clothed in purple.* A purple robe or garment. This colour was expensive as well as splendid, and was chiefly worn by princes, nobles, and those who were very wealthy. Comp. Mat. xxvii. 28. See Notes on Is. i. 18. ¶ *Fine linen.* This linen was chiefly produced of the flax that grew on the banks of the Nile, in Egypt, Pr. vii. 16; Eze. xxvii. 7. It was peculiarly soft and white, and was therefore much sought as an article of luxury, and was so expensive that it could be worn only by princes, by priests, or by those who were very rich, Ge. xli. 42; 1 Ch. xv. 27; Ex. xxviii. 5. ¶ *Fared sumptuously.* Feasted or lived in a splendid manner. ¶ *Every day.* Not merely occasionally, but constantly. This was a mark of great wealth, and, in the view of the world, evidence of great happiness. It is worthy of remark that Jesus did not charge on him any crime. He did not say that he had acquired this property by dishonesty, or even that he was unkind or uncharitable; but simply that he *was a rich man*, and that his riches did not secure him from death and perdition.

20, 21. *Beggar.* Poor man. The original word does not mean *beggar*, but simply that he was *poor*. It should have been so translated to keep up the contrast with the *rich man*. ¶ *Named Lazarus.* The word Lazarus is Hebrew,

21 And desiring to be fed with the crumbs which fell from the rich man's table: moreover, the dogs came and licked his sores.
22 And it came to pass that the beggar died, and was carried by the angels into [n]Abraham's bosom: [o]the rich man also died, and was buried.
23 And[p] in hell he lifted up his

n Mat.8.11. o Pr.14.32. p Re.14.10,11.

and means a man destitute of help, a needy, poor man. It is a name given, therefore, to denote his needy condition. ¶ *Laid at his gate.* At the door of the rich man, in order that he might obtain aid. ¶ *Full of sores.* Covered with ulcers; afflicted not only with poverty, but with loathsome and offensive ulcers, such as often are the accompaniments of poverty and want. These circumstances are designed to show how different was his condition from that of the rich man. *He* was clothed in purple; the poor man was covered with sores; *he* fared sumptuously; the poor man was dependent even for the crumbs that fell from the rich man's table. ¶ *The dogs came.* Such was his miserable condition that even the dogs, as if moved by pity, came and licked his sores in kindness to him. These circumstances of his misery are very touching, and his condition, contrasted with that of the rich man, is very striking. It is not affirmed that the rich man was unkind to him, or drove him away, or refused to aid him. The narrative is designed simply to show that the possession of wealth, and all the blessings of this life, could not exempt from death and misery, and that the lowest condition among mortals may be connected with life and happiness beyond the grave. There was no provision made for the helpless poor in those days, and consequently they were often laid at the gates of the rich, and in places of public resort, for charity. See Ac. iii. 2. The gospel has been the means of all the public charity now made for the needy, as it has of providing hospitals for those who are sick and afflicted. No pagan nation ever had a hospital or an almshouse for the needy, the aged, the blind, the insane. Many heathen nations, as the Hindoos and the Sandwich Islanders, destroyed their aged people; and *all* left their poor to the miseries of public begging, and their sick to the care of their friends or to private charity.

22. *Was carried by the angels.* The Jews held the opinion that the spirits of the righteous were conveyed by angels to heaven at their death. Our Saviour speaks in accordance with this opinion; and as he expressly affirms the fact, it seems as proper that it should be taken literally, as when it is said the rich man died and was buried. Angels are ministering spirits sent forth to minister to those who are heirs of salvation (He. i. 14), and there is no more improbability in the supposition that they attend departing spirits to heaven, than that they attend them while on earth. ¶ *Abraham's bosom.* This is a phrase taken from the practice of reclining at meals, where the head of one lay on the bosom of another, and the phrase therefore denotes intimacy and friendship. See Notes on Mat. xxiii. 6. Also Jn. xiii. 23; xxi. 20. The Jews had no doubt that Abraham was in paradise. To say that Lazarus was in his bosom was therefore the same as to say that he was admitted to heaven and made happy there. The Jews, moreover, boasted very much of being the friends of Abraham and of being his descendants, Mat. iii. 9. To be his friend was, in their view, the highest honour and happiness. Our Saviour therefore showed them that this poor and afflicted man might be raised to the highest happiness, while the rich, who prided themselves on their being descended from Abraham, might be cast away and lost for ever. ¶ *Was buried.* This is not said of the poor man. Burial was thought to be an honour, and funerals were, as they are now, often expensive, splendid, and ostentatious. This is said of the rich man to show that he had *every* earthly honour, and all that the world calls happy and desirable.

23. *In hell.* The word here translated hell (*Hades*) means literally a dark, obscure place; the place where departed spirits go, but especially the place where *wicked* spirits go. See Notes on Job x. 21, 22; Is. xiv. 9. The following circumstances are related of it in this parable: 1st. It is *far off* from the abodes of the righteous. Lazarus was seen *afar off.* 2d. It is a place of torment. 3d. There is a great gulf fixed between that and heaven, ver. 26. 4th. The

eyes, being in torments, and seeth Abraham afar off, and Lazarus in his bosom:

24 And he cried and said, Father Abraham, have mercy on me, and send Lazarus, that he may dip the

suffering is great. It is represented by *torment* in a flame, ver. 24. 5th. There will be no escape from it, ver. 26. The word *hell* here means, therefore, that dark, obscure, and miserable place, far from heaven, where the wicked shall be punished for ever. ¶ *He lifted up his eyes.* A phrase in common use among the Hebrews, meaning *he looked*, Ge. xiii. 10; xviii. 2; xxxi. 10; Da. viii. 3; Lu. vi. 20. ¶ *Being in torment.* The word *torment* means *pain*, *anguish* (Mat. iv. 24); particularly the pain inflicted by the ancients in order to induce men to make confession of their crimes. These *torments* or tortures were the keenest that they could inflict, such as the rack, or scourging, or burning; and the use of the word here denotes that the sufferings of the wicked can be represented only by the extremest forms of human suffering. ¶ *And seeth Abraham*, &c. This was an aggravation of his misery. One of the first things that occurred in hell was to look up, and see the poor man that lay at his gate completely happy. What a contrast! Just now he was rolling in wealth, and the poor man was at his gate. He had no expectation of these sufferings: now they have come upon him, and Lazarus is happy and for ever fixed in the paradise of God. It is more, perhaps, than we are authorized to infer, that the wicked will *see* those who are in paradise. That they will *know* that they are there is certain; but we are not to suppose that they will be so near together as to be seen, or as to make conversation possible. These circumstances mean that there will be a *separation*, and that the wicked in hell will be conscious that the righteous, though on earth they were poor or despised, will be in heaven. Heaven and hell will be far from each other, and it will be no small part of the misery of the one that it is far and for ever removed from the other.

24. *Father Abraham.* The Jews considered it a signal honour that Abraham was their *father*—that is, that they were *descendants* from him. Though this man was now in misery, yet he seems not to have abandoned the idea of his relation to the father of the faithful. The Jews supposed that departed spirits might know and converse with each other. See Lightfoot on this place. Our Saviour speaks in conformity with that prevailing opinion; and as it was not easy to convey ideas about the spiritual world without some such representation, he therefore speaks in the language which was usual in his time. We are not, however, to suppose that this was *literally* true, but only that it was designed to represent more clearly the sufferings of the rich man in hell. ¶ *Have mercy on me.* Pity me. The rich man is not represented as calling on *God*. The mercy of God will be at an end when the soul is lost. Nor did he *ask* to be released from that place. Lost spirits *know* that their sufferings will have no end, and that it would be in vain to ask to escape the place of torment. Nor does he ask to be admitted where Lazarus was. He had no *desire* to be in a holy place, and he well knew that there was no restoration to those who once sink down to hell. ¶ *Send Lazarus.* This shows how low he was reduced, and how the circumstances of men change when they die. Just before, Lazarus was laid at his gate full of sores; now he is happy in heaven. Just before, he had nothing to give, and the rich man could expect to derive no benefit from him; now he asks, as the highest favour, that he might come and render him relief. Soon the poorest man on earth, if he is a friend of God, will have mercies which the rich, if unprepared to die, can never obtain. The rich will no longer despise such men; they would *then* be glad of their friendship, and would beg for the slightest favour at their hands. ¶ *Dip the tip*, &c. This was a small favour to ask, and it shows the greatness of his distress when so small a thing would be considered a great relief. ¶ *Cool my tongue.* The effect of great *heat* on the body is to produce almost insupportable thirst. Those who travel in burning deserts thus suffer inexpressibly when they are deprived of water. So *pain* of any kind produces thirst, and particularly if connected with fever. The sufferings of the rich man are therefore represented as producing burning *thirst*, so much that even a drop of water would be refreshing to his tongue. We can

tip of his finger in water and [q]cool my tongue; for I am [r]tormented in this flame.

25 But Abraham said, Son, remember that thou [s]in thy lifetime receivedst thy good things, and likewise Lazarus evil things; but now he is comforted, and thou art tormented.

26 And beside all this, between us and you there is a great gulf fixed; so that they which would

q Zec.14.12. r Is.66.24; Mar.9.44,&c. s Job 21.13; Ps.73.12-19; ch.6.24.

scarce form an idea of more distress and misery than where this is continued from one day to another without relief. We are not to suppose that he had been guilty of any particular wickedness with his *tongue* as the cause of this. It is simply an idea to represent the natural effect of great suffering, and especially suffering in the midst of great heat. ¶ *I am tormented.* I am in anguish—in insupportable distress. ¶ *In this flame.* The lost are often represented as suffering *in flames*, because *fire* is an image of the severest pain that we know. It is not certain, however, that the wicked will be doomed to suffer in *material* fire. See Notes on Mar. iv. 44.

25. *Son.* This is a representation designed to correspond with the word *father*. He was a descendant of Abraham—a Jew—and Abraham is represented as calling this thing to his remembrance. It would not lessen his sorrows to remember that he was a *son* of Abraham, and that he ought to have lived worthy of that relation to him. ¶ *Remember.* This is a cutting word in this place. One of the chief torments of hell will be the *remembrance* of what was enjoyed and of what was done in this world. Nor will it be any mitigation of the suffering to spend an *eternity* where there will be nothing else to do, day or night, but to *remember* what *was* done, and what *might have been*, if the life had been right. ¶ *Thy good things.* That is, property, splendour, honour. ¶ *Evil things.* Poverty, contempt, and disease. ¶ *But now,* &c. How changed the scene! How different the condition! And how much *better* was the portion of Lazarus, after all, than that of the rich man! It is probable that Lazarus had the most *real* happiness in the land of the living, for riches without the love of God can never confer happiness like the favour of God, even in poverty. But the comforts of the rich man are now gone for ever, and the joys of Lazarus have just commenced. *One* is to be comforted, and *the other* to be tormented, to all eternity. How much better, therefore, is poverty, with the friendship of God, than riches, with all that the world can bestow! And how foolish to seek our chief pleasures only in this life!

26. *A great gulf.* The word translated *gulf* means *chasm*, or the broad, yawning space between two elevated objects. In this place it means that there is no way of passing from one to the other. ¶ *Fixed.* Strengthened—made firm or immovable. It is so established that it will *never* be movable or passable. It will *for ever* divide heaven and hell. ¶ *Which would pass.* We are not to press this passage literally, as if those who are in heaven would *desire* to go and visit the wicked in the world of woe. The simple meaning of the statement is, that there can be no communication between the one and the other—there can be no passing from one to the other. It is impossible to conceive that the righteous would desire to leave their abodes in glory to go and dwell in the world of woe; nor can we suppose that they would wish to go for any reason unless it were possible to furnish relief. That will be out of the question. Not even a drop of water will be furnished as a relief to the sufferer. ¶ *Neither can they pass to us,* &c. There can be no doubt that the wicked will *desire* to pass the gulf that divides them from heaven. They would be glad to be in a state of happiness; but all such wishes will be vain. How, in the face of the solemn statement of the Saviour here, can men believe that there will be a *restoration* of all the wicked to heaven? He solemnly assures us that there can be no passage from that world of woe to the abodes of the blessed; yet, in the face of this, many Universalists hold that hell will yet be vacated of its guilty millions, and that all its miserable inhabitants will be received to heaven! Who shall conduct them across this gulf, when Jesus Christ says it *cannot* be passed? Who shall build a bridge over that yawning chasm which he says is "*fixed?*" No: if there

pass from hence to you cannot;
neither[t] can they pass to us that
would come from thence.
27 Then he said, I pray thee,
therefore, father, that thou wouldest send him to my father's house;
28 For I have five brethren; that
he may testify unto them, lest they
also come into this place of torment.
29 Abraham saith unto him,
[u]They have Moses and the prophets; let them hear them.
30 And he said, Nay, father
Abraham; but if one went unto
them from the dead, they will repent.
31 And he said unto him, [v]If
they hear not Moses and the prophets, [w]neither will they be persuaded though one rose from the
dead.

t Eze.28.24.

u Is.34.16; Jn.5.39. v 2 Co.4.3. w Jn.12.10,11.

is anything certain from the Scripture, it is that they who enter hell return no more; they who sink there sink for ever.

27, 28. *Five brethren.* The number *five* is mentioned merely to preserve the appearance of verisimilitude in the story. It is not to be spiritualized, nor are we to suppose that it has any hidden or inscrutable meaning. ¶ *May testify unto them.* May bear *witness* to them, or may inform them of what is my situation, and the dreadful consequences of the life that I have led. It is remarkable that he did not ask to go himself. He knew that he *could not* be released, even for so short a time. His condition was fixed. Yet he had no wish that his friends should suffer, and he supposed that if one went from the dead they would hear him.

29. *They have Moses.* The writings of Moses. The first five books of the Bible. ¶ *The prophets.* The remainder of the Old Testament. What the prophets had written. ¶ *Hear them.* Hear them speak in the Scriptures. Read them, or hear them read in the synagogues, and *attend* to what they have delivered.

30. *Nay.* No. They will *not hear* Moses and the prophets. They have heard them so long in vain, that there is no prospect now that they will attend to the message; but if one should go to them directly from the eternal world they would hear him. The novelty of the message would attract their attention, and they would listen to what he would say.

31. *Be persuaded.* Be convinced of the truth; of the danger and folly of their way; of the certainty of their suffering hereafter, and be induced to turn from sin to holiness, and from Satan unto God.

From this impressive and instructive parable we may learn—

1st. That the souls of men do not die with their bodies.

2d. That the soul is *conscious* after death; that it does not *sleep*, as some have supposed, till the morning of the resurrection.

3d. That the righteous are taken to a place of happiness immediately at death, and the wicked consigned at once to misery.

4th. That wealth does not secure from death.

"How vain are riches to secure
Their haughty owners from the grave!"

The rich, the beautiful, the gay, as well as the poor, go down to the grave. All their pomp and apparel, all their honours, their palaces, and their gold cannot save them. Death can as easily find his way into the splendid mansions of the rich as into the cottages of the poor; and the rich shall turn to the same corruption, and soon, like the poor, be undistinguished from common dust and be unknown.

5th. We should not envy the condition of the rich.

"On slippery rocks I see them stand,
And fiery billows roll below.

"Now let them boast how tall they rise,
I'll never envy them again;
There they may stand with haughty eyes,
Till they plunge deep in endless pain.

"Their fancied joys how fast they flee!
Like dreams, as fleeting and as vain;
Their songs of softest harmony
Are but a prelude to their pain."

6th. We should strive for a better inheritance than can be possessed in this life.

"Now I esteem their mirth and wine
Too dear to purchase with my blood:
Lord, 'tis enough that *thou* art mine—
My life, my portion, and my God."

7th. The sufferings of the wicked in hell will be indescribably great. Think

CHAPTER XVII.

THEN said he unto the disciples, [a]It is impossible but that offences will come; but woe *unto him* through whom they come!
2 It were better for him that a millstone were hanged about his neck, and he cast into the sea, than that he should offend one of these little ones.
3 Take heed to yourselves: If thy brother trespass against thee, [b]rebuke him; and if he repent, forgive him.
4 And if he trespass against thee seven times in a day, and seven times in a day turn again to thee, saying, I repent, [c]thou shalt forgive him.
5 And the apostles said unto the Lord, [d]Increase our faith.
6 And the Lord said, [e]If ye had

a Mat.18.6,7; Mar.9.42. b Le.19.17. c Mat.6.12,14; Col.3.13. d He.12.2. e Mat.17.20; 21.21; Mar.9.23; 11.23.

what is represented by *torment;* by burning flame; by insupportable thirst; by that state where a single *drop* of water would afford relief. Remember that *all this* is but a representation of the pains of the damned, and that this will have no intermission day or night, but will continue from year to year, and age to age, without any end, and you have a faint view of the sufferings of those who are in hell.

8th. There is a place of sufferings beyond the grave—a hell. If there is not, then this parable has no meaning. It is impossible to make *anything* of it unless it be designed to teach that.

9th. There will never be any escape from those gloomy regions. There is a gulf fixed—*fixed,* not movable. Nor can any of the damned beat a pathway across this gulf to the world of holiness.

10th. We see the amazing folly of those who suppose there may be an *end* to the sufferings of the wicked, and who, on that supposition, seem willing to go down to hell to suffer a long time, rather than go at once to heaven. If man were to suffer but a thousand years, or even *one* year, why should he be so foolish as to choose that suffering rather than go at once to heaven, and be happy at once when he dies?

11th. God gives us sufficient warning to prepare for death. He has sent his Word, his servants, his Son; he warns us by his Spirit and his providence; by the entreaties of our friends and by the death of sinners; he offers us heaven, and he threatens hell. If all this will not move sinners, what *would* do it? There is *nothing* that would.

12th. God will give us nothing farther to warn us. No dead man will come to life to tell us of what he has seen. If he *did,* we would not believe him. Religion appeals to man not by ghosts and frightful apparitions. It appeals to their reason, their conscience, their hopes, their fears. It sets life and death soberly before men, and if they *will not* choose the former, they must die. If you will not hear the Son of God and the warnings of the Scriptures, there is nothing which you *will* or *can* hear. You will *never* be persuaded, and will *never* escape the place of torment.

CHAPTER XVII.

1, 2. *It is impossible.* It cannot but happen. Such is the state of things that *it will be.* See these verses explained in the Notes on Mat. xviii. 6, 7.

3, 4. See Notes on Mat. xviii. 15, 21, 22. *Trespass against thee.* Sin against thee, or does anything that gives you an offence or does you an injury. ¶ *Rebuke.* Reprove. Go and tell him his fault, and seek an explanation. Acquaint him with what has been the effect of his conduct, and the state of your feelings, that he may acknowledge his error and repent.

5. *Increase our faith.* This duty of forgiving offences seemed so difficult to the disciples that they strongly felt the need of an increase of faith. They felt that they were prone themselves to harbour resentments, and that it required an additional increase of true religion to enable them to comply with the requirements of Jesus. We may learn from this—1st. That Jesus has *the power* of increasing the faith of his people. Strength comes from him, and especially strength to believe the gospel. Hence he is called the *Author* and *Finisher* of our faith, He. xii. 2. 2d. The duty of forgiving offences is one of the most difficult duties of the Christian religion. It is so contrary to our natural feelings; it implies such elevation above

faith as a grain of mustard-seed, ye might say unto the sycamine-tree, Be thou plucked up by the root, and be thou planted in the sea, and it should obey you.

7 But which of you, having a servant ploughing, or feeding cattle, will say unto him by and by, when he is come from the field, Go, and sit down to meat?

---

the petty feelings of malice and revenge, and is so contrary to the received maxims of the world, which teach us to *cherish* rather than to forgive the memory of offences, that it is no wonder our Saviour dwells much on this duty, and so strenuously insists on it in order to our having evidence that our hearts have been changed. Some have thought that this prayer that he would increase their faith refers to the power of working miracles, and especially to the case recorded in Mat. xvii. 16–20.

6. See Mat. xvii. 20. *Sycamine-tree.* This name, as well as sycamore, is given, among us, to the large tree commonly called the buttonwood; but the tree here mentioned is different. The Latin Vulgate and the Syriac versions translate it *mulberry-tree.* It is said to have been a tree that commonly grew in Egypt, of the size and appearance of a mulberry-tree, but bearing a species of

Sycamore (*Ficus Sycomorus*).

figs. This tree was common in Palestine. It is probable that our Lord was standing by one as he addressed these words to his disciples. Dr. Thomson (*The Land and the Book*, vol. i. p. 22–24) says of this tree: "It is generally planted by the wayside, in the open space where several paths meet." [Comp. Lu. xix. 4.] "This sycamore is a remarkable tree. It not only bears several crops of figs during the year, but these figs grow on short stems along the trunk and large branches, and not at the end of twigs, as in other fruit-bearing trees. The figs are small, and of a greenish-yellow colour. At Gaza and Askelon I saw them of a purple tinge, and much larger than they are in this part of the country. They were carried to market in large quantities, and appeared to be more valued there than with us. Still, they are, at best, very insipid, and none but the poorer classes eat them. It is easily propagated, merely by planting a stout branch in the ground, and watering it until it has struck its roots into the soil. This it does with great rapidity and to a vast depth. It was with reference to this latter fact that our Lord selected it to illustrate the power of faith. Now, look at this tree—its ample girth, its wide-spread arms branching off from the parent trunk only a few feet from the ground; then examine its enormous roots, as thick, as numerous, and as wide-spread into the deep soil below as the branches extend into the air above—the very best type of invincible steadfastness. What power on earth can pluck up such a tree? Heaven's thunderbolt may strike it down, the wild tornado may tear it to fragments, but nothing short of miraculous power can fairly pluck it up by the roots."

7. *Having a servant*, &c. This parable appears to have been spoken with reference to the rewards which the disciples were expecting in the kingdom of the Messiah. The occasion on which it was spoken cannot be ascertained. It does not seem to have any particular connection with what goes before. It may be supposed that the disciples were somewhat impatient to have the kingdom restored to Israel (Ac. i. 6)—that is, that he would assume his kingly power, and that they were impatient of the *delay*, and anxious to enter on *the rewards* which they expected, and which they not improbably were expecting in consequence of their devotedness to him. In answer to these expectations, Jesus spoke this parable, showing them, 1st. That they should be rewarded as a servant would be provided for; but, 2d. That this was not the *first* thing; that there was a proper *order* of things, and that thus the reward might be delayed,

8 And will not rather say unto him, Make ready wherewith I may sup, and gird thyself, and serve me till I have eaten and drunken; and afterward thou shalt eat and drink?

9 Doth he thank that servant because he did the things that were commanded him? I trow not.

10 So likewise ye, when ye shall have done all those things which are commanded you, say, [f]We are unprofitable servants; we have done that which was our duty to do.

11 And it came to pass, as he went to Jerusalem, that he passed through the midst of [g]Samaria and Galilee.

12 And as he entered into a certain village, there met him ten men that were lepers, which [h]stood afar off:

13 And they lifted up *their* voices, and said, Jesus, Master, have mercy on us.

14 And when he saw *them,* he said unto them, [i]Go show yourselves unto the priests. And it

f Job 22.3; 35.7; Ps.16.2,3; Is.64.6; Ro.11.35; 1 Co. 9.16,17.

g ch.9.51,52; Jn.4.4. h Le.13.46. i Le.13.2; 14.3; Mat.8.4; ch.5.14.

as a servant would be provided for, but at the proper time, and at the pleasure of the master; and, 3d. That this reward was not to be expected as a matter of *merit*, but would be given at the good pleasure of God, for they were but unprofitable servants. ¶ *By and by.* This should have been translated *immediately.* He would not, *as the first thing*, or *as soon as* he returned from the field, direct him to eat and drink. Hungry and weary he might be, yet it would be proper for him first to attend upon his master. So the apostles were not to be *impatient* because they did not *at once* receive the reward for which they were looking. ¶ *To meat.* To eat; or, rather, place thyself at the table.

8. *I may sup.* Make ready my supper. ¶ *Gird thyself.* See Notes on Lu. xii. 37.

9. *I trow not.* I *think* not; or I *suppose* not.

10. *Are unprofitable servants.* We have conferred no favour. We have *merited* nothing. We have not *benefited* God, or laid him under *obligation.* If he rewards us, it will be matter of unmerited favour. This is true in relation to Christians in the following respects: 1st. Our services are not *profitable* to God (Job xxii. 2); he *needs* not our aid, and his essential happiness will not be increased by our efforts. 2d. The grace to do his will comes from him only, and all the praise of that will be due to him. 3d. All that we do is what is our *duty;* we cannot lay claim to having rendered any service that will *bind* him to show us favour; and 4th. Our best services are mingled with imperfections. We come short of his glory (Ro. iii. 23); we do not serve him as sincerely, and cheerfully, and faithfully as we ought; we are far, very far from the example set us by the Saviour; and if we are saved and rewarded, it will be because God will be merciful to our unrighteousness, and will remember our iniquities no more, He. viii. 12.

11. *The midst of Samaria and Galilee.* He went from Galilee, and probably travelled through the chief villages and towns in it and then left it; and as Samaria was situated *between* Galilee and Jerusalem, it was necessary to pass through it; or it may mean that he passed along on the borders of each toward the river Jordan, and so passed in the midst, *i.e. between* Galilee and Samaria. This is rendered more probable from the circumstance that as he went from Galilee, there would have been no occasion for saying that he passed *through it,* unless it be meant through the *confines* or borders of it, or at least it would have been mentioned before Samaria.

12. *There met him.* They were in his way, or in his path, as he was entering the village. They were not allowed to enter the village while they were afflicted with the leprosy, Le. xiii. 46; Nu. v. 2, 3. ¶ *Lepers.* See Notes on Mat. viii. 2. ¶ *Stood afar off.* At a distance, as they were required by law. They were unclean, and it was not lawful for them to come near to those who were in health. As Jesus was travelling, they were also walking in the contrary way, and seeing him, and knowing that they were unclean, they stopped or turned aside, so that they might not expose others to the contagion.

came to pass that, [k]as they went,
they were cleansed.
15 And one of them, when he
saw that he was healed, turned
back, and with a loud voice [l]glorified God.
16 And fell down on *his* face at
his feet, giving him thanks: and
he was a [m]Samaritan.
17 And Jesus answering said,
Were there not ten cleansed? but
where *are* the nine?

k 2 Ki.5.14; Is.65.24. l Ps.30.1,2. m Jn.4.39-42.

14. *Go show yourselves*, &c. See Notes on Mat. viii. 4. By this command he gave them an implied assurance that they would be healed; for the *design* for which they were to go was to exhibit the *evidence* that they were restored, and to obtain permission from the priest to mingle again in society. It may also be observed that this required no small measure of *faith* on their part, for he did not *first* heal them, and then tell them to go; he told them to go without *expressly* assuring them that they would be healed, and without, *as yet*, any evidence to show to the priest. So sinners, defiled with the leprosy of sin, should put faith in the Lord Jesus and obey his commands, with the fullest confidence that he is able to heal them, and that he *will* do it if they follow his directions; and that in due time they shall have the fullest evidence that their peace is made with God, and that their souls shall by him be declared free from the defilement of sin. ¶ *Were cleansed.* Were cured, or made whole.

15, 16. *One of them*, &c. This man, sensible of the power of God and grateful for his mercies, returned to express his gratitude to God for his goodness. Instead of obeying *at once* the *letter* of the command, he *first* expressed his thanks to God and to his Great Benefactor. There is no evidence, however, that he did not, *after* he had given thanks to God, and had poured out his joy at the feet of Jesus, go to the priest as he was directed; indeed, he could not have been restored to society without doing it; but he *first* poured out his thanks to God, and gave him praise for his wonderful recovery. The first duty of sinners, after they have been forgiven and have the hope of eternal life, is to prostrate themselves at the feet of their Great Benefactor, and to consecrate themselves to his service. *Then* let them go and show to others the evidence that they are cleansed. Let them go and mingle, like a restored leper, with their families and friends, and show by the purity and holiness of their lives how great is the mercy that has cleansed them. ¶ *He was a Samaritan.* See Notes on Mat. x. 5. This rendered his conduct more remarkable and striking in the sight of the Jews. *They* considered the Samaritans as peculiarly wicked, and *themselves* as peculiarly holy. This example showed them, like the parable of the good Samaritan, that in this they were mistaken; and one design of this seems to have been to break down the *opposition* between the Jews and Samaritans, and to bring the former to more charitable judgments respecting the latter.

17, 18. *Where* are *the nine?* Jesus had commanded them to go to the priest, and they were probably *literally* obeying the commandment. They were impatient to be healed and *selfish* in wishing it, and had no gratitude to God or their Benefactor. Jesus did not *forbid* their expressing gratitude to him for his mercy; he rather seems to reprove them for *not* doing it. One of the first feelings of the sinner cleansed from sin is a desire to praise his Great Benefactor; and a *real* willingness to obey his commandments is not inconsistent with a wish to render thanks to him for his mercy. With what singular propriety may this question now be asked, *Where are the nine?* And what a striking illustration is this of human nature, and of the ingratitude of man! One had come back to give thanks for the favour bestowed on him; the others were heard of no more. So now. When men are restored from dangerous sickness, here and there one comes to give thanks to God; but "where are the nine?" When men are defended from danger; when they are recovered from the perils of the sea; when a steamboat is destroyed, and a large part of crew and passengers perish, here and there one of those who are saved acknowledges the goodness of God and renders him praise; but where is the mass of them? They give no thanks; they offer no praise. They go about their usual employments, to

18 There are [n]not found that returned to give glory to God, save this stranger.
19 And he said unto him, Arise, go thy way: [o]thy faith hath made thee whole.
20 And when he was demanded of the Pharisees when the kingdom of God should come, he answered them and said, The kingdom of God cometh not [1]with observation.
21 Neither shall they say, Lo here! or, Lo there! for, behold, [p]the kingdom of God is [2]within you.
22 And he said unto the disci-

n Ps.106.13. *o* Mat.9.22.

1 or, *with outward show.* *p* Ro.14.17.
2 or, *among you,* Jn.1.26.

---

mingle in the scenes of pleasure and of sin as if nothing had occurred. Few, few of all who have been rescued from "threatening graves" feel their obligation to God, or ever express it. They forget their Great Benefactor; perhaps the mention of his name is unpleasant, and they scorn the idea that they are under any obligations to him. Such, alas! is man, ungrateful man! ¶ *This stranger.* This foreigner; or, rather, this alien, or this man of another tribe. In the *Syraic* version, "this one who is of a foreign people." This man, who might have been least *expected* to express gratitude to God. The most unlikely characters are often found to be most consistent and grateful. Men from whom we would expect *least* in religion, are often so entirely changed as to disappoint all our expectations, and to put to shame those who have been most highly favoured. The poor often thus put to shame the rich; the ignorant the learned; the young the aged.

19. *Go thy way.* To the *priest;* for without *his* certificate he could not again be restored to the society of his friends, or to the public worship of God. Having now appropriately expressed your gratitude, go to the priest and obey the law of God. Renewed sinners, while their hearts overflow with gratitude to Jesus, *express* that gratitude by obeying God, and by engaging in the appropriate duties of their calling and of religion.

20. *Was demanded.* Was asked. ¶ *Of the Pharisees.* This was a matter of much importance to them, and they had taught that it would come with parade and pomp. It is not unlikely that they asked this merely in *contempt,* and for the purpose of drawing out something that would expose him to ridicule. ¶ *The kingdom of God.* The *reign* of God; or the dispensation under the Messiah. See Notes on Mat. iii. 2. ¶ *With observation.* With scrupulous and attentive looking for it, or with such an appearance as to *attract* observation—that is, with pomp, majesty, splendour. He did not deny that, according to their views, the time was drawing near; but he denied that his kingdom would come in the *manner* in which they expected. The Messiah would *not* come with pomp like an earthly prince; perhaps not in such a manner as to be *discerned* by the eyes of sagacious and artful men, who were expecting him in a way agreeable to their own feelings. The kingdom of God is *within* men, and it makes its way, not by pomp and noise, but by silence, decency, and order, 1 Co. xiv. 40.

21. *Lo here! or, Lo there!* When an earthly prince visits different parts of his territories, he does it with pomp. His movements attract observation, and become the common topic of conversation. The inquiry is, Where is he? which way will he go? and it is a matter of important *news* to be able to say where he is. Jesus says that the Messiah would not come in that manner. It would not be with such pomp and public attention. It would be silent, obscure, and attracting comparatively little notice. Or the passage may have reference to the custom of the *pretended* Messiahs, who appeared in this manner. They said that in this place or in that, in this mountain or that desert, they would show signs that would convince the people that they were the Messiah. Comp. Notes on Ac. v. 36, 37. ¶ *Is within you.* This is capable of two interpretations. 1st. The reign of God is *in the heart.* It does not come with pomp and splendour, like the reign of temporal kings, merely to control the external *actions* and strike the senses of men with awe, but it reigns in the heart by the law of God; it sets up its dominion over the passions, and brings every thought into captivity to the obedience of Christ. 2d. It may mean

ples, [q]The days will come when ye
shall desire to see one of the days
of the Son of man, and ye shall
not see *it*.
23 And [r]they shall say to you,
See here; or, See there: go not
after *them*, nor follow *them*.
24 For as the lightning that
lighteneth out of the one *part* under heaven, shineth unto the other
part under heaven, so shall also
the Son of man be in his day.
25 But[s] first must he suffer many
things, and be rejected of this
generation.
26 And as it was [t]in the days
of Noe, so shall it be also in the
days of the Son of man.
27 They did eat, they drank, they
married wives, they were given in
marriage, until the day that Noe
entered into the ark, and the flood
came and destroyed them all.
28 Likewise also as it was in the
days of Lot; they did eat, they
drank, they bought, they sold, they
planted, they builded:
29 But the same day that [u]Lot
went out of Sodom, it rained fire
and brimstone from heaven, and
destroyed *them* all.
30 Even thus shall it be in the

q Mat.9.15. *r* Mat.24.23,&c.; Mar.13.21; ch.21.8. *s* Mar.8.31; ch.9.22. *t* Ge.7.11,23. *u* Ge.19.23,24.

the new dispensation is *even now among* YOU. The Messiah has come. John has ushered in the kingdom of God, and you are not to expect the appearance of the Messiah with great pomp and splendour, for he is now among you. Most critics at present incline to this latter interpretation. The ancient versions chiefly follow the former.

22. *The days will come.* He here takes occasion to direct the minds of his disciples to the days of vengeance which were about to fall on the Jewish nation. Heavy calamities will befall the Jewish people, and you will desire a deliverer. ¶ *Ye shall desire.* You who now number yourselves among my disciples. ¶ *One of the days of the Son of man.* The Son of man here means *the Messiah*, without affirming that *he* was the Messiah. Such will be the calamities of those times, so great will be the afflictions and persecutions, that you will greatly desire *a deliverer*—one who shall come to you in the character in which *you have expected* the Messiah would come, and who would deliver you from the power of your enemies; and at that time, in the midst of these calamities, men shall rise up pretending *to be* the Messiah, and to be able to deliver you. In view of this, he takes occasion to caution them against being led astray by them. ¶ *Ye shall not see* it. You shall not see such a day of deliverance—such a Messiah as the nation has expected, and such an interposition as you would desire.

23, 24. *And they shall say*, &c. Many false Christs, according to Josephus, appeared about that time, attempting to lead away the people. See Notes on Mat. xxiv. 23-27.

25. See Notes on Mar. viii. 31.

26, 27. See Notes on Mat. xxiv. 37-39.

28-30. *They did eat*, &c. They were busy in the affairs of this life, as if nothing were about to happen. ¶ *The same day*, &c. See Ge. xix. 23-25. ¶ *It rained.* The word here used *might* have been rendered *he* rained. In Genesis it is said that the *Lord* did it. ¶ *Fire and brimstone.* God destroyed Sodom on account of its great wickedness. He took vengeance on it for its sins; and the example of Sodom is set before men to deter them from committing great transgressions, and as a *full proof* that God will punish the guilty. See Jude 7; also Is. i. 10; Je. xxiii. 14. Yet, in overthrowing it, he used natural means. He is not to be supposed to have *created* fire and brimstone for the occasion, but to have *directed* the natural means at his disposal for their overthrow; as he did not *create* the waters to drown the world, but merely broke up the fountains of the great deep and opened the windows of heaven. Sodom and Gomorrah, Admah and Zeboim (De. xxix. 23), were four great cities, on a plain where is now the Dead Sea, at the south-east of Palestine, and into which the river Jordan flows. They were built on ground which abounded, doubtless, as all that region now does, in *bitumen* or *naphtha*, which is easily kindled, and which burns with great intensity. The phrase "fire and brim-

day [v]when the Son of man is revealed.

31 In that day, he which shall be upon the house-top, and his stuff in the house, let him not come down to take it away; and he that is in the field, let him likewise not return back.

32 Remember [w]Lot's wife.

33 Whosoever[x] shall seek to save his life shall lose it; and whosoever shall lose his life, shall preserve it.

34 I tell you, in that night [y]there shall be two *men* in one bed; the one shall be taken, and the other shall be left.

35 Two *women* shall be grinding together; the one shall be taken, and the other left.

36 Two[3] *men* shall be in the field; the one shall be taken, and the other left.

37 And they answered and said unto him, Where, Lord? And he said unto them, [z]Wheresoever the body *is*, thither will the eagles be gathered together.

CHAPTER XVIII.

AND he spake a parable unto them *to this end*, [a]that men ought always to pray, and not to faint;

v 2 Th.1.7. w Ge.19.26. x Mat.16.25; Mar.8.35; ch.9.24; Jn.12.25. y Mat.24.40,41.

3 Verse 36th is wanting in most Greek copies.
z Job 39.30; Mat.24.28.
a Ps.65.2; 102.17; ch.11.8; 21.36; Ro.12.12; Ep.6.18; Phi.4.6.

---

stone" is a Hebrew form of expression, denoting sulphurous fire, or fire having the smell of sulphur; and may denote a volcanic eruption, or any burning like that of naphtha. There is no improbability in supposing either that this destruction was accomplished by lightning, which ignited the naphtha, or that it was a volcanic eruption, which, by direction of God, overthrew the wicked cities. ¶ *From heaven.* By command of God, or from the sky. To the people of Sodom it had *the appearance* of coming from heaven, as all volcanic eruptions would have. Hundreds of towns have been overthrown in this way, and all by the agency of God. He rules the elements, and makes them his instruments, at his pleasure, in accomplishing the destruction of the wicked.

30. *Even thus,* &c. Destruction came upon the old world, and upon Sodom, *suddenly;* when they were engaged in other things, and little expecting this. *So* suddenly and unexpectedly, says he, shall destruction come upon the Jewish people. See Notes on Mat. xxiv.

31. See Notes on Mat. xxiv. 17, 18.

32. *Remember Lot's wife.* See Ge. xix. 26. *She* looked back—she delayed—perhaps she *desired* to take something with her, and God made her a monument of his displeasure. Jesus directed his disciples, when they saw the calamities coming upon the Jews, to flee to the mountains, Mat. xxiv. 16. He here charges them to be in haste—not to look back—not to delay—but to escape quickly, and to remember that by delaying the wife of Lot lost her life.

33. See Notes on Mat. x. 39.

34–36. See Notes on Mat. xxiv. 40, 41.

37. See Notes on Mat. xxiv. 26. ¶ *Where, Lord?* Where, or in what direction, shall these calamities come? The answer implies that it would be where there is the most *guilt* and *wickedness.* Eagles flock where there is prey. So, said he, these armies will flock to the place where there is the most wickedness; and by this their thoughts were directed at once to Jerusalem, the place of eminent wickedness, and the place, therefore, where these calamities might be expected to begin.

CHAPTER XVIII.

1. *A parable.* See Notes on Mat. xiii. 3. ¶ To this end. To show this. ¶ *Always.* At all times. That is, we must not neglect regular stated seasons of prayer; we must seize on occasions of remarkable providences—as afflictions or signal blessings — to seek God in prayer; we must *always* maintain a spirit of prayer, or be in a proper frame to lift up our hearts to God for his blessing, and we must not grow weary though our prayer seems not to be answered. ¶ *Not to faint.* Not to grow weary or give over. The parable is designed to teach us that, though our prayers should long appear to be unanswered, we should persevere, and not grow weary in supplication to God.

2 Saying, There was [1] in a city a
judge, which feared not God, neither regarded man:
3 And there was a widow in that
city; and she came unto him, saying, Avenge me of mine adversary.
4 And he would not for a while:
but afterward he said within himself, Though I fear not God, nor
regard man;
5 Yet, because this widow troubleth me, I will avenge her, lest by
her continual coming she weary me.
6 And the Lord said, Hear what
the unjust judge saith.
7 And shall not God [b] avenge his

1 *in a certain city.*

b Re.6.10.

2. *A judge which feared not God.* One appointed by law to determine causes brought before him. This judge had no reverence for God, and consequently no regard for the rights of man. These two things go together. He that has no regard for God can be expected to have none for man; and our Lord has here indirectly taught us what ought to be the character of a judge—that he *should* fear God and regard the rights of man. Comp. De. i. 16, 17. ¶ *Regarded man.* Cared not for man. Had no respect for the opinions or the rights of man.

3. *A widow.* This is a circumstance that gives increasing interest to the parable. Judges were bound to show peculiar attention to widows, Is. i. 17; Je. xxii. 3. The reason of this was that they were defenceless, were commonly poor, and were liable to be oppressed by those in power. ¶ *Avenge me.* This would have been better translated, "Do me justice against my adversary, or vindicate me from him." It does not denote vengeance or revenge, but simply that she wished to have *justice* done her—a thing which this judge was *bound* to do, but which it seems he had no disposition to do. ¶ *Adversary.* One opposed in law. In this case it seems that the judge was unwilling to do justice, and probably took advantage of her condition to oppress her.

4, 5. *For a while.* Probably this means for a *considerable* time. It was his duty to attend to the claims of justice, but this was long delayed. ¶ *Within himself.* He thought, or came to a conclusion. ¶ *Though I fear not,* &c. This contains the reason why he attended to the case at all. It was not from any regard to justice, or to the duties of his office. It was simply to avoid *trouble.* And yet his conduct in this case might have appeared very upright, and possibly might have been strictly according to law and to justice. How many actions are performed that *appear well,* when the doers of those actions know that they are mere hypocrisy! and how many actions are performed from the basest and lowest motives of *selfishness,* that have the appearance of external propriety and even of goodness! ¶ *She weary me.* The word used here, in the original, is that which was employed to denote the wounds and bruises caused by *boxers,* who beat each other, and blacken their eyes, and disable them. See Notes on 1 Co. ix. 27. Hence it means any vexatious and troublesome importunity that takes the time, and disables from other employment.

6. *Hear,* &c. Give attention to this, and derive from it practical instruction.

7. *Shall not God avenge,* &c. We are not to suppose that the character of God is at all represented by this judge, or that *his* principles of conduct are at all like those of the judge. This parable shows us conclusively that many *circumstances* of a parable are not to be interpreted closely: they are mere appendages to the narrative. The great truth which our Saviour *designed* to teach is what we ought to endeavour to find. In this case there can be no doubt what that truth is. He has himself told us that it is, that *men ought always to pray and not to faint.* This he teaches by the example in the parable; and the argument which it implies is this: 1st. A poor widow, by her perseverance only, obtained from an unjust man what otherwise she would *not* have obtained. 2d. God is not unjust. He is good, and disposed to do justice and to bestow mercy. If, therefore, this *wicked man* by persevering prayer was induced to do justice, how much more shall *God,* who is good, and who is not actuated by any such selfish and base principles, do justice to them who apply to him! ¶ *Avenge.* Do justice to or vindicate them. This may have a twofold reference. 1st. To the disciples

own elect which cry day and night unto him, though he bear long with them?
8 I tell you that [c]he will avenge
them speedily. Nevertheless, when the Son of man cometh, [d]shall he find faith on the earth?
9 And he spake this parable un-

c Ps.46.5; He.10.37; 2 Pe.3.8,9.

d Mat.24.12.

in the time of Jesus, who were about to be oppressed and persecuted, and over whom calamities were about to come, *as if* God did not regard their cries and had forsaken them. To them Jesus gives the assurance that God *would* hear their petitions and come forth to vindicate them; and that, notwithstanding all these calamities, he would yet appear for their deliverance. 2d. It may have a more *general* meaning. The people of God are often oppressed, calumniated, persecuted. They are few in number and feeble. They seem to be almost forsaken and cast down, and their enemies triumph. Yet in due time God will hear their prayers, and will come forth for their vindication. And even if it should not be *in this life*, yet he will do it in the day of judgment, when he will pronounce them blessed, and receive them for ever to himself. ¶ *His own elect.* People of God, saints, Christians; so called because God has *chosen* them to be his. The term is usually given in the Scriptures to the true followers of God, and is a term of affection, denoting his great and peculiar love in choosing them out of a world of sinners, and conferring on them grace, and mercy, and eternal life. See 1 Th. i. 4; Col. iii. 12; 1 Pe. i. 2; Ep. i. 4. It signifies here that they are peculiarly dear to him; that he feels a deep interest in their welfare, and that he will therefore be ready to come forth to their aid. The judge felt no special interest in that widow, yet he heard her; God feels a particular regard, a tender love for his elect, and therefore he will hear and save. ¶ *Which cry day and night.* This expresses one striking characteristic of the elect of God; they pray, and pray constantly. No one can have evidence that he is chosen of God who is not a man of prayer. One of the best marks by which the electing love of God is known is that it disposes us to pray. This passage supposes that when the elect of God are in trouble and pressed down with calamities, they *will* cry unto him; and it affirms that if they do, he will hear their cries and answer their requests. ¶ *Though he bear long with them.* This passage has been variously interpreted, and there is some variety of reading in the manuscripts. Some read, "Will not God avenge his elect? Will he linger in their cause?" But the most natural meaning is, "Although he defers long to avenge them, and greatly tries their patience, yet he will avenge them." He tries their faith; he suffers their persecutions and trials to continue a long time; and it almost *appears* as if he would not interpose. Yet he will do it, and will save them.

8. *Speedily.* Suddenly, unexpectedly. He will surely vindicate them, and that at a time, perhaps, when they were nearly ready to give over and to sink into despair. This may refer to the deliverance of the disciples from their approaching trials and persecutions among the Jews; or, in general, to the fact that God will interpose and aid his people. ¶ *Nevertheless.* But. Notwithstanding this. Though this is true that God will avenge his elect, yet will he find his elect *faithful?* The danger is not that *God* will be unfaithful—he will surely be true to his promises; but the danger is that his elect—his afflicted people—will be discouraged; will not persevere in prayer; will not continue to have confidence in him; and will, under heavy trials, sink into despondency. The sole meaning of this phrase, therefore, is, that *there is more danger that his people would grow weary, than that God would be found unfaithful and fail to avenge his elect.* For this cause Christ spoke the parable, and by the *design* of the parable this passage is to be interpreted. ¶ *Son of man cometh.* This probably refers to the approaching destruction of Jerusalem—the coming of the Messiah, by his mighty power, to abolish the ancient dispensation and to set up the new. ¶ *Faith.* The word *faith* is sometimes taken to denote the *whole* of religion, and it has been understood in this sense here; but there is a close connection in what Christ says, and it should be understood as referring to what he said before. The truth that he had been teaching was, that God would deliver his people from their calamities and save them, though he suffered them to be long tried. He asks

to certain [e]which trusted in themselves [2]that they were righteous, and despised others:

10 Two men went up into the temple to pray; the one a Pharisee, and the other a publican.

11 The Pharisee stood and prayed thus with himself: God, I thank

e ch.10.29. 2 or, *as being righteous.*

---

them here whether, when he came, he should find *this faith*, or a belief of *this truth*, among his followers? Would they be found persevering in prayer, and *believing* that God would yet avenge them; or would they cease to pray *always*, and *faint?* This is not to be understood, therefore, as affirming that when Christ comes to judgment there will be few Christians on the earth, and that the world will be overrun with wickedness. That *may be* true, but it is not the truth taught here. ¶ *The earth.* The land—referring particularly to the land of Judea. The discussion had particular reference to their trials and persecutions in that land. This question implies that *in* those trials many professed disciples might faint and turn back, and many of his *real* followers almost lose sight of this great truth, and begin to inquire whether God would interpose to save them. The same question may be asked respecting any other remarkable visitation of the Son of God in affliction. When tried and persecuted, do *we* believe that God will avenge us? Do *we* pray always and not faint? Have *we* faith to believe that, though clouds and darkness are round about him, yet righteousness and judgment are the habitation of his throne? And when storms of persecution assail us, can *we* go to God and confidently commit our cause to him, and believe that he will bring forth our righteousness as the light, and our judgment as the noon-day?

9. *Unto certain.* Unto some. ¶ *Which trusted in themselves.* Who confided in themselves, or who supposed that they were righteous. They did not trust to God or the Messiah for righteousness, but to their own works. They vainly supposed they had themselves complied with the demands of the law of God. ¶ *Despised others.* Others who were not as externally righteous as themselves. This was the character of the Pharisees. They trusted in their outward conformity to the ceremonies of the law. They considered all who did not do that as sinners. This, moreover, is the true character of self-righteousness. Men of that stamp always despise all others. They think they are far above them in holiness, and are disposed to say to them, Stand by thyself, for I am holier than thou, Is. lxv. 5. True religion, on the contrary, is humble. Those who trust in Christ for righteousness feel that *they* are, in themselves, poor, and miserable, and guilty, and they are willing to admit that others may be much better than themselves. Certain it is, they *despise* no one. They love all men; they regard them, however vile, as the creatures of God and as going to eternity, and are disposed to treat them well, and to aid them in their journey toward another world.

10. *The temple.* Into one of the courts of the temple—the court where prayer was commonly offered. See Notes on Mat. xxi. 12. ¶ *A Pharisee.* See Notes on Mat. iii. 7. ¶ *Publican.* See Notes on Mat. v. 46.

11. *Stood and prayed thus with himself.* Some have proposed to render this, "stood by himself" and prayed. In this way it would be characteristic of the sect of the Pharisees, who dreaded the contact of others as polluting, and who were disposed to say to all, Stand by yourselves. The Syriac so renders it, but it is doubtful whether the Greek will allow this construction. If not, it means, he said over to himself what he had done, and what was the ground on which he expected the favour of God. ¶ *God, I thank thee.* There was still in the prayer of the Pharisee an *appearance* of real religion. He did not profess to claim that he had made himself better than others. He was willing to acknowledge that God had done it for him, and that he had a right to his gratitude for it. Hypocrites are often the most orthodox in opinion of any class of men. They know the truth, and admit it. They use it frequently in their prayers and conversation. They will even persecute those who happen to differ from them in opinion, and who may be really wrong. We are not to judge of the *piety* of men by the fact that they admit the truth, or even that they use it often in their prayers. It is, however, not wrong to thank God that he has kept us from the gross sins which other men commit; but it should

thee that I am [f]not as other men *are*, extortioners, unjust, adulterers, or even as this publican:

12 I fast twice in the week, I give tithes of all that I possess.

13 And the publican, standing afar off, would not lift up so much as *his* eyes unto heaven, but [g]smote upon his breast, saying, God be merciful to me, a sinner.

f Is.65.5; Re.3.17.

g Je.31.19.

---

not be done in an ostentatious manner, nor should it be done forgetting still that we are great sinners and need pardon. These were the faults of the Pharisees. ¶ *Extortioners.* Rapacious; avaricious; who take away the goods of others by force and violence. It means, also, those who take advantage of the necessities of others, the poor and the oppressed, and extort their property. ¶ *Unjust.* They who are not fair and honest in their dealings; who get the property of others by *fraud.* They are distinguished from *extortioners* because they who are unjust may have the *appearance* of honesty; in the other case there is not.

12. *I fast twice*, &c. This was probably the Jewish custom. The Pharisees are said to have fasted regularly on the second and fifth days of every week in private. This was *in addition* to the public days of fasting required in the law of Moses, and they therefore made more a matter of *merit* of it because it was voluntary. ¶ *I give tithes.* A tithe means the tenth part of a thing. A tenth part of the possessions of the Jews was required for the support of the Levites, Nu. xviii. 21. In addition to the tithes required strictly by law, the Pharisees had tithed everything which they possessed—even the smallest matters—as mint, anise, cummin, &c., Lu. xi. 42. It was *this*, probably, on which he so particularly prided himself. As this could not be proved to be strictly *required* in the law, it had more the *appearance* of great piety, and therefore he particularly dwelt on it. ¶ *I possess.* This may mean either all which I *have*, or all which I *gain* or acquire. It is not material which meaning be considered the true one.

The religion of the Pharisee, therefore, consisted—1st. In abstaining from injustice to others; in pretending to live a harmless, innocent, and upright life; and 2d. In a regular observance of all the external duties of religion. His *fault* consisted in relying on this kind of righteousness; in not feeling and acknowledging that he was a sinner; in not seeking a religion that should dwell in the *heart* and regulate the feelings; and in making public and ostentatious professions of his own goodness. Most of all was this abominable in the sight of God, who *looks into the heart*, and who sees wickedness there when the external actions may be blameless. We may learn from the case of the Pharisee—1st. That it is not the man who has the most orthodox belief that has, of course, the most piety; 2d. That men may be externally moral, and not be righteous in the sight of God; 3d. That they may be very exact in the external duties of religion, and even go beyond the strict letter of the law; that they may assume a great appearance of sanctity, and still be strangers to true piety; and 4th. That ostentation in religion, or a *boasting* before God of what we are and of what we have done, is abominable in his sight. This spoils everything, even if the life *should be* tolerably blameless, and if there should be real piety.

13. *Standing afar off.* Afar off from the *temple.* The place where prayer was offered in the temple was the court of women. The Pharisee advanced to the side of the court nearest to the temple, or near as he could; the publican stood on the other side of the same court if he was a Jew, or in the court of the Gentiles if he was a pagan, as far as possible from the temple, being conscious of his unworthiness to approach the sacred place where God had his holy habitation. ¶ *So much as* his *eyes*, &c. Conscious of his guilt. He felt that he was a sinner, and shame and sorrow prevented his looking up. Men who are conscious of guilt always fix their eyes on the ground. ¶ *Smote upon his breast.* An expression of grief and anguish in view of his sins. It is a sign of grief among almost all nations. ¶ *God be merciful*, &c. The prayer of the publican was totally different from that of the Pharisee. He made no boast of his own righteousness toward God or man. He felt that he was a sinner, and, feeling it, was willing to acknowledge it. This is the kind of

14 I tell you, this man went down to his house justified *rather* than the other: [h]for every one that exalteth himself shall be abased; and he that humbleth himself shall be exalted.

15 And[i] they brought unto him also infants, that he would touch them; but when *his* disciples saw *it*, they rebuked them.

16 But Jesus called them *unto him*, and said, Suffer little children to come unto me, and forbid them not; for of such is the kingdom of God.

17 Verily I say unto you, Whosoever shall not receive the kingdom of God [k]as a little child, shall in no wise enter therein.

18 And[l] a certain ruler asked him, saying, Good Master, what shall I do to inherit eternal life?

19 And Jesus said unto him, Why callest thou me good? None *is* good save one, *that is*, God.

20 Thou knowest [m]the commandments, Do not commit adultery, Do not kill, Do not steal, Do not bear false witness, Honour thy father and thy mother.

21 And he said, All these have I kept from my youth up.

22 Now when Jesus heard these things, he said unto him, Yet lackest thou one thing: sell all that thou hast, and distribute unto the poor, and thou shalt have [n]treasure in heaven; and come, follow me.

23 And when he heard this he was very sorrowful; for he was very rich.

24 And when Jesus saw that he was very sorrowful, he said, [o]How hardly shall they that have riches enter into the kingdom of God!

25 For it is easier for a camel to go through a needle's eye, than for a rich man to enter into the kingdom of God.

26 And they that heard *it* said, Who, then, can be saved?

27 And he said, [p]The things which are impossible with men are possible with God.

28 Then Peter said, Lo, we have left all and followed thee.

29 And he said unto them, Verily I say unto you, There is no man that [q]hath left house, or parents, or brethren, or wife, or children, for the kingdom of God's sake,

30 Who shall not receive manifold more in this present time, and in the world to come [r]life everlasting.

31 Then he took *unto him* the

h Job 22.29; Mat.23.12.
i Mat.19.13; Mar.10.13,&c.
k Ps.131.2; Mar.10.15; 1 Pe.1.14.
l Mat.19.16,&c.; Mar.10.17,&c.
m Ex.20.12-16; De.5.16-20; Ro.13.9.
n Mat.6.19,20; 1 Ti.6.19. *o* Pr.11.28; 1 Ti.6.9.
p Je.32.17; Zec.8.6; ch.1.37. *q* De.33.9. *r* Re.2.10.

prayer that will be acceptable to God. When we are willing to confess and forsake our sins, we shall find mercy, Pr. xxviii. 13. The publican was willing to do this in any place; in the presence of any persons; amid the multitudes of the temple, or alone. He felt most that *God* was a witness of his actions, and he was willing, therefore, to confess his sins before him. While we should not *seek* to do this *publicly*, yet we should be willing at all times "to confess our manifold transgressions, to the end that we may obtain forgiveness of the same by God's infinite goodness and mercy." It is not dishonourable to make acknowledgment when we have done wrong. No man is so much dishonoured as he who is a sinner and is not willing to confess it; as he who has done wrong and yet attempts to *conceal* the fault, thus adding hypocrisy to his other crimes.

14. *I tell you.* The Pharisees would have said that the first man here was approved. Jesus assures them that they judged erroneously. God judges of this differently from men. ¶ *Justified.* Accepted or approved of God. The word *justify* means to declare or treat as righteous. In this case it means that in their prayers the one was approved and the other not; the one went down with the favour of God in answer to his petitions, the other not. ¶ *For every one*, &c. See Notes on Lu. xiv. 11.

15–30. See Notes on Mat. xix. 13–30.

twelve, and said unto them, Behold, we go up to Jerusalem, [s]and all things that are written by the prophets concerning the Son of man shall be accomplished.
32 For he shall be [t]delivered unto the Gentiles, and shall be mocked, and spitefully entreated, and spitted on:
33 And they shall scourge *him*, and put him to death; and the third day he shall rise again.
34 And[u] they understood none of these things; and this saying was hid from them, neither knew they the things which were spoken.
35 And[v] it came to pass, that as he was come nigh unto Jericho, a certain blind man sat by the wayside, begging:
36 And hearing the multitude pass by, he asked what it meant.
37 And they told him that Jesus of Nazareth passeth by.
38 And he cried, saying, Jesus, *thou* son of David, [w]have mercy on me.
39 And they which went before rebuked him, that he should hold his peace; but he [x]cried so much the more, *Thou* son of David, have mercy on me.
40 And Jesus stood, and commanded him to be brought unto him; and when he was come near, he asked him,
41 Saying, What wilt thou that I shall do unto thee? And he said, Lord, that I may receive my sight.
42 And Jesus said unto him, Receive thy sight: [y]thy faith hath saved thee.
43 And immediately he [z]received his sight, and followed him, [a]glorifying God: and all the people, when they saw *it*, gave praise unto God.

CHAPTER XIX.

AND *Jesus* entered and passed through [b]Jericho.
2 And, behold, *there was* a man named Zaccheus, which was the chief among the publicans, and he was rich.

s Ps.22.; Is.53.
t Mat.27.2; ch.23.1; Jn.18.28; Ac.3.13.
u Mar.9.32; Jn.12.16.
v Mat.20.29,&c.; Mar.10.46,&c. *w* Ps.62.12.
x Ps.141.1. *y* ch.17.19. *z* Ps.30.2.
a ch.5.26; Ac.4.21; 11.18; Ga.1.24.
b Jos.6.26; 1 Ki.16.34.

31–33. See Notes on Mat. xx. 17–19. ¶ *By the prophets.* Those who foretold the coming of the Messiah, and whose predictions are recorded in the Old Testament. ¶ *Son of man.* The Messiah. They predicted that certain things would take place respecting the Messiah that was to come. See Notes on Da. ix. 25–27; Is. liii. *These things*, Jesus said, would be accomplished *in him*, he being the Son of man, or the Messiah.

34. *Understood none of these things.* Though they were *plainly* revealed, yet such were their prejudices and their unwillingness to believe them that they did not understand them. They expected that he would be a temporal prince and a conqueror, and they were not *willing* to believe that he would be delivered into the hands of his enemies. They did not see how that could be consistent with the prophecies. To us now these things appear plain, and we may hence learn that those things which to us appear most mysterious may yet appear perfectly plain; and we should learn to trust in God, and *believe* just what he has spoken. See Mat. xvi. 21; xvii. 23.

35–43. See this passage explained in the Notes on Mat. xx. 29–34.

CHAPTER XIX.

1. *And* Jesus *entered*, &c. See Notes on Mat. xx. 29. This means, perhaps, *he was passing* through Jericho when Zaccheus saw him. His house was *in* Jericho.

2. *A man named Zaccheus.* The name Zaccheus is Hebrew, and shows that this man was a *Jew*. The Hebrew name properly means *pure*, and is the same as Zacchai in Ezr. ii. 9; Ne. vii. 14. The publicans, therefore, were not all foreigners. ¶ *Chief among the publicans.* Who presided over other tax-gatherers, or who *received* their collections and transmitted them to the Roman govern-

3 And he sought to see Jesus,
who he was; and could not for
the press, because he was little of
stature.
4 And he ran before, and climb-
ed up into a sycamore-tree to see
him; for he was to pass that *way*.
5 And when Jesus came to the
place, he looked up, and [b]saw him,
and said unto him, Zaccheus, make
haste and come down; for to-day
I must [c]abide at thy house.
6 And he made haste, and came
down, and received him joyfully.
7 And when they saw *it*, they
all murmured, saying, [d]That he
was gone to be guest with a man
that is a sinner.
8 And Zaccheus stood, and said
unto the Lord, Behold, Lord, the

b Ps.139.1-3. c Jn.14.23; Re.3.20. d Mat.9.11; ch.5.30.

---

ment. ¶ *He was rich.* Though this class of men was despised and often infamous, yet it seems that they were sometimes wealthy. They sustained, however, the general character of *sinners*, because they were particularly odious in the eyes of the Jews. See ver. 7. The evangelist has thought it worthy of record that he was rich, perhaps, because it was so unlikely that a *rich man* should follow so poor and despised a personage as Jesus of Nazareth, and because it was so unusual a thing during his personal ministry. Not many rich were called, but God chiefly chose the poor of this world. Comp. 1 Co. i. 26–29.

3. *Who he was.* Rather *what sort of person* he was, or how he appeared. He had that curiosity which is natural to men to see one of whom they have heard much. It would seem, also, that in this case mere *curiosity* led to his conversion and that of his family. Comp. 1 Co. xiv. 23–25. God makes use of every principle—of curiosity, or sympathy, or affection, or hope, or fear—to lead men in the way of salvation, and to impress truth on the minds of sinners. ¶ *The press.* The crowd; the multitude that surrounded Jesus. Earthly princes are often borne in splendid equipages, or even carried, as in Eastern nations, in palanquins on the shoulders of men. Jesus mingled with the multitude, not seeking distinctions of that sort, and perhaps, *in appearance*, not distinguished from thousands that followed him. ¶ *Little of stature.* Short. Not a tall man.

4. *A sycamore-tree.* See this described in the Notes on ch. xvii. 6.

5. *Abide at thy house.* Remain there, or put up with him. This was an honour which Zaccheus did not expect. The utmost, it seems, which he aimed at was to *see* Jesus; but, instead of that, Jesus proposed to remain with him, and to give him the benefit of his personal instruction. It is but one among a thousand instances where the Saviour goes, in bestowing mercies, far beyond the desert, the desire, or the expectation of men; and it is not improper to learn from this example that solicitude to behold the Saviour will not pass unnoticed by him, but will meet with his warm approbation, and be connected with his blessing. Jesus was willing to encourage efforts to come to him, and his benevolence prompted him to gratify the desires of the man who was solicitous to see him. He does not disdain the mansions of the rich any more than he does the dwelling-places of the poor, provided there be a humble heart; and he did not suppose there was *less* need of his presence in order to save in the house of the rich man than among the poor. He set an example to all his ministers, and was not afraid or ashamed to proclaim his gospel amid wealth. He was not awed by external splendour or grandeur.

7. *Murmured.* Found fault, complained. ¶ *To be a guest.* To remain with, or to be entertained by. ¶ *A man that is a sinner.* All publicans they regarded as great sinners, and the *chief* of the publicans, therefore, they regarded as peculiarly wicked. It would appear also from Zaccheus' confession that his character *had been* that of an oppressive man. But the people seemed to forget that he might be a penitent, and that the Messiah came to save that which was lost.

8. *The half of my goods I give to the poor.* It is not necessary to understand this as affirming that this *had* been his practice, or that he said this in the way of proclaiming his own righteousness. It may be understood rather as a purpose which he *then* formed under the teach-

half of my goods [e]I give to the poor; and if I have taken any thing from any man [f]by false accusation, I [g]restore *him* four-fold.

9 And Jesus said unto him, This day is salvation come to this house, forasmuch as he also is a [h]son of Abraham.

e Ps.41.1. f Ex.20.16; ch.3.14. g Ex.22.1; 2 Sa.12.6. h ch.13.16.

ing of Christ. He seems to have been sensible that he was a sinner. Of this he was convinced, as we may suppose, by the presence and discourse of Jesus. At first, attracted only by curiosity, or, it may be, by partial conviction that this was the Messiah, he had sought to see the Saviour; but his presence and conversation convinced him of his guilt, and he stood and openly confessed his sins, and expressed his purpose to give half his ill-gotten property to the poor. This was not a proclamation of his *own* righteousness, nor the *ground* of his righteousness, but it was the *evidence* of the sincerity of his repentance, and the confession which with the mouth is made unto salvation, Ro. x. 10. ¶ *And if I have taken.* His office gave him the power of oppressing the people, and it seems that he did not deny that it had been done. ¶ *By false accusation.* This is the same word which in Lu. iii. 14 is rendered "neither accuse any falsely." The accusation seems to have been so made that the person accused was obliged to pay much greater taxes, or so that his property came into the hands of the informer. There are many ways in which this might be done, but we do not know the exact manner. ¶ *I restore* him. We cannot suppose that this had been always his practice, for no man would wantonly extort money from another, and then restore him at once four times as much; but it means that he was made sensible of his guilt; perhaps that his mind had been a considerable time perplexed in the matter, and that now he was resolved to make the restoration. This was the *evidence* of his penitence and conversion. And here it may be remarked that this is *always* an indisputable evidence of a man's conversion to God. A man who has hoarded ill-gotten gold, if he becomes a Christian, will be disposed to do good with it. A man who has injured others—who has cheated them or defrauded them, *even by due forms of law*, must, if he be a Christian, be willing, as far as possible, to make restoration. Zaccheus, for anything that appears to the contrary, may have obtained this property by the decisions of courts of justice, but he now felt that it was wrong; and though the defrauded men could not *legally* recover it, yet his conscience told him that, in order to his being a true penitent, he must make restitution. One of the best evidences of true conversion is when it produces this result; and one of the surest evidences that a *professed* penitent is not a *true* one, is when he is *not* disposed to follow the example of this son of Abraham and make proper restitution. ¶ *Four-fold.* Four times as much as had been unjustly taken. This was the amount that was required in the Jewish law when a sheep had been stolen, and a man was convicted of the theft by trial at law, Ex. xxii. 1. If he *confessed* it himself, without being *detected* and tried, he had only to restore what was stolen, and add to it a fifth part of its value, Nu. v. 6, 7. The sincerity of Zaccheus' repentance was manifest by his being willing to make restoration as great as if it had been proved against him, evincing *his sense* of the wrong, and his purpose to make full restitution. The Jews were allowed to take *no interest* of their brethren (Le. xxv. 35, 36), and this is the reason why that is not mentioned as the measure of the restitution. When injury of this kind is done in other places, the least that is proper is to restore the principal and interest; for the injured person has a right *to all* that his property would have procured him if it had not been unjustly taken away.

9. *Salvation is come to this house.* This family. They have this day received the blessings of the gospel, and become interested in the Messiah's kingdom. Salvation *commences* when men truly receive Christ and their sins are pardoned; it is *completed* when the soul is sanctified and received up into heaven. ¶ *Forasmuch.* Because. For he has given *evidence* that he is a new man, and is disposed to forsake his sins and receive the gospel. ¶ *The son of Abraham.* Hitherto, although a Jew, yet he has been a sinner, and a great sinner. He was not worthy to be called a son of Abraham. Now, by repentance, and

10 For[i] the Son of man is come
to seek and to save [k]that which
was lost.

11 And as they heard these
things, he added and spake a parable, because he was nigh to Jerusalem, and [l]because they thought
that the kingdom of God should
immediately appear.

12 He said, therefore, [m]A certain
nobleman went into a far country,
to receive for himself a kingdom,
and to return.

13 And he called his ten ser-

i Mat.18.11. *k* Eze.34.16; Ro.5.6. *l* Ac.1.6. *m* Mat.25.14,&c.; Mar.13.34.

by receiving the Christ whose day Abraham saw and was glad (Jn. viii. 56), he has shown himself to be worthy to be called his son. Abraham was an example of distinguished piety; the father of the faithful (Ro. iv. 11), as well as the ancestor of the Jews. They were called his sons who were descended from him, and particularly they who *resembled* him. In this place the phrase is used in both senses.

10. See Notes on Mat. xviii. 11.

11. *He spake a parable.* This parable has in some respects a resemblance to the parable of the *talents* in Mat. xxv. 14–28, but it is not the same. They differ in the following respects: That was spoken *after* he had entered Jerusalem; this, while on his way there. That was delivered on the Mount of Olives; this, in the house of Zaccheus. That was delivered to teach them the necessity of *improving* the talents committed to them; this was for a different design. He was now near Jerusalem. A great multitude attended him. His disciples regarded him as the Messiah, and by this they understood a temporal prince who should deliver them from the dominion of the Romans and set them at liberty. They were anxious for that, and supposed that the time was at hand, and that *now*, as soon as he entered Jerusalem, he would assume the appearance of such a prince and set up his kingdom. To *correct that notion* seems to have been the main design of this parable. To do that, he tells them of a man who had a right to the kingdom, yet who, *before* taking possession of it, went into another kingdom to receive a confirmation of his title, thus intimating that *he* would also go away *before* he would completely set up his kingdom (ver. 12); he tells them that this nobleman left to his servants *property* to be improved in his absence, as *he* would leave to his disciples *talents* to be used in his service (ver. 12, 13); he tells them that this nobleman was rejected by his own citizens (ver. 14), as *he* would be by the Jews; and that he received the kingdom and called them to an account, as *he* also would his own disciples. ¶ *Because he was nigh to Jerusalem.* The capital of the country, and where they supposed he would probably set up his kingdom. ¶ *The kingdom of God should immediately appear.* That the reign of the Messiah would immediately commence. He spake the parable to *correct* that expectation.

12. *A certain nobleman.* A prince; a man descended from kings, and having a title, therefore, to succeed in the kingdom. ¶ *Went into a far country,* &c. This expression is derived from the state of things in Judea in the time of the Saviour. Judea was subject to the Romans, having been conquered by Pompey about sixty years before Christ. It was, however, governed by *Jews*, who held the government *under* the Romans. It was necessary that the prince or king should receive a recognition of his right to the kingdom by the Roman emperor, and, in order to this, that he should go to Rome; or, as it is said here, that he might receive to himself a kingdom. This actually occurred several times. Archelaus, a son of Herod the Great, about the time of the birth of Jesus, went to Rome to obtain a confirmation of the title which his father had left him, and succeeded in doing it. Herod the Great, his father, had done the same thing before to secure the aid and countenance of Antony. Agrippa the younger, grandson of Herod the Great, went to Rome also to obtain the favour of Tiberius, and to be confirmed in his government. Such instances, having frequently occurred, would make this parable perfectly intelligible to those to whom it was addressed. By the nobleman, here, is undoubtedly represented the Messiah, the Lord Jesus Christ; by his going into a far country is denoted his going to heaven, to the right hand of his Father, *before* he should *fully* set up his kingdom and establish his reign among men.

vants, and delivered them ten pounds,[1] and said unto them, Occupy till I come.

14 But[n] his citizens hated him, and sent a message after him, saying, We will not have this *man* to reign over us.

15 And it came to pass, that when he was returned, having received the kingdom, then he commanded those servants to be called unto him, to whom he had given the [2]money, that he might know how much every man had gained by trading.

16 Then came the first, saying, Lord, thy pound hath gained ten pounds.

17 And he said unto him, Well, thou good servant; because thou hast been [o]faithful in a very little, have thou authority over ten cities.

18 And the second came, saying, Lord, thy pound hath gained five pounds.

19 And he said likewise to him, Be thou also over five cities.

20 And another came, saying, Lord, behold, *here is* thy pound, which I have kept laid up in a napkin;

21 For I feared thee, because

1 *Mina*, here translated a *pound*, is 12 ounces and a half, which, at 5 shillings the ounce, is £3, 2*s*. 6*d*. *n* Jn.1.11; 15.18. 2 *silver*, and so ver.23.

o ch.16.10.

13. *Ten servants.* Nothing in particular is denoted by the number *ten.* It is a circumstance intended to keep up the narrative. In general, by these servants our Saviour denotes his disciples, and intends to teach us that talents are given us to be improved, for which we must give an account at his return. ¶ *Ten pounds.* The word translated *pound* here denotes the Hebrew *minah*, which was equal to about 15 dollars, or £3. The pounds here denote the talents which God has given to his servants on earth to improve, and for which they must give an account in the day of judgment. ¶ *Occupy till I come.* The word *occupy* here means not merely to *possess*, as it often does in our language, but to *improve*, to employ *in business*, for the purpose of increasing it or of making *profit* on it. The direction was to use this money so as to gain *more* against his return. So Jesus commands his disciples to *improve* their talents; to make the most of them; to increase their capability of doing good, and to do it *until* he comes to call us hence, by death, to meet him. See 1 Co. xii. 7; Ep. iv. 7.

14. *But his citizens.* His *subjects*, or the people whom he was desirous of ruling. ¶ *Hated him.* On account of his character, and their fear of oppression. This was, in fact, the case with regard to Archelaus, the Jewish prince, who went to Rome to be confirmed in his kingdom. ¶ *Sent a message, saying*, &c. His discontented subjects, fearing what would be the character of his reign, sent an embassy to remonstrate against his being appointed as the ruler. This actually took place. Archelaus went to Rome to obtain from Augustus a confirmation of his title to reign over that part of Judea which had been left him by his father, Herod the Great. The Jews, knowing his character (comp. Mat. ii. 22), sent an embassy of fifty men to Rome, to prevail on Augustus *not* to confer the title on him, but they could not succeed. He *received* the kingdom, and reigned in Judea in the place of his father. As this fact was *fresh* in the memory of the Jews, it makes this parable much more striking. By this part of it Christ designed to denote that the Jews would reject *him* —the Messiah, and would say that they did not desire him to reign over them. See Jn. i. 11. So it is true of all sinners that they do not *wish* Jesus to reign over them, and, if it were possible, would cast him off, and never submit to his reign.

15. See Notes on Mat. xxv. 19.

16–19. See Notes on Mat. xxv. 20, 21. ¶ *Ten cities.* We are not to suppose that this will be *literally* fulfilled in heaven. Christ teaches here that our reward in heaven will be *in proportion* to our faithfulness in improving our talents on earth.

20. *A napkin.* A towel. He means by it that he had not wasted it nor thrown it by carelessly, but had been *very careful* of it; so much so as to be at the pains to tie it up in a towel and put it in a safe place, as if he had been *very faithful* to his trust. So many

thou art an austere man: thou
takest up that thou layedst not
down, and reapest that thou didst
not sow.
22 And he saith unto him, [p]Out
of thine own mouth will I judge
thee, *thou* wicked servant. Thou
knewest that I was an austere man,
taking up that I laid not down,
and reaping that I did not sow:
23 Wherefore,[q] then, gavest not
thou my money into the bank, that
at my coming I might have required mine own with usury?
24 And he said unto them that
stood by, Take from him the
pound, and give *it* to him that
hath ten pounds.
25 (And they said unto him,
Lord, he hath ten pounds.)
26 For I say unto you, [r]That unto
every one which hath shall be
given; and from him that hath
not, even that he hath shall be
taken away from him.
27 But those [s]mine enemies,
which would not that I should
reign over them, bring hither, and
slay *them* before me.
28 And when he had thus spoken,
he went before, ascending up to
Jerusalem.

p 2 Sa.1.16; Job 15.6; Mat.12.37; 22.12; Ro.3.19.
q Ro.2.4,5.
r Mat.13.12; 25.29; Mar.4.25; ch.8.18.
s Ps.2.4,5,9; 21.8,9; Is.66.6,14; Na.1.2,8; He.10.13.

men employ their talents, their learning, their property, their influence. They *have* them; they *keep* them; but they never *use* them in the service of the Lord Jesus; and, in regard to their influence on the church or the world, it would be the same if God had never conferred on them these talents.

21. *An austere man.* Hard, severe, oppressive. The word is commonly applied to unripe fruit, and means *sour*, unpleasant, harsh. In this case it means that the man was taking every advantage, and, while *he* lived in idleness, was making his living out of the toils of others. ¶ *Thou takest up*, &c. Thou dost exact of others what thou didst not give. The phrase is applied to a man who *finds* what has been lost by another, and keeps it himself, and refuses to return it to the owner. All this is designed to show the sinner's view of God. He regards him as unjust, demanding more than man has *power* to render, and more, therefore, than God has a *right* to demand. See Notes on Mat. xxv. 24.

22. *Out of thine own mouth.* By your own statement, or your own views of my character. If you *knew* that this was my character, and *knew* that I would be rigid, firm, and even severe, it would have been the part of wisdom in you to have made the best use of the money in your power; but as you *knew* my character beforehand, and was well acquainted with the fact that I should demand a strict compliance with your obligation, you have no right to complain if you are condemned accordingly. We are not to suppose that God is *unjust* or *austere;* but what we are to learn from this is, that as men know that God will be *just*, and will call them to a strict account in the day of judgment, they ought to be prepared to meet him, and that they cannot then complain if God should condemn them.

23. *The bank.* The treasury, or the place of exchange. Why did you not loan it out, that it might be increased? ¶ *Usury.* Interest.

25. *And they said unto him.* Those standing around him said. ¶ *He hath*, &c. This was probably an observation made by some of the by-standers, as if surprised at such a decision. "He has already *ten pounds.* Why take away this *one*, and add to what he already possesses? Why should *his* property be increased at the expense of this man, who has but one pound?" The answer to this is given in the following verse, that every one that hath, to him shall be given; every man who is faithful, and improves what God gives him, shall receive much more.

26, 27. *For I say*, &c. These are the words of the *nobleman* declaring the principles on which he would distribute the rewards of his kingdom. ¶ *But those mine enemies.* By the punishment of those who would not that he should reign over them is denoted the ruin that was to come upon the Jewish nation for rejecting the Messiah, and also upon all sinners for not receiving him as their king. See Notes on the parable of the talents in Mat. xxv.

28–39. See Notes on Mat. xxi. 1–16.

29 And[t] it came to pass, when he was come nigh to Bethphage and Bethany, at the mount called *the mount* of Olives, he sent two of his disciples,

30 Saying, Go ye into the village over against *you;* in the which, at your entering, ye shall find a colt tied, whereon yet never man sat: loose him, and bring *him hither.*

31 And if any man ask you, Why do ye loose *him?* thus shall ye say unto him, [u]Because the Lord hath need of him.

32 And they that were sent went their way, and found even as he had said unto them.

33 And as they were loosing the colt, the owners thereof said unto them, Why loose ye the colt?

34 And they said, The Lord hath need of him.

35 And they brought him to Jesus; and they [v]cast their garments upon the colt, and they [w]set Jesus thereon.

36 And as he went they spread their clothes in the way.

37 And when he was come nigh, even now at the descent of the mount of Olives, the whole multitude of the disciples began to rejoice and praise God with a loud voice, for all the mighty works that they had seen;

38 Saying, [x]Blessed *be* the King that cometh in the name of the Lord; [y]peace in heaven, and glory in the highest.

39 And some of the Pharisees from among the multitude said unto him, Master, rebuke thy disciples.

40 And he answered and said unto them, I tell you, that if these should hold their peace, [z]the stones would immediately cry out.

41 And when he was come near, he beheld the city, and [a]wept over it,

42 Saying, If thou hadst known, even thou, at least in this [b]thy day, the things *which belong* unto thy peace! But now they are hid from thine eyes.

43 For the days shall come upon thee, that thine enemies shall [c]cast a trench about thee, and compass thee round, and keep thee in on every side,

44 And[d] shall lay thee even with the ground, and thy children with-

t Mat.21.1,&c.; Mar.11.1,&c.
u Ps.50.10. *v* 2 Ki.9.13. *w* Jn.12.14.

x Ps.118.26; ch.13.35. *y* ch.2.14; Ro.5.1; Ep.2.14.
z Hab.2.11; Mat.3.9.
a Ps.119.136; Je.9.1; 13.17; 17.16; Jn.11.35.
b Ps.95.7,8; He.3.7,13,15. *c* Is.29.2,3; Je.6.5,6.
d 1 Ki.9.7,8; Mi.3.12; Mat.23.37,38; ch.13.34,35.

40. *The stones would—cry out.* It is *proper* that they should celebrate my coming. Their acclamations *ought* not to be suppressed. So joyful is the event which they celebrate—the coming of the Messiah—that it is not fit that I should attempt to impose silence on them. The expression here seems to be *proverbial*, and is not to be taken literally. Proverbs are designed to express the truth *strongly*, but are not to be taken to signify as much as if they were to be interpreted literally. The sense is, that his coming was an event of so much importance that it *ought* to be celebrated in some way, and *would* be celebrated. It would be impossible to restrain the people, and improper to attempt it. The language here is strong proverbial language to denote that fact. We are not to suppose, therefore, that our Saviour meant to say that the stones were *conscious* of his coming, or that God would *make* them speak, but only that there was *great joy* among the people; that it was *proper* that they should express it in this manner, and that it was not fit that he should attempt to repress it.

41–44. *He wept over it.* Showing his compassion for the guilty city, and his strong sense of the evils that were about to come upon it. See Notes on Mat. xxiii. 37–39. As he entered the city he passed over the Mount of Olives. From that mountain there was a full and magnificent view of the city. See Notes on Mat. xxi. 1. The view of the splendid capital—the knowledge of its crimes—the remembrance of the mercies of God toward it—the certainty that it might have been spared if it had received the

in thee; and [e]they shall not leave in thee one stone upon another; because [f]thou knewest not the time of thy visitation.

45 And[g] he went into the temple, and began to cast out them that sold therein, and them that bought;

46 Saying unto them, It is written, [h]My house is the house of prayer, but ye have made it a [i]den of thieves.

47 And he [k]taught daily in the temple. But the chief priests and the scribes, and the chief of the people, sought to destroy him;

e Mat.24.2; Mar.13.2. f La.1.8; 1 Pe.2.12. g Mat.21.12,13; Mar.11.15-17; Jn.2.15,17. h Is.56.7. i Je.7.11. k Jn.18.20.

prophets and himself—the knowledge that it was about to put *him*, their long-expected Messiah, to death, and *for* that to be given up to utter desolation—affected his heart, and the triumphant King and Lord of Zion wept! Amid all *his* prosperity, and all the acclamations of the multitude, the heart of the Redeemer of the world was turned from the tokens of rejoicing to the miseries about to come on a guilty people. Yet they *might* have been saved. If thou hadst known, says he, even thou, with all thy guilt, the things that make for thy peace; if thou hadst repented, had been righteous, and had received the Messiah; if thou hadst not stained thy hands with the blood of the prophets, and shouldst not with that of the Son of God, then these terrible calamities would not come upon thee. But it is too late. The national wickedness is too great; the cup is full; mercy is exhausted; and Jerusalem, with all her pride and splendour, the glory of her temple, and the pomp of her service, *must perish!* ¶ *For the days shall come*, &c. This took place under Titus, the Roman general, A.D. 70, about thirty years after this was spoken. ¶ *Cast a trench about thee.* The word *trench* now means commonly a *pit* or *ditch*. When the Bible was translated, it meant also *earth thrown up to defend a camp* (Johnson's *Dictionary*). This is the meaning of the original here. It is not a pit or large *ditch*, but a pile of earth, stones, or wood thrown up to guard a camp, and to defend it from the approach of an enemy. This was done at the siege of Jerusalem. Josephus informs us that Titus, in order that he might compel the city to surrender by *famine*, built a wall around the whole circumference of the city. This wall was nearly 5 miles in length, and was furnished with thirteen castles or towers. This work was completed with incredible labour in ten days. The professed design of this wall was *to keep* the city *in on every side*. Never was a prophecy more strikingly accomplished. ¶ *Shall lay thee even with the ground*, &c. This was literally done. Titus caused a plough to pass over the place where the temple stood. See Notes on Mat. xxiv. All this was done, says Christ, because Jerusalem knew not the time of its visitation—that is, did not know, and *would not* know, that the Messiah had come. *His coming* was the time of their merciful visitation. That time had been predicted, and invaluable blessings promised as the result of his advent; but they would not know it. They rejected him, they put him to death, and it was just that they should be destroyed.

45, 46. See Notes on Mat. xxi. 12, 13.

47. *Daily in the temple.* That is, for five or six days before his crucifixion.

48. *Could not find*, &c. Were not able to accomplish their purpose; they did not know *how* to bring it about. ¶ *Very attentive.* Literally, *hung upon him* to hear him. The word denotes an anxious desire, a fixed attention, a cleaving to him, and an unwillingness to *leave* him, so that they might hear his words. This is always the case when men become anxious about their salvation. They manifest it by hanging on the preaching of the gospel; by fixed attention; and by an unwillingness to leave the place where the word of God is preached. In view of the fact that the Lord Jesus wept over Jerusalem, we may remark:

(1.) It was on account of the sins and danger of the inhabitants, and of the fact that they had rejected offered mercy.

(2.) There was *occasion* for weeping. Jesus would not have wept had there been no cause for it. If they were in no danger, if there was no punishment in the future world, why should he have wept? When the Lord Jesus weeps over sinners, it is the fullest proof that they are in danger.

48 And could not find what they
might do; for all the people [3]were
very attentive to hear him.

CHAPTER XX.

AND[a] it came to pass, *that* on
one of those days, as he
taught the people in the temple,
and preached the gospel, the chief
priests and the scribes came upon
him, with the elders,
2 And spake unto him, saying,
Tell us, [b]by what authority doest
thou these things? or who is he
that gave thee this authority?
3 And he answered and said
unto them, I will also ask you one
thing; and answer me:
4 The baptism of John, was it
from heaven or of men?
5 And they reasoned with themselves, saying, If we shall say, From
heaven, he will say, Why, then,
believed ye him not?
6 But and if we say, Of men,
all the people will stone us; [c]for
they be persuaded that John was
a prophet.
7 And they answered that they
could not tell whence *it was*.
8 And Jesus said unto them,

[3] or, *hanged on him*.
a Mat.21.23,&c.; Mar.11.27,&c.
b Ac.4.7-10; 7.27. *c* Mat.14.5.

Neither tell I you by what authority I do these things.
9 Then began he to speak to the
people this parable: [d]A certain
man [e]planted a vineyard, and let
it forth to husbandmen, and went
into a far country for a long time.
10 And at the season he sent a
servant to the husbandmen, that
they should give him of the [f]fruit
of the vineyard; but the husbandmen beat him, and sent *him* away
empty.
11 And again he sent another
servant; and they beat him also,
and entreated *him* shamefully, and
sent *him* away empty.
12 And again he sent a third;
and they wounded him also, and
cast *him* out.
13 Then said the lord of the
vineyard, What shall I do? I will
send my beloved son: it may be
they will reverence *him*, when they
see him.
14 But when the husbandmen
saw him, they reasoned among
themselves, saying, This is [g]the
heir: come, [h]let us kill him, that
the inheritance may be ours.

d Mat.21.33,&c.; Mar.12.1,&c.
e Ca.8.11,12; Is.5.1-7. *f* Jn.15.16; Ro.7.4.
g Ps.2.8; Ro.8.17; He.1.2.
h Mat.27.21-25; Ac.2.23; 3.15.

(3.) Sinners are in the same danger now. They reject Christ as sinners did then. They despise the gospel as they did then. They refuse now to come to him as the inhabitants of Jerusalem did. Why are they not then in the same danger?

(4.) Deep feeling, gushing emotions, lively affections, are proper in religion. If the Saviour wept, it is not improper for us to weep—it is right. Nay, can it be right *not* to weep over the condition of lost man.

(5.) Religion is tenderness and love. It led the Saviour to weep, and it teaches us to sympathize and to feel deeply. Sin hardens the heart, and makes it insensible to every pure and noble emotion; but religion teaches us to feel "for others' woes," and to sympathize in the danger of others.

(6.) Christians and Christian ministers should weep over lost sinners. They have souls just as precious as they had then; they are in the same danger; they are going to the judgment-bar; they are wholly insensible to their danger and their duty.

"Did Christ o'er sinners weep?
And shall our cheeks be dry?
Let floods of penitential grief
Burst forth from every eye.

"The Son of God in tears,
Angels with wonder see!
Be thou astonished, O my soul;
He shed those tears for thee.

"He wept that we might weep;
Each sin demands a tear;
In heaven alone no sin is found,
And there's no weeping there."

CHAPTER XX.

1-9. See this passage explained in the Notes on Mat. xxi. 23-27.

9-19. See this parable explained in the Notes on Mat. xxi. 33-45.

15 So they cast him out of the vineyard, and killed *him*. What, therefore, shall the lord of the vineyard do unto them?

16 He shall come and destroy these husbandmen, and shall [i]give the vineyard to others. And when they heard *it*, they said, God forbid.

17 And he beheld them, and said, What is this, then, that is written, The[k] stone which the builders rejected, the same is become the head of the corner?

18 Whosoever shall fall upon that stone shall be broken; [l]but on whomsoever it shall fall, it will grind him to powder.

19 And the chief priests and the scribes the same hour sought to lay hands on him; and they feared the people; for they perceived that he had spoken this parable against them.

20 And they watched *him*, and sent forth spies, which should feign themselves just men, [m]that they might take hold of his words, that so they might deliver him unto the power and authority of the governor.

21 And they asked him, saying, Master, we know that thou sayest and teachest rightly, neither acceptest thou the person *of any*, but teachest the way of God [1]truly:

22 Is it lawful for us to give tribute unto Cæsar, or no?

23 But he perceived their craftiness, and said unto them, Why tempt ye me?

24 Show me a [2]penny. Whose image and superscription hath it? They answered and said, Cæsar's.

25 And he said unto them, Render,[n] therefore, unto Cæsar the things which be Cæsar's, and unto God the things which be God's.

i Ne.9.36,37. *k* Ps.118.22. *l* Da.2.34,35. *m* Mat.22.15,&c.; Mar.12.13. 1 or, *of a truth*. 2 See Mat.18.28. *n* Ro.13.7.

20–38. See this explained in the Notes on Mat. xxii. 15–33, and Mar. xii. 13–27.

26 And they could not take hold of his words before the people; and they marvelled at his answer, and [o]held their peace.

27 Then[p] came to *him* certain of the [q]Sadducees, which deny that there is any resurrection; and they asked him,

28 Saying, Master, Moses wrote unto us, [r]If any man's brother die, having a wife, and he die without children, that his brother should take his wife, and raise up seed unto his brother.

29 There were therefore seven brethren; and the first took a wife and died without children.

30 And the second took her to wife, and he died childless.

31 And the third took her; and in like manner the seven also; and they left no children, and died.

32 Last of all the woman died also.

33 Therefore in the resurrection whose wife of them is she? for seven had her to wife.

34 And Jesus answering said unto them, The children of this world marry, and are given in marriage;

35 But they which shall be [s]accounted worthy to obtain that world, and the resurrection from the dead, neither marry nor are given in marriage:

36 Neither[t] can they die any more; for they are [u]equal unto the angels, and are [v]the children of God, being the children of the resurrection.

37 Now that the dead are raised, even Moses [w]showed at the bush, when he calleth the Lord the God of Abraham, and the God of Isaac, and the God of Jacob.

o Tit.1.10,11. *p* Mat.22.23,&c.; Mar.12.18,&c. *q* Ac.23.6,8. *r* De.25.5-8. *s* ch.21.36; Re.3.4. *t* Re.21.4. *u* 1 Co.15.49,52; 1 Jn.3.2. *v* Ro.8.17. *w* Ex.3.2-6.

39. See Notes on Mar. xii. 32.
40–44. See Notes on Mat. xxii. 41–46.
45–47. See Notes on Mat. xxiii. 1.

38 For he is not a God of the
dead, but of the living; [x]for all
live unto him.
39 Then certain of the scribes
answering, said, Master, thou hast
well said.
40 And after that they durst
not ask him any *question at all.*
41 And[y] he said unto them,
How say they that Christ is
David's son?
42 And David himself saith in
the book of Psalms, [z]The Lord
said unto my Lord, Sit thou on
my right hand,
43 Till I make thine enemies
thy footstool.
44 David therefore calleth him
Lord; how is he then his son?
45 Then, in the audience [a]of
all the people, he said unto his
disciples,
46 Beware[b] of the scribes, which
desire to walk in long robes, and
love [c]greetings in the markets, and
the highest seats in the synagogues,
and the chief rooms at feasts;
47 Which[d] devour widows'
houses, and for a [e]show make long
prayers: the same shall [f]receive
greater damnation.

CHAPTER XXI.

AND he looked up, [a]and saw
the rich men casting their
gifts into the treasury.
2 And he saw also a certain
poor widow casting in thither two
[1]mites.
3 And he said, Of a truth I
say unto you, that this poor
widow hath cast in [b]more than
they all;
4 For all these have of their
abundance cast in unto the offerings of God, but she of her penury
hath cast in all the living that
she had.
5 And[c] as some spake of the
temple, how it was adorned with
goodly stones and gifts, he said,
6 *As for* these things which ye
behold, the days will come in the
which [d]there shall not be left one
stone upon another that shall not
be thrown down.
7 And they asked him, saying,
Master, but when shall these things
be? and what sign *will there be*
when these things shall come to
pass?
8 And he said, [e]Take heed that
ye be not deceived; for many shall
come in my name, saying, I am
Christ; and [f]the time draweth near:
go ye not, therefore, after them.
9 But when ye shall hear of wars
and commotions, [g]be not terrified;
for these things must first come to
pass, but the end *is* not by and by.
10 Then said he unto them,
[h]Nation shall rise against nation,
and kingdom against kingdom;

x Ro.14.8,9. y Mat.22.42; Mar.12.35,&c. z Ps.110.1; Ac.2.34. a 1 Ti.5.20. b Mar.12.38,&c. c ch.11.43. d Is.10.2; Mat.23.14; 2 Ti.3.6. e 1 Th.2.5. f ch.10.12,14; Ja.3.1. a Mar.12.41.

1 See Mar.12.42. b 2 Co.8.12. c Mat.24.1,&c.; Mar.13.1,&c. d ch.19.44,&c. e 2 Th.2.3,9,10; 1 Jn.4.1; 2 Jn.7. f Re.1.3. g Pr.3.25,26. h Hag.2.22.

CHAPTER XXI.

1-4. See this explained in the Notes on Mar. xii. 41-44.

4. *Penury.* Poverty.

5. *Goodly stones.* Beautiful stones. Either referring to the large, square, and well-finished stones of which the eastern wall was built, or to the precious stones which might have been used in decorating the temple itself. See Notes on Mar. xiii. 1. ¶ *Gifts.* This word properly denotes anything devoted or dedicated to God. Anciently warriors dedicated to their gods the spoils of war—the shields, and helmets, and armour, and garments of those slain in battle. These were suspended in the temples. It would seem that something of this kind had occurred in the temple of Jerusalem, and that the people, to express their gratitude to God, had suspended on the pillars and porches of the temple gifts and offerings. Josephus mentions particularly a golden *vine* with which Herod the Great had adorned the columns of the temple (*Antiq.* xiii. 8). See also 2 Mac. v. 16; ix. 16.

11 And great earthquakes shall
be in divers places, and famines,
and pestilences; and fearful sights
and great signs shall there be from
heaven.
12 But before all these they shall
lay their hands on you, and persecute
you, delivering *you* up to the synagogues, and [i]into prisons, being
brought[k] before kings and rulers
for my name's sake.
13 And[l] it shall turn to you for
a testimony.
14 Settle *it*, therefore, in your
hearts [m]not to meditate before
what ye shall answer;
15 For I will give you a mouth and
wisdom which all your adversaries
shall [n]not be able to gainsay nor
resist.
16 And[o] ye shall be betrayed both
by parents, and brethren, and kins-
folks, and friends; [p]and *some* of you
shall they cause to be put to death.
17 And ye shall be [q]hated of all
men for my name's sake.
18 But[r] there shall not a hair of
your head perish.
19 In[s] your patience possess ye
your souls.
20 And when ye shall see Jerusalem compassed with armies, then
know that the desolation thereof is
nigh.
21 Then let them which are in
Judea flee to the mountains; and
let them which are in the midst of
it depart out; and let not them that
are in the countries enter thereinto.
22 For these be the days of vengeance, that [t]all things which are
written may be fulfilled.
23 But woe unto [u]them that are
with child, and to them that give

i Ac.4.3; 5.18; 12.4; 16.24; Re.2.10. *k* Ac.25.23.
l Phi.1.28; 2 Th.1.5. *m* Mat.10.19; ch.12.11.
n Ac.6.10. *o* Mi.7.5,6.
p Ac.7.59; 12.2; 26.10; Re.2.13; 6.9; 12.11.
q Jn.17.14. *r* Mat.10.30.
s Ro.5.3; He.10.36; Ja.1.4.
t De.28.25,48; Da.9.26,27; Zec.11.6; 14.1,2.
u La.4.10.

---

6. See Notes on Mat. xxiv. 2.

7–36. The account of the destruction of Jerusalem contained in this chapter has been fully considered in the Notes on Mat. xxiv. All that will be necessary here will be an explanation of a few words that did not occur in that chapter.

9. *Commotions.* Insurrections. Subjects rising against their rulers.

11. *Fearful sights.* See Mat. xxiv. 7.

12, 13. *Synagogues, and into prisons.* See Notes on Mar. xiii. 9, 10.

14. *Settle it, therefore, in your hearts.* Fix it firmly in your minds—so firmly as to become a settled principle—that you are always to depend on God for aid in all your trials. See Mar. xiii. 11.

15. *A mouth.* Eloquence, ability to speak as the case may demand. Comp. Ex. iv. 11. ¶ *Gainsay.* Speak against. They will not be able to *reply* to it, or to *resist* the force of what you shall say.

18. *A hair of your head perish.* This is a proverbial expression, denoting that they should not suffer any essential injury. This was strikingly fulfilled in the fact that in the calamities of Jerusalem there is reason to believe that no Christian suffered. Before those calamities came on the city they had fled to *Pella*, a city on the east of the Jordan. See Notes on Mat. xxiv. 18.

19. *In your patience.* Rather by your perseverance. The word *patience* here means constancy or perseverance in sustaining afflictions. ¶ *Possess ye your souls.* Some read here the *future* instead of the *present* of the verb rendered *possess.* The word *possess* means here to *preserve* or keep, and the word *souls* means *lives.* This passage may be thus translated: By persevering in bearing these trials you *will* save your lives, or you will be safe; or, by persevering *preserve* your lives; that is, do not yield to these calamities, but bear up under them, for he that endureth to the end, the same shall be saved. Comp. Mat. xxiv. 13.

22. *All things which are written may be fulfilled.* Judgment had been threatened by almost all the prophets against that wicked city. They had spoken of its crimes and threatened its ruin. Once God had destroyed Jerusalem and carried the people to Babylon; but their crimes had been repeated when they returned, and God had again threatened their ruin. Particularly was this very destruction foretold by Daniel,

suck in those days! for there shall
be great distress in the land, and
wrath upon this people.
24 And they shall fall by the
edge of the sword, and shall be led
away captive into all nations; [v]and
Jerusalem shall be trodden down
of the Gentiles [w]until the times of
the Gentiles be fulfilled.
25 And there shall be signs in
the sun, and in the moon, and in
the stars; and upon the earth [x]distress
of nations, with perplexity;
the sea and the waves roaring;

v Da.12.7; Re.11.2. w Ro.11.25. x Da.12.1.

---

ch. ix. 26, 27: "And after threescore and two weeks shall Messiah be cut off, but not for himself; and the people of the prince that shall come *shall destroy the city and the sanctuary;* and the end thereof shall be with a flood, and unto the end of the war desolations are determined." See Notes on that passage.

24. *Shall fall*, &c. No less than one million one hundred thousand perished in the siege of Jerusalem. ¶ *Shall be led away captive.* More than ninety thousand were led into captivity. See Notes on Mat. xxiv. ¶ *Shall be trodden down by the Gentiles.* Shall be in possession of the Gentiles, or be subject to them. The expression also implies that it would be an *oppressive* subjection, as when a captive in war is trodden down under the feet of the conqueror. Anciently conquerors *trod on* the necks of those who were subdued by them, Jos. x. 24; 2 Sa. xxii. 41; Eze. xxi. 29. The bondage of Jerusalem has been long and very oppressive. It was for a long time under the dominion of the Romans, then of the Saracens, and is now of the Turks, and is aptly represented by a captive stretched on the ground whose neck is *trodden* by the foot of the conqueror. ¶ *Until the times of the Gentiles be fulfilled.* This passage has been understood very differently by different expositors. Some refer it to the time which the Romans who conquered it had dominion over it, as signifying that *they* should keep possession of it until a part of the pagans should be converted, when it should be rebuilt. Thus it was rebuilt by the Emperor Adrian. Others suppose that it refers to the end of the world, when all the Gentiles shall be converted, and they shall *cease* to be Gentiles by becoming Christians, meaning that it should *always* be desolate. Others, that Christ meant to say that in the times of the millennium, when the gospel should spread universally, he would reign personally on the earth, and that the *Jews* would return and rebuild Jerusalem and the temple. This is the opinion of the Jews and of many Christians. The meaning of the passage clearly is, 1st. That Jerusalem would be completely destroyed. 2d. That this would be done by Gentiles—that is, by the Roman armies. 3d. That this desolation would continue as long as God should judge it proper in a fit manner to express his abhorrence of the crimes of the nation—that is, until the times allotted to *them* by God for this desolation should be accomplished, without specifying how long that would be, or what would occur to the city after that. It *may* be rebuilt, and inhabited by converted Jews. Such a thing is *possible*, and the Jews naturally seek that as their home; but whether this be so or not, the time when the *Gentiles*, as such, shall have dominion over the city is limited. Like all other cities on the earth, it will yet be brought under the influence of the gospel, and will be inhabited by the true friends of God. Pagan, infidel, anti-Christian dominion shall cease there, and it will be again a place where God will be worshipped in sincerity—a place *even then* of peculiar interest from the recollection of the events which have occurred there. *How long* it is to be before this occurs is known only to Him "who hath put the times and seasons in his own power," Ac. i. 7.

25. See Notes on Mat. xxiv. 29. ¶ *Upon the earth distress of nations.* Some have proposed to render the word *earth* by *land*, confining it to Judea. It often has this meaning, and there seems some propriety in so using it here. The word translated *distress* denotes anxiety of mind—such an anxiety as men have when they do not know what to do to free themselves from calamities; and it means here that the calamities would be so great and overwhelming that they would not know what to do to escape. There would be a want of counsel, and deep anxiety at the impending evils. ¶ *With perplexity.* Rather *on account* of their perplexity,

26 Men's hearts failing them for fear, and for looking after those things which are coming on the earth; for [y]the powers of heaven shall be shaken.

27 And then shall they [z]see the Son of man coming in a cloud with power and great glory.

28 And when these things begin to come to pass, then look up and lift up your heads, for [a]your redemption draweth nigh.

29 And[b] he spake to them a parable: Behold the fig-tree, and all the trees;

30 When they now shoot forth, ye see and know of your own selves that summer is now nigh at hand.

31 So likewise ye, when ye see these things come to pass, know ye that the kingdom of God is nigh at hand.

32 Verily I say unto you, This generation shall not pass away till all be fulfilled.

33 Heaven[c] and earth shall pass away, but my word shall not pass away.

34 And[d] take heed to yourselves, lest at any time your hearts be overcharged with [e]surfeiting, and drunkenness, and cares of this life,

y 2 Pe.3.10-12. *z* Re.1.7; 14.14. *a* Ro.8.23. *b* Mat.24.32; Mar.13.28.

c Is.40.8; 51.6. *d* Ro.13.12,13; 1 Th.5.6-8; 1 Pe.4.7. *e* Is.28.1-3; 1 Co.6.10.

or the desperate state of their affairs. The Syriac has it, "perplexity or *wringing of hands*," which is a sign of deep distress and horror. ¶ *The sea and the waves roaring.* This is not to be understood literally, but as an image of great distress. Probably it is designed to denote that these calamities would come upon them like a deluge. As when in a storm the ocean roars, and wave rolls on wave and dashes against the shore, and each succeeding surge is more violent than the one that preceded it, so would the calamities come upon Judea. They would roll over the whole land, and each wave of trouble would be more violent than the one that preceded it, until the whole country would be desolate. The same image is also used in Is. viii. 7, 8, and Re. xviii. 15.

26. *Men's hearts failing them.* This is an expression denoting the highest terror. The word rendered *failing* commonly denotes *to die*, and here it means that the terror would be so great that men would faint and be ready to die in view of the approaching calamities. And if this was true in respect to the judgments about to come upon Judea, how much more so will it be in the day of judgment, when the wicked will be arraigned before the Son of God, and when they shall have before them the prospect of the awful sufferings of hell—the pains and woes which shall continue for ever! It will be no wonder, then, if they call on the rocks and mountains to hide them from the face of God, and if their hearts sink within them at the prospect of eternal suffering.

28. *Your redemption draweth nigh.* See Notes on Mat. xxiv. 33. This is expressed in the 31st verse thus: "the kingdom of God is nigh at hand"—that is, from that time God will signally build up his kingdom. It shall be fully established when the Jewish policy shall come to an end; when the temple shall be destroyed, and the Jews scattered abroad. Then the power of the Jews shall be at an end; they shall no longer be able to persecute you, and you shall be completely delivered from all these trials and calamities in Judea.

34. *Lest at any time your hearts be overcharged,* &c. The meaning of this verse is, "Be continually expecting these things. Do not forget them, and do not be *secure* and satisfied with this life and the good things which it furnishes. Do not suffer yourselves to be drawn into the fashions of the world; to be conformed to its customs; to partake of its feasts and revelry; and so these calamities shall come upon you when you least expect them." And from this we may learn—what alas! we may from the *lives* of many professing Christians—that there is need of cautioning the disciples of Jesus now that they do not indulge in the festivities of this life, and *forget* that they are to die and come to judgment. How many, alas! who bear the Christian name, have forgotten this caution of the Saviour, and live as if their lives were secure; as if they feared not death; as if there were no heaven and no judgment! Christians

and *so* that day come upon you
unawares.
35 For[f] as a snare shall it come
on all them that dwell on the face
of the whole earth.
36 Watch[g] ye, therefore, and pray
always, that ye may be [h]accounted
worthy to escape all these things
that shall come to pass, and [i]to stand
[k]before the Son of man.
37 And in the day-time he was
teaching in the temple; and at
night he went out, and abode in
the [l]mount that is called *the mount*
of Olives.
38 And all the people came
early in the morning to him in
the temple, for to hear him.

f 1 Th.5.2; 2 Pe.3.10; Re.16.15. g Mat.25.13. h ch.20.35. i Ps.1.5. k Jude 24. l Jn.8.1,2.

should feel that they are soon to die, and that their portion is not in this life; and, feeling this, they should be *looking for and hasting unto the coming of the day of God.* ¶ *Overcharged.* Literally, *be made heavy*, as is the case with those who have eaten and drunken too much. ¶ *Surfeiting.* Excessive eating and drinking, so as to oppress the body; indulgence in the pleasures of the table. This word does not include *intoxication*, but merely indulgence in food and drink, though the food and drink should be in themselves lawful. ¶ *Drunkenness.* Intoxication, intemperance in drinking. The ancients were not acquainted with the poison that we chiefly use on which to become drunk. They had no distilled spirits. They became intoxicated on wine, and strong drink made of a mixture of dates, honey, &c. All nations have contrived some way to become intoxicated—to bring in folly, and disease, and poverty, and death, by drunkenness; and in nothing is the depravity of men more manifest than in thus endeavouring to hasten the ravages of crime and death.

35. *As a snare.* In Matthew and Mark Jesus compares the suddenness with which these calamities would come to the deluge coming in the days of Noah. Here he likens it to a snare. Birds are caught by a snare or net. It is sprung on them quickly, and when they are not expecting it. So, says he, shall these troubles come upon Judea. The figure is often used to denote the suddenness of calamities, Ps. lxix. 22; Ro. xi. 9; Ps. cxxiv. 7; Is. xxiv. 17.

36. *To stand before the Son of man.* These approaching calamities are represented as the *coming of the Son of man* to judge Jerusalem for its crimes. Its inhabitants were so wicked that they were not worthy to stand before him and would be condemned, and the city would be overthrown. To *stand before him* here denotes approbation, acquittal, favour, and is equivalent to saying that *they* would be free from these calamities, while they should come upon others. See Ro. xiv. 4; Ps. i. 5; cxxx. 3; Re. vi. 17. Perhaps, also, there is a reference here to the day of judgment. See Notes on Matthew xxiv.

37, 38. See Notes on Mat. xxi. 17. ¶ *Came early in the morning.* He returned early from the Mount of Olives, and taught in the temple. Our Saviour did not waste his mornings in idleness or sleep. He rose early and repaired to the temple. The people, also, flocked to the sanctuary to hear him. This example is at once an encouragement to early rising and to the early worship of God. It is a reproof of those who spend the part of the day best fitted for devotion in unnecessary sleep; and it shows the propriety, where it can be done, of assembling early in the morning for prayer and the worship of God. Early prayer-meetings have the countenance of the Saviour, and will be found to be eminently conducive to the promotion of religion. The whole example of Jesus goes to show the importance of beginning the day with God, and of lifting up the heart to him for direction, for the supply of our wants, and for preservation from temptation, before the mind is engrossed by the cares, and distracted by the perplexities, and led away by the temptations of this life. Commencing the day with God is like arresting evil at the fountain; prayer at any other time, without this, is an attempt to arrest it when it has swollen to a stream and rolls on like a torrent. Let the day be begun with God, and the work of piety is easy. Let the world have the ascendency in the morning, and it will be likely to have it also at noonday and at evening.

CHAPTER XXII.

NOW[a] the feast of unleavened
bread drew nigh, which is
called the Passover.
2 And[b] the chief priests and
scribes sought how they might kill
him; for they feared the people.
3 Then[c] entered Satan into Judas, surnamed Iscariot, being of the
number of the twelve.
4 And he went his way, and
communed with the chief priests
and captains how he might betray
him unto them.
5 And they were glad, [d]and
covenanted to give him money.
6 And he promised, and sought
opportunity to betray him unto
them [1]in the absence of the multitude.
7 Then came the [e]day of unleavened bread, when the passover must
be killed.
8 And he sent Peter and John,
saying, Go and prepare us the
passover, that we may eat.
9 And they said unto him,
Where wilt thou that we prepare?
10 And he said unto them, Behold, when ye are entered into the
city, there shall a man meet you,
bearing a pitcher of water: follow
him into the house where he entereth in.
11 And ye shall say unto the goodman of the house, The Master saith
unto thee, Where is the guest-
chamber, where I shall eat the
passover with my disciples?
12 And he shall show you a large
upper room furnished: there make
ready.
13 And they went, and found as
he had said unto them; and they
made ready the passover.
14 And[f] when the hour was

a Mat.26.2; Mar.14.1,&c. b Ps.2.2; Ac.4.27. c Mat.26.14; Mar.14.10,&c.; Jn.13.2,27. d Zec.11.12. 1 or, *without tumult.* e Ex.12. f Mat.26.20; Mar.14.17.

CHAPTER XXII.

1, 2. See Notes on Mat. xxvi. 1, 2.

3. *Then entered Satan into Judas.* It is not necessary to suppose that Satan entered personally into the body of Judas, but only that he brought him under his influence; he filled his mind with an evil passion, and led him on to betray his Master. The particular passion of which Satan made use was *avarice*—probably the besetting sin of Judas. To show its exceeding evil and baseness, it is only necessary to say that when it produced its *appropriate* effect in this case, it led to the betraying and crucifixion of the Son of God. We may learn, also, that when Satan *tempts* men, he commonly does it by exciting and raising to the highest pitch their native passions. He does not make them act contrary to their nature, but leads them on to *act out* their proper disposition. ¶ *Satan.* This word properly means an adversary or an accuser. It is the name which in the Scriptures is commonly given to the prince or leader of evil spirits, and is given to him because he is the *accuser* or *calumniator* of the righteous (see Re. xii. 10; comp. Job i. 6–9), as well as because he is the *adversary* of God. ¶ *Being of the number of the twelve.* One of the twelve apostles. This greatly aggravated his crime. He should have been bound by most tender ties to Jesus. He was one of his family—long with him, and treated by him with every mark of kindness and confidence; and nothing could more enhance his guilt than thus to make use of this confidence for the commission of one of the basest crimes.

4–6. *Chief priests and captains.* See Notes on Mat. xxvi. 14. See the account of the bargain which Judas made with them explained in the Notes on Mat. xxvi. 14–16, and Mar. xiv. 10, 11. ¶ *Absence of the multitude.* The multitude, *the people,* were then favourable to Jesus. He had preached in the temple, and many of them believed that he was the Messiah. It was a hazardous thing, therefore, to take him by force, and in their presence, as they might rise and rescue him. Hence they sought to take him when *he* was away from the multitude; and as Judas knew of a place where he could be found *alone,* they were glad of the opportunity of so easily securing him.

7–13. See this passage explained in the Notes on Mat. xxvi. 17–19, and Mar. xiv. 12–16.

come, he sat down, and the twelve apostles with him.

15 And he said unto them, [2]With desire I have desired to eat this passover with you before I suffer.

16 For I say unto you, I will not any more eat thereof, [g]until it be fulfilled in the kingdom of God.

17 And he took the cup, and gave thanks, and said, Take this and divide *it* among yourselves;

18 For I say unto you, I will not drink of the fruit of the vine until the kingdom of God shall come.

19 And[h] he took bread, and gave thanks, and brake *it*, and gave unto them, saying, This is my body, which is given for you: this do in remembrance of me.

20 Likewise also the cup after supper, saying, This cup *is* the new testament in my blood, which is shed for you.

21 But, behold, the hand of him that betrayeth me *is* [i]with me on the table.

22 And truly the Son of man goeth [k]as it was determined; but woe unto that man by whom he is betrayed!

23 And they began to inquire among themselves which of them it was that should do this thing.

24 And[l] there was also a strife

2 or, *I have heartily desired.*
g ch.14.15; 1 Co.5.7,8; Re.19.9.
h 1 Co.10.16; 11.24,&c.
i Ps.41.9; Jn.13.26.
k ch.24.46; Ac.2.23; 4.28; 1 Co.15.3.
l Mar.9.34; ch.9.46.

---

14. *When the hour was come.* The hour of eating the paschal lamb, which was in the evening. See Notes on Mat. xxvi. 20.

15. *With desire I have desired.* This is a Hebrew form of expression, and means *I have greatly desired.* The reasons why he desired this we may suppose to have been—1st. That, as he was about to leave them, he was desirous once of seeing them together, and of partaking with them of one of the religious privileges of the Jewish dispensation. Jesus was *man* as well as God, and he never undervalued the religious rites of his country, or the blessings of social and religious intercourse; and there is no impropriety in supposing that even *he* might feel that his human nature might be prepared by the service of religion for his great and terrible sufferings. 2d. He doubtless wished to take an opportunity to prepare *them* for his sufferings, and to impress upon them more fully the certainty that he was about to leave them, that they might be prepared for it. 3d. We may also suppose that he particularly desired it that he might institute for *their* use, and for the edification of all Christians, the supper which is called by his name—*the Lord's Supper.* All his sufferings were the expression of love to his people, and he was desirous of testifying *always* his regard for their comfort and welfare. ¶ *Before I suffer.* Before I die.

16. *Until it be fulfilled.* See Notes on Mat. xxvi. 29.

17. *And he took the cup and gave thanks.* This was not the *sacramental* cup, for that was taken *after* supper, ver. 20. This was one of the cups which were usually taken during the celebration of the Passover, and pertained to that observance. *After* he had kept this in the usual manner, he instituted the supper which bears his name, using the bread and wine which had been prepared for the Passover; and thus ingrafted the Lord's Supper on the Passover, or superseded the Passover by another ordinance, which was intended to be perpetual.

19, 20. See Notes on Mat. xxvi. 26–28.

21–23. See Notes on Mat. xxvi. 21–25.

24. *A strife.* A contention or debate. ¶ *Which of them should be the greatest.* The apostles, in common with the Jews generally, had supposed that the Messiah would come as a temporal prince, and in the manner of other princes of the earth—of course, that he would have officers of his government, ministers of state, &c. Their contention was founded on this expectation, and they were disputing which of them should be raised to the highest office. They had before had a similar contention. See Mat. xviii. 1; xx. 20–28. Nothing can be more humiliating than that the disciples should have had *such* contentions, and in such a time and place. That just as Jesus was contemplating his own death, and labouring to prepare them for it, they should strive and contend about office and rank,

among them which of them should
be accounted the greatest.
25 And he said unto them, [m]The
kings of the Gentiles exercise lord-
ship over them; and they that exercise authority upon them are
called benefactors.
26 But[n] ye *shall* not *be so;* but
he that is greatest among you, let
him be as the younger; and he
that is chief, as he that doth serve.
27 For whether *is* greater, he that
sitteth at meat, or he that serveth?
is not he that sitteth at meat? [o]but
I am among you as he that serveth.
28 Ye are they which have continued with me in [p]my temptations.
29 And I appoint unto you [q]a
kingdom, as my Father hath appointed unto me;
30 That[r] ye may eat and drink
at my table in my kingdom, and
sit on thrones, [s]judging the twelve
tribes of Israel.
31 And the Lord said, Simon, Simon, behold, [t]Satan hath desired

m Mat.20.25; Mar.10.42. *n* 1 Pe.5.3; 3 Jn.9,10.
o Jn.13.13,14; Phi.2.7. *p* He.4.15. *q* Mat.25.34; ch.12.32; 1 Co.9.25; 1 Pe.5.4. *r* Re.19.9. *s* Mat.19.28; 1 Co.6.2; Re.3.21. *t* 1 Pe.5.8.

shows how deeply seated is the love of power; how ambition will find its way into the most secret and sacred places; and how even the disciples of the meek and lowly Jesus are sometimes actuated by this most base and wicked feeling.

25. *The kings of the Gentiles.* The kings of the *nations,* or of the earth. They do this, and it is to be expected of them, and it is right. Our Lord does not mean to say that it was wrong that there should be such authority, but that *his* kingdom was to be of a different character, and they were not to expect it there. ¶ *Over them.* That is, over the *nations.* ¶ *Are called benefactors.* The word *benefactor* is applied to one who bestows *favour* on another. It was applied to kings by way of *compliment* or *flattery.* Some of them might have been truly benefactors of their people, but this was by no means true of *all.* Yet it was applied to all, and especially to the Roman emperors. It is found applied to them often in the writings of Josephus and Philo.

26, 27. *But ye* shall *not* be so. Christ here takes occasion to explain the nature of his kingdom. He assures them that it is established on different principles from those of the world; that his subjects were not to expect titles, and power, and offices of pomp in his kingdom. He that would be most advanced in *his* kingdom would be he that was most humble; and in order to show them this, he took a towel and girded himself after the manner of a servant, and washed their feet, to show them what ought to be their feelings toward each other. See Jn. xiii. 4–17. ¶ *He that sitteth at meat.* The master of the feast, or one of his guests. ¶ *But I am among you,* &c. This was said in connection with his washing their feet. He *showed* them how they ought to feel and act toward each other. *They* ought, therefore, not to aim at office and power, but to be humble, and serve and aid one another.

28. *My temptations.* My trials, my humiliations, and my assaults from the power of Satan and a wicked world. ¶ *And I appoint unto you a kingdom.* He assures them here that they should *have* a kingdom — their expectations would be realized. They had continued with him; they had seen how *he* had lived, and to what trials he had been subjected; they had all along expected a kingdom, and he assures them that they should not be disappointed. ¶ *As my Father,* &c. They had seen how God had appointed a kingdom to *him.* It was not with pomp, and splendour, and external glory, but it was in poverty, want, persecution, and trial. So would *he* appoint to them a kingdom. They should *surely* possess it; but it would be not with external splendour, but by poverty and toil. The original word *appoint* has the force of a *covenant* or compact, and means that it should be *surely* or certainly done, or that he pledged himself to do it. All Christians must enter into the kingdom of heaven after the manner of their Lord—through much tribulation; but, though it must be, as it was with him, by many tears and sorrows, yet they shall surely reach the place of their rest and the reward of heaven, for it is secured to them by the covenant pledge and faithfulness of their Lord and King.

30. See Notes on Mat. xix. 28.

31. *Simon.* Peter. Jesus, foreseeing the danger of Peter, and knowing that

to have you, that he may [u]sift *you*
as wheat;
32 But [v]I have prayed for thee,
that thy faith fail not; and when
thou art converted, [w]strengthen
thy brethren.
33 And he said unto him, Lord,
I am ready to go with thee both
into prison and to death.
34 And he said, I tell thee,
Peter, the cock shall not crow this
day before that thou shalt thrice
deny that thou knowest me.
35 And he said unto them, [x]When
I sent you without purse, and
scrip, and shoes, lacked ye any
thing? And they said, Nothing.
36 Then said he unto them, But

u Am.9.9. *v* Jn.17.9,15; He.7.25; 1 Jn.2.1. *w* Ps.51.13; Jn.21.15-17. *x* ch.9.3.

he was about to deny him, took occasion to forewarn him and put him on his guard, and also to furnish him with a solace when he should be brought to repentance. ¶ *Satan hath desired.* Satan is the prince of evil. One of his works is to try the faith of believers—to place temptations and trials in their way, that they may be tested. Thus God gave Job into his hands, that it might be seen whether he would be found faithful, or would apostatize. See Notes on Job i. 7-12. So Satan desired to have Peter in his hands, that he might also try him. ¶ *May sift* you *as wheat.* Grain was agitated or shaken in a kind of fan or sieve. The grain remained in the fan, and the chaff and dust were thrown off. So Christ says that Satan desired to try Peter; to place trials and temptations before him; *to agitate him;* to see whether anything of faith would remain, or whether all would not be found to be chaff—mere natural ardour and false professions.

32. *That thy faith fail not.* The word *faith,* here, seems to be used in the sense of religion, or attachment to Christ, and the words *fail not* mean *utterly fail* or fail altogether—that is, apostatize. It is true that the *courage* of Peter failed; it is true that he had not that immediate confidence in Jesus and reliance on him which he had before had; but the prayer of Jesus was that he might not altogether apostatize from the faith. God heard Jesus *always* (Jn. xi. 42); it follows, therefore, that *every* prayer which he ever offered was answered; and it follows, as he asked here for a specific thing, that that thing was granted; and as he prayed that Peter's faith might not utterly fail, so it follows that there was no time in which Peter was not really a pious man. Far as he wandered, and grievously as he sinned, yet he well knew that Jesus was the Messiah. He *did know* the man; and though his fears overcame him and led him to aggravated sin, yet the prayer of Christ was prevalent, and he was brought to true repentance. ¶ *When thou art converted.* The word *converted* means turned, changed, recovered. The meaning is, when thou art turned from this sin, when thou art recovered from this heinous offence, then use *your* experience to warn and strengthen those who are in danger of like sins. A man may be *converted* or *turned* from any sin, or any evil course. He is *regenerated* but once—at the beginning of his Christian life; he may be *converted* as often as he falls into sin. ¶ *Strengthen thy brethren.* Confirm them, warn them, encourage them. They are in continual danger, also, of sinning. Use your experience to warn them of their danger, and to comfort and sustain them in their temptations. And from this we learn—1st. That one design of permitting Christians to fall into sin is to show their own weakness and dependence on God; and, 2d. That they who have been overtaken in this manner should make use of their experience to warn and preserve others from the same path. The two epistles of Peter, and his whole life, show that *he* was attentive to this command of Jesus; and in his death he manifested his deep abhorrence of this act of dreadful guilt in denying his blessed Lord, by requesting to be crucified with his head downward, as unworthy to suffer in the same manner that Christ did. Comp. Notes on Jn. xxi. 18.

33, 34. See Notes on Mat. xxvi. 33-35.

35. *When I sent you,* &c. See Notes on Mat. x. 9, 10. ¶ *Lacked ye,* &c. Did you want anything? Did not God fully provide for you? He refers to this to convince them that his words were true; that their past experience should lead them to put confidence in him and in God.

now he that hath a purse, let him take *it*, and likewise *his* scrip; and he that hath no sword, let him sell his garment and buy one.

37 For I say unto you, that this that is written must yet be accomplished in me, [y] And he was reckoned among the transgressors; for the things concerning me have an end.

y Is.53.12.

36. *But now.* The Saviour says the times are changed. *Before*, he sent them out only for a little time. They were in their own country. Their journeys would be short, and there was no need that they should make preparation for a long absence, or for encountering great dangers. But *now* they were to go into the wide world, among strangers, trials, dangers, and wants. And as the time was near; as he was about to die; as these dangers pressed on, it was proper that they should make provision for what was before them. ¶ *A purse.* See Notes on Mat. x. 9. He intimates that they should *now* take money, as it would be necessary to provide for their wants in travelling. ¶ *Scrip.* See Notes on Mat. x. 10. ¶ *And he that hath no sword.* There has been much difficulty in understanding why Jesus directed his disciples to arm themselves, as if it was his purpose to make a defence. It is certain that the spirit of his religion is against the use of the sword, and that it was not his purpose to defend himself against Judas. But it should be remembered that these directions about the purse, the scrip, and the sword were not made with reference to his *being taken* in the garden, but with reference *to their future life.* The time of the trial in Gethsemane was just at hand; nor was there *time* then, if no other reason existed, to go and make the purchase. It altogether refers to their future life. They were going into the midst of dangers. The country was infested with robbers and wild beasts. It was customary to go armed. He tells them of those dangers—of the necessity of being prepared in the usual way to meet them. This, then, is not to be considered as a specific, positive *command* to procure a sword, but an intimation that great dangers were before them; that their manner of life would be changed, and that they would need the provisions *appropriate to that kind of life.* The *common* preparation for that manner of life consisted in money, provisions, and arms; and he foretells them of that manner of life by giving them directions commonly understood to be appropriate to it. It amounts, then, to a *prediction* that they would soon leave the places which they had been accustomed to, and go into scenes of poverty, want, and danger, where they would feel the necessity of money, provisions, and the means of defence. All, therefore, that the passage justifies is—1st. That it is proper for men to provide beforehand for their wants, and for ministers and missionaries as well as any others. 2d. That self-defence is lawful. Men encompassed with danger may lawfully *defend* their lives. It does not prove that it is lawful to make *offensive* war on a nation or an individual. ¶ *Let him sell his garment.* His *mantle* or his outer garment. See Notes on Mat. v. 40. The meaning is, let him procure one at any expense, even if he is obliged to sell his clothes for it—intimating that the danger would be very great and pressing.

37. *This that is written.* See Notes on Is. liii. 12. ¶ *Was reckoned among the transgressors.* Not reckoned *as* a transgressor, but *among* or *with* them—that is, he was treated as transgressors are. He was put to death in their company, and as he *would have been* if he had been a transgressor. He was innocent, holy, harmless, and undefiled, He. vii. 26. God knew this always, and could not *think* of him, or make him *to be* otherwise than he was; yet it pleased him to bruise him, and to give him into the hands of men who did reckon him as a transgressor, and who treated him accordingly. ¶ *Have an end.* This may either mean, "shall be surely accomplished," or "they are *about* to be fulfilled," or "are *now* fulfilled." The former is probably the meaning, denoting that *every* prophecy in regard to him would certainly be accomplished.

38. Are *two swords.* The Galileans, it is said, often went armed. The Essenes did so also. The reason was that the country was full of robbers and wild beasts, and it was necessary to carry, in their travels, some means of defence. It seems that the disciples followed the customs of the country, and had with

38 And they said, Lord, behold,
here *are* two swords; and he said
unto them, It is enough.
39 And[z] he came out, and went,
as he was wont, to the mount of
Olives, and his disciples also followed him.
40 And when he was at the
place, he said unto them, Pray
that ye enter not into temptation.
41 And he was withdrawn from
them about a stone's cast, and
kneeled down and prayed,
42 Saying, Father, if thou be
willing,[3] remove this cup from me;
nevertheless, not my will, but thine
be done.
43 And there appeared [a]an angel
unto him from heaven, strengthening him.
44 And[b] being in an agony, he
prayed more earnestly; and his
sweat was as it were great drops of
blood falling down to the ground.
45 And when he rose up from
prayer, and was come to his disciples, he found them sleeping for
sorrow,
46 And said unto them, Why
sleep ye? rise and [c]pray, lest ye
enter into temptation.
47 And while he yet spake, [d]behold, a multitude, and he that was
called Judas, one of the twelve,
went before them, and drew near
unto Jesus to kiss him.

z Mat.26.36; Mar.14.32,&c.; Jn.18.1,&c.
3 *willing to remove.* a Mat.4.11.

b La.1.12; Jn.12.27; He.5.7. c ver.40.
d Mat.26.47,&c.; Mar.14.43,&c.; Jn.18.3,&c.

---

them some means of defence, though they had but two swords among the twelve. ¶ *It is enough.* It is difficult to understand this. Some suppose that it is spoken *ironically;* as if he had said, "You are bravely armed indeed, with two swords among twelve men, and to meet such a host!" Others, that he meant to reprove them for understanding him *literally*, as if he meant that they were *then* to procure swords for *immediate* battle. As if he had said, "This is absurd, or a perversion of my meaning. I did not *intend this*, but merely to foretell you of impending dangers *after* my death." It is to be observed that he did not say "*the two swords* are enough," but "*it* is enough;" perhaps meaning simply, enough has been said. Other matters press on, and you will yet understand what I mean.

39-46. See Notes on Mat. xxvi. 30-46; Mar. xiv. 26-42.

43. *Strengthening him.* His human nature, to sustain the great burden that was upon his soul. Some have supposed from this that he was not divine as well as human; for if he was *God*, how could an angel give any strength or comfort? and why did not the divine nature *alone* sustain the human? But the fact that he was *divine* does not affect the case at all. It might be asked with the same propriety, If he was, as all admit, the friend of God, and beloved of God, and holy, why, if he was a mere man, did not *God* sustain him alone, without an angel's intervening? But the objection in neither case would have any force. The *man, Christ Jesus*, was suffering. His human nature was in agony, and it is the *manner* of God to sustain the afflicted by the intervention of others; nor was there any more *unfitness* in sustaining the human nature of his Son in this manner than any other sufferer.

44. *In an agony.* See this verse explained in the Notes on Mat. xxvi. 42-44.

45. *Sleeping for sorrow.* On account of the greatness of their sorrow. See Notes on Mat. xxvi. 40.

47-53. See this explained in Mat. xxvi. 48-56.

48. *Betrayest thou the Son of man with a kiss?* By the *Son of man* was evidently meant *the Messiah.* Judas had had the most satisfactory evidence of that, and did not doubt it. A kiss was the sign of affection. By that slight artifice Judas thought to conceal his base purpose. Jesus with severity reproaches him for it. Every word is emphatic. *Betrayest* thou—dost thou violate all thy obligations of fidelity, and deliver thy Master up to death? Betrayest *thou*—thou, so long with him, so much favoured, so sure that this is the Messiah? Betrayest thou *the Son of man*—the Messiah, the hope of the nations, the desire of all people, the world's Redeemer? Betrayest thou the Son of man *with a kiss*—the sign of friendship

48 But Jesus said unto him, Judas, betrayest thou the Son of man with a kiss?

49 When they which were about him saw what would follow, they said unto him, Lord, shall we smite with the sword?

50 And one of them smote the servant of the high-priest, and cut off his right ear.

51 And Jesus answered and said, Suffer ye thus far. And he touched his ear, and healed him.

52 Then Jesus said unto the chief priests, and captains of the temple, and the elders, which were come to him, Be ye come out, as against a thief, with swords and staves?

53 When I was daily with you in the temple, ye stretched forth no hands against me; [e]but this is your hour and the power of darkness.

54 Then they took him, and led *him*, and brought him into the high-priest's house. And Peter followed afar off.

55 And when they had kindled a fire in the midst of the hall, and were set down together, Peter sat down among them.

56 But[f] a certain maid beheld him as he sat by the fire, and earnestly looked upon him, and said, This man was also with him.

57 And he denied him, saying, Woman, I know him not.

58 And[g] after a little while another saw him, and said, Thou art also of them. And Peter said, Man, I am not.

59 And about the space of one hour after, [h]another confidently affirmed, saying, Of a truth this *fellow* also was with him, for he is a Galilean.

60 And Peter said, Man, I know not what thou sayest. And immediately, while he yet spake, the cock crew.

61 And the Lord turned and looked upon Peter. And[i] Peter remembered the word of the Lord, how he had said unto him, [k]Before the cock crow, thou shalt deny me thrice.

62 And[l] Peter went out and wept bitterly.

63 And[m] the men that held Jesus mocked him and smote *him*.

64 And when they had blindfolded him, they struck him on the face, and asked him, saying, Prophesy, who is it that smote thee?

65 And many other things blasphemously spake they against him.

66 And[n] as soon as it was day, the elders of the people and the chief priests and the scribes came together, and led him into their council, saying,

67 Art[o] thou the Christ? tell us. And he said unto them, If I tell you, ye will not believe:

68 And if I also ask *you*, ye will not answer me nor let *me* go.

69 Hereafter shall the Son of man sit on the [p]right hand of the power of God.

70 Then said they all, Art thou, then, the Son of God? And he said unto them, Ye say that I am.

71 And they said, What need we any further witness? for we ourselves have heard of his own mouth.

e Job 20.5; Jn.12.27.
f Mat.26.69; Mar.14.66,69; Jn.18.17.
g Mat.26.71; Mar.14.69; Jn.18.25.
h Mat.26.73; Mar.14.70; Jn.18.26.
i Mat.26.75; Mar.14.72. k ver.34.
l Ps.130.1-4; 143.1-4; Je.31.18; Eze.7.16; 1 Co.10.12; 2 Co.7.10,11. m Mat.26.67,68; Mar.14.65.
n Mat.27.1; Ac.4.26-28.
o Mat.26.63,&c.; Mar.14.61,&c.
p He.1.3; 8.1; Re.3.21.

---

and affection employed in a base and wicked purpose, intending to add deceit, disguise, and the prostitution of a mark of affection to the *crime of treason*? Every word of this must have gone to the very soul of Judas. Perhaps few reproofs of crime more resemble the awful searchings of the souls of the wicked in the day of judgment.

54–62. See Notes on Mat. xxvi. 57–75.

63–71. See Notes on Mat. xxvi. 57–68.

CHAPTER XXIII.

AND[a] the whole multitude of them arose, and led him unto Pilate.

2 And they began to [b]accuse him, saying, [c]We found this *fellow* perverting the nation, and [d]forbidding to give tribute to Cæsar, saying that [e]he himself is Christ a king.

3 And Pilate asked him, saying, Art thou the King of the Jews? And[f] he answered him, and said, Thou sayest *it*.

4 Then said Pilate to the chief priests and *to* the people, [g]I find no fault in this man.

5 And they were the [h]more fierce, saying, He stirreth up the people, teaching throughout all Jewry, beginning from Galilee to this place.

6 When Pilate heard of Galilee, he asked whether the man were a Galilean.

7 And as soon as he knew that he belonged unto [i]Herod's jurisdiction, he sent him to Herod, who himself also was at Jerusalem at that time.

a Mat.27.2,11,&c.; Mar.15.1,&c.; Jn.18.28, &c.
b Zec.11.8. *c* ver.5; Ac.16.20,21; 17.6,7.
d Mat.17.27; 22.21; Mar.12.17.
e Jn.18.36; 19.12. *f* 1 Ti.6.13.
g Jn.18.38; 19.4; He.7.26; 1 Pe.2.22.
h Ps.57.4. *i* ch.3.1.

CHAPTER XXIII.

1. See Notes on Mat. xxvii. 1, 2.

2. *This* fellow. The word *fellow* is not in the original. It conveys a notion of *contempt*, which no doubt they *felt*, but which is not expressed in the *Greek*, and which it is not proper should be expressed in the translation. It might be translated, "We found this man." ¶ *Perverting the nation.* That is, exciting them to sedition and tumults. This was a mere wanton accusation, but it was plausible before a Roman magistrate; for, 1st. The Galileans, as Josephus testifies, were prone to seditions and tumults. 2d. Jesus drew multitudes after him, and they thought it was easy to show that this was itself promoting tumults and seditions. ¶ *Forbidding,* &c. About their charges they were very cautious and cunning. They did not say that he *taught* that men should not give tribute—that would have been too gross a charge, and would have been easily refuted; but it was an *inference* which they drew. They said it *followed* from his doctrine. He professed to be a king. They *inferred*, therefore, if *he* was *a king*, that he must hold that it was not right to acknowledge allegiance to any foreign prince; and if they could make *this* out, they supposed that Pilate *must* condemn him of course. ¶ *Tribute.* Taxes. ¶ *Cæsar.* The Roman emperor, called also Tiberius. The name *Cæsar* was common to the Roman emperors, as *Pharaoh* was to the Egyptian kings. *All* the kings of Egypt were called Pharaoh, or *the* Pharaoh; so all the Roman emperors were called *Cæsar*.

3. See Notes on Mat. xxvii. 11.

4. *I find no fault.* I see no evidence that he is guilty of what you charge him with. This was *after* Pilate had taken Jesus into the judgment-hall by himself and examined him *privately*, and had been satisfied in regard to the nature of his kingdom. See Jn. xviii. 33–38. He was *then* satisfied that though he claimed to be *a king*, yet his kingdom was not of this world, and that *his* claims did not interfere with those of Cæsar.

5. *The more fierce.* The more urgent and pressing. They saw that there was a prospect of losing their cause, and they attempted to press on Pilate the point that would be most likely now to affect him. Pilate had, in fact, acquitted him of the charge of being an enemy to Cæsar, and they therefore urged the other point more vehemently. ¶ *Stirreth up the people.* Excites them to tumult and sedition. ¶ *All Jewry.* All Judea. ¶ *From Galilee to this place.* To Jerusalem—that is, throughout the whole country. It is not merely in one place, but from one end of the land to the other.

6. *Whether he were a Galilean.* He asked this because, if he was, he properly belonged to Herod's jurisdiction, who reigned over Galilee.

7. *Herod's jurisdiction.* Herod Antipas, a son of Herod the Great. This was the same Herod that put John the Baptist to death. Jesus had passed the most of his life in the part of the country where he ruled, and it was therefore considered that he belonged to his jurisdiction—that is, that it belonged to Herod, not to Pilate, to try this cause.

8 And when Herod saw Jesus
he was exceeding glad, [k]for he was
desirous to see him of a long *season*, [l]because he had heard many
things of him; [m]and he hoped to
have seen some miracle done by
him.
9 Then he questioned with him
in many words; [n]but he answered
him nothing.
10 And the chief priests and
scribes stood and vehemently accused him.
11 And Herod with his men of
war [o]set him at nought, and mocked *him*, and arrayed him in a [p]gorgeous robe, and sent him again to
Pilate.

k ch.9.9. l Mat.14.1; Mar.6.14. m 2 Ki.5.11. n Ps.38.13,14; 39.1,9; Is.53.7. o Is.49.7; 53.3. p Jn.19.5.

12 And the same day [q]Pilate and
Herod were made friends together;
for before they were at enmity between themselves.
13 And Pilate, when he had
called together the chief priests,
and the rulers, and the people,
14 Said unto them, Ye have
brought this man unto me as one
that perverteth the people; and,
behold, [r]I, having examined *him*
before you, have found no fault in
this man touching those things
whereof ye accuse him:
15 No, nor yet Herod; for I sent
you to him; and, lo, nothing worthy
of death is done unto him.
16 I will therefore [s]chastise him,
and release *him*.

q Ac.4.27. r ver.4. s Is.53.5.

10. *Vehemently accused him.* Violently or unjustly accused him, endeavouring to make it appear that he had been guilty of sedition in Herod's province.

11. *Herod with his men of war.* With his soldiers, or his body-guard. It is probable that in travelling he had *a guard* to attend him constantly. ¶ *Set him at nought.* Treated him with contempt and ridicule. ¶ *A gorgeous robe.* A white or shining robe, for this is the meaning of the original. The Roman princes wore *purple* robes, and *Pilate* therefore put such a robe on Jesus. The Jewish kings wore a *white* robe, which was often rendered very shining or gorgeous by much tinsel or silver interwoven. Josephus says that the robe which Agrippa wore was so bright with silver that when the sun shone on it, it so dazzled the eyes that it was difficult to look on it. The Jews and Romans therefore decked him in the manner appropriate to their own country, for purposes of mockery. All this was unlawful and malicious, as there was not the least evidence of his guilt. ¶ *Sent him to Pilate.* It was by the interchange of these civilities that they were made friends. It would seem that Pilate sent him to Herod as a token of civility and respect, and with a design, perhaps, of putting an end to their quarrel. Herod returned the civility, and it resulted in their reconciliation.

12. *Made friends together*, &c. What had been the cause of their quarrel is unknown. It is commonly supposed that it was Pilate's slaying the Galileans in Jerusalem, as related in Lu. xiii. 1, 2. The occasion of their reconciliation seems to have been the civility and respect which Pilate showed to Herod in this case. It was not because they were united in *hating* Jesus, as is often the case with wicked men, for Pilate was certainly desirous of releasing him, and *both* considered him merely as an object of ridicule and sport. It is true, however, that wicked men, at variance in other things, are often united in opposing and ridiculing Christ and his followers; and that enmities of long standing are sometimes made up, and the most opposite characters brought together, simply to oppose religion. Comp. Ps. lxxxiii. 5-7.

15. *Nothing worthy of death is done unto him.* Deserving of death. The charges are not proved against him. They had had every opportunity of proving them, first before Pilate and then before Herod, unjustly subjecting him to trial before *two* men in succession, and thus giving them a double opportunity of condemning him, and yet, after all, he was declared by both to be innocent. There could be no better evidence that he *was* innocent.

16. *I will therefore chastise him.* The word *chastise* here means to *scourge* or to *whip*. This was usually done before capital punishment, to increase the sufferings of the man condemned. It is

17 (For of necessity he must release one unto them at the feast.)
18 And they cried out all at once,
saying, Away with this *man*, and
release unto us Barabbas:
19 (Who for a certain sedition
made in the city, and [t]for murder,
was cast into prison.)
20 Pilate therefore, willing to release Jesus, spake again to them.
21 But they cried, saying, Crucify *him*, crucify him.
22 And he said unto them the
third time, Why, what evil hath
he done? I have found no cause
of death in him: I will therefore
chastise him and let *him* go.
23 And they were [u]instant with
loud voices, requiring that he
might be crucified. And the voices
of them and of the chief priests
prevailed.
24 And Pilate [1]gave sentence
that it should be [v]as they required.
25 And he released [w]unto them
him that for sedition and murder
was cast into prison, whom they
had desired; but he delivered Jesus
to their will.
26 And[x] as they led him away,
they laid hold upon one Simon, a
Cyrenian, coming out of the country, and on him they laid the cross,
that he might bear *it* after Jesus.
27 And there followed him a
great company of people, and of
women, which also bewailed and
lamented him.
28 But Jesus, turning unto them,
said, Daughters of Jerusalem, weep
not for me, but weep for yourselves
and for your children:
29 For, behold, [y]the days are
coming, in the which they shall
say, Blessed *are* the barren, and
the wombs that never bare, and
the paps which never gave suck.
30 Then[z] shall they begin to say
to the mountains, Fall on us; and
to the hills, Cover us.

t Ac.3.14. *u* Ps.22.12; ver.5.
1 or, *assented*. *v* Ex.23.2. *w* Ac.3.14.
x Mat.27.32,&c.; Mar.15.21,&c.; Jn.19.17.
y Mat.24.19; ch.21.23.
z Is.2.19; Ho.10.8; Re.6.16; 9.6.

---

not easy to see the reason why, if Pilate supposed Jesus to be *innocent*, he should propose publicly to scourge him. It was as *really* unjust to do that as it was to crucify him. But probably he expected by this to conciliate the minds of his accusers; to show them that he was willing to gratify them if it *could* be done with propriety; and perhaps he expected that by seeing him whipped and disgraced, and condemned to ridicule, to contempt, and to suffering, they would be satisfied. It is farther remarked that among the Romans it was competent for a magistrate to inflict a *slight* punishment on a man when a charge of gross offence was not fully made out, or where there was not sufficient testimony to substantiate the precise charge alleged. All this shows, 1st, the palpable *injustice* of our Lord's condemnation; 2d, the persevering malice and obstinacy of the Jews; and, 3d, the want of firmness in Pilate. He should have released him at once; but the love of *popularity* led him to the murder of the Son of God. Man should do his duty in all situations; and he that, like Pilate, seeks only for public favour and popularity, will assuredly be led into crime.

17. See Notes on Mat. xxvii. 15.

18–23. See Notes on Mat. xxvii. 20–23.

23–25. See Notes on Mat. xxvii. 26.

26. See Notes on Mat. xxvii. 32. ¶ *After Jesus.* Probably to bear one end of the cross. Jesus was feeble and unable to bear it alone, and they compelled Simon to help him.

28. *Daughters of Jerusalem.* Women of Jerusalem. This was a common mode of speaking among the Hebrews. ¶ *Weep for yourselves*, &c. This refers to the calamities that were about to come upon them in the desolation of their city by the Romans.

30. *To the mountains, Fall on us*, &c. This is an image of great calamities and judgments. So great will be the calamities that they will seek for shelter from the storm, and will call on the hills to protect them. The same figure is used respecting the wicked in the day of judgment in Re. vi. 16, 17. Compare also Is. ii. 21.

31. *For if they do these things in a green tree*, &c. This seems to be a pro-

31 For[a] if they do these things in a green tree, what shall be done in the dry?

32 And there were also two others, [b]malefactors, led with him to be put to death.

33 And when they were come to the place which is called [2]Calvary, there they crucified him, and the malefactors; one on the right hand, and the other on the left.

34 Then said Jesus, [c]Father, for-

a Pr.11.31; Je.25.29; Eze.20.47; 21.4; 1 Pe.4.17. b Is.53.12.

2 or, *the place of a skull.* c Mat.5.44; Ac.7.60; 1 Co.4.12.

---

verbial expression. A *green* tree is not easily set on fire; a dry one is easily kindled and burns rapidly; and the meaning of the passage is—"If they, the Romans, do these things to *me*, who am innocent and blameless; if they punish me in this manner in the face of justice, what will they *not* do in relation to this guilty nation? What security have *they* that heavier judgments will not come upon them? What desolations and woes may not be expected when *injustice* and oppression have taken the place of justice, and have set up a rule over this wicked people?" Our Lord alludes, evidently, to the calamities that would come upon them by the Romans in the destruction of their city and temple. The passage may be applied, however, without impropriety, and with great beauty and force, to the punishment of the wicked in the future world. Thus applied, it means that the sufferings of the Saviour, as compared with the sufferings of the guilty, were like the burning of a green tree as compared with the burning of one that is dry. A green tree is not adapted to burn; a dry one is. So the Saviour—innocent, pure, and holy—stood in relation to suffering. There were sufferings which an innocent being could not endure. There was remorse of conscience, the sense of guilt, punishment properly so called, and the eternity of woes. He had the consciousness of innocence, and he would not suffer for ever. He had no passions to be enkindled that would rage and ruin the soul. The sinner is *adapted* to sufferings, like a dry tree to the fire. He is guilty, and will suffer all the horrors of remorse of conscience. He will be punished literally. He has raging and impetuous passions, and they will be enkindled in hell, and will rage for ever and ever. The meaning is, that if the innocent Saviour suffered *so much*, the sufferings of the sinner for ever in hell must be more unspeakably dreadful. Yet who could endure the sufferings of the Redeemer on the cross for a single day? Who could bear them for ever and ever, aggravated by all the horrors of a guilty conscience, and all the terrors of unrestrained anger, and hate, and fear, and wrath? *Why* WILL *the wicked die?*

32, 33. See Notes on Mat. xxvii. 35, 38.

34. *Father, forgive them.* This is a fulfilment of the prophecy in Is. liii. 12: *He made intercession for the transgressors.* The prayer was offered for those who were guilty of putting him to death. It is not quite certain whether he referred to the *Jews* or *to the Roman soldiers.* Perhaps he referred to both. The Romans knew not what they did, as they were really ignorant that he was the Son of God, and as they were merely obeying the command of their rulers. The Jews knew, indeed, that he was *innocent*, and they had evidence, if they would have looked at it, that he was the Messiah; but they did not know what would be the effect of their guilt; they did not know what judgments and calamities they were bringing down upon their country. It may be added, also, that, though they had abundant evidence, if they would look at it, that he was the Messiah, and enough to leave them without excuse, yet they did not, *in fact*, believe that he was the Saviour promised by the prophets, and had not, *in fact*, any proper sense of his rank and dignity as "the Lord of glory." If they had had, they would not have crucified him, as we cannot suppose that they would knowingly put to death their own Messiah, the hope of the nation, and him who had been so long promised to the fathers. See Notes on 1 Co. ii. 8. We may learn from this prayer—1st. The duty of praying for our enemies, even when they are endeavouring most to injure us. 2d. The thing for which we should pray for them is that *God* would pardon them and give them better minds. 3d. The power and excellence of the Christian religion. No other

give them, for they know not what they do. And they parted his raiment, and cast lots.
35 And the people stood beholding. And the [d]rulers also with them, derided *him*, saying, He saved others; let him save himself, if he be Christ, the chosen of God.
36 And the soldiers also mocked him, coming to him and offering him vinegar,
37 And saying, If thou be the King of the Jews, save thyself.
38 And a superscription also was written over him, in letters of Greek, and Latin, and Hebrew, THIS IS THE KING OF THE JEWS.
39 And [e]one of the malefactors which were hanged railed on him, saying, If thou be Christ, save thyself and us.
40 But the other answering, rebuked him, saying, [f]Dost not thou fear God, seeing thou art [g]in the same condemnation?
41 And we indeed justly; for we receive the due reward of our

d Ps.22.7. e ch.17.34-36. f Ps.36.1. g Je.5.3.

religion *teaches* men to pray for the forgiveness of enemies; no other *disposes* them to do it. Men of the world seek for *revenge;* the Christian bears reproaches and persecutions with patience, and prays that God would pardon those who injure them, and save them from their sins. 4th. The greatest sinners, through the intercession of Jesus, may obtain pardon. God heard him, and still hears him *always*, and there is no reason to doubt that many of his enemies and murderers obtained forgiveness and life. Comp. Ac. ii. 37, 42, 43; vi. 7; xiv. 1. ¶ *They know not what they do.* It was done through ignorance, Ac. iii. 17. Paul says that, "had they known it, they would not have crucified the Lord of glory," 1 Co. ii. 8. Ignorance does not excuse altogether a crime if the ignorance be wilful, but it diminishes its guilt. They *had* evidence; they *might* have learned his character; they *might* have known what they were doing, and they *might* be held answerable for all this. But Jesus here shows the compassion of his heart, and as they were *really* ignorant, whatever might have been the cause of their ignorance, he implores God to pardon them. He even urges it as a *reason* why they should be pardoned, that they were ignorant of what they were doing; and though men are often guilty for their ignorance, yet God often in compassion overlooks it, averts his anger, and grants them the blessings of pardon and life. So he forgave Paul, for he "did it in ignorance, in unbelief," 1 Ti. i. 13. So God *winked at* the ignorance of the Gentiles, Ac. xvii. 30. Yet this is no excuse, and no evidence of safety, for those who in our day contemptuously put away from them and their children the means of instruction.

35–39. See Notes on Mat. xxvii. 41–44.

38. *In letters of Greek*, &c. See Notes on Mat. xxvii. 37.

39. *One of the malefactors.* Matthew (ch. xxvii. 44) says "*the thieves—cast the same in his teeth.*" See the apparent contradiction in these statements reconciled in the Notes on that place. ¶ *If thou be Christ.* If thou art the Messiah; if thou art what thou dost pretend to be. This is a taunt or reproach of the same kind as that of the priests in ver. 35. ¶ *Save thyself and us.* Save our lives. Deliver us from the cross. This man did not seek for salvation truly; he asked not to be delivered from his sins; if he had, Jesus would also have heard him. Men often, in sickness and affliction, call upon God. They are earnest in prayer. They ask of God to save them, but it is only to save them from *temporal* death. It is not to be saved from their sins, and the consequence is, that when God *does* raise them up, they forget their promises, and live as they did before, as this robber *would* have done if Jesus had heard his prayer and delivered him from the cross.

40. *Dost not thou fear God*, &c. You are condemned to die as well as he. It is improper for you to rail on him as the rulers and Romans do. God is just, and you are hastening to his bar, and you should therefore fear him, and fear that he will punish you for railing on this innocent man. ¶ *Same condemnation.* Condemnation to death; not death for the same thing, but the same *kind* of death.

41. *Due reward of our deeds.* The pro-

deeds; but this man [h]hath done nothing amiss.
42 And he said unto Jesus, [i]Lord, remember me when thou comest into thy kingdom.
43 And Jesus said unto him,

h 1 Pe.1.19. i Ps.106.4,5; Ro.10.9,10; 1 Co.6.10,11.

per punishment for our crimes. They had been highwaymen, and it was just that they should die.

42. *Remember me.* This is a phrase praying for favour, or asking him to grant him an *interest* in his kingdom, or to acknowledge him as one of his followers. It implied that he believed that Jesus was what he claimed to be—the Messiah; that, though he was dying with them, yet he would set up his kingdom; and that he had full power to bless him, though about to expire. It is possible that this man might have heard him preach before his crucifixion, and have learned there the nature of his kingdom; or it may have been that while on the cross Jesus had taken occasion to acquaint them with the nature of his kingdom. While he might have been doing this, one of the malefactors may have continued to rail on him while the other became truly penitent. Such a result of preaching the gospel would not have been unlike what has often occurred since, where, while the gospel has been proclaimed, one has been "taken and another left;" one has been melted to repentance, another has been more hardened in guilt. The promise which follows shows that this prayer was answered. This was a case of repentance in the last hour, the trying hour of death; and it has been remarked that *one* was brought to repentance there, to show that no one should *despair* on a dying bed; and *but* one, that none should be presumptuous and delay repentance to that awful moment. ¶ *When thou comest*, &c. It is impossible now to fix the precise idea which this robber had of Christ's coming. Whether it was that he expected that he would rise from the dead, as some of the Jews supposed the Messiah would; or whether he referred to the day of judgment; or whether to an immediate translation to his kingdom in the heavens, we cannot tell. All that we know is, that he fully believed him to be the Messiah, and that he desired to obtain an interest in that kingdom which he knew he would establish.

43. *To-day*, &c. It is not probable that the dying thief expected that his prayer would be so soon answered. It is rather to be supposed that he looked to some *future* period when the Messiah would rise or would return; but Jesus told him that his prayer would be answered that very day, implying, evidently, that it would be *immediately* at death. This is the more remarkable, as those who were crucified commonly lingered for several days on the cross before they died; but Jesus foresaw that measures would be taken to *hasten* their death, and assured him that *that* day he should receive an answer to his prayer and be with him in his kingdom. ¶ *Paradise.* This is a word of *Persian* origin, and means *a garden*, particularly a garden of pleasure, filled with trees, and shrubs, and fountains, and flowers. In hot climates such gardens were peculiarly pleasant, and hence they were attached to the mansions of the rich and to the palaces of princes. The word came thus to denote any place of happiness, and was used particularly to denotes the abodes of the blessed in another world. The Romans spoke of their Elysium, and the Greeks of the gardens of Hesperides, where the trees bore golden fruit. The garden of Eden means, also, the garden of *pleasure*, and in Ge. ii. 8 the Septuagint renders the word *Eden* by *Paradise.* Hence this name in the Scriptures comes to denote the abodes of the blessed in the other world. See Notes on 2 Co. xii. 4. The Jews supposed that the souls of the righteous would be received into such a place, and those of the wicked cast down to Gehenna until the time of the judgment. They had many fables about this state which it is unnecessary to repeat. The plain meaning of the passage is, "To-day thou shalt be made happy, or be received to a state of blessedness with me after death." It is to be remarked that Christ says nothing about the *place where* it should be, nor of the condition of those there, excepting that it is a place of blessedness, and that its happiness is to commence immediately after death (see also Phi. i. 23); but from the narrative we may learn—1st. That the soul will exist separately from the body; for, while the thief and the Saviour would be in Paradise, their *bodies* would be on the cross or in the grave. 2d. That immediately after

Verily[k] I say unto thee, To-day
shalt thou be with me in [l]paradise.
44 And it was about the sixth
hour, and there was darkness over
all the [3]earth until the ninth hour.
45 And the sun was darkened,
and the veil of the temple was
rent in the midst.
46 And when Jesus had cried
with a loud voice, he said, [m]Father,
into thy hands I commend my
spirit; [n]and having said thus, he
gave up the ghost.
47 Now when the centurion saw
what was done, he glorified God,
saying, Certainly this was a righteous man.
48 And all the people that came
together to that sight, beholding
the things which were done, smote
their breasts and returned.
49 And all his acquaintance, and
the women that followed him from
Galilee, [o]stood afar off, beholding
these things.
50 And, behold, *there was* a man
named Joseph, a counsellor; *and
he was* a good man, and a just:
51 (The same had not consented
to the counsel and deed of them:)
he was of Arimathea, a city of the
Jews; [p]who also himself waited
for the kingdom of God.
52 This *man* went unto Pilate
and begged the body of Jesus.
53 And he took it down, and
wrapped it in linen, and laid it [q]in
a sepulchre that was hewn in
stone, wherein man never before
was laid.
54 And that day was [r]the preparation, and the sabbath drew on.
55 And the [s]women also, which
came with him from Galilee, followed after, and beheld the sepulchre, and how his body was laid.
56 And they returned, and [t]pre-
pared spices and ointments; and
rested the sabbath-day, [u]accord-
ing to the commandment.

CHAPTER XXIV.

NOW[a] upon the first *day* of the
week, very early in the morning, they came unto the sepulchre,
bringing the spices which they had
prepared, and certain *others* with
them.
2 And they found the stone
rolled away from the sepulchre.

k Ro.5.20,21. l 2 Co.12.4; Re.2.7. 3 or, *land.* m Ps.31.5; 1 Pe.2.23. n Mat.27.50,&c.; Mar.15.37,&c.; Jn.19.30. o Ps.38.11; 142.4.

p Mar.15.43; ch.2.25,38. q Is.53.9. r Mat.27.62. s ch.8.2; ver.49. t Mar.16.1. u Ex.20.8-10. a Mat.28.1,&c.; Mar.16.2,&c.; Jn.20.1,&c.

death—the same day—the souls of the righteous will be made happy. They will feel that they are secure; they will be received among the just; and they will have the assurance of a glorious immortality. 3d. That state will differ from the condition of the wicked. The promise was made to but one on the cross, and there is no evidence whatever that the other entered there. See also the parable of the rich man and Lazarus, Lu. xvi. 19-31. 4th. It is the chief glory of this state and of heaven to be permitted to see Jesus Christ and to be with him: "Thou shalt be *with me.*" "I desire to depart and *to be with Christ,*" Phi. i. 23. See also Re. xxi. 23; v. 9-14.

44-46. See Notes on Mat. xxvii. 45-50.

47-49. See Notes on Mat. xxvii. 52-55.

48. *The things which were done.* The earthquake, the darkness, and the sufferings of Jesus. ¶ *Smote their breasts.* In token of alarm, fear, and anguish. They saw the judgments of God; they saw the guilt of the rulers; and they feared the farther displeasure of the Almighty.

50-56. See Notes on Mat. xxvii. 57-61; Mar. xv. 42-47.

CHAPTER XXIV.

1-12. See Notes on Mat. xxviii. 1-11.

13. *Two of them.* Two of the disciples. The name of one of them was *Cleopas,* ver. 18. Many have supposed that the other was Luke, and that he omitted his own name from modesty. Others have supposed that it was Peter. See ver. 34; 1 Co. xv. 5. There is no evidence to guide us here. Dr. Lightfoot has shown that *Cleopas* is the same

3 And they entered in, and
found not the body of the Lord
Jesus.
4 And it came to pass, as they
were much perplexed thereabout,
behold, [b]two men stood by them
in shining garments:
5 And, as they were afraid, and
bowed down *their* faces to the
earth, they said unto them, Why
seek ye [1]the living among the
dead?
6 He is not here, but is risen:
remember how he [c]spake unto you
when he was yet in Galilee,
7 Saying, The Son of man
must be delivered into the hands
of sinful men, and be crucified,
and the third day rise again.
8 And they remembered his
words,
9 And returned from the sepulchre, and told all these things unto
the eleven, and to all the rest.
10 It was Mary Magdalene,
and [d]Joanna, and Mary *the mother*
of James, and other *women that
were* with them, which told these
things unto the apostles.
11 And their words [e]seemed
to them as idle tales, and they
believed them not.
12 Then[f] arose Peter, and ran
unto the sepulchre; and stooping
down, he beheld the linen clothes
laid by themselves, and departed,
wondering in himself at that which
was come to pass.
13 And, behold, [g]two of them
went that same day to a village
called Emmaus, which was from
Jerusalem *about* threescore furlongs.
14 And they talked together of

b Jn.20.12; Ac.1.10.
1 or, *him that liveth*, Re.1.18.
c Mat.16.21; 17.23; Mar.8.31; 9.31; ch.9.22; Jn.2.22.
d ch.8.3.
e Ge.19.14; 2 Ki.7.2; Job 9.16; Ps.126.1; Ac.12.9,15.
f Jn.20.3,6. g Mar.16.12.

name as *Alpheus*, who was the father of the apostle James, Mat. x. 3. ¶ *Emmaus.* In regard to the locality of Emmaus, it seems quite probable that it is the same village which is referred to by Josephus (*Jewish Wars*, vii. 6, § 6), who states that, after the destruction of Jerusalem, Titus gave *Emmaus*, distant from Jerusalem threescore furlongs, to eight hundred of his troops, whom he had dismissed from his army, for their habitation. Dr. Thomson (*The Land and the Book*, vol. ii. p. 307, 540) regards it as the present Kuriet el 'Aineb, which Dr. Robinson identifies with Kirjath-jearim. Of this place he says: "Kuriet el 'Aineb itself would be the proper distance from Jerusalem, and being on the road to Jaffa, and on the dividing ridge between the plain and the mountains, the Roman emperor might have deemed it an advantageous post for a colony made up of his disbanded soldiers, who could keep in check the surrounding country. Certain it is that in these later ages the occupants of this place have controlled the whole adjacent region, and for many a generation exercised their lawless tyranny upon helpless pilgrims.

"It took just three hours' moderate riding from Kuriet el 'Aineb to Jerusalem: first, a long descent into Wady Hanîna, which passes between it and Soba; then a similar ascent, succeeded by a very steep pass, and a very slippery path down to Kulonia. At this place are some heavy foundations of church, convent, or castle by the road-side, which may be of almost any age, and also gardens of fruit-trees, irrigated by a fountain of excellent water. Kulonia is on a hill north of the road, and appears in a fair way to become a ruin itself before long. The path then winds up a valley, and stretches over a dreary waste of bare rocks until within a mile of the city, when the view opens upon its naked ramparts and the mysterious regions toward the Dead Sea." ¶ *Threescore furlongs.* Sixty furlongs, or about seven or eight miles. It is not certain that these were apostles, but the contrary seems to be implied in ver. 33. See Notes on that verse. If they were not, it is probable that they were intimate disciples, who may have been much with the Saviour during the latter part of his ministry and the closing scenes of his life. But it is wholly unknown why they were going to Emmaus. It may have been that this was their native place, or that they had friends in the vicinity. They seem to have

all these things which had happened.
15 And it came to pass that,
while they [h]communed *together*
and reasoned, Jesus himself drew
near and went with them.
16 But their [i]eyes were holden,
that they should not know him.
17 And he said unto them,
What manner of communications
are these that ye have one to
another, as ye walk and are sad?
18 And the one of them, whose
name was [k]Cleopas, answering,
said unto him, Art thou only a
stranger in Jerusalem, and hast
not known the things which are
come to pass there in these days?
19 And he said unto them,
What things? And they said unto

h Mal.3.16; Mat.18.20; ver.36. *i* Jn.20.14,15; 21.4.

k Jn.19.25.

given up all for lost, and to have come to the conclusion that Jesus was not the Messiah, though they naturally conversed about it, and there were many things which they could not explain. Their Master had been crucified contrary to their expectation, their hopes dashed, their anticipation disappointed, and they were now returning in sadness, and very naturally conversed, in the way, of the things which had happened in Jerusalem.

15. *Communed* together. Talked together. ¶ *And reasoned.* They reasoned, doubtless, about the probability or improbability that Jesus was the Messiah; about the evidence of his resurrection; about what was to be done in the present state of things. ¶ *Jesus himself drew near*, &c. The disciples were properly employed. Their minds were anxious about the state of things, and they endeavoured to arrive at the truth. In this state of things Jesus came to solve their doubts, and to establish them in the belief that he was the Christ; and we may learn from this that Christ will guide those who are sincerely endeavouring to know the truth. They who candidly and seriously endeavour to ascertain what is true and right he will direct; and often in an unexpected manner he will appear, to dissipate their doubts and to scatter all their perplexities. *Our* duty is sincerely to strive to ascertain the truth, and to do his will; and if his people do this, he will not leave them to perplexity and wandering.

16. *Their eyes were holden.* This expression is used merely to denote that they did not *know* who he was. It does not appear that there was anything supernatural or miraculous in it, or that God used any power to blind them. It may easily be accounted for without any such supposition; for, 1st. Jesus appeared *in another form* (Mar. xvi. 12)—that is, different from his *usual* appearance. 2d. They were not *expecting* to see him—indeed, they did not suppose that he was alive, and it required the strongest evidence to convince them that he was really risen from the dead.

17. *What manner of communications*, &c. What is the subject of your conversation? What is it that has so much affected your minds? They were deeply affected in the recollection of the death of Jesus; and, as became all Christians, they were conversing about him, and were sad at the overwhelming events that had come upon them.

18. *Art thou only a stranger?* &c. This is an expression of surprise that he should be unacquainted with an affair that had made so much noise, and that had been attended with so remarkable circumstances. The word *stranger* here denotes one who had come to reside at a place only for a *time*, not a permanent inhabitant. Many Jews came up from all parts of the world to Jerusalem, to keep the Passover there. They appear to have taken Jesus to be such a stranger or foreigner. The meaning of this verse may be thus expressed: "The affair concerning which we are sad has been well known, and has made a great talk and noise, so that all, even the strangers who have come up to remain there but a little time, are well acquainted with it. Art thou the *only one* of them who has not heard it? Is everybody so well acquainted with it, and thou hast not heard of it? It is a matter of surprise, and we cannot account for it."

19. *A prophet.* A teacher sent from God. They did not now call him the *Messiah*, for his *death* had led them to doubt that, but they had no doubt that he was a distinguished *prophet.* The

him, Concerning Jesus of Nazareth, which was [l]a prophet [m]mighty in deed and word before God and all the people;

20 And [n]how the chief priests and our rulers delivered him to be condemned to death, and have crucified him.

21 But we trusted that [o]it had been he which should have redeemed Israel; and, beside all this, to-day is the third day since these things were done.

22 Yea, and [p]certain women also of our company made us astonished, which were early at the sepulchre;

23 And when they found not his body, they came, saying that they had also seen a vision of angels, which said that he was alive.

24 And [q]certain of them which were with us went to the sepulchre, and found *it* even so as the women had said; but him they saw not.

25 Then he said unto them, [r]O fools, and slow of heart to believe all that the prophets have spoken!

26 Ought[s] not Christ to have

l ch.7.16; Jn.3.2; Ac.2.22. *m* Ac.7.22. *n* ch.23.1; Ac.13.27,28. *o* ch.1.68; Ac.1.6. *p* ver.9,10.

q ver.12. *r* He.5.11,12. *s* ver.46; Ac.17.3; He.9.22,23.

---

evidence of that was so clear that they *could* not call it in question. ¶ *Mighty in deed.* Powerful in working miracles, in raising the dead, healing the sick, &c. ¶ *In word.* In teaching. ¶ *Before God and all the people.* Manifestly; publicly. So that *God* owned him, and the people regarded him as a distinguished teacher.

20. See Notes on Mat. xxvi. 59–66.

21. *We trusted.* We hoped and expected. ¶ *Should have redeemed Israel.* That he was the Messiah, who would have delivered the nation from the Romans. ¶ *Besides all this.* It is to be observed that Cleopas states things just as they occurred to his own mind. There is little connection. His mind is confused and distracted. There were so many things that were remarkable in Jesus; there was so much evidence that he was the Messiah; their hopes had been so suddenly dashed by his death, and the succeeding events had been so wonderful, that his mind was confused, and he knew not what to think. The things which he now stated served to increase his perplexity. The expressions here are perfectly natural. They bespeak an agitated mind. They are simple touches of nature, which show that the book was not forged. If the book had been the work of imposture, this artless and perplexed narrative would not have been thought of. ¶ *To-day is the third day,* &c. Jesus had foretold them that he would rise on the third day. This they did not understand; but it is not improbable that they looked to this day expecting something wonderful, and that the visit to the sepulchre had called it to their recollection, and they were more and more amazed when they put all these things together. As if they had said, "The third day is come, and we have not seen him. Yet we begin to remember his promise—the angels have informed us that he is alive—but we do not know how to put these things together, or what to make of them."

22, 23. *Certain women.* See Mat. xxviii. 1–7; Jn. xx. 12. ¶ *A vision of angels.* An appearance of angels, or they had seen angels. See Jn. xx. 12.

24. *Certain of them which were with us.* Peter and John. See Jn. xx. 2–9.

25. *O fools.* The word *fool* sometimes is a term of reproach denoting *wickedness.* In this sense we are forbidden to employ it in addressing another, Mat. v. 22. That, however, is a different word in the Greek from the one which occurs here. The one there used implies contempt, but the one employed in this place denotes *weakness* or *dulness.* He reproached them for not seeing what he had himself so clearly predicted, and what had been foretold by the prophets. The word used in the original does not imply as much *reproach* as the word *fool* does among us. It was not an expression of *contempt;* it was an expression denoting merely that they were *thoughtless,* and that they did not properly *attend to* the evidence that he must die and rise again. ¶ *Slow of heart to believe.* Not quick to perceive. Dull of learning. They had suffered their previous opinions and prejudices to prevent their seeing the evidence that he must die

suffered these things, [t]and to enter into his glory?

27 And beginning at [u]Moses, and all [v]the prophets, he expounded unto them in all the scriptures the things concerning himself.

28 And they drew nigh unto the village whither they went; [w]and he made as though he would have gone further.

29 But they constrained him, saying, Abide with us; for it is toward evening, and the day is far spent. And he went in to tarry with them.

30 And it came to pass as he sat at meat with them, [x]he took bread, and blessed *it*, and brake, and gave to them.

31 And their eyes were opened,

t 1 Pe.1.3,11. *u* ver.44; Ac.3.22. *v* Ac.10.43; 26.22. *w* Ge.32.26; Mar.6.48. *x* Mat.14.19.

and rise from the dead. ¶ *All that the prophets have spoken.* Respecting the character and sufferings of the Messiah. See Notes on ver. 27.

26. *Ought not Christ*, &c. Ought not the *Messiah.* Was there not evidence that he would do it? and was it not indispensable that he should, in order to fulfil the prophecies? The *necessity* of his suffering these things referred to *here* was that it was foretold that he *would.* The reason why it was predicted, and why it was necessary that it should occur, was that it was proper that God should manifest his justice, and do honour to his law, and secure the due regard for his government, while he pardoned the guilty.

27. *Beginning at Moses.* At the *writings* of Moses, or at the beginning of the Old Testament; or rather the word *beginning* should be separated from what follows, denoting simply that he *commenced* his discourse, and not that he began at the prophets as well as at Moses; thus, "And commencing his discourse, or replying to them, he expounded from Moses and the prophets," &c. ¶ *All the prophets.* The books of the Old Testament generally. ¶ *He expounded.* He explained or interpreted it to them. Probably he showed them that *their* notions of the Messiah were not according to the Scriptures. *They* expected a temporal prince; they were perplexed because Jesus had not assumed the regal power, but had been put to death. He showed them that according to the prophecies he ought to suffer, and that his *death*, therefore, was no argument that he was not the Messiah. ¶ *In all the scriptures.* In all the *writings* of the Old Testament. They were called *scriptures* because they were *written*, the art of printing being then unknown. ¶ *The things concerning himself.* Concerning the Messiah. It does not appear that he *applied* them to himself, but left them, probably, to make the application. He showed what the Scriptures foretold, and *they* saw that these things applied to Jesus of Nazareth, and began to be satisfied that he was the Messiah. The most striking passages foretelling the character and sufferings of Christ are the following, which we may suppose it possible our Saviour dwelt upon to convince them that, though he was crucified, yet he was the Christ: Ge. iii. 15; De. xviii. 15; Ge. xlix. 10; Nu. xxi. 8, 9; Is. liii.; Da. ix. 25–27; Is. ix. 6, 7; Ps. cx.; xvi.; xxii.; Mal. iv. 2–6.

28. *He made as though he would have gone further.* He did not *say* he would go farther, but he kept on as if it was not his intention to stop, and doubtless he *would* have gone on if they had not constrained him to tarry.

29. *Constrained him.* They urged him, or pressingly invited him. They did not yet perceive that it was Jesus, but they had been charmed and delighted with his discourse, and they wished to hear him farther. Christians are delighted with communion with the Saviour. They seek it as the chief object of their desire, and they find their chief pleasure in fellowship with him. The two disciples felt it a privilege to entertain the stranger, as they supposed, who had so charmed them with his discourse; and so those to whom the gospel is preached, and who love it, feel it a privilege, and not a burden, to show kindness to those who bear to them the message of salvation. ¶ *Abide with us.* Remain with us, or pass the night in our house.

30. *Sat at meat.* Reclined at the table, or while he was at supper. ¶ *He took bread and blessed* it, &c. This was the office of the master of a feast, and perhaps this first attracted particularly their attention. Though he was in *their*

and they knew him; and he [2]vanished out of their sight.

32 And they said one to another,
Did not our heart [y]burn within us
while he talked with us by the
way, and while he opened to us
the scriptures?

33 And they rose up the same
hour and returned to Jerusalem,
and found the eleven gathered

2 or, *ceased to be seen of them.*
y Ps.39.3; Je.20.9; 23.29.

house, yet he acted as *master* of the feast, as he used to do with them before his death. Perhaps, also, as he *gave* them the bread, they observed the *prints* in his hands, and they knew that it was Jesus. This was not a *sacramental*, but a common supper; yet our Saviour sought a blessing on the food, and thus set an example to all his followers to acknowledge God in their daily gifts, and to seek his benediction in all their enjoyments.

31. *Their eyes were opened.* The obscurity was removed. They saw him to be the Messiah. Their doubts were gone, and they saw clearly that he was risen, and was truly, as they had long hoped, the Saviour of men. It is not meant that they were before *blind*, but that they did not know till then who he was. ¶ *He vanished out of their sight.* He suddenly departed. It does not appear that there was anything miraculous in this, but, during their surprise, he took the opportunity suddenly to withdraw from them.

32. *Our heart burn within us.* This is an expression denoting the deep interest and pleasure which they had felt in his discourse before they knew who he was. They now recalled his instruction; they remembered how his words reached the *heart* as he spoke to them; how convincingly he had showed them that the Messiah ought to suffer, and how, while he talked to them of the Christ that they so much loved, their hearts glowed with intense love. This feeling was not confined to them alone. All the followers of Jesus know how precious and tender are the communications of the Saviour, and how the heart glows with love as they think or hear of his life, and sufferings, and death. ¶ *He opened to us.* He *explained* to us the Scriptures. See ver. 27.

This narrative shows us, 1st. How blind men may be to the plainest doctrines of the Scriptures until they are explained to them. These disciples had often read or heard the Scriptures, but never, till then, did they fully understand that the Messiah must suffer. 2d. It is proper there should be those whose office it is to explain the Scriptures. Jesus did it while on earth; he does it now by his Spirit; and he has appointed his ministers, whose business it is to explain them. 3d. If men attempt to explain the Bible, they should themselves understand it. They should give their time and talents to a suitable preparation to understand the sacred volume. Preaching should consist in *real*, and not *fancied* explanations of the Scriptures; the real doctrines which *God* has taught in his word, and not the doctrines that *men* have taught in their systems. 4th. Here was convincing evidence that Jesus was the Messiah. This was but one of many instances where Jesus convinced his disciples, contrary to their previous belief. In this case the evidence was abundant. He first satisfied them from the Old Testament that the very things which had happened were foretold; he then dissipated every doubt by showing *himself* to them and convincing them that he was truly the Christ. There was no chance here for deception and juggling. Who would have met them and talked with them in this way but the real Saviour? Who would have thought of writing this narrative to help an imposture? What impostor would have recorded the dulness of the disciples as to the plain declarations of the Old Testament, and *then* have thought of this device to prop up the narrative? Everything about this narrative—its simplicity—its tenderness—its particularity—its perfect nature—its freedom from all appearance of trick—shows that it was taken from real life; and if so, then the Christian religion is true, for here is evidence that Jesus rose from the dead.

33. *The same hour.* Though it was late, and they had stopped, as they thought, for the night, yet such was their joy that they hastened to tell it to their companions and friends. This was natural and proper, and it shows how quick and ready they who have found the Saviour are to tell it to others. Comp. Jn. i. 41-45. Young converts to Christ *should* hasten to tell

together, and them that were with them,
34 Saying, The Lord is risen indeed, and [z]hath appeared to Simon.
35 And they told what things *were done* in the way, and how he was known of them in breaking of bread.
36 And[a] as they thus spake, Jesus himself stood in the midst of them, and saith unto them, Peace *be* unto you.

37 But they were terrified and affrighted, and [b]supposed that they had seen a spirit.
38 And he said unto them, Why are ye troubled? and why do thoughts arise in your hearts?
39 Behold my hands and my feet, that it is I myself: handle me, and see; for a spirit hath not flesh and bones, as ye see me have.
40 And when he had thus spoken, he showed them *his* hands and *his* feet.

z 1 Co.15.5. a Mar.16.14,&c.; Jn.20.19,&c. b Mar.6.49.

---

their joy, and should not shrink at self-denial to proclaim to others what God hath done for the soul, Ps. lxvi. 16.

"My lips and cheerful heart, prepare
To make his mercies known:
Come, ye that fear my God, and hear
The wonders he hath done.

"When on my head huge sorrows fell,
I sought his heavenly aid;
He saved my sinking soul from hell,
And death's eternal shade."

¶ *The eleven.* The eleven apostles. Judas was now dead. This shows that the two that went to Emmaus were not apostles.

34. *Saying.* The eleven said this. ¶ *Hath appeared to Simon.* To Peter. It is not known precisely when this happened, as the time and place are not mentioned. Paul has referred to it in 1 Co. xv. 5, from which it appears that he appeared to *Cephas* or *Peter* before he did to any other of the apostles. This was a mark of special love and favour, and particularly, after Peter's denial, it showed how ready he was to pardon, and how willing to impart comfort to those who are penitent, though their sins are great.

36, 37. *Jesus stood in the midst of them.* This was when the apostles were assembled, and when they had closed the doors for fear of the Jews, Jn. xx. 19. It was this fact, as well as his sudden and unexpected appearance, that alarmed them. The doors were shut, and the suddenness of his appearance led them to suppose they had seen a spirit. ¶ *Peace* be *unto you.* This was a form of salutation among the Hebrews denoting a wish of peace and prosperity. See Ge. xliii. 23. It was peculiarly appropriate for Jesus, as he had said before his death that he left *his peace* with them as their inheritance (Jn. xiv. 27), and as they were now alarmed and fearful at their state, and trembling for fear of the Jews, Jn. xx. 19.

38. *Why are ye troubled?* Why are you alarmed or frightened? ¶ *And why do thoughts,* &c. The word *thoughts* here means *doubts* or suspicions. It is used in this sense also in 1 Ti. ii. 8. The doubts which they had were whether he was the Christ. He reproves them for doubting this; for, 1st. The Scriptures had foretold his death; 2d. He had himself repeatedly done it; and, 3d. They had now the testimony of Peter that he had seen Jesus alive, and of the angels that he was risen. After all this evidence, Jesus reproves them for doubting whether he was truly the Messiah.

39–43. *Behold my hands,* &c. Jesus proceeds to give them evidence that he was truly the same person that had been crucified. He first showed them his hands and his feet—still pierced, and with the wounds made by the nails still open. Comp. Jn. xx. 27. He told them to handle him and see him. He ate before them. All this was to satisfy them that be was not, as they supposed, a spirit. Nor could better evidence have been given. He appealed to their senses, and peformed acts which a disembodied spirit could not do. ¶ *Handle me.* Or touch me; feel of me. Comp. Jn. xx. 27. ¶ *And see.* Be convinced, for you could not thus handle a spirit. The object here was to convince them that his body had really come to life. ¶ *For a spirit,* &c. He appeals here to what they well knew; and this implies that the spirit may exist separate from the body. That was the view of the apostles, and our Saviour distinctly countenances that belief.

41 And while they yet [c]believed
not for joy, and wondered, he said
unto them, [d]Have ye here any
meat?
42 And they gave him a piece
of a broiled fish, and of an honey-
comb.
43 And he took *it,* and did [e]eat
before them.
44 And he said unto them, [f]These
are the words which I spake unto
you while I was yet with you, [g]that
all things must be fulfilled which
were written in the law of Moses,
and *in* [h]the prophets, and *in* [i]the
psalms, concerning me.
45 Then opened he their understanding, that they might understand the scriptures,
46 And said unto them, Thus it

c Ge.45.26. d Jn.21.5,&c. e Ac.10.41. f Mat.16.21.

g ch.21.22; Ac.3.18; 13.27,33. h ver.27. i Ps.22.1,&c.

41. *Believed not for joy.* Their joy was so great, and his appearance was so sudden and unexpected, that they were bewildered, and still sought more evidence of the truth of what they *wished* to believe. This is nature. We have similar expressions in our language. *The news is too good to be true;* or, *I cannot believe it; it is too much for me.* ¶ *Any meat.* This word does not mean *meat* in our sense of it, but in the old English sense, denoting *anything to eat.*

42. *Honey-comb.* Honey abounded in Palestine, and was a very common article of food. Bees lived in caves of the rocks, in the hollows of trees, and were also kept as with us. The disciples gave, probably, just what was their own common fare, and what was ready at the time.

44. *These* are *the words.* Or this is the *fulfilment* of what I before told you respecting my death. See Lu. xviii. 33; Mar. x. 33. ¶ *While I was yet with you.* Before my death. While I was with you as a teacher and guide. ¶ *In the law of Moses.* The five books of Moses—Genesis, Exodus, Leviticus, Numbers, Deuteronomy. Among the Jews this was the first division of the Old Testament, and was called the *law.* ¶ *The prophets.* This was the second and largest part of the Hebrew Scriptures. It comprehended the books of Joshua, Judges, 1st and 2d Samuel, 1st and 2d Kings, which were called the *former prophets;* and Isaiah, Jeremiah, Ezekiel, and the twelve smaller books from Daniel to Malachi, which were called the *latter prophets.* ¶ *The psalms.* The word here used probably means what were comprehended under the name of *Hagiographa,* or holy writings. This consisted of the Psalms, Proverbs, Job, Song of Solomon, Ruth, Lamentations, Ecclesiastes, Esther, Daniel, Ezra, and Nehemiah, and the two books of Chronicles. This division of the Old Testament was in use long before the time of Christ, and was what he referred to here; and he meant to say that in *each of* these divisions of the Old Testament there were prophecies respecting himself. The *particular* subject before them was his *resurrection from the dead.* A most striking prediction of this is contained in Ps. xvi. 9–11. Compare it with Ac. ii. 24–32; xiii. 35–37.

45. *Opened he their understanding.* Enabled them fully to comprehend the meaning of the prophecies which foretold his death and resurrection. They had seen him die, they now saw him risen. Their prejudices were now, by his instructions, and by the facts which they could no longer call in question, removed, and they no longer doubted that he was the Messiah, and that all the *facts* in the case which had before confounded them could be easily accounted for. Hence we may learn—1st. That *facts,* or the farther disclosure of truth, will yet remove the *mysteries* that we now see in religion. 2d. That our prejudices and our preconceived opinions are one cause of our seeing so many mysteries in the Bible. If a man is willing to take the plain declarations of the Bible, he will commonly be little perplexed with mysteries. 3d. That God only can open the mind so as fully to comprehend the Scriptures. He only can overcome our prejudices, open our hearts, and dispose us to receive the ingrafted word with meekness, and with the simplicity of a child. See Ac. xvi. 14; Ja. i. 21; Mar. x. 15. 4th. The design of God's opening the understanding is that we may be acquainted with the Scriptures. It is not that we may be made wise above what is written, but that we may submit ourselves wholly to the Word of God.

46. *It behoved.* It became; it was

is written, and thus [k]it behoved
Christ to suffer, and [l]to rise from
the dead the third day;
47 And that [m]repentance and remission of sins should be preached
in his name among all nations, beginning at Jerusalem.
48 And ye are [n]witnesses of these
things.
49 And, behold, I send the promise of my Father upon you; but
tarry ye in the city of Jerusalem
until ye be [o]endued with power
from on high.
50 And he led them out as far
as to Bethany; and he lifted up
his hands and blessed them.
51 And it came to pass, while
he blessed them, he was parted
from them, and [p]carried up into
heaven.
52 And[q] they worshipped him,

k Is.53.3,5; Ac.4.12. *l* 1 Pe.1.3. *m* Ac.5.31; 13.38. *n* Ac.1.8.
o Is.44.3; Joel 2.28,&c.; Ac.2.1-21; 1.8. *p* Ac.1.9; He.4.14. *q* Mat.28.9,17.

proper or necessary that the Messiah should thus suffer. It was predicted of him, and all things have happened as it was foretold.

47. *Repentance.* Sorrow for sin and forsaking of it. It was proper that the *necessity* of repentance should be preached among all nations, for all were sinners. See Ac. xvii. 30. ¶ *Remission of sins.* Pardon or forgiveness of sins. It should be proclaimed that all men should repent, and that those who are penitent may be pardoned. ¶ *In my name.* By my command it should be proclaimed that men should repent, and by my merit that they may be pardoned. Pardon is offered by the authority of Christ to ALL nations, and this is a sufficient warrant to offer the gospel *to every man.* ¶ *Beginning at Jerusalem.* This was the dwelling of his murderers, and it shows his readiness to forgive the vilest sinners. It was the holy place of the temple, the habitation of God, the place of the solemnities of the ancient dispensation, and it was proper that pardon should be first proclaimed there. This was done—the gospel was first preached there. See Ac. ii. Paul also, in his travels, preached the gospel *first* to the Jews, the ancient people of God, offering them pardon through their own Messiah; and, when *they* rejected it, turned to the Gentiles, Ac. xiii. 46.

48. *Are witnesses of these things.* Of my life, my sufferings, my death, and my resurrection. How solemn was their office—to *testify* these things to the world, and, in the face of suffering and death, to go and proclaim them to all nations! In like manner, *all* Christians are witnesses for Christ. They are the *evidences* of his mercy and his love, and they should so live that others may be brought to see and love the Saviour.

49. *The promise of my Father.* The promise which the Father had made to them *through* the Saviour. See Mat. x. 19; Jn. xiv. 16, 17, 26. The promise was, that they should be aided by the power of the Holy Ghost. He also doubtless referred to the promise of God, made in the days of Joel, respecting the outpouring of the Holy Ghost. See Joel ii. 28, 29, compared with Ac. ii. 16–21. ¶ *Endued with power from on high.* The power which would be given them by the descent of the Holy Ghost—the power of speaking with tongues, of working miracles, and of preaching the gospel with the attending blessing and aid of the Holy Ghost. This was accomplished in the gift of the Holy Spirit on the day of Pentecost. See Ac. ii.

50, 51. *To Bethany.* See Notes on Mar. xvi. 19. Bethany was on the eastern declivity of the Mount of Olives, from which our Lord was taken up to heaven, Ac. i. 12. Bethany was a favoured place. It was the abode of Martha, and Mary, and Lazarus, and our Saviour delighted to be there. From this place, also, he ascended to his Father and our Father, and to his God and our God. ¶ *While he blessed them.* While he commanded his benediction to rest upon them; while he assured them of his favour, and commended them to the protection and guidance of God, in the dangers, trials, and conflicts which they were to meet in a sinful and miserable world.

52. *They worshipped him.* The word *worship* does not *always* denote religious homage. See Notes on Mat. ii. 11. Comp. Lu. xiv. 10. But here it is to be remarked, 1st. That they offered this worship to an *absent* Saviour. It was *after* he left them and had vanished out of their sight. It was therefore an act of religion, and was the *first* religious

and returned to Jerusalem with great joy;
53 And were continually in the temple, [r]praising and blessing God. Amen.

r Ac.2.46,47; 5.42.

homage that was paid to Jesus after he had left the world. 2d. If *they* worshipped an absent Saviour—a Saviour unseen by the bodily eye, it is right for *us* to do it. It was an example which we *may* and *should* follow. 3d. If worship may be rendered to Jesus, he is divine. See Ex. xx. 4, 5.

53. *Were continually in the temple.* Until the day of Pentecost—that is, about ten days after. See Ac. ii. ¶ *Praising and blessing God.* Chiefly for the full proof that the Messiah had come; had redeemed them, and had ascended to heaven. "Thus the days of their mourning were ended." They were filled with happiness at the assurance of redemption, and expressed what every Christian should feel—fulness of joy at the glad tidings that a Saviour has died, and risen, and ascended to God; and an earnest desire to pour forth in the sanctuary prayers and thanksgivings to the God of grace for his mercy to a lost and ruined world.

PREFACE

TO THE GOSPEL ACCORDING TO JOHN.

JOHN, the writer of this Gospel, was the son of Zebedee and Salome; compare Mat. xxvii. 56 with Mar. xv. 40, 41. His father was a fisherman of Galilee, though it would appear that he was not destitute of property, and was not in the lowest condition of life. He had hired men in his employ, Mar. i. 20. Salome is described as one who attended our Saviour in his travels, and ministered to his wants, Mat. xxvii. 55; Mar. xv. 41. Jesus commended his own mother Mary, on the cross, to John, and he took her to his own home (Jn. xix. 26, 27), with whom, history informs us, she lived until her death, about fifteen years after the crucifixion of Christ; and John was known to Caiaphas, the high-priest, Jn. xviii. 15. From all this it would seem not improbable that John had some property, and was better known than any of the other apostles.

He was the youngest of the apostles when called, and lived to the greatest age, and is the only one who is supposed to have died a peaceful death. He was called to be a follower of Jesus while engaged with his father and his elder brother James mending their nets at the Sea of Tiberias, Mat. iv. 21; Mar. i. 19; Lu. v. 10.

John was admitted by our Saviour to peculiar favour and friendship. One of the ancient fathers (Theophylact) says that he was related to him. "Joseph," he says, "had seven children by a former wife, four sons and three daughters, Martha, Esther, and *Salome*, whose son John was; therefore Salome was reckoned our Lord's sister, and John was his nephew." If this was the case it may explain the reason why James and John sought and expected the first places in his kingdom, Mat. xx. 20, 21. These may also possibly be the persons who were called our Lord's "brethren" and "sisters," Mat. xiii. 55, 56. This may also explain the reason why our Saviour committed his mother to the care of John on the cross, Jn. xix. 27.

The two brothers, James and John, with Peter, were several times admitted to peculiar favours by our Lord. They were the only disciples that were permitted to be present at the raising of the daughter of Jairus, Mar. v. 37; Lu. viii. 51; they only were permitted to attend the Saviour to the mount where he was transfigured, Mat. xvii. 1; Mar. ix. 2. The same three were permitted to be present at his sufferings in the garden of Gethsemane, Mat. xxvi. 36–45; Mar. xiv. 32–42. And it was to *these* disciples, together with Andrew, to whom the Saviour specially addressed himself when he made known the desolations that were coming upon Jerusalem and Judea; compare Mat. xxiv. 12; Mar. xiii. 3, 4. John was also admitted to *peculiar* friendship with the Lord Jesus. Hence he is mentioned as "that disciple whom Jesus loved" (Jn. xix. 26), and he is represented (Jn. xiii. 23) as leaning on his bosom at the institution of the Lord's Supper—an evidence of peculiar friendship. See Notes on that place. Though the Redeemer was attached to *all* his disciples, yet there is no improbability in supposing that *his* disposition was congenial with that of the meek and amiable John—thus authorizing and setting the example of special friendships among Christians.

To John was committed the care of Mary, the mother of Jesus. After the ascension of Christ he remained some time at Jerusalem, Ac. i. 14; iii. 1; iv. 13. John is also mentioned as having been sent down to Samaria to preach the gospel there with Peter (Ac. viii. 14–25); and from Ac. xv. it appears that he was present at the council at Jerusalem, A.D. 49 or 50. All this agrees with what is said by Eusebius, that he lived at Jerusalem till the death of Mary, fifteen years after the crucifixion of Christ. Till this time it is probable that he had not been engaged in preaching the gospel among the Gentiles.

At what time he went first among the Gentiles to preach the gospel is not certainly known. It has commonly been supposed that he resided in Judea and the neighbourhood until the war broke out with the Romans, and that he came into Asia Minor about the year 69 or 70. It is clear that he was not at Ephesus at the time that Paul visited those regions, as in all the travels of Paul and Luke there is no mention made of John.

Ecclesiastical history informs us that he spent the latter part of his life in Asia Minor, and that he resided chiefly at Ephesus, the chief city of that country. Of his residence there little is certainly known. In the latter part of his life he was banished to Patmos, a small desolate island in the Ægean Sea, about twenty miles in circumference. This is commonly supposed to have been during the persecution of Domitian, in the latter part of his reign. Domitian died A.D. 96. It is probable that he returned soon after that, in the reign of the Emperor Trajan. In that island he wrote the book of Revelation. See Notes on Rev. i. 9. After his return from Patmos he lived peaceably at Ephesus until his death, which is supposed to have occurred not long after. He was buried at Ephesus; and it has been commonly thought that he was the only one of the apostles who did not suffer martyrdom. It is evident that he lived to a very advanced period of life. We know not his age, indeed, when Christ called him to follow him, but we cannot suppose it was less than twenty-five or thirty. If so, he must have been not far from one hundred years old when he died.

Many anecdotes are related of him while he remained at Ephesus, but there is no sufficient evidence of their truth. Some have said that he was taken to Rome in a time of persecution and thrown into a caldron of boiling oil, and came out uninjured. It has been said also that, going into a bath one day at Ephesus, he perceived *Cerinthus*, who denied the divinity of the Saviour, and that he fled from him hastily, to express his disapprobation of his doctrine. It is also said, and of this there can be no doubt, that during his latter years he was not able to make a long discourse. He was carried to the church, and was accustomed to say nothing but this, "Little children, love one another." At length his disciples asked him why he always dwelt upon the same thing. He replied, "Because it is the Lord's command; and if this be done, it is sufficient."

Learned men have been much divided about the *time* when this Gospel was written. Wetstein supposed it was written just after our Saviour's ascension; Mill and Le Clerc, that it was written in 97; Dr. Lardner, that it was about the year 68, just before the destruction of Jerusalem. The common opinion is that it was written at Ephesus after his return from Patmos, and of course as late as the year 97 or 98. Nothing can be determined with certainty on the subject, and it is a matter of very little consequence.

There is no doubt that it was written by John. This is abundantly confirmed by the ancient fathers, and was not questioned by Celsus, Porphyry, or Julian, the acutest enemies of revelation in the early ages. It has never been extensively questioned to have been the work of John, and is one of the books of the New Testament whose canonical authority was never disputed. See Lardner, or Paley's *Evidences.*

The design of writing it John himself states, ch. xx. 31. It was to show that Jesus was the Christ, the Son of God, and that those who believed might have life through his name. *This design is kept in view through the whole Gospel, and should be remembered in our attempts to explain it.* Various attempts have been made to show that he wrote it to confute the followers of Cerinthus and the Gnostics, but no satisfactory evidence of such a design has been furnished.

As he wrote after the other evangelists, he has recorded many things which they omitted. He dwells much more fully than they do on the *divine character* of Jesus; relates many things pertaining to the early part of his ministry which they had omitted; records many more of his discourses than they have done, and particularly the interesting discourse at the institution of the Supper. See ch. xiv. xv. xvi. xvii.

It has been remarked that there are evidences in this Gospel that it was not written for the Jews. The author explains words and customs which to a Jew would have needed no explanation. See ch. i. 38, 41; v. 1, 2; vii. 2; iv. 9. The style in the Greek indicates that he was an unlearned man. It is simple, plain, unpolished, such as we should *suppose* would be used by one in his circumstances. At the same time it is dignified, containing pure and profound sentiments, and is on many accounts the most difficult of all the books of the New Testament to interpret. It contains more about *Christ,* his person, design, and work, than any of the other Gospels. The other evangelists were employed more in recording the *miracles,* and giving *external* evidence of the divine mission of Jesus. John is employed chiefly in telling us what he was, and what was his peculiar doctrine. His aim was to show, 1st, That Jesus was the Messiah. 2d. To show, *from the words of Jesus himself,* what the Messiah was. The other evangelists record his parables, his miracles, his debates with the Scribes and Pharisees; John records chiefly his discourses about *himself.* If anyone wishes to learn the true doctrine respecting the *Messiah, the Son of God,* expressed in simple language, but with most sublime conceptions; to learn the true nature and character of God, and the way of approach to his mercy-seat; to see the true nature of Christian piety, or the source and character of religious consolation; to have perpetually before him the purest model of character the world has seen, and to contemplate the purest precepts that have ever been delivered to man, he cannot better do it than by a prayerful study of the Gospel by John. It may be added that this Gospel is of itself proof that cannot be overthrown of the truth of revelation. John was a fisherman, unhonoured and unlearned, Ac. iv. 13. What man in that rank of life *now* could compose a book like this? Can it be conceived that any man of that rank, unless under the influence of inspiration, could conceive so sublime notions of God, could present so pure views of morals, and could draw a character so inimitably lovely and pure as that of Jesus Christ? To ask these questions is to answer them. And this Gospel will stand to the end of time as an unanswerable demonstration that the fisherman who wrote it was under a more than human guidance, and was, according to the promise that he has recorded (xvi. 13; comp. xiv. 26), *guided into all truth*. It will also remain as an unanswerable proof that the character which he has described—the character of the Lord Jesus—was real. It is a perfect character. It has not a flaw. How has this happened? The attempt has often been made to draw a perfect character—and as often, in every other instance, failed. How is it, when Homer and Virgil, and the ancient historians, have all failed to describe a perfect character, with the purest models before them, and with all the aid of imagination, that in every instance they have failed? How is it that this has at last been accomplished only by a Jewish fisherman? The difficulty is vastly increased if another idea is borne in mind. John describes one who he believed had a divine nature, ch. i. 1. It is an attempt to describe *God in human nature*, or to show how the Divine Being acts when united with man, or when appearing in human form. And the description is complete. There is not a word expressed by the Lord Jesus, or an emotion ascribed to him, inconsistent with such a supposition. But this same attempt was often made, and as often failed. Homer and Virgil, and all the ancient poets, have undertaken to show what the gods would be if they came down and conversed with man. And what were they? What were Jupiter, and Juno, and Venus, and Mars, and Vulcan? Beings of lust, and envy, and contention, and blood. How has it happened that the only successful account which has been given of the divine nature united with the human, and of living and acting as became such a union, has been given by a Jewish fisherman? How, unless the character was *real*, and the writer under a guidance far superior to the genius of Homer and the imagination of Virgil—the guidance of the Holy Spirit?

THE
GOSPEL ACCORDING TO JOHN.

CHAPTER I.

IN[a] the beginning was the [b]Word, and the Word was [c]with God, and the Word [d]was God.

a Pr.8.22-31; Col.1.16,17; 1 Jn.1.1. *b* Re.19.13. *c* ch.17.5. *d* Phi.2.6; He.1.8-13; 1 Jn.5.7.

2 The same was in the beginning with God.

3 All[e] things were made by him; and without him was not any thing made that was made.

e Ps.33.6; Ep.3.9.

1. *In the beginning.* This expression is used also in Ge. i. 1. To that place John evidently has allusion here, and means to apply to "the Word" an expression which is there applied *to God.* In both places it clearly means "before creation," "before the world was made," "when as yet there was nothing." The meaning is, that the *Word* had an existence before the world was created. This is not spoken of the *man* Jesus, but of that which *became* a man, or was incarnate, ver. 14. The Hebrews, by expressions like this, commonly denoted eternity. Thus the *eternity* of God is described (Ps. xc. 2): *Before the mountains were brought forth,* &c.; and eternity is commonly expressed by the phrase, *before the foundation of the world.* Whatever is meant by the term "Word," it is clear that it had an existence before *creation.* It is not, then, a *creature* or created being, and must be, therefore, uncreated and eternal. There is but *one* Being that is uncreated, and Jesus must be therefore divine. Compare the Saviour's own declarations respecting himself in the following places: Jn. viii. 58; xvii. 5; vi. 62; iii. 13; vi. 46; viii. 14; xvi. 28. ¶ *Was the Word.* Greek, "was the *Logos.*" This name is given to him who afterward became *flesh,* or was incarnate (ver. 14)—that is, to the Messiah. Whatever is meant by it, therefore, is applicable to the Lord Jesus Christ. There have been many opinions about the reason why this name was given to the Son of God. Those opinions it is unnecessary to repeat. The opinion which seems most plausible may be expressed as follows: 1st. A *word* is that by which we communicate our will; by which we convey our thoughts; or by which we issue commands—the medium of communication with others. 2d. The Son of God may be called "the Word," because he is the medium by which God promulgates his will and issues his commandments. See He. i. 1–3. 3d. This term was in use before the time of John. (*a*) It was used in the Chaldee translation of the Old Testament, as, *e. g.*, Is. xlv. 12: "I have made the earth, and created man upon it." In the Chaldee it is, "I, *by my word,* have made," &c. Is. xlviii. 13: "Mine hand also hath laid the foundation of the earth." In the Chaldee, "*By my word* I have founded the earth." And so in many other places. (*b*) This term was used by the Jews as applicable to the Messiah. In their writings he was commonly known by the term "Mimra"—that is, "Word;" and no small part of the interpositions of God in defence of the Jewish nation were declared to be by "the Word of God." Thus, in their Targum on De. xxvi. 17, 18, it is said, "Ye have appointed THE WORD OF GOD a king over you this day, that he may be your God." (*c*) The term was used by the Jews who were scattered among the Gentiles, and especially those who were conversant with the Greek philosophy. (*d*) The term was used by the followers of Plato among the Greeks, to denote the second person of the *Trinity.* The term *nous,* or *mind,* was commonly given to this second person, but it was said that this *nous* was *the word* or *reason* of the first person. The term was therefore extensively in use among the Jews and Gentiles before John wrote his Gospel, and it was certain that it *would be* applied to the second person of the Trinity by Christians, whether converted from Judaism or Paganism. It was important, therefore, that the *meaning* of the term should be settled by an inspired man, and accordingly John, in the com-

mencement of his Gospel, is at much pains to state clearly what is the true doctrine respecting the Logos, or Word. It is *possible*, also, that the doctrines of the Gnostics had begun to spread in the time of John. They were an Oriental sect, and held that the *Logos* or *Word* was one of the *Æons* that had been created, and that this one had been united to the man Jesus. If that doctrine had begun then to prevail, it was of the more importance for John to settle the truth in regard to the rank of the Logos or Word. This he has done in such a way that there need be no doubt about its meaning. ¶ *Was with God.* This expression denotes friendship or intimacy. Comp. Mar. ix. 19. John affirms that he was *with God* in the beginning—that is, before the world was made. It implies, therefore, that he was partaker of the divine glory; that he was blessed and happy with God. It proves that he was intimately united with the Father, so as to partake of his glory and to be appropriately called by the name God. He has himself explained it. See Jn. xvii. 5: *And now, O Father, glorify thou me with thine own self, with the glory which I had with thee before the world was.* See also Jn. i. 18: *No man hath seen God at any time; the only-begotten Son, which* IS IN THE BOSOM OF THE FATHER, *he hath declared him.* See also Jn. iii. 13: *The Son of man, which is in heaven.* Comp. Phi. ii. 6, 7. ¶ *Was God.* In the previous phrase John had said that the Word was *with God.* Lest it should be supposed that he was a different and *inferior* being, he here states that *he was God.* There is no more unequivocal declaration in the Bible than this, and there *could* be no stronger proof that the sacred writer meant to affirm that the Son of God was equal with the Father; for, 1st. There is no doubt that by the *Logos* is meant Jesus Christ. 2d. This is not an *attribute* or quality of God, but is a real subsistence, for it is said that the Logos was made *flesh*—that is, became a man. 3d. There is no variation here in the manuscripts, and critics have observed that the Greek will bear no other construction than what is expressed in our translation—that the Word *was God.* 4th. There is no evidence that John intended to use the word *God* in an *inferior* sense. It is not "the Word was *a* god," or "the Word was *like* God," but the Word *was God.* He had just used the word *God* as evidently applicable to Jehovah, the true God; and it is absurd to suppose that he would *in the same verse*, and without any indication that he was using the word in an inferior sense, employ it to denote a being altogether inferior to the true God. 5th. The name *God* is elsewhere given to him, showing that he is the supreme God. See Ro. ix. 5; He. i. 8, 9, 10–12; 1 Jn. v. 20; Jn. xx. 28. The meaning of this important verse may then be thus summed up: 1st. The name Logos, or Word, is given to Christ in reference to his becoming the Teacher or Instructor of mankind; the medium of communication between God and man. 2d. The name was in use at the time of John, and it was his design to state the correct doctrine respecting the Logos. 3d. The *Word*, or Logos, existed *before creation*—of course was not a *creature*, and must have been, therefore, from eternity. 4th. He was *with God*—that is, he was united to him in a most intimate and close union *before* the creation; and, as it could not be said that God was *with himself*, it follows that the Logos was in some sense *distinct* from God, or that there was a *distinction* between the Father and the Son. When we say that one is *with another*, we imply that there is some sort of distinction between them. 5th. Yet, lest it should be supposed that he was a *different* and *inferior* being—a creature—he affirms that he was God—that is, was equal with the Father. This is the foundation of the doctrine of the Trinity: 1. That the second person is in some sense *distinct* from the first. 2. That he is intimately united with the first person in essence, so that there are not two or more Gods. 3. That the second person may be called by the same name; has the same attributes; performs the same works; and is entitled to the same honours with the first, and that therefore he is "the same in substance, and equal in power and glory," with God.

2. *The same.* The Word, or the Logos, ¶ *Was in the beginning with God.* This seems to be a repetition of what was said in the first verse; but it is stated over again *to guard the doctrine*, and to prevent the possibility of a mistake. John had said that he existed before the creation, and that he was *with God;* but he had *not* said in the first verse *that the union with God existed in the beginning.* He now expresses that idea,

4 In[f] him was life; and the life was [g]the light of men.

f ch.5.26; 1 Jn.5.11. *g* ch.8.12.

5 And the light shineth [h]in darkness, and the darkness [i]comprehended it not.

h ch.3.19. *i* 1 Co.2.14.

and assures us that that *union* was not one which was commenced *in time*, and which might be, therefore, a mere union of *feeling*, or a *compact*, like that between any other beings, but was one which existed in *eternity*, and which was therefore a union of *nature or essence*.

3. *All things.* The universe. The expression cannot be limited to any part of the universe. It appropriately expresses everything which exists—all the vast masses of material worlds, and all the animals and things, great or small, that compose those worlds. See Re. iv. 11; He. i. 2; Col. i. 16. ¶ *Were made.* The original word is from the verb *to be*, and signifies "*were*" by him; but it expresses the idea of creation here. It does not alter the sense whether it is said "*were* by him," or "were *created* by him." The word is often used in the sense of *creating*, or forming from nothing. See Ja. iii. 9; and Ge. ii. 4, Is. xlviii. 7, in the Septuagint. ¶ *By him.* In this place it is affirmed that *creation* was effected by *the Word*, or the Son of God. In Ge. i. 1, it is said that the Being who created the heavens and the earth was God. In Ps. cii. 25–28, this work is ascribed to Jehovah. The *Word*, or the Son of God, is therefore appropriately called *God*. The work of *creation* is uniformly ascribed in the Scriptures to the second person of the Trinity. See Col. i. 16; He. i. 2, 10. By this is meant, evidently, that he was the agent, or the efficient cause, by which the universe was made. There is no higher proof of *omnipotence* than the work of *creation;* and hence God often appeals to that work to prove that he is the *true* God, in opposition to idols. See Is. xl. 18–28; Je. x. 3–16; Ps. xxiv. 2; xxxix. 11; Pr. iii. 19. It is absurd to say that God can invest a creature with *omnipotence*. If he can make a *creature omnipotent*, he can make him *omniscient*, and can in the same way make him omnipresent, and infinitely wise and good; that is, he can invest a creature with all his own attributes, or make another being like himself, or, which is the same thing, there could be two Gods, or as many Gods as he should choose to make. But this is absurd. The Being, therefore, that *created* all things must be divine; and as this work is ascribed to Jesus Christ, and as it is uniformly in the Scriptures declared to be the work of God, Jesus Christ is therefore *equal with the Father*. ¶ *Without him.* Without his agency; his notice; the exertion of his power. Comp. Mat. x. 29. This is a strong way of speaking, designed to confirm, beyond the possibility of doubt, what he had just said. He says, therefore, in general, that all things were made by Christ. In this part of the verse he shuts out all doubt, and affirms that there was *no exception;* that there was not a single thing, however minute or unimportant, which was not made by him. In this way he confirms what he said in the first verse. Christ was not merely *called* God, but he did the *works* of God, and therefore the name is used in its proper sense as implying supreme divinity. To this same test Jesus himself appealed as proving that he was divine. Jn. x. 37: *If I do not* THE WORKS *of my Father, believe me not.* Jn. v. 17: MY FATHER *worketh hitherto, and I work.*

4. *In him was life.* The evangelist had just affirmed (ver. 3) that by the *Logos* or *Word* the world was originally created. One part of that creation consisted in *breathing into man the breath of life*, Ge. ii. 7. God is declared to be *life*, or the *living* God, because he is the source or fountain of life. This attribute is here ascribed to Jesus Christ. He not merely made the *material* worlds, but he also gave *life*. He was the agent by which the *vegetable* world became animated; by which *brutes* live; and by which *man* became a living soul, or was endowed with immortality. This was a *higher* proof that the "Word was God," than the creation of the material worlds; but there is another sense in which he was *life*. The *new creation*, or the renovation of man and his restoration from a state of sin, is often compared with the *first creation;* and as the Logos was the source of *life* then, so, in a similar but higher sense, he is the source of life to the soul dead in trespasses and sins, Ep. ii. 1. And it is probably in reference to this that he is so often called *life* in the writings of John. "For as the Father hath life in himself, so hath

6 There was a [k]man sent from God, whose name *was* John.

7 The same came for a witness, to bear witness of the Light, that

k Lu.3.2,3.

he given to the Son to have life in himself," Jn. v. 26; "He giveth life unto the world," Jn. vi. 33; "I am the resurrection and the life," Jn. xi. 25; "This is the true God and eternal life," 1 Jn. v. 20. See also 1 Jn. i. 1, 2; v. 11; Ac. iii. 15; Col. iii. 4. The meaning is, that he is the source or the fountain of both natural and spiritual life. Of course he has the attributes of God. ¶ *The life was the light of men. Light* is that by which we see objects distinctly. The light of the sun enables us to discern the form, the distance, the magnitude, and the relation of objects, and prevents the perplexities and dangers which result from a state of darkness. Light is in all languages, therefore, put for *knowledge*—for whatever enables us to discern our duty, and that saves us from the evils of ignorance and error. "Whatsoever doth make manifest is light," Ep. v. 13. See Is. viii. 20; ix. 2. The Messiah was predicted as the *light* of the world, Is. ix. 2, compared with Mat. iv. 15, 16; Is. lx. 1. See Jn. viii. 12: "I am the light of the world;" xii. 35, 36, 46: "I am come a light into the world." The meaning is, that the Logos or Word of God is the *instructor* or *teacher* of mankind. This was done before his advent by his direct agency in giving man reason or understanding, and in giving his law, for the "law was ordained by angels *in the hand of a mediator*" (Ga. iii. 19); after his advent by his personal ministry when on earth, by his Spirit (Jn. xiv. 16, 26), and by his ministers since, Ep. iv. 11; 1 Co. xii. 28.

5. *The light shineth in darkness.* Darkness, in the Bible, commonly denotes ignorance, guilt, or misery. See Is. ix. 1, 2; Mat. iv. 16; Ac. xxvi. 18; Ep. v. 8, 11; Ro. xiii. 12. It refers here to a wicked and ignorant people. When it is said that "the light shineth in darkness," it is meant that the Lord Jesus came to teach an ignorant, benighted, and wicked world. This has always been the case. It was so when he sent his prophets; so during his own ministry; and so in every age since. His efforts to enlighten and save men have been like light struggling to penetrate a thick, dense cloud; and though a few rays may pierce the gloom, yet the great mass is still an impenetrable shade. ¶ *Comprehended it not.* This word means *admitted* it not, or *received* it not. The word *comprehend*, with us, means to *understand.* This is not the meaning of the original. The darkness did not *receive* or *admit* the rays of light; the shades were so thick that the light could not penetrate them; or, to drop the figure, men were so ignorant, so guilty, so debased, that they did not appreciate the value of his instructions; they despised and rejected him. And so it is still. The great mass of men, sunk in sin, will not receive his teachings, and be enlightened and saved by him. Sin always blinds the mind to the beauty and excellency of the character of the Lord Jesus. It indisposes the mind to receive his instructions, just as *darkness* has no affinity for *light;* and if the one exists, the other must be displaced.

6. *A man sent from God.* See Mat. iii. The evangelist proceeds now to show that John the Baptist was not the Messiah, and to state the true nature of his office. Many had supposed that he was the Christ, but this opinion he corrects; yet he admits that he was *sent from God*—that he was divinely commissioned. Though he denied that he was *the Messiah*, yet he did not deny that he was sent from or by heaven on an important errand to men. Some have supposed that the sole design of this gospel was to show that John the Baptist was not the Messiah. Though there is no foundation for this opinion, yet there is no doubt that *one* object was to show this. The *main* design was to show that *Jesus was the Christ*, ch. xx. 31. To do this, it was proper, in the beginning, to prove that *John* was not the Messiah; and this might have been at that time an important object. John made many disciples, Mat. iii. 5. Many persons supposed that he might be the Messiah, Lu. iii. 15; Jn. i. 19. *Many of these disciples of John remained* AT EPHESUS, *the very place where John is supposed to have written this gospel, long after the ascension of Jesus*, Ac. xix. 1–3. It is not improbable that there might have been many others who adhered to John, and perhaps many who supposed that he was the Messiah. On these accounts it was important for the evan-

all *men* through him might believe.

8 He[l] was not that Light, but *was sent* to bear witness of that Light.

9 *That* was the true [m] Light,

l Ac.19.4.

m Is.49.6.

gelist to show that John *was not the Christ*, and to show, also, that he, who was extensively admitted to be a prophet, was an important *witness* to prove that Jesus of Nazareth was the Christ. The evangelist in the first four verses stated that "the Word" was divine; he now proceeds to state the proof that he was *a man*, and was the Messiah. The *first* evidence adduced is the testimony of John the Baptist.

7, 8. *For a witness.* To give testimony. He came to prepare the minds of the people to receive him (Mat. iii.; Lu. iii.); to lead them by repentance to God; and to point out the Messiah to Israel when he came, Jn. i. 31. ¶ *Of the Light.* That is, of the Messiah. Comp. Is. lx. 1. ¶ *That all* men, &c. It was the object of John's testimony that *all* men might believe. He designed to prepare them for it; to announce that the Messiah was about to come, to direct the minds of men *to* him, and thus to fit them to believe on him when he came. Thus he baptized them, saying "That they should believe on him who should come after him" (Ac. xix. 4), and thus he produced a very general expectation that the Messiah was about to come. The testimony of John was peculiarly valuable on the following accounts: 1st. It was made when he had no *personal* acquaintance with Jesus of Nazareth, and of course there could have been no *collusion* or agreement to deceive them, Jn. i. 31. 2d. It was sufficiently long before he came to excite general attention, and to fix the mind on it. 3d. It was that of a man acknowledged by all to be a prophet of God—"for all men held John to be a prophet," Mat. xxi. 26. 4th. It was *for the express purpose* of declaring beforehand that he was about to appear. 5th. It was *disinterested.* He was himself extremely popular. Many were disposed to receive *him* as the Messiah. It was evidently in his *power* to form a large party, and to be regarded extensively as the Christ. This was the highest honour to which a Jew could aspire; and it shows the value of John's testimony, that he was willing to lay all his honours at the feet of Jesus, and to acknowledge that he was unworthy to perform for him the office of the humblest servant, Mat. iii. 11. ¶ *Through him.* Through John, or by means of his testimony. ¶ *Was not that Light.* Was not *the Messiah.* This is an explicit declaration designed to satisfy the disciples of John. The *evidence* that he was not the Messiah he states in the following verses.

From the conduct of John here we may learn, 1st. The duty of laying *all* our honours at the feet of Jesus. 2d. As John came that all might believe, so it is no less true of the ministry of Jesus himself. He came for a similar purpose, and we may ALL, therefore, trust in him for salvation. 3d. We should not rely too much on ministers of the gospel. They cannot save us any more than John could; and *their* office, as *his* was, is simply to direct men *to the Lamb of God that taketh away the sin of the world.*

9. That *was the true Light.* Not John, but the Messiah. He was not a false, uncertain, dangerous guide, but was one that was true, real, steady, and worthy of confidence. A false light is one that leads to danger or error, as a false beacon on the shores of the ocean may lead ships to quicksands or rocks; or an *ignis fatuus* to fens, and precipices, and death. A true light is one that does not deceive us, as the true beacon may guide us into port or warn us of danger. Christ does not lead astray. All false teachers do. ¶ *That lighteth.* That enlightens. He removes darkness, error, ignorance, from the mind. ¶ *Every man.* This is an expression denoting, in general, the whole human race—Jews and Gentiles. John preached to the Jews. Jesus came *to be a light to lighten the Gentiles*, as well as to be the *glory of the people of Israel*, Lu. ii. 32. ¶ *That cometh into the world.* The phrase in the original is ambiguous. The word translated "that cometh" may either refer to the *light*, or to the word *man;* so that it may mean either "this *true light that cometh* into the world enlightens all," or "it enlightens every *man that cometh* into the world." Many critics, and, among the fathers, Cyril and Augustine, have preferred the former, and translated it, "The true light was he who, coming into the world, enlightened

which lighteth every man that cometh into the world.

10 He was in the world, and the world was made by him, [n]and the world knew him not.

11 He[o] came unto his own, and his own received him not.

12 But [p]as many as received him, to them gave he [1]power to become

n ver.5.

o Ac.3.26; 13.46. p Is.56.4,5; Ro.8.15; 1 Jn.3.1.
1 or, *the right;* or, *privilege.*

every man." The principal reasons for this are, 1st. That the Messiah is often spoken of as he that cometh into the world. See ch. vi. 14; xviii. 37. 2d. He is often distinguished as "*the light that cometh into the world.*" Ch. iii. 19: "This is the condemnation, that *light* is come into the world." Ch. xii. 46: "I am come *a light* into the world." Christ may be said *to do* what is accomplished by his command or appointment. This passage means, therefore, that by his own personal ministry, and by his Spirit and apostles, light or teaching is afforded to all. It does not mean that every individual of the human family is enlightened with the knowledge *of the gospel*, for this never yet *has been;* but it means, 1st. That this light is not confined to the *Jews*, but is extended to *all*—Jews and Gentiles. 2d. That it is provided for all and offered to all. 3d. It is not affirmed that at the time that John wrote all *were actually enlightened*, but the word "lighteth" has the form of the *future*. *This is that light so long expected and predicted, which, as the result of its coming into the world, will ultimately enlighten all nations.*

10. *He was in the world.* This refers, probably, not to his pre-existence, but to the fact that he became incarnate; that he dwelt among men. ¶ *And the world was made by him.* This is a repetition of what is said in ver. 3. Not only *men*, but all material things, were made by him. These facts are mentioned here to make what is said immediately after more striking, to wit, that men did not receive him. The proofs which he furnished that they *ought* to receive him were, 1st. Those given while he was *in the world*—the miracles that he wrought and his instructions; and, 2d. The fact that the *world was made by him.* It was remarkable that the world did not *know* or approve its own maker. ¶ *The world knew him not.* The word *knew* is sometimes used in the sense of *approving* or *loving*, Ps. i. 6; Mat. vii. 23. In this sense it may be used here. The world did not love or approve him, but rejected him and put him to death. Or it may mean that they did not understand or know that he was the Messiah; for had the Jews *known* and *believed* that he was the Messiah, they would not have put him to death, 1 Co. ii. 8: "Had they known it, they would not have crucified the Lord of glory." Yet they *might* have known it, and therefore they were not the less to blame.

11. *He came unto his own.* His own *land* or *country*. It was called *his* land because it was the place of his birth, and also because it was the chosen land where God delighted to dwell and to manifest his favour. See Is. v. 1–7. Over that land the laws of God had been extended, and that land had been regarded as peculiarly his, Ps. cxlvii. 19, 20. ¶ *His own.* His own *people*. There is a distinction here in the original words which is not preserved in the translation. It may be thus expressed: "He came to his own *land*, and his own people received him not." They were *his* people, because God had chosen them to be his above all other nations; had given to them his laws; and had signally protected and favoured them, De. vii. 6; xiv. 2. ¶ *Received him not.* Did not acknowledge him to be the Messiah. They rejected him and put him to death, agreeably to the prophecy, Is. liii. 3, 4. From this we learn, 1st. That it is reasonable to expect that those who have been peculiarly favoured should welcome the message of God. God had a right to expect, after all that had been done for the Jews, that they would receive the message of eternal life. So he has a right to expect that *we* should embrace him and be saved. Yet, 2d. It is not the abundance of mercies that incline men to seek God. The Jews had been signally favoured, but they rejected him. So, many in Christian lands live and die rejecting the Lord Jesus. 3d. Men are alike in every age. All would reject the Saviour if left to themselves. All men are by nature wicked. There is no more certain and universal proof of this than the universal rejection of the Lord Jesus.

12. *To as many as received him.* The great mass; the people; the scribes and

the sons of God, *even* to [q]them that believe on his name:
13 Which were [r]born, not of
blood, nor of the will of the flesh, nor of the will of man, but of God.
14 And the [s]Word was made

q Ga.3.26. r Ja.1.18. s Lu.1.35; 1 Ti.3.16.

Pharisees rejected him. A few in his lifetime received him, and many more after his death. To *receive him*, here, means to *believe* on him. This is expressed at the end of the verse. ¶ *Gave he power.* This is more appropriately rendered in the margin by the word *right* or *privilege.* Comp. Ac. i. 7; v. 4; Ro. ix. 21; 1 Co. vii. 37; viii. 9; ix. 4, 5. ¶ *Sons of God.* Children of God by adoption. See Notes on Mat. i. 1. Christians are called sons of God—1st. Because they are *adopted* by him, 1 Jn. iii. 1. 2d. Because they are *like him;* they resemble him and have his spirit. 3d. They are united to the Lord Jesus, the Son of God—are regarded by *him* as his brethren (Mat. xxv. 40), and are therefore regarded as the children of the Most High. ¶ *On his name.* This is another way of saying believeth in *him.* The *name* of a person is often put for the person himself, ch. ii. 23; iii. 18; 1 Jn. v. 13. From this verse we learn, 1st. That to be a child of God is a privilege—far more so than to be the child of any man, though in the highest degree rich, or learned, or honoured. Christians are therefore more honoured than any other men. 2d. God *gave* them this privilege. It is not by their own works or deserts; it is because God chose to impart this blessing to them, Ep. ii. 8; Jn. xv. 16. 3d. This favour is given only to those who believe on him. All others are the children of the wicked one, and no one who has not *confidence in God* can be regarded as his child. No parent would acknowledge one for his child, or approve of him, who had no *confidence* in him, who *doubted* or denied all he said, and who despised his character. Yet this the sinner constantly does toward God, and he cannot, therefore, be called his son.

13. *Which were born.* This doubtless refers to the *new birth,* or to the great change in the sinner's mind called regeneration or conversion. It means that they did not become the children of God in virtue of their natural birth, or because they were the children of *Jews,* or because they were descended from pious parents. The term "to be born" is often used to denote this change. Comp. Jn. iii. 3–8; 1 Jn. ii. 29. It illustrates clearly and beautifully this great change. The natural birth introduces us to life. The new birth is the beginning of spiritual life. Before, the sinner is *dead* in sins (Ep. ii. 1); now he begins truly to live. And as the natural birth is the beginning of life, so to be born of God is to be introduced to *real* life, to light, to happiness, and to the favour of God. The term expresses at once the *greatness* and the *nature* of the change. ¶ *Not of blood.* The Greek word is plural; not of *bloods*—that is, not of *man.* Comp. Mat. xxvii. 4. The Jews prided themselves on being the descendants of Abraham, Mat. iii. 9. They supposed that it was proof of the favour of God to be descended from such an illustrious ancestry. In this passage this notion is corrected. It is not because men are descended from an illustrious or pious parentage that they are entitled to the favour of God; or perhaps the meaning may be, not because there is a *union* of illustrious lines of ancestry or *bloods* in them. The law of Christ's kingdom is different from what the Jews supposed. Comp. 1 Pe. i. 23. It was necessary to be *born of God* by regeneration. Possibly, however, it may mean that they did not become children of God by the bloody rite of *circumcision,* as many of the Jews supposed they did. This is agreeable to the declaration of Paul in Ro. ii. 28, 29. ¶ *Nor of the will of the flesh.* Not by natural generation. ¶ *Nor of the will of man.* This *may* refer, perhaps, to the will of man in *adopting* a child, as the former phrases do to the natural birth; and the design of using these three phrases *may* have been to say that they became the children of God neither in virtue of their descent from illustrious parents like Abraham, nor by their natural birth, nor by being *adopted* by a pious man. None of the ways by which we become entitled to the privileges of *children* among men can give us a title to be called the sons of God. It is not by human power or agency that men become children of the Most High. ¶ *But of God.* That is, God produces the change, and confers the privilege of being called his children.

flesh, and dwelt among us, ([t]and we beheld his glory, the glory as of the only-begotten of the Father,) [u]full of grace and truth.

t 2 Pe.1.17; 1 Jn.1.1,2. *u* Ps.45.2; Col.2.3,9.

The heart is changed by his power. No unaided effort of man, no works of ours, can produce this change. At the same time, it is true that no man is renewed who does not himself *desire* and *will* to be a believer; for the effect of the change is on his *will* (Ps. cx. 3), and no one is changed who does not strive to enter in at the strait gate, Phi. ii. 12. This important verse, therefore, teaches us, 1st. That if men are saved they must be born again. 2d. That their salvation is not the result of their birth, or of any honourable or pious parentage. 3d. That the children of the rich and the noble, as well as of the poor, must be born of God if they will be saved. 4th. That the children of pious parents must be born again, or they cannot be saved. None will go to heaven simply because their *parents* are Christians. 5th. That this work is the work of God, and *no man* can do it for us. 6th. That we should forsake all human dependence, cast off all confidence in the flesh, and go at once to the throne of grace, and beseech of God to adopt us into his family and save our souls from death.

14. *And the Word was made flesh.* The word *flesh*, here, is evidently used to denote *human nature* or *man.* See Mat. xvi. 17; xix. 5; xxiv. 22; Lu. iii. 6; Ro. i. 3; ix. 5. The "Word" was made *man.* This is commonly expressed by saying that he became *incarnate.* When we say that a being becomes *incarnate*, we mean that one of a higher order than man, and of a different nature, assumes the appearance of man or becomes a man. Here it is meant that "the Word," or the second person of the Trinity, whom John had just proved to be equal with God, became a man, or was united with the man Jesus of Nazareth, so that it might be said that he *was made flesh.* ¶ *Was made.* This is the same word that is used in ver. 3: "All things *were made* by him." It is not simply affirmed that he *was* flesh, but that he was *made* flesh, implying that he had pre-existence, agreeably to ver. 1. This is in accordance with the doctrine of the Scriptures elsewhere. He. x. 5: "A *body* hast thou prepared me." He. ii. 14: "As the children are partakers of flesh and blood, he also himself likewise took part of the same." 1 Jn. iv. 2: "Jesus Christ is come in the flesh." See also 1 Ti. iii. 16; Phi. ii. 6; 2 Co. viii. 9; Lu. i. 35. The expression, then, means that he became a man, and that he became such by the power of God providing for him a body. It cannot mean that the divine nature was *changed* into the human, for that could not be; but it means that the Logos, or "Word," became so intimately *united* to Jesus that it might be said that the Logos, or "Word" *became* or *was* a man, as the *soul* becomes so *united* to the body that we may say that it is *one person* or *a man.* ¶ *And dwelt among us.* The word in the original denotes "dwelt as in a tabernacle or tent;" and some have supposed that John means to say that the human body was a tabernacle or tent for the Logos to abide in, in allusion to the tabernacle among the Jews, in which the Shechinah, or visible symbol of God, dwelt; but it is not necessary to suppose this. The object of John was to prove that "the Word" became *incarnate.* To do this he appeals to various evidences. One was that he *dwelt* among them; sojourned with them; ate, drank, slept, and was with them for years, so that they "saw him with their eyes, they looked upon him, and their hands handled him," 1 Jn. i. 1. To *dwell in a tent with one* is the same as to be in his family; and when John says he *tabernacled* with them, he means that he was with them as a friend and as one of a family, so that they had full opportunity of becoming familiarly acquainted with him, and could not be mistaken in supposing that *he was really a man.* ¶ *We beheld his glory.* This is a new proof of what he was affirming—*that* THE WORD OF GOD *became man.* The first was, that they had seen him *as a man.* He now adds that they had seen him in his proper glory *as God and man united in one person*, constituting him the unequalled Son of the Father. There is no doubt that there is reference here to the transfiguration on the holy mount. See Mat. xvii. 1–9. To this same evidence Peter also appeals, 2 Pe. i. 16–18. John was one of the witnesses of that scene, and hence he says, "WE *beheld his glory*," Mar. ix. 2. The word *glory* here means majesty, dignity,

15 John[v] bare witness of him, and cried, saying, This was he of whom I spake, He that cometh after me is preferred before me; for he was before me.

v Mat.3.13,&c.

splendour. ¶ *The glory as of the only-begotten of the Father.* The dignity which was appropriate to the only-begotten Son of God; such glory or splendour as could belong to no other, and as properly expressed his rank and character. This glory was seen eminently on the mount of transfiguration. It was also seen in his miracles, his doctrine, his resurrection, his ascension; all of which were such as to illustrate the perfections, and manifest the glory that belongs only to the Son of God. ¶ *Only-begotten.* This term is never applied by John to any but Jesus Christ. It is applied by him five times to the Saviour, ch. i. 14, 18; iii. 16, 18; 1 Jn. iv. 9. It means literally an only child. Then, as an only child is peculiarly dear to a parent, it means one that is especially beloved. Comp. Ge. xxii. 2, 12, 16; Je. vi. 26; Zec. xii. 10. On *both* these accounts it is bestowed on the Saviour. 1st. As he was eminently the Son of God, sustaining a peculiar relation to him in his divine nature, exalted above all men and angels, and thus worthy to be called, by way of eminence, his only Son. Saints are called his *sons* or children, because they are born of his Spirit, or are like him; but the Lord Jesus is exalted far above all, and deserves eminently to be called his only-begotten Son. 2d. He was peculiarly dear to God, and therefore this appellation, implying tender affection, is bestowed on him. ¶ *Full of grace and truth.* The word *full* here refers to the *Word made flesh*, which is declared to be full of grace and truth. The word *grace* means *favours*, gifts, acts of beneficence. He was kind, merciful, gracious, doing good to all, and seeking man's welfare by great sacrifices and love; so much so, that it might be said to be characteristic of him, or he *abounded* in favours to mankind. He was also *full of truth.* He declared the truth. In him was no falsehood. He was not like the false prophets and false Messiahs, who were wholly impostors; nor was he like the emblems and shadows of the old dispensation, which were only types of the true; but he was truth itself. He *represented things as they are*, and thus became the *truth* as well as *the way and the life.*

15. *John bare witness of him.* The evangelist now returns to the testimony of John the Baptist. He had stated that the Word became incarnate, and he now appeals to the testimony of John to show that, thus incarnate, he was the Messiah. ¶ *He that cometh after me.* He of whom I am the forerunner, or whose way I am come to prepare. See Notes on Mat. iii. 3. ¶ *Is preferred before me.* Is superior to me. Most critics have supposed that the words translated "is preferred" relate to *time*, and not to *dignity;* meaning that though he came *after* him publicly, being six months younger than John, as well as entering on his work *after* John, yet that he had existed long before him. Most, however, have understood it more correctly, as our translators seem to have done, as meaning, He was worthy of more *honour* than I am. ¶ *He was before me.* This can refer to nothing but his pre-existence, and can be explained only on the supposition that he *existed* before John, or, as the evangelist had before shown, from the beginning. He came *after* John in his public ministry and in his human nature, but in his divine nature he had existed long before John had a being—from eternity. We may learn here that it is one mark of the true spirit of a minister of Christ to desire and feel that Christ is always to be preferred to ourselves. We should keep ourselves out of view. The great object is to hold up the Saviour; and however much ministers may be honoured or blessed, yet they should lay all at the feet of Jesus, and direct all men to him as the undivided object of affection and honour. It is the business of every Christian, as well as of every Christian minister, to be a *witness* for Christ, and to endeavour to convince the world that he is worthy of confidence and love.

16. *Of his fulness.* In the 14th verse the evangelist has said that Christ was *full of grace and truth.* Of that *fulness* he now says that all the disciples had received; that is, they derived from his abundant truth and mercy grace to understand the plan of salvation, to preach the gospel, to live lives of holiness; they *partook* of the numerous blessings which he came to impart by his instructions

16 And of his [w]fulness have all
we received, and grace for grace.
17 For the law was given by
Moses, *but* [x]grace and truth came
by Jesus Christ.
18 No[y] man hath seen God at

w ch.3.34.

x Ps.85.10; Ro.5.21. y Ex.33.20; 1 Ti.6.16.

---

and his death. These are undoubtedly not the words of John the Baptist, but of the evangelist John, the writer of this gospel. They are a continuation of what he was saying in the 14th verse, the 15th verse being evidently thrown in as a parenthesis. The declaration had not exclusive reference, probably, to the apostles, but it is extended to *all* Christians, for all believers have received of the *fulness of grace and truth* that is in Christ. Comp. Ep. i. 23; iii. 19; Col. i. 19; ii. 9. In all these places our Saviour is represented as the fulness of God—as *abounding* in mercy, as exhibiting the divine attributes, and as possessing in himself all that is necessary to fill his people with truth, and grace, and love. ¶ *Grace for grace.* Many interpretations of this phrase have been proposed. The chief are briefly the following: 1st. "We have received, under the gospel, grace or favour, *instead* of those granted under the law; and God has *added* by the gospel important favours to those which he gave under the law." This was first proposed by Chrysostom. 2d. "We, Christians, have received grace *answering to*, or corresponding to that which is in Jesus Christ. We are *like* him in meekness, humility," &c. 3d. "We have received grace *as grace*—that is, freely. We have not purchased it nor deserved it, but God has conferred it on us *freely*" (Grotius). 4th. The meaning is, probably, simply that we have received through him *abundance* of grace or favour. The Hebrews, in expressing the *superlative* degree of comparison, used simply to *repeat* the word—thus, "pits, pits," meaning many pits (Hebrew in Ge. xiv. 10). So here grace for grace may mean *much* grace; superlative favours bestowed on man; favours superior to all that had been under the law—superior to all other things that God can confer on men. These favours consist in pardon, redemption, protection, sanctification, peace here, and heaven hereafter.

17. *The law was given.* The Old Testament economy. The institutions under which the Jews lived. ¶ *By Moses.* By Moses, as the servant of God. He was the great legislator of the Jews, by whom, under God, their polity was formed. The *law* worketh wrath (Ro. iv. 15); it was attended with many burdensome rites and ceremonies (Ac. xv. 10); it was preparatory to another state of things. The gospel succeeded that and took its place, and thus showed the *greatness* of the gospel economy, as well as its grace and truth. ¶ *Grace and truth came by Jesus Christ.* A system of religion full of favours, and the *true* system, was revealed by him. The old system was one of *law*, and *shadows*, and *burdensome rites; this* was full of mercy to mankind, and was true in all things. We may learn from these verses—1st. That all our mercies come from Jesus Christ. 2d. "All true believers receive from Christ's fulness; the best and greatest saints cannot live without him, the meanest and weakest may live by him. This excludes proud boasting that we have nothing but *we have received it*, and silenceth perplexing fears that we want nothing but *we may receive it.*"

18. *No man hath seen God at any time.* This declaration is probably made to show the superiority of the revelation of Jesus above that of any previous dispensation. It is said, therefore, that Jesus *had an intimate knowledge of God*, which neither Moses nor any of the ancient prophets had possessed. God is invisible; no human eyes have seen him; but Christ had a knowledge of God which might be expressed to *our* apprehension by saying that he *saw* him. He knew him intimately and completely, and was therefore fitted to make a fuller manifestation of him. See Jn. v. 37; vi. 46; 1 Jn. iv. 12; Ex. xxxiii. 20; Jn. xiv. 9. This passage is not meant to deny that men had witnessed *manifestations* of God, as when he appeared to Moses and the prophets (comp. Nu. xii. 8; Is. vi.); but it is meant that no one has seen the essence of God, or has *fully known God.* The prophets delivered what they *heard* God speak; Jesus what he *knew* of God as his equal, and as understanding fully his nature. ¶ *The only-begotten Son.* See Notes on ver. 14. This verse shows John's sense of the meaning of that phrase, as denoting an intimate and

any time; [z]the only-begotten Son,
which is in the bosom of the Father, he hath declared *him.*

19 And this is [a]the record of
John, when the Jews sent priests and Levites from Jerusalem to ask him, Who art thou?

20 And he confessed, and denied
not; but confessed, I am not the Christ.

21 And they asked him, What
then? Art thou Elias? And he saith, I am not. Art thou [2]that prophet? And he answered, No.

22 Then said they unto him,
Who art thou? that we may give

z 1 Jn.4.9. a Lu.3.15,&c.

2 or, *a prophet.*

full knowledge of God. ¶ *In the bosom of the Father.* This expression is taken from the custom among the Orientals of reclining at their meals. See Notes on Mat. xxiii. 6. It denotes intimacy, friendship, affection. Here it means that Jesus had a knowledge of God such as one friend has of another—knowledge of his character, designs, and nature which no other one possesses, and which renders him, therefore, qualified above all others to make him known. ¶ *Hath declared* him. Hath fully revealed him or made him known. Comp. He. i. 1, 4. This verse proves that Jesus had a knowledge of God above that which any of the ancient prophets had, and that the fullest revelations of his character are to be expected in the gospel. By his Word and Spirit he can enlighten and guide us, and lead us to the true knowledge of God; and there is no true and full knowledge of God which is not obtained through his Son. Comp. ch. xiv. 6; 1 Jn. ii. 22, 23.

19. *This is the record.* The word *record* here means *testimony*, in whatever way given. The word *record* now commonly refers to *written* evidence. This is not its meaning here. John's testimony was given without writing. ¶ *When the Jews sent.* John's fame was great. See Mat. iii. 5. It spread from the region of Galilee to Jerusalem, and the nation seemed to suppose, from the character of his preaching, that he was the Messiah, Lu. iii. 15. The great council of the nation, or the Sanhedrim, had, among other things, the charge of religion. They felt it to be their duty, therefore, to inquire into the character and claims of John, and to learn whether he was the Messiah. It is not improbable that they *wished* that he might be the long-expected Christ, and were prepared to regard him as such. ¶ *When the Jews sent priests and Levites.* See Notes on Lu. x. 31, 32. These were probably members of the Sanhedrim.

20. *I am not the Christ.* This confession proves that John was not an impostor. He had a wide reputation. The nation was expecting that the Messiah was about to come, and multitudes were ready to believe that John was he, Lu. iii. 15. If John had been an impostor he would have taken advantage of this excited state of public feeling, proclaimed himself to be the Messiah, and formed a large party in his favour. The fact that he did *not* do it is full proof that he did not intend to *impose* on men, but came only as the forerunner of Christ; and his example shows that all Christians, and especially all Christian ministers, however much they may be honoured and blessed, should be willing to lay all their honours at the feet of Jesus; to keep *themselves* back and to hold up before the world only the Son of God. To do this is one eminent mark of the true spirit of a minister of the gospel.

21. *Art thou Elias?* This is the Greek way of writing Elijah. The Jews expected that Elijah would appear before the Messiah came. See Notes on Mat. xi. 14. *They* supposed that it would be the *real* Elijah returned from heaven. In this sense John denied that he *was* Elijah; but he did not deny that he was the Elias or Elijah which the prophet intended (Mat. iii. 3), for he immediately proceeds to state (ver. 23) that he was sent, as it was predicted that Elijah would be, to prepare the way of the Lord; so that, while he corrected their false notions about Elijah, he so clearly stated to them his true character that they might understand that he was really the one predicted as Elijah. ¶ *That prophet.* It is possible that the Jews supposed that not only *Elijah* would reappear before the coming of the Messiah, but also *Jeremiah.* See Notes on Mat. xvi. 14. Some have supposed, however, that this question has reference to the prediction of Moses in De. xviii. 15.

an answer to them that sent us.
What sayest thou of thyself?
23 He[b] said, I *am* the voice of
one crying in the wilderness, Make
straight the way of the Lord, as
said the prophet [c]Esaias.
24 And they which were sent
were of the Pharisees.
25 And they asked him, and said
unto him, Why baptizest thou
then, if thou be not that Christ,
nor Elias, neither that prophet?
26 John answered them, saying,
I baptize with water; but [d]there
standeth one among you whom ye
know not:

b Mat.3.3; Mar.1.3; Lu.3.4; ch.3.28. c Is.40.3. d Mal.3.1.

23. *I* am *the voice*, &c. See Notes on Mat. iii. 3.

24. *Were of the Pharisees.* For an account of this sect, see Notes on Mat. iii. 7. Why *they* are particularly mentioned is not certainly known. Many of the *Sadducees* came to his baptism (Mat. iii. 7), but it seems that they did not join in sending to him to know what was the design of John. This circumstance is one of those incidental and delicate allusions which would occur to no impostor in forging a book, and which show that the writers of the New Testament were honest men and knew what they affirmed. For, 1st. The Pharisees composed a great part of the Sanhedrim, Ac. xxiii. 6. It is probable that a deputation from the Sanhedrim would be of that party. 2d. The Pharisees were very tenacious of rites and customs, of traditions and ceremonies. They observed many. They believed that they were lawful, Mar. vii. 3, 4. Of course, they believed that those rites might be increased, but they did not suppose that it could be done except by the authority of a prophet or of the Messiah. When, therefore, John came *baptizing*—adding a rite to be observed by his followers—baptizing not only *Gentiles*, but also *Jews*—the question was whether he had *authority* to institute a new rite; whether it was to be received among the ceremonies of religion. In this question the *Sadducees* felt no interest, for they rejected *all* such rites at once; but the *Pharisees* thought it was worth inquiry, and it was a question on which *they* felt themselves specially called on to act as the guardians of the ceremonies of religion.

25. *Why baptizest thou then*, &c. Baptism on receiving a proselyte from *heathenism* was common before the time of John, but it was not customary to baptize a *Jew*. John had changed the custom. He baptized *all*, and they were desirous of knowing by what authority he made such a change in the religious customs of the nation. They presumed, from the fact that he *introduced* that change, that he claimed to be a prophet or the Christ. They supposed that no one would attempt it without *pretending*, at least, authority from heaven. As he disclaimed the character of Christ and of the prophet Elijah, they asked whence he derived his authority. As he had just before applied to himself a prediction that they all considered as belonging to the forerunner of Christ, they *might* have understood *why* he did it; but they were blind, and manifested, as all sinners do, a remarkable slowness in understanding the plainest truths in religion.

26. *I baptize.* He did not deny it; nor did he condescend to state his authority. *That* he had given. He *admitted* that he had introduced an important *change* in the rites of religion, and he goes on to tell them that *this* was not all. Greater and more important changes would soon take place without *their* authority. The Messiah was about to come, and the *power* was about to depart from *their* hands. ¶ *There standeth one.* There *is* one. ¶ *Among you.* In the midst of you. He is undistinguished among the multitude. The Messiah had already come, and was about to be manifested to the people. It was not until the next day (ver. 29) that Jesus was manifested or proclaimed as the Messiah; but it is not improbable that he was *then* among the people that were assembled near the Jordan, and mingled with them, though he was undistinguished. He had gone there, probably, with the multitudes that had been drawn thither by the fame of John, and had gone without attracting attention, though his real object was to receive baptism in this public manner, and to be exhibited and proclaimed as the Messiah. ¶ *Whom ye know not.* Jesus was not yet declared publicly to be the Christ. Though it is probable

27 He it is, who, coming after
me, is preferred before me, whose
shoe's latchet I am not worthy to
unloose.
28 These things were done [e]in
Bethabara, beyond Jordan, where
John was baptizing.
29 The next day John seeth
Jesus coming unto him, and saith,
Behold the [f]Lamb of God, [g]which
[3]taketh away the sin of the world!
30 This is he of whom I said,
After me cometh a man which is
preferred before me; for he was
before me.
31 And I knew him not; but

e Ju.7.24.
f Ex.12.3; Is.53.7,11; Re.5.6.
g Ac.13.39; 1 Pe.2.24; Re.1.5. 3 or, *beareth*, He.9.28.

that he was then among the multitude, yet he was not known as the Messiah. We may hence learn, 1st. That there is often great excellency in the world that is obscure, undistinguished, and unknown. Jesus was *near* to all that people, but they were not conscious of his presence, for he was retired and obscure. Though the greatest personage ever in the world, yet he was not externally distinguished from others. 2d. Jesus may be near to men of the world, and yet they know him not. He is everywhere by his Spirit, yet few know it, and few are *desirous* of knowing it.

27. *Whose shoe's latchet.* See Notes on Mat. iii. 11. The *latchet* of sandals was the string or thong by which they were fastened to the feet. To unloose them was the office of a servant, and John means, therefore, that he was unworthy to perform the lowest office for the Messiah. This was remarkable humility. John was well known; he was highly honoured; thousands came to hear him. Jesus was at that time unknown; but John says that he was unworthy to perform the humblest office for Jesus. So we all should be willing to lay all that we have at the feet of Christ, and feel that we are unworthy to be his lowest servants.

28. *In Bethabara.* Almost all the ancient manuscripts and versions, instead of *Bethabara* here, have *Bethany*, and this is doubtless the true reading. There was a Bethany about 2 miles east of Jerusalem, but there is said also to have been another in the tribe of Reuben, on the east side of the river Jordan, and in this place, probably, John was baptizing. It is about 12 miles above Jericho. The word *Bethabara* means *house* or *place of a ford.* The reading *Bethabara,* instead of *Bethany*, seems to have arisen from the conjecture of Origen, who found in his day no such place as *Bethany*, but saw a town called *Bethabara,* where John was said to have baptized, and therefore took the liberty of changing the former reading.—Rob., *Lex.* ¶ *Beyond Jordan.* On the east side of the river Jordan.

29. *The next day.* The day after the Jews made inquiry whether he was the Christ. ¶ *Behold the Lamb of God.* A *lamb*, among the Jews, was killed and eaten at the Passover to commemorate their deliverance from Egypt, Ex. xii. 3–11. A lamb was offered in the tabernacle, and afterward in the temple, every morning and evening, as a part of the daily worship, Ex. xxix. 38, 39. The Messiah was predicted as a lamb led to the slaughter, to show his patience in his sufferings, and readiness to die for man, Is. liii. 7. A lamb, among the Jews, was also an emblem of patience, meekness, gentleness. On *all* these accounts, rather than on any one of them alone, Jesus was called *the Lamb.* He was innocent (1 Pe. ii. 23–25); he was a sacrifice for sin—the substance represented by the daily offering of the lamb, and slain at the usual time of the evening sacrifice (Lu. xxiii. 44–46); and he was what was represented by the Passover, turning away the anger of God, and saving sinners by his blood from vengeance and eternal death, 1 Co. v. 7. ¶ *Of God.* Appointed by God, approved by God, and most dear to him; the sacrifice which he *chose*, and which he *approves* to save men from death. ¶ *Which taketh away.* This denotes his *bearing* the sins of the world, or the sufferings which made an atonement for sin. Comp. Is. liii. 4; 1 Jn. iii. 5; 1 Pe. ii. 24. He takes away sin by *bearing* in his own body the sufferings which God appointed to show his sense of the evil of sin, thus magnifying the law, and rendering it consistent for him to pardon. See Notes on Ro. iii. 24, 25. ¶ *Of the world.* Of all mankind, Jew and Gentile. His work was not to be confined to the Jew, but was also to

that he should be made manifest
to Israel, therefore am I come baptizing with water.
32 And John bare record, saying,
I saw the Spirit descending from
heaven like a dove, and it abode
upon him.
33 And I knew him not: but he
that sent me to baptize with water, the same said unto me, Upon
whom thou shalt see the Spirit descending and [h]remaining on him,
the same is he which [i]baptizeth
with the Holy Ghost.
34 And I saw, and bare record
that this is the Son of God.
35 Again, the next day after,
John stood, and two of his disciples;
36 And looking upon Jesus as
he walked, he saith, Behold the
Lamb of God!
37 And the two disciples heard

h ch.3.34.

i Ac.1.5; 2.4.

benefit the Gentile; it was not confined to any one part of the world, but was designed to open the way of pardon to all men. He was the propitiation for the sins of the whole world, 1 Jn. ii. 2. See Notes on 2 Co. v. 15.

31. *I knew him not.* John was not *personally* acquainted with Jesus. Though they were remotely related to each other, yet it seems that they had had heretofore no personal acquaintance. John had lived chiefly in the hill country of Judea. Jesus had been employed with Joseph at Nazareth. Until Jesus came to be baptized (Mat. iii. 13, 14), it seems that John had no acquaintance with him. He understood that he was to announce that the Messiah was about to appear. He was sent to proclaim his coming, but he did not personally know Jesus, or that *he* was to be the Messiah. This proves that there could have been no *collusion* or *agreement* between them to impose on the people. ¶ *Should be made manifest.* That the Messiah should be *exhibited*, or made known. He came to prepare the way for the Messiah, and it *now* appeared that the Messiah was Jesus of Nazareth. ¶ *To Israel.* To the Jews.

32. *Bare record.* Gave testimony. ¶ *I saw the Spirit*, &c. See Notes on Mat. iii. 16, 17.

33, 34. *The same said*, &c. This was the sign by which he was to know the Messiah. He was to see the Spirit descending like a dove and abiding on him. It does not follow, however, that he had no *intimation* before this that Jesus was the Christ, but it means that by this he should *infallibly know it.* From Mat. iii. 13, 14, it seems that John supposed, before the baptism of Jesus, that he *claimed* to be the Messiah, and that he believed it; but the *infallible*, *certain* testimony in the case was the descent of the Holy Spirit on him at his baptism. ¶ *That this is the Son of God.* This was distinctly declared by a voice from heaven at his baptism, Mat. iii. 17. This John heard, and he testified that he had heard it.

35. *The next day.* The day after his remarkable testimony that Jesus was the Son of God. This testimony of John is reported because it was the main design of this evangelist to show that Jesus was the Messiah. See the Introduction. To do this, he adduces the decided and repeated testimony of John the Baptist. This was impartial evidence in the case, and hence he so particularly dwells upon it. ¶ *John stood.* Or was standing. This was probably apart from the multitude. ¶ *Two of his disciples.* One of these was Andrew (ver. 40), and it is not improbable that the other was the writer of this gospel.

36. *Looking upon Jesus*, &c. Fixing his eyes intently upon him. Singling him out and regarding him with special attention. Contemplating him as the long-expected Messiah and Deliverer of the world. In this way should all ministers fix the eye on the Son of God, and direct all others to him. ¶ *As he walked.* While *Jesus* was walking.

37. *They followed Jesus.* They had been the disciples of John. *His* office was to point out the Messiah. When that was done, they left at once their master and teacher, John, and followed the long-expected Messiah. This shows that John was sincere; that he was not desirous of forming a party or of building up a sect; that he was willing that all those whom he had attracted to himself by his ministry should become followers of Christ. The object of minis-

him speak, and they followed Jesus.

38 Then Jesus turned, and saw them following, and saith unto them, What seek ye? They said unto him, Rabbi, (which is to say, being interpreted, Master,) where dwellest[4] thou?

39 He saith unto them, Come and see. They came and saw where he dwelt, and abode with him that day; for it was [5]about the tenth hour.

40 One of the two which heard John *speak*, and followed him, was Andrew, Simon Peter's brother.

[4] or, *abidest*.

[5] *That was two hours before night.*

ters should *not* be to build up their own interests or to extend their own fame. It is to point men to the Saviour. Ministers, however popular or successful, should be willing that their disciples should look to Christ rather than to them; nay, should *forget* them and look away from them, to tread in the footsteps of the Son of God; and the conduct of these disciples shows us that we should forsake *all* and follow Jesus when he is pointed out to us as the Messiah. We should not delay nor debate the matter, but leave at once all our old teachers, guides and companions, and follow the Lamb of God. And we should do that, too, though *to the world* the Lord Jesus may appear, as he did to the multitude of the Jews, as poor, unknown, and despised. Reader, have *you* left all and followed him? Have you forsaken the guides of false philosophy and deceit, of sin and infidelity, and committed yourself to the Lord Jesus Christ.

38. *What seek ye?* This was not asked to obtain *information*. Comp. ver. 48. It was not a harsh reproof, forbidding them to follow him. Comp. Mat. xi. 28–30. It was a kind inquiry respecting their desires; an invitation to lay open their minds, to state their wishes, and to express all their feelings respecting the Messiah and their own salvation. We may learn, 1st. That Jesus regards the first inclinations of the soul to follow him. He *turned* toward these disciples, and he will incline his ear to all who begin to approach him for salvation. 2d. Jesus is ready to hear their requests and to answer them. 3d. Ministers of the gospel, and all other Christians, should be accessible, kind, and tender toward all who are inquiring the way to life. In conformity with their Master, they should be willing to aid all those who look to them for guidance and help in the great work of their salvation. ¶ *Rabbi*. This was a Jewish title conferred somewhat as literary degrees now are, and meaning literally *a great one*, and was applied to a teacher or master in the Jewish schools. It corresponded with the title *Doctor*. Our Saviour solemnly forbade his disciples to wear that title. See Notes on Mat. xxiii. 8. The fact that John *interpreted* this word shows that he wrote his gospel not for the Jews only, but for those who did not understand the Hebrew language. It is supposed to have been written at Ephesus. ¶ *Where dwellest thou?* This question they probably asked him in order to signify their wish to be with him and to be instructed by him. They desired more fully to listen to him than they could now by the wayside. They were unwilling to interrupt him in his travelling. Religion teaches men true politeness, or a disposition to consult the convenience of others, and not improperly to molest them, or to break in upon them when engaged. It also teaches us to *desire to be with Christ;* to seek every opportunity of communion with him, and chiefly to desire *to be with him where he is* when we leave this world. Comp. Phi. i. 23.

39. *Come and see.* This was a kind and gracious answer. He did not put them off to some future period. Then, as now, he was willing that they should come at once and enjoy the full opportunity which they desired of his conversation. Jesus is ever ready to admit those who seek him to his presence and favour. ¶ *Abode with him.* Remained with him. This was probably the dwelling of some friend of Jesus. His usual home was at Nazareth. ¶ *The tenth hour*. The Jews divided their day into twelve equal parts, beginning at sunrise. If John used their mode of computation, this was about four o'clock P.M. The Romans divided time as we do, beginning at midnight. If John used their mode, it was about ten o'clock in the forenoon. It is not certain which he used.

41. *He first findeth.* He found him

41 He first findeth his own
brother Simon, and saith unto him,
We have found the Messias, which
is, being interpreted, [6]the Christ.
42 And he brought him to Jesus.
And when Jesus beheld him he
said, Thou art Simon, the son of
Jonas: [k]thou shalt be called Cephas,
which is, by interpretation, [7] A
stone.
43 The day following, Jesus
would go forth into Galilee, and
findeth Philip, and saith unto
him, Follow me.
44 Now Philip was of Bethsaida, the city of Andrew and
Peter.
45 Philip findeth Nathanael,
and saith unto him, We have
found him of whom [l]Moses in the
law, and the prophets, did write,
Jesus of Nazareth, the son of
Joseph.
46 And Nathanael said unto

6 or, *the anointed.* k Mat.16.18. 7 or, *Peter.* l Lu.24.27,44.

and *told him about Jesus* before he brought him to Jesus. ¶ *We have found the Messias.* They had learned from the testimony of John, and now had been more fully convinced from conversation with Jesus, that he was the Messiah. The word Messiah, or Messias, is Hebrew, and means the same as the Greek word Christ, *anointed.* See Notes on Mat. i. 1. From the conduct of Andrew we may learn that it is the nature of religion to desire that others may possess it. It does not lead us to monopolize it or to hide it under a bushel, but it seeks that others also may be brought to the Saviour. It does not *wait* for them to come, but it goes *for* them; it seeks them out, and tells them that a Saviour is found. Young converts should *seek* their friends and neighbours, and tell them of a Saviour; and not only their relatives, but all others as far as possible, that all may come to Jesus and be saved.

42. *Cephas.* This is a Syriac word, meaning the same as the Greek word Peter, a stone. See Notes on Mat. xvi. 17. The stone, or rock, is a symbol of firmness and steadiness of character—a trait in Peter's character *after* the ascension of Jesus that was very remarkable. *Before* the death of Jesus he was rash, headlong, variable; and it is one proof of the omniscience of Jesus that he saw that Peter *would* possess a character that would be expressed appropriately by the word *stone* or *rock.* The word *Jonas* is a Hebrew word, whose original signification is *a dove.* It may be that Jesus had respect to that when he gave Simon the name Peter. "You now bear a name emblematic of timidity and inconstancy. You shall be called by a name denoting firmness and constancy."

43. *Would go forth.* Was about to go. ¶ *Into Galilee.* He was now in Judea, where he went to be baptized by John. He was now about to return to his native country. ¶ *Findeth Philip.* This does not refer to his calling these disciples to be *apostles,* for that took place at the Sea of Tiberias (Mat. iv. 18), but it refers to their being convinced that he was the Christ. This is the object of this evangelist, to show how and when they were convinced of this. Matthew states the time and occasion in which they were called to be *apostles;* John, the time in which they first became acquainted with Jesus, and were convinced that he was the Messiah. There is, therefore, no contradiction in the evangelists.

44. *Of Bethsaida.* See Notes on Mat. xi. 21. ¶ *The city of.* The place where Andrew and Peter dwelt.

45. *Moses, in the law.* Moses, in that part of the Old Testament which he wrote, called by the Jews *the law.* See De. xviii. 15, 18; Ge. xlix. 10; iii. 15. ¶ *And the prophets,* Is. liii.; ix. 6, 7; Da. ix. 24-27; Je. xxiii. 5, 6; &c. ¶ *Jesus of Nazareth,* &c. They spoke according to common apprehension. They spoke of him as the son of Joseph because he was commonly supposed to be. They spoke of him as dwelling at Nazareth, though they might not have been ignorant that he was born at Bethlehem.

46. *Can any good thing,* &c. The character of Nazareth was proverbially bad. To be a Galilean or a Nazarene was an expression of decided contempt, Jn. vii. 52. See Notes on Mat. ii. 23. Nathanael asked, therefore, whether it was possible that the Messiah should come from a place proverbially wicked. This was a mode of judging in the case not uncommon. It is not by examining *evidence,* but by prejudice. Many per-

him, [m]Can there any good thing come out of Nazareth? Philip saith unto him, Come and see.
47 Jesus saw Nathanael coming to him, and saith of him, [n]Behold, an Israelite indeed, in whom is no guile!
48 Nathanael saith unto him, Whence knowest thou me? Jesus answered and said unto him, Before that Philip called thee, when thou wast under the fig-tree, [o]I saw thee.
49 Nathanael answered and

m ch.7.41. *n* Ps.32.2; Ro.2.28,29. *o* Ps.139.1,2.

sons suffer their minds to be filled with prejudice against religion, and then pronounce at once without examination. They refuse to examine the subject, for they have set it down that it *cannot* be true. It matters not where a teacher comes from, or what is the place of his birth, provided he be authorized of God and qualified for his work. ¶ *Come and see.* This was the best way to answer Nathanael. He did not sit down to *reason* with him, or speculate about the possibility that a good thing could come from Nazareth; but he asked him to go and examine for himself, to see the Lord Jesus, to hear him converse, to lay aside his prejudice, and to judge from a fair and candid personal inquiry. So we should beseech sinners to lay aside their prejudices against religion, and *to be Christians*, and thus make trial for themselves. If men can be persuaded to come to Jesus, all their petty and foolish objections against religion will vanish. They will be satisfied from their *own experience* that it is true, and in this way only *will* they ever be satisfied.

47. *An Israelite indeed.* One who is really an Israelite—not by birth only, but one worthy of the name. One who possesses the spirit, the piety, and the integrity which become a man who is really a Jew, who fears God and obeys his law. Comp. Ro. ix. 6; ii. 28, 29. ¶ *No guile.* No deceit, no fraud, no hypocrisy. He is really what he professes to be—a Jew, a descendant of the patriarch Jacob, fearing and serving God. He makes no profession which he does not live up to. He does not say that Nathanael was without guilt or sin, but that he had no disguise, no trick, no deceit—he was sincere and upright. This was a most honourable testimony. How happy would it be if he, who knows the hearts of all as he did that of Nathanael, could bear the same testimony of all who profess the religion of the gospel!

48. *Whence knowest thou me?* Nathanael was not yet acquainted with the divinity of Christ, and supposed that he had been a stranger to him. Hearing him express a favourable opinion of him, he naturally inquired by what means he had any knowledge of him. His conscience testified to the truth of what Jesus said—that he had no guile, and he was anxious to know whence he had learned his character. ¶ *Before that Philip called thee.* See ver. 45. ¶ *When thou wast under the fig-tree.* It is evident that it was from something that had occurred under the fig-tree that Jesus judged of his character. What that was is not recorded. It is not improbable that Nathanael was accustomed to retire to the shade of a certain tree, perhaps in his garden or in a grove, for the purpose of meditation and prayer. The Jews were much in the habit of selecting such places for private devotion, and in such scenes of stillness and retirement there is something peculiarly favourable for meditation and prayer. Our Saviour also worshipped in such places. Comp. Jn. xviii. 2; Lu. vi. 12. In that place of retirement it is not improbable that Nathanael was engaged in private devotion. ¶ *I saw thee.* It is clear, from the narrative, that Jesus did not mean to say that he was bodily present with Nathanael and saw him; but he knew his thoughts, his desires, his secret feelings and wishes. In this sense Nathanael understood him. We may learn —1st. That Jesus sees what is done in secret, and is therefore divine. 2d. That he sees us when we little think of it. 3d. That he sees us especially in our private devotions, hears our prayers, and marks our meditations. And 4th. That he judges of our *character* chiefly by our private devotions. Those are secret; the world sees them not; and in our closets we show what we are. How does it become us, therefore, that our secret prayers and meditations should be without *guile* and hypocrisy, and such as Jesus will approve!

saith unto him, Rabbi, thou art the[p] Son of God; thou art [q]the King of Israel.

50 Jesus answered and said unto him, Because I said unto thee, I saw thee under the fig-tree, believest thou? Thou shalt see greater things than these.

51 And he saith unto him, Verily, verily, I say unto you,

p Mat.14.33; ch.20.28,29. *q* Mat.21.5; 27.11.

---

49. *Rabbi.* Master. Applied appropriately to Jesus, and to no one else, Mat. xxiii. 10. ¶ *The Son of God.* By this title he doubtless meant that he was the Messiah. His conscience told him that he had judged right of his character, and that therefore he must know the heart and the desires of the mind. If so, he could not be a mere man, but must be the long-expected Messiah. ¶ *The King of Israel.* This was one of the titles by which the Messiah was expected, and this was the title which was affixed to his cross, Jn. xix. 18. This case of Nathanael John adduces as another evidence that Jesus was the Christ. The great object he had in view in writing this gospel was to collect the evidence that he was the Messiah, ch. xx. 31. A case, therefore, where Jesus searched the heart, and where his knowledge of the heart convinced a pious *Jew* that he was the Christ, is very properly adduced as important testimony.

50. *Greater things.* Fuller proof of his Messiahship, particularly what is mentioned in the following verse.

51. *Verily, verily.* In the Greek, *Amen, amen.* The word *amen* means *truly, certainly, so be it*—from the verb to confirm, to establish, to be true. It is often used in this gospel. When repeated it expresses the speaker's sense of the *importance* of what he is saying, and the *certainty* that it is as he affirms. ¶ *Ye shall see.* Not, perhaps, with the bodily eyes, but you shall have *evidence* that it is so. The thing shall take place, and you shall be a witness of it. ¶ *Heaven open.* This is a figurative expression, denoting *the conferring of favours.* Ps. lxxviii. 23, 24: "He opened the doors of heaven, and had rained down manna." It also denotes that God was about to work a miracle in attestation of a particular thing. See Mat. iii. 16. In the *language*, here, there is an evident allusion to the ladder that Jacob saw in a dream, and to the angels ascending and descending on it, Ge. xxviii. 12. It is not probable that Jesus referred to any particular instance in which Nathanael should literally see the heavens opened. The baptism of Jesus had taken place, and no other instance occurred in his life in which it is said that the *heavens were* opened. ¶ *Angels of God.* Those pure and holy beings that dwell in heaven, and that are employed as ministering spirits to our world, He. i. 14. Good men are represented in the Scriptures as being under their protection, Ps. xci. 11, 12; Ge. xxviii. 12. They are the agents by which God often expressed his will to men, He. ii. 2; Ga. iii. 19. They are represented as strengthening the Lord Jesus, and ministering unto him. Thus they aided him in the wilderness (Mar. i. 13), and in the garden (Lu. xxii. 43), and they were present when he rose from the dead, Mat. xxviii. 2–4; Jn. xx. 12, 13. By their ascending and descending upon him it is probable that he meant that Nathanael would have evidence that they came to his aid, and that he would have *the* KIND of protection and assistance from God which would show *more fully that he was the Messiah.* Thus his life, his many deliverances from dangers, his wisdom to confute his skilled and cunning adversaries, the scenes of his death, and the attendance of angels at his resurrection, may all be represented by the angels descending upon him, and *all* would show to Nathanael and the other disciples most clearly that he was the Son of God. ¶ *The Son of man.* A term by which he often describes himself. It shows his humility, his love for man, his willingness to be esteemed *as a man*, Phi. ii. 6, 7.

From this interview with Nathanael we may learn, 1st. That Jesus searches the heart. 2d. That he was truly the Messiah. 3d. That he was under the protection of God. 4th. That if we have faith in Jesus, it will be continually strengthened—the evidence will grow brighter and brighter. 5th. That if we believe his *word*, we shall yet see full proof that his word is true. 6th. As Jesus was under the protection of God, so will all his friends be. God will defend and save us also if we put our trust in him. 7th. Jesus applied to himself terms expressive of humility. He was not solicitous even to be called by titles

Hereafter ye shall see [r]heaven
open, and [s]the angels of God ascending and descending upon the
Son of man.

CHAPTER II.

AND the third day there was
a marriage in [a]Cana of Galilee; and the mother of Jesus was
there:
2 And both Jesus was called,
and his disciples, to [b]the marriage.
3 And [c] when they wanted
wine, the mother of Jesus saith
unto him, They have no wine.
4 Jesus saith unto her, Woman,

r Eze.1.1. s Ge.28.12; Da.7.9,10; Ac.1.10,11. a Jos.19.28; ch.4.46. b He.13.4. c Ec.10.19; Is.24.11.

which he *might* claim. So we should not be ambitious of titles and honours. Ministers of the gospel most resemble him when they seek for the fewest titles, and do not aim at distinctions from each other or their brethren. See Notes on Mat. xxiii. 8.

CHAPTER II.

1. *And the third day.* On the third day after his conversation with Nathanael. ¶ *Cana.* This was a small town about 15 miles north-west of Tiberias and 6 miles north-east of Nazareth. It is now called Kefr Kenna, is under the government of a Turkish officer, and contains perhaps three hundred inhabitants, chiefly Catholics. The natives still pretend to show the place where the water was turned into wine, and even one of the large stone water-pots. "A Greek church," says Professor Hackett (*Illustrations of Scripture*, p. 322), "stands at the entrance of the town, deriving its special sanctity, as I understood, from its being supposed to occupy the site of the house in which the marriage was celebrated to which Jesus and his friends were invited. A priest to whom we were referred as the custodian soon arrived, in obedience to our call, and unlocked the doors of the church. It is a low stone building, wretchedly neglected and out of repair." "The houses," says Dr. Thomson (*The Land and the Book*, vol. ii. p. 126), "were built of limestone, cut and laid up after the fashion still common in this region, and some of them may have been inhabited within the last fifty years. There are many ancient cisterns about it, and fragments of water-jars in abundance, and both reminded us of the 'beginning of miracles.' Some of my companions gathered bits of these water-jars as mementoes—witnesses they could hardly be, for those of the narrative were of *stone*, while these were baked earth." The place is now quite deserted. Dr. Thomson (*ibid.*) says: "There is not now a habitable house in the humble village where our blessed Lord sanctioned, by his presence and miraculous assistance, the all-important and world-wide institution of marriage." It was called *Cana of Galilee* to distinguish it from another Cana in the tribe of Ephraim, Jos. xvi. 9. This was the native place of Nathanael, Jn. xxi. 2. ¶ *The mother of Jesus.* Mary. It is not improbable that she was a relative of the family where the marriage took place.

2. *His disciples.* Those that he had made when in Judea. These were Peter, Andrew, Philip, and Nathanael. They were not yet called to be *apostles*, but they believed that he was the Messiah. The miracle wrought here was doubtless to convince them more fully that he was the Christ.

3. *When they wanted wine.* A marriage feast among the Jews was commonly observed for seven or eight days. It is not probable that there would be a want of wine at the marriage itself, and it is possible, therefore, that Jesus came there some time during the marriage feast. ¶ *They have no wine.* It is not known why Mary told this to Jesus. It would seem that she had a belief that he was able to supply it, though he had as yet worked no miracle.

4. *Woman.* This term, as used here, seems to imply reproof, as if she was interfering in that which did not properly concern her; but it is evident that no such reproof or disrespect was intended by the use of the term *woman* instead of *mother*. It is the same term by which he tenderly addressed Mary Magdalene after his resurrection (ch. xx. 15), and his mother when he was on the cross, ch. xix. 26. Comp. also Mat. xv. 28; Jn. iv. 21; 1 Co. vii. 16. ¶ *What have I to do with thee?* See Notes on Mat. viii. 29. This expression is sometimes used to denote indignation or contempt. See Ju. xi. 12; 2 Sa. xvi.

what have I to do with thee?
Mine hour is not yet come.
5 His mother saith unto the
servants, [d] Whatsoever he saith
unto you, do *it*.
6 And there were set there
six water-pots of stone, after the
manner of the purifying of the
Jews, containing two or three
firkins apiece.
7 Jesus saith unto them, Fill
the water-pots with water. And
they filled them up to the brim.
8 And he saith unto them,

d Lu.5.5,6.

10; 1 Ki. xvii. 18. But it is not probable that it denoted either in this place; if it did, it was a mild reproof of Mary for attempting to control or direct him in his power of working miracles. Most of the ancients supposed this to be the intention of Jesus. The words sound to us harsh, but they might have been spoken in a *tender* manner, and not have been intended as a reproof. It is clear that he did not intend to *refuse* to provide wine, but only to *delay* it a little; and the design was, therefore, to compose the anxiety of Mary, and to prevent her being solicitous about it. It may, then, be thus expressed: "My mother, be not anxious. To you and to me this should not be a matter of solicitude. The proper time of my interfering has not yet come. When that is come I will furnish a supply, and in the meantime neither you nor I should be solicitous." Thus understood, it is so far from being *a harsh reproof*, that it was a mild exhortation for her to dismiss her fears and to put proper trust in him. ¶ *Mine hour*, &c. My time. The proper time for my interposing. Perhaps the wine was not yet *entirely* exhausted. The wine had begun to fail, but he would not work a miracle until it was entirely gone, that the miracle might be free from all possibility of suspicion. It does not mean that the proper time for his working a miracle, or entering on his public work had not come, but that the proper time for his interposing *there* had not arrived.

5. *His mother saith*, &c. It is evident from this verse that his mother did not understand what he had said as a harsh reproof and repulse, but as an indication of his willingness at the proper time to furnish wine. In all this transaction he evinced the appropriate feelings of a son toward a mother.

6. *Six water-pots of stone.* Made of stone; or, as we should say, stoneware. ¶ *After the manner.* After the usual custom. ¶ *Of the purifying.* Of the *washings* or ablutions of the Jews. They were for the purpose of washing the hands before and after eating (Mat. xv. 2), and for the formal washing of vessels, and even articles of furniture, Lu. xi. 39; Mar. vii. 3, 4. ¶ *Two or three firkins.* It is not quite certain what is meant here by the word *firkins.* It is probable that the measure intended is the Hebrew *bath*, containing about 7½ gallons.

7. *With water.* This was done by the servants employed at the feast. It was done by *them*, so that there might be no opportunity of saying that the disciples of Jesus had filled them with wine to produce the *appearance* of a miracle. In this case there could be no deception. The quantity was very considerable. The servants would know whether the *wine* or *water* had been put in these vessels. It could not be believed that *they* had either the power or the disposition to impose on others in this manner, and the way was therefore clear for the proof that Jesus had really changed what was known to be *water* into *wine.* ¶ *To the brim.* To the top. So full that no *wine* could be *poured in* to give the *appearance* of a mixture. Farther, vessels were used for this miracle in which wine had not been kept. These pots were never used to put wine in, but simply to keep *water* in for the various purposes of ablution. A large number was used on this occasion, because there were many guests.

8. *Draw out now.* This command was given to the servants. It showed that the miracle had been *immediately* wrought. As soon as they were filled the servants were directed to take to the governor of the feast. Jesus made no parade about it, and it does not even appear that he approached the water-pots. He willed it, and it was done. This was a clear exertion of divine power, and made in such a manner as to leave no doubt of its reality. ¶ *The governor.* One who presided on the occasion. The one who stood at the *head* or upper end of the table. He had the charge of the entertainment,

Draw[e] out now and bear unto the governor[f] of the feast. And they bare *it*.

9 When the ruler of the feast had tasted the water that was made wine, and knew not whence it was, (but the [g]servants which drew the water knew,) the governor of the feast called the bridegroom,

10 And saith unto him, Every man at the beginning doth set forth good wine; and when men have well drunk, then that which

e Ec.9.7. f Ro.13.7. g Ps.119.100; ch.7.17.

provided the food, gave directions to the servants, &c.

9. *And knew not whence it was.* This is said, probably, to indicate that his judgment was not biased by any favour, or any *want* of favour, toward Jesus. Had he known what was done, he would have been less likely to have judged impartially. As it is, we have his testimony that this was *real* wine, and of so fine a body and flavour as to surpass that which had been provided for the occasion. Everything in this miracle shows that there was no collusion or understanding between Jesus and any of the persons at the feast.

10. *Every man.* It is customary, or it is generally done. ¶ *When men have well drunk.* This word does not of necessity mean that they were *intoxicated,* though it is usually employed in that sense. It may mean when they have drunk sufficient, or to satiety; or have drunk so much as to produce hilarity, and to destroy the keenness of their taste, so that they could not readily distinguish the good from that which was worse. But this cannot be adduced in favour of drunkenness, even if it means to be intoxicated; for, 1st. It is not said of those who were present *at that feast*, but of what *generally* occurred. For anything that appears, at that feast all were perfectly temperate and sober. 2d. It is not the saying of Jesus that is here recorded, but of the governor of the feast, who is declaring what usually occurred as a fact. 3d. There is not any expression of opinion in regard to its *propriety*, or in approval of it, even by that governor. 4th. It does not appear that our Saviour even *heard* the observation. 5th. Still less is there any evidence that he *approved* such a state of things, or that he designed that it should take place here. Farther, the word translated "well drunk" cannot be shown to mean intoxication; but it *may* mean when they had drunk as much as they judged proper or as they desired, then the other was presented. It is clear that neither our Saviour, nor the sacred writer, nor the speaker here expresses any *approbation* of intemperance, nor is there the least evidence that anything of the kind occurred here. It is not proof that *we* approve of intemperance when we mention, as this man did, what occurs usually among men at feasts. ¶ *Is worse.* Is of an inferior quality. ¶ *The good wine.* This shows that this had all the qualities of real wine. We should not be deceived by the phrase "*good wine.*" *We* often use the phrase to denote that it is good in proportion to its strength and its power to intoxicate; but no such sense is to be attached to the word here. Pliny, Plutarch, and Horace describe wine as *good*, or mention that as *the best wine*, which was *harmless* or *innocent*—poculo vini *innocentis.* The most useful wine—*utilissimum vinum*—was that which had little strength; and the most wholesome wine—*saluberrimum vinum*—was that which had not been adulterated by "the addition of anything to the *must* or juice." Pliny expressly says that a "good wine" was one that was destitute of spirit (lib. iv. c. 13). It should not be assumed, therefore, that the "good wine" was *stronger* than the other: it is rather to be presumed that it was milder. The wine referred to here was doubtless such as was commonly drunk in Palestine. That was the pure juice of the grape. It was not brandied wine, nor drugged wine, nor wine compounded of various substances, such as we drink in this land. The common wine drunk in Palestine was that which was the simple juice of the grape. *We* use the word *wine* now to denote the kind of liquid which passes under that name in this country—always containing a considerable portion of alcohol—not only the alcohol produced by fermentation, but alcohol *added* to keep it or make it stronger. But we have no right to take *that* sense of the word, and go with it to the interpretation of the Scriptures. We should endeavour to place ourselves in

is worse; *but* thou hast kept [h]the good wine until now.

11 This beginning of miracles did Jesus in Cana of Galilee, [i]and

h Ps.104.15; Pr.9.2,5.

i ch.1.14.

the exact circumstances of those times, ascertain precisely what idea the word would convey to those who used it then, and apply *that* sense to the word in the interpretation of the Bible; and there is not the slightest evidence that the word so used would have conveyed any idea but that of the pure juice of the grape, nor the slightest circumstance mentioned in this account that would not be fully met by such a supposition. No man should adduce *this* instance in favour of drinking wine unless he can prove that the wine made in the "water-pots" of Cana was *just like* the wine which he proposes to drink. The Saviour's example may be always pleaded JUST AS IT WAS; but it is a matter of obvious and simple justice that we should find out exactly what the example was before we plead it. There is, moreover, no evidence that any other part of the water was converted into wine than that which was *drawn out* of the water-casks for the use of the guests. On this supposition, certainly, all the circumstances of the case are met, and the miracle would be more striking. All that was needed was to furnish a *supply* when the wine that had been prepared was nearly exhausted. The object was not to furnish a large quantity for future use. The miracle, too, would in this way be more apparent and impressive. On this supposition, the casks would *appear* to be filled with water *only;* as it was drawn out, it was pure wine. Who could doubt, then, that there was the exertion of miraculous power? All, therefore, that has been said about the Redeemer's furnishing a large quantity of wine for the newly-married pair, and about his benevolence in doing it, is wholly gratuitous. There is no evidence of it whatever; and it is not necessary to suppose it in order to an explanation of the circumstances of the case.

11. *This beginning of miracles.* This his first public miracle. This is declared by the sacred writer to be a *miracle*—that is, an exertion of divine power, producing a change of the substance of water into wine, which no human power could do. ¶ *Manifested forth.* Showed; exhibited. ¶ *His glory.* His power, and proper character as the Messiah; showed that he had divine power, and that God had certainly commissioned him. This is shown to be a *real* miracle by the following considerations: 1st. Real water was placed in the vessels. This the servants believed, and there was no possibility of deception. 2d. The water was placed where it was not *customary* to keep wine. It could not be *pretended* that it was merely a *mixture* of water and wine. 3d. It was judged to be wine without knowing whence it came. There was no agreement between Jesus and the governor of the feast to impose on the guests. 4th. It was a change which nothing but divine power could effect. He that can change *water* into a substance like the juice of the grape must be clothed with divine power. ¶ *Believed on him.* This does not mean that they did not *before* believe on him, but that their faith was *confirmed* or strengthened. They saw a miracle, and it satisfied them that he was the Messiah. *Before this* they *believed* on the testimony of John, and from conversation with Jesus (ch. i. 35–51); *now* they saw that he was invested with almighty power, and their faith was established.

From this narrative we may learn, 1st. That marriage is honourable, and that Jesus, if sought, will not refuse his presence and blessing on such an occasion. 2d. On such an occasion the presence and approbation of Christ *should* be sought. No compact formed on earth is more important; none enters so deeply into our comfort in this world; perhaps none will so much affect our destiny in the world to come. It should be entered into, then, in the fear of God. 3d. On all such occasions our conduct should be such that the presence of Jesus would be no interruption or disturbance. He is holy. He is always present in every place; and on all festival occasions our deportment should be such as that we should welcome the presence of the Lord Jesus Christ. *That is not a proper state of feeling or employment which would be interrupted by the presence of the Saviour.* 4th. Jesus delighted to do good. In the very beginning of his ministry he worked a miracle to show his benevolence. This was the appropriate commencement of a life in which he was to go about doing

manifested forth his glory; [k]and
his disciples believed on him.
12 After this he went down to
Capernaum, he, and his mother,
and his brethren, and his disciples;
and they continued there not many
days.

13 And the Jews' [l]passover was
at hand, and [m]Jesus went up to
Jerusalem,
14 And[n] found in the temple
those that sold oxen, and sheep,
and doves, and the changers of
money sitting;

k 1 Jn.5.13.

l Ex.12.14. m ver.23; ch.5.1; 6.4; 11.55. n Mat.21.12; Mar.11.15; Lu.19.45.

good. He seized every opportunity of doing it; and at a marriage feast, as well as among the sick and poor, he showed the character which he always sustained—that of a benefactor of mankind. 5th. An argument *cannot* be drawn from this instance in favour of intemperate drinking. There is no evidence that any who were present on that occasion drank too freely. 6th. Nor can an argument be drawn from this case in favour even of drinking wine such as we have. The common wine of Judea was the pure juice of the grape, without any mixture of alcohol, and was harmless. It was the common drink of the people, and did not tend to produce intoxication. *Our* wines are a *mixture* of the juice of the grape and of brandy, and often of infusions of various substances to give it colour and taste, and the appearance of wine. Those wines are little less injurious than brandy, and the habit of drinking them should be classed with the drinking of all other liquid fires.

The following table will show the danger of drinking the wines that are in common use:—

Brandy has fifty-three parts and 39 hundredths in a hundred of alcohol, or	53·39	per cent.
Rum	53·68	„
Whisky, Scotch	54·32	„
Holland Gin	51·60	„
Port Wine, highest kind	25·83	„
„ lowest „	21·40	„
Madeira, highest „	29·42	„
„ lowest „	19·34	„
Lisbon	18·94	„
Malaga	17·26	„
Red Champagne	11·30	„
White „	12·80	„
Currant Wine	20·25	„

It follows that a man who drinks two glasses of most of the wines used has taken as much alcohol as if he had taken one glass of brandy or whisky, and why should he not as well drink the alcohol in the brandy as in the wine? What difference can it make in morals? what difference in its effects on his system? The experience of the world has shown that water, pure water, is the most wholesome, safe, and invigorating drink for man.

12. *To Capernaum.* See Notes on Mat. iv. 13. ¶ *Not many days.* The reason why he remained there no longer was that the Passover was near, and they went up to Jerusalem to attend it.

13. *The Jews' passover.* The feast among the Jews called the Passover. See Notes on Mat. xxvi. 2-17. ¶ *And Jesus went up to Jerusalem.* Every male among the Jews was required to appear at this feast. Jesus, in obedience to the law, went up to observe it. This is the *first* Passover on which he attended after he entered on the work of the ministry. It is commonly supposed that he observed three others—one recorded Lu. vi. 1, another Jn. vi. 4, and the last one on the night before he was crucified, Jn. xi. 55. As his baptism when he entered on his ministry had taken place some time before this—probably not far from six months—it follows that the period of his ministry was not far from three years and a half, agreeably to the prophecy in Da. ix. 27.

14. *Found in the temple,* &c. The transaction here recorded is in almost all respects similar to that which has been explained in the Notes on Mat. xxi. 12. This took place at the *commencement* of his public ministry; that *at the close.* On each occasion he showed that his great regard was for the *pure worship* of his Father; and one great design of his coming was to reform the abuses which had crept into that worship, and to bring man to a proper regard for the glory of God. If it be asked how it was that those engaged in this traffic so readily *yielded* to Jesus of Nazareth, and that they left their gains and their property, and fled from the temple at the command of one so obscure as he was, it may be replied, 1st. That their *consciences* reproved them for their impiety, and they could not set up the *appearance* of self-defence. 2d. It was customary in the nation to cherish a profound regard for the authority of a

15 And when he had made a scourge of small cords, he drove them all out of the temple, and the sheep, and the oxen; and poured out the changers' money, and overthrew the tables;

16 And said unto them that sold doves, Take these things hence; make not my Father's house an house of merchandise.

17 And his disciples remembered that it was written, [o] The zeal of thine house hath eaten me up.

18 Then answered the Jews

o Ps.69.9.

prophet; and the appearance and manner of Jesus—so fearless, so decided, so authoritative—led them to suppose *he* was a prophet, and they were afraid to resist him. 3d. He *had* even then a wide reputation among the people, and it is not improbable that many supposed him to be the Messiah. 4th. Jesus on all occasions had a most wonderful control over men. None could resist him. There was something in his *manner*, as well as in his doctrine, that awed men, and made them tremble at his presence. Comp. Jn. xviii. 5, 6. On this occasion he had the *manner* of a prophet, the authority of God, and the testimony of their own consciences, and they could not, therefore, resist the authority by which he spoke.

Though Jesus thus purified the temple at the commencement of his ministry, yet in three years the same scene was to be repeated. See Mat. xxi. 12. And from this we may learn, 1st. How soon men forget the most solemn reproofs, and return to evil practices. 2d. That no sacredness of time or place will guard them from sin. In the very temple, under the very eye of God, these men soon returned to practices for which their consciences reproved them, and which they knew God disapproved. 3d. We see here how strong is the love of gain—the ruling passion of mankind. Not even the sacredness of the temple, the presence of God, the awful ceremonials of religion, deterred them from this unholy traffic. So wicked men and hypocrites will always turn *religion*, if possible, into gain; and not even the sanctuary, the Sabbath, or the most awful and sacred scenes, will deter them from schemes of gain. Comp. Am. viii. 5. So strong is this grovelling passion, and so deep is that depravity which fears not God, and regards not his Sabbaths, his sanctuary, or his law.

15. *A scourge.* A whip. ¶ *Of small cords.* This whip was made as an emblem of authority, and also for the purpose of driving from the temple the cattle which had been brought there for sale. There is no evidence that he used any violence to the men engaged in that unhallowed traffic. The original word implies that these *cords* were made of twisted *rushes* or *reeds*—probably the ancient material for making ropes.

17. *It was written*, &c. This is recorded in Ps. lxix. 9. Its meaning is, that he was affected with great zeal or concern for the pure worship of God. ¶ *The zeal of thine house. Zeal* is intense ardour in reference to any object. The *zeal of thine house* means extraordinary concern for the temple of God; intense solicitude that the worship there should be pure, and such as God would approve. ¶ *Hath eaten me up.* Hath absorbed me, or engaged my entire attention and affection; hath surpassed all other feelings, so that it may be said to be the one great absorbing affection and desire of the mind. Here is an example set for ministers and for all Christians. In Jesus this was the great commanding sentiment of his life. In us it should be also. In this manifestation of zeal he began and ended his ministry. In this we should begin and end our lives. We learn, also, that ministers of religion should aim to purify the church of God. Wicked men, conscience-smitten, will tremble when they see proper zeal in the ministers of Jesus Christ; and there is no combination of wicked men, and no form of depravity, that can stand before the faithful, zealous, pure preaching of the gospel. The preaching of every minister should be such that wicked men will feel that they must either become Christians or leave the house of God, or spend their lives there in the consciousness of guilt and the fear of hell.

18. *What sign*, &c. What *miracle* dost thou work? He assumed the character of a prophet. He was reforming, by his authority, the temple. It was natural to ask by what *authority* this was done; and as they had been accustomed

and said unto him, [p] What sign showest thou unto us, seeing that thou doest these things?
19 Jesus answered and said unto them, [q] Destroy this temple, and in three days I will raise it up.
20 Then said the Jews, Forty

p Mat.12.38,&c.; ch.6.30.

q Mat.26.61; 27.40.

to miracles in the life of Moses, and Elijah, and the other prophets, so they demanded evidence that *he* had authority thus to cleanse the house of God. ¶ *Seeing that thou doest.* Rather "by what *title* or *authority* thou doest these things." Our translation is ambiguous. They wished to know *by what miracle* he had shown, or could show, his right to do those things.

19. *Destroy this temple.* The evangelist informs us (ver. 21) that by *temple*, here, he meant his body. It is not improbable that he pointed with his finger to his body as he spoke. The word *destroy*, used here in the *imperative*, has rather the force of the *future.* Its meaning may thus be expressed: "You are now profaners of the temple of God. You have defiled the sanctuary; you have made it a place of traffic. You have also despised my authority, and been unmoved by the miracles which I have already wrought. But your wickedness will not end here. You will oppose me more and more; you will reject and despise me, until in your wickedness you will take my life and *destroy* my body." Here was therefore a distinct prediction both of his death and the cause of it. The word *temple*, or *dwelling*, was not unfrequently used by the Jews to denote the *body* as being the residence of the spirit, 2 Co. v. 1. Christians are not unfrequently called the temple of God, as being those in whom the Holy Spirit dwells on earth, 1 Co. iii. 16, 17; vi. 19; 2 Co. vi. 16. Our Saviour called his body a temple in accordance with the common use of language, and more particularly because *in him the fulness of the Godhead dwelt bodily*, Col. ii. 9. The *temple* at Jerusalem was the appropriate dwelling-place of God. His visible presence was there peculiarly manifested, 2 Ch. xxxvi. 15; Ps. lxxvi. 2. As the Lord Jesus was divine—as the fulness of the Godhead dwelt in him—so his body might be called a *temple.* ¶ *In three days I will raise it up.* The Jews had asked a *miracle* of him in proof of his authority—that is, a proof that he was the Messiah. He tells them that a full and decided proof of that would be his *resurrection from the dead.* Though they would not be satisfied by any other miracle, yet by this they ought to be convinced that he came from heaven, and was the long-expected Messiah. To the same evidence that he was the Christ he refers them on other occasions. See Mat. xii. 38, 39. Thus early did he foretell his death and resurrection, for at the beginning of his work he had a clear foresight of all that was to take place. This knowledge shows clearly that he came from heaven, and it evinces, also, the extent of his love—that he was *willing* to come to save us, knowing clearly what it would cost him. Had he come *without* such an expectation of suffering, his love might have been far less; but when he fully knew all that was before him, when he saw that it would involve him in contempt and death, it shows compassion "worthy of a God" that he was willing to endure the load of all our sorrows, and die to save us from death everlasting. When Jesus says, "*I* will raise it up," it is proof, also, of divine power. A mere *man* could not say this. No deceased *man* can have such power over his body; and there must have been, therefore, in the person of Jesus a nature superior to human to which the term "I" could be applied, and which had power to raise the dead—that is, which was divine.

20. *Then said the Jews*, &c. The Jews, either from the ambiguity of his language, or more probably from a design to cavil, understood him as speaking of the temple at Jerusalem. What he said here is all the evidence that they could adduce on his trial (Mat. xxvi. 61; Mar. xiv. 58), and they reproached him with it when on the cross, Mat. xxvii. 40. The Jews frequently perverted our Saviour's meaning. The language which he used was often that of parables or metaphor; and as they *sought* to misunderstand him and pervert his language, so he often left them to their own delusions, as he himself says, "that seeing they might not see, and hearing they might not understand," Mat. xiii. 13. This was a case

and six years was this temple in
building, and wilt thou rear it up
in three days?

21 But he spake of the [r]temple
of his body.

22 When, therefore, he was risen
from the dead, [s]his disciples remembered that he had said this
unto them; and they believed the
scripture, and the word which Jesus had said.

23 Now when he was in Jerusalem, at the passover, in the feast-
day, many believed in his name

r Ep.2.21,22; Col.2.9; He.8.2. s Lu.24.8.

which they *might*, if they had been disposed, have easily understood. They were in the temple; the conversation was about the temple; and though he probably pointed to his body, or designated it in some plain way, yet they *chose* to understand him as referring to the temple itself; and as it appeared so improbable that he could raise up that in three days, they sought to pervert his words and pour ridicule on his pretensions. ¶ *Forty and six years*, &c. The temple in which they then were was that which was commonly called *the second temple*, built after the return of the Jews from Babylon. See Notes on Mat. xxi. 12. This temple Herod the Great commenced repairing, or began to rebuild, in the eighteenth year of his reign—that is, *sixteen years* before the birth of Christ (Jos. *Ant.*, b. xv. § 1). The main body of the temple he completed in *nine years and a half* (Jos. *Ant.*, xv. 5, 6), yet the temple, with its outbuildings, was not entirely complete in the time of our Saviour. Herod continued to ornament it and to perfect it even till the time of Agrippa (Jos. *Ant.*, b. xx. ch. viii. § 11). As Herod began to rebuild the temple sixteen years before the birth of Jesus, and as what is here mentioned happened in the thirtieth year of the age of Jesus, so the time which had been occupied in it was *forty-six years.* This circumstance is one of the many in the New Testament which show the accuracy of the evangelists, and which prove that they were well acquainted with what they recorded. It demonstrates that their narration is true. Impostors do not trouble themselves to be very accurate about names and dates, and there is nothing in which they are more liable to make mistakes. ¶ *Wilt thou*, &c. This is an expression of contempt. Herod, with all his wealth and power, had been engaged in this work almost half a century. Can you, an obscure and unknown Galilean, accomplish it in three days? The thing, in their judgment, was ridiculous, and showed, as *they* supposed, that he had no authority to do what he had done in the temple.

22. *When he was risen from the dead*, &c. This saying of our Saviour at that time seemed obscure and difficult. The disciples did not understand it, but they treasured it up in their memory, and the event showed what was its true meaning. Many prophecies are obscure when spoken which are perfectly plain when the event takes place. We learn from this, also, the importance of treasuring up the truths of the Bible *now*, though we may not perfectly understand them. Hereafter they may be plain to us. It is therefore important that *children* should learn the truths of the sacred Scriptures. Treasured up in their memory, they may not be understood *now*, but hereafter they may be clear to them. Every one engaged in teaching a Sunday-school, therefore, may be imparting instruction which may be understood, and may impart comfort, long after the teacher has gone to eternity. ¶ *They believed.* That is, *after* he rose from the dead. ¶ *The scripture.* The Old Testament, which predicted his resurrection. Reference here must be made to Ps. xvi. 10, comp. Ac. ii. 27–32, xiii. 35–37; Ps. ii. 7, comp. Ac. xiii. 33. They understood those Scriptures in a sense different from what they did before. ¶ *The word which Jesus had said.* The prediction which he had made respecting his resurrection in this place and on other occasions. See Mat. xx. 19; Lu. xviii. 32, 33.

23. *Feast*-day. Feast. During the celebration of the Passover, which continued eight days. ¶ *Miracles which he did.* These miracles are not particularly recorded. Jesus took occasion to work miracles, and to preach at that time, for a great multitude were present from all parts of Judea. It was a favourable opportunity for making known his doctrines and showing the evidence that he was the Christ, and he embraced it.

when they saw the miracles which
he did.
24 But Jesus did not commit
himself unto them, because [t]he
knew all *men*,
25 And needed not that any
should testify of man; for he knew
what was in man.

t 1 Sa.16.7; 1 Ch.28.9; 29.17; Je.17.9,10; Mat.9.4; ch. 16.30; Ac.1.24; Re.2.23.

CHAPTER III.

THERE was a man of the Pharisees, named [a]Nicodemus, a
ruler of the Jews:
2 The same came to Jesus by
night, and said unto him, Rabbi,
we know that thou art a teacher
come from God; [b]for no man can

a ch.7.50,51; 19.39. *b* ch.9.16,33; Ac.2.22.

We should always seek and embrace opportunities of doing good, and we should not be *deterred*, but rather *excited*, by the multitude around us to make known our real sentiments on the subject of religion.

24. *Did not commit himself.* The word translated *commit* here is the same which in ver. 23 is translated *believed.* It means to put *trust* or *confidence in.* Jesus did not put *trust* or *reliance* in them. He did not leave himself in their hands. He acted cautiously and prudently. The proper time for him to die had not come, and he secured his own safety. The *reason* why he did not commit himself to them is *that he knew all men.* He knew the *inconstancy* and *fickleness* of the multitude. He knew how easily they might be turned against him by the Jewish leaders, and how unsafe he would be if they should be moved to sedition and tumult.

25. *Should testify of man.* Should give him the character of any man. ¶ *He knew what was in man.* This he did because he had made all (ch. i. 3), and because he was God, ch. i. 1. There can be no higher evidence than this that he was omniscient, and was therefore divine. To search the heart is the prerogative of God alone (Je. xvii. 10); and as Jesus knew what was in *these disciples*, and as it is expressly said that he knew what was in *man*—that is, in *all men*—so it follows that he must be equal with God. As he knows *all*, he is acquainted with the *false* pretentions and professions of hypocrites. None can deceive him. He also knows the wants and desires of all his *real* friends. He hears their groans, he sees their sighs, he counts their tears, and in the day of need will come to their relief.

CHAPTER III.

1. *A man of the Pharisees.* A Pharisee. See Notes on Mat. iii. 7. ¶ *Nicodemus, a ruler of the Jews.* One of the *Sanhedrim*, or great council of the nation. He is twice mentioned after this as being friendly to our Saviour; in the first instance as advocating his cause, and defending him against the unjust suspicion of the Jews (ch. vii. 50), and in the second instance as one who came to aid in embalming his body, ch. xix. 39. It will be recollected that the design of *John* in writing this gospel was to show that Jesus was the *Messiah.* To do this he here adduces the testimony of one of the *rulers* of the Jews, who early became convinced of it, and who retained the belief of it until the death of Jesus.

2. *The same came to Jesus.* The design of his coming seems to have been to inquire more fully of Jesus what was the doctrine which he came to teach. He seems to have been convinced that he was the Messiah, and desired to be farther instructed *in private* respecting his doctrine. It was not usual for a man of rank, power, and riches to come to inquire of Jesus in this manner; yet we may learn that the most favourable opportunity for teaching such men the nature of personal religion is when they are alone. Scarcely any man, of any rank, will refuse to converse on this subject when addressed respectfully and tenderly *in private.* In the midst of their companions, or engaged in business, they may refuse to listen or may cavil. When *alone*, they will hear the voice of entreaty and persuasion, and be willing to converse on the great subjects of judgment and eternity. Thus Paul says (Ga. ii. 2), "*privately to them which are of reputation;*" evincing his consummate prudence, and his profound knowledge of human nature. ¶ *By night.* It is not mentioned why he came by night. It might have been that, being a member of the Sanhedrim, he was engaged all the day; or it may have been because the Lord Jesus was occupied all the day in teaching publicly and in working miracles, and that there was no oppor-

do these miracles that thou doest except [c]God be with him.

3 Jesus answered and said unto him, Verily, verily, I say unto thee,

c Ac.10.38.

tunity for conversing with him as freely as he desired; or it may have been that he was afraid of the ridicule and contempt of those in power, and fearful that it might involve him in danger if publicly known; or it may have been that he was afraid that if it were publicly known that he was disposed to favour the Lord Jesus, it might provoke more opposition against *him* and endanger his life. As no *bad* motive is imputed to him, it is most in accordance with Christian charity to suppose that his motives were such as God would approve, especially as the Saviour did not reprove him. We should not be disposed to blame men where Jesus did not, and we should desire to find *goodness* in every man rather than be ever on the search for evil motives. See 1 Co. xiii. 4–7. We may learn here, 1st. That our Saviour, though engaged during the day, did not refuse to converse with an inquiring sinner at night. Ministers of the gospel at all times should welcome those who are asking the way to life. 2d. That it is *proper* for men, even those of elevated rank, to *inquire* on the subject of religion. Nothing is so important as religion, and no temper of mind is more lovely than a disposition to ask the way to heaven. *At all times* men should seek the way of salvation, and especially in times of great religious excitement they should make inquiry. At Jerusalem, at the time referred to here, there was great solicitude. Many believed on Jesus. He wrought miracles, and preached, and many were converted. There was what would now be called *a revival of religion*, having all the features of a work of grace. At such a season it was proper, as it is now, that not only the poor, but the rich and great, should inquire the path to life. ¶ *Rabbi.* This was a title of respect conferred on distinguished Jewish teachers, somewhat in the way that the title *doctor of divinity* is now conferred. See Notes on ch. i. 38. Our Saviour forbade his disciples to wear that title (see Notes on Mat. xxiii. 8), though it was proper for *him* to do it, as being the great *Teacher* of mankind. It literally signifies *great*, and was given by Nicodemus, doubtless, because Jesus gave distinguished proofs that he came as a teacher from God. ¶ *We know.* I know, and those with whom I am connected. Perhaps he was acquainted with some of the Pharisees who entertained the same opinion about Jesus that he did, and *he* came to be more fully confirmed in the belief. ¶ *Come from God.* Sent by God. This implies his *readiness* to hear him, and his *desire* to be instructed. He acknowledges the divine mission of Jesus, and delicately asks him to instruct him in the truth of religion. When we read the words of Jesus in the Bible, it should be with a belief that he came from God, and was therefore qualified and authorized to teach us the way of life. ¶ *These miracles.* The miracles which he wrought in the temple and at Jerusalem, ch. ii. 23. ¶ *Except God be with him.* Except God *aid* him, and except his instructions are *approved* by God. Miracles show that a prophet or religious teacher comes from God, because God would not work a miracle in attestation of a falsehood or to give countenance to a false teacher. If God gives a man power to work a miracle, it is proof that he approves the teaching of that man, and the miracle is the proof or the credential that he came from God.

3. *Verily, verily.* An expression of strong affirmation, denoting the *certainty* and the *importance* of what he was about to say. Jesus proceeds to state one of the fundamental and indispensable doctrines of his religion. It may seem remarkable that he should introduce this subject in this manner; but it should be remembered that Nicodemus acknowledged that he was a *teacher* come from God; that he *implied* by that his readiness and desire to receive instruction; and that it is not wonderful, therefore, that Jesus should *commence* with one of the fundamental truths of his religion. It is no part of Christianity to *conceal* anything. Jesus declared to every man, high or low, rich or poor, the most humbling truths of the gospel. Nothing was kept back for fear of offending men of wealth or power; and for them, as well as the most poor and lowly, it was declared to be indispensable to experience, as the first thing in religion, a change of heart and of life. ¶ *Except a man.* This is a universal form of expression de-

Except[d] a man be born [1]again, he cannot see the kingdom of God.

4 Nicodemus saith unto him, How can a man be born when he

d ch.1.13; Ga.6.15; Ep.2.1; Tit.3.5; Ja.1.18; 1 Pe.1. 23; 1 Jn.2.29; 3.9. [1] or, *from above.*

signed to include all mankind. Of *each and every* man it is certain that unless he is born again he cannot see the kingdom of God. It includes, therefore, men of every character and rank, and nation, moral and immoral, rich and poor, in office and out of office, old and young, bond and free, the slave and his master, Jew and Gentile. It is clear that our Saviour intended to convey to *Nicodemus* the idea, also, that *he* must be born again. It was not sufficient to be a Jew, or to acknowledge him to be a teacher sent by God—that is, the Messiah; it was necessary, in addition to this, to experience in his own soul that great change called the *new birth* or regeneration. ¶ *Be born again.* The word translated here *again* means also *from above*, and is so rendered in the margin. It is evident, however, that Nicodemus understood it not as referring to a birth *from above*, for if he had he would not have asked the question in ver. 4. It is probable that in the language which he used there was not the same ambiguity that there is in the Greek. The ancient versions all understood it as meaning *again*, or *the second time.* Our natural birth introduces us to light, is the commencement of life, throws us amid the works of God, and is the beginning of our existence; but it also introduces us to a world of sin. We early go astray. All men transgress. The imagination of the thoughts of the heart is evil from the youth up. We are conceived in sin and brought forth in iniquity, and there is none that doeth good, no, not one. The carnal mind is enmity against God, and by nature we are dead in trespasses and sins, Ge. viii. 21; Ps. xiv. 2, 3; li. 5; Ro. i. 29-32; iii. 10-20; viii. 7. All sin exposes men to misery here and hereafter. To escape from sin, to be happy in the world to come, it is necessary that man should be changed in his principles, his feelings, and his manner of life. This change, or the beginning of this new life, is called the *new birth*, or *regeneration.* It is so called because in many respects it has a striking analogy to the natural birth. It is the beginning of spiritual life. It introduces us to the light of the gospel. It is the moment when we really begin to live to any purpose. It is the moment when God reveals himself to us as our reconciled Father, and we are adopted into his family as his sons. And as every man is a sinner, it is necessary that each one should experience this change, or he cannot be happy or saved. This doctrine was not unknown to the Jews, and was particularly predicted as a doctrine that would be taught in the times of the Messiah. See De. x. 16; Je. iv. 4; xxxi. 33; Eze. xi. 19; xxxvi. 25; Ps. li. 12. The change in the New Testament is elsewhere called the *new creation* (2 Co. v. 17; Ga. vi. 15), and *life from the dead*, or a resurrection, Ep. ii. 1; Jn. v. 21, 24. ¶ *He cannot see.* To *see*, here, is put evidently for enjoying—or he cannot be fitted for it and partake of it. ¶ *The kingdom of God.* Either in this world or in that which is to come—that is, heaven. See Notes on Mat. iii. 2. The meaning is, that the kingdom which Jesus was about to set up was so pure and holy that it was indispensable that every man should experience this change, or he could not partake of its blessings. This is solemnly declared by the Son of God by an affirmation equivalent to an oath, and there can be no possibility, therefore, of entering heaven without experiencing the change which the Saviour contemplated by the *new birth.* And it becomes every man, as in the presence of a holy God before whom he must soon appear, to ask himself whether he has experienced this change, and if he has not, to give no rest to his eyes until he has sought the mercy of God, and implored the aid of his Spirit that his heart may be renewed.

4. *How can a man*, &c. It may seem remarkable that Nicodemus understood the Saviour *literally*, when the expression *to be born again* was in common use among the Jews to denote a change from *Gentilism* to *Judaism* by becoming a proselyte by *baptism.* The word with them meant a change from the state of a heathen to that of a Jew. But they never used it as applicable to *a Jew*, because they supposed that by his birth every Jew was entitled to all the privileges of the people of God. When, therefore, our Saviour used it of *a Jew*, when he affirmed its necessity of *every*

is old? Can he enter the second time into his mother's womb and be born?

5 Jesus answered, Verily, verily, I say unto thee, Except a man be born of [e]water and *of* [f]the Spirit, he cannot enter into the kingdom of God.

6 That[g] which is born of the

e Mar.16.16; Ac.2.38. f Ro.8.2; 1 Co.2.12. g 1 Co.15.47-49; 2 Co.5.17.

man, Nicodemus supposed that there was an absurdity in the doctrine, or something that surpassed his comprehension, and he therefore asked whether it was possible that Jesus could teach so absurd a doctrine—as he could conceive no other sense as applicable to a Jew—as that he should, when old, enter a second time into his mother's womb and be born. And we may learn from this—1st. That prejudice leads men to misunderstand the plainest doctrines of religion. 2d. That things which are at first incomprehensible or apparently absurd, may, when explained, become clear. The doctrine of regeneration, so difficult to Nicodemus, is plain to a *child* that is born of the Spirit. 3d. Those in high rank in life, and who are learned, are often most ignorant about the plainest matters of religion. It is often wonderful that they exhibit so little acquaintance with the most simple subjects pertaining to the soul, and so much absurdity in their views. 4th. A doctrine is not to be *rejected* because the rich and the great do not believe or understand it. The doctrine of regeneration was not *false* because Nicodemus did not comprehend it.

5. *Be born of water*. By *water*, here, is evidently signified *baptism*. Thus the word is used in Ep. v. 26; Tit. iii. 5. Baptism was practised by the Jews in receiving a Gentile as a proselyte. It was practised by John among the Jews; and Jesus here says that it is an ordinance of his religion, and the sign and seal of the renewing influences of his Spirit. So he said (Mar. xvi. 16), "He that believeth *and is baptized* shall be saved." It is clear from these places, and from the example of the apostles (Ac. ii. 38, 41; viii. 12, 13, 36, 38; ix. 18; x. 47, 48; xvi. 15, 33; xviii. 8; xxii. 16; Ga. iii. 27), that they considered this ordinance as binding on all who professed to love the Lord Jesus. And though it cannot be said that none who are not baptized can be saved, yet Jesus meant, undoubtedly, to be understood as affirming that this was to be the regular and uniform way of entering into his church; that it was the appropriate mode of making a profession of religion; and that a man who neglected this, when the duty was made known to him, neglected a plain command of God. It is clear, also, that any other command of God might as well be neglected or violated as this, and that it is the duty of everyone not only to love the Saviour, but to make an acknowledgment of that love by being baptized, and by devoting himself thus to his service. But, lest Nicodemus should suppose that this was all that was meant, he added that it was necessary that he should *be born of the Spirit* also. This was predicted of the Saviour, that he should *baptize with the Holy Ghost and with fire*, Mat. iii. 11. By this is clearly intended that the heart must be changed by the agency of the Holy Spirit; that the love of sin must be abandoned; that man must repent of crime and turn to God; that he must renounce all his evil propensities, and give himself to a life of prayer and holiness, of meekness, purity, and benevolence. This great change is in the Scripture ascribed uniformly to the Holy Spirit, Tit. iii. 5; 1 Th. i. 6; Ro. v. 5; 1 Pe. i. 22. ¶ *Cannot enter into*. This is the way, the appropriate way, of entering into the kingdom of the Messiah here and hereafter. He cannot enter into the true church here, or into heaven in the world to come, except in connection with a change of heart, and by the proper expression of that change in the ordinances appointed by the Saviour.

6. *That which is born of the flesh*. To show the *necessity* of this change, the Saviour directs the attention of Nicodemus to the natural condition of man. By *that which is born of the flesh* he evidently intends man as he is by nature, in the circumstances of his natural birth. Perhaps, also, he alludes to the question asked by Nicodemus, whether a man could be born when he was old? Jesus tells him that if this could be, it would not answer any valuable purpose; he would still have the same propensities and passions. Another change was therefore indispensable. ¶ *Is flesh*.

flesh is flesh; and that which is born of the Spirit is spirit.

7 Marvel not that I said unto thee, Ye must be born [2]again.

8 The wind bloweth where it listeth, and thou hearest the sound thereof, but canst not tell whence it cometh and whither it goeth; [h]so is every one that is born of the Spirit.

2 or, *from above*.

h 1 Co.2.11.

Partakes of the nature of the parent. Comp. Ge. v. 3. As the parents are corrupt and sinful, so will be their descendants. See Job xiv. 4. And as the parents are *wholly* corrupt by nature, so their children will be the same. The word *flesh* here is used as meaning *corrupt, defiled, sinful.* The *flesh* in the Scriptures is often used to denote the sinful propensities and passions of our nature, as those propensities are supposed to have their seat in the animal nature. "The works of the flesh are manifest, which are these: adultery, fornication, uncleanness, lasciviousness," &c., Ga. v. 19, 20. See also Ep. ii. 3; 1 Pe. iii. 21; ii. 18; 1 Jn. ii. 16; Ro. viii. 5. ¶ *Is born of the Spirit.* Of the Spirit of God, or by the agency of the Holy Ghost. ¶ *Is spirit.* Is spiritual, *like* the spirit, that is, holy, pure. Here we learn, 1st. That all men are by nature sinful. 2d. That none are renewed but by the Spirit of God. If man did the work himself, it would be still carnal and impure. 3d. That the effect of the new birth is to make men *holy.* And, 4th. That no man can have evidence that he is born again who is not holy, and just in proportion as he becomes pure in his life will be the evidence that he is born of the Spirit.

7. *Marvel not.* Wonder not. It is possible that Nicodemus in some way still expressed a doubt of the doctrine, and Jesus took occasion in a very striking manner to illustrate it.

8. *The wind bloweth,* &c. Nicodemus had objected to the doctrine because he did not understand how it *could be.* Jesus shows him that he ought not to reject it on that account, for he constantly believed things quite as difficult. It might appear incomprehensible, but it was to be judged of by its *effects.* As in this case of the wind, the *effects* were seen, the sound was heard, important *changes* were produced by it, trees and clouds were moved, yet the wind is *not seen,* nor do we know whence it comes, nor by what laws it is governed; so it is with the operations of the Spirit. We see the changes produced. Men just now sinful become holy; the thoughtless become serious; the licentious become pure; the vicious, moral; the moral, religious; the prayerless, prayerful; the rebellious and obstinate, meek, and mild, and gentle. When we see such changes, we ought no more to doubt that they are produced by some *cause*—by some mighty agent, than when we see the trees moved, or the waters of the ocean piled on heaps, or feel the cooling effects of a summer's breeze. In those cases we attribute it to the *wind,* though we see it not, and though we do not understand its operations. We may learn, hence, 1st. That the proper evidence of conversion is the *effect* on the life. 2d. That we are not too curiously to search for the *cause* or *manner* of the change. 3d. That God has power over the most hardened sinner to change him, as he has power over the loftiest oak, to bring it down by a sweeping blast. 4th. That there may be great *variety* in the modes of the operation of the Spirit. As the *wind* sometimes sweeps with a tempest, and prostrates all before it, and sometimes breathes upon us in a mild evening zephyr, so it is with the operations of the Spirit. The sinner sometimes trembles and is prostrate before the truth, and sometimes is sweetly and gently drawn to the cross of Jesus. ¶ *Where it listeth.* Where it *wills* or *pleases.* ¶ *So is every one,* &c. Every one that is born of the Spirit is, in some respects, like the effects of the wind. You see it not, you cannot discern its laws, but you see *its effects,* and you know therefore that it does exist and operate. Nicodemus's objection was, that he could not *see* this change, or perceive *how* it could be. Jesus tells him that he should not reject a doctrine merely because he could not understand it. Neither could the *wind* be seen, but its effects were well known, and no one doubted the existence or the power of the agent. Comp. Ec. xi. 5.

9. *How can these things be?* Nicodemus was still unwilling to admit the doctrine unless he understood it; and we have here an instance of a man of rank stum-

9 Nicodemus answered and said unto him, How can these things be?

10 Jesus answered and said unto him, Art thou a master of Israel, and knowest not these things?

11 Verily, verily, I say unto thee, [i]We speak that we do know, and

i 1 Jn.1.1-3.

bling at one of the plainest doctrines of religion, and unwilling to admit a truth because he could not understand *how* it could be, when he daily admitted the truth of facts in other things which he could as little comprehend. And we may learn, 1st. That men will often admit facts on other subjects, and be greatly perplexed by similar facts in religion. 2d. That no small part of men's difficulties are because they cannot understand *how* or *why* a thing is. 3d. That men of rank and learning are as likely to be perplexed by these things as those in the obscurest and humblest walks of life. 4th. That this is one reason why such men, particularly, so often reject the truths of the gospel. And, 5th. That this is a very *unwise* treatment of truth, and a way which they do not apply to other things. If the wind cools and refreshes me in summer—if it prostrates the oak or lashes the sea into foam—if it destroys my house or my grain, it matters little *how* it does this; and so of the Spirit. If it renews my heart, humbles my pride, subdues my sin, and comforts my soul, it is a matter of little importance *how* it does all this. Sufficient for me is it to know that it *is* done, and to taste the blessings which flow from the renewing and sanctifying grace of God.

10. *A master of Israel.* A *teacher* of Israel; the same word that in the second verse is translated *teacher*. As such a *teacher* he ought to have understood this doctrine. It was not *new*, but was clearly taught in the Old Testament. See particularly Ps. li. 10, 16, 17; Eze. xi. 19; xxxvi. 26. It may seem surprising that a man whose business it was to teach the people should be a stranger to so plain and important a doctrine; but when worldly-minded men are placed in offices of religion—when they seek those offices for the sake of ease or reputation, it is no wonder that they are strangers to the plain truths of the Bible; and there have been many, and there are still, who are in the ministry itself, to whom the plainest doctrines of the gospel are obscure. No man can understand the Bible fully unless he is a humble Christian, and the easiest way to comprehend the truths of religion is to give the heart to God and live to his glory. A child thus may have more *real* knowledge of the way of salvation than many who are pretended masters and teachers of Israel, Jn. vii. 17; Mat. xi. 25; Ps. viii. 2, compared with Mat. xxi. 16. ¶ *Of Israel.* Of the Jews; of the Jewish nation.

11. *We speak.* Jesus here speaks in the *plural* number, including himself and those engaged with him in preaching the gospel. Nicodemus had said (ver. 2), "*We* know that thou art," &c., including himself and those with whom he acted. Jesus in reply said, *We*, who are engaged in spreading the new doctrines about which you have come to inquire, speak what we know. We do not deliver doctrines which we do not *practically* understand. This is a positive affirmation of Jesus, which he had a right to make about his new doctrine. *He* knew its truth, and those who came into his kingdom knew it also. We learn here, 1st. That the Pharisees taught doctrines which they did not practically understand. They taught much truth (Mat. xxiii. 2), but they were deplorably ignorant of the plainest matters in their practical application. 2d. Every minister of the gospel ought to be able to appeal to his own experience, and to say that he *knows* the truth which he is communicating to others. 3d. Every Sunday-school teacher should be able to say, "I *know* what I am communicating; I have experienced what is meant by the new birth, and the love of God, and the religion which I am teaching." ¶ *Testify.* Bear witness to. ¶ *That we have seen.* Jesus had seen by his omniscient eye all the operations of the Spirit on the hearts of men. His ministers have seen its effects as we see the effects of the wind, and, having seen men changed from sin to holiness, they are qualified to bear witness to the truth and reality of the change. Every successful minister of the gospel thus becomes a witness of the saving power of the gospel. ¶ *Ye receive not.* Ye Pharisees. Though we give evidence of the truth of the new religion; though miracles are wrought, and proof is given that this doctrine

testify that we have seen; and ye receive not our witness.

12 If I have told you earthly things and ye believe not, how shall ye believe if I tell you *of* heavenly things?

13 And[k] no man hath ascended up to heaven, but he that came

k Ep.4.9,10.

came from heaven, yet you reject it. ¶ *Our witness.* Our testimony. The *evidence* which is furnished by miracles and by the saving power of the gospel. Men reject revelation though it is attested by the strongest evidence, and though it is constantly producing the most desirable changes in the hearts and lives of men.

12. *If I have told you earthly things.* Things which *occur* on earth. Not *sensual* or *worldly* things, for Jesus had said nothing of these; but he had told him of *operations of the Spirit* which had occurred *on earth*, whose effects were visible, and which *might* be, therefore, believed. These were the *plainest* and most obvious of the doctrines of religion. ¶ *How shall ye believe.* How *will* you believe. Is there any probability that you will understand them? ¶ *Heavenly things.* Things pertaining to the government of God and his doings in the heavens; things which are removed from human view, and which cannot be subjected to human sight; the more profound and inscrutable things pertaining to the redemption of men. Learn hence, 1st. The height and depth of the doctrines of religion. There is much that we cannot yet understand. 2d. The feebleness of our understandings and the corruptions of our hearts are the real causes why doctrines of religion are so little understood by us. 3d. There is before us a vast eternity, and there are profound wonders of God's government, to be the study of the righteous, and to be seen and admired by them for ever and ever.

13. *And no man hath ascended into heaven.* No man, therefore, is qualified to speak of heavenly things, ver. 12. To speak of those things requires intimate acquaintance with them—demands that we have *seen* them; and as no one has ascended into heaven and returned, so no one is qualified to speak of them but He who came down from heaven. This does not mean that no one had *gone* to heaven or had been saved, for Enoch and Elijah had been borne there (Ge. v. 24; comp. He. xi. 5; 2 Ki. ii. 11), and Abraham, Isaac, and Jacob, and others were there; but it means that no one had ascended and *returned*, so as to be qualified to speak of the things there. ¶ *But he that came down*, &c. The Lord Jesus. He is represented as coming down, because, being equal with God, he took upon himself our nature, Jn. i. 14; Phi. ii. 6, 7. He is represented as *sent* by the Father, Jn. iii. 17, 34; Ga. iv. 4; 1 Jn. iv. 9, 10. ¶ *The Son of man.* Called thus from his being *a man;* from his interest in man; and as expressive of his regard for man. It is a favourite title which the Lord Jesus gives to himself. ¶ *Which is in heaven.* This is a very remarkable expression. Jesus, the Son of man, was then bodily on earth conversing with Nicodemus; yet he declares that he is *at the same time* in heaven. This can be understood only as referring to the fact that he had two natures—that his *divine nature* was in heaven, and his *human nature* on earth. Our Saviour is frequently spoken of in this manner. Comp. Jn. vi. 62; xvii. 5; 2 Co. viii. 9. As Jesus was *in* heaven—as his proper abode was there—he was fitted to speak of heavenly things, and to declare the will of God to man. And we may learn, 1st. That the truth about the deep things of God is not to be learned of *men.* No one has ascended to heaven and returned to tell us what is there; and no infidel, no mere man, no prophet, is qualified of himself to speak of them. 2d. That all the light which we are to expect on those subjects is to be sought in the Scriptures. It is only Jesus and his inspired apostles and evangelists that can speak of those things. 3d. It is not wonderful that some things in the Scriptures are mysterious. They are about things which we have not seen, and we must receive them on the *testimony* of one who *has* seen them. 4th. The Lord Jesus is divine. He was in heaven while on earth. He had, therefore, a nature far above the human, and is equal with the Father, ch. i. 1.

14. *And as Moses.* Jesus proceeds in this and the following verses to state the reason why he came into the world; and, in order to this, he illustrates his design, and the efficacy of his coming, by a reference to the case of the brazen

down from heaven, *even* the Son of man which is in heaven.

14 And[l] as Moses lifted up the serpent in the wilderness, even so must the Son of man be lifted up;

15 That[m] whosoever believeth in him should not perish, but have eternal life.

16 For[n] God so loved the world that he gave his only-begotten

l Nu.21.9. *m* ver.36; He.7.25. *n* 1 Jn.4.9.

serpent, recorded in Nu. xxi. 8, 9. The people were bitten by flying fiery serpents. There was no cure for the bite. Moses was directed to make an *image* of the serpent, and place it in sight of the people, that they might look on it and be healed. There is no evidence that this was intended to be a *type* of the Messiah, but it is used by Jesus as strikingly *illustrating* his work. Men are sinners. There is no cure by human means for the maladies of the soul; and as the people who were bitten might look on the image of the serpent and be healed, so may sinners look to the Saviour and be cured of the moral maladies of our nature. ¶ *Lifted up.* Erected on a pole. Placed on high, so that it might be seen by the people. ¶ *The serpent.* The *image* of a serpent made of brass. ¶ *In the wilderness.* Near the land of Edom. In the desert and desolate country to the south of Mount Hor, Nu. xxi. 4. ¶ *Even so.* In a similar *manner* and with a similar *design.* He here refers, doubtless, to his own death. Comp. Jn. xii. 32; viii. 28. The points of resemblance between *his* being lifted up and that of the brazen serpent seem to be these: 1st. In each case those who are to be benefited can be aided in no other way. The bite of the serpent was deadly, and could be healed only by looking on the brazen serpent; and sin is deadly in its nature, and can be removed only by looking on the cross. 2d. The mode of their being lifted up. The brazen serpent was in the sight of the people. So Jesus was exalted from the earth—raised on a tree or cross. 3d. The design was similar. The one was to save the life, the other the soul; the one to save from temporal, the other from eternal death. 4th. The manner of the cure was similar. The people of Israel were *to look* on the serpent and be healed, and so sinners are to look on the Lord Jesus that they may be saved. ¶ *Must.* It is proper; necessary; indispensable, if men are saved. Comp. Lu. xxiv. 26; xxii. 42. ¶ *The Son of man.* The Messiah.

15. *That whosoever.* This shows the fulness and freeness of the gospel. All may come and be saved. ¶ *Believeth in him.* Whosoever puts *confidence* in him as able and willing to save. All who feel that they are sinners, that they have no righteousness of their own, and are willing to look to him as their only Saviour. ¶ *Should not perish.* They are in danger, by nature, of *perishing*—that is, of sinking down to the pains of hell; of "being *punished with everlasting destruction* from the presence of the Lord and from the glory of his power," 2 Th. i. 9. All who believe on Jesus shall be saved from this condemnation and be raised up to eternal life. And from this we learn, 1st. That there is salvation in no other. 2d. That salvation is here full and free for all who will come. 3d. That it is easy. What was more easy for a poor, wounded, dying Israelite, bitten by a poisonous serpent, than to *look up* to a brazen serpent? So with the poor, lost, dying sinner. And what more foolish than for such a wounded, dying man to *refuse* to look on a remedy so easy and effectual? So nothing is more foolish than for a lost and dying sinner to *refuse* to look on God's only Son, exalted on a cross to die for the sins of men, and able to save to the uttermost *all* who come to God by him.

16. *For God so loved.* This does not mean that God *approved* the conduct of men, but that he had *benevolent* feelings toward them, or was *earnestly desirous* of their happiness. God hates wickedness, but he still desires the happiness of those who are sinful. *He hates the sin, but loves the sinner.* A parent may love his child and desire his welfare, and yet be strongly opposed to the conduct of that child. When we approve the *conduct* of another, this is the love of *complacency;* when we desire simply their *happiness*, this is the love of *benevolence.* ¶ *The world.* All mankind. It does not mean any particular *part* of the world, but *man as man—the race* that had rebelled and that deserved to die. See Jn. vi. 33; xvii. 21. His love for the world, or for all mankind, in giving his Son, was shown by these circumstances: 1st. All the world was in

Son, that whosoever believeth in him should not perish, but have everlasting life.

17 For[o] God sent not his Son into the world to condemn the world, but that the world through him might be saved.

18 He[p] that believeth on him is not condemned; but he that believeth not is condemned already,

o Lu.9.56.

p ch.6.40,47.

ruin, and exposed to the wrath of God. 2d. All men were in a hopeless condition. 3d. God *gave* his Son. Man had no *claim* on him; it was a gift—an undeserved gift. 4th. He gave him up to extreme sufferings, even the bitter pains of death on the cross. 5th. It was for all the world. He tasted "death for every man," He. ii. 9. He "died for all," 2 Co. v. 15. "He is the propitiation for the sins of the whole world," 1 Jn. ii. 2. ¶ *That he gave.* It was a free and unmerited gift. Man had no claim; and when there was no eye to pity or arm to save, it pleased God to *give* his Son into the hands of men to die in their stead, Ga. i. 4; Ro. viii. 32; Lu. xxii. 19. It was the mere movement of love; the expression of eternal compassion, and of a desire that sinners should not perish for ever. ¶ *His only-begotten Son.* See Notes on Jn. i. 14. This is the highest expression of love of which we can conceive. A parent who should give up his only son to die for others who are guilty—if this could or might be done—would show higher love than could be manifested in any other way. So it shows the depth of the love of God, that he was willing to give his only Son into the hands of sinful men that he might be slain, and thus redeem them from eternal sorrow.

17. *To condemn the world.* Not to *judge*, or pronounce sentence on mankind. God *might* justly have sent him for this. Man deserved condemnation, and it would have been right to have pronounced it; but God was willing that there should be an offer of pardon, and the sentence of condemnation was delayed. But, although Jesus did not come *then* to condemn mankind, yet the time is coming when he will return to judge the living and the dead, Ac. xvii. 31; 2 Co. v. 10; Mat. xxv. 31-46.

18. *He that believeth.* He that has confidence in him; that relies on him; that trusts to his merits and promises for salvation. To believe on him is to *feel* and *act* according to truth—that is, to go as lost sinners, and act toward him as a Saviour from sins; relying on him, and looking to him *only* for salvation. See Notes on Mar. xvi. 16. ¶ *Is not condemned.* God pardons sin, and delivers us from deserved punishment, *because* we believe on him. Jesus died in our stead; he suffered for us, and by his sufferings our sins are expiated, and it is *consistent* for God to forgive. When a sinner, therefore, believes on Jesus, he trusts in him as having died in his place, and God having accepted the offering which Christ made in our stead, as being an equivalent for *our* sufferings in hell, there is now no farther condemnation, Ro. viii. 1. ¶ *He that believeth not.* All who do not believe, whether the gospel has come to them or not. All men by nature. ¶ *Is condemned already.* By conscience, by law, and in the judgment of God. God disapproves of their character, and this feeling of disapprobation, and the expression of it, is the condemnation. There is no condemnation so terrible as this—that *God disapproves* our conduct, and that he will *express* his disapprobation. He will judge according to truth, and woe to that man whose conduct God *cannot* approve. ¶ *Because.* This word does not imply that the *ground* or *reason* of their condemnation is that they have not believed, or that they are condemned *because* they do not believe on him, for there are millions of sinners who have never heard of him; but the meaning is this: There is but *one* way by which men can be freed from condemnation. All men without the gospel are condemned. They who do not believe are still under this condemnation, not having embraced the *only way* by which they can be delivered from it. The verse may be thus paraphrased: "All men are by nature condemned. There is but one way of being delivered from this state—by believing on the Son of God. They who do *not* believe or *remain* in that state are still condemned, FOR they have not embraced the only way in which they can be freed from it." Nevertheless, those to whom the gospel comes greatly heighten their guilt and condemnation by rejecting the offers of mercy, and trampling under foot the blood of the

because he hath not believed in
the name of the only-begotten Son
of God.

19 And this is the condemnation, that [q]light is come into the world, and men loved darkness rather than light, because their deeds were evil.

20 For every one that doeth evil hateth the light, [r]neither cometh to the light, lest his deeds should be [3]reproved.

21 But he that [s]doeth truth cometh to the light, that his deeds may be made manifest that [t]they are wrought in God.

q ch.1.4,9-11.

r Job 24.13,17; Pr.4.18,19.
3 or *discovered*. s 1 Jn.1.6. t 3 Jn.11.

Son of God, Lu. xii. 47; Mat. xi. 23; He. x. 29; Pr. i. 24–30. And there are thousands going to eternity under this *double* condemnation—1st. For positive, open sin; and, 2d. For rejecting God's mercy, and despising the gospel of his Son. This it is which will make the doom of sinners in Christian lands so terrible.

19. *This is the condemnation.* This is the *cause* of condemnation; or this is the reason why men are punished. ¶ *That light is come.* Light often denotes instruction, teaching, doctrine, as that by which we see clearly the path of duty. *All* the instruction that God gives us by conscience, reason, or revelation may thus be called light; but this word is used peculiarly to denote the Messiah or the Christ, who is often spoken of as *the light.* See Is. lx. 1; ix. 2. Compare Mat. iv. 16; also Notes on Jn. i. 4. It was doubtless this light to which Jesus had particular reference here. ¶ *Men loved darkness.* Darkness is the emblem of ignorance, iniquity, error, superstition—whatever is opposite to truth and piety. Men are said to love darkness more than they do light when they are better pleased with error than truth, with sin than holiness, with Belial than Christ. ¶ *Because their deeds are evil.* Men who commit crime commonly choose to do it in the night, so as to escape detection. So men who are wicked prefer false doctrine and error to the truth. Thus the Pharisees cloaked their crimes under the errors of their system; and, amid their false doctrines and superstitions, they attempted to convince others that they had great zeal for God. ¶ *Deeds.* Works; actions.

20. *That doeth evil.* Every wicked man. ¶ *Hateth the light.* This is true of all wicked men. They choose to practise their deeds of wickedness in darkness. They are afraid of the light, because they could be easily detected. Hence most crimes are committed in the night. So with the sinner against God. He hates the gospel, for it condemns his conduct, and his conscience would trouble him if it were enlightened. ¶ *His deeds should be reproved.* To *reprove* here means not only to *detect* or make manifest, but also includes the idea of *condemnation* when his deeds are detected. The gospel would make his wickedness manifest, and his conscience would condemn him. We learn from this verse, 1st. That one design of the gospel is *to reprove* men. It convicts them of sin in order that it may afford consolation. 2d. That men by nature *hate* the gospel. No man who is a sinner loves it; and no man by nature is disposed to come to it, any more than an adulterer or thief is disposed to come to the daylight, and do his deeds of wickedness there. 3d. The reason why the gospel is hated is that men are sinners. "Christ is hated because sin is loved." 4th. The sinner must be convicted or convinced of sin. If it be not in this world, it will be in the next. There is no escape for him; and the only way to avoid condemnation in the world to come is to come humbly and acknowledge sin here, and seek for pardon.

21. *He that doeth truth.* He who does right, or he that *obeys* the truth. *Truth* here is opposed to error and to evil. The sinner acts from falsehood and error. The good man acts according to truth. The sinner believes a lie—that God will not punish, or that there is no God, or that there is no eternity and no hell. The Christian believes all these, and acts *as if* they were true. This is the difference between a Christian and a sinner. ¶ *Cometh to the light.* Loves the truth, and seeks it more and more. By prayer and searching the Scriptures he endeavours to ascertain the truth, and yield his mind to it. ¶ *May be made manifest.* May be made clear or plain; or that it may be made plain that his deeds *are* wrought

22 After these things came Jesus and his disciples into the land of Judea; and there he tarried with them, [u]and baptized.

23 And John also was baptizing in Enon, near to [v]Salim, because there was much water there; [w]and they came and were baptized:

u ch.4.2. v 1 Sa.9.4. w Mat.3.5,6.

in God. He searches for truth and light that he may have evidence that his actions are right. ¶ *Wrought in God.* That they are performed according to the will of God, or perhaps by the assistance of God, and are such as God will approve. The actions of good men are performed by the influence and aid of God, Phi. ii. 12. Of course, if they are performed by his aid, they are such as he will approve. Here is presented the character of a good man and a sincere Christian. We learn respecting that character, 1st. He does truth. He loves it, seeks it, follows it. 2d. He comes to the light. He does not attempt to deceive himself or others. 3d. He is willing to know himself, and aims to do it. He desires to know the true state of his heart before God. 4th. An especial object of his efforts is that his deeds may be *wrought in God.* He *desires* to be a good man; to receive continual aid from God, and to perform such actions as he will approve.

This is the close of our Lord's discourse with Nicodemus—a discourse condensing the gospel, giving the most striking exhibition and illustration of truth, and representing especially the fundamental doctrine of regeneration and the evidence of the change. It is clear that the Saviour regarded this as lying at the foundation of religion. Without it we cannot possibly be saved. And now it becomes every reader, as in the presence of God, and in view of the judgment-seat of Christ, solemnly to ask himself whether he has experienced this change? whether he knows by experience what it is to be born of that Spirit? If he does he will be saved. If not, he is in the gall of bitterness and in the bond of iniquity, and should give no sleep to his eyes till he has made his peace with God.

22. *Land of Judea.* The region round about Jerusalem. ¶ *And baptized.* Jesus did not *himself* administer the ordinance of baptism, but his disciples did it by his direction and authority, Jn. iv. 2.

23. *In Enon.* The word *Enon,* or *Ænon,* means *a fountain,* and was doubtless given to this place because of the *fountains* there. On the situation of the place nothing certain has been determined. Eusebius places it 8 Roman miles south of Scythopolis or Bethshan, and 53 north-east of Jerusalem. ¶ *Near to Salim.* It would seem from this that Salim was better known then than Enon, but nothing can be determined now respecting its site. These places are believed to have been on the west side of the Jordan. ¶ *Because there was much water there.* John's preaching attracted great multitudes. It appears that they remained with him probably many days. In many parts of that country, particularly in the hilly region near where John preached, it was difficult to find water to accommodate the necessities of the people, and perhaps, also, of the camels with which those from a distance would come. To meet their necessities, as well as for the purpose of baptizing, he selected a spot that was well watered, probably, with springs and rivulets. Whether the ordinance of baptism was performed by immersion or in any other mode, the selection of a place well watered was proper and necessary. The mention of the fact that there was much water there, and that John selected that as a convenient place to perform his office as a baptizer, proves nothing in regard to the *mode* in which the ordinance was administered, since he would naturally select such a place, whatever was the mode. Where numbers of people came together to remain any time, it is necessary to select such a place, whatever their employment. An encampment of soldiers is made on the same principles, and in every camp-meeting that I have ever seen, a place is selected where there is a good supply of water, though not one person should be *immersed* during the whole services. As all the facts in the case are fully met by the supposition that John might have baptized in some other way besides immersion, and as it is easy to conceive *another* reason that is sufficient to account for the fact that such a place was selected, *this* passage certainly should not be adduced to prove that he performed baptism only in that manner.

24 For[x] John was not yet cast into prison.
25 Then there arose a question between *some* of John's disciples and the Jews about purifying.
26 And they came unto John, and said unto him, Rabbi, he that was with thee beyond Jordan, [y]to whom thou barest witness, behold, the same baptizeth, and [z]all *men* come to him.
27 John answered and said, [a]A

x Mat.14.3.

y ch.1.7,15,&c. z Ps.65:2; Is.45.23. a 1,Co.2.12-14; 4.7; He.5.4; Ja.1.17.

24. *For John was not yet cast into prison.* See Lu. iii. 20. The mention of this shows that John was not imprisoned till some time after our Lord entered on his ministry. The design of John was to call men to repentance, and to prepare them for the Messiah, and this he continued to do after our Saviour commenced *his* work. It shows that a minister of religion should be industrious to the day of his death. John still toiled in his work not the *less* because the Messiah had come. So ministers should not labour less when Christ appears by his Spirit, and takes the work into his own hands, and turns many to himself.

25. *A question.* Rather a controversy —a dispute. ¶ *John's disciples.* Those who had been baptized by him, and who attached great efficacy and importance to the teaching of their master. Comp. Notes on Ac. xix. 1–5. ¶ *And the Jews.* Many manuscripts, some of the fathers, and the ancient Syriac version, read this in the singular number— "with *a Jew*," one who, it is commonly supposed, had been baptized by the disciples of Jesus. ¶ *About purifying.* What the precise subject of this dispute was we do not know. From what follows, it would seem probable that it was about the comparative value and efficacy of the baptism performed by John and by the disciples of Jesus. The word *purifying* may be applied to baptism, as it was an emblem of repentance and purity, and was thus used by the Jews, by John, and by Jesus. About this subject it seems that a dispute arose, and was carried to such a length that complaint was made to John. From this we may learn, 1st. That even in the time of Jesus, when the gospel began to be preached, there was witnessed—what has been ever since —unhappy disputings on the subject of religion. Even young converts may, by overheated zeal and ignorance, fall into angry discussion. 2d. That such discussions are commonly about some unimportant matter of religion—something which they may not yet be qualified to understand, and which does not materially affect them if they could. 3d. That such disputes are often connected with a spirit of proselytism— with boasting of the superior excellence of the sect with which *we* are connected, or in connection with whom *we* have been converted, and often with a desire to persuade others to join with us. 4th. That such a spirit is eminently improper on such occasions. Love should characterize the feelings of young converts; a disposition to *inquire* and not to *dispute;* a willingness that all should follow the dictates of their own consciences, and not a desire to *proselyte* them to *our* way of thinking or to *our* church. It may be added that there is scarcely anything which so certainly and effectually arrests a revival of religion as such a disposition to *dispute,* and to make proselytes to particular modes of faith, and of administering the ordinances of the gospel.

26. *Came unto John.* Came to him with their complaint; envious and jealous at the success of Jesus, and evidently irritated from the discussion, as if their master was about to lose his popularity. ¶ *Rabbi.* Master. See Notes on Mat. xxiii. 7. Acknowledging him as their master and teacher. ¶ *That was with thee.* Who was baptized by thee. ¶ *Thou barest witness.* See ch. i. 29–35. ¶ *All* men *come to him.* This was the source of their difficulty. It was that Jesus was gaining popularity; that the people flocked to him; that they feared that John would be forsaken, and his followers be diminished in numbers and influence. Thus many love their *sect* more than they do Christ, and would be more rejoiced that a man became a Presbyterian, a Methodist, a Baptist, than that he became a sincere and humble Christian. This is not the spirit of the gospel. True piety teaches us to rejoice that sinners turn to Christ and become holy, whether they follow *us* or not. See Mar. ix. 38, 39. Let Jesus be exalted, and let men turn to *him,* is the

man can [4]receive nothing, except it be given him from heaven.

28 Ye yourselves bear me witness that I said, [b]I am not the Christ, but that [c]I am sent before him.

29 He that hath the [d]bride is the bridegroom; but the [e]friend of the bridegroom, which standeth and heareth him, rejoiceth greatly because of the bridegroom's voice. This my joy, therefore, is fulfilled.

30 He must increase, but I *must* decrease.

31 He that cometh [f]from above is above all: [g]he that is of the earth is earthly, and speaketh of

4 or, *take unto himself*. b ch.1.20,27. c Lu.1.17. d Ca.4.8-12; Je.2.2; Eze.16.8; Ho.2.19,20; Mat.22.2; 2 Co.11.2; Ep.5.25,27; Re.21.9. e Ca.5.1.

f ch.6.33; 8.23; Ep.1.20,21. g 1 Co.15.47.

language of religion, whatever denomination they may feel it their duty to follow.

27. *John answered*, &c. John did not enter into their feelings or sympathize with their love of party. He came to honour Jesus, not to build up a sect. He rejoiced at the success of the Messiah, and began to teach them to rejoice in it also. ¶ *A man can receive nothing*, &c. All success is from heaven. All *my* success was from God. All the success of Jesus is from God. As success comes from the *same* source, we ought not to be envious. It is designed to answer the same end, and, by whomsoever accomplished, the hand of God is in it, and we should rejoice. If Jesus and his disciples are successful, if all men flee to him, it is proof that God favours him, and you should rejoice.

28. *Bear me witness.* You remember that at first I told you I was not the Messiah. As he had been *witness* to Jesus—as he came for no other end but to point him out to the Jews, they ought not to suppose that he was his superior. It was but reasonable to expect that Christ himself would be more successful than his forerunner. "I came, not to form *a separate party*, a peculiar sect, but to prepare the way that *he* might be more successful, and that the people might be ready for his coming, and that he might have the success which he has actually met with. You should rejoice, therefore, at that success, and not envy it, for *his success* is the best proof of the greatness of *my* word, and of *its success* also."

29. *He that hath the bride*, &c. This is an illustration drawn from marriage. The bride belongs to her husband. So the church, the bride of the Messiah, belongs to him. It is *to be expected*, therefore, and *desired*, that the people should flock to him. ¶ *But the friend of the bridegroom.* He whose office it is to attend him on the marriage occasion. This was commonly the nearest friend, and was a high honour. ¶ *Rejoiceth greatly.* Esteems himself highly honoured by the proof of friendship. ¶ *The bridegroom's voice.* His commands, requests, or conversation. ¶ *This my joy*, &c. "I sustain to the Messiah the relation which a groomsman does to the groom. The chief honour and the chief joy is not mine, but his. It is to be expected, therefore, that the people will come to him, and that his success will be great." The relation of Christ to the church is often compared with the marriage relation, denoting the tenderness of the union, and his great love for his people. Comp. Is. lxii. 5; Re. xxi. 2, 9; xxii. 17; Ep. v. 26, 27, 32; 2 Co. xi. 2.

30. *He must increase. His* authority and influence among the people must grow. *His* doctrine shall continue to spread till it extends through all the earth. ¶ *I* must *decrease.* "The purpose of my ministry is to point men to him. When that is done my work is done. I came not to form a party of my own, nor to set up a religion of my own; and my teaching must *cease* when he is fully established, as the light of the morning star fades away and is lost in the beams of the rising sun." This evinced John's humility and willingness to be esteemed as nothing if he could honour Christ. It shows us, also, that it is sufficient honour for man if he may be permitted to point sinners to the Lord Jesus Christ. No work is so honourable and joyful as the ministry of the gospel; none are so highly honoured as those who are permitted to stand near the Son of God, to hear his voice, and to lead perishing men to his cross. Comp. Da. xii. 3.

31. *He that cometh from above.* The Messiah, represented as coming down from heaven. See ver. 13; ch. vi. 33; viii. 23. It has been doubted whether the remainder of this chapter contains

the earth: he that cometh from heaven is above all.

32 And what he hath seen and heard, that he testifieth; and [h]no man receiveth his testimony.

33 He that hath received his testimony hath [i]set to his seal that God is true.

34 For[k] he whom God hath sent speaketh the words of God; [l]for God giveth not the Spirit by measure *unto him*.

h ch.1.11.

i 1 Jn.5.10. k ch.7.16.
l Ps.45.7; Is.11.2; 59.21; ch.1.16; Col.1.19.

the words of *John the Baptist* or of *the evangelist.* The former is the more probable opinion, but it is difficult to decide it, and it is of very little consequence. ¶ *Is above all.* In nature, rank, and authority. Is *superior to all prophets* (He. i. 1, 2); *to all angels* (He. i. 4–14), *and is over all the universe as its sovereign Lord,* Ro. ix. 5; Ep. i. 21, 22; Col. i. 15–19; 1 Co. xv. 25. ¶ *He that is of the earth.* He who has no higher nature than the human nature. The prophets, apostles, and John were men like others, born in the same way, and sinking, like others, to the dust. See Ac. xiv. 15. Jesus had a nature superior to man, and *ought*, therefore, to be exalted above all. ¶ *Is earthly.* Is human. Is *inferior* to him who comes from heaven. Partakes of his *origin*, which is inferior and corrupt. ¶ *Speaketh of the earth.* His teaching is inferior to that of him who comes from heaven. It is comparatively obscure and imperfect, not full and clear, like the teaching of him who is from above. This was the case with all the prophets, and even with John the Baptist, as compared with the teaching of Christ.

32. *And what he hath seen,* &c. See ver. 11. ¶ *No man receiveth his testimony.* The words *no man* are here to be understood in the sense of *few.* Though his doctrine is pure, plain, sublime, yet *few*, comparatively, received it in faith. Though multitudes came to him, drawn by various motives (Jn. vi. 26), yet *few* became his *real* disciples, Mat. xxvi. 56; vii. 22. ¶ *His testimony.* His doctrine. The truth to which he bears *witness* as having *seen* and *known* it, ver. 11. Often many persons *appear* for a time to become the followers of Christ, who in the end are seen to have known nothing of religion, Mat. xiii. 6; Lu. viii. 13.

33. *He that hath received his testimony.* Hath received and fully believed his doctrine. Hath yielded his heart to its influence. ¶ *Hath set to his seal.* To *seal* an instrument is to make it sure; to acknowledge it as *ours;* to pledge our veracity that it is true and binding, as when a man seals a bond, a deed, or a will. Believing a doctrine, therefore, in the heart, is expressed by *sealing it,* or by believing it we express *our firm conviction* that it is true, and that God who has spoken it is true. We vouch for the veracity of God, and assume *as our own* the proposition that it is the truth of God. ¶ *God is true.* Is faithful; is the author of the system of doctrines, and will fulfil all that he has promised. We learn here, 1st. That to be a true believer is something more than to hold a mere speculative belief of the truth. 2d. That to be a believer is to *pledge ourselves* for the truth, to seal it as our own, to adopt it, to choose it, and solemnly assent to it, as a man does in regard to an instrument of writing that is to convey his property, or that is to dispose of it when he dies. 3d. Every Christian is a witness for God, and it is his business to show by his life that he believes that God is true to his threatenings and to his promises. See Notes on Is. xliii. 10. 4th. It is a solemn act to become a Christian. It is a surrender of all to God, or giving away body, soul, and spirit to him, with a belief that he is *true*, and alone is able to save. 5th. The man that does not do this—that is not willing to pledge his belief that God is true, sets to *his* seal that God is *a liar* and unworthy of confidence, 1 Jn. v. 10.

34. *Whom God hath sent.* The Messiah. ¶ *Speaketh the words of God.* The *truth*, or commands of God. ¶ *For God giveth not the Spirit.* The Spirit of God. Though Jesus was God as well as man, yet, *as Mediator*, God anointed him, or endowed him with the influences of his Spirit, so as to be completely qualified for his great work. ¶ *By measure.* Not in a small degree, but fully, completely. The prophets were inspired on *particular* occasions to deliver special messages. The Messiah was *continually* filled with the Spirit of God. "The Spirit dwelt in him, not as a vessel, but

35 The[m] Father loveth the Son, and hath given all things into his hand.

36 He[n] that believeth on the Son hath everlasting life; and he that believeth not the Son shall not see life, but the [o]wrath of God abideth on him.

m Mat.28.18. *n* Hab.2.4; ver.15,16. *o* Ro.1.18.

as in a fountain, as in a bottomless ocean" (Henry).

35. *Loveth the Son.* Loves him eminently, above all the prophets and all the other messengers of God. ¶ *Hath given all things into his hand.* See Notes on Mat. xxviii. 18.

36. *Hath everlasting life.* Has or is in possession of that which is a recovery from spiritual death, and which will result in eternal life in heaven. Piety here is the same that it will be there, except that it will be expanded, matured, purified, made more glorious. It is here life begun—the first breathings and pantings of the soul for immortality; yet it is life, though at first feeble and faint, which is eternal in its nature, and which shall be matured in the full and perfect bliss of heaven. The Christian here has a foretaste of the world of glory, and enjoys the same *kind* of felicity, though not the same *degree*, that he will there. ¶ *Shall not see life.* Shall neither enjoy true *life* or happiness here nor in the world to come. Shall never enter heaven. ¶ *The wrath of God.* The anger of God for sin. His opposition to sin, and its terrible effects in this world and the next. ¶ *Abideth on him.* This implies that he is *now* under the wrath of God, or under condemnation. It implies, also, that it will *continue* to remain on him. It will *abide* or *dwell* there as its appropriate habitation. As there is no way of escaping the wrath of God but by the Lord Jesus Christ, so those who will not believe must go to eternity *as they are*, and bear alone and unpitied all that God may choose to inflict as the expression of *his* sense of sin. Such is the miserable condition of the sinner! Yet thousands choose to remain in this state, and to encounter *alone* all that is terrible in the wrath of Almighty God, rather than come to Jesus, who has borne their sins in his own body on the tree, and who is willing to bless them with the peace, and purity, and joy of immortal life.

CHAPTER IV.

WHEN, therefore, the Lord knew how the Pharisees had heard that Jesus made and [a]baptized more disciples than John,

2 (Though Jesus himself baptized not, but his disciples,)

a ch.3.22,26.

CHAPTER IV.

1. *The Lord knew.* When Jesus knew. *How* he knew this we are not informed; whether by that power of omniscience by which he knew all things, or whether some person had informed him of it. ¶ *How the Pharisees had heard.* The *Pharisees*, here, seem to denote either the members of the Sanhedrim or those who were in authority. They claimed the authority to regulate the rites and ceremonies of religion, and hence they supposed they had a right to inquire into the conduct of both John and our Lord. They had on a former occasion sent to inquire of John to know by what authority he had introduced such a rite into the religion of the Jewish people. See Notes on ch. i. 25. ¶ *More disciples than John.* Though many of the Pharisees came to his baptism (Mat. iii.), yet those who were in authority were displeased with the success of John, Jn. i. 25. The reasons of this were, probably, the severity and justness of his reproofs (Mat. iii. 7), and the fact that by drawing many after him he weakened their authority and influence. As they were displeased with *John*, so they were with *Jesus*, who was doing the same thing on a larger scale—not only making disciples, but *baptizing* also without their authority, and drawing away the people after him.

2. *Though Jesus himself baptized not.* The reason why Jesus did not baptize was probably because, if *he* had baptized, it might have made unhappy divisions among his followers: those might have considered themselves most worthy or honoured who had been baptized by *him.* Comp. 1 Co. i. 17.

3. *He left Judea.* The envy and malice of the Pharisees he might have known were growing so rapidly as to endanger his life. As his time to die had not yet come, he retired to Galilee, a country farther from Jerusalem, and much less under their control than Judea. See

3 He left Judea, and departed
again into Galilee.
4 And he [b]must needs go through
Samaria.
5 Then cometh he to a city of
Samaria which is called Sychar,
near to the parcel of ground that
Jacob [c]gave to his son Joseph.
6 Now Jacob's well was there.
Jesus therefore, being wearied with
his journey, sat thus on the well;
and it was about the sixth hour.
7 There cometh a woman of
Samaria to draw water. Jesus
saith unto her, Give me to drink.
8 For his disciples were gone
away unto the city to buy meat.
9 Then saith the woman of

b Lu.2.49. *c* Ge.33.19; 48.22; Jos.24.32.

Mar. ii. 22; Lu. iii. 1. Though he feared not death and did not shrink from suffering, yet he did not *needlessly* throw himself into danger or provoke opposition. He could do as much *good* in Galilee, probably, as in Judea, and he therefore withdrew himself from immediate danger.

4. *And he must needs go through Samaria.* Samaria was between Judea and Galilee. The *direct* and usual way was to pass through Samaria. Sometimes, however, the Jews took a circuitous route on the east side of the Jordan, See Notes on Mat. ii. 22.

5. *Sychar.* This city stood about eight miles south-east of the city called Samaria, between Mount Ebal and Mount Gerizim. It was one of the oldest cities of Palestine, and was formerly known by the name of *Shechem*, or Sichem, Ge. xxxiii. 18; xii. 6. The city was in the tribe of Ephraim, Jos. xxi. 21. It was at this place that Joshua assembled the people before his death, and here they renewed their covenant with the Lord, Jos. xxiv. After the death of Gideon it became a place of idolatrous worship, the people worshipping *Baal-berith*, Ju. ix. 46. It was destroyed by Abimelech, who beat down the city and sowed it with salt, Ju. ix. 45. It was afterward rebuilt, and became the residence of Jeroboam, the King of Israel, 1 Ki. xii. 25. It was called by the Romans *Flavia Neapolis*, and this has been corrupted by the Arabs into *Nablûs*, its present name. It is still a considerable place, and its site is remarkably pleasant and productive. ¶ *The parcel of ground.* The *piece* of ground; or the *land*, &c. ¶ *That Jacob gave*, &c. Jacob bought one piece of ground near to Shalem, a city of Shechem, of the children of Hamor, the father of Shechem, for an hundred pieces of silver, Ge. xxxiii. 19. In this place the bones of Joseph were buried when they were brought up from Egypt, Jos. xxiv. 32. He also gave to Joseph an additional piece of ground which he took from the hand of the Amorite by his own valour, "with his sword and his bow," as a portion above that which was given to his brethren, Ge. xlviii. 22. Possibly these pieces of ground lay near together, and were a part of the *homestead* of Jacob. The well was "near" to this. There is now, the Rev. E. Smith mentioned to me in conversation, a place near this well called *Shalem*.

6. *Jacob's well.* This is not mentioned in the Old Testament. It was called *Jacob's well*, probably, either because it was handed down by tradition that he dug it, or because it was near to the land which he gave to Joseph. There is still a well a few miles to the east of Nablûs, which is said by the people there to be the same. The Rev. Eli Smith, missionary to Syria, stated to me that he had visited this well. It is about 100 feet deep. It is cut through solid rock of limestone. It is now dry, probably from having been partly filled with rubbish, or perhaps because the water has been diverted by earthquakes. The well is covered with a large stone, which has a hole in the centre large enough to admit a man. It is at the foot of Mount Gerizim, and has a plain on the east. ¶ *Sat thus.* Jesus was weary, and, being *thus* weary, sat down on the well. The word translated *on* here may denote also *by*—he sat down *by* the well, or near it. ¶ *The sixth hour.* About twelve o'clock. This was the common time of the Jewish meal, and this was the reason why his disciples were gone away to buy food.

7. *Of Samaria.* Not of the *city* of Samaria, for this was at a distance of 8 miles, but a woman who was a Samaritan, and doubtless from the city of Sychar. ¶ *Give me to drink.* This was in the heat of the day, and when Jesus was weary with his journey. The request was also made that it might give him occasion to discourse with her on

Samaria unto him, How is it that thou, being a Jew, askest drink of me, which am a woman of Samaria? [d]for the Jews have no dealings with the Samaritans.

10 Jesus answered and said unto her, If thou knewest [e]the gift of God, and who it is that saith to thee, Give me to drink; thou wouldest have asked of him, and he would have given thee [f]living water.

11 The woman saith unto him, Sir, thou hast nothing to draw with, and the well is deep; from whence, then, hast thou that living water?

12 Art thou greater than our

d Ac.10.28. e Ep.2.8. f Is.12.3; 41.17,18; Je.2.13; Zec.13.1; 14.8; Re.22.17.

---

the subject of religion, and in this instance we have a specimen of the remarkably happy manner in which he could lead on a conversation so as to introduce the subject of religion.

8. *Buy meat.* Buy food.

9. *No dealings with the Samaritans.* For an account of the Samaritans, and of the differences between them and the Jews, see Notes on Mat. x. 5.

10. *The gift of God.* The word *gift*, here denotes *favour.* It may refer to Jesus *himself*, as the *gift* of God to the world, given to save men from death (ch. iii. 16; 2 Co. ix. 15), or it may refer to the *opportunity* then afforded her of seeking salvation. If thou knewest how favourable an opportunity God now gives thee to gain a knowledge of himself, &c. ¶ *And who it is*, &c. If thou knewest that the Messiah was speaking. ¶ *Living water.* The Jews used the expression *living water* to denote springs, fountains, or running streams, in opposition to dead and stagnant water. Jesus here means to denote by it his doctrine, or his grace and religion, in opposition to the impure and dead notions of the Jews and the Samaritans. See ver. 14. This was one of the many instances in which he took occasion from common topics of conversation to introduce religious discourse. None ever did it so happily as he did, but, by studying his example and manner, *we* may learn also to do it. One way to acquire the art is to have the mind *full* of the subject; to make religion our first and main thing; to carry it with us into all employments and into all society; to look upon everything in a religious light, and out of the abundance of the heart the mouth will speak, Mat. xii. 34.

11. *Hast nothing to draw with.* It seems that there were no means of drawing water *affixed* to the well, as with us. Probably each one took a pail or pitcher and a cord for the purpose. In travelling this was indispensable. The woman, seeing that Jesus had no *means* of drawing water, and not yet understanding his design, naturally inquired whence he could obtain the water. ¶ *The well is deep.* If the same one that is there now, it was about 100 feet deep.

12. *Art thou greater?* Art thou wiser, or better able to find water, than Jacob was? It seems that she supposed that he meant that he could direct her to some living spring, or to some better well in that region, and that this implied more knowledge or skill than Jacob had. To find water and to furnish a good well was doubtless considered a matter of signal skill and success. It was a subject of great importance in that region. This shows how ready sinners are to misunderstand the words of Christ, and to pervert the doctrines of religion. If she had had any proper anxiety about her soul, she would at least have *suspected* that he meant to direct her thoughts to spiritual objects. ¶ *Our father Jacob.* The Samaritans were composed partly of the remnant of the ten tribes, and partly of people sent from Chaldea; still, they considered themselves descendants of Jacob. ¶ *Which gave us.* This was doubtless the tradition, though there is no evidence that it was true. ¶ *And drank thereof*, &c. This was added in commendation of the water of the well. A well from which Jacob, and his sons, and cattle had drank must be pure, and wholesome, and honoured, and quite as valuable as any that Jesus could furnish. Men like to commend that which their ancestors used as superior to anything else. The world over, people love to speak of that which *their* ancestors have done, and boast of titles and honours that have been handed down from them, even if it is nothing better than existed here—because Jacob's *cattle* had drunk of the water.

father Jacob, which gave us the well, and drank thereof himself, and his children, and his cattle?

13 Jesus answered and said unto her, Whosoever drinketh of this water shall thirst again;

14 But[g] whosoever drinketh of the water that I shall [h]give him shall never thirst; but the water that I shall give him shall be [i]in him a well of water springing up into everlasting life.

15 The woman saith unto him, Sir, give me this water, that I thirst not, neither come hither to draw.

16 Jesus saith unto her, Go call thy husband, and come hither.

17 The woman answered and

g ch.6.35,58. h ch.17.2,3; Ro.6.23. i ch.7.38.

13. *Shall thirst again.* Jesus did not directly answer her question, or say that he was *greater* than Jacob, but he gave her an answer by which she might infer that he was. He did not despise or undervalue Jacob or his gifts; but, however great might be the value of that well, the water could not altogether remove thirst.

14. *The water that I shall give him.* Jesus here refers, without doubt, to his own *teaching*, his *grace*, his *spirit*, and to the benefits which come into the soul that embraces his gospel. It is a striking image, and especially in Eastern countries, where there are vast deserts, and often a great want of water. The soul by nature is like such a desert, or like a traveller wandering through such a desert. It is thirsting for happiness, and seeking it everywhere, and finds it not. It looks in all directions and tries all objects, but in vain. Nothing meets its desires. Though a sinner seeks for joy in wealth and pleasures, yet he is not satisfied. He still thirsts for more, and seeks still for happiness in some new enjoyment. To such a weary and unsatisfied sinner the grace of Christ is *as cold waters to a thirsty soul.* ¶ *Shall never thirst.* He shall be *satisfied* with this, and will not have a sense of want, a distressing feeling that it is not adapted to him. He who drinks this will not wish to seek for happiness in other objects. *Satisfied* with the grace of Christ, he will not desire the pleasures and amusements of this world. And this will be for ever—in this world and the world to come. *Whosoever* drinketh of this—all who partake of the gospel—shall be *for ever* satisfied with its pure and rich joys. ¶ *Shall be in him.* The grace of Christ shall be in his heart; or the principles of religion shall abide with him. ¶ *A well of water.* There shall be a constant supply, an unfailing fountain; or religion shall *live* constantly with him. ¶ *Springing up.* This is a beautiful image. It shall bubble or spring up like a fountain. It is not like a stagnant pool—not like a deep well, but like an ever-living fountain, that flows at all seasons of the year, in heat and cold, and in all external circumstances of weather, whether foul or fair, wet or dry. So religion always lives; and, amid all changes of external circumstances—in heat and cold, hunger and thirst, prosperity and adversity, life, persecution, contempt, or death—it still lives on, and refreshes and cheers the soul. ¶ *Into everlasting life.* It is not *temporary*, like the supply of our natural wants; it is not changing in its nature; it is not like a natural fountain or spring of water, to play a while and then die away, as all natural springs will at the end of the world. It is eternal in its nature and supply, and will continue to live on for ever. We may learn here—1st. That the Christian has a never-failing source of consolation adapted to all times and circumstances. 2d. That religion has its seat in the heart, and that it should constantly *live* there. 3d. That it sheds its blessings on a world of sin, and is manifest by a continual *life* of piety, like a constant flowing spring. 4th. That its end is everlasting life. It will continue for ever; and *whosoever drinks of this shall never thirst*, but his piety shall be in his heart a pure fountain *springing up to eternal joy.*

15. *The woman said*, &c. It may seem strange that the woman did not yet understand him, but it shows how slow sinners are to understand the doctrines of religion.

16. *Go call thy husband.* We may admire the manner which our Saviour took to lead her to perceive that he was the Christ. His instructions she did not understand. He therefore proceeded to show her that he was acquainted with her life and with her sins. His object, here, was to lead her

said, I have no husband. Jesus said unto her, Thou hast well said, I have no husband;

18 For thou hast had five husbands; and he whom thou now hast is not thy husband: in that saidst thou truly.

19 The woman saith unto him, Sir, I [k]perceive that thou art a prophet.

20 Our fathers worshipped in [l]this mountain; and ye say that in [m]Jerusalem is the place where men ought to worship.

k ch.1.48,49. l Ju.9.7. m De.12.5-11; 1 Ki.9.3.

to consider her own state and sinfulness—a delicate and yet pungent way of making her see that she was a sinner. By showing her, also, that he knew her life, though a stranger to her, he convinced her that he was qualified to teach her the way to heaven, and thus prepared her to admit that he was the Messiah, ver. 29.

17. *I have no husband.* This was said, evidently, to evade the subject. Perhaps she feared that if she came there with the man that she lived with, the truth might be exposed. It is not improbable that by this time she began to suspect that Jesus was a prophet. ¶ *Hast well said.* Hast said the truth.

18. *Hast had five husbands.* Who have either died; or who, on account of your improper conduct, have divorced you; or whom you have left improperly, without legal divorce. Either of these might have been the case. ¶ *Is not thy husband.* You are not lawfully married to him. Either she might have left a former husband without divorce, and thus her marriage with this man was unlawful, or she was living with him without the form of marriage, in open guilt.

19. *A prophet.* One sent from God, and who understood her life. The word here does not denote one who *foretells future events*, but one who *knew her heart* and life, and who must therefore have come from God. She did not yet suppose him to be the Messiah, ver. 25. Believing him now to be a man sent from God, she proposed to him a question respecting the proper place of worship. This point had been long a matter of dispute between the Samaritans and the Jews. She submitted it to him because she thought he could settle the question, and perhaps because she wished to divert the conversation from the unpleasant topic respecting her husbands. The conversation about her manner of life was a very unpleasant topic to her—as it is always unpleasant to sinners to talk about their lives and the necessity of religion—and she was glad to *turn the conversation* to something else. Nothing is more common than for sinners to *change* the conversation when it begins to bear too hard upon their consciences; and no way of doing it is more common than to direct it to some *speculative* inquiry having *some sort of connection with religion*, as if to show that they are willing to talk *about* religion, and do not wish to appear to be opposed to it. Sinners do not love direct religious conversation, but many are too well-bred to refuse altogether to talk about it; yet they choose to converse about some speculative matter, or something pertaining to the mere *externals* of religion, rather than the salvation of their own souls. So sinners often now change the conversation to some inquiry about a preacher, or about some doctrine, or about building or repairing a place of worship, or about a Sabbath-school, in order to *seem* to talk *about* religion, and yet to evade close and faithful appeals to their own consciences.

20. *Our fathers.* The Samaritans; perhaps also meaning to intimate that the patriarchs had done it also. See Ge. xii. 6; xxxiii. 20. ¶ *Worshipped.* Had a place of worship. ¶ *In this mountain. Mount Gerizim*, but a little way from Sychar. On this mountain they had built a temple somewhat similar to the one in Jerusalem. This was one of the main subjects of controversy between them and the Jews. The old Samaritan Pentateuch, or five books of Moses, has the word *Gerizim* instead of *Ebal* in De. xxvii. 4. On this account, as well as because the patriarchs are mentioned as having worshipped in Shechem, they supposed that that was the proper place on which to erect the temple. ¶ *Ye say.* Ye Jews. ¶ *In Jerusalem.* The place where the temple was built. This was built in accordance with the promise and command of God, De. xii. 5, 11. In building this, David and Solomon were under the divine direction, 2 Sa. vii. 2, 3, 13; 1 Ki. v. 5, 12; viii. 15-22.

21 Jesus saith unto her, Woman, believe me, the hour cometh [n]when ye shall neither in this mountain, nor yet at Jerusalem, worship the Father.

22 Ye[o] worship ye know not what: we know what we worship; [p]for salvation is of the Jews.

23 But the hour cometh, and now is, when the true worshippers

n Mal.1.11; Mat.18.20. *o* 2 Ki.17.29. *p* Is.2.3; Ro.9.5.

As it was contemplated in the law of Moses that there should be but *one* place to offer sacrifice and to hold the great feasts, so it followed that the Samaritans were in error in supposing that *their* temple was the place. Accordingly, our Saviour decided in favour of the Jews, yet in such a manner as to show the woman that the question was of much *less* consequence than *they* supposed it to be.

21. *Believe me.* As she had professed to believe that he was a prophet, it was right to require her to put faith in what he was about to utter. It also shows the importance of what he was about to say. ¶ *The hour cometh.* The *time* is coming, or is near. ¶ *When neither in this mountain*, &c. Hitherto the public solemn worship of God has been confined to one place. It has been a matter of dispute whether that place should be Jerusalem or Mount Gerizim. That controversy is to be of much less importance than you have supposed. The old dispensation is about to pass away. The *peculiar* rites of the Jews are to cease. The worship of God, so long confined to a single place, is soon to be celebrated everywhere, and with as much acceptance in one place as in another. He does not say that there would be *no* worship of God in that place or in Jerusalem, but that the worship of God would not be *confined* there. He would be worshipped in other places as well as there.

22. *Ye worship ye know not what.* This probably refers to the comparative ignorance and corruption of the Samaritan worship. Though they received the five books of Moses, yet they rejected the prophets, and of course all that the prophets had said respecting the true God. Originally, also, they had joined the worship of idols to that of the true God. See 2 Ki. xvii. 26–34. They had, moreover, no *authority* for building their temple and conducting public worship by sacrifices there. On all these accounts they were acting in an unauthorized manner. They were not obeying the true God, nor offering the worship which he had commanded or would approve. Jesus thus *indirectly* settled the question which she had proposed to him, yet in such a way as to show her that it was of much less importance than she had supposed. ¶ *We know.* We Jews. This they knew because God had commanded it; because they worshipped in a place appointed by God, and because they did it in accordance with the direction and teaching of the prophets. ¶ *Salvation is of the Jews.* They have the true religion and the true form of worship; and the *Messiah*, who will bring salvation, is to proceed from them. See Lu. ii. 30; iii. 6. Jesus thus affirms that the Jews had the true form of the worship of God. At the same time he was sensible how much they had corrupted it, and on various occasions reproved them for it.

23. *But the hour cometh, and now is.* The old dispensation is about to pass away, and the new one to commence. *Already* there is so much light that God may be worshipped acceptably in any place. ¶ *The true worshippers.* All who truly and sincerely worship God. They who do it with the *heart*, and not merely *in form.* ¶ *In spirit.* The word *spirit*, here, stands opposed to rites and ceremonies, and to the pomp of external worship. It refers to the *mind*, the *soul*, the *heart.* They shall worship God with a sincere *mind;* with the simple offering of gratitude and prayer; with a *desire* to glorify him, and without external pomp and splendour. *Spiritual* worship is that where the *heart* is offered to God, and where we do not depend on external forms for acceptance. ¶ *In truth.* Not through the medium of shadows and types, not by means of sacrifices and bloody offerings, but in the manner represented or typified by all these, He. ix. 9, 24. In the *true* way of direct access to God through Jesus Christ. ¶ *For the Father seeketh*, &c. Jesus gives two reasons why this kind of worship should take place. *One* is that God *sought* it, or desired it. He had appointed the old mode, but he did it because he sought to lead the mind to himself even *by those forms*, and to pre-

shall worship the Father [q]in spirit and in truth; for the Father seeketh such to worship him.

24 God[r] *is* a spirit; and they that worship him must worship *him* in spirit and in truth.

25 The woman saith unto him, I know that Messias cometh, which is called Christ: when he is come, he will tell us all things.

26 Jesus saith unto her, [s]I that speak unto thee am *he*.

27 And upon this came his disciples, and marvelled that he

q Phi.3.3. r 2 Co.3.17. s ch.9.37.

pare the people for the purer system of the gospel, and *now* he sought or *desired* that those who worshipped him should worship him in that manner. He intimated his will by Jesus Christ.

24. *God* is *a spirit.* This is the *second* reason why men should worship him in spirit and in truth. By this is meant that God is without a body; that he is not material or composed of parts; that he is invisible, in every place, pure and holy. This is one of the first truths of religion, and one of the sublimest ever presented to the mind of man. Almost all nations have had some idea of God as gross or material, but the Bible declares that he is a pure spirit. As he is such a spirit, he dwells not in temples made with hands (Ac. vii. 48), neither is worshipped with men's hands as though he needed anything, seeing he giveth to all life, and breath, and all things, Ac. xvii. 25. A pure, a holy, a spiritual worship, therefore, is such as he seeks—the offering of the *soul* rather than the formal offering of *the body*—the homage of the *heart* rather than that of the *lips.*

25. *I know that Messias cometh.* As the Samaritans acknowledged the five books of Moses, so they expected, also, the coming of the Messiah. ¶ *Which is called Christ.* These are probably the words of the evangelist, as it is not likely that the woman would explain the name on such an occasion. ¶ *Will tell us all things.* Jesus had decided the question proposed to him (ver. 20) in favour of the Jews. The woman does not seem to have been satisfied with this answer, and said that the Messiah would tell them all about this question. Probably she was expecting that he would soon appear.

26. *I that speak unto thee am* he. I am the Messiah. This was the first time that he openly professed it. He did not do it yet to the Jews, for it would have excited envy and opposition. But nothing could be apprehended in Samaria; and as the woman seemed reluctant to listen to him as a prophet, and professed her willingness to listen to the Messiah, he openly declared that he was the Christ, that by some means he might save her soul. From this we may learn, 1st. The great wisdom of the Lord Jesus in leading the thoughts along to the subject of practical personal religion. 2d. His knowledge of the heart and of the life. He must be therefore divine. 3d. He gave evidence here that he was the Messiah. This was the design of John in writing this gospel. He has therefore recorded this narrative, which was omitted by the other evangelists. 4th. We see *our* duty. It is to seize on all occasions to lead sinners to the belief that Jesus is the Christ, and to make use of all topics of conversation to teach them the nature of religion. There never was a model of so much wisdom in this as the Saviour, and we shall be successful only as we diligently study his character. 5th. We see the nature of religion. It does not consist merely in external forms. It is pure, spiritual, active—an ever-bubbling fountain. It is the worship of a pure and holy God, where the *heart* is offered, and where the desires of an humble soul are breathed out for salvation.

27. *Upon this.* At this time. ¶ *Marvelled.* Wondered. They wondered because the Jews had no intercourse with the Samaritans, and they were surprised that Jesus was engaged with her in conversation. ¶ *Yet no man said.* No one of the disciples. They had such respect and reverence for him that they did not dare to ask him the reason of his conduct, or even to appear to reprove him. We should be confident that Jesus is right, even if we cannot fully understand all that he does.

28. *Left her water-pot.* Her mind was greatly excited. She was disturbed, and hastened to the city in great agitation to make this known. She seems to have been convinced that he was the Messiah, and went immediately to make

talked with the woman; yet no
man said, What seekest thou? or,
Why talkest thou with her?
28 The woman then left her
water-pot, and went her way into
the city, and saith to the men,
29 Come, see a man which told
me all things that ever I did. Is
not this the Christ?
30 Then they went out of the
city and came unto him.
31 In the mean while his disciples
prayed him, saying, Master, eat.
32 But he said unto them, I have
meat to eat that ye know not of.
33 Therefore said the disciples
one to another, Hath any man
brought him *aught* to eat?
34 Jesus saith unto them, [t]My
meat is to do the will of him that
sent me, and to [u]finish his work.
35 Say not ye, There are yet four

t Job 23.12; ch.6.38. u ch.17.4.

it known to others. Our first business, when we have found the Saviour, should be to make him known also to others.

29. *Is not this the Christ?* Though she probably believed it, yet she proposed it modestly, lest she should appear to dictate in a case which was so important, and which demanded so much attention. The evidence on which *she* was satisfied that he was the Messiah was that he had told her all things that she had done—perhaps much more than is here recorded. The question which she submitted to them was whether this was not satisfactory proof that he was the Messiah.

30. *They went out of the city.* The men of the city left it and went to Jesus, to hear and examine for themselves.

31. *Prayed him.* Asked him.

32. *I have meat to eat.* See ver. 34.

33. *Hath any man brought him,* &c. This is one of the many instances in which the disciples were slow to understand the Saviour.

34. *My meat,* &c. Jesus here explains what he said in ver. 32. His great object—the great design of his life—was to do the will of God. He came to that place weary and thirsty, and at the usual time of meals, probably an hungered; yet an opportunity of doing good presented itself, and he forgot his fatigue and hunger, and found comfort and joy in doing good—in seeking to save a soul. This one great object absorbed all his powers, and made him forget his weariness and the wants of nature. The mind may be so absorbed in doing the will of God as to forget all other things. Intent on this, we may rise above fatigue, and hardship, and want, and bear all with pleasure in seeing the work of God advance. See Job xxiii. 12: "I have esteemed the words of his mouth more than my necessary food." We may learn, also, that the main business of life is not to avoid fatigue or to seek the supply of our temporal wants, but to do the will of God. The mere supply of our temporal necessities, though most men make it an object of their chief solicitude, is a small consideration in the sight of him who has just views of the great design of human life. ¶ *The will of him that sent me.* The will of God in regard to the salvation of men. See Jn. vi. 38. ¶ *To finish his work.* To *complete* or fully to do the work which he has commanded in regard to the salvation of men. It is *his* work to provide salvation, and his to redeem, and his to apply the salvation to the heart. Jesus came to *do it* by teaching, by his example, and by his death as an expiation for sin. And he shows us that *we* should be diligent. If *he* was so diligent for *our* welfare, if he bore fatigue and want to benefit *us,* then *we* should be diligent, also, in regard to our *own* salvation, and also in seeking the salvation of others.

35. *Say not ye.* This seems to have been a proverb. Ye say—that is, men say. ¶ *Four months and,* &c. The common time from sowing the seed to the harvest, in Judea, was about *four months.* The meaning of this passage may be thus expressed: "The husbandman, when he sows his seed, is compelled to wait a considerable period before it produces a crop. He is encouraged in sowing it; he expects fruit; his labour is lightened by that expectation; but it is not *immediate*—it is remote. But it is not so with *my* preaching. The seed has already sprung up. Scarce was it sown before it produced an abundant harvest. The gospel was just preached to a woman, and see how many of the Samaritans come to hear

months, and *then* cometh harvest?
Behold, I say unto you, Lift up
your eyes, and look on the fields,
for they are [v]white already to
harvest.
36 And he that reapeth receiveth
wages, and [w]gathereth fruit unto
life eternal; that [x]both he that
soweth and he that reapeth may
rejoice together.
37 And herein is that saying true,
[y]One soweth, and another reapeth.
38 I sent you to reap that whereon
ye bestowed no labour: [z]other men

v Mat.9.37. w Ro.6.22. x 1 Co.3.5-9. y Mi.6.15. z 1 Pe.1.12.

---

it also. There is therefore more encouragement to labour in this field than the farmer has to sow his grain." ¶ *Lift up your eyes.* See the Samaritans coming to hear the gospel. ¶ *They are white.* Grain, when ripe, turns from a green to a yellow or light colour, indicating that it is time to reap it. So here were indications that the gospel was effectual, and that the harvest was to be gathered in. Hence we may learn, 1st. That there is as much encouragement to attempt to save souls as the farmer has to raise a crop. 2d. That the gospel is fitted to make an *immediate* impression on the minds of men. We are to expect that it will. We are not to *wait* to some future period, as if we could not expect immediate results. This wicked and ignorant people—little likely, apparently, to be affected—turned to God, heard the voice of the Saviour, and came in multitudes to him. 3d. We are to expect *revivals* of religion. Here was one instance of it under the Saviour's own preaching. Multitudes were excited, moved, and came to learn the way of life. 4th. We know not how much good may be done by conversation with even a single individual. This conversation with a woman resulted in a deep interest felt throughout the city, and in the conversion of many of them to God. So a single individual may often be the means, in the hand of God, of leading many to the cross of Jesus. 5th. What evils may follow from *neglecting* to do our duty! How easily might Jesus have alleged, if he had been like many of his professed disciples, that he was weary, that he was hungry, that it was esteemed improper to converse with a woman alone, that she was an abandoned character, and there could be little hope of doing her good! How many consciences of ministers and Christians would have been satisfied with reasoning like this? Yet Jesus, in spite of his fatigue and thirst, and all the difficulties of the case, seriously set about seeking the conversion of this woman. And behold what a glorious result! The city was moved, and a great harvest was found ready to be gathered in! *Let us not be weary in well-doing, for in due season we shall reap if we faint not.*

36. *He that reapeth.* He that gathers the harvest, or he who so preaches that souls are converted to Christ. ¶ *Receiveth wages.* The labourer in the harvest receives his hire. Jesus says it shall be thus with those who labour in the ministry—he will not suffer them to go unrewarded. See Da. xii. 3; Mat. xix. 28. ¶ *Gathereth fruit unto life eternal.* Converts souls, who shall inherit eternal life. The harvest is not temporary, like gathering grain, but shall result in eternal life. ¶ *That both he that soweth,* &c. It is a united work. It matters little whether we sow the seed or whether we reap the harvest. It is part of the same work, and whatever part we may do, we should rejoice. God gives the increase, while Paul may plant and Apollos water. The teacher in the Sunday-school, who sows the seed in early life, shall rejoice with the minister of the gospel who may gather in the harvest, and both join in giving all the praise to God.

37. *That saying.* That proverb. This proverb is found in some of the *Greek* writers (Grotius). Similar proverbs were in use among the Jews. See Is. lxv. 21, 22; Le. xxvi. 16; Mi. vi. 15. ¶ *One soweth,* &c. One man may preach the gospel, and with little apparent effect; another, succeeding him, may be crowned with eminent success. The seed, long buried, may spring up in an abundant harvest.

38. *I sent you.* In the commission given you to preach the gospel. You have not laboured or toiled in preparing the way for the great harvest which is now to be gathered in. ¶ *Other men laboured.* (1.) The prophets, who long laboured to prepare the way for the coming of the Messiah. (2.) The teachers among the Jews, who have read and

laboured, and ye are entered into their labours.

39 And many of the Samaritans of that city believed on him [a]for the saying of the woman, which testified, He told me all that ever I did.

40 So when the Samaritans were come unto him, they besought him that he would tarry with them; and he abode there two days.

41 And many more believed because of his own word;

42 And said unto the woman, Now we believe, not because of thy saying; [b]for we have heard *him* ourselves, and know that this is indeed the Christ, the Saviour of the world.

43 Now after two days he departed thence, and went into Galilee.

44 For Jesus himself testified that [c]a prophet hath no honour in his own country.

45 Then, when he was come into Galilee, the Galileans received him, [d]having seen all the things that he did at Jerusalem at the feast; [e]for they also went unto the feast.

46 So Jesus came again into Cana of Galilee, where he [f]made

a ver.29. *b* ch.17.8; 1 Jn.4.14.

c Mat.13.57; Mar.6.4; Lu.4.24. *d* ch.2.23. *e* De.16.16. *f* ch.2.1,11.

explained the law and taught the people. (3.) John the Baptist, who came to prepare the way. And, (4.) The Saviour himself, who by his personal ministry taught the people, and prepared them for the success which was to attend the preaching of the apostles. Especially did Jesus lay the foundation for the rapid and extensive spread of the gospel. *He* saw comparatively little fruit of his ministry. He confined his labours to Judea, and even there he was occupied in sowing seed which chiefly sprang up after his death. From this we may learn, 1st. That the man who is crowned with eminent success has no cause of *boasting* over others, any more than the man who *reaps* a field of grain should *boast* over the man who sowed it. The labour of both is equally necessary, and the labour of both would be useless if GOD did not give the increase. Comp. 1 Co. iii. 6. 2d. We should not be discouraged if we do not meet with immediate success. The man that *sows* is not disheartened because he does not see the harvest *immediately* spring up. We are to sow our seed in the morning, and in the evening we are not to withhold our hand, for we know not whether shall prosper, this or that; and we are to go forth bearing precious seed, though *weeping*, knowing that we shall come again rejoicing, bearing our sheaves with us, Ec. xi. 4; Ps. cxxvi. 6. 3d. Every part of the work of the ministry and of teaching men is needful, and we should rejoice that we are permitted to bear any part, however humble, in bringing sinners to the knowledge of our Lord and Saviour Jesus Christ, 1 Co. xii. 21–24.

39–42. *And many of the Samaritans of that city believed on him*, &c. There is seldom an instance of so remarkable success as this. From a single conversation, in circumstances, in a place, and with an individual little likely to be attended with such results, many sinners were converted; many believed on the testimony of the woman; many more came to hear, and believed because they heard him themselves. We should never despair of doing good in the most unpromising circumstances, and we should seize upon every opportunity to converse with sinners on the great subject of their souls' salvation.

43. *Into Galilee.* Into some of the parts of Galilee, though evidently not into Nazareth, but probably direct to *Cana*, ver. 46.

44. *For Jesus himself testified*, &c. See Notes on Mat. xiii. 57. The connection of this verse with the preceding may be thus explained: "Jesus went to Galilee, *but not* to Nazareth, for he testified," &c. Or, "Jesus went to Galilee, *although* he had said that a prophet had no honour in his own country; yet, because he foreknew that the Galileans would many of them believe on him, he went at this time."

45. *Received him.* Received him kindly, or as a messenger of God. They had seen his miracles, and believed on him.

46. *A certain nobleman.* One who was of the royal family, connected by

the water wine. And there was
a certain [1]nobleman, whose son
was sick at Capernaum.
47 When he heard that Jesus
was come out of Judea into
Galilee, he went unto him, and
besought him that he would come
down and heal his son, for he was
at the point of death.
48 Then said Jesus unto him,
Except ye see [g]signs and wonders,
ye will not believe.
49 The nobleman saith unto him,
Sir, come down ere my child die.
50 Jesus saith unto him, [h]Go
thy way; thy son liveth. And the
man believed the word that Jesus
had spoken unto him, and he went
his way.
51 And as he was now going
down, his servants met him, and
told *him*, saying, Thy son liveth.
52 Then inquired he of them the
hour when he began to amend.
And they said unto him, Yesterday at the seventh hour the fever
left him.
53 So the father knew that

1 or, *courtier*; or, *ruler*. g 1 Co.1.22.

h Mat.8.13; Mar.7.29,30; Lu.17.14.

birth with Herod Antipas; or one of the officers of the court, whether by birth allied to him or not. It seems that his ordinary residence was at Capernaum. Capernaum was about a day's journey from Cana, where Jesus then was.

47. *He went unto him.* Though high in office, yet he did not refuse to go personally to Jesus to ask his aid. He felt as a father; and believing, after all that Jesus had done, that he could cure his son, he travelled to meet him. If men receive benefits of Christ, they must come in the same manner. The rich and the poor, the high and the low, must come personally as humble suppliants, and must be willing to bear all the reproach that may be cast on them for thus coming to him. This man showed strong faith in being willing thus to *go* to Jesus, but he erred in supposing that Jesus could heal only by his being present with his son. ¶ *Would come down.* It is probable that the miracles of Jesus heretofore had been performed only on those who were *present* with him, and this nobleman seems to have thought that this was necessary. One design of Jesus in working this miracle was to show him that this was not necessary. Hence he did not go down to Capernaum, but healed him where he was.

48. *Except ye see signs,* &c. This was spoken not to the nobleman only, but to the Galileans generally. The Samaritans had believed without any miracle. The Galileans, he said, were less disposed to believe him than even they were; and though he had wrought miracles *enough* to convince them, yet, unless they continually saw them, they would not believe.

49. *Come down,* &c. The earnestness of the nobleman evinces the deep and tender anxiety of a father. So anxious was he for his son that he was not willing that Jesus should delay a moment—not even to address the people. He still seems to have supposed that Jesus had no power to heal his son except he was *present* with him.

50. *Go thy way.* This was a kind and tender address. It was designed to convince him that he could word a miracle though not personally present. ¶ *Thy son liveth.* Thy son shall recover; or he shall be restored to health, according to thy request. ¶ *The man believed.* The manner in which Jesus spoke it, and the assurance which he gave, convinced the man that he could heal him there as well as to go to Capernaum to do it. This is an instance of the power of Jesus to convince the mind, to soothe doubts, to confirm faith, and to meet our desires. He blesses not always in the *manner* in which we ask, but he grants us our *main* wish. The father wished his son healed by Jesus *going down* to Capernaum. Jesus healed him, but not in *the way* in which he asked it to be done. God will hear our prayers and grant our requests, but often not in the precise *manner* in which we ask it. It is *his* to judge of the best way of doing us good.

52. *The seventh hour.* About one o'clock in the afternoon.

53. *The same hour.* The very time when Jesus spoke. ¶ *The fever left him.* It seems that it left him suddenly and entirely; so much so that his friends went to inform the father, and to comfort him, and also, doubtless, to apprise him that it was not necessary to ask aid

it was at the [i]same hour in the which Jesus said unto him, Thy son liveth: [k]and himself believed, and his whole house.

54 This *is* again the second miracle *that* Jesus did when he was come out of Judea into Galilee.

i Ps.107.20. *k* Ac.16.34; 18.8.

CHAPTER V.

AFTER this there was a [a]feast of the Jews; and Jesus went up to Jerusalem.

2 Now there is at Jerusalem, by the sheep-[1]*market*, a pool, which is called in the Hebrew

a Le.23.2,&c.; De.16.16; ch.2.13.
1 or, gate, Ne.3.1; 12.39.

---

from Jesus. From this miracle we may learn, 1st. That Jesus has an intimate knowledge of all things. He knew the case of this son—the extent of his disease—where he was—and thus had power to heal him. 2d. That Jesus has almighty power. Nothing else could have healed this child. Nor could it be pretended that he did it by any natural means. He was far away from him, and the child knew not the source of the power that healed him. It could not be pretended that there was any collusion or jugglery. The father came in deep anxiety. The servants saw the cure. Jesus was at a distance. Everything in the case bears the mark of being the simple energy of God—put forth with equal ease to heal, whether far or near. Thus he can save the sinner. 3d. We see the benevolence of Jesus. Ever ready to aid, to heal, or to save, he may be called on at all times, and will never be called on in vain. ¶ *Himself believed.* This miracle removed all his doubts, and he became a real disciple and friend of Jesus. ¶ *His whole house.* His whole family. We may learn from this, 1st. That sickness or any deep affliction is often the means of great good. Here the sickness of the son resulted in the faith of all the family. God often takes away earthly blessings that he may impart rich spiritual mercies. 2d. The father of a family may be the means of the salvation of his children. Here the effort of a parent resulted in their conversion to Christ. 3d. There is great beauty and propriety when sickness thus results in piety. For that it is sent. God does not willingly grieve or afflict the children of men; and when afflictions thus terminate, it will be cause of eternal joy, of ceaseless praise. 4th. There is a peculiar charm when piety thus comes into the families of the rich and the noble. It is so unusual; their example and influence go so far; it overcomes so many temptations, and affords opportunities of doing so much good, that there is no wonder that the evangelist selected this instance as one of the effects of the power and of the preaching of the Lord Jesus Christ.

CHAPTER V.

1. *A feast.* Probably the Passover, though it is not certain. There were two other feasts—the Pentecost and the Feast of Tabernacles—at which all the males were required to be present, and it might have been one of them. It is of no consequence, however, which of them is intended.

2. *The sheep*-market. This might have been rendered the *sheep-gate*, or the gate through which the sheep were taken into the city for sacrifice. The marginal rendering is *gate*, and the word "*market*" is not in the original, nor is a "*sheep-market*" mentioned in the Scriptures or in any of the Jewish writings. A *sheep-gate* is repeatedly mentioned by Nehemiah (ch. iii. 1, 32; xii. 39), being that by which sheep and oxen were brought into the city. As these were brought mainly for sacrifice, the gate was doubtless near the temple, and near the present place which is shown as the pool of Bethesda. ¶ *A pool.* This word may either mean a small lake or pond in which one can swim, or a place for fish, or any waters collected for bathing or washing. ¶ *Hebrew tongue.* Hebrew language. The language then spoken, which did not differ essentially from the ancient Hebrew. ¶ *Bethesda.* The house of mercy. It was so called on account of its strong healing properties—the property of restoring health to the sick and infirm. ¶ *Five porches.* The word *porch* commonly means a covered place surrounding a building, in which people can walk or sit in hot or wet weather. Here it probably means that there were five covered places, or apartments, in which the sick could remain, from each one of which they could have access to the water. This "pool" is thus described by Professor Hackett (*Illustra-*

tongue Bethesda, having five porches.

3 In these lay a great multitude of impotent folk, of blind, halt, withered, waiting for the moving of the water.

4 For an angel went down at a certain season into the pool,

---

tions of Scripture, p. 291, 292): "Just to the east of the Turkish garrison, and under the northern wall of the mosque, is a deep excavation, supposed by many to be the ancient pool of Bethesda, into which the sick descended 'after the troubling of the water,' and were healed, Jn. v. 1, sq. It is 360 feet long, 130 feet wide, and 75 deep. The evangelist says that this pool was near the sheep-gate, as the Greek probably signifies, rather than sheep-market, as rendered in the English version. That gate, according to Ne. iii. 1, sq., was on the north side of the temple, and hence the situation of this reservoir would agree with that of Bethesda. The present name, Birket Israil, Pool of Israil, indicates the opinion of the native inhabitants in regard to the object of the excavation. The general opinion of the most accurate travellers is that the so-called pool was originally part of a trench or fosse which protected the temple on the north. Though it contains no water at present except a little which trickles through the stones at the west end, it has evidently been used at some period as a reservoir. It is lined with cement, and adapted in other respects to hold water." Dr. Robinson established by personal inspection the fact of the subterranean connection of the pool of *Siloam* with the *Fountain of the Virgin*, and made it probable that the fountain under the mosque of Omar is connected with them. This spring is, as he himself witnessed, an *intermittent* one, and there *may* have been some artificially constructed basin in connection with this spring to which was given the name of *Bethesda*. He supposes, however, that there is not the slightest evidence that the place or reservoir now pointed out as *Bethesda* was the Bethesda of the New Testament (*Bib. Res.*, i. 501, 506, 509). In the time of Sandys (1611) the spring was found running, but in small quantities; in the time of Maundrell (1697) the stream did not run. Probably in his time, as now, the water which had formerly filtered through the rocks was dammed up by the rubbish.

3. *Impotent folk.* Sick people; or people who were *weak* and feeble by long disease. The word means those who were *feeble* rather than those who were afflicted with *acute* disease. ¶ *Halt.* Lame. ¶ *Withered.* Those who were afflicted with one form of the palsy that *withered* or dried up the part affected. See Notes on Mat. iv. 24. ¶ *Moving of the water.* It appears that this pool had medicinal properties only when it was *agitated* or *stirred.* It is probable that at regular times or intervals the fountain put forth an unusual quantity of water, or water of peculiar properties, and that *about* these times the people assembled in multitudes who were to be healed.

4. *An angel.* It is not affirmed that the angel did this *visibly*, or that they *saw* him do it. They judged by the *effect*, and when they saw the waters agitated, they concluded that they had healing properties, and descended to them. The Jews were in the habit of attributing all favours to the ministry of the angels of God, Ge. xix. 15; He. i. 14; Mat. iv. 11; xviii. 10; Lu. xvi. 22; Ac. vii. 53; Ga. iii. 19; Ac. xii. 11. This fountain, it seems, had strong medicinal properties. Like many other waters, it had the property of healing certain diseases that were incurable by any other means. Thus the waters of Bath, of Saratoga, &c., are found to be highly medicinal, and to heal diseases that are otherwise incurable. In the case of the waters of Bethesda there does not appear to have been anything *miraculous*, but the waters seem to have been endued with strong medicinal properties, especially after a periodical agitation. All that is peculiar about them in the record is that this was produced by the ministry of an angel. This was in accordance with the common sentiment of the Jews, the common doctrine of the Bible, and the belief of the sacred writers. Nor can it be shown to be absurd or improbable that such blessings should be imparted to man by the ministry of an angel. There is no more absurdity in the belief that a pure spirit or holy *angel* should aid man, than that a physician or a parent should; and no more absurdity in supposing that the healing

and troubled the water: whosoever then [b]first after the troubling of the water stepped in, [c]was made whole of whatsoever disease he had.

5 And a certain man was there which [d]had an infirmity thirty and eight years.

6 When Jesus saw him lie, [e]and knew that he had been now a long time in *that case*, he saith unto him, Wilt thou be made whole?

7 The impotent man answered him, Sir, [f]I have no man, when the water is troubled, to put me

b Pr.8.17; Ec.9.10; Mat.11.12.
c Eze.47.8,9; Zec.13.1. d Lu.8.43; 13.16.
e Ps.142.3.
f De.32.36; Ps.72.12; 142.4; Ro.5.6; 2 Co.1.9,10.

properties of such a fountain should be produced by his aid, than that any other blessing should be, He. i. 12. What man can *prove* that all his temporal blessings do not come to him through the medium of others—of parents, of teachers, of friends, of *angels?* And who can prove that it is unworthy the *benevolence* of angels to minister to the wants of the poor, the needy, and the afflicted, when *man* does it, and Jesus Christ did it, and God himself does it daily? ¶ *Went down.* Descended to the pool. ¶ *At a certain season.* At a certain time; periodically. The people knew *about* the time when this was done, and assembled in multitudes to partake of the benefits. Many medicinal springs are more strongly impregnated at some seasons of the year than others. ¶ *Troubled the water.* Stirred or *agitated* the water. There was probably an increase, and a bubbling and agitation produced by the admission of a fresh quantity. ¶ *Whosoever then first.* This does not mean that but *one* was healed, and that the *first* one, but that those who first descended into the pool were healed. The strong medicinal properties of the waters soon subsided, and those who could not at first enter into the pool were obliged to wait for the return of the agitation. ¶ *Stepped in.* Went in. ¶ *Was made whole.* Was healed. It is not implied that this was done *instantaneously* or *by a miracle.* The water had such properties that he was healed, though probably gradually. It is not less the gift of God to suppose that this fountain restored gradually, and in accordance with what commonly occurs, than to suppose, what is not affirmed, that it was done at once and in a miraculous manner.

In regard to this passage, it should be remarked that the account of the angel in the 4th verse is wanting in many manuscripts, and has been by many supposed to be spurious. There is not conclusive evidence, however, that it is not a part of the genuine text, and the best critics suppose that it should not be rejected. One difficulty has been that no such place as this spring is mentioned by Josephus. But John is as good a historian, and as worthy to be believed as Josephus. Besides, it is known that many important places and events have not been mentioned by the Jewish historian, and it is no evidence that there was no such place as this because *he* did not mention it. When this fountain was discovered, or how long its healing properties continued to be known, it is impossible now to ascertain. All that we know of it is what is mentioned here, and conjecture would be useless. We may remark, however, that *such* a place anywhere is an evidence of the great goodness of God. Springs or fountains having healing properties abound on earth, and nowhere more than in our own country. Diseases are often healed in such places which no human skill could remove. The Jews regarded such a provision as proof of the mercy of God. They gave this healing spring the name of a "house of mercy." They regarded it as under the care of an angel. And there is no place where man should be more sensible of the goodness of God, or be more disposed to render him praise as *in* a "house of mercy," than when at such a healing fountain. And *yet* how lamentable is it that such places—watering places—should be mere places of gaiety and thoughtlessness, of balls, and gambling, and dissipation! How melancholy that amid the very places where there is most evidence of the goodness of God, and of the misery of the poor, the sick, the afflicted, men should forget all the goodness of their Maker, and spend their time in scenes of dissipation, folly, and vice!

5. *An infirmity.* A weakness. We know not what his disease was. We

into the pool; but while I am
coming, another steppeth down
before me.
8 Jesus saith unto him, [g]Rise,
take up thy bed, and walk.
9 And immediately the man was
made whole, and took up his bed,
and walked; [h]and on the same day
was the sabbath.
10 The Jews therefore said unto
him that was cured, [i]It is the sabbath-day; it is not lawful for thee
to carry *thy* bed.
11 He answered them, He that

g Mat.9.6; Mar.2.11; Lu.5.24.

h ch.9.14. i Je.17.21,&c.; Mat.12.2,&c.

know only that it disabled him from walking, and that it was of very long standing. It was doubtless regarded as incurable.

7. *Sir, I have no man*, &c. The answer of the man implied that he *did* wish it, but, in addition to all his other trials, he had no *friend* to aid him. This is an additional circumstance that heightened his affliction.

8. *Rise, take up*, &c. Jesus not only restored him to health, but he gave evidence to those around him that this was a real miracle, and that he was really healed. For almost forty years he had been afflicted. He was not even able to walk. Jesus commanded him not only to *walk*, but to take up his *bed* also, and carry that as proof that he was truly made whole. In regard to this we may observe, 1st. That it was a remarkable command. The poor man had been long infirm, and it does not appear that he expected to be healed except by being put into the waters. Yet Jesus, when he gives a commandment, can give strength to obey it. 2d. It is our business to obey the commands of Jesus, however feeble we feel ourselves to be. His grace will be sufficient for us, and his burden will be light. 3d. The weak and helpless sinner should put forth his efforts in obedience to the command of Jesus. Never was a sinner more *helpless* than was this man. If God gave *him* strength to do his will, so he can all others; and the plea that we can do nothing could have been urged with far more propriety by this man than it can be by any impenitent sinner. 4th. This narrative should not be *abused*. It should not be supposed as intended to teach that a sinner should delay repentance, as if *waiting for God*. The narrative neither teaches nor implies *any such thing*. It is a simple record *of a fact* in regard to a man who had no power to heal himself, and who was under no obligation to heal himself. There is no reference in the narrative to the difficulties of a sinner—no intimation that it was intended to refer to his condition; and to make this example an excuse for *delay*, or an argument for *waiting*, is to abuse and pervert the Bible. Seldom is more mischief done than by attempting to draw from the Bible what it was not intended to teach, and by an effort to make that convey spiritual instruction which God has not declared designed for that purpose. ¶ *Thy bed.* Thy couch; or the mattress or clothes on which he lay.

9. *The Sabbath.* To carry burdens on the Sabbath was forbidden in the Old Testament, Je. xvii. 21; Ne. xiii. 15; Ex. xx. 8–10. If it be asked, then, why Jesus commanded a man to do on the Sabbath what was understood to be a violation of the day, it may be answered, 1st. That the Son of man was Lord of the Sabbath, and had a right to declare what *might* be done, and even to dispense with a *positive* law of the Jews, Mat. xii. 8; Jn. v. 17. 2d. This was a poor man, and Jesus directed him to secure his property. 3d. The Jews extended the obligation of the Sabbath beyond what was intended by the appointment. They observed it superstitiously, and Jesus took every opportunity to convince them of their error, and to restore the day to its proper observance, Mat. xii. 6–11; Lu. vi. 9; xiii. 14; xiv. 5. This method he took to show them what the law of God really *permitted* on that day, and that works of necessity and mercy were lawful.

10. *Not lawful.* It was forbidden, they supposed, in the Old Testament. The Jews were very strenuous in the observation of the external duties of religion.

11. *He that made me whole.* The man reasoned correctly. If Jesus had power to work so signal a miracle, he had a right to explain the law. If he had conferred so great a favour on him, he had a right to expect obedience; and we may learn that the mercy of God

made me whole, the same said unto me, Take up thy bed and walk.

12 Then asked they him, What man is that which said unto thee, Take up thy bed and walk?

13 And he that was healed wist[k] not who it was; [l]for Jesus had conveyed himself away, [2]a multitude being in *that* place.

14 Afterward Jesus findeth him in the temple, and said unto him, Behold, thou art made whole: [m]sin no more, lest a worse thing come unto thee.

15 The man departed, and told

k ch.14.9. *l* Lu.4.30. 2 or, *from the multitude that was.* *m* ch.8.11.

---

in pardoning our sins, or in bestowing any signal blessing, imposes the obligation to obey him. We should yield obedience to him according to what we *know* to be his will, whatever may be the opinions of men, or whatever interpretation *they* may put on the law of God. *Our* business is a simple, hearty, child-like obedience, let the men of the world say or think of us as they choose.

12. *What man is he*, &c. In this verse there is a remarkable instance of the *perverseness* of men, of their want of candour, and of the manner in which they often look at a subject. Instead of looking at the *miracle*, and at the man's statement of the manner in which he was healed, they look only at what they thought to be a violation of the law. They assumed it as certain that nothing could make his conduct, in carrying his bed on the Sabbath-day, proper; and they meditated vengeance, not only on the man who was carrying his bed, but on him, also, who had told him to do it. Thus men often assume that a certain course or opinion is proper, and when anyone differs from them they look only *at the difference*, but not *at the reasons* for it. One great source of dispute among men is that they look only at the points in which they *differ*, but are unwilling to listen to the reasons why others do not believe as they do. It is always enough to condemn one in the eyes of a bigot that he differs from *him*, and he looks upon him who holds a different opinion, as the Jews did at this man, *as certainly wrong;* and such a bigot looks at the reasons why others differ from him just as the Jews did at the reason why this man bore his bed on the Sabbath—as not worth regarding or hearing, or as if they could not possibly be right.

13. *Wist not.* Knew not. ¶ *Had conveyed himself away.* Was lost in the crowd. He had silently mingled with the multitude, or had passed on with the crowd unobserved, and the man had been so rejoiced at his cure that he had not even inquired the *name* of his benefactor.

14. *Findeth him.* Fell in with him, or saw him. ¶ *In the temple.* The man seems to have gone at once to the temple—perhaps a privilege of which he had been long deprived. They who are healed from sickness should seek the sanctuary of God and give him thanks for his mercy. Comp. Notes on Is. xxxviii. 20. There is nothing more improper, when we are raised up from a bed of pain, than to forget God our benefactor, and neglect to praise him for his mercies. ¶ *Thou art made whole.* Jesus calls to his remembrance the fact that he was healed, in order that he might admonish him not to sin again. ¶ *Sin no more.* By this expression it was implied that the infirmity of this man was caused by sin—perhaps by vice in his youth. His crime or dissipation had brought on him this long and distressing affliction. Jesus shows him that he knew the *cause* of his sickness, and takes occasion to warn him not to repeat it. No man who indulges in vice can tell what may be its consequences. It must always end in evil, and not unfrequently it results in loss of health, and in long and painful disease. This is always the case with intemperance and all gross pleasures. Sooner or later, sin will always result in misery. ¶ *Sin no more.* Do not repeat the vice. You have had dear-bought experience, and if repeated it will be worse. When a man has been restored from the effects of sin, he should learn to avoid the very appearance of evil. He should shun the place of temptation; he should not mingle again with his old companions; he should touch not, taste not, handle not. God visits with heavier judgment those who have been once restored from the ways of sin and who return again to it. The drunkard that has been reformed, and

the Jews that it was Jesus which had made him whole.

16 And therefore did the Jews persecute Jesus, and sought to slay him, because he had done these things on the sabbath-day.

17 But Jesus answered them, [n]My Father worketh hitherto, and I work.

18 Therefore the Jews sought the more [o]to kill him, because he not only had broken the sabbath,

n ch.9.4; 14.10. *o* ch.7.19.

that returns to his habits of drinking, becomes more beastly; the man that professes to have experienced a change of heart, and who then indulges in sin, sinks deeper into pollution, and is seldom restored. The only way of safety in all such cases is to *sin no more;* not to be in the way of temptation; not to expose ourselves; not to touch or approach that which came near to working our ruin. The man who has been intemperate and is reformed, if he tastes the poison *at all*, may expect to sink deeper than ever into drunkenness and pollution. ¶ *A worse thing.* A more grievous disease, or the pains of hell. "The doom of apostates is a worse thing than thirty-eight years' lameness" (Henry).

16. *Persecuted Jesus.* They opposed him; attempted to ruin his character; to destroy his popularity; and probably held him up before the people as a violator of the law of God. Instead of making inquiry whether he had not given proof that he was the Messiah, they *assumed* that he must be wrong, and ought to be punished. Thus every bigot and persecutor does in regard to those who differ from them. ¶ *To slay him.* To put him to death. This they attempted to do because it was directed in the law of Moses, Ex. xxxi. 15; xxxv. 2. See Lu. vi. 7, 11; xiii. 14. We see here, 1st. How full of enmity and how bloody was the purpose of the Jews. All that Jesus had done was to restore an infirm man to health—a thing which *they* would have done for their cattle (Lu. vi. 7), and yet they sought his life because he had done it for a sick *man*. 2d. Men are often extremely envious because good is done by others, especially if it is not done according to the way of *their* denomination or party. 3d. Here was an instance of the common feelings of a hypocrite. He often covers his enmity against the *power* of religion by great zeal for the *form* of it. He hates and persecutes those who do good, who seek the conversion of sinners, who love revivals of religion and the spread of the gospel, because it is not according to some matter of form which has been established, and on which he supposes the whole safety of the church to hang. There was nothing that Jesus was more opposed to than hypocrisy, and nothing that he set himself more against than those who suppose all goodness to consist in *forms*, and all piety in the *shibboleths* of a party.

17. *My Father.* God. ¶ *Worketh hitherto.* Worketh *until now*, or till this time. God has not ceased to work on the Sabbath. He makes the sun to rise; he rolls the stars; he causes the grass, the tree, the flower to grow. He has not suspended his operations on the Sabbath, and the obligation to *rest* on the Sabbath does not extend to him. He *created* the world in six days, and ceased the work of *creation;* but he has not ceased to *govern* it, and to carry forward, by his providence, his great plans on the Sabbath. ¶ *And I work.* "As God does good on that day; as he is not bound by the law which requires his creatures to rest on that day, so *I* do the same. The law on that subject may be dispensed with, also, in my case, for the Son of man is Lord of the Sabbath." In this reply it is implied that he was equal with God from two circumstances: 1st. Because he called God his Father, ver. 18. 2d. Because he claimed the same *exemption* from law which God did, asserting that the law of the Sabbath did not bind him or his Father, thus showing that he had a right to impose and repeal laws in the same manner as God. He that has a right to do this must be God.

18. *The more to kill him.* The answer of Jesus was fitted greatly to irritate them. He did not *deny* what he had done, but he *added* to that what he well knew would highly offend them. That he should claim the right of *dispensing* with the law, and affirm that, in regard to its observance, he was in the same condition with God, was eminently fitted to enrage them, and he doubtless knew that it might endanger his life. We may learn from his answer, 1st.

but said also that God was his
Father, [p] making himself equal
with God.

19 Then answered Jesus and
said unto them, Verily, verily, I
say unto you, [q] The Son can do
nothing of himself, but what he
seeth the Father do; for what
things soever he doeth, these also
doeth the Son likewise.

20 For[r] the Father loveth the
Son, and showeth him all things

p Zec.13.7; ch.10.30,33; Phi.2.6. q ver.30.

r Mat.3.17; ch.3.35; 17.26.

That we are not to keep back truth because it may endanger us. 2d. That we are not to keep back truth because it will irritate and enrage sinners. The fault is not in the *truth*, but in the *sinner*. 3d. That when any one portion of truth enrages hypocrites, they will be enraged the more they hear. ¶ *Had broken the sabbath.* They *supposed* he had broken it. ¶ *Making himself equal with God.* This shows that, in the view of the Jews, the name Son of God, or that calling God his Father, implied equality with God. The Jews were the best interpreters of their own language, and as Jesus did not deny the correctness of their interpretations, it follows that he meant to be so understood. See ch. x. 29-38. The interpretation of the Jews was a very natural and just one. He not only said that God was his Father, but he said that he had the same right to work on the Sabbath that God had; that by the same authority, and in the same manner, he could dispense with the obligation of the day. They had now *two* pretences for seeking to kill him—one for making himself equal with God, which they considered blasphemy, and the other for violating the Sabbath. For each of these the law denounced death, Nu. xv. 35; Le. xxiv. 11-14.

19. *The Son can do nothing of himself.* Jesus, having stated the *extent* of his authority, proceeds here to show its *source and nature*, and to *prove* to them that what he had said was true. The first explanation which he gives is in these words: *The Son*—whom he had just impliedly affirmed to be equal with God—did nothing *of himself;* that is, nothing without the appointment of the Father; nothing contrary to the Father, as he immediately explains it. When it is said that he CAN *do nothing* OF HIMSELF, it is meant that such is the union subsisting between the Father and the Son that he can do nothing *independently* or separate from the Father. Such is the nature of this union that he can do nothing which has not the concurrence of the Father, and which he does not command. In all things he must, from the necessity of his nature, act in accordance with the nature and will of God. Such is the intimacy of the union, that the fact that *he* does anything is proof that it is by the concurring agency of God. There is no separate action—no separate existence; but, alike in being and in action, there is the most perfect oneness between him and the Father. Comp. Jn. x. 30; xvii. 21. ¶ *What he seeth the Father do.* In the works of creation and providence, in making laws, and in the government of the universe. There is a peculiar force in the word *seeth* here. No *man* can see God acting in his works; but the word here implies that the Son sees him act, as we see our fellow-men act, and that he has a knowledge of him, therefore, which no mere mortal could possess. ¶ *What things soever.* In the works of creation and of providence, and in the government of the worlds. The word is without limit—ALL that the Father does the Son likewise does. This is as high an assertion as possible of his being *equal* with God. If one does *all* that another does or can do, then there must be equality. If the Son does all that the Father does, then, like him, he must be almighty, omniscient, omnipresent, and infinite in every perfection; or, in other words, he must be God. If he had *this* power, then he had authority, also, to do on the Sabbath-day what God did.

20. *The Father loveth the Son.* This authority he traces to the love which the Father has for him—that peculiar, ineffable, infinite love which God has for his only-begotten Son, feebly and dimly illustrated by the love which an earthly parent has for an only child. ¶ *Showeth him.* Makes him acquainted with. Conceals nothing from him. From apostles, prophets, and philosophers no small part of the doings of God are concealed. From the *Son* nothing is. And as God shows him *all* that he does, he must be possessed of omniscience, for to no finite mind could be imparted a

that himself doeth; and he will show him greater works than these, that ye may marvel.

21 For as the Father raiseth up the dead, and quickeneth *them*, even so [s]the Son quickeneth whom he will.

22 For the Father judgeth no man, but [t]hath committed all judgment unto the Son;

23 That all *men* should honour the Son, even as they honour the Father. He that honoureth not

s Lu.8.54; ch.11.25; 17.2.

t Mat.11.27; Ac.17.31; 2 Co.5.10.

knowledge of *all* the works of God. ¶ *Will show him.* Will appoint and direct him to do greater works than these. ¶ *Greater works than these.* Than healing the impotent man, and commanding him to carry his bed on the Sabbath-day. The greater works to which he refers are those which he proceeds to specify--he will raise the dead and judge the world, &c. ¶ *May marvel.* May wonder, or be amazed.

21. *As the Father raiseth up the dead.* God has power to raise the dead. By his power it had been done in at least two instances—by the prophet Elijah, in the case of the son of the widow of Sarepta (1 Ki. xvii. 22), and by the prophet Elisha, in the case of the Shunamite's son, 2 Ki. iv. 32–35. The Jews did not doubt that God had power to raise the dead. Jesus here expressly affirms it, and says he has the same power. ¶ *Quickeneth* them. Gives them *life.* This is the sense of the word *quickeneth* throughout the Bible. ¶ *Even so.* In the same manner. By the same authority and power. The power of raising the dead must be one of the highest attributes of the divinity. As Jesus affirms that he has the power to do this *in the same manner* as the Father, so it follows that he must be equal with God. ¶ *The Son quickeneth.* Gives life to. This may either refer to his raising the dead from their graves, or to his giving spiritual life to those who are dead in trespasses and sins. The former he did in the case of Lazarus and the widow's son at Nain, Jn. xi. 43, 44; Lu. vii. 14, 15. The latter he did in the case of all those who were converted by his power, and still does it in any instance of conversion. ¶ *Whom he will.* It was in the power of Jesus to raise up any of the dead as well as Lazarus. It depended on his will whether Lazarus and the widow's son should come to life. So it depends on his will whether sinners shall live. He has power to renew them, and the renewing of the heart is as much the result of his *will* as the raising of the dead.

22. *Judgeth no man.* Jesus in these verses is showing his *equality with God.* He affirmed (ver. 17) that he had the same power over the Sabbath that his Father had; in ver. 19, that he *did* the same things as the Father; in ver. 21 particularly that he had the same power to raise the dead. He now adds that God has given him the authority to *judge* men. The Father pronounces judgment on no one. This office he has committed to the Son. The power of judging the world implies ability to search the heart, and omniscience to understand the motives of all actions. This is a work which none but a divine being can do, and it shows, therefore, that the Son is equal to the Father. ¶ *Hath committed,* &c. Hath appointed him to be the judge of the world. In the previous verse he had said that he had power *to raise the dead;* he here adds that it will be his, also, to *judge* them when they are raised. See Mat. xxv.; Ac. xvii. 31.

23. *That all* men *should honour,* &c. To honour is to esteem, reverence, praise, do homage to. We honour one when we ascribe to him in our hearts, and words, and actions the praise and obedience which are due to him. We honour God when we obey him and worship him aright. We honour the Son when we esteem him to be as he is; when we have right views and feelings toward him. As he is declared to be God (Jn. i. 1), as he here says he has power and authority equal with God, so we honour him when we regard him as such. The primitive Christians are described by Pliny, in a letter to the Emperor Trajan, as meeting together to sing hymns to Christ *as God.* So we honour him aright when we regard him as possessed of wisdom, goodness, power, eternity, omniscience — equal with God. ¶ *Even as.* To the same extent; in the same manner. Since the Son is to be honoured EVEN AS the Father, it follows that he must be equal

the Son, honoureth not the Father which hath sent him.

24 Verily, verily, I say unto you, [u]He that heareth my word, and believeth on him that sent me, hath everlasting life, and shall

u ch.6.40,47.

with the Father. To *honour the Father* must denote *religious* homage, or the rendering of that honour which is due to God; so to honour the Son must also denote *religious* homage. If our Saviour here did not intend to teach that he ought to be *worshipped*, and to be esteemed as *equal* with God, it would be difficult to teach it by any language which we could use. ¶ *He that honoureth not the Son.* He that does not believe on him, and render to him the homage which is his due as the equal of God. ¶ *Honoureth not the Father.* Does not worship and obey the Father, the first person of the Trinity—that is, does not worship *God.* He may imagine that he worships God, but there *is* no God but the God subsisting as Father, Son, and Holy Ghost. He that withholds proper homage from one, withholds it from all. He that should refuse to honour *the Father*, could not be said to honour *God;* and in the like manner, he that honoureth not *the Son*, honoureth not *the Father.* This appears farther from the following considerations:—1st. The Father wills that the Son should be honoured. He that refuses to do it disobeys the Father. 2d. They are equal. He that denies the one denies also the other. 3d. The same feeling that leads us to honour the *Father* will also lead us to honour the *Son*, for he is "the brightness of his glory, and the express image of his person," He. i. 3. 4th. The evidence of the existence of the Son is the same as that of the Father. He has the same wisdom, goodness, omnipresence, truth, power.

And from these verses we may learn —1st. That those who do not render proper homage to Jesus Christ do not worship the true God. 2d. There is no such God as the infidel professes to believe in. There can be but one God; and if the God of the Bible be the true God, then all other gods are false gods. 3d. Those who withhold proper homage from Jesus Christ, who do not honour him EVEN AS they honour the Father, cannot be Christians. 4th. One evidence of piety is when we are willing to render proper praise and homage to Jesus Christ —to love him, and serve and obey him, with all our hearts. 5th. *As a matter of fact*, it may be added that they who do not honour the Son do not worship God at all. The infidel has no form of worship; he has no place of secret prayer, no temple of worship, no family altar. Who ever yet heard of an infidel that prayed? Where do such men build houses of worship? Where do they meet to praise God? Nowhere. As certainly as we hear the name *infidel*, we are certain at once that we hear the name of a man who has no form of religion in his family, who never prays in secret, and who will do nothing to maintain the public worship of God. Account for it as men may, it is a fact that no one can dispute, that it is only they who do honour to the Lord Jesus that have any form of the worship of God, or that honour him; *and their veneration for God is just in proportion to their love for the Redeemer—just as they honour him.*

24. *He that heareth my word.* To *hear*, in this place, evidently denotes not the outward act of hearing, but to receive in a proper manner; to suffer it to make its proper impression on the mind; to obey. The word *hear* is often used in this sense, Mat. xi. 15; Jn. viii. 47; Ac. iii. 23. Many persons outwardly hear the gospel who neither understand nor obey it. ¶ *My word.* My doctrine, my teaching. All that Jesus taught about *himself*, as well as about the Father. ¶ *On him that sent me.* On the Father, who, in the plan of redemption, is represented as *sending* his Son to save men. See Jn. iii. 17. Faith in God, who sent his Son, is here represented as being connected with everlasting life; but there can be no faith in him who *sent* his Son, without faith also in him who is *sent.* The belief of *one* of the true doctrines of religion is connected with, and will lead to, the belief of *all.* ¶ *Hath everlasting life.* The state of man by nature is represented as death in sin, Ep. ii. 1. Religion is the opposite of this, or is *life.* The *dead* regard not anything. They are unaffected by the cares, pleasures, amusements of the world. They hear neither the voice of merriment nor the tread of the living over their graves. So with sinners. They are unmoved with the things of

not come into condemnation, but is[v] passed from death unto life.

25 Verily, verily, I say unto you, The hour is coming, and now is, when [w]the dead shall hear the voice of the Son of God; and they that hear shall live.

26 For as the Father hath life

v 1 Jn.3.14.

w ver.28; Ep.2.1.

religion. They hear not the voice of God; they see not his loveliness; they care not for his threatenings. But religion is *life*. The Christian *lives* with God, and feels and acts as if there was a God. Religion, and its blessings here and hereafter, are one and the same. The happiness of heaven is *living* unto God—being sensible of his presence, and glory, and power—and rejoicing in that. There shall be no more *death* there, Re. xxi. 4. This *life*, or this religion, whether on earth or in heaven, is the same—the same joys extended and expanded for ever. Hence, when a man is converted, it is said that he *has* everlasting life; not merely *shall have*, but is already *in possession* of that life or happiness which shall be everlasting. It is life begun, expanded, ripening for the skies. He has already entered on his inheritance—that inheritance which is everlasting. ¶ *Shall not come into condemnation.* He was by nature under condemnation. See Jn. iii. 18. Here it is declared that he shall not return to that state, or he will not be again condemned. This promise is sure; it is made by the Son of God, and there is no one that can pluck them out of his hand, Jn. x. 28. Comp. Notes on Ro. viii. 1. ¶ *But is passed from death unto life.* Has *passed over* from a state of spiritual death to the life of the Christian. The word translated *is passed* would be better expressed by *has passed.* It implies that he has done it voluntarily; that none compelled him; and that the passage is made unto *everlasting* life. Because Christ is the *author* of this life in the soul, he is called the *life* (Jn. i. 4); and as he has *always* existed, and is the source of *all life*, he is called the *eternal life*, 1 Jn. v. 20.

25. *The hour.* The time. ¶ *Is coming.* Under the preaching of the gospel, as well as in the resurrection of the dead. ¶ *Now is.* It is now taking place. Sinners were converted under his ministry and brought to spiritual life. ¶ *The dead.* Either the dead in sins, or those that are in their graves. The words of the Saviour will apply to either. Language, in the Scriptures, is often so used as to describe two *similar* events. Thus the destruction of Jerusalem and the end of the world are described by Jesus in the same language, Mat. xxiv. xxv. The return of the Jews from Babylon, and the coming of the Messiah, and the spread of his gospel, are described in the same language by Isaiah, Is. xl.–lxi. Comp. Notes on Is. vii. 14. The renewal of the heart, and the raising of the dead at the judgment, are here also described in similar language, because they so far resemble each other that the same language will apply to both. ¶ *The voice of the Son of God.* The voice is that by which we give command. Jesus raised up the dead by his command, or by his authority. When he did it he spoke, or commanded it to be done. Mar. v. 41: "He took the damsel by the hand, and *said*, Talitha cumi." Lu. vii. 14: "And he came and touched the bier, and *said*, Young man, I say unto thee, Arise." Jn. xi. 43: "He cried with a loud voice, Lazarus, come forth." So it is by his command that those who are dead in sins are quickened or made alive, ver. 21. And so at the day of judgment the dead will be raised by his command or voice, though there is no reason to think that his voice will be audibly heard, ver. 28. ¶ *Shall live.* Shall be restored to life.

26. *As the Father hath life.* God is the source of all life. He is thence called the *living* God, in opposition to idols which have no life. Ac. xiv. 15: "We preach unto you that ye should turn from these vanities (idols) *unto the living God*," Jos. iii. 10; 1 Sa. xvii. 26; Je. x. 10. See also Is. xl. 18–31. ¶ *In himself.* This means that life in God, or existence, is not *derived* from any other being. *Our* life is derived from God. Gen. ii. 7: God "breathed into his nostrils the breath of life, and man became a living soul"—that is, a living being. All other creatures derive their life from him. Ps. civ. 30, 29: "Thou sendest forth thy spirit, they are created; thou takest away their breath, they die and return to their dust." But God is underived. He always existed as he is. Ps. xc. 2: "From everlasting to everlasting thou art God." He is unchangeably the same, Ja. i. 17. It

in himself, so hath he given to the Son to have [x]life in himself;

x 1 Co.15.45.

27 And hath given him [y]authority to execute judgment also, because he is the Son of man.

y ver.22.

cannot be said that he is *self-existent*, because that is an absurdity; no being can originate or create himself; but he is not dependent on any other for *life.* Of course, no being can take away his existence; and of course, also, no being can take away his *happiness.* He has *in himself* infinite sources of happiness, and no other being, no change in his universe can destroy that happiness. ¶ *So.* In a manner like his. It corresponds to the first "as," implying that one is the same as the other; life in the one is the *same*, and possessed in the *same manner*, as in the other. ¶ *Hath he given.* This shows that the power or authority here spoken of was *given* or committed to the Lord Jesus. This evidently does not refer to the manner in which the second person of the Trinity exists, for the power and authority of which Christ here speaks is that which he exercises as *Mediator*. It is the power of raising the dead and judging the world. In regard to his *divine nature*, it is not affirmed here that it is in any manner derived; nor does the fact that God is said to have *given* him this power prove that he was inferior in his nature or that his existence was derived. For, 1st. It has reference merely *to office.* As Mediator, he may be said to have been appointed by the Father. 2d. Appointment to office does not prove that the one who is appointed is inferior in nature to him who appoints him. A son may be appointed to a particular work by a parent, and yet, in regard to talents and every other qualification, may be equal or superior to the father. He sustains the relation of a son, and in this relation there is an official inferiority. General Washington was not inferior in nature and talents to the men who commissioned him. He simply derived *authority* from them to do what he was otherwise fully *able* to do. So the Son, *as Mediator*, is subject to the Father; yet this proves nothing about *his nature.* ¶ *To have life.* That is, the right or authority of imparting life to others, whether dead in their graves or in their sins. ¶ *In himself.* There is much that is remarkable in this expression. It is IN *him* as it is IN *God.* He has the control of it, and can exercise it as he will. The prophets and apostles are never represented as having such power in themselves. They were dependent; they performed miracles in the name of God and of Jesus Christ (Ac. iii. 6; iv. 30; xvi. 18); but Jesus did it by his own name, authority, and power. He had but to speak, and it was done, Mar. v. 41; Lu. vii. 14; Jn. xi. 43. This wonderful commission he bore from God to raise up the dead as he pleased; to convert sinners when and where he chose; and finally to raise up *all* the dead, and pronounce on them an eternal doom according to the deeds done in the body. None could do this but he who had the power of creation—equal in omnipotence to the Father, and the power of searching *all* hearts—equal in omniscience to God.

27. *Hath given him authority.* Hath appointed him to do this. Has made him to be judge of all. This is represented as being the appointment of the Father, Ac. xvii. 31. The word *authority* here (commonly rendered *power*) implies all that is necessary to execute judgment—all the physical power to raise the dead, and to investigate the actions and thoughts of the life; and all the *moral right* or authority to sit in judgment on the creatures of God, and to pronounce their doom. ¶ *To execute judgment.* To *do* judgment—that is, to judge. He has appointment to *do justice;* to see that the universe suffers no wrong, either by the escape of the guilty or by the punishment of the innocent. ¶ *Because he is the Son of man.* The phrase *Son of man* here seems to be used in the sense of "because he is a man," or because he has human nature. The term is one which Jesus often gives to himself, to show his union with man and his interest in man. See Notes on Mat. viii. 19, 20. It is to be remarked here that the word *son* has not the article before it in the original: "Because he is *a* Son of man"—that is, because he is a man. It would seem from this that there is a propriety that one in our nature should judge us. What this propriety is we do not certainly know. It may be, 1st. Because one who has experienced our infirmities, and who possesses our nature, may be supposed by those *who are judged* to be

28 Marvel not at this; for the
hour is coming, in the which all
that are in the graves shall hear
his voice,
29 And shall come forth; [z]they
that have done good unto the
resurrection of life, and they that
have done evil unto [a]the resurrection of damnation.
30 I[b] can of mine own self do

z Da.12.2. a Mat.25.46. b ver.19.

better qualified than one in a different nature. 2d. Because he is to decide between *man* and *God*, and it is proper that *our* feelings, and nature, and views should be represented in the judge, as well as those of God. 3d. Because Jesus has all the feelings of compassion we could ask—all the benevolence we could desire in a judge; because he has *shown* his disposition to defend us by giving his life, and it can never be alleged by those who are condemned that their judge was a distant, cold, and unfriendly being. Some have supposed that the expression *Son of man* here means the same as *Messiah* (see Da. vii. 13, 14), and that the meaning is that God hath made him judge because he was the Messiah. Some of the ancient versions and fathers connected this with the following verse, thus: "Marvel not because I am a man, or because this great work is committed to a man apparently in humble life. You shall see greater things than these." Thus the Syriac version reads it, and Chrysostom, Theophylact, and some others among the fathers.

28. *Marvel not.* Do not wonder or be astonished at this. ¶ *The hour is coming.* The *time* is approaching or will be. ¶ *All that are in the graves.* All the dead, of every age and nation. They are described as *in the graves.* Though many have turned to their native dust and perished from human view, yet God sees them, and can regather their remains and raise them up to life. The phrase *all that are in the graves* does not prove that the same particles of matter will be raised up, but it is equivalent to saying *all the dead.* See Notes on 1 Co. xv. 35–38. ¶ *Shall hear his voice.* He will restore them to life, and command them to appear before him. This is a most sublime description, and this will be a wonderful display of almighty power. None but God can *see* all the dead, none but he could remould their frames, and none else could command them to return to life.

29. *Shall come forth.* Shall come out of their graves. This was the language which he used when he raised up Lazarus, Jn. xi. 43, 44. ¶ *They that have done good.* That is, they who are righteous, or they who have by their good works *shown* that they were the friends of Christ. See Mat. xxv. 34–36. ¶ *Resurrection of life.* Religion is often called life, and everlasting life. See Notes on ver. 24. In the resurrection the righteous will be raised up to the full enjoyment and perpetual security of that life. It is also called the resurrection of life, because there shall be no more *death*, Re. xxi. 4. The enjoyment of God himself and of his works; of the society of the angels and of the redeemed; freedom from sickness, and sin, and dying, will constitute the *life* of the just in the resurrection. The resurrection is also called the resurrection of the just (Lu. xiv. 14), and the first resurrection, Re. xx. 5, 6. ¶ *The resurrection of damnation.* The word *damnation* means the sentence passed on one by a judge—judgment or condemnation. The word, as we use it, applies only to the judgment pronounced by God on the wicked; but this is not its meaning always in the Bible. Here it has, however, that meaning. Those who have done evil will be raised up *to be condemned* or *damned.* This will be the object in raising them up—this the sole design. It is elsewhere said that they shall then be condemned to everlasting punishment (Mat. xxv. 46), and that they shall be punished with everlasting destruction (2 Th. i. 8, 9); and it is said of the unjust that they are reserved unto the day of judgment to be punished, 2 Pe. ii. 9. That this refers to the future judgment—to the resurrection then, and not to anything that takes place in this life—is clear from the following considerations: 1st. Jesus had just spoken of what would be done in this life—of the power of the gospel, ver. 25. He adds here that something still more wonderful—something *beyond* this—would take place. *All that are in the graves* shall hear his voice. 2d. He speaks of those who are in their graves, evidently referring to the dead. Sinners are sometimes said to be dead

nothing: as I hear I judge; and my judgment is just, because I seek not mine own will, but [c]the will of the Father which hath sent me.

31 If[d] I bear witness of myself, my witness is not true.

32 There is [e]another that beareth witness of me; and I know that the witness which he witnesseth of me is true.

33 Ye sent unto John, and [f]he bare witness unto the truth.

34 But I receive not testimony

c Ps.40.7,8; Mat.26.39; ch.4.34; 6.38.
d Ps.27.2; ch.8.14; Re.3.14.
e ch.8.18; Ac.10.43; 1 Jn.5.7-9. f ch.1.7,32.

in sin, but sinners are not said to be *in a grave.* This is applied in the Scriptures only to those who are deceased. 3d. The language used here of the *righteous* cannot be applied to anything in this life. When God converts men, it is not because they *have been good.* 4th. Nor is the language employed of the evil applicable to anything here. In what condition among men can it be said, with any appearance of sense, that they are brought forth from their graves to the resurrection of damnation? The doctrine of those Universalists who hold that all men will be saved immediately at death, therefore, cannot be true. This passage proves that at the day of judgment the wicked will be condemned. Let it be added that if *then* condemned they will be lost for ever. Thus (Mat. xxv. 46) it is said to be *everlasting* punishment; 2 Th. i. 8, 9, it is called *everlasting* destruction. There is no account of redemption in hell—no Saviour, no Holy Spirit, no offer of mercy there.

30. *Of mine own self.* See ver. 19. The Messiah, the Mediator, does nothing without the concurrence and the authority of God. Such is the nature of the union subsisting between them, that he does nothing *independently* of God. Whatever he does, he does according to the will of God. ¶ *As I hear I judge.* To *hear* expresses the condition of one who is commissioned or instructed. Thus (Jn. viii. 26), "I speak to the world those things which I have *heard* of him;" viii. 28, "As the Father hath taught me, I speak those things." Jesus here represents himself as commissioned, taught, or sent of God. When he says, "as I *hear*," he refers to those things which the Father had *showed* him (ver. 20)—that is, he came to communicate the will of God; to show to man what God wished man to know. ¶ *I judge.* I determine or decide. This was true respecting the institutions and doctrines of religion, and it will be true respecting the sentence which he will pass on mankind at the day of judgment. He will decide their destiny according to what the Father wills and wishes—that is, according to justice. ¶ *Because I seek,* &c. This does not imply that his own judgment would be wrong if he sought his own will, but that he had no *private* ends, no selfish views, no improper bias. He came not to aggrandize himself, or to promote his own views, but he came to do the will of God. Of course his decision would be impartial and unbiased, and there is every security that it will be according to truth. See Lu. xxii. 42, where he gave a memorable instance, in the agony of the garden, of his submission to his Father's will.

31. *If I bear witness of myself.* If I have no other evidence than my own testimony about myself. ¶ *My witness.* My testimony; my evidence. The proof would not be decisive. ¶ *Is not true.* The word *true,* here, means worthy of belief, or established by suitable evidence. See Mat. xxii. 16: "We *know* that thou art *true*"—that is, worthy of confidence, or that thou hast been truly sent from God, Lu. xx. 21; Jn. viii. 13, 17. The law did not admit a man to testify in his own case, but required *two* witnesses, De. xvii. 6. Though what Jesus said was *true* (ch. viii. 13, 17), yet he admitted it was not sufficient testimony *alone* to claim their belief. They had a right to expect that his statement that he came from God would be confirmed by other evidence. This evidence he gave in the miracles which he wrought as proof that God had sent him.

32. *There is another.* That is, God. See ver. 36.

33. *Ye sent unto John.* See ch. i. 19. ¶ *He bare witness,* &c. See ch. i. 26, 29, 36. This testimony of John *ought* to have satisfied them. John was an eminent man; many of the Pharisees believed on him; he was candid, unambitious, sincere, and his evidence was impartial. On this Jesus *might* have

from man; [g]but these things I say that ye might be saved.
35 He was a burning and a shining light, and [h]ye were willing for a season to rejoice in his light.
36 But I have greater witness than *that* of John; for [i]the works which [k]the Father hath given me to finish, the same works that I do, bear witness of me that the Father hath sent me.
37 And [l] the Father himself,

g ch.20.31; Ro.3.3. h Mat.21.26; Mar.6.20. i ch.10.25; 15.24; Ac.2.22. k ch.17.4. l Mat.3.17; 17.5.

rested the proof that he was the Messiah, but he was willing, also, to adduce evidence of a higher order.

34. *I receive not testimony from men.* I do not depend for proof of my Messiahship on the testimony of men, nor do I pride myself on the commendations or flattery of men. ¶ *But these things*, &c. "This testimony of John I adduce that you might be convinced. It was evidence of your own seeking. It was clear, full, explicit. You *sent* to make inquiry, and he gave you a candid and satisfactory answer. Had you believed that, you would have believed in the Messiah and been saved." Men are often dissatisfied with the very evidence of the truth of religion which they sought, and on which they professed themselves willing to rely.

35. *He was.* It is probable that John had been cast into prison before this. Hence his public ministry had ceased, and our Saviour says he *was* such a light. ¶ *Light.* The word in the original properly means a *lamp*, and is not the same which in Jn. i. 4, 5 is translated *light.* That is a word commonly applied to the sun, the fountain of light; this means a *lamp*, or a light that is lit up or kindled artificially from oil or tallow. A teacher is often called a *light*, because he guides or illuminates the minds of others. Ro. ii. 19: "Thou art confident that thou art a guide of the blind, *a light* of them that sit in darkness;" Jn. viii. 12; xii. 46; Mat. v. 14. ¶ *A burning.* A lamp lit up that burns with a steady lustre. ¶ *Shining.* Not dim, not indistinct. The expression means that he was an eminent teacher; that his doctrines were clear, distinct, consistent. ¶ *Ye were willing.* You willed, or you chose; you went out voluntarily. This shows that some of those whom Jesus was now addressing were among the great multitudes of Pharisees that came unto John in the wilderness, Mat. iii. 7. As *they* had at one time admitted John to be a prophet, so Jesus might with great propriety adduce his testimony in his favour. ¶ *For a season.* In the original, for an *hour*—denoting only a short time. They did it, as many others do, while he was popular, and it was the *fashion* to follow him. ¶ *To rejoice in his light.* To rejoice in his doctrines, and in admitting that he was a distinguished prophet; perhaps, also, to rejoice that he professed to be sent to introduce the Messiah, until they found that he bore testimony to Jesus of Nazareth.

36. *Greater witness.* Stronger, more decisive evidence. ¶ *The works.* The miracles—healing the sick and raising the dead. ¶ *Hath given me.* Hath committed to me, or appointed me to do. Certain things he intrusted in his hands to accomplish. ¶ *To finish.* To do or to perform until the task is completed. The word is applied to the *termination* of anything, as we say a task is *ended* or a work is completed. So Jesus said, when he expired, It is "*finished*," Jn. xix. 30. From this it appears that Jesus came to *accomplish* a certain work; and hence we see the reason why he so often guarded his life and sought his safety until the task was fully completed. These works or miracles bore witness of him; that is, they showed that he was sent from God, because none but God could perform them, and because God would not give such power to any whose life and doctrines he did not approve. They were more decisive proof than the testimony of John, because, 1st. John worked no miracles, Jn. x. 41. 2d. It was possible that *a man* might be deceived or be an impostor. It was *not* possible for *God* to deceive. 3d. The miracles which Jesus wrought were such as no *man* could work, and no angel. He that could raise the dead must have all power, and he who commissioned Jesus, therefore, must be God.

37. *The Father himself—hath borne witness of me.* This God had done, 1st. By the miracles which Jesus had wrought, and of which he was conversing. 2d. At the baptism of Jesus, where he said, "This is my beloved

which hath sent me, hath borne
witness of me. Ye[m] have neither
heard his voice at any time, nor
seen his shape.
38 And[n] ye have not his word
abiding in you; for whom he hath
sent, him ye believe not.
39 Search[o] the scriptures; for in

m De.4.12; 1 Ti.6.16. n 1 Jn.2.14. o Is.8.20; 34.16; Lu.16.29.

Son," Mat. iii. 17. 3d. In the prophecies of the Old Testament. It is not easy to say here to which of these he refers. Perhaps he has reference to all. ¶ *Ye have neither heard his voice.* This difficult passage has been interpreted in various ways. The main design of it seems to be clear—to reprove the Jews for not believing the evidence that he was the Messiah. In doing this he says that they were indisposed to listen to the testimony of God. He affirmed that God had given sufficient evidence of his divine mission, but they had disregarded it. The *first thing* that he notices is that they had not heard his voice. The word *hear*, in this place, is to be understood in the sense of *obey* or listen to. See Notes on ver. 25. The voice of God means his *commands* or his declarations, however made; and the Saviour said that it had been the *characteristic* of the Jews that they had not listened to the voice or command of God. As this had been their *general* characteristic, it was not wonderful that they disregarded now his testimony in regard to the Messiah. The voice of God *had been* literally heard on the mount. See De. iv. 12: "Ye heard the voice of the words." ¶ *At any time.* This has been the uniform characteristic of the nation that they have disregarded and perverted the testimony of God, and it was as true of that generation as of their fathers. ¶ *Nor seen his shape.* No man hath seen *God* at any time, Jn. i. 18. But the word *shape*, here, does not mean *God himself.* It refers to the visible *manifestation* of himself; to the *appearance* which he assumed. It is applied in the Septuagint to his manifesting himself to Moses, Nu. xii. 8: "With him will I speak mouth to mouth, *even apparently;*" in Greek, *in a form* or *shape*—the word used here. It is applied to the visible symbol of God that appeared in the cloud and that rested on the tabernacle, Nu. ix. 15, 16. It is the same word that is applied to the Holy Spirit appearing in bodily *shape* like a dove, Lu. iii. 22. Jesus does not here deny that God had *appeared* in this manner, but he says they had not seen—that is, had not *paid attention to*, or *regarded*, the appearance of God. He had manifested himself, but they disregarded it, and, in particular, they had disregarded his manifestations in attestation of the Messiah. As the word *hear* means to obey, to listen to, so the word *see* means to pay attention to, to regard (2 Jn. 8; 1 Jn. iii. 6), and thus throws light on Jn. xiv. 9: "He that hath seen me hath seen the Father." "I am a *manifestation* of God—God appearing in human flesh, as he appeared formerly in the symbol of the cloud; and he that *regards me*, or attends to me, regards the Father."

38. *His word abiding in you.* His law does not abide in you—that is, you do not regard or obey it. This was the *third* thing that he charged them with. 1st. They had not obeyed the command of God. 2d. They had not regarded his manifestations, either in the times of the old dispensation, or now through the Messiah. 3d. They did not yield to what he had said in the revelation of the Old Testament. ¶ *For whom he hath sent.* God had foretold that the Messiah would come. He had now given evidence that Jesus was he; but now they rejected him, and this was proof that they did not regard the word of God.

39. *Search the scriptures.* The word translated *search* here means to *search diligently* or anxiously. It is applied to miners, who search for precious metals—who look anxiously for the *bed* of the ore with an intensity or anxiety proportionate to *their sense* of the value of the metal. Comp. Notes on Job xxviii. 3. It is applied by Homer to a lioness robbed of her whelps, and who *searches* the plain to *trace out* the footsteps of the man who has robbed her. It is also applied by him to dogs tracing their game by searching them out by the scent of the foot. It means a diligent, faithful, anxious investigation. The word *may be* either in the indicative or imperative mood. In our translation it is in the imperative, as if Jesus *commanded* them to search the Scriptures. Cyril, Erasmus, Beza, Bengel,

them ye think ye have eternal life; and [p] they are they which testify of me.

40 And [q] ye will not come to me, that ye might have life.

41 I receive not honour [r] from men.

42 But I know you, that ye have not the love of God in you.

43 I am come in my Father's name, and ye receive me not: if another shall come in his own name, him ye will receive.

44 How can ye believe, [s] which

p Lu.24.27; 1 Pe.1.10,11. q ch.3.19. r ver.34; 1 Th.2.6. s ch.12.43.

Kuinoel, Tholuck, De Wette, and others, give it as in the indicative; Chrysostom, Augustine, Luther, Calvin, Wetstein, Stier, Alford, and others, regard it as in the imperative, or as a command. It is impossible to determine which is the true interpretation. Either of them makes good sense, and it is proper to use the passage in either signification. There is abundant evidence that the Jews *did* search the books of the Old Testament. It is equally clear that all men *ought* to do it. ¶ *The scriptures.* The writings or books of the Old Testament, for those were all the books of revelation that they then possessed. ¶ *In them ye think ye have eternal life.* The meaning of this is: "Ye think that by studying the Scriptures you will obtain eternal life. You suppose that they teach the way to future blessedness, and that by diligently studying them you will attain it." We see by this—1. That the Jews in the time of Jesus were expecting a future state. 2. The Scriptures teach the way of life, and it is our duty to study them. The Bereans are commended for searching the Scriptures (Ac. xvii. 11); and Timothy is said from a child to have "known the holy scriptures, which are able to make us wise unto salvation," 2 Ti. iii. 15. Early life is the proper time to search the Bible, for they who seek the Lord early shall find him. ¶ *They are they,* &c. They bear witness to the Messiah. They predict his coming, and the manner of his life and death, Is. liii.; Da. ix. 26, 27, &c. See Notes on Lu. xxiv. 27.

40. *And ye will not come,* &c. Though the Old Testament bears evidence that I am the Messiah; though you professedly search it to learn the way to life, and though my works prove it, yet you will not come to me to obtain life. From this we may learn, 1st. That life is to be obtained in Christ. He is the way, the truth, and the life, and he only can save us. 2d. That, in order to do that, we must *come to him*—that is, must come in the way appointed, as lost sinners, and be willing to be saved by him alone. 3d. That the reason why sinners are not saved lies in the will. "The only reason why sinners die is because *they will not come* to Christ for life and happiness: it is not because they *cannot,* but because they *will not*" (Henry). 4th. Sinners have a particular opposition to going to *Jesus Christ* for eternal life. They would prefer any other way, and it is commonly not until all other means are tried that they are willing to submit to him.

41, 42. *I receive not honour,* &c. "I do not say these things because I am desirous of human applause, but to account for the fact that you do not believe on me. The reason is, that you have not the love of God in you." In this passage we see, 1st. That we should not seek for human applause. It is of very little value, and it often keeps men from the approbation of God, ver. 44. 2d. They who will not believe on Jesus Christ give evidence that they have no love for God. 3d. The reason why they do not believe on him is because they have no regard for his character, wishes, or law. ¶ *Love of God.* Love to God. ¶ *In you.* In your hearts. You do not love God.

43. *I am come in my Father's name.* By the authority of God; or giving proof that I am sent by him. ¶ *If another shall come in his own name.* A false teacher setting up himself, and not even pretending to have a divine commission. The Jews were much accustomed to receive and follow particular teachers. In the time of Christ they were greatly divided between the schools of Hillel and Shammai, two famous teachers. ¶ *Ye will receive.* You will follow, or obey him as a teacher.

44. *Which receive honour one of another.* Who are studious of praise, and live for pride, ambition, and vainglory. This desire, Jesus says, was the great reason why they would not believe on him.

receive honour one of another,
and[t] seek not the honour that
cometh from God only?
45 Do not think that I will
accuse you to the Father: [u]there
is *one* that accuseth you, *even*
Moses, in whom ye trust.
46 For had ye believed Moses,
ye would have believed me; for
[v]he wrote of me.

t Ro.2.10. *u* Ro.2.12. *v* Ge.3.15; 22.18; De.18.15,18; Ac.26.22.

They were unwilling to renounce their worldly honours, and become the followers of one so humble and unostentatious as he was. They expected a Messiah of pomp and splendour, and would not submit to one so despised and of so lowly a rank. Had the Messiah come, as they expected, with pomp and power, it would have been an honour, in their view, to follow him; as it was, they despised and rejected him. The great reason why multitudes do not believe is their attachment to human honours, or their pride, and vanity, and ambition. These are so strong, that while they continue they cannot and will not believe. They might, however, renounce these things, and then, the obstacles being removed, they would believe. Learn, 1. A man *cannot* believe the gospel while he is wholly under the influence of ambition. The two are not compatible. The religion of the gospel is humility, and a man who has not that *cannot* be a Christian. 2. Great numbers are deterred from being Christians by pride and ambition. Probably there is no single thing that prevents so many young men from becoming Christians as this passion. The proud and ambitious heart refuses to bow to the humiliating terms of the gospel. 3. Though while a man is under this governing principle he *cannot* believe the gospel, yet this proves nothing about his *ability* to lay that aside, and to yield to truth. *That* is another question. A child CANNOT open a trunk when he gets on the lid and attempts to raise his own weight and the cover of the trunk too; but that settles nothing about the inquiry whether he might not get off and then open it. The true question is whether a man can or cannot lay aside his ambition and pride, and about that there ought not to be any dispute. No one doubts that it may be done; and if that can be done, he can become a Christian. ¶ *Seek not the honour.* The praise, the glory, the approbation of God. The honour which comes from men is their praise, flattery, commendation; the honour that comes from God is his approbation for doing his will. God alone can confer the honours of heaven—the reward of having done our duty here. That we should seek, and if we seek that, we shall come to Christ, who is the way and the life.

45, 46. *Do not think that I will accuse you.* Do not suppose that I intend to follow your example. They had accused Jesus of breaking the law of God, ver. 16. He says that he will not imitate their example, though he implies that he *might* accuse them. ¶ *To the Father.* To God. ¶ *There is* one *that accuseth you.* Moses might be said to accuse or reprove them. He wrote of the Messiah, clearly foretold his coming, and commanded them to hear him. As they did *not* do it, it might be said that they had disregarded his command; and as Moses was divinely commissioned and had a right to be obeyed, so his command reproved them: they were disobedient and rebellious. ¶ *He wrote of me.* He wrote of the Messiah, and I am the Messiah, Ge. iii. 15; xii. 3; comp. Jn. viii. 56; Ge. xlix. 10; De. xviii. 15.

47. *If ye believe not his writings.* If you do not credit what he has written which you *profess* to believe, it is not to be expected that you will believe my declarations. And from this we may learn, 1st. That many men who *profess* to believe the Bible have really no regard for it when it crosses their own views and inclinations. 2d. It is our duty to study the Bible, that we may be established in the belief that Jesus is the Messiah. 3d. The prophecies of the Old Testament are conclusive proofs of the truth of the Christian religion. 4th. He that rejects one part of the Bible, will, for the same reason, reject all. 5th. The Saviour acknowledged the truth of the writings of Moses, built his religion upon them, appealed to them to prove that he was the Messiah, and commanded men to search them. We have the testimony of Jesus, therefore, that the Old Testament is a revelation from God. He that rejects his testimony on *this* subject must reject his authority altogether; and it is vain for any man to profess to believe in

47 But[w] if ye believe not his writings, how shall ye believe my words?

CHAPTER VI.

AFTER[a] these things Jesus went over the sea of Galilee, which is *the sea* of Tiberias.

2 And a great multitude followed him, because they saw his miracles which he did on them that were diseased.

3 And Jesus went up into a mountain, and there he sat with his disciples.

4 And the passover, a feast of the Jews, was nigh.

5 When Jesus then lifted up *his* eyes, and saw a great company come unto him, he saith unto Philip, Whence shall we buy bread, that these may eat?

6 And this he said to prove him; for he himself knew what he would do.

7 Philip answered him, [b]Two hundred pennyworth of bread is not sufficient for them, that every one of them may take a little.

8 One of his disciples, Andrew, Simon Peter's brother, saith unto him,

9 There is a lad here which hath five barley-loaves and two small fishes; but what are they among so many?

10 And Jesus said, Make the men sit down. Now there was much grass in the place. So the men sat down, in number about five thousand.

11 And Jesus took the loaves; and when he had given thanks, he distributed to the disciples, and the disciples to them that were set down; and likewise of the fishes as much as they would.

12 When they were [c]filled, he said unto his disciples, Gather up the fragments that remain, [d]that nothing be lost.

13 Therefore they gathered *them*

w Lu.16.31.
a Mat.14.15,&c.; Mar.6.34,&c.; Lu.9.12,&c.
b Nu.11.21,22; 2 Ki.4.43.
c Ne.9.25. d Ne.8.10.

---

the New Testament, or in the Lord Jesus, without also acknowledging the authority of the Old Testament and of Moses.

We have in this chapter an instance of the profound and masterly manner in which Jesus could meet and silence his enemies. There is not anywhere a more conclusive argument, or a more triumphant meeting of the charges which they had brought against him. No one can read this without being struck with his profound wisdom; and it is scarcely possible to conceive that there could be a more distinct declaration and proof that he was equal with God.

CHAPTER VI.

1. *Jesus went over.* Went to the east side of the sea. The place to which he went was Bethsaida, Lu. ix. 10. The account of this miracle of feeding the five thousand is recorded also in Mat. xiv. 13-21; Mar. vi. 32-44; Lu. ix. 10-17. John has added a few circumstances omitted by the other evangelists.

2. *Because they saw his miracles*, &c. They saw that he had the power to supply their wants, and they therefore followed him. See ver. 26. Comp. also Mat. xiv. 14.

4. *The passover.* See Notes on Mat. xxvi. 2, 17. ¶ *A feast of the Jews.* This is one of the circumstances of explanation thrown in by John which show that he wrote for those who were unacquainted with Jewish customs.

6. *To prove him.* To try him; to see if he had faith, or if he would show that he believed that Jesus had power to supply them.

12. *Gather up the fragments.* This command is omitted by the other evangelists. It shows the care of Jesus that there should be no waste. Though he had power to provide any quantity of food, yet he has here taught us that the bounties of Providence are not to be squandered. In all things the Saviour set us an example of frugality, though he had an infinite supply at his disposal; he was himself economical, though he was Lord of all. If *he* was thus saving, it becomes *us* dependent creatures not to waste the bounties of a

together, and filled twelve baskets
with the fragments of the five
barley-loaves, which remained over
and above unto them that had
eaten.
14 Then those men, when they
had seen the miracle that Jesus
did, said, This is of a truth [e]that
Prophet that should come into the
world.
15 When Jesus therefore perceived that they would come and
take him by force, to make him
a king, he departed again into a
mountain himself alone.
16 And[f] when even was *now*
come, his disciples went down unto
the sea,
17 And entered into a ship, and
went over the sea toward Capernaum. And it was now dark, and
Jesus was not come to them.
18 And[g] the sea arose, by reason
of a great wind that blew.
19 So when they had rowed
about five and twenty or thirty
furlongs, they see Jesus walking
on the sea, and drawing nigh unto
the ship; and they were afraid.
20 But he saith unto them, [h]It
is I; be not afraid.
21 Then they willingly received
him into the ship; and immediately the ship was at the land
whither they went.
22 The day following, when the
people which stood on the other
side of the sea saw that there was

e Ge.49.10; De.18.15-18. f Mat.14.23; Mar.6.47,&c. g Ps.107.25. h Ps.35.3; Is.43.1,2; Re.1.17,18.

---

beneficent Providence. And it especially becomes the rich not to squander the bounties of Providence. They often *feel* that they are rich. They have enough. They have no fear of want, and they do not feel the necessity of studying economy. Yet let them remember that what they have is the gift of God—just as certainly as the loaves and fishes created by the Saviour were his gift. It is not given them to waste, nor to spend in riot, nor to be the means of injuring their health or of shortening life. It is given to sustain life, to excite gratitude, to fit for the active service of God. Everything should be applied to its appropriate end, and nothing should be squandered or lost.

14. *That Prophet*, &c. The Messiah. The *power* to work the miracle, and the benevolence manifested in it, showed that he was the long-expected Messiah.

15. *When Jesus perceived*, &c. They were satisfied by the miracle that he was the Messiah. They supposed that the Messiah was to be a temporal prince. They saw that Jesus was retiring, unambitious, and indisposed to assume the ensigns of office. They thought, therefore, that they would proclaim him as the long-expected king, and constrain him to assume the character and titles of an earthly prince. Men often attempt to dictate to God, and suppose that they understand what is right better than he does. They are fond of pomp and power, but Jesus sought retirement, and evinced profound humility. Though he had *claims* to the honour and gratitude of the nation, yet he sought it not in this way; nor did it evince a proper spirit in his followers when they sought to advance him to a place of external splendour and regal authority.

16–21. See this miracle of walking on the sea explained in the Notes on Mat. xiv. 22–33. Comp. Mar. vi. 45–52.

21. *Immediately*. Quickly. Before a long time. How far they were from the land we know not, but there is no evidence that there was a *miracle* in the case. The word translated *immediately* does not of necessity imply that there was no interval of time, but that there was not a long interval. Thus in Mat. xiii. 5, in the parable of the sower, "and *forthwith* (the same word in Greek) they sprung up," &c., Mar. iv. 17; Mat. xxiv. 29; 3 Jn. 14.

22. *The people which stood on the other side of the sea*. That is, on the *east* side, or on the same side with Jesus. The country was called the region *beyond* or *on the other side* of the sea, because the writer and the people lived on the west side. ¶ *Jesus went not with his disciples*. He had gone into a mountain to pray alone, ver. 15. Comp. Mar. vi. 46.

23. *There came other boats*. After the disciples had departed. This is added because, from what follows, it appears that they supposed that he had entered one of those boats and gone to Capernaum after his disciples had departed.

none other boat there, save that
one whereinto his disciples were
entered, and that Jesus went not
with his disciples into the boat,
but *that* his disciples were gone
away alone:
23 (Howbeit there came other
boats from Tiberias, nigh unto [i]the
place where they did eat bread,
after that the Lord had given
thanks:)
24 When the people, therefore,
saw that Jesus was not there, neither his disciples, they also took
shipping and came to Capernaum,
seeking for Jesus.
25 And when they had found
him on the other side of the sea,
they said unto him, Rabbi, when
camest thou hither?
26 Jesus answered them and
said, Verily, verily, I say unto you,

i ver.11.

¶ *From Tiberias.* This town stood on the western borders of the lake, not far from where the miracle had been wrought. It was so called in honour of the Emperor Tiberius. It was built by Herod Antipas, and was made by him the capital of Galilee. The city afterward became a celebrated seat of Jewish learning. It is now called *Tabaria*, and is a considerable place. It is occupied chiefly by Turks, and is very hot and unhealthy. Mr. Fisk, an American missionary, was at Tiberias (Tabaria) in 1823. The old town is surrounded by a wall, but within it is very ruinous, and the plain for a mile or two south is strewed with ruins. The Jordan, where it issues from the lake, was so shallow that cattle and asses forded it easily. Mr. Fisk was shown a house called the house of Peter, which is used as the Greek Catholic church, and is the only church in the place. The number of Christian families is thirty or forty, all Greek Catholics. There were two sects of Jews, each of whom had a synagogue. The Jewish population was estimated at about one thousand. On the 1st of January, 1837, Tiberias was destroyed by an earthquake. Dr. Thomson (*The Land and the Book*, vol. ii. p. 76, 77) says of this city: "Ever since the destruction of Jerusalem, it has been chiefly celebrated in connection with the Jews, and was for a long time the chief seat of rabbinical learning. It is still one of their four holy cities. Among the Christians it also early rose to distinction, and the old church, built upon the spot where our Lord gave his last charge to Peter, is a choice bit of ecclesiastical antiquity. The present city is situated on the shore, at the north-east corner of this small plain. The walls inclose an irregular parallelogram, about 100 rods from north to south, and in breadth not more than 40. They were strengthened by ten round towers on the west, five on the north, and eight on the south. There were also two or three towers along the shore to protect the city from attack by sea. Not much more than one-half of this small area is occupied by buildings of any kind, and the north end, which is a rocky hill, has nothing but the ruins of the old palace. The earthquake of 1837 prostrated a large part of the walls, and they have not yet been repaired, and perhaps never will be. There is no town in Syria so utterly filthy as Tiberias, or so little to be desired as a residence. Being *600 feet* below the level of the ocean, and overhung on the west by a high mountain, which effectually shuts off the Mediterranean breezes, it is fearfully hot in summer. The last time I was encamped at the Baths the thermometer stood at 100° *at midnight*, and a steam went up from the surface of the lake as from some huge smouldering volcano. Of course it swarms with all sorts of vermin. What can induce human beings to settle down in such a place? And yet some two thousand of our race make it their chosen abode. They are chiefly Jews, attracted hither either to cleanse their leprous bodies in her baths, or to purify their unclean spirits by contact with her traditionary and ceremonial holiness."

24. *Took shipping.* Went into the boats. ¶ *Came to Capernaum.* This was the ordinary place of the residence of Jesus, and they therefore expected to find him there.

26. *Ye seek me, not because*, &c. The *miracles* which Jesus wrought were proofs that he came from God. To seek him because they had seen them, and were convinced by them that he was the Messiah, would have been proper; but to follow him simply because

Ye seek me, not because ye saw the miracles, but because ye did eat of the loaves and were filled.

27 Labour[1] not for the meat which perisheth, but for [k]that meat which endureth unto everlasting life, which the Son of man shall give unto you; for [l]him hath God the Father sealed.

28 Then said they unto him, What shall we do, that we might work the works of God?

29 Jesus answered and said unto them, [m]This is the work of God, that ye believe on him whom he hath sent.

30 They said, therefore, unto him, What [n]sign showest thou

1 or, *Work not.* *k* Je.15.16; ch.4.14; ver.54,58. *l* Ps.2.7; 40.7; Is.42.1; ch.8.18; Ac.2.22; 2 Pe.1.17.

m 1 Jn.3.23. *n* Mat.12.38; 1 Co.1.22.

their wants were supplied was mere selfishness of a gross kind. Yet, alas! many seek religion from no better motive than this. They suppose that it will add to their earthly happiness, or they seek *only* to escape from suffering or from the convictions of conscience, or they seek for heaven *only* as a place of enjoyment, and regard religion as valuable *only* for this. All this is mere selfishness. Religion does not *forbid* our regarding our own happiness, or seeking it in any proper way; but when this is the *only* or the *prevailing* motive, it is evident that we have never yet sought God aright. We are aiming at the loaves and fishes, and not at the honour of God and the good of his kingdom; and if this is the only or the main motive of our entering the church, we *cannot* be Christians.

27. *Labour not.* This does not mean that we are to make *no effort* for the supply of our wants (comp. 1 Ti. v. 1; 2 Th. iii. 10), but that we are not to manifest anxiety, we are not to make this the main or supreme object of our desire. See Notes on Mat. vi. 25. ¶ *The meat that perisheth.* The food for the supply of your natural wants. It perishes. The strength you derive from it is soon exhausted, and your wasted powers need to be reinvigorated. ¶ *That meat which endureth.* The supply of your spiritual wants; that which supports, and nourishes, and strengthens the soul; the doctrines of the gospel, that are to a weak and guilty soul what needful food is to the weary and decaying body. ¶ *To everlasting life.* The strength derived from the doctrines of the gospel is not exhausted. It endures without wasting away. It nourishes the soul to everlasting life. "They that wait upon the Lord shall renew their strength; they shall run and not be weary, and shall walk and not faint," Is. xl. 31. ¶ *Him hath God the Father sealed.* To *seal* is to confirm or approve as *ours.* This is done when we set our seal to a compact, or deed, or testament, by which we ratify it as *our act.* So God the Father, by the miracles which had been wrought by Jesus, had shown that he had sent him, that he approved his doctrines, and ratified his works. The *miracles* were to his doctrine what *a seal* is to a written instrument. See Notes on Jn. iii. 33.

28. *What shall we do, that we might work the works of God?* That is, such things as God will approve. This was the earnest inquiry of men who were seeking to be saved. They had crossed the Sea of Tiberias to seek him; they supposed him to be the Messiah, and they sincerely desired to be taught the way of life; yet it is observable that they expected to find that way as other sinners commonly do—by *their works.* The idea of doing something to *merit* salvation is one of the last that the sinner ever surrenders.

29. *This is the work of God.* This is the thing that will be acceptable to God, or which you are to do in order to be saved. Jesus did not tell them they had *nothing to do*, or that they were to sit down and wait, but that there *was* a work to perform, and that was a duty that was imperative. It was to believe on the Messiah. This is the work which sinners are to do; and doing this they will be saved, for Christ is the end of the law for righteousness to every one that believeth, Ro. x. 4.

30. *What sign showest thou?* On the word *sign*, comp. Notes on Is. vii. 14. What miracle dost thou work to prove that thou art the Messiah? They had just seen the miracle of the loaves in the desert, which was sufficient to show that he was the Messiah, and it would seem from the preceding narrative that those who crossed the lake to see him supposed that he was the Christ. It seems wonderful that they should so

then, that we may see and believe
thee? what dost thou work?
31 Our[o] fathers did eat manna
in the desert; as it is written, [p]He
gave them bread from heaven to
eat.
32 Then Jesus said unto them,
Verily, verily, I say unto you, Moses gave you not that bread from
heaven; but [q]my Father giveth
you the true bread from heaven.
33 For the [r]bread of God is he
which cometh down from heaven,
and giveth life unto the world.

o Ex.16.15; Nu.11.7; 1 Co.10.3. *p* Ne.9.15; Ps.78.24,25. *q* Ga.4.4. *r* ver.48,58.

---

soon ask for farther evidence that he was sent from God; but it is not improbable that this question was put by *other Jews*, rulers of the synagogue, who happened to be present, and who had not witnessed his miracles. Those men were continually asking for *signs* and proofs that he was the Messiah. See Mat. xii. 38, 39; Mar. viii. 11; Lu. xi. 29. As Jesus claimed the right of teaching them, and as it was manifest that he would teach them differently from what *they* supposed Moses to teach, it was natural to ask him by what authority he claimed the right to be heard.

31. *Our fathers.* The Jews who were led by Moses through the wilderness. ¶ *Did eat manna.* This was the name given by the Jews to the food which was furnished to them by God in their journey. It means literally, "What is this?" and was the question which they asked when they first saw it, Ex. xvi. 14, 15. It was small like frost, and of the size of coriander-seed, and had a sweetish taste like honey. It fell in great quantities, and was regarded by the Jews as proof of a continued miracle during forty years, and was incontestable evidence of the interposition of God in favour of their fathers. The manna which is sold in the shops of druggists is a different substance from this. It is obtained from the bark of certain trees in Armenia, Georgia, Persia, and Arabia. It is procured, as resin is, by making an incision in the bark, and it flows out or distils from the tree. ¶ *As it is written.* The substance of this is written in Ps. lxxviii. 24, 25. ¶ *He gave them.* This was regarded as a miraculous interference in their behalf, and an attestation of the divine mission of Moses, and hence they said familiarly that *Moses* gave it to them. ¶ *Bread from heaven.* The word *heaven*, in the Scriptures, denotes often the region of the *air*, the atmosphere, or that region in which the clouds are. See Mat. xvi. 3: "The sky (heaven) is red and lowering." Also Mat. iii. 16; Lu. iv. 15; v. 18. The Jews, as appears from their writings (see Lightfoot), expected that the Messiah would provide his followers with plenty of delicious food; and as *Moses* had provided for the Jews in the wilderness, so they supposed that Christ would make provision for the temporal wants of his friends. This was *the sign*, probably, which they were now desirous of seeing.

32. *Moses gave you not that bread from heaven.* This might be translated, "Moses gave you not *the* bread of heaven." The word "that," which makes some difference in the sense, is not necessary to express the meaning of the original. It does not appear that Jesus intended to call in question the fact that their fathers were fed by the instrumentality of Moses, but to state that he did not give them the true bread that was adapted to the wants of the *soul.* He fed the body, although his food did not keep the body alive (ver. 49), but he did not give that which would preserve the soul from death. God gave, in his Son Jesus, the true bread from heaven which was fitted to man, and of far more value than any supply of their temporal wants. He tells them, therefore, that they are not to seek from him any such supply of their temporal wants as they had supposed. A better gift had been furnished in *his* being given for the life of the world. ¶ *My father giveth you.* In the gospel; in the gift of his Son. ¶ *The true bread.* The *true* or *real* support which is needed to keep the soul from death. It is not false, deceitful, or perishing. Christ is called *bread*, because, as bread supports life, so his doctrine supports, preserves, and saves the soul from death. He is the *true* support, not only in opposition to the mere supply of *temporal* wants such as Moses furnished, but also in opposition to all false religion which deceives and destroys the soul.

33. *The bread of God.* The means of

34 Then said they unto him, Lord, evermore give us this bread.
35 And Jesus said unto them, I am the bread of life: [s]he that cometh to me shall never hunger, and [t]he that believeth on me shall never thirst.
36 But I said unto you, [u]That ye also have seen me, and believe not.
37 All[v] that the Father giveth me shall come to me; and [w]him that cometh to me I will in no wise cast out.

s Re.7.16. t ch.4.14; 7.38.

u ver.64. v ver.45; ch.17.6,8,&c. w Ps.102.17; Is.1.18; 55.7; Mat.11.28; Lu.23.42,43; 1 Ti.1.15,16; Re.22.17.

support which God furnishes. That which, in his view, is needful for man. ¶ *Is he*, &c. Is the Messiah who has come from heaven. ¶ *And giveth life*, &c. See Notes on Jn. i. 4.

35. *I am the bread of life.* I am the *support* of spiritual life; or my doctrines will give life and peace to the soul. ¶ *Shall never hunger.* See Notes on Jn. iv. 14.

36. *But I said unto you.* This he said, not in so many words, but *in substance*, in ver. 26. Though they saw him, and had full proof of his divine mission, yet they did not believe. Jesus then proceeds to state that, although *they* did not believe on him, yet his work would not be in vain, for others would come to him and be saved.

37. *All.* The original word is in the neuter gender, but it is used, doubtless, for the masculine, or perhaps refers to his people considered as a *mass* or *body*, and means that *every individual* that the Father had given him should come to him. ¶ *The Father giveth me.* We here learn that those who come to Christ, and who will be saved, are *given* to him by God. 1st. God promised him that he should see of the travail of his soul—that is, "the fruit of his wearisome toil" (Lowth), and should be satisfied, Is. liii. 11. 2d. All men are sinners, and none have any *claim* to mercy, and he may therefore bestow salvation on whom he pleases. 3d. All men of themselves are disposed to reject the gospel, Jn. v. 40. 4th. God enables those who do believe to do it. He draws them to him by his Word and Spirit; he opens their hearts to understand the Scriptures (Ac. xvi. 14); and he grants to them repentance, Ac. xi. 18; 2 Ti. ii. 25. 5th. All those who become Christians may therefore be said to be *given* to Jesus as the reward of his sufferings, for his death was the price by which they were redeemed. Paul says (Ep. i. 4, 5) that, "he hath chosen us in him (that is, in Christ) before the foundation of the world, that we should be holy and without blame before him in love; having predestinated us unto the adoption of children to himself, according to the good pleasure of his will." ¶ *Shall come to me.* This is an expression denoting that they would *believe* on him. To *come to* one implies our need of help, our confidence that he can aid us, and our readiness to trust to him. The sinner comes to Jesus feeling that he is poor, and needy, and wretched, and casts himself on his mercy, believing that he alone can save him. This expression also proves that men are not *compelled* to believe on Christ. Though they who believe are *given* to him, and though his Spirit works in them faith and repentance, yet they are made *willing* in the day of his power, Ps. cx. 3. No man is *compelled* to go to heaven against his will, and no man is *compelled* to go to hell against his will. The Spirit of God inclines the will of one, and he *comes* freely as a moral agent. The other *chooses* the way to death; and, though God is constantly using means to save him, yet he prefers the path that leads down to woe. ¶ *Him that cometh.* Every one that comes—that is, every one that comes in a proper manner, feeling that he is a lost and ruined sinner. This invitation is wide, and full, and free. It shows the unbounded mercy of God; and it shows, also, that the reason, and the only reason, why men are not saved, is that they will not come to Christ. Of any sinner it may be said that if he had been willing to come to Christ he *might* have come and been saved. As he *chooses not* to come, he cannot blame God because he saves others who *are* willing, no matter from what cause, and who thus are made partakers of everlasting life. ¶ *In no wise.* In no manner, or at no time. The original is simply, "I will *not* cast out." ¶ *Cast out.* Reject, or refuse to save. This expression does not refer to the doctrine of perseverance of the saints, but

38 For I came down from heaven, not to do mine own will, [x]but the will of him that sent me.

39 And this is the [y]Father's will which hath sent me, that of all which he hath given me I should lose nothing, but should raise it up again at the last day.

40 And this is the will of him that sent me, [z]that every one which seeth the Son, and believeth on him, may have everlasting life; and [a]I will raise him up at the last day.

41 The Jews then murmured at him because he said, I am the

x Ps.40.7,8; ch.5.30.
y Mat.18.14; ch.10.28; 17.12; 18.9; 2 Ti.2.19.
z ver.47,54; ch.3.15,16. a ch.11.25.

to the fact that Jesus will not *reject* or *refuse* any sinner who comes to him.

38. *For I came down*, &c. This verse shows that he came for a specific purpose, which he states in the next verse, and means that, as he came to do his Father's will, he would be faithful to the trust. Though his hearers should reject him, yet the will of God would be accomplished in the salvation of some who should come to him. ¶ *Mine own will.* See Notes on Jn. v. 30.

39. *Father's will.* His purpose; desire; intention. As this is the Father's will, and Jesus came to execute his will, we have the highest security that it will be done. God's will is always right, and he has power to execute it. Jesus was always faithful, and all power was given to him in heaven and on earth, and he will therefore most certainly accomplish the will of God. ¶ *Of all which.* That is, of every one who believes on him, or of all who become Christians. See ver. 37. ¶ *I should lose nothing.* Literally, "I should not *destroy.*" He affirms here that he will keep it to life eternal; that, though the Christian will die, and his body return to corruption, yet he will not be *destroyed.* The Redeemer will watch over him, though in his grave, and keep him to the resurrection of the just. This is affirmed of all who are given to him by the Father; or, as in the next verse, "*Every one* that believeth on him shall have everlasting life." ¶ *At the last day.* At the day of judgment. The Jews supposed that the *righteous* would be raised up at the appearing of the Messiah. See Lightfoot. Jesus directs them to a *future* resurrection, and declares to them that they will be raised at the *last* day—the day of judgment. It is also supposed and affirmed by some Jewish writers that they did not believe that the *wicked* would be raised. Hence, to speak of being raised up in the last day was the same as to say that one was righteous, or it was spoken of as the peculiar privilege of the righteous. In accordance with this, Paul says, "If by any means I might attain *unto the resurrection of the dead*," Phi. iii. 11.

40. *Every one which seeth the Son, and believeth on him.* It was not sufficient to see him and hear him, but it was necessary, also, to *believe* on him. Many of the Jews had *seen* him, but few believed on him. Jesus had said in the previous verse that all that the Father *had given him* should be saved. But he never left a doctrine so that men *must* misunderstand it. Lest it should be supposed that if a man was *given* to him this was all that was needful, and lest anyone should say, "If I am to be saved I shall be, and my efforts will be useless," he states here that it is necessary that a man should *believe* on him. This would be the *evidence* that he was given to God, and this would be evidence conclusive that he would be saved. If this explanation of the Saviour had always been attended to, the doctrine of election would not have been abused as it has been. Sinners would not sit down in unconcern, saying that if they are *given* to Christ all will be well. They would have arisen like the prodigal, and would have gone to God; and, having *believed* on the Saviour, they would *then* have had evidence that they were *given* to him—the evidence resulting from an humble, penitent, believing heart—and *then* they might rejoice in the assurance that Jesus would lose none that were given to him, but would raise it up at the last day. All the doctrines of Jesus, as *he* preached them, are safe, and pure, and consistent; as *men* preach them, they are, unhappily, often inconsistent and open to objection, and are either fitted to produce despair on the one hand, or presumptuous self-confidence on the other. Jesus teaches men to strive to enter heaven, as if they could do the work themselves; and yet to depend on the help

bread which came down from heaven.

42 And they said, [b]Is not this Jesus, the son of Joseph, whose father and mother we know? How is it then that he saith, I came down from heaven?

43 Jesus therefore answered and said unto them, Murmur not among yourselves.

44 No man can come to me except the Father, which hath sent me, [c]draw him; and I will raise him up at the last day.

45 It is written [d]in the prophets, And they shall be all taught of God. Every[e] man, therefore, that hath heard, and hath learned of the Father, cometh unto me.

46 Not[f] that any man hath seen

b Mat.13.55; Mar.6.3; Lu.4.22.

c Ca.1.4. d Is.54.13; Je.31.34; Mi.4.2. e Mat.11.27. f ch.5.37.

of God, and give the glory to him, as if he had done it all.

44. *No man can come to me.* This was spoken by Jesus to reprove their murmurings—"Murmur not among yourselves." They objected to his doctrine, or murmured against it, because he claimed to be greater than Moses, and because they supposed him to be a mere man, and that what he said was impossible. Jesus does not deny that these things appeared difficult, and hence he said that if any man believed, it was proof that God had inclined him. It was not to be expected that *of themselves* they would embrace the doctrine. If any man believed, it would be because he had been influenced by God. When we inquire what the reasons were why they did not believe, they appear to have been—1st. Their improper regard for Moses, as if no one could be superior to him. 2d. Their unwillingness to believe that Jesus, whom they knew to be the reputed son of a carpenter, should be superior to Moses. 3d. The difficulty was explained by Jesus (Jn. v. 40) as consisting in the opposition of their will; and (Jn. v. 44) when he said that their love of *honour* prevented their believing on him. The difficulty in the case was not, therefore, a want of natural faculties, or of power to do their duty, but erroneous opinions, pride, obstinacy, self-conceit, and a deep-felt contempt for Jesus. The word "*cannot*" is often used to denote a strong and violent opposition of the *will.* Thus we say a man is so great a liar that he cannot speak the truth, or he is so profane that he cannot but swear. We mean by it that he is so wicked that while he has that disposition the other effects will follow, but we do not mean to say that he could not break off from the habit. Thus it is said (Ge. xxxvii. 4) of the brethren of Joseph that they *hated him, and could not speak peaceably to him.* Thus (Mat. xii. 34), "How *can* ye, being evil, speak good things?" See Lu. xiv. 33; 1 Sa. xvi. 2. ¶ *Come to me.* The same as believe on me. ¶ *Draw him.* This word is used here, evidently, to denote such an influence from God as to secure the result, or as to incline the mind to believe; yet the *manner* in which this is done is not determined by the use of the word. It is used in the New Testament six times. Once it is applied to a compulsory drawing of Paul and Silas to the market-place, Ac. xvi. 19. Twice it is used to denote the drawing of a net, Jn. xxi. 6, 11. Once to the drawing of a sword (Jn. xviii. 10); and once in a sense similar to its use here (Jn. xii. 32): "And I, if I be lifted up from the earth, will *draw* all men unto me." What is its meaning here must be determined by the *facts* about the sinner's conversion. See Notes on ver. 40. In the conversion of the sinner God enlightens the mind (ver. 45), he inclines the will (Ps. cx. 3), and he influences the soul by motives, by just views of his law, by his love, his commands, and his threatenings; by a desire of happiness, and a consciousness of danger; by the Holy Spirit applying truth to the mind, and urging him to yield himself to the Saviour. So that, while God inclines him, and will have all the glory, man yields without compulsion; the obstacles are removed, and he becomes a willing servant of God.

45. *In the prophets.* Is. liv. 13. A similar sentiment is found in Mi. iv. 1–4, and Je. xxxi. 34; but by the *prophets,* here, is meant *the book of the prophets,* and it is probable that Jesus had reference only to the place in Isaiah, as this was the usual way of quoting the prophets. ¶ *Shall be all taught of God.*

the Father, [g]save he which is of
God; he hath seen the Father.
47 Verily, verily, I say unto you,
He[h] that believeth on me hath
everlasting life.
48 I[i] am that bread of life.
49 Your fathers did eat manna
in the wilderness, and [k]are dead.
50 This is the bread which
cometh down from heaven, that a
man may eat thereof, and [l]not die.
51 I am the living bread which
came down from heaven. If any
man eat of this bread he shall live
for ever; and the bread that I will
give is [m]my flesh, which I will give
for [n]the life of the world.
52 The Jews therefore strove
among themselves, saying, [o]How
can this man give us *his* flesh to
eat?
53 Then Jesus said unto them,

g Lu.10.22. h ver.40. i ver.33,35,51. k Zec.1.5. l ver.58. m He.10.5,10,20. n ch.3.16; 1 Jn.2.2. o ch.3.9.

This explains the preceding verse. It is by the *teaching* of his Word and Spirit that men are *drawn* to God. This shows that it is not *compulsory*, and that there is no obstacle in the way but a strong voluntary ignorance and unwillingness.

46. *Not that any man hath seen the Father.* Jesus added this, evidently, to guard against mistake. He had said that all who came to him were *taught* of God. The *teacher* was commonly *seen* and *heard* by the pupil; but, lest it should be supposed that he meant to say that a man to come to him must *see* and *hear* God, visibly and audibly, he adds that he did not intend to affirm this. It was still true that no man had seen God at any time. They were not, therefore, to *expect* to see God, and his words were not to be *perverted* as if he meant to teach that. ¶ *Save he which is of God.* Jesus here evidently refers to himself as the Son of God. He had just said that no *man* had seen the Father. When he affirms that *he* has seen the Father, it implies that he is more than man. He is the only-begotten Son who is in the bosom of the Father, Jn. i. 18; the brightness of his glory, and the express image of his person, He. i. 3; God over all, blessed for ever, Ro. ix. 5. By his being *of God* is meant that he is the only-begotten Son of God, and sent as the Messiah into the world. ¶ *Hath seen.* Hath intimately known or perceived him. He knows his nature, character, plans. This is a claim to knowledge superior to what man possesses, and it cannot be understood except by supposing that Jesus is equal with God.

48. *I am that bread of life.* My doctrines and the benefits of my mediation are that *real* support of spiritual life of which the manna in the wilderness was the faint emblem. See ver. 32, 33.

49. *Your fathers did eat manna.* There was a real miracle wrought in their behalf; there was a perpetual interposition of God which showed that they were his chosen people. ¶ *And are dead.* The bread which they ate could not save them from death. Though God interfered in their behalf, yet they died. We may learn, 1st. That that is not the most valuable of God's gifts which merely satisfies the temporal wants. 2d. That the most distinguished temporal blessings will not save from death. Wealth, friends, food, raiment, will not preserve life. 3d. There is need of something better than mere earthly blessings; there is need of that bread which cometh down from heaven, and which giveth life to the world.

51. *The bread that I will give is my flesh.* That is, his body would be offered as a sacrifice for sin, agreeably to his declaration when he instituted the Supper: "This is my body which is broken for you," 1 Co. xi. 24. ¶ *Life of the world.* That sinners might, by his atoning sacrifice, be recovered from spiritual death, and be brought to eternal life. The use of the word *world* here shows that the sacrifice of Christ was full, free, ample, and designed for all men, as it is said in 1 Jn. ii. 2, "He is the propitiation for our sins, and not for ours only, but also for the sins of the whole world." In this verse Jesus introduces the subject of his *death* and atonement. It may be remarked that in the language which he used the transition from *bread* to his *flesh* would appear more easy than it does in our language. The same word which in Hebrew means *bread*, in the Syriac and Arabic means also *flesh*.

53–55. In these verses Jesus repeats

Verily, verily, I say unto you, [p]Except ye eat the flesh of the Son of man, and drink his blood, ye have no life in you.

54 Whoso[q] eateth my flesh, and drinketh my blood, hath eternal life, and I will raise him up at the last day.

55 For my flesh is [r]meat indeed, and my blood is drink indeed.

56 He that [s]eateth my flesh, and drinketh my blood, [t]dwelleth in me, and I in him.

57 As the living Father hath sent me, and I live by the Father, [u]so he that eateth me, even he shall live by me.

58 This is that bread which came down from heaven: [v]not as your fathers did eat manna, and are dead: he that eateth of this bread shall live for ever.

p Mat.26.26,28. *q* ver.40. *r* Ps.4.7. *s* La.3.24. *t* ch.15.4; 1 Jn.3.24; 4.15,16. *u* 1 Co.15.22. *v* ver.49-51.

---

what he had in substance said before. ¶ *Except ye eat the flesh,* &c. He did not mean that this should be understood *literally,* for it was never done, and it is absurd to suppose that it was intended to be so understood. Nothing can *possibly* be more absurd than to suppose that when he instituted the Supper, and gave the bread and wine to his disciples, they literally ate his flesh and drank his blood. Who *can* believe this? There he stood, a living man—his body yet alive, his blood flowing in his veins; and how can it be believed that this body was eaten and this blood drunk? Yet this absurdity must be held by those who hold that the bread and wine at the communion are "changed into the body, blood, and *divinity* of our Lord." So it is taught in the decrees of the Council of Trent; and to such absurdities are men driven when they depart from the simple meaning of the Scriptures and from common sense. It may be added that if the bread and wine used in the Lord's Supper were not changed into his literal body and blood when it was first instituted, they have never been since. The Lord Jesus would institute it just as he meant it should be observed, and there is nothing *now* in that ordinance which there was not when the Saviour first appointed it. His body was offered on the cross, and was raised up from the dead and received into heaven. Besides, there is no evidence that he had any reference in this passage to the Lord's Supper. That was not yet instituted, and in that there was no literal eating of his flesh and drinking of his blood. The plain meaning of the passage is, that by his bloody death—his body and his blood offered in sacrifice for sin—he would procure pardon and life for man; that they who partook of that, or had an interest in that, should obtain eternal life. He uses the figure of eating and drinking because that was the subject of discourse; because the Jews prided themselves much on the fact that their fathers had eaten *manna;* and because, as he had said that he was the *bread* of life, it was natural and easy, especially in the language which he used, to *carry out the figure,* and say that bread must be eaten in order to be of any avail in supporting and saving men. To eat and to drink, among the Jews, was also expressive of *sharing in* or *partaking of* the privileges of friendship. The happiness of heaven and all spiritual blessings are often represented under this image, Mat. viii. 11; xxvi. 29; Lu. xiv. 15, &c.

55. *Is meat indeed.* Is truly food. My doctrine is truly that which will give life to the soul.

56. *Dwelleth in me.* Is truly and intimately connected with me. To dwell or abide in him is to remain in the belief of his doctrine, and in the participation of the benefits of his death. Comp. Jn. xv. 1-6; xvii. 21-23. ¶ *I in him.* Jesus dwells in believers by his Spirit and doctrine. When his Spirit is given them to sanctify them; when his temper, his meekness, his humility, and his love pervade their hearts; when his doctrine is received by them and influences their life, and when they are supported by the consolations of the gospel, it may be said that he *abides* or dwells in them.

57. *I live by the Father.* See Notes on Jn. v. 26.

58. *This is that bread,* &c. This is *the* true bread that came down. The word "that" should not be in the translation. ¶ *Shall live for ever.* Not on

59 These things said he in the synagogue, as he taught in Capernaum.

60 Many, therefore, of his disciples, when they had heard *this*, said, This is an hard saying; who can hear it?

61 When Jesus knew in himself that his disciples murmured at it, he said unto them, Doth this offend you?

62 *What* and if ye shall see the Son of man [w]ascend up where he was before?

63 It[x] is the Spirit that quickeneth; the flesh profiteth nothing: the words that I speak unto you, *they* are spirit and *they* are life.

w ch.3.13; Mar.16.19; Ep.4.8-10. x 2 Co.3.6.

the earth, but in the enjoyments of a better world.

60. *Many of his disciples.* The word *disciple* means *learner*. It was applied to the followers of Christ because they were *taught* by him. It does not imply, of necessity, that those to whom it was given were real Christians, but simply that they were under his *teaching*, and were professed learners in his school. See Mat. xvii. 16; Mar. ii. 18; Jn. ix. 28; Mat. x. 24. It is doubtless used in this sense here. It is, however, often applied to those who are real Christians. ¶ *This is an hard saying.* The word *hard* here means *offensive*, *disagreeable*—that which they could not bear. Some have understood it to mean "difficult to be understood," but this meaning does not suit the connection. The doctrine which he delivered was opposed to their prejudices; it seemed to be absurd, and they therefore rejected it. ¶ *Saying.* Rather *doctrine* or *speech*—Greek, *logos.* It does not refer to any *particular part* of the discourse, but includes the whole. ¶ *Who can hear it?* That is, who can hear it *patiently*—who can stay and listen to such doctrine or believe it. The effect of this is stated in ver. 66. The doctrines which Jesus taught that were so offensive appear to have been, 1st. That he was superior to Moses. 2d. That God would save all that he had chosen, and those only. 3d. That he said he was the bread that came from heaven. 4th. That it was necessary to partake of that; or that it was necessary that an *atonement* should be made, and that they should be saved by that. These doctrines have always been among the most offensive that men have been called on to believe, and many, rather than trust in them, have chosen to draw back to perdition.

62. What *and if*, &c. Jesus does not say that those who were then present would see him ascend, but he implies that he would ascend. They had taken offence because he said he came down from heaven. Instead of explaining that away, he proceeds to state another doctrine quite as offensive to them—that he would reascend to heaven. The apostles only were present at his ascension, Ac. i. 9. As Jesus was to *ascend* to heaven, it was clear that he could not have intended *literally* that they should eat his flesh.

63. *It is the Spirit that quickeneth.* These words have been understood in different ways. The word "Spirit," here, evidently does not refer to the Holy Ghost, for he adds, "The words that I speak unto you, they are *spirit*." He refers here, probably, to the doctrine which *he* had been teaching in opposition to *their* notions and desires. "*My* doctrine is spiritual; it is fitted to quicken and nourish the soul. It is from heaven. Your doctrine or your views are *earthly*, and may be called *flesh*, or fleshly, as pertaining only to the support of the body. You place a great value on the doctrine that Moses fed the *body;* yet that did not permanently *profit*, for your fathers are dead. You seek also food from me, but your views and desires are gross and earthly." ¶ *Quickeneth.* Gives life. See Notes on ch. v. 21. ¶ *The flesh.* Your carnal views and desires, and the *literal* understanding of my doctrine. By this Jesus shows them that he did not intend that his words should be taken literally. ¶ *Profiteth nothing.* Would not avail to the *real* wants of man. The bread that Moses gave, the food which you seek, would not be of *real* value to man's highest wants. ¶ They *are spirit.* They are spiritual. They are not to be understood *literally*, as if you were really to eat my flesh, but they are to be understood as denoting the need of that provision for the soul which God has made by my coming into the world. ¶ *Are life.* Are fitted to produce or give life to the soul dead in sins.

64 But there are some of you that believe not. For Jesus [y]knew from the beginning who they were that believed not, and who should betray him.

65 And he said, Therefore [z]said I unto you, that no man can come unto me except it were given unto him of my Father.

66 From that *time* many of his disciples [a]went back, and walked no more with him.

67 Then said Jesus unto the twelve, Will ye also go away?

68 Then Simon Peter answered him, Lord, to whom shall we go? thou hast [b]the words of eternal life.

y Ro.8.29; 2 Ti.2.19. *z* ver.44,45.

a Zep.1.6; Lu.9.62; He.10.38. *b* Ac.5.20; 7.38.

64. *Jesus knew from the beginning*, &c. As this implied a knowledge of the *heart*, and of the secret principles and motives of men, it shows that he must have been omniscient.

66. *Many of his disciples.* Many who had followed him professedly as his disciples and as desirous of learning of him. See Notes on ver. 60. ¶ *Went back.* Turned away from him and left him. From this we may learn, 1st. Not to wonder at the apostasy of many who profess to be followers of Christ. Many are induced to become his professed followers by the prospect of some temporal benefit, or under some public excitement, as these were; and when that temporal benefit is not obtained, or that excitement is over, they fall away. 2d. Many may be expected to be offended by the doctrines of the gospel. Having no spirituality of mind, and really understanding nothing of the gospel, they may be expected to take offence and turn back. The best way to understand the doctrines of the Bible is to be a sincere Christian, and aim to do the will of God, Jn. vii. 17. 3d. We should examine ourselves. We should honestly inquire whether we have been led to make a profession of religion by the hope of any temporal advantage, by any selfish principle, or by mere excited animal feeling. If we have it will profit us nothing, and we shall either *fall away* of ourselves, or be *cast away* in the great day of judgment.

67. *The twelve.* The twelve apostles. ¶ *Will ye also go away?* Many apostatized, and it was natural now for Jesus to submit the question to the twelve. "Will *you*, whom I have chosen, on whom I have bestowed the apostleship, and who have seen the evidence of my Messiahship, will you now also leave me?" This was the time to try them; and it is always a time to try *real* Christians when many professed disciples become cold and turn back; and *then* we may suppose Jesus addressing *us*, and saying, Will ye ALSO go away? Observe here, it was submitted to their choice. God compels none to remain with him against their will, and the question in such trying times is submitted to every man whether he will or will not go away.

68. *Simon Peter answered him.* With characteristic ardour and promptness. Peter was probably one of the oldest of the apostles, and it was his character to be *first* and most ardent in his professions. ¶ *To whom shall we go?* This implied their firm conviction that Jesus was the Messiah, and that he alone was able to save them. It is one of Peter's noble confessions—the instinctive promptings of a pious heart and of ardent love. There was no one else who could teach them. The Pharisees, the Sadducees, and the scribes were corrupt, and unable to guide them aright; and, though the doctrines of Jesus were mysterious, yet they were the *only* doctrines that could instruct and save them. ¶ *Thou hast*, &c. The meaning of this is, *thou teachest the doctrines which lead to eternal life.* And from this we may learn, 1st. That we are to expect that some of the doctrines of the Bible will be mysterious. 2d. That, though they are difficult to be understood, yet we should not therefore reject them. 3d. That nothing would be *gained* by rejecting them. The atheist, the infidel —nay, the philosopher, believes, or professes to believe, propositions quite as mysterious as any in the Bible. 4th. That poor, lost, sinful man has nowhere else to go but to Jesus. He is the way, the truth, and the life, and if the sinner betakes himself to any other way he will wander and die. 5th. We should, therefore, on no account forsake the teachings of the Son of God. The words that he speaks are spirit and are life.

69. *We are sure*, &c. See a similar confession of Peter in Mat. xvi. 16, and

69 And[c] we believe and are sure that thou art that Christ, the Son of the living God.
70 Jesus answered them, Have not I chosen you twelve, and one of you is [d]a devil?
71 He spake of Judas Iscariot, *the son* of Simon; for he it was that should betray him, being one of the twelve.

c Mat.16.16; ch.1.29; 11.27.

d ch.13.27.

the Notes on that place. Peter says *we* are sure, in the name of the whole of the apostles. Jesus immediately cautions him, as he did on other occasions, not to be too confident, for *one* of them actually had no such feelings, but was a traitor.

70. *Have not I chosen you twelve?* There is much emphasis in these words. Have not *I*—I, the Saviour, the Messiah, chosen you in mercy and in love, and therefore it will be a greater sin to betray me? *Chosen.* Chosen to the apostolic office; conferred on you marks of peculiar favour, and treason is therefore the greater sin. *You twelve.* So small a number. Out of such a multitude as follow for the loaves and fishes, it is to be expected there should be apostates; but when the number is so small, chosen in such a manner, then it becomes every one, however confident he may be, to be on his guard and examine his heart. ¶ *Is a devil.* Has the spirit, the envy, the malice, and the treasonable designs of a devil. The word *devil* here is used in the sense of an *enemy*, or one hostile to him.

71. *He spake of Judas*, &c. There is no evidence that Jesus *designated* Judas so that the disciples *then* understood that it was he. It does not appear that the apostles even suspected Judas, as they continued to treat him afterward with the same confidence, for he carried the *bag*, or the purse containing their little property (Jn. xii. 6; xiii. 29); and at the table, when Jesus said that one of them would betray him, the rest did not suspect Judas until Jesus pointed him out particularly, Jn. xiii. 26. Jesus spoke of *one*, to put them on their guard, to check their confidence, and to lead them to self-examination. So in every church, or company of professing Christians, we may know that it is probable that there may be some one or more deceived; but we may not know who it may be, and should therefore inquire prayerfully and honestly, "Lord, is it *I*?" ¶ *Should betray.* Would betray. If it be asked why Jesus called a man to be an apostle who he knew had no love for him, who would betray him, and who had from the beginning the spirit of a "devil," we may reply, 1st. It was that Judas might be an important witness for the innocence of Jesus, and for the fact that he was not an impostor. Judas was with him more than three years. He was treated with the same confidence as the others, and in some respects even with superior confidence, as he had "the bag" (Jn. xii. 6), or was the treasurer. He saw the Saviour in public and in private, heard his public discourses and his private conversation, and he would have been just the witness which the high-priests and Pharisees would have desired, if he had known any reason why he should be condemned. Yet he alleged nothing against him. Though he betrayed him, yet he afterward said that he was *innocent*, and, under the convictions of conscience, committed suicide. If Judas had known anything *against* the Saviour he would have alleged it. If he had known that he was an impostor, and had alleged it, he would have saved his own life and been rewarded. If Jesus was an impostor, he *ought* to have made it known, and to have been rewarded for it. 2d. It *may* have been, also, with a foresight of the necessity of having such a man among his disciples, in order that his own death might be brought about in the manner in which it was predicted. There were several prophecies which would have been unfulfilled had there been no such man among the apostles. 3d. It showed the knowledge which the Saviour had of the human heart, that he could thus discern character before it was developed, and was able so distinctly to predict that he would betray him. 4th. We may add, what benevolence did the Saviour evince—what patience and forbearance—that he had with him for more than three years a man who he knew hated him at heart, and who would yet betray him to be put to death on a cross, and that during all that time he treated him with the utmost kindness!

CHAPTER VII.

AFTER these things Jesus walked in Galilee; for he would not walk in Jewry, because the Jews sought to kill him.

2 Now the Jews' [a]feast of tabernacles was at hand.

3 His brethren therefore said unto him, Depart hence, and go into Judea, that thy disciples also may see the works that thou doest.

4 For *there is* no man *that* doeth any thing in secret, and he himself seeketh to be known openly. If thou do these things, show thyself to the world.

5 For neither did his [b]brethren believe in him.

6 Then Jesus said unto them, [c]My time is not yet come; but your time is alway ready.

7 The[d] world cannot hate you;

a Le.23.34. *b* Mar.3.21. *c* ch.2.4; 8.20; ver.8,30. *d* ch.15.19.

CHAPTER VII.

1. *After these things.* After the transactions which are recorded in the last chapters had taken place, and after the offence he had given the Jews. See ch. v. 18. ¶ *Jesus walked.* Or Jesus *lived*, or *taught*. He travelled around Galilee teaching. ¶ *In Jewry.* In Judea, the southern division of Palestine. Comp. Notes on ch. iv. 3. ¶ *The Jews sought.* That is, the *rulers* of the Jews. It does not appear that the common people ever attempted to take his life.

2. *The Jews' feast of tabernacles.* Or the feast of *tents*. This feast was celebrated on the fifteenth day of the month *Tisri*, answering to the last half of our month September and the first half of October, Nu. xxix. 12; De. xvi. 13-15. It was so called from the *tents* or tabernacles which on that occasion were erected in and about Jerusalem, and was designed to commemorate their dwelling in *tents* in the wilderness, Ne. viii. 16-18. During the continuance of this feast they dwelt in *booths* or tents, as their fathers did in the wilderness, Le. xxiii. 42, 43. The feast was continued *eight* days, and the eighth or last day was the most distinguished, and was called the *great day* of the feast, ver. 37; Nu. xxix. 35. The Jews on this occasion not only dwelt in *booths*, but they carried about the branches of palms, willows, and other trees which bore a thick foliage, and also branches of the olive-tree, myrtle, &c., Ne. viii. 15. Many sacrifices were offered on this occasion (Nu. xxix. 12-39; De. xvi. 14-16), and it was a time of general joy. It is called by Josephus and Philo the *greatest* feast, and was one of the three feasts which every male among the Jews was obliged to attend.

3. *His brethren.* See Notes on Mat. xii. 47. ¶ *Thy disciples.* The disciples which he had made when he was before in Judea, Jn. iv. 1-3. ¶ *The works.* The miracles.

4, 5. *For* there is *no man*, &c. The brethren of Jesus supposed that he was influenced as others are. As it is a common thing among men to seek popularity, so they supposed that he would also seek it; and as a great multitude would be assembled at Jerusalem at this feast, they supposed it would be a favourable time to make himself known. What follows shows that this was said, probably, not in sincerity, but in derision; and to the other sufferings of our Lord was to be added, what is so common to Christians, *derision* from his relatives and friends on account of his pretensions. If our Saviour was derided, we also may expect to be by our relatives; and, having his example, we should be content to bear it. ¶ *If thou do*, &c. It appears from this that they did not really believe that he wrought miracles; or, if they *did* believe it, they did not suppose that he was the Christ. Yet it seems hardly credible that they could suppose that his miracles were *real*, and yet not admit that he was the Messiah. Besides, there is no evidence that these relatives had been present at any of his miracles, and all that they knew of them might have been from report. See Notes on Mar. iii. 21. On the word *brethren* in ver. 5, see Notes on Mat. xiii. 55, and Ga. i. 19.

6. *My time*, &c. The proper time for my going up to the feast. We know not *why* it was not yet a proper time for him to go. It might be because if he went *then*, in their company, while multitudes were going, it would have too much the appearance of parade and ostentation; it might excite too much notice, and be more likely to expose him to the envy and opposition of the

but me it hateth, because I testify
of it, that the works thereof are
evil.
8 Go ye up unto this feast: I
go not up yet unto this feast; for
my time is not yet full come.
9 When he had said these words
unto them he abode *still* in Galilee.
10 But when his brethren were
gone up, then went he also up unto
the feast, not openly, but as it were
in secret.
11 Then[e] the Jews sought him
at the feast, and said, Where
is he?

e ch.11.56.

12 And[f] there was much murmuring among the people concerning him; for some said, He
is a good man; others said, Nay,
but he deceiveth the people.
13 Howbeit, no man spake
openly of him, for fear of the
Jews.
14 Now about the midst of
the feast, Jesus went up into
the temple and taught.
15 And[g] the Jews marvelled,
saying, How knoweth this man
[1]letters, having never learned?

f ch.9.16. g Mat.13.54. 1 or, *learning*.

rulers. ¶ *Your time*, &c. It makes no difference to you when you go up. Your going will excite no tumult or opposition; it will not attract attention, and will not endanger your lives. Jesus therefore chose to go up more privately, and to remain until the multitude had gone. They commonly travelled to those feasts in large companies, made up of most of the families in the neighbourhood. See Notes on Lu. ii. 44.

7. *The world cannot hate you.* You profess no principles in opposition to the world. You do not excite its envy, or rouse against you the civil rulers. As you possess the same spirit and principles with the men of the world, they cannot be expected to hate you. ¶ *I testify of it.* I bear witness against it. This was the main cause of the opposition which was made to him. He proclaimed that men were depraved, and the result was that they hated him. We may expect that all who preach faithfully against the wickedness of men will excite opposition. Yet this is not to deter us from doing our duty, and, after the example of Jesus, from proclaiming to men their sins, whatever may be the result.

8. *I go not up yet.* Jesus remained until about the middle of the feast, ver. 14. That is, he remained about four days after his brethren had departed, or until the mass of the people had gone up, so that his going might excite no attention, and that it might not be said he chose such a time to excite a tumult. We have here a signal instance of our Lord's prudence and opposition to parade. Though it would have been *lawful* for him to go up at that time, and though it would have been a favourable period to make himself known, yet he chose to forego these advantages rather than to afford an occasion of envy and jealousy to the rulers, or to *appear* even to excite a tumult among the people.

12. *Murmuring.* Contention, disputing. ¶ *He deceiveth the people.* That is, he is *deluding* them, or drawing them away by pretending to be the Messiah.

13. *Spake openly of him.* The word translated *openly*, here, is commonly rendered *boldly*. This refers, doubtless, to those who really believed on him. His enemies were not silent; but his friends had not confidence to speak of him *openly* or *boldly*—that is, to speak what they really thought. Many supposed that he was the Messiah, yet even this they did not dare to profess. All that they could say in his favour was that he *was a good man*. There are always many such friends of Jesus in the world who are desirous of saying *something* good about him, but who, from fear or shame, refuse to make a full acknowledgement of him. Many will praise his *morals*, his *precepts*, and his *holy life*, while they are ashamed to speak of his *divinity* or his *atonement*, and still more to acknowledge that they are dependent on him for salvation.

14. *About the midst.* Or about the middle of the feast. It continued eight days. ¶ *The temple.* See Notes on Mat. xxi. 12. ¶ *And taught.* Great multitudes were assembled in and around the temple, and it was a favourable time and place to make known his doctrine.

15. *Knoweth this man letters.* The

16 Jesus answered them and
said, My doctrine is [h]not mine,
but his that sent me.
17 If[i] any man will do his will,
he shall know of the doctrine
whether it be of God, or *whether*
I speak of myself.
18 He[k] that speaketh of him-

h ch.8.28; 12.49. *i* ch.8.43. *k* ch.8.50.

Jewish *letters* or science consisted in the knowledge of their Scriptures and traditions. Jesus exhibited in his discourses such a profound acquaintance with the Old Testament as to excite their amazement and admiration. ¶ *Having never learned.* The Jews taught their law and tradition in celebrated schools. As Jesus had not been instructed in those schools, they were amazed at his learning. What early human teaching the Saviour had we have no means of ascertaining, farther than that it was customary for the Jews to teach their children to read the Scriptures. 2 Ti. iii. 15: "From a child thou (Timothy) hast known the holy scriptures."

16. *My doctrine.* My *teaching*, or what I teach. This is the proper meaning of the word *doctrine.* It is what is *taught* us, and, as applied to religion, it is what is *taught* us by God in the holy Scriptures. ¶ *Is not mine.* It is not *originated* by me. Though I have not learned in your schools, yet you are not to infer that the doctrine which I teach is *devised* or *invented* by me. I teach nothing that is contrary to the will of God, and which he has not appointed me to teach. ¶ *His that sent me.* God's. It is such as he approves, and such as he has commissioned me to teach. The doctrine is divine in its origin and in its nature.

17. *If any man will do his will.* Literally, if any man *wills* or is *willing* to do the will of God. If there is a *disposition* in anyone to do that will, though he should not be able perfectly to keep his commandments. To do the *will* of God is to obey his commandments; to yield our hearts and lives to his requirements. A disposition to do his will is a readiness to yield our intellects, our feelings, and all that we have entirely to him, to be governed according to his pleasure. ¶ *He shall know.* He shall have *evidence*, in the very attempt to do the will of God, of the truth of the doctrine. This evidence is *internal*, and to the individual it is satisfactory and conclusive. It is of two kinds. 1st. He will find that the doctrines which Jesus taught are such as commend themselves to his reason and conscience, and such as are consistent with all that we know of the perfections of God. His doctrines commend themselves to us as fitted to make us pure and happy, and of course they are such as must be from God. 2d. An honest desire to obey God will lead a man to embrace the great doctrines of the Bible. He will find that his heart is depraved and inclined to evil, and he will see and feel the truth of the doctrine of *depravity;* he will find that he is a sinner and needs to be *born again;* he will learn his own weakness, and see his need of *a Saviour*, of an atonement, and of pardoning mercy; he will feel that he is polluted, and needs the purifying influence of the Holy Spirit. Thus we may learn, 1st. That an honest effort to obey God is the easiest way to become acquainted with the doctrines of the Bible. 2d. Those who *make* such an effort will not *cavil* at *any* of the doctrines of the Scriptures. 3d. This is evidence of the truth of revelation which every man can apply to his own case. 4th. It is such evidence as to lead to *certainty.* No man who has ever made an honest effort to live a pious life, and to do all the will of God, has ever had any doubt of the truth of the Saviour's doctrines, or any doubt that his religion is true and is fitted to the nature of man. They only doubt the truth of religion who wish to live in sin. 5th. We see the goodness of God in giving us evidence of his truth that may be within every man's reach. It does not require great learning to be a Christian, and to be convinced of the truth of the Bible. It requires an *honest* heart, and a willingness to obey God. ¶ *Whether it be of God.* Whether it be *divine.* ¶ Or whether *I speak of myself.* Of myself without being commissioned or directed by God.

18. *That speaketh of himself.* This does not mean *about* or *concerning* himself, but he that speaks by *his own authority*, without being sent by God, as mere human teachers do. ¶ *Seeketh his own glory.* His own *praise*, or seeks for reputation and applause. This is the case with mere human teachers,

self seeketh his own glory; [l]but he that seeketh his glory that sent him, the same is true, and no unrighteousness is in him.

19 Did not [m]Moses give you the law, and *yet* [n]none of you keepeth the law? Why go ye about [o]to kill me?

20 The people answered and said, [p]Thou hast a devil; who goeth about to kill thee?

21 Jesus answered and said unto them, I have done one work, and ye all marvel.

22 Moses[q] therefore gave unto you circumcision; (not because it is of Moses, [r]but of the fathers;) and ye on the sabbath-day circumcise a man.

23 If a man on the sabbath-day receive circumcision, [2]that the law of Moses should not be

l Pr.25.27. *m* Jn.1.17; Ga.3.19. *n* Ro.3.10-19. *o* Mat.12.14; ch.5.16,18. *p* ch.8.48.

q Le.12.3. *r* Ge.17.10.
[2] or, *without breaking the law of Moses.*

---

and as Jesus in his discourses manifestly sought to honour *God,* they ought to have supposed that he was sent by him. ¶ *No unrighteousness.* This word here means, evidently, there is no *falsehood,* no *deception* in him. He is not an impostor. It is used in the same sense in 2 Th. ii. 10-12. It is true that there was no *unrighteousness,* no *sin* in Jesus Christ, but that is not the truth taught here. It is that he was not an *impostor,* and the evidence of this was that he sought not his own glory, but the honour of God. This evidence was furnished, 1st. In his retiring, unobtrusive disposition; in his not seeking the applause of men. 2d. In his teaching such doctrines as tended to exalt God and humble man. 3d. In his ascribing all glory and praise to God.

19. *Did not Moses give you the law?* This they admitted, and on this they prided themselves. Every violation of that law they considered as deserving of death. They had accused Jesus of violating it because he had healed a man on the Sabbath, and for that they had sought his life, ch. v. 10-16. He here recalls that charge to their recollection, and shows them that, though they pretended great reverence for that law, yet they were really its violators in having sought his life. ¶ *None of you,* &c. None of you Jews. They had sought to kill him. This was a pointed and severe charge, and shows the great faithfulness with which he was accustomed to proclaim the truth. ¶ *Why go ye about to kill me?* Why do ye *seek* to kill me? See ch. v. 16.

20. *The people.* Perhaps some of the people who were not aware of the designs of the rulers. ¶ *Thou hast a devil.* Thou art deranged or mad. See ch. x. 20. As they saw no effort to kill him, and as they were ignorant of the designs of the rulers, they supposed that this was the effect of derangement.

21. *One work.* The healing of the man on the Sabbath, Jn. v. ¶ *Ye all marvel.* You all wonder or are amazed, and particularly that it was done on the Sabbath. This was the *particular* ground of astonishment, that he should dare to do what they esteemed a violation of the Sabbath.

22. *Moses therefore gave unto you circumcision.* Moses commanded you to circumcise your children, Le. xii. 3. The word "therefore" in this place—literally "*on account of this*"—means, "Moses *on this account* gave you circumcision, not because it is of Moses, but of the fathers;" that is, the reason was not that he himself appointed it as a new institution, but he found it already in existence, and incorporated it in his institutions and laws. ¶ *Not because,* &c. Not *that* it is of Moses. Though Jesus spoke in accordance with the custom of the Jews, who ascribed the appointment of circumcision to Moses, yet he is careful to remind them that it was in observance long before Moses. So, also, the *Sabbath* was kept before Moses, and alike in the one case and the other they ought to keep in mind the *design* of the appointment. ¶ *Of the fathers.* Of the patriarchs, Abraham, Isaac, and Jacob, Ge. xvii. 10. ¶ *Ye on the sabbath-day,* &c. The law required that the child should be circumcised on the *eighth* day. If that day happened to be the *Sabbath,* yet they held that he was to be circumcised, as there was a positive law to that effect; and as this was *commanded,* they did not consider it a breach of the Sabbath. ¶ *A man.* Not an *adult* man, but a man-child. See Jn. xvi. 21:

broken, are ye angry at me [s]because I have made a man every
whit whole on the sabbath-day?
24 Judge[t] not according to the
appearance, but judge righteous
judgment.
25 Then said some of them of

s Jn.5.8. t De.1.16,17.

Jerusalem, Is not this he whom
they seek to kill?
26 But, lo, he speaketh boldly,
and they say nothing unto him.
Do[u] the rulers know indeed that
this is the very Christ?
27 Howbeit[v] we know this man

u ver.48. v Mat.13.55.

"She remembereth no more the anguish, for joy that *a man* is born into the world."

23. *That the law of Moses should not be broken.* In order that the law requiring it to be done at a specified time, though that might occur on the Sabbath, should be kept. ¶ *Are ye angry,* &c. The argument of Jesus is this: "You yourselves, in interpreting the law about the Sabbath, allow a work of necessity to be done. You do that which is necessary as an ordinance of religion denoting *separation* from other nations, or external purity. As you allow this, you ought also, for the same reason, to allow that a man should be completely restored to health—that a work of much more importance should be done." We may learn here that it would be happy for all if they would not condemn others in that thing which they allow. Men often accuse others of doing things which they themselves do in other ways. ¶ *Every whit whole.* Literally, "I have restored the whole man to health," implying that the man's *whole body* was diseased, and that he had been *entirely* restored to health.

24. *Judge not according to the appearance.* Not as a thing first offers itself to you, without reflection or candour. In *appearance*, to circumcise a child on the Sabbath might be a violation of the law; yet you do it, and it is right. So, to *appearance*, it might be a violation of the Sabbath to heal a man, yet it is right to do works of necessity and mercy. ¶ *Judge righteous judgment.* Candidly; looking at the law, and inquiring what its *spirit* really requires.

26. *Do the rulers know indeed,* &c. It seems from this that they supposed that the *rulers* had been convinced that Jesus was the Messiah, but that from some cause they were not willing yet to make it known to the people. The reasons of this opinion were these: 1st. They knew that they *had* attempted to kill him. 2d. They now saw him speaking boldly to the people without interruption from the rulers. They concluded, therefore, that some change had taken place in the sentiments of the rulers in regard to him, though they had not yet made it public. ¶ *The rulers.* The members of the *Sanhedrim*, or great council of the nation, who had charge of religious affairs. ¶ *Indeed.* Truly; certainly. Have they certain evidence, as would appear from their suffering him to speak without interruption? ¶ *The very Christ.* Is *truly* or *really* the Messiah.

27. *Howbeit.* But. They proceeded to state a reason why *they* supposed that he could *not* be the Messiah, whatever the *rulers* might think. ¶ *We know this man whence he is.* We know the place of his birth and residence. ¶ *No man knoweth whence he is.* From Mat. ii. 5, it appears that the common expectation of the Jews was that the Messiah would be born at Bethlehem; but they had also feigned that after his birth he would be *hidden* or taken away in some mysterious manner, and appear again from some unexpected quarter. We find allusions to this expectation in the New Testament, where our Saviour *corrects* their common notions, Mat. xxiv. 23: "Then if any man shall say unto you, Lo, here is Christ, or there, believe it not." And again (ver. 26), "If they shall say unto you, Behold, he is in the desert, go not forth; behold, he is in the secret chambers, believe it not." The following extracts from Jewish writings show that this was the common expectation: "The Redeemer shall manifest himself, and afterward be hid. So it was in the redemption from Egypt. Moses showed himself and then was hidden." So on the passage, Ca. ii. 9—"My beloved is like a roe or a young hart"—they say: "A roe appears and then is hid; so the Redeemer shall first appear and then be concealed, and then again be concealed and then again appear." "So the Redeemer shall first appear and then be hid, and then, at the end of forty-five days, shall reap-

whence he is; but when Christ
cometh, no man knoweth whence
he is.
28 Then cried Jesus in the
temple as he taught, saying, Ye
both know me, and ye know
whence I am; [w]and I am not
come of myself, but [x]he that sent
me is true, [y]whom ye know not.
29 But[z] I know him; for I am
from him, and he hath sent me.
30 Then[a] they sought to take
him, but no man laid hands on
him, because his hour was not yet
come.
31 And [b]many of the people
believed on him, and said, When
Christ cometh, will he do more
miracles than these which this
man hath done?
32 The Pharisees heard that
the people murmured such things
concerning him; and the Pharisees
and the chief priests sent officers
to take him.
33 Then said Jesus unto them,
[c]Yet a little while am I with
you, and *then* I go unto him that
sent me.
34 Ye[d] shall seek me, and shall

w ch.5.43. x Ro.3.4. y ch.1.18; 8.55. z Mat.11.27; ch.10.15. a Mar.11.18; Lu.20.19; ch.8.37.

b ch.4.39. c ch.13.33; 16.16. d Ho.5.6; ch.8.21.

pear, and cause *manna* to descend." See Lightfoot. Whatever may have been the source of this opinion, it explains this passage, and shows that the writer of this gospel was well acquainted with the opinions of the Jews, however improbable those opinions were.

28. *Ye know whence I am.* You have sufficient evidence of my divine mission, and that I am the Messiah. ¶ *Is true.* Is worthy to be believed. He has given evidence that I came from him, and he is worthy to be believed. Many read this as a question—Do ye know me, and know whence I am? I am not come of myself, &c.

30. *Then they sought to take him.* The rulers and their friends. They did this—1st. Because of his reproof; and, 2d. For professing to be the Messiah. ¶ *His hour.* The proper and the appointed *time* for his death. See Mat. xxi. 46.

31. *Will he do more miracles?* It was a common expectation that the Messiah would work many miracles. This opinion was founded on such passages as Is. xxxv. 5, 6, &c.: "Then the eyes of the blind shall be opened, and the ears of the deaf shall be unstopped; then shall the lame man leap as an hart," &c. Jesus had given abundant evidence of his power to work such miracles, and they therefore believed that he was the Messiah.

32. *The people murmured such things.* That is, that the question was agitated whether he was the Messiah; that it excited debate and contention; and that the consequence was, he made many friends. They chose, therefore, if possible, to remove him from them.

33. *Yet a little while am I with you.* It will not be long before my death. This is supposed to have been about six months before his death. This speech of Jesus is full of tenderness. They were seeking his life. He tells them that he is fully aware of it; that he will not be long with them; and *implies* that they should be diligent to seek him while he was yet with them. He was about to die, but they might now seek his favour and find it. When we remember that this was said to his persecutors and murderers; that it was said even while they were seeking his life, we see the peculiar tenderness of his love. Enmity, and hate, and persecution did not prevent his offering salvation to them. ¶ *I go unto him that sent me.* This is one of the intimations that he gave that he would *ascend* to God. Comp. ch. vi. 62.

34. *Ye shall seek me.* This probably means simply, Ye shall seek *the Messiah.* Such will be your troubles, such the calamities that will come on the nation, that you will earnestly desire the coming of *the Messiah.* You will seek for a deliverer, and will look for *him* that he may bring deliverance. This does not mean that they would seek for *Jesus* and not be able to find him, but that they would desire the aid and comfort of *the Messiah,* and would be disappointed. Jesus speaks of *himself* as the Messiah, and his own name as synonymous with the Messiah. See Notes on Mat. xxiii. 39. ¶ *Shall not find* me. Shall not find the Messiah. He will not come, according to your expectations, to aid you. See Notes on Mat. xxiv. ¶ *Where I am.* This whole

not find *me;* and where I am, *thither* ye cannot come.

35 Then said the Jews among themselves, Whither will he go, that we shall not find him? Will he go unto the [e]dispersed among the [3]Gentiles, and teach the Gentiles?

36 What *manner of* saying is this that he said, Ye shall seek me, and shall not find *me;* and where I am, *thither* ye cannot come?

37 In the [f]last day, that great *day* of the feast, Jesus stood and cried, saying, [g]If any man thirst, let him come unto me and drink.

38 He that believeth on me, as

e Is.11.12; Ja.1.1; 1 Pe.1.1. 3 or, *Greeks.* f Le.23.36. g Is.55.1; Re.22.17.

clause is to be understood as future, though the words "am" and "cannot" are both in the present tense. The meaning is, Where I shall be you will not be able to come. That is, he, the Messiah, would be in heaven; and though they would earnestly desire his presence and aid to save the city and nation from the Romans, yet they would not be able to obtain it—represented here by their not being able to *come to him.* This does not refer to their *individual* salvation, but to the deliverance of their nation. It is not true of individual sinners that they seek Christ in a proper manner and are not able to find him; but it *was* true of the Jewish nation that they *looked for* the Messiah, and sought his coming to deliver them, but he did not do it.

35. *The dispersed among the Gentiles.* To the *Jews* scattered among the Gentiles, or living in distant parts of the earth. It is well known that at that time there were Jews dwelling in almost every land. There were multitudes in Egypt, in Asia Minor, in Greece, in Rome, &c., and in all these places they had synagogues. The question which they asked was whether he would leave an ungrateful country, and go into those distant nations and teach them. ¶ *Gentiles.* In the original, *Greeks.* All those who were not *Jews* were called *Greeks,* because they were chiefly acquainted with those heathens only who spake the Greek language. It is remarkable that Jesus returned no answer to these inquiries. He rather chose to turn off their minds from a speculation about the place to which he was going, to the great affairs of their own personal salvation.

37. *In the last day.* The eighth day of the festival. ¶ *That great* day. The day of the holy convocation or solemn assembly, Le. xxiii. 36. This seems to have been called the *great* day, 1st. Because of the solemn assembly, and because it was the closing scene. 2d. Because, according to their traditions, on the previous days they offered sacrifices for the *heathen* nations as well as for themselves, but on this day for the Jews only (Lightfoot). 3d. Because on this day they abstained from all servile labour (Le. xxiii. 39), and regarded it as a *holy* day. 4th. On this day they finished the reading of the law, which they commenced at the beginning of the feast. 5th. Because on this day probably occurred the ceremony of drawing water from the pool of Siloam. On the last day of the feast it was customary to perform a solemn ceremony in this manner: The priest filled a golden vial with water from the fount of Siloam (see Notes on Jn. ix. 7), which was borne with great solemnity, attended with the clangour of trumpets, through the gate of the temple, and being mixed with wine, was poured on the sacrifice on the altar. What was the origin of this custom is unknown. Some suppose, and not improbably, that it arose from an improper understanding of the passage in Is. xii. 3: "With joy shall ye draw water out of the wells of salvation." It is certain that no such ceremony is commanded by Moses. It is supposed to be probable that Jesus *stood and cried* while they were performing this ceremony, that he might, 1st, *illustrate* the nature of his doctrine by this; and 2d, call off their attention from a rite that was uncommanded, and that could not confer eternal life. ¶ *Jesus stood.* In the temple, in the midst of thousands of the people. ¶ *If any man thirst.* Spiritually. If any man feels his need of salvation. See Jn. iv. 13, 14; Mat. v. 6; Re. xxii. 17. The invitation is full and free to all. ¶ *Let him come unto me,* &c. Instead of depending on *this* ceremony of drawing water let him come to me, the Messiah, and he shall find an ever-abundant supply for all the wants of his soul.

the scripture hath said, [h]out of
his belly shall flow rivers of living
water.
39 (But this he spake of [i]the
Spirit, which they that believe on
him should receive; for the Holy
Ghost was not yet *given*, because
that Jesus was not yet glorified.)
40 Many of the people, therefore,
when they heard this saying, said,
Of a truth this is [k]the Prophet.
41 Others said, This is [l]the

h Pr.18.4; Is.58.11; ch.4.14.
i Is.44.3; Joel 2.28; ch.16.7; Ac.2.17,33.
k De.18.15,18; ch.6.14. *l* ch.4.42; 6.69.

---

38. *He that believeth on me.* He that acknowledges me as the Messiah, and trusts in me for salvation. ¶ *As the scripture hath said.* This is a difficult expression, from the fact that no such expression as follows is to be found literally in the Old Testament. Some have proposed to connect it with what precedes—"He that believeth on me, as the Old Testament has *commanded* or required"—but to this there are many objections. The natural and obvious meaning here is, doubtless, the true one; and Jesus probably intended to say, not that there was any *particular* place in the Old Testament that affirmed this in so many words, but that this was the *substance* of what the Scriptures taught, or this was the *spirit* of their declarations. Hence the *Syriac* translates it in the plural—the *Scriptures.* Probably there is a reference more particularly to Is. lviii. 11, than to any other single passage: "Thou shalt be like a watered garden, and like a spring of water whose waters fail not." See also Is. xliv. 3, 4; Joel iii. 18. ¶ *Out of his belly.* Out of his midst, or out of his heart. The word belly is often put for the midst of a thing, the centre, and the heart, Mat. xii. 40. It means here that from the *man* shall flow; that is, his piety shall be of such a nature that it will extend its blessings to others. It shall be like a running fountain—perhaps in allusion to statues or ornamented reservoirs in gardens, in which pipes were placed from which water was continually flowing. The Jews used the same figure: "His two reins are like fountains of water, from which the law flows." And again: "When a man turns himself to the Lord, he shall be as a fountain filled with living water, and his streams shall flow to all the nations and tribes of men" (Kuinoel). ¶ *Rivers.* This word is used to express *abundance*, or a full supply. It means here that those who are Christians shall diffuse large, and liberal, and constant blessings on their fellow-men; or, as Jesus immediately explains it, that they shall be the *instruments* by which the Holy Spirit shall be poured down on the world. ¶ *Living water.* Fountains, ever-flowing streams. That is, the gospel shall be constant and life-giving in its blessings. We learn here, 1st. That it is the nature of Christian piety to be diffusive. 2d. That no man can believe on Jesus who does not desire that others should also, and who will not seek it. 3d. That the desire is large and liberal—that the Christian desires the salvation of all the world. 4th. That the *faith* of the believer is to be connected with the influence of the Holy Spirit, and *in that way* Christians are to be like rivers of living water.

39. *Of the Spirit.* Of the Holy Spirit, that should be sent down to attend their preaching and to convert sinners. ¶ *For the Holy Ghost was not yet given.* Was not given in such full and large measures as should be after Jesus had ascended to heaven. Certain measures of the influences of the Spirit had been always given in the conversion and sanctification of the ancient saints and prophets; but that *abundant* and *full* effusion which the apostles were permitted afterward to behold had not yet been given. See Ac. ii.; x. 44, 45. ¶ *Jesus was not yet glorified.* Jesus had not yet ascended to heaven—to the glory and honour that awaited him there. It was a part of the arrangement in the work of redemption that the influences of the Holy Spirit should descend chiefly after the death of Jesus, as that death was the procuring cause of this great blessing. Hence he said (Jn. xvi. 7), "It is expedient for you that I go away; for if I go not away the Comforter will not come unto you; but if I depart I will send him unto you." See also ver. 8–12, and ch. xiv. 15, 16, 26. Comp. Ep. iv. 8–11.

40. *The Prophet.* That is, the prophet whom they expected to *precede* the coming of the Messiah—either Elijah or Jeremiah. See Mat. xvi. 14.

41, 42. See Notes on Mat. ii. 4–6. ¶ *Where David was.* 1 Sa. xvi. 1–4.

Christ. But some said, [m]Shall Christ come out of Galilee?

42 Hath not the scripture said, That [n]Christ cometh of the seed of David, and out of [o]the town of Bethlehem, [p]where David was?

43 So there was a division among the people because of him.

44 And some of them would have taken him, but no man laid hands on him.

45 Then came the officers to the chief priests and Pharisees; and they said unto them, Why have ye not brought him?

46 The officers answered, [q]Never man spake like this man.

47 Then answered them the Pharisees, Are ye also deceived?

48 Have any of [r]the rulers or of the Pharisees believed on him?

m ch.1.46; ver.52. *n* Ps.132.11; Je.23.5. *o* Mi.5.2; Lu.2.4. *p* 1 Sa.16.1,4.

q Lu.4.22. *r* Je.5.4,5; ch.12.42; 1 Co.1.26.

45, 46. *The officers.* Those who had been appointed (ver. 32) to take him. It seems that Jesus was in the midst of the people addressing them, and that they happened to come at the very time when he was speaking. They were so impressed and awed with what he said that they dared not take him. There have been few instances of eloquence like this. His speaking had so much evidence of truth, so much proof that he was from God, and was so impressive and persuasive, that they were convinced of his innocence, and they *dared* not touch him to execute their commission. We have here, 1st. A remarkable testimony to the commanding eloquence of Jesus. 2d. Wicked men may be awed and restrained by the presence of a good man, and by the evidence that he speaks that which is true. 3d. God can preserve his friends. Here were men sent for a particular purpose. They were armed with power. They were commissioned by the highest authority of the nation. On the other hand, Jesus was without arms or armies, and without external protection. Yet, in a manner which the officers and the high-priests would have little expected, he was preserved. So, in ways which *we* little expect, God will defend and deliver us when in the midst of danger. 4th. No prophet, apostle, or minister has ever spoken the truth with as much power, grace, and beauty as Jesus. It should be *ours*, therefore, to listen to his words, and to sit at his feet and learn heavenly wisdom.

47. *Are ye also deceived?* They set down the claims of Jesus as of course an imposture. They did not examine, but were, like thousands, determined to believe that he was a deceiver. Hence they did not ask them whether they were *convinced*, or had seen evidence that he was the Messiah; but, with mingled contempt, envy, and anger, they asked if they were also *deluded*. Thus many assume religion to be an imposture; and when one becomes a Christian, they *assume* at once that he is deceived, that he is the victim of foolish credulity or superstition, and treat him with ridicule or scorn. Candour would require them to inquire whether such changes were not proof of the *power* and *truth* of the gospel, as candour in the case of the rulers required them to inquire whether Jesus had not given them evidence that he was from God.

48. *The rulers.* The members of the Sanhedrim, who were supposed to have control over the religious rites and doctrines of the nation. ¶ *The Pharisees.* The sect possessing wealth, and office, and power. The name *Pharisees* sometimes denotes those who were high in honour and authority. ¶ *Believed on him.* Is there any instance in which those who are high in rank or in office have embraced him as the Messiah? This shows the rule by which *they* judged of religion. 1st. They claimed the right of regulating the doctrines and rites of religion. 2d. They repressed the liberty of private judgment, stifled investigation, assumed that a *new* doctrine *must* be heresy, and laboured to keep the people in inglorious bondage. 3d. They treated the new doctrine of Jesus with *contempt*, and thus attempted to put it down, not by argument, but by *contempt*, and especially because it was embraced by the common people. This is the way in which doctrines contrary to the truth of God have been uniformly supported in the world; this is the way in which new views of truth are met; and this the way in which those in ecclesiastical power often attempt to *lord it over*

49 But this people, who knoweth not the law, are cursed.

50 Nicodemus saith unto them, ([s]he that came [4]to Jesus by night, being one of them,)

51 Doth[t] our law judge *any man* before it hear him, and know what he doeth?

52 They answered and said unto him, Art thou also of Galilee?

s ch.3.2. 4 *to him.* t De.17.8; Pr.18.13.

God's heritage, and to repress the investigation of the Bible.

49. *This people.* The word here translated *people* is the one commonly rendered *the multitude.* It is a word expressive of contempt, or, as we would say, *the rabble.* It denotes the scorn which they felt that the *people* should presume to judge for themselves in a case pertaining to their own salvation. ¶ *Who knoweth not the law.* Who have not been *instructed* in the schools of the Pharisees, and been taught to interpret the Old Testament as they had. They supposed that any who believed on the humble and despised Jesus must be, *of course*, ignorant of the true doctrines of the Old Testament, as they held that a very *different* Messiah from him was foretold. Many instances are preserved in the writings of the Jews of the great contempt in which the Pharisees held the common people. It may here be remarked that Christianity is the only system of religion ever presented to man that in a proper manner regards the poor, the ignorant, and the needy. Philosophers and Pharisees, in all ages, have looked on them with contempt. ¶ *Are cursed.* Are execrable; are of no account; are worthy only of contempt and perdition. Some suppose that there is reference here to their being worthy to be cut off from the people for believing on him, or worthy to be put out of the synagogue (see ch. ix. 22); but it seems to be an expression only of *contempt;* a declaration that they were a rabble, ignorant, unworthy of notice, and going to ruin. Observe, however, 1st. That of this despised people were chosen most of those who became Christians. 2d. That if the people were ignorant, it was the fault of the Pharisees and rulers. It was their business to see that they were taught. 3d. There is no way so common of attempting to oppose Christianity as by ridiculing its friends as poor, and ignorant, and weak, and credulous. As well might food, and raiment, and friendship, and patriotism be held in contempt because the poor need the one or possess the other.

50. *Nicodemus.* See ch. iii. 1. ¶ *One of them.* That is, one of the great council or Sanhedrim. God often places one or more pious men in legislative assemblies to vindicate his honour and his law; and he often gives a man grace on such occasions boldly to defend his cause; to put men *upon their proof*, and to confound the proud and the domineering. We see in this case, also, that a man, at one time timid and fearful (comp. ch. iii. 1), may on other occasions be bold, and fearlessly defend the truth as it is in Jesus. This example should lead every man intrusted with authority or office fearlessly to defend the truth of God, and, when the rich and the mighty are pouring contempt on Jesus and his cause, to stand forth as its fearless defender.

51. *Doth our law*, &c. The law required *justice* to be done, and gave every man the right to claim a fair and impartial trial, Le. xix. 15, 16; Ex. xxiii. 1, 2; De. xix. 15, 18. Their condemnation of Jesus was a violation of every rule of right. He was not arraigned; he was not heard in self-defence, and not a single witness was adduced. Nicodemus demanded that *justice* should be done, and that he should not be condemned until he had had a fair trial. Every man should be presumed to be innocent until he is proved to be guilty. This is a maxim of law, and a most just and proper precept in our judgments in private life.

52. *Art thou also of Galilee?* Here is another expression of contempt. To be a *Galilean* was a term of the highest reproach. They knew well that he was not of Galilee, but they meant to ask whether *he* also had become a follower of the despised Galilean. Ridicule is not argument, and there is no demonstration in a gibe; but, unhappily, this is the only weapon which the proud and haughty often use in opposing religion. ¶ *Ariseth no prophet.* That is, there is no prediction that any prophet should come out of Galilee, and especially no

Search and look; for [u]out of Galilee ariseth no prophet.

53 And every man went unto his own house.

CHAPTER VIII.

JESUS went unto the mount of Olives.

2 And early in the morning he came again into the temple, and all the people came unto him; and he sat down and taught them.

3 And the scribes and Pharisees brought unto him a woman taken in adultery; and when they had set her in the midst,

4 They say unto him, Master, this woman was taken in adultery, in the very act.

5 Now[a] Moses in the law commanded us that such should be stoned; but what sayest thou?

6 This they said, tempting him, that they might have to accuse him.

u Is.9.1,2.

a Le.20.10.

---

prophet that was to attend or precede the Messiah. Comp. Jn. i. 46. They assumed, therefore, that Jesus could not be the Christ.

53. *And every man went unto his own house.* There is every mark of confusion and disorder in this breaking up of the Sanhedrim. It is possible that some of the Sadducees might have joined Nicodemus in opposing the Pharisees, and thus increased the disorder. It is a most instructive and melancholy exhibition of the influence of pride, envy, contempt, and anger, when brought to bear on an inquiry, and when they are manifestly opposed to candour, to argument, and to truth. So wild and furious are the passions of men when they oppose the person and claims of the Son of God! It is remarkable, too, how God accomplishes his purposes. *They* wished to destroy Jesus. God suffered their passions to be excited, a tumult to ensue, the assembly thus to break up in disorder, and Jesus to be safe, for his time had not yet come. "The wrath of man shall praise thee; the remainder of wrath shalt thou restrain," Ps. lxxvi. 10.

CHAPTER VIII.

1. *Mount of Olives.* The mountain about a mile directly east of Jerusalem. See Notes on Mat. xxi. 1. This was the place in which he probably often passed the night when attending the feasts at Jerusalem. The Garden of Gethsemane, to which he was accustomed to resort (ch. xviii. 2), was on the western side of that mountain, and Bethany, the abode of Martha and Mary, on its east side, ch. xi. 1.

5. *Moses in the law,* &c. The punishment of adultery commanded by Moses was death, Le. xx. 10; De. xxii. 22. The particular manner of the death was not specified in the law. The Jews had themselves, in the time of Christ, determined that it should be by stoning. See this described in the Notes on Mat. xxi. 35, 44. The punishment for adultery varied. In some cases it was strangling. In the time of Ezekiel (ch. xvi. 38-40) it was stoning and being thrust through with a sword. If the adulteress was the daughter of a priest, the punishment was being burned to death.

6. *Tempting him.* Trying him, or laying a plan that they might have occasion to accuse him. If he decided the case, they expected to be able to bring an accusation against him; for if he decided that she ought to die, they might accuse him of claiming power which belonged to the Romans—the power of life and death. They might allege that it was not the giving an opinion about an abstract case, but that she was formally before him, that he decided her case *judicially*, and that without authority or form of trial. If he decided otherwise, they would have alleged that he denied the authority of the law, and that it was his intention to abrogate it. They had had a controversy with him about the authority of the Sabbath, and they perhaps supposed that he would decide this case as he did that—against them. It may be farther added that they knew that Jesus admitted publicans and sinners to eat with him; that one of their charges was that he was friendly to sinners (see Lu. xv. 2); and they wished, doubtless, to make it appear that he was *gluttonous*, and a *winebibber*, and a *friend of sinners*, and disposed to relax all the laws of morality, even in the case of adultery. Seldom was there a plan more artfully laid, and *never* was more wisdom and knowledge

But Jesus stooped down, and with
his finger wrote on the ground, *as*
though he heard them not.
7 So when they continued asking him, he lifted up himself, and
said unto them, [b]He that is without sin among you, let him first
cast a stone at her.
8 And again he stooped down
and wrote on the ground.
9 And they which heard *it*, being convicted by *their own* conscience, went out one by one, beginning at the eldest, *even* unto the
last; and Jesus was left alone, and
the woman standing in the midst.
10 When Jesus had lifted up
himself, and saw none but the
woman, he said unto her, Woman,
where are those thine accusers?
Hath no man condemned thee?
11 She said, No man, Lord. And

b De.17.7; Ro.2.1,22.

of human nature displayed than in the manner in which it was met. ¶ *Wrote on the ground.* This took place in the *temple.* The "ground," here, means the *pavement*, or the dust on the pavement. By this Jesus showed them clearly that he was not *solicitous* to pronounce an opinion in the case, and that it was not his wish or intention to intermeddle with the civil affairs of the nation. ¶ As though he heard them not. This is added by the translators. It is not in the original, and should not have been added. There is no intimation in the original, as it seems to be implied by this addition, that the *object* was to convey the impression that he did not hear them. What was his object is unknown, and conjecture is useless. The most probable reason seems to be that he did not wish to intermeddle; that he designed to show no solicitude to decide the case; and that he did not mean to decide it unless he was *constrained* to.

7. *They continued asking him.* They pressed the question upon him. They were determined to extort an answer from him, and showed a perseverance in evil which has been unhappily often imitated. ¶ *Is without sin.* That is, without this particular sin; he who has not himself been guilty of this very crime—for in this place the connection evidently demands this meaning. ¶ *Let him first cast a stone at her.* In the punishment by death, one of the witnesses threw the culprit from the scaffold, and the other threw the first stone, or rolled down a stone to crush him. See De. xvii. 6, 7. This was in order that the witness might feel his responsibility in giving evidence, as he was also to be the executioner. Jesus therefore put them to the test. Without pronouncing on her case, he directed them, if any of them were innocent, to perform the office of executioner. This was said, evidently, well knowing their guilt, and well knowing that no one would dare to do it.

9. *Beginning at the eldest.* As being conscious of more sins, and, therefore, being desirous to leave the Lord Jesus. The word *eldest* here probably refers not to *age*, but to *honour*—from those who were in highest reputation to the lowest in rank. This consciousness of crime showed that the state of the public morals was exceedingly corrupt, and justified the declaration of Jesus that it was an *adulterous and wicked generation*, Mat. xvi. 4. ¶ *Alone.* Jesus *only* was left with the woman, &c. ¶ *In the midst.* Her *accusers* had gone out, and left Jesus and the woman; but it is by no means probable that *the people* had left them; and, as this was in the temple on a public occasion, they were doubtless surrounded still by many. This is evident from the fact that Jesus immediately (ver. 12) addressed a discourse to the people present.

10. *Hath no man condemned thee?* Jesus had directed them, if innocent, to cast a stone, thus *to condemn her*, or to use the power which he gave them to condemn her. No one of them had done that. They had *accused* her, but they had not proceeded to the act expressive of *judicial condemnation.*

11. *Neither do I condemn thee.* This is evidently to be taken in the sense of *judicial* condemnation, or of passing sentence as a *magistrate*, for this was what they had arraigned her for. It was not to obtain his *opinion* about adultery, but to obtain the *condemnation* of the woman. As he claimed no *civil* authority, he said that he did not exercise it, and should not *condemn her to die.* In this sense the word is used in the previous verse, and this is the only

Jesus said unto her, [c]Neither do I
condemn thee; go, [d]and sin no
more.
12 Then spake Jesus again unto
them, saying, [e]I am the light of the
world. He[f] that followeth me
shall not walk in darkness, but
shall have the light of life.
13 The Pharisees therefore said

c ch.3.17. d ch.5.14.
e ch.1.4; 9.5. f ch.12.35,46.

unto him, [g]Thou bearest record of
thyself; thy record is not true.
14 Jesus answered and said unto
them, Though I bear record of myself, *yet* my record is true; for I
know whence I came, and whither
I go; [h]but ye cannot tell whence
I come, and whither I go.
15 Ye judge after the flesh; [i]I
judge no man.

g ch.5.31. h ch.7.28; 9.29,30. i ch.3.17; 12.47.

---

sense which the passage demands. Besides, what follows shows that this was his meaning. ¶ *Go, and sin no more.* You have sinned. You have been detected and accused. The sin is great. But I do not claim power to condemn you to die, and, as your *accusers* have left you, my direction to you is that you *sin* no more. This passage therefore teaches us, 1st. That Jesus claimed no *civil* authority. 2d. That he regarded the action of which they accused her as *sin*. 3d. That he knew the *hearts* and *lives* of men. 4th. That men are often very zealous in accusing others of that of which they themselves are guilty. And, 5th. That Jesus was endowed with wonderful wisdom in meeting the devices of his enemies, and eluding their deep-laid plans to involve him in ruin.

It should be added that this passage, together with the last verse of the preceding chapter, has been by many critics thought to be spurious. It is wanting in many of the ancient manuscripts and versions, and has been rejected by Erasmus, Calvin, Beza, Grotius, Wetstein, Tittman, Knapp, and many others. It is not easy to decide the question whether it be a genuine part of the New Testament or not. Some have supposed that it was not *written* by the evangelists, but was often *related* by them, and that after a time it was recorded and introduced by Papias into the sacred text.

12. *I am the light of the world.* See Notes on ch. i. 4, 9.

13. *Thou bearest record of thyself.* Thou art a *witness* for thyself, or in thy own case. See ch. v. 31. The law required two witnesses in a criminal case, and they alleged that as the only evidence which Jesus had was his own assertion, it could not be entitled to belief. ¶ *Is not true.* Is not worthy of belief, or is not substantiated by sufficient evidence.

14. *Jesus answered*, &c. To this objection Jesus replied by saying, first, that the case was such that his testimony *alone* ought to be received; and, secondly, that he had the evidence given him by his Father. Though, in common life, in courts, and in mere human transactions, it was true that a man ought not to give evidence in his own case, yet in this instance, such was the nature of the case that his word was worthy to be believed. ¶ *My record.* My evidence, my testimony. ¶ *Is true.* Is worthy to be believed. ¶ *For I know whence I came—but ye*, &c. I know by what authority I act; I know by whom I am sent, and what commands were given me; but you cannot determine this, for you do not know these unless *I* bear witness of them to you. We are to remember that Jesus came not of himself (ch. vi. 38); that he came not to do his own will, but the will of his Father. He came as a *witness* of those things which he had seen and known (ch. iii. 11), and no man could judge *of those things*, for no man had seen them. As he came from heaven; as he knew his Father's will; as he had *seen* the eternal world, and known the counsels of his Father, so his testimony was worthy of confidence. As *they* had not seen and known these things, they were not qualified to judge. An ambassador from a foreign court knows the will and purposes of the sovereign who sent him, and is competent to bear witness of it. The court to which he is sent has no way of judging but by *his* testimony, and he is therefore competent to testify in the case. All that can be demanded is that he give his *credentials* that he is appointed, and this Jesus had done both by the nature of his doctrine and his miracles.

15. *After the flesh.* According to appearance; according to your carnal and corrupt mode; not according to the

16 And yet, if I judge, [k]my judgment is true; [l]for I am not alone, but I and the Father that sent me.

17 It is also [m]written in your law that the testimony of two men is true.

18 I am one that bear witness of myself, and [n]the Father that sent me beareth witness of me.

19 Then said they unto him, Where is thy Father? Jesus answered, [o]Ye neither know me, nor

k 1 Sa.16.7; Ps.45.6,7; 72.2. *l* ver.29; ch.16.32. *m* De.17.6; 19.15. *n* ch.5.37. *o* ver.55; ch.16.3; 17.25.

spiritual nature of the doctrines. By your preconceived opinions and prejudices you are determined not to believe that I am the Messiah. ¶ *I judge no man.* Jesus came not to *condemn* the world, ch. iii. 17. *They* were in the habit of judging rashly and harshly of all; but this was not the purpose or disposition of the Saviour. This expression is to be understood as meaning that he judged no one *after their manner;* he did not come to censure and condemn men *after the appearance*, or in a harsh, biassed, and unkind manner.

16. *And yet, if I judge.* If I should express my judgment of men or things. He was not *limited*, nor forbidden to do it, nor restrained by any fear that his judgment would be erroneous. ¶ *My judgment is true.* Is worthy to be regarded. ¶ *For I am not alone.* I concur with the Father who hath sent me. His judgment *you* admit would be right, and *my* judgment would accord with his. He was commissioned by his Father, and his judgment would coincide with all that God had purposed or revealed. This was shown by the evidence that God gave that he had sent him into the world.

17. *In your law.* De. xvii. 6; xix. 15. Comp. Mat. xviii. 16. This related to cases in which the life of an individual was involved. Jesus says that if, in such a case, the testimony of two men were sufficient to *establish* a fact, his own testimony and that of his Father ought to be esteemed ample evidence in the case of religious doctrine. ¶ *Two men.* If two *men* could confirm a case, the evidence of *Jesus* and of *God* ought not to be deemed insufficient. ¶ *Is true.* In Deuteronomy, "*established.*" This means the same thing. It is confirmed; is worthy of belief.

18. *I am one that bear witness of myself.* In human courts a man is not allowed to bear witness of himself, because he has a personal interest in the case, and the court could have no proof of the *impartiality* of the evidence; but in the case of Jesus it was otherwise. When one has no party ends to serve; when he is willing to deny himself; when he makes great sacrifices; and when, by his life, he gives every evidence of sincerity, his own testimony may be admitted in evidence of his motives and designs. This was the case with Jesus and his apostles. And though in a *legal* or *criminal* case such testimony would not be admitted, yet, in an argument on *moral* subjects, about the will and purpose of him who sent him, it would not be right to reject the testimony of one who gave so many proofs that he came from God. ¶ *The Father—beareth witness of me.* By the voice from heaven at his baptism (Mat. iii. 17), and by the miracles which Jesus wrought, as well as by the prophecies of the Old Testament. We may here remark, 1st. That there is a distinction between the Father and the Son. They are both represented as bearing testimony; yet, 2d. They are not divided. They are not different beings. They bear testimony to the same thing, and are *one* in counsel, in plan, in essence, and in glory.

19. *Where is thy Father?* This question was asked, doubtless, in derision. Jesus had often given them to understand that by his Father he meant God, ch. v. vi. They *professed* to be ignorant of this, and probably looked round in contempt for his Father, that he might adduce him as a witness in the case. ¶ *If ye had known me,* &c. If you had listened to my instructions, and had received me as the Messiah, you would also, at the same time, have been acquainted with God. We may here observe, 1st. The *manner* in which Jesus answered them. He gave no heed to their cavil; he was not *irritated* by their contempt; he preserved his *dignity*, and gave them an answer worthy of the Son of God. 2d. We should meet the *cavils* and sneers of sinners in the same manner. We should not render railing for railing, but "in meekness instruct those that oppose themselves, if God peradventure will give them repentance to the acknow-

my Father: [p]if ye had known me,
ye should have known my Father
also.
20 These words spake Jesus in
the [q]treasury, as he taught in the
temple; and no man laid hands on
him, [r]for his hour was not yet come.
21 Then said Jesus again unto
them, I go my way, and [s]ye shall
seek me, [t]and shall die in your
sins: whither I go [u]ye cannot come.
22 Then said the Jews, Will he
kill himself? because he saith,
Whither I go ye cannot come.
23 And he said unto them, Ye
are from beneath, I am from above;
ye are of this world, I am not of
this world.
24 I [v]said therefore unto you,
that ye shall die in your sins; [w]for
if ye believe not that I am *he*, ye
shall die in your sins.
25 Then said they unto him,
Who art thou? And Jesus saith

p ch.14.7,9. q Mar.12.41. r ch.7.30. s ch.7.34. t Job 20.11; Ps.73.18-20; Pr.14.32; Is.65.20; Ep.2.1. u Lu.16.26. v ver.21. w Mar.16.16.

ledging of the truth," 2 Ti. ii. 25. 3d. The way to know God is to know Jesus Christ. "No man hath seen God at any time. The only-begotten Son which is in the bosom of the Father, he hath *declared* him," Jn. i. 18. No sinner can have just views of God but in Jesus Christ, 2 Co. iv. 6.

20. *The treasury.* See Notes on Mat. xxi. 12. ¶ *His hour was not yet come.* The time for him to die had not yet arrived, and God restrained them, and kept his life. This proves that God has power over wicked men to control them, and to make them accomplish his own purposes.

21. *I go my way.* See Notes on ch. vii. 33. ¶ *Ye shall die in your sins.* That is, you will seek the Messiah; you will desire his coming, but the Messiah that *you* expect will not come; and, as you have rejected me, and there is no other Saviour, you must die in your sins. You will die unpardoned, and as you did not seek me where you might find me, you cannot come where I shall be. Observe, 1st. All those who reject the Lord Jesus must die unforgiven. There is no way of pardon but by him. See Notes on Ac. iv. 12. 2d. There will be a time when sinners will seek for a Saviour but will find none. Often this is done too late, in a dying moment, and in the future world they may seek a deliverer, but not be able to find one. 3d. Those who reject the Lord Jesus *must* perish. Where he is they cannot come. Where he is is heaven. Where he is not, with his favour and mercy, there is hell; and the sinner that has *no Saviour* must be wretched for ever.

22. *Will he kill himself?* It is difficult to know whether this question was asked from ignorance or malice. Self-murder was esteemed then, as it is now, as one of the greatest crimes; and it is not improbable that they asked this question with mingled hatred and contempt. "He is a *deceiver;* he has broken the law of Moses; he is mad, and it is probable he *will* go on and kill himself." If this was their meaning, we see the wonderful patience of Jesus in enduring the contradiction of sinners; and as *he* bore contempt without rendering railing for railing, so should we.

23. *Ye are from beneath.* The expression *from beneath*, here, is opposed to the phrase *from above.* It means, You are *of the earth*, or are influenced by earthly, sensual, and corrupt passions. You are governed by the lowest and vilest views and feelings, such as are opposed to heaven, and such as have their origin in earth or in hell. ¶ *I am from above.* From heaven. My views are heavenly, and my words should have been so interpreted. ¶ *Ye are of this world.* You think and act like the corrupt men of this world. ¶ *I am not of this world.* My views are above these earthly and corrupt notions. The meaning of the verse is: "Your reference to *self-murder* shows that you are earthly and corrupt in your views. You are governed by the mad passions of men, and can think only of these." We see here how difficult it is to excite wicked men to the contemplation of heavenly things. They interpret all things in a low and corrupt sense, and suppose all others to be governed as they are themselves.

24. *That I am* he. That I am the Messiah.

25. *Who art thou?* As Jesus did not *expressly* say in the previous verse that he was the Messiah, they professed still

unto them, Even *the same* that I said unto you from the beginning.
26 I have many things to say and to judge of you; but [x]he that sent me is true, and I speak to the world those things which I have heard of him.
27 They understood not that he spake to them of the Father.

x ch.7.28.

28 Then said Jesus unto them, When ye have [y]lifted up the Son of man, then shall ye know that I am *he*, and *that* I do nothing of myself; but as my Father hath taught me, I speak these things.
29 And he that sent me is with me: the Father hath not left me

y ch.3.14; 12.32.

not to understand him. In great contempt, therefore, they asked him who *he* was. As if they had said, "Who art thou that undertakest to threaten us in this manner?" When we remember that they regarded him as a mere pretender from Galilee; that he was poor and without friends; and that he was persecuted by those in authority, we cannot but admire the patience with which all this was borne, and the coolness with which he answered them. ¶ *Even* the same, &c. What he had professed to them was that he was the light of the world; that he was the bread that came down from heaven; that he was sent by his Father, &c. From all this they might easily gather that he claimed to be the Messiah. He assumed no *new* character; he made no *change* in his professions; he is the same yesterday, to-day, and for ever; and as he had once professed to be the light of the world, so, in the face of contempt, persecution, and death, he adhered to the profession. ¶ *The beginning.* From his first discourse with them, or *uniformly.*

26. *I have many things to say.* There are many things which I *might* say to reprove and expose your pride and hypocrisy. By this he implied that he understood *well* their character, and that he was able to expose it. This, indeed, he had shown them in his conversations with them. ¶ *And to judge of you.* To reprove in you. There are many things in you which I might condemn. ¶ *But he that sent me is true.* Is worthy to be believed, and his declarations about men are to be credited. The meaning of this verse may be thus expressed: "I have indeed many things to say blaming or condemning you. I have already said many such things, and there are many more that I might say; but I speak only those things which God has commanded. I speak not of myself I come to execute his commission, and he is worthy to be heard and feared. Let it not be thought, therefore, that my judgment is rash or harsh. It is such as is commanded by God."

27. *They understood not.* They knew not, or they were unwilling to receive him as a messenger from God. They doubtless understood that he *meant* to speak of God, but they were unwilling to acknowledge that he *really* came from God.

28. *When ye have lifted up.* When you have crucified. See Notes on ch. iii. 14; also ch. xii. 32. ¶ *The Son of man.* See Notes on Mat. viii. 19, 20. ¶ *Then shall ye know.* Then shall you have *evidence* or *proof.* ¶ *That I am* he. Am the Messiah, which I have professed to be. ¶ *And* that *I do nothing of myself.* That is, you shall have proof that God has sent me; that I am the Messiah; and that God concurs with me and approves my doctrine. This proof was furnished by the miracles that attended the death of Jesus —the earthquake and darkness; but chiefly by his resurrection from the dead, which proved, beyond a doubt, that he was what he affirmed he was—the Messiah.

29. *Is with me.* In working miracles, &c. ¶ *Hath not left me alone.* Though *men* had forsaken and rejected him, yet God attended him. ¶ *Those things that please him.* See Mat. iii. 17: "This is my beloved Son, in whom I am well pleased," Phi. ii. 8; Is. liii. 10, 11, 12; 2 Pe. i. 17; Lu. iii. 22; Mat. xvii. 5. His *undertaking* the work of redemption was pleasing to God, and he had the consciousness that in *executing* it he did those things which God approved. It is a small matter to have *men* opposed to us, if we have a conscience void of offence, and evidence that we please God. Comp. He. xi. 5: "Enoch —before his translation had this testimony that he *pleased* God." See also 1 Co. iv. 3.

alone, for I do always those things that please him.

30 As he spake these words many[z] believed on him.

31 Then said Jesus to those Jews which believed on him, If ye [a]continue in my word, *then* are ye my disciples indeed;

32 And ye shall [b]know the truth, and [c]the truth shall make you free.

33 They answered him, We be Abraham's seed, and were [d]never in

z ch.10.42. a Ro.2.7; Col.1.23; He.10.38,39.

b Ho.6.3.
c Ps.119.45; ch.17.17; Ro.6.14,18,22; Ja.1.25; 2.12.
d Le.25.42.

30. *Many believed on him.* Such was the convincing nature and force of the truths which he presented, that they believed he was the Messiah and received his doctrine. While there were many that became more obstinate and hardened under his preaching, there were many, also, who by the same truth were made penitent and believing. "The same sun that hardens the clay, softens the wax" (Clarke).

31. *If ye continue in my word.* If you continue to obey my commandments and to receive my doctrines. ¶ Then *are ye*, &c. This is the true test of Christian character. Jn. xiv. 21: "He that hath my commandments and keepeth them, he it is that loveth me." See 1 Jn. ii. 4; iii. 24; 2 Jn. 6. In this place Jesus cautions them against *too much confidence* from their present feelings. They were just converted—converted under a single sermon. They had had no time to test their faith. Jesus assures them that if their faith should abide the test, if it should produce obedience to his commandments and a holy life, it would be proof that their faith was genuine, for the tree is known by its fruit. So we may say to all new converts, Do not repress your love or your joy, but do not be too confident. Your faith has not yet been tried, and if it does not produce a holy life it is vain, Ja. ii. 17–26.

32. *Shall know the truth.* See Notes on ch. vii. 17. ¶ *The truth shall make you free.* The *truth* here means the Christian religion. Comp. Ga. iii. 1; Col. i. 6. The doctrines of the true religion shall make you free—that is, it will free you from the *slavery* of evil passions, corrupt propensities, and grovelling views. The condition of a sinner is that of a *captive* or a *slave* to sin. He is one who serves and obeys the dictates of an evil heart and the promptings of an evil nature, Ro. vi. 16, 17: "Ye were the *servants* of sin;" —19: "Ye have yielded your members *servants* unto iniquity;"—20; vii. 6, 8, 11; viii. 21; Ac. viii. 23: "Thou art in the —*bond* of iniquity;" Ga. iv. 3, 9. The effect of the gospel is to break this hard bondage to sin and to set the sinner free. We learn from this that religion is not slavery or oppression. It is true freedom.

"He is the freeman whom the truth makes free,
And all are slaves beside."—*Cowper.*

The service of God is freedom from degrading vices and carnal propensities; from the slavery of passion and inordinate desires. It is a cheerful and delightful surrender of ourselves to Him whose yoke is easy and whose burden is light.

33. *They answered him.* Not those who believed on him, but some who stood by and heard him. ¶ *We be Abraham's seed.* We are the children or descendants of Abraham. Abraham was not a slave, and they pretended that they were his real descendants, inheriting his freedom as well as his spirit. They meant that they were the direct descendants of Abraham by Isaac, his heir. Ishmael, also Abraham's son, was the son of a bond-woman (Ga. iv. 21–23), but *they* were descended in a direct line from the acknowledged heir of Abraham. ¶ *Were never in bondage to any man.* This is a most remarkable declaration, and one evidently false. Their fathers had been slaves in Egypt; their nation had been enslaved in Babylon; it had repeatedly been subject to the Assyrians; it was enslaved by Herod the Great; and was, at the very time they spoke, groaning under the grievous and insupportable bondage of the Romans. But we see here, 1st. That Jesus was right when he said (ver. 44), "Ye are of your father the devil; he is a liar, and the father of it." 2d. Men will say anything, however false or ridiculous, to avoid and oppose the truth. 3d. Men groaning under the most oppressive bondage are often unwilling to acknowledge it in any manner, and are indignant at being charged with it. This is the case with all sinners. 4th. Sin, and the bondage

bondage to any man; how sayest thou, Ye shall be made free?

34 Jesus answered them, Verily, verily, I say unto you, [e]Whosoever committeth sin is the servant of sin.

35 And the [f]servant abideth not in the house for ever, *but* the Son abideth ever.

36 If[g] the Son, therefore, shall make you free, [h]ye shall be free indeed.

37 I know that ye are Abraham's seed; but ye seek to kill me, because my word hath no place in you.

38 I[i] speak that which I have seen with my Father, and ye do that which ye have seen with your father.

e Ro.6.16,20; 2 Pe.2.19. f Ga.4.30. g Is.61.1. h Ro.8.2; Ga.5.1. i ch.14.10,24.

---

to sin, produces passion, irritation, and a troubled soul; and a man under the influence of passion regards little what he says, and is often a liar. 5th. There is need of the gospel. That only can make men free, calm, collected, meek, and lovers of truth; and as every man is by nature the servant of sin, he should without delay seek an interest in that gospel which can alone make him free.

34. *Whosoever committeth sin*, &c. In this passage Jesus shows them that he did not refer to *political* bondage, but to the slavery of the soul to evil passions and desires. ¶ *Is the servant.* Is the *slave* of sin. He is bound to it as a slave is to his master.

35. *The servant abideth not*, &c. The servant does not, of course, remain for ever, or till his death, with his master. If he is disobedient and wicked, the master sells him or turns him away. He is not the heir, and may at any time be expelled from the house of his master. But a son is the heir. He cannot be in this manner cast off or sold. He is privileged with the right of remaining in the family. This takes place in common life. So said the Saviour to the Jews: "You, if you are disobedient and rebellious, may at any time be rejected from being the people of God, and be deprived of your peculiar privileges as a nation. You are in the condition of servants, and unless you are made *free* by the gospel, and become entitled to the privilege of the sons of God, you will be cast off like an unfaithful slave." Comp. He. iii. 5, 6. ¶ *Abideth not.* Remains not, or has not the legal right to remain. He may at any time be rejected or sold. ¶ *In the house.* In the family of his master. ¶ *For ever.* During the whole time of his life. ¶ *The Son.* The heir. He remains, and cannot be sold or cast off. ¶ *Ever.* Continually. Till the day of his death. This is the privilege of a son, to inherit and dispose of the property.

36. *If the Son*, &c. The Son of God —heir of all things—who is for ever with God, and who has therefore the right and power to liberate men from their thraldom. ¶ *Shall make you free.* Shall deliver you from the bondage and dominion of sin. ¶ *Free indeed.* Truly and really free. You shall be blessed with the most valuable freedom; not from the chains and oppressions of earthly masters and monarchs, but from the bondage of sin.

37. *I know*, &c. I admit that you are the descendants of Abraham. Jesus did not wish to call that in question, but he endeavoured to show them that they might be his descendants and still lack entirely his spirit. See Notes on Mat. iii. 9. ¶ *Ye seek to kill me.* Ch. v. 16; vii. 32. ¶ *Because my word.* My *doctrine;* the principles of my religion. You have not the spirit of my doctrine; you hate it, and you therefore seek to kill me. ¶ *Hath no place.* That is, you do not embrace my doctrine, or it exerts no influence over you. The original word conveys the notion that there was no *room* for his doctrine in their minds. It met with *obstructions*, and did not penetrate into their hearts. They were so filled with pride, and prejudice, and false notions, that they would not receive his truth; and as they had not his truth or spirit, and could not bear it, they sought to kill him.

38. *I speak*, &c. Jn. iii. 11–13. ¶ *My Father.* God. ¶ *Your father.* The devil. See ver. 44. To *see* here means *to learn of.* They had learned of or been taught by the devil, and *imitated* him.

39. *Abraham is our father.* We are descended from Abraham. Of this the Jews boasted much, as being descended from such an illustrious man. See

39 They answered and said unto
him, [k]Abraham is our father. Jesus saith unto them, [l]If ye were
Abraham's children, ye would do
the works of Abraham.
40 But now ye seek to kill me, a
man that hath told you the truth,
which I have heard of God: [m]this
did not Abraham.

k Mat.3.9. *l* Ro.2.28,29; 9.7; Ga.3.7,29. *m* Ro.4.12.

41 Ye do the deeds of your father. Then said they to him, We
be not born of fornication; [n]we
have one Father, *even* God.
42 Jesus said unto them, [o]If God
were your Father, ye would love
me; for I proceeded forth and
came from God; neither came I of
myself, but [p]he sent me.

n Is.63.16; 64.8. *o* Mal.1.6; 1 Jn.5.1. *p* ch.17.8,25.

Notes on Mat. iii. 9. As Jesus did not expressly say who he meant (ver. 38) when he said they did the works of their father, they obstinately persisted in pretending not to understand him, as if they had said, "We acknowledge no other father but Abraham, and to charge us with being the offspring of another is slander and calumny." ¶ *If ye were Abraham's children.* The words *sons* and *children* are often used to denote those who *imitate* another or who have his spirit. See Notes on Mat. i. 1. Here it means, "if you were worthy to be called the children of Abraham, or if you had his spirit."

40. *Ye seek to kill me.* See ver. 37. ¶ *This did not Abraham.* Or *such* things Abraham did not do. There are two things noted here in which they differed from Abraham: 1st. In seeking to kill him, or in possessing a murderous and bloody purpose. 2d. In rejecting the truth as God revealed it. Abraham was distinguished for love to man as well as God. He liberated the captives (Ge. xiv. 14–16); was distinguished for hospitality to strangers (Ge. xviii. 1–8); and received the revelations of God to him, however mysterious, or however trying their observance, Ge. xii. 1–4; xv. 4–6; xxii. It was for these things that he is so much commended in the New Testament (Ro. iv. 9; ix. 9; Ga. iii. 6); and, as the Jews sought to *kill* Jesus instead of treating him hospitably and kindly, they showed that they had none of the spirit of Abraham.

41. *The deeds of your father.* See ver. 38. Jesus repeats the charge, and yet repeats it as if unwilling to *name* Satan as their father. He chose that they should *infer* whom he meant, rather than bring a charge so direct and repelling. When the Saviour delivered an awful or an offensive truth, he always approached the mind so that the truth might make the deepest impression. ¶ *We be not born of fornication.* The people still professed not to understand him; and since Jesus had denied that they were the children of *Abraham*, they affected to suppose that he meant they were a mixed, spurious race; that they had no right to the covenant privileges of the Jews; that they were not worshippers of the true God. Hence they said, We are not thus descended. We have the evidence of our genealogy. We are worshippers of the true God, descended from those who acknowledged him, and we acknowledge no other God and Father than him. To be *children of fornication* is an expression denoting in the Scriptures *idolatry*, or the worship of other gods than the true God, Is. i. 21; lvii. 3; Ho. i. 2; ii. 4. This they denied. They affirmed that they acknowledged no God for their Father but the true God.

42. *If God were your Father.* If you had the spirit of God, or love to him, or were worthy to be called his children. ¶ *Ye would love me.* Jesus was "the brightness of the Father's glory and the express image of his person," He. i. 3. "Every one that loveth him that begat, loveth him also that is begotten of him," 1 Jn. v. 1. From this we see, 1st. That all who truly love God, love his Son Jesus Christ. 2d. That men that *pretend* that they love God, and reject his Son, have no evidence that they are the friends of God. 3d. That those who reject the Bible cannot be the friends of God. If they loved God, they would love Him who came from him, and who bears his image.

43. *Why do ye not,* &c. My meaning is clear, if you were disposed to understand me. ¶ Even *because ye cannot hear my word.* The word "hear" in this place is to be understood in the sense of *bear* or *tolerate*, as in ch. vi. 60. His doctrine was offensive to them. They hated it, and hence they perverted his meaning, and were resolved *not* to understand him. Their pride, vanity,

43 Why do ye not understand
my speech? *even* [q]because ye cannot hear my word.
44 Ye[r] are of *your* father the
devil, and the lusts of your father
ye will do. He was a murderer
from the beginning, and [s]abode
not in the truth, because there is
no truth in him. When he speaketh a lie, he speaketh of his own;
for he is a liar, and the father of it.
45 And [t]because I tell *you* the
truth, ye believe me not.
46 Which of you [u]convinceth me

q Is.6.9. r Mat.13.38; 1 Jn.3.8. s Jude 6. t Ga.4.16; 2 Th.2.10. u He.4.15.

and wickedness opposed it. The reason why sinners do not understand the Bible and its doctrines is because they cannot *bear* them. They hate them, and their hatred produces want of candour, a disposition to cavil and to pervert the truth, and an obstinate purpose that it *shall not* be applied to their case. Hence they embrace every form of false doctrine, and choose error rather than truth, and darkness rather than light. A *disposition to believe God* is one of the best helps for understanding the Bible.

44. *Ye are of* your *father the devil.* That is, you have the temper, disposition, or spirit of the devil. You are influenced by him, you imitate him, and ought therefore to be called his children. See also 1 Jn. iii. 8, 9, 10; Ac. xiii. 10: "Thou child of the devil." ¶ *The devil.* See Notes on Mat. iv. 1. ¶ *The lusts.* The *desires* or *the wishes.* You do what pleases him. ¶ *Ye will do.* The word *will*, here, is not an auxiliary verb. It does not simply express *futurity*, or that such a thing *will* take place, but it implies an act of *volition.* This you *will* or *choose* to do. The same mode of speech occurs in Jn. v. 40. In what *respects* they showed that they were the children of the devil he proceeds to state: 1st, in their murderous disposition; 2d, in rejecting the truth; 3d, in being favourable to falsehood and error. ¶ *He was a murderer from the beginning.* That is, from the beginning of the world, or in the first records of him he is thus represented. This refers to the seduction of Adam and Eve. Death was denounced against sin, Ge. ii. 17. The devil deceived our first parents, and they became subject to death, Ge. iii. As he was the *cause* why death came into the world, he may be said to have been a *murderer* in that act, or from the beginning. We see here that the tempter mentioned in Ge. iii. was Satan or the devil, who is here declared to have been the murderer. Comp. Ro. v. 12, and Re. xii. 9: "And the great dragon was cast out, that old serpent called the devil, and Satan, which deceiveth the whole world." Besides, Satan has in all ages *deceived* men, and been the cause of their spiritual and eternal death. His work has been to destroy, and in the worst sense of the word he may be said to have been *a murderer.* It was by his instigation, also, that Cain killed his brother, 1 Jn. iii. 12: "Not as Cain, who was of that wicked one, and slew his brother." As the Jews endeavoured to *kill* the Saviour, so they showed that they had the spirit of the devil. ¶ *Abode not in the truth.* He departed from the truth, or was false and a liar. ¶ *No truth in him.* That is, he is a liar. It is his nature and his work to deceive. ¶ *He speaketh of his own.* The word "own" is in the *plural* number, and means *of the things that are appropriate to him*, or that belong to his nature. His speaking falsehood is originated by his own propensities or disposition; he utters the expressions of his genuine character. ¶ *He is a liar.* As when he *deceived* Adam, and in his deceiving, as far as possible, the world, and dragging man down to perdition. ¶ *The father of it.* The father or *originator of falsehood.* The word "it" refers to *lie* or *falsehood* understood. From him falsehood first proceeded, and all liars possess his spirit and are under his influence. As the Jews refused to hear the truth which Jesus spoke, so they showed that they were the children of the father of lies.

46. *Which of you convinceth me?* To *convince*, with us, means to satisfy a *man's own mind* of the truth of anything; but this is not its meaning here. It rather means to *convict.* Which of you can *prove* that I am guilty of sin? ¶ *Of sin.* The word *sin* here evidently means *error*, *falsehood*, or *imposture.* It stands opposed to *truth.* The argument of the Saviour is this: A doctrine might be rejected if it could be proved that he that delivered it was an *impostor;*

of sin? And if I say the truth, why do ye not believe me?

47 He that is of God heareth God's words; ye, therefore, hear *them* not, because ye are not of God.

48 Then answered the Jews and said unto him, Say we not well, that thou art a Samaritan, [v]and hast a devil?

49 Jesus answered, I have not a devil; but I honour my Father, and ye do dishonour me.

50 And [w]I seek not mine own glory: there is one that seeketh and judgeth.

v ch.7.20. w ch.5.41.

---

but as you cannot prove this of me, you are bound to receive my words.

47. *He that is of God.* He that loves, fears, and honours God. ¶ *Heareth God's words.* Listens to, or attends to the doctrines or commandments of God, as a child who loves his parent will regard and obey his commandments. This is an evidence of true piety. A willingness to receive all that God teaches us, and to obey all his commandments, is an undoubted proof that we are his friends, Jn. xiv. 21; 1 Jn. ii. 4; iii. 24. As the Jews did *not* show a readiness to obey the commands of God, it proved that they were not of him, and to this was owing their rejection of the Lord Jesus.

48. *Say we not well.* Say we not *truly.* ¶ *Thou art a Samaritan.* This was a term of contempt and reproach. See Notes on ch. iv. 9. It had the force of charging him with being a *heretic* or a *schismatic*, because the Samaritans were regarded as such. ¶ *And hast a devil.* See ch. vii. 20. This charge they brought against him because he had said that they were not of God, or were not the friends of God. This they regarded as the same as taking sides with the Samaritans, for the question between the Jews and Samaritans was, which of them worshipped God aright, ch. iv. 20. As Jesus affirmed that the *Jews* were not of God, and as he, contrary to all *their* views, had gone and preached to the Samaritans (ch. iv.), they regarded it as a proof that he was disposed to take part with them. They also regarded it as evidence that he had a devil. The *devil* was an *accuser* or *calumniator;* and as Jesus charged them with being opposed to God, they considered it as proof that he was influenced by such an evil spirit. ¶ *Devil.* In the original, *demon.* Not the prince or chief of the devils, but an evil spirit.

49. *I have not a devil.* To the first part of the charge, that he was a Samaritan, he did not reply. To the other part he replied by saying that he *honoured his Father.* He taught the doctrines that tended to exalt God. He taught that he was holy and true. He sought that men should love him and obey him. All his teaching proved this. An evil spirit would not do this, and this was sufficient proof that he was not influenced by such a spirit.

50. *Mine own glory.* My own praise or honour. In all his teaching this was true. He did not seek to exalt or to vindicate himself. He was willing to lie under reproach and to be despised. He regarded little, therefore, their taunts and accusations; and *even now,* he says, he would not seek to *vindicate himself.* ¶ *There is one that seeketh and judgeth.* God will take care of my reputation. He seeks my welfare and honour, and I may commit my cause into his hands without attempting my own vindication. From these verses (46–50) we may learn—1st. That where men have no sound arguments, they attempt to overwhelm their adversaries by calling odious and reproachful names. Accusations of heresy and schism, and the use of reproachful terms, are commonly proof that men are not only under the influence of unchristian feeling, but that they have no sound reasons to support their cause. 2d. It is right to vindicate ourselves from such charges, but it should not be done by rendering railing for railing. "In meekness we should instruct those that oppose themselves, if God peradventure will give them repentance to the acknowledging of the truth," 2 Ti. ii. 25. 3d. We should not regard it as necessarily dishonourable if we lie under reproach. If we have a good conscience, if we have examined for ourselves, if we are conscious that we are seeking the glory of God, we should be willing, as Jesus was, to bear reproach, believing that God will in due time avenge us, and bring forth our righteousness as the light, and our judgment as the noonday, Ps. xxxvii. 6.

51 Verily, verily, I say unto you, If a man keep my saying, he shall never see death.

52 Then said the Jews unto him, Now we know that thou hast a devil. Abraham [x]is dead, and the prophets; and thou sayest, If a man keep my saying, he shall never taste of death.

53 Art thou greater than our father Abraham, which is dead? And the prophets are dead: whom makest thou thyself?

54 Jesus answered, [y]If I honour myself, my honour is nothing: [z]it is my Father that honoureth me, of whom ye say that he is your God;

55 Yet ye have not known him; but I know him; and if I should say I know him not, I shall be a liar like unto you; but I know him, and keep his saying.

56 Your father Abraham rejoiced to see my day, and [a]he saw *it* and was glad.

x Zec.1.5. *y* ch.5.31,41. *z* ch.17.1. *a* Ge.22.13,14; He.11.13.

---

51. *If a man keep my saying.* If he believes on me and obeys my commandments. ¶ *He shall never see death.* To *see death*, or to *taste of death*, is the same as *to die*, Lu. ii. 26; Mat. xvi. 28; Mar. ix. 1. The sense of this passage is, "He shall obtain eternal life, or he shall be raised up to that life where there shall be no death." See ch. vi. 49, 50; iii. 36; v. 24; xi. 25, 26.

52. *Hast a devil.* Art deranged. Because he affirmed a thing which they supposed to be contrary to all experience, and to be impossible.

53. *Whom makest thou thyself?* Or, who dost thou pretend to be? Although the greatest of the prophets have died, yet *thou*—a Nazarene, a Samaritan, and a devil—pretendest that thou canst keep thy followers from dying! It would have been scarcely possible to ask a question implying more contempt and scorn.

54. *If I honour myself.* If I commend or praise myself. If I had no other honour and sought no other honour than that which proceeds from a desire to glorify myself. ¶ *My honour is nothing.* My commendation or praise of myself would be of no value. See Notes on ch. v. 31.

56. *Your father Abraham.* The testimony of Abraham is adduced by Jesus because the Jews considered it to be a signal honour to be his descendants, ver. 39. As they regarded the sayings and deeds of Abraham as peculiarly illustrious and worthy of their imitation, so they were bound, in consistency, to listen to what he had said of the Messiah. ¶ *Rejoiced.* This word includes the notion of *desire* as well as *rejoicing.* It denotes that act when, impelled with strong desire for an object, we *leap forward* toward its attainment with joy; and it expresses—1st. The fact that this was an object that filled the heart of Abraham with joy; and 2d. That he *earnestly desired* to see it. We have no single word which expresses the meaning of the original. In Mat. v. 12 it is rendered "be exceeding glad." ¶ *To see.* Rather, he earnestly and joyfully desired *that he might see.* To see here means to have *a view* or *distinct conception of.* It does not imply that Abraham *expected* that the Messiah would appear during his life, but that he might have a representation of, or a clear description and foresight of the times of the Messiah. ¶ *My day.* The day of the Messiah. The word "day," here, is used to denote the *time*, the appearance, the advent, and the manner of life of the Messiah. Lu. xvii. 26: "As it was in the *days* of Noah, so shall it be also *in the days* of the Son of man." See Jn. ix. 4; Mat. xi. 12. The day of judgment is also called *the day* of the Son of man, because it will be a remarkable *time* of his manifestation. Or perhaps in both those cases it is called HIS *day* because *he* will act the most conspicuous part; his person and work will *characterize the times;* as we speak of the *days* of Noah, &c., because he was the most conspicuous person of the age. ¶ *He saw* it. See He. xi. 13: "These all died in faith, not having received (obtained the fulfilment of) the promises, *but having seen them afar off*, and were persuaded of them," &c. Though Abraham was not permitted to live to see the times of the Messiah, yet he was permitted to have a prophetic view of him, and also of the design of his coming; for, 1st. God foretold his

57 Then said the Jews unto him, Thou art not yet fifty years old, and hast thou seen Abraham?

58 Jesus said unto them, Verily, verily, I say unto you, Before Abraham was, [b]I am.

b Ex.3.14; Is.43.13; ch.1.1,2; Col.1.17; Re.1.8.

advent clearly to him, Ge. xii. 3; xviii. 18. Comp. Ga. iii. 16: "Now to Abraham and his seed were the promises made. He saith not, And to seeds, as of many; but as of one, and to thy seed, which is Christ." 2d. Abraham was permitted to have a view of the death of the Messiah as a sacrifice for sin, represented by the command to offer Isaac, Ge. xxii. 1-13. Comp. He. xi. 19. The death of the Messiah as a sacrifice for the sins of men was that which characterized his work—which distinguished his times and his advent, and this was represented to Abraham clearly by the command to offer his son. From this arose the proverb among the Jews (Ge. xxii. 14), "In the mount of the Lord it shall be seen," or it shall be provided for; a proverb evidently referring to the offering of the Messiah on the mount for the sins of men. By this event Abraham was impressively told that a parent would not be required to offer in sacrifice his sons for the sins of his soul—a thing which has often been done by heathen; but that God would provide a victim, and in due time an offering would be made for the world. ¶ *Was glad.* Was glad in view of the promise, and that he was permitted so distinctly to see it represented. If the father of the faithful rejoiced so much to see him afar off, how should we rejoice that he has come; that we are not required to look into a distant futurity, but know that he has appeared; that we may learn clearly the manner of his coming, his doctrine, and the design of his death! Well might the eyes of a patriarch rejoice to be permitted to look in any manner on the sublime and glorious scene of the Son of God dying for the sins of men. And *our* chief honour and happiness is to contemplate the amazing scene of man's redemption, where the Saviour groaned and died to save a lost and ruined race.

57. *Fifty years old.* Jesus is supposed to have been at this time about thirty-three. It is remarkable that when he was so young they should have mentioned the number fifty, but they probably designed to prevent the possibility of a reply. Had they said *forty* they might have apprehended a reply, or could not be so certain that they were correct. ¶ *Hast thou seen Abraham?* It is remarkable, also, that they perverted his words. His affirmation was not that *he* had seen Abraham, but that *Abraham* had seen his day. The design of Jesus was to show that he was greater than Abraham, ver. 53. To do this, he says that Abraham, great as he was, earnestly desired to see his time, thus acknowledging his *inferiority* to the Messiah. The Jews perverted this, and affirmed that it was impossible that he and Abraham should have seen each other.

58. *Verily, verily.* This is an expression used only in John. It is a strong affirmation denoting particularly the great importance of what was about to be affirmed. See Notes on ch. iii. 5. ¶ *Before Abraham was.* Before Abraham *lived.* ¶ *I am.* The expression I *am,* though in the *present* tense, is clearly designed to refer to a *past* time. Thus, in Ps. xc. 2, "From everlasting to everlasting thou *art* God." Applied to God, it denotes *continued* existence without respect to time, so far as *he* is concerned. *We* divide time into the past, the present, and the future. The expression, applied to God, denotes that *he* does not measure his existence in this manner, but that the word by which we express the *present* denotes his *continued* and *unchanging* existence. Hence he assumes it as his name, "I AM," and "I AM THAT I AM," Ex. iii. 14. Comp. Is. xliv. 6; xlvii. 8. There is a remarkable similarity between the expression employed by Jesus in this place and that used in Exodus to denote the name of God. The *manner* in which Jesus used it would strikingly *suggest* the application of the same language to God. The question here was about his pre-existence. The objection of the Jews was that he was not fifty years old, and could not, therefore, have seen Abraham. Jesus replied to that that he *existed before Abraham.* As in his human nature he was *not* yet fifty years old, and could not, as a man, have existed before Abraham, this declaration must be referred to another nature; and the passage proves that, while he was *a man,* he was also endowed with *another nature*

59 Then took they up stones to cast at him; but Jesus hid himself and went out of the temple, going through the midst of them, and so passed by.

CHAPTER IX.

AND as *Jesus* passed by, he saw a man which was blind from *his* birth.

2 And his disciples asked him, saying, Master, who did sin, this man, or his parents, that he was born blind?

3 Jesus answered, Neither hath this man sinned, nor his parents, but [a]that the works of God should be made manifest in him.

4 I must work the works of him that sent me while it is day: the

a ch.11.4.

---

existing before Abraham, and to which he applied the term (familiar to the Jews as expressive of the existence of God) I AM; and this declaration corresponds to the affirmation of John (ch. i. 1), that he was in the beginning with God, and was God. This affirmation of Jesus is one of the proofs on which John relies to prove that he was the Messiah (ch. xx. 31), to establish which was the design of writing this book.

59. *Then took they up stones.* It seems *they* understood him as blaspheming, and proceeded, even without a form of trial, to stone him as such, because this was the punishment prescribed in the law for blasphemy, Le. xxiv. 16. See ch. x. 31. The fact that the *Jews* understood him in this sense is strong proof that his words *naturally* conveyed the idea that he was divine. This was in the temple. Herod the Great had not yet completed its repairs, and Dr. Lightfoot has remarked that stones would be lying around the temple in repairing it, which the people could easily use in their indignation. ¶ *Jesus hid himself.* See Lu. iv. 30. That is, he either by a miracle rendered himself invisible, or he so mixed with the multitude that he was concealed from them and escaped. Which is the meaning cannot be determined.

CHAPTER IX.

1. *As* Jesus *passed by.* As he was leaving the temple, ch. viii. 59. This man was in the way in which Jesus was going to escape from the Jews.

2. *Master, who did sin?* &c. It was a universal opinion among the Jews that *calamities* of all kinds were the effects of sin. See Notes on Lu. xiii. 1-4. The case, however, of this man was that of one that was blind from his *birth*, and it was a question which the disciples could not determine whether it was *his* fault or that of his parents. Many of the Jews, as it appears from their writings (see Lightfoot), believed in the doctrine of the *transmigration* of souls; or that the soul of a man, in consequence of sin, might be compelled to pass into other bodies, and be punished there. They also believed that an infant might sin before it was born (see Lightfoot), and that consequently this blindness might have come upon the child as a consequence of that. It was also a doctrine with many that the crime of the parent might be the cause of deformity in the child, particularly the violation of the command in Le. xx. 18.

3. *Neither hath this man sinned,* &c. That is, his blindness is not the effect of his sin, or that of his parents. Jesus did not, evidently, mean to affirm that he or his parents were without any sin, but that this blindness was not the effect of sin. This answer is to be interpreted by the nature of the question submitted to him. The sense is, "his blindness is not to be traced to any fault of his or of his parents." ¶ *But that the works of God.* This thing has happened that it might appear how great and wonderful are the works of God. By the *works of God*, here, is evidently intended the miraculous power which God would put forth to heal the man, or rather, perhaps, the *whole* that happened to him in the course of divine providence—first his blindness, as an act of his providence, and then his *healing* him, as an act of mercy and power. It has *all* happened, not by the fault of his parents or of himself, but by the wise arrangement of God, that it *might be seen* in what way calamities come, and in what way God meets and relieves them. And from this we may learn, 1st. To pity and not to despise and blame those who are afflicted with any natural deformity or calamity. While the Jews regarded it as the effect of *sin*, they looked upon it without compassion. Jesus tells us that it

night cometh, when no man can work.

5 As long as I am in the world, I[b] am the light of the world.

b ch.1.5,9; 8.12; 12.35,46.

6 When he had thus spoken, [c]he spat on the ground, and made clay of the spittle, and he [1]anointed

c Mar.8.23.
1 or, *spread the clay upon the eyes of the blind man.*

is not the fault of man, but proceeds from the wise arrangement of God. 2d. All suffering in the world is not the effect of sin. In this case it is expressly so declared; and there may be many modes of suffering that cannot be traced to any particular transgression. We should be cautious, therefore, in affirming that there can be no calamity in the universe but by transgression. 3d. We see the wise and wonderful arrangement of Divine Providence. It is a part of his great plan to adapt his mercies to the woes of men; and often calamity, want, poverty, and sickness are permitted, that he may show the provisions of his mercy, that he may teach us to prize his blessings, and that deep-felt gratitude for deliverance may bind us to him. 4th. Those who are afflicted with blindness, deafness, or any deformity, should be submissive to God. It is his appointment, and is right and best. God does no wrong, and the universe will, when *all* his works are seen, feel and know that he is just.

4. *The works of him*, &c. The works of beneficence and mercy which God has commissioned me to do, and which are expressive of his goodness and power. This was on the Sabbath-day (ver. 14); and though Jesus had endangered his life (ch. v. 1–16) by working a similar miracle on the Sabbath, yet he knew that this was the will of God that he should do good, and that he would take care of his life. ¶ *While it is day.* The *day* is the proper time for work—night is not. This is the general, the universal sentiment. While the day lasts it is proper to labour. The term *day* here refers to the *life* of Jesus, and to the opportunity thus afforded of working miracles. His life was drawing to a close. It was probably but about six months after this when he was put to death. The meaning is, My life is near its close. While it continues I must employ it in doing the works which God has appointed. ¶ *The night cometh. Night* here represents death. It was drawing near, and he must therefore do what he had to do soon. It is not improbable, also, that this took place near the close of the Sabbath, as the sun was declining, and the shades of evening about to appear. This supposition will give increased beauty to the language which follows. ¶ *No man can work.* It is literally true that *day* is the appropriate time for toil, and that the *night of death* is a time when nothing can be done. Ec. ix. 10: "There is no work, nor device, nor knowledge, nor wisdom in the grave." From this we may learn, 1st. That it is our duty to employ all our time in doing the will of God. 2d. That we should seek for opportunities of doing good, and suffer none to pass without improving it. *We go but once through the world, and we cannot return to correct errors, and recall neglected opportunities of doing our duty.* 3d. We should be especially diligent in doing our Lord's work from the fact that the night of death is coming. This applies to the aged, for they *must* soon die; and to the young, for they *may* soon be called away from this world to eternity.

5. *As long as I am in the world*, &c. As the sun is the natural light of the world, even while it sinks away to the west, so am I, although my days are drawing to a close, the light of the spiritual world. What a sublime description is this! Jesus occupied the same place, filled the same space, shed his beams as far, in the moral world, as the sun does on natural objects; and as all is dark when that sun sinks to the west, so when he withdraws from the souls of men all is midnight and gloom. When we look on the sun in the firmament or in the west, let us remember that such is the great Sun of Righteousness in regard to our souls; that his shining is as necessary, and his beams as mild and lovely on the soul, as is the shining of the natural sun to illumine the material creation. See Notes on ch. i. 4.

6. *And made clay*, &c. Two reasons may be assigned for making this clay, and anointing the eyes with it. One is, that the Jews regarded *spittle* as medicinal to the eyes when diseased, and that they forbade the use of medicines

the eyes of the blind man with
the clay,
7 And said unto him, Go, wash
in the [d]pool of Siloam, (which is,
by interpretation, Sent.) He[e] went
his way, therefore, and washed, and
came seeing.
8 The neighbours, therefore,
and they which before had seen
him that he was blind, said, Is
not this he that sat and begged?

9 Some said, This is he; others
said, He is like him; *but* he said,
I am *he*.
10 Therefore said they unto
him, How were thine eyes opened?
11 He answered and said,[f]A man
that is called Jesus made clay, and
anointed mine eyes, and said unto
me, Go to the pool of Siloam, and
wash; and I went and washed, and
I received sight.

d Ne.3.15. *e* 2 Ki.5.14. *f* ver.6,7.

---

on the Sabbath. They regarded the Sabbath so strictly that they considered the preparation and use of medicines as contrary to the law. Especially it was particularly forbidden among them to use spittle on that day to heal diseased eyes. See instances in Lightfoot. Jesus, therefore, by making this spittle, showed them that their manner of keeping the day was superstitious, and that he dared to do a thing which they esteemed unlawful. He showed that *their* interpretation of the law of the Sabbath was contrary to the intention of God, and that his disciples were not bound by *their* notions of the sacredness of that day. Another reason may have been that it was common for prophets to use some symbolical or expressive action in working miracles. Thus Elisha commanded his *staff* to be laid on the face of the child that he was about to restore to life, 2 Ki. iv. 29. Compare Notes on Is. viii. 18. In such instances the prophet showed that the miracle was wrought by power communicated through *him;* so, in this case, Jesus by this act showed to the blind man that the power of *healing* came from him who anointed his eyes. He could not *see* him, and the act of anointing convinced him of what might have been known without such an act, could he have *seen* him—that Jesus had power to give sight to the blind.

7. *Wash in the pool.* In the *fountain.* ¶ *Of Siloam.* See Notes on Lu. xiii. 4. ¶ *By interpretation, Sent.* From the Hebrew verb *to send*—perhaps because it was regarded as a blessing *sent* or *given* by God. *Why* Jesus sent him to wash there is not known. It is clear that the waters had no efficacy themselves to open the eyes of a blind man, but it is probable that he directed him to go there to *test his obedience*, and to see whether he was disposed to obey him in a case where he could not see the reason of it. An instance somewhat similar occurs in the case of Naaman, the Syrian leper, 2 Ki. v. 10. The proud Syrian despised the direction; the humble blind man obeyed and was healed. This case shows us that we should obey the commands of God, however unmeaning or mysterious they may appear. God has always a reason for all that he directs us to do, and our faith and willingness to obey him are often tried when we can see little of the reason of his requirements. In the first edition of these Notes it was remarked that the word *Siloam* is from the same verb as *Shiloh* in Ge. xlix. 10. "The sceptre shall not depart from Judah—until Shiloh (that is, the Sent of God; the Messiah) come," and that John in this remark probably had reference to this prophecy. This was incorrect; and there is no evidence that John in this passage had reference to that prophecy, or that this fountain was emblematic of the Messiah. The original words *Siloam* and *Shiloh* are from different roots and mean different things. The former, *Siloam* (שִׁלֹחַ), is derived from שָׁלַח (*to send*); the latter, *Shiloh* (שִׁילֹה), means *rest* or *quiet*, and was given to the Messiah, probably, because he would bring *rest*—that is, he would be the "prince of peace." Comp. Is. ix. 6.

8. *The neighbours*, &c. This man seems to have been one who attracted considerable attention. The number of persons totally blind in any community is very small, and it is possible that this was the only blind beggar in Jerusalem. The case was one, therefore, likely to attract attention, and one where there

12 Then said they unto him,
Where is he? He said, I know
not.
13 They brought to the Pharisees him that aforetime was blind.
14 And it was the sabbath-day
when Jesus made the clay and
opened his eyes.
15 Then again the Pharisees
also asked him how he had received his sight. He said unto
them, He put clay upon mine
eyes, and I washed, and do see.
16 Therefore said some of the
Pharisees, This man is not of
God, because he keepeth not the
sabbath-day. Others said, [g]How
can a man that is a sinner do
such miracles? And[h] there was
a division among them.
17 They say unto the blind
man again, What sayest thou of

g ver.31; ch.3.2. *h* ch.7.12,43.

could be no imposture, as he was generally known.

13. *To the Pharisees.* To the members of the Sanhedrim. They did this, doubtless, to accuse Jesus of having violated the Sabbath, and not, as they ought to have done, to examine into the evidence that he was from God.

15. *The Pharisees asked him how,* &c. The proper question to have been asked in the case was whether he had *in fact* done it, and not *in what way.* The question, also, about a sinner's conversion is whether in fact it has been done, and not about the *mode* or *manner* in which it is effected; yet it is remarkable that no small part of the disputes and inquiries among men are about the *mode* in which the Spirit renews the heart, and not about the evidence that it is done.

16. *This man is not of God.* Is not *sent* by God, or cannot be a *friend* of God. ¶ *Because he keepeth not the sabbath-day.* They assumed that *their views* of the Sabbath were correct, and by *those views* they judged others. It did not occur to them to inquire whether the interpretation which they put on the law might not be erroneous. Men often assume their own interpretations of the Scriptures to be infallible, and then judge and condemn all others by those interpretations. ¶ *A sinner.* A deceiver; an impostor. They reasoned conclusively that God would not give the power of working such miracles to an impostor. The miracles were such as could not be denied, nor did even the enemies of Jesus attempt to deny them or to explain them away. They were open, public, frequent. And this shows that they *could* not deny their reality. Had it been possible, they would have done it; but the reality and power of those miracles had already made a party in favour of Jesus, even in the Sanhedrim (ch. vii. 50; xii. 42), and those opposed to them could not deny their reality. It may be added that the early opponents of Christianity never denied the *reality* of the miracles performed by the Saviour and his apostles. Celsus, Porphyry, and Julian—as acute foes of the gospel as perhaps have ever lived—never call this in question. They attempted to show that it was by some evil influence, or to account for the miracles in some other way than by admitting the divine origin of the Christian religion, but about the *facts* they had no question. Were they not as well qualified to judge about those *facts* as men are now? They lived near the time; had every opportunity to examine the evidence; were skilful and talented disputants; and if they *could* have denied the reality of the miracles they would have done it. It is scarcely possible to conceive of more conclusive proof that those miracles were really performed, and, if so, then the Lord Jesus was sent by God. ¶ *A division.* Greek, "*A schism.*" A separation into two parties.

17. *What sayest thou of him?* &c. The translation here expresses the sense obscurely. The meaning is, "What sayest thou of him for giving thee sight?" (Campbell); or, "What opinion of him hath this work of power and mercy to thee wrought in thee?" (Hammond). ¶ *He is a prophet.* That is, "I think that the power to work such a miracle proves that he is sent from God. And though this has been done on the Sabbath, yet it proves that he must have been sent by God, for such a power could never have proceeded from man." We see here, 1st. A noble confession made by the man who was healed, in the face of the rulers of the people, and when he doubtless knew

him, that he hath opened thine
eyes? He said, [i]He is a prophet.
18 But the Jews [k]did not believe
concerning him, that he had been
blind, and received his sight, until
they called the parents of him that
had received his sight.
19 And they asked them, saying,
Is this your son, who ye say was
born blind? How then doth he
now see?
20 His parents answered them
and said, We know that this is
our son, and that he was born
blind;
21 But by what means he now
seeth we know not, or who hath
opened his eyes we know not: he
is of age, ask him; he shall speak
for himself.
22 These *words* spake his parents,
because [l]they feared the Jews; for
the Jews had agreed already that
if any man did confess that he was
Christ, [m]he should be put out of the
synagogue.
23 Therefore said his parents,
He is of age, ask him.
24 Then again called they the
man that was blind, and said unto

i ch.4.19. *k* Is.26.11. *l* Pr.29.25; ch.7.13; 12.42. *m* ver.34; ch.16.2.

that they were opposed to Jesus. We should never be ashamed, before any class of men, to acknowledge the favours which we have received from Christ, and to express our belief of his power and of the truth of his doctrine. 2d. The works of Jesus were such as to prove that he came from God, however much he may have appeared to oppose the previous notions of men, the interpretation of the law by the Pharisees, or the deductions of reason. Men should *yield* their own views of religion to the teachings of God, and believe that he that could open the eyes of the blind and raise the dead was fitted to declare his will.

18, 19. *Is this your son?* &c. The Pharisees proposed *three* questions to the parents, by which they hoped to convict the man of falsehood. 1st. Whether he was their son? 2d. Whether they would affirm that he was *born* blind? and, 3d. Whether they knew by what means he now saw? They evidently intended to intimidate the parents, so that they might give an answer to *one* of these questions that would convict the man of deception. We see here the *art* to which men will resort rather than admit the truth. Had they been half as much *disposed* to believe on Jesus as they were to disbelieve, there would have been no difficulty in the case. And so with all men: were they as much *inclined* to embrace the truth as they are to reject it, there would soon be an end of cavils.

20-22. *His parents answered*, &c. To the first *two* questions they answered without hesitation. They knew that he was their son, and that he was born blind. The third question they *could not* positively answer, as they had not witnessed the means of the cure, and were afraid to express their belief. It appears that they had themselves no doubt, but they were not eye-witnesses, and could not be therefore legal evidence. ¶ *He is of age.* He is of sufficient age to give testimony. Among the Jews this age was fixed at thirteen years. ¶ *If any man did confess that he was Christ.* Did acknowledge that he was *the Messiah.* They had prejudged the case, and were determined to put down all free inquiry, and *not* to be convinced by *any* means. ¶ *Put out of the synagogue.* This took place in the *temple*, or near the temple. It does not refer, therefore, to any *immediate* and violent putting forth from the place where they were. It refers to *excommunication* from the synagogue. Among the Jews there were two grades of excommunication; the one for lighter offences, of which they mentioned twenty-four causes; the other for greater offences. The first excluded a man for thirty days from the privilege of entering a synagogue, and from coming nearer to his wife or friends than 4 cubits. The other was a solemn exclusion for ever from the worship of the synagogue, attended with awful maledictions and curses, and an exclusion from all intercourse with the people. This was called *the curse*, and so thoroughly excluded the person from all communion whatever with his countrymen, that they were not allowed to sell to him anything, even the necessaries of life (Buxtorf). It is probable that this *latter* punishment was what they intended to inflict if anyone should

him, [n]Give God the praise: we know that this man is a sinner.
25 He answered and said, Whether he be a sinner *or no*, I know not: one thing I know, that whereas I was blind, now I see.
26 Then said they to him again, What did he to thee? how opened he thine eyes?
27 He answered them, I have told you already, and ye did not hear; wherefore would ye hear *it* again? will ye also be his disciples?
28 Then they [o]reviled him, and

n Jos.7.19; Ps.50.14,15.

o 1 Pe.2.23.

---

confess that Jesus was the Messiah; and it was the fear of this terrible punishment that deterred his parents from expressing their opinion.

24. *Give God the praise.* This expression seems to be a form of administering an oath. It is used in Jos. vii. 19, when Achan was put on his oath and entreated to confess his guilt. Joshua said, "My son, give, I pray thee, glory to the Lord God of Israel (in the Greek of the Septuagint, the very expression used in John, 'Give God the praise'), and make confession unto him." It is equivalent to an adjuration in the presence of God to acknowledge the truth; as the *truth* would be giving God praise, confessing the case before him, and trusting to his mercy. Comp. 1 Sa. vi. 5. The meaning here is not "give God praise for *healing* you," for they were not willing to admit that *he had been cured* (ver. 18), but *confess* that there is imposture in the case; that you have declared to us a falsehood, that you have endeavoured to impose on us; and by *thus* confessing your sin, give praise and honour to God, who condemns all imposture and falsehood, and whom you will thus acknowledge to be *right* in your condemnation. To induce him to do this, they added that they *knew*, or were satisfied that Jesus was a sinner. As they considered *that point* settled, they urged him to confess that *he* had attempted to impose on them. ¶ *We know.* We have settled that. He has broken the Sabbath, and that leaves no doubt. ¶ *A sinner.* A violator of the law respecting the Sabbath, and an impostor. See ver. 16.

25. *Whether he be a sinner* or no, *I know not.* The man had just said that he believed Jesus to be *a prophet*, ver. 17. By his saying that he did not know whether he was a sinner *may be* meant that *though* he might be a prophet, yet that he might not be perfect; or that it did not become him, being an obscure and unlearned man, to attempt to determine that question. What follows shows that he did not believe that he was a sinner, and these words were probably spoken in *irony* to deride the Pharisees. They were perverse and full of cavils, and were determined not to believe. The man reminded them that the question was not whether Jesus was a sinner; that, though that *might* be, yet it did not settle the other question about opening his eyes, which was the chief point of the inquiry. ¶ *One thing I know*, &c. About this *he* could have no doubt. He disregarded, therefore, their cavils. We may learn, also, here, 1st. That this declaration may be made by every converted sinner. He may not be able to meet the cavils of others. He may not be able to tell *how* he was converted. It is enough if he can say, "I *was* a sinner, but now love God; I *was* in darkness, but have now been brought to the light of truth." 2d. We should not be *ashamed* of the fact that we are made to see by the Son of God. No cavil or derision of men should deter us from such an avowal. 3d. Sinners are perpetually shifting the *real* point of inquiry. They do not inquire into *the facts*. They *assume* that a thing *cannot* be true, and then argue as if *that* was a conceded point. The proper way in religion is first to inquire *into the facts*, and then account for them as we can.

26. *How opened he thine eyes?* The reason why they asked this so often was doubtless to attempt to draw him into a contradiction; either to intimidate him, or throw him off his guard, so that he might be detected in denying what he had before affirmed. But God gave to this poor man grace and strength to make a bold confession of the truth, and sufficient common sense completely to confound his proud and subtle examiners.

28. *Thou art his disciple.* This they cast at him as a reproach. His defence of Jesus they regarded as proof that he was his follower, and this they now attempted to show was inconsistent with being a friend of Moses and his law. Moses had given the law respecting the

said, Thou art his disciple, but we
are Moses' disciples.
29 We[p] know that God spake
unto Moses; *as for* this *fellow*,
we[q] know not from whence he is.
30 The man answered and said
unto them, [r]Why, herein is a marvellous thing, that ye know not
from whence he is, and *yet* [s]he
hath opened mine eyes.
31 Now we know that [t]God
heareth not sinners; [u]but if any
man be a worshipper of God, and
doeth his will, him he heareth.
32 Since the world began was it

p Ps.103.7; He.3.5. q ch.8.14. r ch.3.10.
s Ps.119.18; Is.29.18,19; 35.5; 2 Co.4.6.
t Job 27.9; Ps.66.18; Pr.28.9; Is.1.15; Je.11.11; Eze. 8.18; Mi.3.4; Zec.7.13. u Ps.34.15; Pr.15.29.

Sabbath; Jesus had healed a man contrary, in *their* view, to the law of Moses. They therefore held Jesus to be a violater and contemner of the law of Moses, and of course that his followers were also. ¶ *We are Moses' disciples.* We acknowledge the authority of the law of Moses, which they alleged Jesus has broken by healing on that day.

29. *We know*, &c. We know that God commanded Moses to deliver the law. In that they were correct; but they assumed *their* interpretation of the law to be infallible, and hence condemned Jesus. ¶ As for *this* fellow. The word *fellow* is not in the original. It is simply "*this.*" The word *fellow* implies contempt, which it cannot be proved they intended to express. ¶ *Whence he is.* We know not his origin, his family, or his home. The contrast with the preceding member of the sentence shows that they intended to express their belief that he was not from God. They knew not whether he was mad, whether he was instigated by the devil, or whether he spoke of himself. See ch. vii. 27; viii. 48–52.

30. *A marvellous thing.* This is wonderful and amazing. ¶ *Know not from whence he is.* That you cannot perceive that he who has wrought such a miracle *must* be from God.

31. *Now we know.* That is, it is an admitted or conceded point. No one calls it into question. ¶ *God heareth not.* When a miracle was performed it was customary to invoke the aid of God. Jesus often did this himself, and it was by his power only that prophets and apostles could perform miracles. The word "*heareth*" in this place is to be understood as referring to such cases. God will not *hear*—that is, answer. ¶ *Sinners.* Impostors. False prophets and pretenders to divine revelation. See ver. 24. The meaning of this verse is, therefore, "It is well understood that God will not give miraculous aid to impostors and false prophets." We may remark here, 1st. That the passage has no reference to the prayers which *sinners* make for salvation. 2d. If it had it would not be of course true. It was the mere opinion of this man, in accordance with the common sentiment of the Jews, and there is no evidence that *he* was inspired. 3d. The only prayers which God will not hear are those which are offered in mockery, or when the man loves his sins and is unwilling to give them up. Such prayers God will not hear, Ps. lxvi. 18: "If I regard iniquity in my heart, the Lord will not hear me;" Is. i. 14, 15; Job xxvii. 9; Je. xi. 11; Eze. viii. 18; Mi. iii. 4; Zec. vii. 13. ¶ *A worshipper.* A sincere worshipper; one who fears, loves, and adores him. ¶ *Doeth his will.* Obeys his commandments. This is infallibly true. The Scripture abounds with promises to such that God will hear their prayer. See Ps. xxxiv. 15; Mat. vii. 7, 8.

32. *Since the world began.* Neither Moses nor any of the prophets had ever done this. No instance of this kind is recorded in the Old Testament. As this was a miracle which had *never* been performed, the man argued justly that he who had done it must be from God. As Jesus did it not by surgical operations, but by *clay*, it showed that he had power of working miracles by any means. It may be also remarked that the restoration of sight to the blind by surgical operations was never performed until the year 1728. Dr. Cheselden, an English surgeon, was the first who attempted it successfully, who was enabled to remove a *cataract* from the eye of a young man, and to restore sight. This fact shows the difficulty of the operation when the most skilful natural means are employed, and the greatness of the miracle performed by the Saviour.

33. *Could do nothing.* Could do no such work as this. This reasoning was conclusive. The fact that Jesus could

not heard that any man opened the
eyes of one that was born blind.
33 If this man were not of God,
he could do nothing.
34 They answered and said unto
him, [v]Thou wast altogether born
in sins, and dost thou teach us?
And [w]they [2]cast him out.
35 Jesus heard that they had
cast him out; and when he had
found him, he said unto him,
Dost thou [x]believe on the Son of
God?
36 He answered and said, Who
is he, Lord, that I might believe
on him?
37 And Jesus said unto him,
Thou hast both seen him, [y]and it
is he that talketh with thee.
38 And he said, Lord, I believe.
And[z] he worshipped him.
39 And Jesus said, [a]For judg-

v ver.2. w Is.66.5. 2 or, *excommunicated him.*

x 1 Jn.5.13. y ch.4.26. z Mat.14.33. a ch.5.22,27; 12.47.

---

perform miracles like this was full proof that he was commissioned by God—proof that never has been and never can be refuted. One such miracle proves that he was from God. But Jesus gave *many* similar proofs, and thus put his divine mission beyond the possibility of doubt.

34. *Wast born in sins.* That is, thou wast born in a state of blindness—a state which proved that either thou or thy parents had sinned, and that this was the punishment for it. See ver. 2. Thou wast cursed by God with blindness for crime, and yet thou dost set up for a religious teacher! When men have no arguments, they attempt to supply their place by revilings. When they are *pressed* by argument, they reproach their adversaries with crime, and especially with being *blind, perverse, heretical, disposed to speculation, and regardless of the authority of God.* And especially do they consider it great presumption that one of an inferior *age* or *rank* should presume to advance an argument in opposition to prevailing opinions. ¶ *They cast him out.* Out of the synagogue. They *excommunicated* him. See Notes on ver. 22.

35. *Dost thou believe on the Son of God?* Hitherto he had understood little of the true character of Jesus. He believed that he had *power* to heal him, and he *inferred* that he must be a prophet, ver. 17. He believed according to the *light he had*, and he *now* showed that he was prepared to believe *all* that Jesus said. This is the nature of true faith. It believes all that God *has* made known, and it is *prepared* to receive all that he *will* teach. The phrase *Son of God* here is equivalent to *the Messiah.* See Notes on Mat. viii. 29.

36. *Who is he?* It is probable that the man did not know that he who now addressed him was the same who had healed him. He had not yet *seen him* (ver. 7), but he was prepared to acknowledge him when he did see him. He inquired, therefore, *who* the person was, or wished that he might be pointed out to him, that he *might* see him. This passage shows that he was *disposed* to believe, and had a strong desire to see and hear the Son of God. ¶ *Lord.* This word here, as in many other instances in the New Testament, means "Sir." It is clear that the man did not know that it was the *Lord Jesus* that addressed him, and he therefore replied to him in the common language of respect, and asked him to point out to him the Son of God. The word translated "Lord" here is rendered "Sir" in Jn. iv. 11; xx. 15; xii. 21; Ac. xvi. 30; Mat. xxvii. 63. It should have been also here, and in many other places.

38. *I believe.* This was the overflowing expression of gratitude and faith. ¶ *And he worshipped him.* He did homage to him as the Messiah and as his gracious benefactor. See Notes on Mat. ii. 2. This shows, 1st. That it is right and natural to express thanks and praise for mercies. 2d. All blessings should lead us to pour out our gratitude to Jesus, for it is from him that we receive them. 3d. Especially is this true when the *mind* has been enlightened, when our spiritual eyes have been opened, and we are permitted to see the glories of the heavenly world. 4th. It is right to pay homage or worship to Jesus. He forbade it not. He received it on earth, and for all mercies of providence and redemption we should pay to him the tribute of humble and grateful hearts. The Syriac renders the phrase, "he worshipped him," thus: "and, casting himself down, he adored him." The Persic, "and he bowed

ment I am come into this world, that [b]they which see not might see, and that [c]they which see might be made blind.

40 And *some* of the Pharisees which were with him heard these words, and said unto him, [d]Are we blind also?

41 Jesus said unto them, [e]If ye were blind, ye should have no sin: but now ye say, We see; [f]therefore your sin remaineth.

CHAPTER X.

VERILY, verily, I say unto you, [a]He that entereth not

b 1 Pe.2.9. *c* Mat.13.13; ch.3.19. *d* Ro.2.19; Re.3.17.
e ch.15.22,24. *f* Is.5.21; Lu.18.14; 1 Jn.1.8-10.
a Ro.10.15; He.5.4.

down and adored Christ." The Arabic, "and he adored him." The Latin Vulgate, "and, falling down, he adored him."

39. *For judgment.* The word *judgment*, here, has been by some understood in the sense of *condemnation*—"The effect of my coming is to condemn the world." But this meaning does not agree with those places where Jesus says that he came not to condemn the world, Jn. iii. 17; xii. 47; v. 45. To *judge* is to express *an opinion in a judicial manner*, and also to express any sentiment about any person or thing, Jn. vii. 24; v. 30; Lu. viii. 43. The meaning here may be thus expressed: "I came to *declare the condition* of men; to show them their duty and danger. My coming will have this effect, that some will be reformed and saved, and some more deeply condemned." ¶ *That they*, &c. The Saviour does not affirm that this was the *design* of his coming, but that such would be the *effect* or *result.* He came to declare the truth, and the effect *would be*, &c. Similar instances of expression frequently occur. Comp. Mat. xi. 25; x. 34: "I came not to send peace, but a sword"—that is, such will be the effect of my coming. ¶ *That they which see not.* Jesus took this illustration, as he commonly did, from the case before him; but it is evident that he meant it to be taken in a *spiritual* sense. He refers to those who are blind and ignorant by sin; whose minds have been darkened, but who are desirous of seeing. ¶ *Might see.* Might discern the path of truth, of duty, and of salvation, ch. x. 9. ¶ *They which see.* They who *suppose* they see; who are proud, self-confident, and despisers of the truth. Such were evidently the Pharisees. ¶ *Might be made blind.* Such would be *the effect* of his preaching. It would exasperate them, and their pride and opposition to him would confirm them more and more in their erroneous views. This is always the effect of truth. Where it does not *soften* it *hardens* the heart; where it does not convert, it sinks into deeper blindness and condemnation.

41. *If ye were blind.* If you were *really* blind—had had no *opportunities* of learning the truth. If you were truly ignorant, and were willing to confess it, and to come to me for instruction. ¶ *No sin.* You would not be guilty. Sin is measured by the *capacities* or *ability* of men, and by their opportunities of knowing the truth. If men had no *ability* to do the will of God, they could incur no blame. If they have all proper *ability*, and no *disposition*, God holds them to be guilty. This passage teaches conclusively, 1st. That men are not condemned for what they cannot do. 2d. That the reason why they are condemned is that they are not disposed to receive the truth. 3d. That pride and self-confidence are the sources of condemnation. 4th. That if men are condemned, they, and not God, will be to blame. ¶ *We see.* We have knowledge of the law of God. This they had pretended when they professed to understand the law respecting the Sabbath better than Jesus, and had condemned him for healing on that day. ¶ *Your sin remaineth.* You *are* guilty, and your sin is unpardoned. Men's sins will *always* be unpardoned while they are proud, and self-sufficient, and confident of their own wisdom. If they will come with humble hearts and confess their ignorance, God will forgive, enlighten, and guide them in the path to heaven.

CHAPTER X.

1. *Verily, verily.* See Notes on Jn. iii. 3. ¶ *I say unto you.* Some have supposed that what follows here was delivered on some other occasion than the one mentioned in the last chapter; but the expression *verily, verily*, is one which is not used at the *commencement*

by the door into the sheepfold, but climbeth up some other way, the same is a thief and a robber.

2 But he that entereth in by [b]the door is the shepherd of the sheep.

3 To[c] him the porter openeth, and the sheep hear his voice; and

b ver.7,9. c Re.3.20.

of a discourse, and the discourse itself seems to be a continuation of what was said before. The Pharisees professed to be the *guides* or *shepherds* of the people. Jesus, in the close of the last chapter, had charged them with being *blind*, and of course of being unqualified to lead the people. He proceeds here to state the character of a *true* shepherd, to show what was a hireling, and to declare that *he* was the true shepherd and guide of his people. This is called (ver. 6) *a parable*, and it is an eminently beautiful illustration of the office of the Messiah, drawn from an employment well known in Judea. The Messiah was predicted under the image of a *shepherd*, Eze. xxxiv. 23; xxxvii. 24; Zec. xiii. 7. Hence at the close of the discourse they asked him whether he were the Messiah, ver. 24. ¶ *Into the sheepfold.* The sheepfold was an inclosure made in fields where the sheep were collected by night to defend them from robbers, wolves, &c. It was not commonly covered, as the seasons in Judea were mild. By the figure here we are to understand the Jewish people, or the church of God, which is often likened to a flock, Eze. xxxiv. 1–19; Je. xxiii. 1–4; Zec. xiii. By the *door*, here, is meant the Lord Jesus Christ, ver. 7, 9. He is "the way, the truth, and the life," Jn. xiv. 6. And, as the only proper way of entering the fold was by the door, so the only way of entering the church of God is by believing on him and obeying his commandments. The particular application of this place, however, is to *religious teachers*, who cannot enter properly on the duties of teaching and guarding the flock except by the Lord Jesus—that is, in the way which he has appointed. The Pharisees claimed to be *pastors*, but not under his appointment. They entered some other way. The true *pastors* of the church are those who enter by the influences of the Spirit of Jesus, and in the manner which he has appointed. ¶ *Some other way.* Either at a window or over the wall. ¶ *A thief.* One who *silently* and *secretly* takes away the property of another. ¶ *A robber.* One who does it by *violence* or *bloodshed.* Jesus here designates those pastors or ministers of religion who are influenced not by love to *him*, but who seek the office from ambition, or the love of power, or wealth, or ease; who come, not to promote the welfare of the church, but to promote their own interests. Alas! in all churches there have been many—many who for no better ends have sought the pastoral office. To all such Jesus gives the names of *thieves* and *robbers.*

2. *He that entereth by the door.* This was the way in which a *shepherd* had access to his flock. In ver. 7 Jesus says *he* is the door. In this place he refers to those who *by him*—that is, in accordance with his spirit and law—become ministers of religion. ¶ *Is the shepherd of the sheep.* Christ does not here refer *to himself*, for he is the way or door by which *others* enter; but he refers to all the ministers of the gospel who have access to the church *by* him. In the original, the article "the" is wanting before the word shepherd—"is *a* shepherd." By his entering in this manner he shows that he is a *shepherd*—one who cares for his flock, and does not come to kill and destroy.

3. *To him the porter openeth.* The *porter* is the *doorkeeper.* It seems that the more wealthy Jews who owned flocks employed some person to take charge of the flock. At first *all* shepherds attended their flocks personally by day and by night, and this continued to be commonly the practice, but not always. ¶ *The sheep hear his voice.* The voice of the shepherd. A flock will readily discern the well-known voice of one who is accustomed to attend them. The meaning is, that the people of God will be found disposed to listen to the instructions of those who are appointed by Christ, who preach his pure doctrines, and who show a real love for the church of God. There is scarcely any better test of fidelity in the pastoral office than the approbation of the humble and obscure people of God, when they discern in the preacher the very manner and spirit of the doctrines of the Bible. ¶ *He calleth his own sheep by name.* It was customary, and is still, we are told by travellers, for shepherds to give particular *names* to their sheep,

he [d]calleth his own sheep by name, and [e]leadeth them out.

4 And when he putteth forth his own sheep, he goeth before them, and the sheep follow him, for [f]they know his voice.

5 And a stranger will they not follow, [g]but will flee from him;

d Eze.34.11; Ro.8.30. e Is.40.11. f Ca.2.8; 5.2. g 2 Ti.3.5; Re.2.2.

by which they soon learned to regard the voice of the shepherd. By this our Saviour indicates, doubtless, that it is the duty of a minister of religion to seek an intimate and personal acquaintance with the people of his charge; to feel an interest in them as *individuals*, and not merely to address them *together;* to learn their private wants; to meet them in their individual trials, and to administer to them personally the consolations of the gospel. ¶ *Leadeth them out.* He leads them from the fold to pasture or to water. Perhaps there is here intended the care of a faithful pastor to provide suitable *instruction* for the people of his charge, and to feed them with the bread of life. See a beautiful and touching description of the care of the Great Shepherd in Ps. xxiii.

4. *He putteth forth.* Or leads them out of the fold. ¶ *He goeth before them.* He leads them, and guides them, and does not leave them. A shepherd spent his time with his flocks. He went before them to seek the best pastures and watering-places, and to defend them from danger. In this is beautifully represented the tender care of him who watches for souls as one that must give account.

5. *A stranger*, &c. This was literally true of a flock. Accustomed to the voice and presence of a kind shepherd, they would not regard the command of a stranger. It is also true spiritually. Jesus by this indicates that the true people of God will not follow false teachers—those who are proud, haughty, and self-seeking, as were the Pharisees. Many *may* follow such, but humble and devoted Christians seek those who have the mild and self-denying spirit of their Master and Great Shepherd. It is also true in reference to those who are *pastors* in the churches. They have an influence which no stranger or wandering minister can have. A church learns to put confidence in a pastor; he knows the wants of his people, sees their danger, and can adapt his instructions to them. A stranger, however eloquent, pious, or learned, can have few of these advantages; and it is more absurd to commit the churches to the care of wandering strangers, of those who have no permanent relation to the church, than it would be for a flock to be committed to a foreigner who knew nothing of it, and who had no particular interest in it. The *pastoral office* is one of the wisest institutions of heaven. The following extract from *The Land and the Book* (Thomson) will show how strikingly this whole passage accords with what actually occurs at this day in Palestine: "This is true to the letter. They are so tame and so trained that they *follow* their keeper with the utmost docility. He leads them forth from the fold, or from their houses in the villages, just where he pleases. As there are many flocks in such a place as this, each one takes a different path, and it is his business to find pasture for them. It is necessary, therefore, that they should be taught to follow, and not to stray away into the unfenced fields of corn which lie so temptingly on either side. Any one that thus wanders is sure to get into trouble. The shepherd calls sharply from time to time to remind them of his presence. They know his voice and follow on; but if a stranger call, they stop short, lift up their heads in alarm, and, if it is repeated, they turn and flee, because they know not the voice of a stranger. This is not the fanciful costume of a parable; it is simple fact. I have made the experiment repeatedly. The shepherd goes before, not merely to point out the way, but to see that it is practicable and safe. He is armed in order to defend his charge, and in this he is very courageous. Many adventures with wild beasts occur not unlike that recounted by David, and in these very mountains; for, though there are now no lions here, there are wolves in abundance; and leopards and panthers, exceedingly fierce, prowl about these wild wadies. They not unfrequently attack the flock in the very presence of the shepherd, and he must be ready to do battle at a moment's warning. I have listened with intense interest to their graphic descriptions of downright and desperate fights with these savage beasts. And when

for they know not the voice of strangers.

6 This parable spake Jesus unto them; but they understood not what things they were which he spake unto them.

7 Then said Jesus unto them again, Verily, verily, I say unto you, [h]I am the door of the sheep.

8 All that ever came before me are thieves and robbers; but the sheep did not hear them.

9 I am the door: by me, if any man enter in, he shall be saved, and shall go in and out, and find pasture.

10 The thief cometh not but for to steal, and to kill, and to destroy; I am come that they

h Ep.2.18.

---

the thief and the robber come (and come they do), the faithful shepherd has often to put his life in his hand to defend his flock. I have known more than one case in which he had literally to lay it down in the contest. A poor faithful fellow last spring, between Tiberias and Tabor, instead of fleeing, actually fought three Bedawin robbers until he was hacked to pieces with their khanjars, and died among the sheep he was defending."

6. *This parable.* See Notes on Mat. xiii. 3. ¶ *They understood not,* &c. They did not understand the *meaning* or *design* of the illustration.

7. *I am the door.* I am the way by which ministers and people enter the true church. It is by his merits, his intercession, his aid, and his appointment that they enter. ¶ *Of the sheep.* Of the church.

8. *All that ever came before me.* This does not refer to the prophets, but to those who came *pretending* to be the pastors or guides of the people. Some have supposed that he referred to those who pretended to be the Messiah before him; but there is not evidence that *any* such person appeared before the coming of Jesus. It is probable that he rather refers to the scribes and Pharisees, who claimed to be instructors of the people, who claimed the right to regulate the affairs of religion, and whose only aim was to aggrandize themselves and to oppress the people. See Notes on Jn. i. 18. When the Saviour says that "*all*" were thieves, he speaks in a popular sense, using the word "all" as it is often used in the New Testament, to denote the great *mass* or the *majority.* ¶ *Thieves and robbers.* See ver. 1; also Je. xxiii. 1: "Woe be unto the pastors that destroy and scatter the sheep of my pasture;" Eze. xxxiv. 2, 3: "Woe be to the shepherds of Israel that do feed themselves! Ye eat the fat, and ye clothe you with the wool, ye kill them that are fed; but ye feed not the flock." This had been the *general* character of the Pharisees and scribes. They sought wealth, office, ease at the expense of the people, and thus deserved the character of thieves and robbers. They insinuated themselves slyly as a *thief,* and they oppressed and spared not, like a robber. ¶ *The sheep.* The people of God—the pious and humble portion of the Jewish nation. Though the great *mass* of the people were corrupted, yet there were always *some* who were the humble and devoted people of God. Comp. Ro. xi. 3, 4. So it will be always. Though the great mass of teachers may be corrupt, yet the true friends of God will mourn in secret places, and refuse to "listen to the instruction that causeth to err."

9. *By me.* By my instruction and merits. ¶ *Shall be saved.* See ch. v. 24. ¶ *Shall go in and out,* &c. This is language applied commonly to flocks. It meant that he shall be well supplied, and defended, and led "beside the still waters of salvation."

10. *The thief cometh not,* &c. The thief has no other design in coming but to plunder. So false teachers have no other end in view but to enrich or aggrandize themselves. ¶ *I am come that they might have life.* See Notes on Jn. v. 24. ¶ *Might have* it *more abundantly.* Literally, that they may have *abundance,* or that which abounds. The word denotes that which is not absolutely essential to *life,* but which is superadded to make life happy. They shall not merely have *life*—simple, bare *existence*—but they shall have all those superadded things which are needful to make that life eminently blessed and happy. It would be vast mercy to keep men merely from annihilation or hell; but Jesus will give them eternal joy, peace, the society of the blessed, and all those exalted means of felicity which are prepared for them in the world of glory.

might have life, and that they might have *it* more abundantly.

11 I[i] am the good shepherd: the good shepherd giveth his life for the sheep.

12 But he that is an hireling, and not the shepherd, whose own the sheep are not, seeth the wolf coming, and [k]leaveth the sheep, and fleeth; and the wolf catcheth them, and scattereth the sheep.

13 The hireling fleeth because he is an hireling, and careth not for the sheep.

14 I am the good shepherd, [l]and know my *sheep*, [m]and am known of mine.

15 As[n] the Father knoweth me, even so know I the Father; and [o]I lay down my life for the sheep.

16 And[p] other sheep I have, which are not of this fold: them also I must bring, and they shall

i He.13.20; 1 Pe.2.25. *k* Eze.34.2-6; Zec.11.17. *l* 2 Ti.2.19. *m* 1 Jn.5.20. *n* Mat.11.27. *o* ch.15.13; Is.53.4,5. *p* Is.49.6; 56.8.

11. *The good shepherd.* The faithful and true shepherd, willing to do *all* that is necessary to defend and save the flock. ¶ *Giveth his life.* A shepherd that regarded his flock would hazard his own life to defend them. When the wolf comes, he would still remain to protect them. To *give his life*, here, means the same as *not to fly*, or to forsake his flock; to be willing to expose his life, if necessary, to defend them. Comp. Ju. xii. 3: "I put my life in my hands and passed over," &c.; 1 Sa. xix. 5; xxviii. 21. See ver. 15. The Messiah was often predicted under the character of a shepherd.

12. *A hireling.* A man employed to take care of the sheep, to whom wages is paid. As he does not *own* the sheep, and guards them merely for pay, rather than risk his life he would leave the flock to the ravages of wild beasts. The word translated *hireling* is often employed in a good sense; but here it denotes one who is unfaithful to his trust; and especially those ministers who preach *only* for support, and who are unwilling to encounter any danger or to practise any self-denial for the welfare of the church of God. They are those who have no *boldness* in the cause of their Master, but who, rather than lose their reputation or place, would see the church corrupted and wasted by its spiritual foes. ¶ *Whose own the sheep are not.* Who does not own the sheep.

13. *Because he is a hireling.* Because he regards only his wages. He feels no special interest in the flock.

14. *Know my* sheep. Know my people, or my church. The word *know* here is used in the sense of *affectionate regard* or *love.* It implies such a knowledge of their wants, their dangers, and their characters, as to result in a *deep interest* in their welfare. Thus the word "knoweth," in ver. 15, is in ver. 17 explained by the word "loveth." Jesus *knows* the hearts, the dangers, and the wants of his people, and his kindness as their shepherd prompts him to defend and aid them. ¶ *Am known of mine.* That is, he is known and loved as their Saviour and Friend. They have seen their sins, and dangers, and wants; they have felt their need of a Saviour; they have come to him, and they have found him and his doctrines to be such as they need, and they have loved him. And as a flock follows and obeys its kind shepherd, so they follow and obey him who leads them beside the still waters, and makes them to lie down in green pastures.

15. *As the Father knoweth me*, &c. See Notes on Mat. xi. 27; also Lu. x. 22. ¶ *I lay down my life for the sheep.* That is, I give my life as an atoning sacrifice for their sins. I die in their place, to redeem them from sin, and danger, and death. See ver. 17, 18.

16. *Other sheep.* There are others who shall be members of my redeemed church. ¶ *I have.* This does not imply that they were *then* his friends, but that they *would* be. There were others whom it was his *purpose* and *intention* to call to the blessings of the gospel and salvation. The purpose was so sure, and the fact that they would believe on him so certain, that he could use the present tense as if they were already his own. This purpose was in accordance with the promise (Is. liii. 11), "He shall see of the travail of his soul, and shall be satisfied." An instance of a parallel expression occurs in Ac. xviii. 10, "I *have much people* in this city" (Corinth). That is, it was the *purpose* of God to bless the preaching of Paul, and give

hear my voice; [q]and there shall be one fold *and* one shepherd.

17 Therefore doth my Father love me, [r]because I lay down my life, that I might take it again.

18 No man taketh it from me, but [s]I lay it down of myself. I have power to lay it down, and [t]I have power to take it again. [u]This commandment have I received of my Father.

19 There was a division, there-

q Eze.37.22; Ep.2.14. r Is.53.7-12; He.2.9. s Phi.2.6-8. t ch.2.19. u ch.6.38.

---

him many souls as the seals of his ministry. It was so *certain* that they would believe in the Saviour, that it could be spoken of as if it were already done. This certainty could have existed only in consequence of the *intention* of God that it *should be* so. It did not consist in any disposition to embrace the gospel which was foreseen, for they were the most corrupt and licentious people of antiquity, and it must have been because God *meant* that it should be so. Declarations like these are full proof that God has a *plan* in regard to the salvation of men, and that the number is known and determined by him. Learn—1. That it is not a question of chance or uncertainty whether men shall be saved. 2. That there is encouragement for preaching the gospel. There are those whom God *means* to save, and if he *intends* to do it it will be done. ¶ *Not of this fold.* Not Jews. This is a distinct intimation that the gospel was to be preached to the Gentiles—a doctrine extremely offensive to the Jews. This prediction of the Saviour has been strikingly confirmed in the conversion of millions of the Gentiles to the gospel. ¶ *Them also I must bring.* Bring into the church and kingdom of heaven. This was to be done, not by his personal ministry, but by the labour of his apostles and other ministers. ¶ *One fold.* One church; there shall be no distinction, no peculiar national privileges. The partition between the Jews and the Gentiles shall be broken down, and there shall be no pre-eminence of rank or honour, Ep. ii. 14: "Christ hath broken down the middle wall of partition between us;" Ro. x. 12: "There is no difference between the Jew and the Greek." ¶ *One shepherd.* That is, the Lord Jesus—the common Saviour, deliverer, and friend of all true believers, in whatever land they were born and whatever tongue they may speak. This shows that Christians of all denominations and countries should feel that they are *one*—redeemed by the same blood, and going to the same eternal home. Comp. 1 Co. xii. 13; Ga. iii. 28; Col. iii. 11; Ac. xvii. 26.

17. *I lay down my life.* I give myself to die for my people, in Jewish and pagan lands. I offer myself a sacrifice to show the willingness of my Father to save them; to provide an atonement, and thus to open the way for their salvation. This proves that the salvation of man was an object dear to God, and that it was a source of peculiar gratification to him that his Son was *willing* to lay down his life to accomplish his great purposes of benevolence. ¶ *That I might take it again.* Be raised up from the dead, and glorified, and still carry on the work of redemption. See this same sentiment sublimely expressed in Phi. ii. 5–11.

18. *No man taketh it from me.* That is, no one could take it by force, or unless I was willing to yield myself into his hands. He had power to preserve his life, as he showed by so often escaping from the Pharisees; he voluntarily went up to Jerusalem, knowing that he would die; he knew the approach of Judas to betray him; and he expressly told Pilate at his bar that he could have no power at all against him except it were given him by his Father, Jn. xix. 11. Jesus had a right to lay down his life for the good of men. The patriot dies for his country on the field of battle; the merchant exposes his life for gain; and the Son of God had a right to put himself in the way of danger and of death, when a dying world *needed* such an atoning sacrifice. This shows the peculiar love of Jesus. His death was voluntary. His *coming* was voluntary—the fruit of love. His death was the fruit of love. He was permitted to choose the *time* and *mode* of his death. He did. He chose the most painful, lingering, ignominious manner of death then known to man, and THUS showed his love. ¶ *I have power.* This word often means *authority.* It includes all necessary power in the case, and the commission or *authority* of his Father

fore, again among the Jews for these sayings.
20 And many of them said, He[v] hath a devil, and is mad; why hear ye him?
21 Others said, These are not the words of him that hath a devil. Can a devil [w]open the eyes of the blind?
22 And it was at Jerusalem the feast of the dedication, and it was winter.
23 And Jesus walked in the temple, in [x]Solomon's porch.
24 Then came the Jews round about him, and said unto him, How long dost thou [1]make us to doubt? If thou be the Christ, tell us plainly.
25 Jesus answered them, I told

v ch.7.20. w ch.9.6,&c. x Ac.3.11; 5.12. 1 or, *hold us in suspense.*

to do it. ¶ *Power to take it again.* This shows that he was divine. A *dead* man has no power to raise himself from the grave. And as Jesus had this power *after* he was deceased, it proves that there was some other nature than that which had expired, to which the term "I" might be still applied. None but God can raise the dead; and as Jesus had this power over his own body it proves that he was divine. ¶ *This commandment.* My Father has appointed this, and commissioned me to do it.

20. *He hath a devil.* Ch. vii. 20. ¶ *Is mad.* Is deranged, or a maniac. His words are incoherent and unintelligible.

21. *Not the words,* &c. His words are sober, grave, pious, full of wisdom. The preaching of Jesus always produced effect. It made bitter enemies or decided friends. So will all faithful preaching. It is not the fault of the *gospel* that there are divisions, but of the unbelief and mad passions of men.

22. *The feast of the dedication.* Literally, the feast of the *renewing*, or of the *renovation.* This feast was instituted by Judas Maccabæus, in the year 164 B.C. The temple and city were taken by Antiochus Epiphanes in the year 167 B.C. He slew forty thousand inhabitants, and sold forty thousand more as slaves. In addition to this, he sacrificed a sow on the altar of burnt-offerings, and a broth being made of this, he sprinkled it all over the temple. The city and temple were recovered three years afterward by Judas Maccabæus, and the temple was *purified* with great pomp and solemnity. The ceremony of purification continued through eight days, during which Judas presented magnificent victims, and celebrated the praise of God with hymns and psalms (Josephus, *Ant.*, b. xii. ch. 11). "They decked, also, the forefront of the temple with crowns of gold and with shields, and the gates and chambers they *renewed* and hanged doors upon them," 1 Mac. iv. 52–59. On this account it was called the feast of renovation or dedication. Josephus calls it the feast of *lights*, because the city was illuminated, as expressive of joy. The feast began on the twenty-fifth day of *Chisleu*, answering to the fifteenth day of December. The festival continued for eight days, with continued demonstrations of joy. ¶ *It was winter.* The feast was celebrated in the winter. The word here implies that it was cold and inclement, and it is given as a reason why he walked in Solomon's porch. ¶ *Solomon's porch.* The porch or covered way on the east of the temple. See Notes on Mat. xxi. 12.

24. *Tell us plainly.* The Messiah was predicted as a *shepherd.* Jesus had applied that prediction to himself. They supposed that that was an evidence that he claimed to be the Messiah. He also wrought miracles, which they considered as evidence that he was the Christ, ch. vii. 31. Yet the rulers made a difficulty. They alleged that he was from Galilee, and that the Messiah could not come from thence, ch. vii. 52. He was poor and despised. He came contrary to the common expectation. A splendid prince and conqueror had been expected. In this perplexity they came to him for a plain and positive declaration that he was the Messiah.

25. *I told you.* It is not recorded that Jesus had told them in so many words that he was the Christ, but he had used expressions designed to convey the same truth, and which many of them understood as claiming to be the Messiah. See ch. v. 19; viii. 36, 56; x. 1. The expression "the Son of God" they understood to be equivalent to the Messiah. This he had often used of himself in a sense not to be mistaken. ¶ *The works.* The

you, and ye believed not: [y]the
works that I do in my Father's
name, they bear witness of me.
26 But[z] ye believe not, because
ye are not of my sheep, as I said
unto you.
27 My[a] sheep hear my voice,
and I know them, and they follow me;
28 And I give unto them eternal
life; and [b]they shall never perish,
neither shall any *man* pluck them
out of my hand.
29 My[c] Father, which [d]gave

y ch.5.36. z ch.8.47; 1 Jn.4.6. a ver.4. b ch.17.12; 18.9; He.7.25. c ch.14.28. d ch.17.2.

miracles, such as restoring the blind, curing the sick, &c. ¶ *In my Father's name.* By the power and command of God. Jesus was either the Messiah or an impostor. The Pharisees charged him with being the latter (Mat. xxvi. 60, 61; xxvii. 63; Jn. xviii. 36); but God would not give such power to an impostor. The power of working miracles is an attestation of God to what is taught. See Notes on Mat. iv. 24.

26. *Are not of my sheep.* Are not my people, my followers. You do not possess the spirit of meek and humble disciples. Were it not for pride, and prejudice, and vainglory—for your false notions of the Messiah, and from a determination *not* to believe, you would have learned from my declarations and works that I am the Christ. ¶ *As I said unto you.* Comp. ch. viii. 47.

27. *My sheep.* My church, my people, those who have the true spirit of my followers. The name is given to his people because it was an illustration which would be well understood in a country abounding in flocks. There is also a striking resemblance, which he proceeds to state, between them. ¶ *Hear my voice.* See ver. 3, 4. Applied to Christians, it means that they hear and obey his commandments. ¶ *I know them.* See ver. 14. ¶ *They follow me.* A flock follows its shepherd to pastures and streams, ver. 3. Christians not only *obey* Christ, but they *imitate* him; they go where his Spirit and providence lead them; they yield themselves to his guidance, and seek to be led by him. When Jesus was upon earth many of his disciples *followed* or *attended* him from place to place. Hence Christians are called his *followers*, and in Re. xiv. 4 they are described as "they that follow the Lamb."

28. *I give unto them eternal life.* See ch. v. 24. ¶ *Shall never perish.* To *perish* here means to be *destroyed*, or to be punished in hell. Mat. x. 28: "Which is able to *destroy* (the same word) both soul and body in hell." Mat. xviii. 14: "It is not the will of your Father which is in heaven that one of these little ones should *perish.*" Jn. iii. 15: "That whosoever believeth in him should not *perish.*" Ro. ii. 12: "They who have sinned without law shall also *perish* without law." Jn. xvii. 12; 1 Co. i. 18. In all these places the word refers to *future punishment*, and the declaration of the Saviour is that his followers, his true disciples, shall never be cast away. The original is expressed with remarkable strength: "They shall not be destroyed for ever." Syriac: "They shall not perish to eternity." This is spoken of all Christians—that is, of all who ever possess the character of true followers of Christ, and who can be called his flock. ¶ *Shall any.* The word *any* refers to any power that might *attempt* it. It will apply either to men or to devils. It is an affirmation that no man, however eloquent in error, or persuasive in infidelity, or cunning in argument, or mighty in rank; and that no devil with all his malice, power, cunning, or allurements, shall be able to pluck them from his hand. ¶ *Pluck them.* In the original to *rob;* to seize and bear away as a robber does his prey. Jesus holds them so secure and so certainly that no foe can *surprise* him as a robber does, or overcome him *by force.* ¶ *My hand.* The *hand* is that by which we *hold* or *secure* an object. It means that Jesus has them safely in his own care and keeping. Comp. Ro. viii. 38, 39.

29. *Which gave* them *me.* See ch. vi. 37. ¶ *Is greater.* Is more powerful. ¶ *Than all.* Than all others—men, angels, devils. The word includes *everything*—everything that could *attempt* to pluck them away from God; in other words, it means that God is *supreme.* It implies, farther, that God will keep them, and will so control *all* other beings and things that they shall be safe. ¶ *None is able.* None has power to do it. In these two verses we are taught the following important truths:

them me, is greater than all, and no *man* is able to pluck *them* out of my Father's hand.

30 I[e] and *my* Father are one.

31 Then[f] the Jews took up stones again to stone him.

32 Jesus answered them, Many good works have I showed you from my Father; for which of those works do ye stone me?

33 The Jews answered him, saying, For a good work we stone

e ch.17.11,22. f ch.8.59.

1st. That Christians are *given* by God the Father to Christ. 2d. That *Jesus* gives to them eternal life, or *procures* by his death and intercession, and *imparts* to them by his Spirit, that religion which shall result in eternal life. 3d. That both the Father and the Son are pledged to keep them so that they shall never fall away and perish. It would be impossible for any language to teach more explicitly that the saints will persevere. 4th. That there is no power in man or devils to defeat the purpose of the Redeemer to save his people. We also see our safety, if we truly, humbly, cordially, and *daily* commit ourselves to God the Saviour. In no other way can we have evidence that we are his people than by such a persevering resignation of ourselves to him, to obey his law, and to follow him through evil report or good report. If we do that we are safe. If we do not that we have no evidence of piety, and are not, cannot be safe.

30. *I and* my *Father are one.* The word translated "one" is not in the *masculine*, but in the *neuter* gender. It expresses *union*, but not the precise nature of the union. It *may* express any union, and the particular kind intended is to be inferred from the connection. In the previous verse he had said that he and his Father were *united* in the same object—that is, in redeeming and preserving his people. It was *this* that gave occasion for this remark. Many interpreters have understood this as referring to union of design and of plan. The words may bear this construction. In this way they were understood by Erasmus, Calvin, Bucer, and others. Most of the Christian fathers understood them, however, as referring to the *oneness* or *unity of nature* between the Father and the Son; and that this was the design of Christ appears probable from the following considerations: 1st. The question in debate was not about his being united with the Father in *plan* and *counsel*, but in *power*. He affirmed that he was able to rescue and keep his people from *all* enemies, or that he had *power* superior to men and devils—that is, that he had *supreme* power over all creation. He affirmed the same of his Father. *In this*, therefore, they were *united.* But this was an attribute only of God, and they thus understood him as claiming equality to God in regard to *omnipotence.* 2d. The Jews understood him as affirming his equality with God, for they took up stones to punish him for blasphemy (ver. 31, 33), and they said *to him* that they understood him as affirming that he was God, ver. 33. 3d. Jesus did not *deny* that it was his intention to be so understood. See Notes on ver. 34–37. 4th. He *immediately* made another declaration implying the same thing, leaving the same impression, and which they attempted to punish in the same manner, ver. 37–39. If Jesus had not *intended* so to be understood, it cannot be easily reconciled with moral honesty that he did not distinctly *disavow* that such was his intention. The Jews were well acquainted with their own language. They understood him in this manner, and he left this impression on their minds.

31. *The Jews took up stones.* Stoning was the punishment of a blasphemer, Le. xxiv. 14–16. They considered him guilty of blasphemy because he made himself equal with God, ver. 33. ¶ *Again.* They had before plotted against his life (ch. v. 16, 18), and once at least they had taken up stones to destroy him, ch. viii. 59.

32. *Many good works.* Many miracles of benevolence—healing the sick, &c. His miracles were *good works,* as they tended to promote the happiness of men, and were proofs of his benevolence. He had performed no other works than those of benevolence; he knew that they could charge him with no other, and he confidently appealed to *them* as witnesses of that. Happy would it be if all, when they are opposed and persecuted, could appeal even to their persecutors in proof of their own innocence.

33. *For blasphemy.* See Notes on Mat.

thee not; but for blasphemy; [g] and because that thou, being a man, makest thyself God.

34 Jesus answered them, Is it not written in your law, I said, Ye are gods?

35 If he called them gods, unto whom the word of God came, and the scripture cannot be broken;

36 Say ye of him, whom the Father [h] hath sanctified and sent into the world, Thou blasphemest; because I said, [i] I am the Son of God?

g ch.5.18; ver.30; Ps.82.6; Ro.13.1.

h Is.11.2,3; 49.1,3; ch.6.27. *i* Phi.2.6.

ix. 3. ¶ *Makest thyself God.* See Notes on ch. v. 18. This shows how *they* understood what he had said. ¶ *Makest thyself.* Dost *claim* to be God, or thy language implies this.

34–38. *Jesus answered them.* The answer of Jesus consists of two parts. The first (ver. 34–36) shows that *they* ought not to object to his use of the word God, *even if* he were no more than a man. The second (ver. 37, 38) repeats substantially what he had before said, left the same impression, and in proof of it he appealed to his works.

34. *In your law.* Ps. lxxxii. 6. The word *law* here, is used to include the Old Testament. ¶ *I said.* The Psalmist said, or God said by the Psalmist. ¶ *Ye are gods.* This was said of *magistrates* on account of the dignity and honour of their office, and it shows that the word translated "god" in that place *might* be applied to man. Such a use of the word is, however, rare. See instances in Ex. vii. 1; iv. 16.

35. *Unto whom the word of God came.* That is, who were his servants, or who received their dignity and honour *only* because the law of God was intrusted to them. The *word of God* here means the *command of God;* his commission to them to do justice. ¶ *The scripture cannot be broken.* See Mat. v. 19. The authority of the Scripture is final; it *cannot be set aside.* The meaning is, "If, therefore, the Scripture uses the word *god* as applied to magistrates, it settles the question that it is *right* to apply the term to those in office and authority. If applied to *them,* it may be to others in similar offices. It cannot, therefore, be *blasphemy* to use this word as applicable to a personage so much more exalted than mere magistrates as the Messiah."

36. *Whom the Father hath sanctified.* The word *sanctify* with us means to *make holy;* but this is not its meaning here, for the Son of God was always holy. The original word means to set apart from a common to a sacred use; to devote to a sacred purpose, and to designate or consecrate to a holy office. This is the meaning here. God has *consecrated* or appointed his Son to be his Messenger or Messiah to mankind. See Ex. xxviii. 41; xxix. 1, 44; Le. viii. 30. ¶ *And sent into the world.* As the Messiah, an office far more exalted than that of magistrates. ¶ *I am the Son of God.* This the Jews evidently understood as the same as saying that he was equal with God. This expression he had often applied to himself. The meaning of this place may be thus expressed: "You charge me with blasphemy. The foundation of that charge is the use of the name *God,* or the *Son of God,* applied to myself; yet *that same term* is applied in the Scriptures to magistrates. The use of it there shows that it is *right* to apply it to those who sustain important offices. And especially *you,* Jews, ought not to attempt to found a charge of blasphemy on the application of a word to the *Messiah* which in *your own Scriptures* is applied to *all* magistrates." And we may remark here, 1st. That Jesus did not deny that he meant to apply the term to himself. 2d. He did not deny that it was *properly* applied to him. 3d. He did not deny that it implied that he *was* God. He affirmed only that *they* were *inconsistent,* and *were not authorized* to bring a charge of blasphemy for the application of the *name* to himself.

37. *The works of my Father.* The very works that my Father does. See ch. v. 17: "My Father worketh hitherto, and I work." See the Note on that place. *The works of his Father* are those which God only can do. As Jesus *did* them, it shows that the *name* "*Son of God,*" implying *equality* with God, was properly applied to him. This shows conclusively that he *meant* to be understood as claiming to be equal with God. So the Jews naturally understood him (ver. 39), and they were left with this impression on their minds.

38. *Believe the works.* Though you do

37 If[k] I do not the works of my Father, believe me not.
38 But if I do, though ye believe not me, believe the works; that ye may know and believe that the Father *is* in me, and I in him.
39 Therefore they sought again to take him; but he escaped out of their hand,
40 And went away again beyond Jordan, into [l]the place where John at first baptized; and there he abode.
41 And many resorted unto him, and said, John did no miracle; but [m]all things that John spake of this man were true.
42 And many believed on him there.

CHAPTER XI.

NOW a certain *man* was sick, *named* Lazarus, of Bethany, the town of [a]Mary and her sister Martha.
2 (It was *that* Mary [b]which anointed the Lord with ointment, and wiped his feet with her hair, whose brother Lazarus was sick.)
3 Therefore his sisters sent unto

k ch.14.10,11; 15.24. *l* ch.1.28. *m* ch.3.30-36. *a* Lu.10.38,39. *b* Mar.14.3; ch.12.3.

---

not credit *me*, yet consider my *works*, for they prove that I came from God. No one could do them unless he was sent of God. ¶ *Father* is *in me*, &c. Most intimately connected. See Jn. v. 36. This expression denotes most intimate union—such as can exist in no other case. See Mat. xi. 27. Notes on Jn. xvii. 21.

39. *Sought again to take him.* They evidently understood him as still claiming equality with God, and under this impression Jesus left them. Nor can it be doubted that he *intended* to leave them with this impression; and if so, then he is divine. ¶ *He escaped.* See ch. viii. 59.

40. *Where John at first baptized.* At Bethabara, or Bethany, ch. i. 28.

41. *No miracle.* He did not confirm his mission by working *miracles*, but he showed that he was a *prophet* by foretelling the character and success of Jesus. Either miracle or prophecy is conclusive proof of a divine mission, for no man can foretell a future event, or work a miracle, except by the special aid of God. It may be remarked that the people of that place were properly prepared by the ministry of John for the preaching of Jesus. The persecution of the Jews was the occasion of his going there, and thus the wrath of man was made to praise him. It has commonly happened that the opposition of the wicked has resulted in the increased success of the cause which they have persecuted. God takes the wise in their own craftiness, and brings glory to himself and salvation to sinners out of the pride, and passions, and rage of wicked men.

CHAPTER XI.

1. *A certain* man *was sick.* The resurrection of Lazarus has been recorded only by John. Various reasons have been conjectured why the other evangelists did not mention so signal a miracle. The most probable is, that at the time they wrote Lazarus was still living. The miracle was well known, and yet to have recorded it might have exposed Lazarus to opposition and persecution from the Jews. See ch. xii. 10, 11. Besides, John wrote for Christians who were out of Palestine. The other gospels were written chiefly for those who were in Judea. There was the more need, therefore, that he should enter minutely into the account of the miracle, while the others did not deem it necessary or proper to record an event so well known. ¶ *Bethany.* A village on the eastern declivity of the Mount of Olives. See Notes on Mat. xxi. 1. ¶ *The town of Mary.* The place where she lived. At that place also lived Simon the leper (Mat. xxvi. 6), and there our Lord spent considerable part of his time when he was in Judea. The transaction recorded in this chapter occurred nearly four months after those mentioned in the previons chapter. Those occurred in December, and these at the approach of the Passover in April.

2. *It was* that *Mary*, &c. See Notes on Mat. xxvi. 6; Lu. vii. 36-50.

3. *Whom thou lovest*, ver. 5. The members of this family were among the few peculiar and intimate friends of our Lord. He was much with them, and showed them marks of special friendship (Lu. x. 38-42), and they bestowed upon him peculiar proofs of affection in

him, saying, Lord, behold, [c]he whom
thou lovest is sick.
4 When Jesus heard *that*, he said,
This sickness is not unto death,
but [d]for the glory of God, that
the Son of God might be glorified
thereby.
5 Now Jesus loved Martha, and
her sister, and Lazarus.
6 When he had heard, therefore,
that he was sick, he abode two
days still in the same place where
he was.
7 Then after that saith he to *his*
disciples, Let us go into Judea
again.
8 *His* disciples say unto him,
Master, the Jews [e]of late sought
to stone thee; and [f]goest thou
thither again?
9 Jesus answered, Are there not
twelve hours in the day? If[g] any
man walk in the day he stumbleth
not, because he seeth the light of
this world.

c He.12.6; Re.3.19. d ch.9.3; ver.40. e ch.10.31. f Ac.20.24. g ch.12.35.

return. This shows that *special* attachments are lawful for Christians, and that those friendships are peculiarly lovely which are tempered and sweetened with the spirit of Christ. *Friendships* should always be cemented by religion, and one main end of those attachments should be to aid one another in the great business of preparing to die. ¶ *Sent unto him.* They believed that he had power to heal him (ver. 21), though they did not *then* seem to suppose that he could raise him if he died. Perhaps there were two reasons why they sent for him; one, because they supposed he would be desirous of *seeing* his friend; the other, because they supposed he could restore him. In sickness we should implore the aid and presence of Jesus. He only can restore us and our friends; he only can perform for us the office of a friend when all other friends fail; and he only can cheer us with the hope of a blessed resurrection.

4. *This sickness is not unto death.* The word *death* here is equivalent to *remaining under death*, Ro. vi. 23: "The wages of sin is *death*"—permanent or unchanging death, opposed to *eternal* life. Jesus evidently did not intend to deny that he would die. The words which he immediately adds show that he would expire, and that he would raise him up to show forth the power and glory of God. Comp. ver. 11. Those words cannot be understood on any other supposition than that he *expected* to raise him up. The Saviour often used expressions similar to this to fix the attention on what he was about to say in explanation. The sense may be thus expressed: "His sickness is not *fatal.* It is not *designed* for his death, but to furnish an opportunity for a signal display of the glory of God, and to furnish a standing proof of the truth of religion. It is intended to exhibit the power of the Son of God, and to be a proof at once of the truth of his mission; of his friendship for this family; of his mild, tender, peculiar love as a man; of his power and glory as the Messiah; and of the great doctrine that the dead will rise. ¶ *For the glory of God.* That God may be honoured. See ch. ix. 3. ¶ *That the Son of God*, &c. The glory of God and of his Son is the same. That which promotes the one promotes also the other. Few things could do it more than the miracle which follows, evincing at once the lovely and tender character of Jesus as a man and a friend, and his power as the equal with God.

6. *He abode two days.* Probably Lazarus died soon after the messengers left him. Jesus knew that (ver. 11), and did not hasten to Judea, but remained two days longer where he was, that there might not be the possibility of doubt that he was dead, so that when he came there he had been dead four days, ver. 39. This shows, moreover, that he *intended* to raise him up. If he had not, it could hardly be reconciled with friendship thus to remain, without any reason, away from an afflicted family. ¶ *Where he was.* At Bethabara (ch. i. 28; x. 40), about 30 miles from Bethany. This was about a day's journey, and it renders it probable that Lazarus died soon after the message was sent. One day would be occupied before the message came to him; two days he remained; one day would be occupied by him in going to Bethany; so that Lazarus had been dead four days (ver. 39) when he arrived.

8. *Of late.* About four months before, ch. x. 31.

10 But if a man [h]walk in the
night, he stumbleth, because there
is no light in him.
11 These things said he; and
after that he saith unto them,
Our friend Lazarus [i]sleepeth; but
I go that I may awake him out of
sleep.
12 Then said his disciples, Lord,
if he sleep, he shall do well.
13 Howbeit Jesus spake of his
death; but they thought that he
had spoken of taking of rest in
sleep.
14 Then said Jesus unto them
plainly, Lazarus is dead;

h Ec.2.14. *i* De.31.16; Ac.7.60; 1 Co.15.18,51.

9, 10. *Twelve hours.* The Jews divided the day from sunrise to sunset into twelve equal parts. A similar illustration our Saviour uses in ch. ix. 4, 5. See the Notes on that place. ¶ *If any man walk.* If any man *travels.* The illustration here is taken from a *traveller.* The conversation was respecting a *journey* into Judea, and our Lord, as was his custom, took the illustration from the case before him. ¶ *He stumbleth not.* He is able, having light, to make his journey safely. He sees the obstacles or dangers and can avoid them. ¶ *The light of this world.* The light by which the world is illuminated —that is, the light of the sun. ¶ *In the night.* In darkness he is unable to see danger or obstacles, and to avoid them. His journey is unsafe and perilous, or, in other words, it is not a proper time to travel. ¶ *No light in him.* He sees no light. It is dark; his eyes admit no light within him to direct his way. This description is figurative, and it is difficult to fix the meaning. Probably the intention was the following: 1st. Jesus meant to say that there was an allotted or appointed time for him to live and do his Father's will, represented here by the *twelve hours of the day.* 2d. Though his life was *nearly* spent, yet it was not entirely; a remnant of it was left. 3d. A traveller journeyed on till night. It was as proper for him to travel the *twelfth* hour as any other. 4th. So it was proper for Jesus to labour until the close. It was the proper time for him to work. The night of death was coming, and no work could then be done. 5th. God would defend him in this until the appointed time of his death. He had nothing to fear, therefore, in Judea from the Jews, until it was the will of God that he should die. He was safe in his hand, and he went fearlessly into the midst of his foes, trusting in him. This passage teaches us that we should be diligent to the end of life; fearless of enemies when we know that God requires us to labour, and confidently committing ourselves to Him who is able to shield us, and in whose hand, if we have a conscience void of offence, we are safe.

11. *Lazarus sleepeth.* Is dead. The word *sleep* is applied to death, 1st. Because of the *resemblance* between them, as sleep is the "*kinsman of death.*" In this sense it is often used by pagan writers. But, 2d. In the Scriptures it is used to intimate that death will not be *final:* that there will be an awaking out of this sleep, or a resurrection. It is a beautiful and tender expression, removing all that is dreadful in death, and filling the mind with the idea of calm repose after a life of toil, with a reference to a future resurrection in increased vigour and renovated powers. In this sense it is applied in the Scriptures usually to the saints, 1 Co. xi. 30; xv. 51; 1 Th. iv. 14; v. 10; Mat. ix. 24.

12. *If he sleep, he shall do well.* Sleep was regarded by the Jews, in sickness, as a favourable symptom; hence it was said among them, "Sleep in sickness is a sign of recovery, because it shows that the violence of the disease has abated" (Lightfoot). This seems to have been the meaning of the disciples. They intimated that if he had *this* symptom, there was no need of his going into Judea to restore him.

15. *I am glad,* &c. The meaning of this verse may be thus expressed: "If I had been there during his sickness, the entreaties of his sisters and friends would have prevailed with me to restore him to health. I could not have refused them without appearing to be unkind. Though a restoration to *health* would have been a miracle, and sufficient to convince you, yet the miracle of raising him after being four days dead will be far more impressive, and on that account I rejoice that an opportunity is thus given so strikingly to confirm your faith." ¶ *To the intent.* To furnish you *evidence* on which you might be

15 And I am glad for your sakes that I was not there, to the intent ye may believe; nevertheless, let us go unto him.
16 Then said Thomas, which is called Didymus, unto his fellow-disciples, Let us also go, that we may die with him.
17 Then when Jesus came, he found that he had *lain* in the grave four days already.
18 Now Bethany was nigh unto Jerusalem, [1]about fifteen furlongs off;
19 And many of the Jews came to Martha and Mary, [k]to comfort them concerning their brother.
20 Then Martha, as soon as she

1 i.e. *about two miles.*
k 1 Ch.7.22; Job 2.11; 42.11; Ro.12.15; 1 Th.4.18.

established in the belief that I am the Messiah.

16. *Thomas, which is called Didymus.* These names express the same thing. One is Hebrew and the other Greek. The name means *a twin.* ¶ *Die with him.* It has been much doubted by critics whether the word *him* refers to Lazarus or to Jesus. They who refer it to *Lazarus* suppose this to be the meaning: "Let us go and die, for what have we to hope for if Jesus returns into Judea? Lately they attempted to stone him, and now they will put him to death, and *we* also, like Lazarus, shall be dead." This expression is supposed to be added by John to show the *slowness* with which Thomas believed, and his readiness to doubt without the fullest evidence. See ch. xx. 25. Others suppose, probably more correctly, that it refers to Jesus: "He is about to throw himself into danger. The Jews lately sought his life, and will again. They will put him to death. But let us not forsake him. Let us attend him and die with him." It may be remarked that this, not less than the other mode of interpretation, expresses the *doubts* of Thomas about the *miracle* which Jesus was about to work.

17. *In the grave.* It was sometimes the custom to *embalm* the dead, but in this case it does not seem to have been done. He was probably buried soon after death.

18. *Nigh unto Jerusalem.* This is added to show that it was easy for many of the Jews to come to the place. The news that Jesus was there, and the account of the miracle, would also be easily carried to the Sanhedrim. ¶ *Fifteen furlongs.* Nearly two miles. It was directly east from Jerusalem. Dr. Thomson (*The Land and the Book*, vol. ii. p. 599) says of Bethany: "It took half an hour to walk over Olivet to Bethany this morning, and the distance from the city, therefore, must be about two miles. This agrees with what John says: 'Now Bethany was nigh unto Jerusalem, about fifteen furlongs off.' The village is small, and appears never to have been large, but it is pleasantly situated near the south-eastern base of the mount, and has many fine trees about and above it. We, of course, looked at the remains of those old edifices which may have been built in the age of Constantine, and repaired or changed to a convent in the time of the Crusades. By the dim light of a taper we also descended very cautiously, by twenty-five slippery steps, to the reputed sepulchre of Lazarus, or El Azariyeh, as both tomb and village are now called. But I have no description of it to give, and no questions about it to ask. It is a wretched cavern, every way unsatisfactory, and almost disgusting."

19. *Many of the Jews.* Probably their distant relatives or their friends. ¶ *To comfort.* These visits of consolation were commonly extended to seven days (Grotius; Lightfoot).

20. *Then Martha,* &c. To Martha was intrusted the management of the affairs of the family, Lu. x. 40. It is probable that she first heard of his coming, and, without waiting to inform her sister, went immediately out to meet him. See ver. 28. ¶ *Sat* still *in the house.* The word *still* is not in the original. It means that she remained sitting in the house. The common posture of grief among the Jews was that of *sitting*, Job ii. 8; Eze. viii. 14. Often this grief was so excessive as to fix the person in astonishment, and render him immovable, or prevent his being affected by any external objects. It is possible that the evangelist meant to intimate this of Mary's grief. Comp. Ezr. ix. 3, 4; Ne. i. 4; Is. xlvii. 1.

22. *Whatsoever thou wilt ask of God.* Whatever is necessary to our consolation that thou wilt ask, thou canst ob-

heard that Jesus was coming, went
and met him; but Mary sat *still* in
the house.
21 Then said Martha unto Jesus,
Lord, if thou hadst been here, my
brother had not died.
22 But I know that even now,
whatsoever[l] thou wilt ask of God,
God will give *it* thee.
23 Jesus saith unto her, Thy
brother shall rise again.
24 Martha saith unto him, I know
that he shall rise again [m]in the
resurrection at the last day.
25 Jesus said unto her, I am
[n]the resurrection and [o]the life: he
that believeth in me, [p]though he
were dead, yet shall he live;
26 And [q]whosoever liveth and
believeth in me shall never die.
Believest thou this?
27 She saith unto him, Yea,
Lord; I believe that thou art
the Christ, the Son of God, which
should come into the world.
28 And when she had so said,
she went her way, and [r]called Mary
her sister secretly, saying, [s]The

l ch.9.31. *m* ch.5.29.

n ch.6.40,44. *o* Is.38.16; ch.14.6; 1 Jn.1.2. *p* Job 19.26; Is.26.19; Ro.4.17. *q* ch.3.15; 4.14. *r* ch.21.7. *s* ch.13.13.

tain. It is possible that she meant gently to intimate that he could raise him up and restore him again to them.

23. *Thy brother shall rise again.* Martha had spoken of the power of Jesus. He said nothing of *himself* in reply. It was not customary for him to speak of himself, unless it was demanded by necessity. It cannot be doubted that by *rising again*, here, Jesus referred to the act which he was about to perform; but as Martha understood it, referring to the future resurrection, it was full of consolation. The idea that departed friends shall rise to glory is one that fills the mind with joy, and one which we owe only to the religion of Christ.

24. *At the last day.* The day of judgment. Of this Martha was fully convinced; but this was not all which she desired. She in this manner delicately hinted what she did not presume expressly to declare—her wish that Jesus might even *now* raise him up.

25. *I am the resurrection.* I am the *author* or the *cause* of the resurrection. It so depends on my power and will, that it may be said that I *am* the resurrection itself. This is a most expressive way of saying that the whole doctrine of the resurrection came from him, and the whole power to effect it was his. In a similar manner he is said to be made of God unto us "*wisdom, and righteousness, and sanctification, and redemption,*" 1 Co. i. 30. ¶ *And the life.* Jn. i. 4. As the resurrection of *all* depends on him, he intimated that it was not indispensable that it should be deferred to the *last day.* He had power to do it now as well as then. ¶ *Though he were dead.* Faith does not save from *temporal* death; but although the believer, as others, will die a temporal death, yet he will hereafter have life. *Even if he dies,* he shall hereafter live. ¶ *Shall he live.* Shall be restored to life in the resurrection.

26. *Whosoever liveth.* He had just spoken of the prospects of the pious dead. He now says that the same prospects are before the living who have like faith. Greek, "Every one living and believing on me." ¶ *Shall never die.* As the dead, though dead, shall yet *live,* so the living shall have the same kind of life. They shall never come into eternal death. See ch. vi. 50, 51, 54, 58. Greek, "Shall by no means die for ever." ¶ *Believest thou this?* This question was doubtless asked because it implied that he was then able to raise up Lazarus, and because it was a proper time for her to test her own faith. The time of affliction is a favourable period to try ourselves to ascertain whether we have faith. If we still have confidence in God, if we look to him for comfort in such seasons, it is good evidence that we are his friends. He that loves God when he takes away his comforts, has the best evidence possible of true attachment to him.

27. *Yea, Lord.* This was a noble confession. It showed her full confidence in him as the Messiah, and her full belief that all that he said was true. See Mat. xvi. 16.

28. *She went her way.* Jesus probably directed her to go, though the evangelist has not recorded it, for she said to Mary, *The Master calleth for thee.* ¶ *Secretly.* Privately. So that the others did not hear her. This was done, per-

Master is come, and [t] calleth for
thee.
29 As soon as she heard *that*, she
arose quickly and came unto him.
30 Now Jesus was not yet come
into the town, but was in that
place where Martha met him.
31 The[u] Jews, then, which were
with her in the house, and comforted
her, when they saw Mary
that she rose up hastily and went
out, followed her, saying, She goeth
unto the grave, to weep there.
32 Then when Mary was come
where Jesus was, and saw him, she
fell down at his feet, saying unto
him, [v] Lord, if thou hadst been
here, my brother had not died.
33 When Jesus therefore saw
her weeping, and the Jews also
weeping which came with her,
he groaned in the spirit and [2] was
troubled,
34 And said, Where have ye
laid him? They say unto him,
Lord, come and see.
35 Jesus[w] wept.

t Mar.10.49. *u* ver.19.

v ch.4.49; ver.21,37. 2 *he troubled himself.* *w* Is.63.9; Lu.19.41; He.2.16,17.

haps, to avoid confusion, or because it was probable that if they knew Jesus was coming they would have made opposition. Perhaps she doubted whether Jesus desired it to be known that he had come. ¶ *The Master is come.* This appears to have been the appellation by which he was known to the family. It means, literally, *teacher*, and was a title which he claimed for himself: "One is your Master, even Christ," Mat. xxiii. 8, 10. The Syriac has it, "*Our* Master."

31. *Saying, She goeth unto the grave.* Syriac, "They *thought* that she went to weep." They had not heard Martha call her. The first days of mourning among the Jews were observed with great solemnity and many ceremonies of grief.

33. *He groaned in the spirit.* The word rendered *groaned*, here, commonly denotes to be angry or indignant, or to reprove severely, denoting violent agitation of mind. Here it also evidently denotes violent agitation — not from *anger*, but from *grief*. He saw the sorrow of others, and he was also moved with sympathy and love. The word *groan* usually, with us, denotes an *expression* of internal sorrow by a peculiar sound. The word here, however, does not mean that *utterance* was given to the internal emotion, but that it was deep and agitating, though internal. ¶ *In the spirit.* In the mind. See Ac. xix. 21: "Paul purposed *in the spirit*"—that is, in his mind, Mat. v. 3. ¶ *Was troubled.* Was affected with grief. Perhaps this expression denotes that his countenance was troubled, or gave indications of sorrow (Grotius).

34. *Where have ye laid him?* Jesus spoke as a man. In all this transaction he manifested the deep sympathies of a man; and though he who could raise the dead man up could also know where he was, yet he chose to lead them to the grave by inducing them to point the way, and hence he asked this question.

35. *Jesus wept.* It has been remarked that this is the shortest verse in the Bible; but it is exceedingly important and tender. It shows the Lord Jesus as a friend, a tender friend, and evinces his character as a man. And from this we learn, 1st. That the most tender personal friendship is not inconsistent with the most pure religion. Piety binds stronger the ties of friendship, makes more tender the emotions of love, and seals and sanctifies the affections of friends. 2d. It is right, it is natural, it is indispensable for the Christian to sympathize with others in their afflictions. Ro. xii. 15: "Rejoice with them that do rejoice, and weep with them that weep." 3d. Sorrow at the death of friends is not improper. It is right to weep. It is the expression of nature, and religion does not forbid or condemn it. All that religion does in the case is to *temper* and chasten our grief; to teach us to mourn with submission to God; to weep without murmuring, and to seek to banish tears, not by *hardening the heart* or forgetting the friend, but by bringing the soul, made tender by grief, to receive the sweet influences of religion, and to find calmness and peace in the God of all consolation. 4th. We have here an instance of the tenderness of the character of Jesus. The same Saviour *wept* over Jerusalem, and felt deeply for poor dying sinners. To the same tender and compassionate Saviour Christians may now come (He. iv. 15);

36 Then said the Jews, Behold,
how he loved him!
37 And some of them said, Could
not this man, [x]which opened the
eyes of the blind, have caused that
even this man should not have
died?
38 Jesus therefore, again groaning in himself, cometh to the
grave. It was a cave, and a stone
lay upon it.
39 Jesus said, [y]Take ye away
the stone. Martha, the sister of
him that was dead, saith unto him,
Lord, [z]by this time he stinketh;
for he hath been *dead* four days.

x ch.9.6. *y* Mar.16.3. *z* Ps.49.7,9; Ac.2.27.

40 Jesus saith unto her, [a]Said I
not unto thee, that if thou wouldest
believe, thou shouldest see the glory
of God?
41 Then they took away the
stone *from the place* where the dead
was laid. And Jesus lifted up *his*
eyes, and said, [b]Father, I thank
thee that thou hast heard me.
42 And I knew that thou hearest
me always; but because of the
people which stand by, I said *it*,
that they may believe that thou
hast sent me.
43 And when he thus had spoken, he cried with a loud voice,
Lazarus, come forth!

a ver.4,23. *b* ch.12.28-30.

---

and to him the penitent sinner may also come, knowing that he will not cast him away.

38. *It was a cave.* This was a common mode of burial. See Notes on Mat. viii. 28. ¶ *A stone lay upon it.* Over the mouth of the cave. See Mat. xxvii. 60.

39. *Four days.* This proves that there could be no deception, for it could not have been a case of suspended animation. All these circumstances are mentioned to show that there was no imposture. Impostors do not mention minute *circumstances* like these. They deal in *generals* only. Every part of this narrative bears the marks of truth.

40. *Said I not unto thee.* This was *implied* in what he had said about the resurrection of her brother, ver. 23-25. There would be a manifestation of the glory of God in raising him up which *she* would be permitted, with all others, to behold. ¶ *The glory of God.* The power and goodness displayed in the resurrection. It is probable that Martha did not really expect that Jesus would raise him up, but supposed that he went there merely to see the corpse. Hence, when he directed them to take away the stone, she suggested that by that time the body was offensive.

41. *Lifted up* his *eyes.* In an attitude of prayer. See Lu. xviii. 13; Mat. xiv. 19. ¶ *I thank thee that thou hast heard me.* It is possible that John has recorded only the sum or substance of the prayer on this occasion. The thanks which Jesus renders here are evidently in view of the fact that power had been committed to him to raise up Lazarus. On account of the people, and the signal proof which would be furnished of the truth of his mission, he expressed his thanks to God. In all his doings he recognized his *union* to the Father, and his dependence on him as Mediator.

42. *And I knew.* "As for me. So far as *I* am concerned. I had no anxiety, no doubt as to myself, that I should always be heard; but the particular ground of gratitude is the benefit that will result to those who are witnesses." Jesus never prayed in vain. He never attempted to work a miracle in vain; and in all his miracles the ground of his joy was, not that *he* was to be praised or honoured, but that *others* were to be benefited and God glorified.

43. *A loud voice.* Greek, "A *great* voice." Syriac, "A *high* voice." This was distinctly asserting *his* power. He uttered a distinct, audible voice, that there might be no suspicion of charm or *incantation.* The ancient magicians and jugglers performed their wonders by whispering and muttering. See Notes on Is. viii. 19. Jesus spake openly and audibly, and asserted thus his power. So, also, in the day of judgment he will call the dead with a *great sound* of a trumpet, Mat. xxiv. 31; 1 Th. iv. 16. ¶ *Lazarus, come forth!* Here we may remark, 1st. That Jesus did this by his own power. 2d. The power of raising the dead is the highest of which we can conceive. The ancient heathen declared it to be even beyond the power of God. It implies not merely giving life to the deceased body, but the power of enter-

44 And[c] he that was dead came forth, bound hand and foot with grave-clothes; and [d]his face was bound about with a napkin. Jesus saith unto them, Loose him, and let him go.

45 Then many of the Jews which came to Mary, and [e]had seen the

c 1 Ki.17.22; 2 Ki.4.34,35; Lu.7.14,15; Ac.20.9-12. d ch.20.7.

e ch.2.23; 10.41,42; 12.11,18.

ing the world of spirits, of recalling the departed soul, and of reuniting it with the body. He that could do this must be omniscient as well as omnipotent; and if Jesus did it by his own power, it proves that he was divine. 3d. This is a striking illustration of the general resurrection. In the same manner Jesus will raise *all* the dead. This miracle shows that it is possible; shows the way in which it will be done—by the voice of the Son of God; and demonstrates the certainty that he will do it. Oh how important it is that *we* be prepared for that moment when his voice shall be heard in *our* silent tombs, and he shall call *us* forth again to life!

44. *He that was dead.* The same man, body and soul. ¶ *Bound hand and foot.* It is not certain whether the whole body and limbs were bound together, or each limb separately. When they embalmed a person, the whole body and limbs were *swathed* or bound together by strips of linen, involved around it to keep together the aromatics with which the body was embalmed. This is the condition of Egyptian mummies. See Ac. v. 6. But it is not certain that this was always the mode. Perhaps the body was simply involved in a winding-sheet. The custom still exists in western Asia. No coffins being used, the body itself is more carefully and elaborately wrapped and swathed than is common or desirable where coffins are used. In this method the body is stretched out and the arms laid straight by the sides, after which the whole body, from head to foot, is wrapped round tightly in many folds of linen or cotton cloth; or, to be more precise, a great length of cloth is taken and rolled around the body until the whole is enveloped, and every part is covered with several folds of the cloth. The ends are then sewed, to keep the whole firm and compact; or else a narrow bandage is wound over the whole, forming, ultimately, the exterior surface. The body, when thus enfolded and swathed, retains the profile of the human form; but, as in the Egyptian mummies, the legs are not folded separately, but together; and the arms also are not distinguished, but confined to the sides in the general envelope. Hence it would be clearly impossible for a person thus treated to move his arms or legs, if restored to existence.

The word rendered "grave-clothes" denotes also the bands or clothes in which new-born infants are involved. He went forth, but his walking was impeded by the bands or clothes in which he was involved. ¶ *And his face,* &c. This was a common thing when they buried their dead. See ch. xx. 7. It is not known whether the whole face was covered in this manner, or only the forehead. In the Egyptian mummies it is only the forehead that is thus bound. ¶ *Loose him.* Remove the bandages, so that he may walk freely. The effect of this miracle is said to have been that many believed on him. It may be remarked in regard to it that there could not be a more striking proof of the divine mission and power of Jesus. There could be here no possibility of deception. 1st. The friends of Lazarus *believed* him to be dead. In this they could not be deceived. There *could* have been among them no design to deceive. 2d. He was four days dead. It could not be a case, therefore, of suspended animation. 3d. Jesus was at a distance at the time of his death. There was, therefore, no *agreement* to attempt to impose on others. 4th. No higher power can be conceived than that of raising the dead. 5th. It was not *possible* to impose on his sisters, and to convince them that he was restored to life, if it was not really so. 6th. There were *many* present who were convinced also. God had so ordered it in his providence that to this miracle there should be many witnesses. There was no concealment, no jugglery, no secrecy. It was done publicly, in open day, and was witnessed by many who followed them to the grave, ver. 31. 7th. Others, who saw it, and did not believe that Jesus was the Messiah, went and told it to the Pharisees. But they did not *deny* that Jesus had raised up Lazarus. They could not deny it. The very ground of their alarm—the very *reason* why they went—was that he had *actually done it.*

things which Jesus did, believed on him.

46 But some of them went their ways to the Pharisees, and told them what things Jesus had done.

47 Then[f] gathered the chief priests and the Pharisees a council,

and said, [g]What do we? for this man doeth many miracles.

48 If we let him thus alone, [h]all *men* will believe on him; and the Romans shall come, and take away both our place and nation.

49 And one of them, [i]*named*

f Ps.2.2. g Ac.4.16. h ch.12.19. i Lu.3.2; ch.18.14; Ac.4.6.

Nor did the Pharisees dare to call the fact in question. If they *could* have done it, they would. But it was not possible; for, 8th. Lazarus was yet alive (ch. xii. 10), and the fact of his resurrection could not be denied. Every circumstance in this account is plain, simple, consistent, bearing all the marks of truth. But if Jesus performed this miracle his religion is true. God would not give such power to an impostor; and unless it can be *proved* that this account is false, the Christian religion *must be* from God.

46. *Some of them*, &c. We see here the different effect which the word and works of God will have on different individuals. Some are converted and others are hardened; yet the *evidence* of this miracle was as clear to the one as the other. But they *would not* be convinced.

47. *A council.* A meeting of the Sanhedrim, or great council of the nation. See Notes on Mat. ii. 4. They claimed the right of regulating all the affairs of religion. See Notes on Jn. i. 19. ¶ *What do we?* What measures are we taking to arrest the progress of his sentiments? ¶ *For this man doeth many miracles.* If they admitted that he performed *miracles*, it was clear what they *ought* to do. They should have received him as the Messiah. It may be asked, If they really believed that he worked miracles, why did they not believe on him? To this it may be replied that they did not doubt that *impostors* might work miracles. See Mat. xxiv. 24. To this opinion they were led, probably, by the wonders which the magicians performed in Egypt (Ex. vii., viii.), and by the passage in De. xiii. 1. As they regarded the tendency of the doctrines of Jesus to draw off the people from the worship of God, and from keeping his law (ch. ix. 16), they did not suppose themselves bound to follow him, even *if he did* work miracles.

48. *All* men. That is, all men among the Jews. The whole nation. ¶ *And the Romans shall come.* They were then subject to the Romans—tributary and dependent. Whatever privileges they had they held at the will of the Roman emperor. They believed, or feigned to believe, that Jesus was intending to set up a *temporal* kingdom. As he claimed to be the Messiah, so they supposed, of course, that he designed to be a temporal prince, and they professed to believe that this claim was, *in fact*, hostility to the Roman emperor. They supposed that it would involve the nation in war if he was not arrested, and that the effect would be that they would be vanquished and destroyed. It was on this charge that they at last arraigned him before Pilate, Lu. xxiii. 2, 3. ¶ *Will take away.* This expression means to *destroy*, to ruin, to overthrow, Lu. viii. 12; Ac. vi. 13, 14. ¶ *Our place.* This probably refers to the *temple*, Ac. vi. 13, 14. It was called "*the place*" by way of eminence, as being the chief or principal place on earth—being the seat of the peculiar worship of God. This place *was* utterly destroyed by the Romans. See Notes on Mat. xxiv. ¶ *And nation.* The nation or *people* of the Jews.

49. *Caiaphas.* See Notes on Lu. iii. 2. ¶ *Being high-priest that same year.* It is probable that the office of high-priest was at first for life, if there was no conduct that rendered the person unworthy the office. In that case the incumbent was removed. Thus Abiathar was removed by Solomon, 1 Ki. ii. 27. Subsequently the kings, and especially the conquerors of Judea, claimed and exercised the right of removing the high priest at pleasure, so that, in the time of the Romans, the office was held but a short time. (See the Chronological Table at the end of this volume.) Caiaphas held the office about ten years. ¶ *Ye know nothing at all.* That is, you know nothing respecting the subject under consideration. You are fools to *hesitate* about so plain a case. It is probable that there was a party, even in

Caiaphas, being the high-priest that same year, said unto them, Ye know nothing at all,

50 Nor consider that [k]it is expedient for us that one man should die for the people, and that the whole nation perish not.

51 And this spake he not of himself; but, being high-priest that year, he prophesied that Jesus should die for that nation;

k Lu.24.46.

---

the Sanhedrim, that was secretly in favour of Jesus as the Messiah. Of that party Nicodemus was certainly one. See ch. iii. 1; vii. 50, 51; xi. 45; xii. 42: "Among the chief rulers, also, many believed on him," &c.

50. *It is expedient for us.* It is *better* for us. Literally, "It is *profitable* for us." ¶ *That one man should die.* Jesus they regarded as promoting sedition, and as exposing the nation, if he was successful, to the vengeance of the Romans, ver. 48. If *he* was put to death they supposed *the people* would be safe. This is all, doubtless, that he meant by his dying for the people. He did not *himself* intend to speak of his dying as an *atonement* or a *sacrifice;* but his *words* might also express that, and, though he was unconscious of it, he was expressing a *real truth.* In the sense in which *he* intended it there was no truth in the observation, nor occasion for it, but in the sense which the words *might convey* there was *real* and most important truth. It *was* expedient, it was infinitely desirable, that Jesus should die for that people, and for all others, to save them from perishing.

51. *Not of himself.* Though he uttered what proved to be a *true prophecy*, yet it was accomplished in a way which *he* did not intend. He had a wicked design. He was plotting murder and crime. Yet, wicked as he was, and little as he intended it, God so ordered it that he delivered a most precious truth respecting the atonement. Remark, 1st. God may fulfil the words of the wicked in a manner which they do not wish or intend. 2d. He may make even *their* malice and wicked plots the very means of accomplishing his purposes. What they regard as the fulfilment of *their* plans God may make the fulfilment of *his*, yet so as directly to overthrow *their* designs, and prostrate *them* in ruin. 3d. Sinners should tremble and be afraid when they lay plans against God, or seek to do unjustly to others. ¶ *Being high-priest that year.* It is not to be supposed that Caiaphas was a *true prophet*, or was conscious of the meaning which John has affixed to his words; but his words *express* the truth about the atonement of Jesus, and John records it *as a remarkable circumstance* that the high-priest of the nation should unwittingly deliver a sentiment which turned out to be the truth about the death of Jesus. Great importance was attached to the opinion of the high-priest by the Jews, because it was by him that the judgment by Urim and Thummim was formerly declared in cases of importance and difficulty, Nu. xxvii. 21. It is not certain or probable that the high-priest ever was endowed with the gift of prophecy; but he sustained a high office, the authority of his name was great, and it was thence remarkable that he uttered a declaration which the result showed to be *true*, though not in the sense that he intended. ¶ *He prophesied.* He uttered words which proved to be prophetic; or he expressed at that time a sentiment which turned out to be true. It does not mean that he was *inspired*, or that he deserved to be ranked among the true prophets; but his words were such that they accurately expressed a future event. The word *prophecy* is to be taken here not in the strict sense, but in a sense which is not uncommon in the sacred writers. Ac. xxi. 9: "And the same man had four daughters, virgins, which did *prophesy.*" See Notes on Ro. xii. 6; 1 Co. xiv. 1; comp. Mat. xxvi. 68; Lu. xxii. 64. ¶ *That Jesus should die.* Die in the *place* of men, or as an atonement for sinners. This is evidently the meaning which John attaches to the words. ¶ *For that nation.* For the Jews. As a sacrifice for their sins. In no other sense whatever could it be said that he died for them. His death, so far from *saving* them in the sense in which the high-priest understood it, was the very occasion of their destruction. They invoked the vengeance of God when they said, "His blood be on us and on our children" (Mat. xxvii. 25), and all these calamities came upon them because they *would*

52 And [l]not for that nation only,
but that also he should gather together in one the children of God
that were [m]scattered abroad.
53 Then from that day forth
they[n] took counsel together for to
put him to death.
54 Jesus therefore walked no
more [o]openly among the Jews, but
went thence into a country near to
the wilderness, into a city called
Ephraim,[p] and there continued
with his disciples.
55 And[q] the Jews' passover was
nigh at hand; and many went out
of the country up to Jerusalem
before the passover to purify themselves.
56 Then[r] sought they for Jesus,
and spake among themselves as
they stood in the temple, What
think ye, that he will not come to
the feast?
57 Now both the chief priests
and the Pharisees had given a
commandment, that if any man
knew where he were, he should
show *it,* that they might take him.

l Is.49.6; Ro.3.29; 1 Jn.2.2. *m* ch.10.16; Ep.2.14-17. *n* Ps.109.4,5. *o* ch.7.1; 18.20. *p* 2 Sa.13.23; 2 Ch.13.19. *q* ch.2.13; 5.1; 6.4.

r ch.5.16,18; ver.8.

not come to him and be saved—that is, because they rejected him and put him to death, Mat. xxiii. 37–39.

52. *Should gather together in one.* All his chosen among the Jews and Gentiles. See ch. x. 16. ¶ *The children of God.* This is spoken not of those who *were then* Christians, but of all whom God should bring to him; all who *would be,* in the mercy of God, called, chosen, sanctified among all nations, ch. x. 16.

53. *They took counsel.* The judgment of the high-priest silenced opposition, and they began to devise measures to put him to death without exciting tumult among the people. Comp. Mat. xxvi. 5.

54. *No more openly.* No more publicly, in the cities and towns. Jesus never exposed his life unnecessarily to hazard. Although the time of his death was determined in the counsel of God, yet this did not prevent his using proper means to preserve his life. ¶ *The wilderness.* See Notes on Mat. iii. 1. ¶ *A city called Ephraim.* This was probably a small town in the tribe of Ephraim, about five miles west of Jericho.

55. *Jews' passover.* See Notes on Mat. xxvi. 2–17. Its being called the *Jews'* Passover shows that John wrote this gospel among people who were not Jews, and to whom it was necessary, therefore, to explain their customs. ¶ *To purify themselves.* This purifying consisted in preparing themselves for the proper observation of the Passover, according to the commands of the law. If any were defiled in any manner by contact with the dead or by any other ceremonial uncleanness, they were required to take the prescribed measures for purification, Le. xxii. 1–6. For want of this, great inconvenience was sometimes experienced. See 2 Ch. xxx. 17, 18. Different periods were necessary in order to be cleansed from ceremonial pollution. For example, one who had been polluted by the touch of a dead body, of a sepulchre, or by the bones of the dead, was sprinkled on the third and seventh days, by a clean person, with hyssop dipped in water mixed in the ashes of the red heifer. After washing his body and clothes he was then clean. These persons who went up *before* the Passover were doubtless those who had in some manner been ceremonially polluted.

56. *Will not come to the feast?* They doubted whether he would come. On the one hand, it was required by law that all males should come. On the other, his coming was attended with great danger. This was the cause of their doubting. It was in this situation that our Saviour, like many of his followers, was called to act. Danger was on the one hand, and duty on the other. He chose, as all should, to do his duty, and leave the event with God. He preferred to do it, though he *knew* that death was to be the consequence; and we should not shrink, when we have reason to apprehend danger, persecution, or death, from an honest attempt to observe all the commandments of God.

CHAPTER XII.

1. *Then Jesus came to Bethany.* This was near to Jerusalem, and it was from

CHAPTER XII.

THEN Jesus, six days before the passover, came to Bethany, where [a]Lazarus was which had been dead, whom he raised from the dead.

2 There they made him a supper, and [b]Martha served; but Lazarus was one of them that sat at the table with him.

3 Then[c] took Mary a pound of ointment of spikenard, very costly, and anointed the feet of Jesus, and wiped his feet with her hair; and the house was filled with the odour of the ointment.

4 Then saith one of his disciples, Judas Iscariot, Simon's *son*, which should betray him,

5 Why was not this ointment sold for three hundred pence, and given to the poor?

6 This he said, not that he cared for the poor, but because [d]he was a thief, and [e]had the bag, and bare what was put therein.

a ch.11.1,43. *b* Lu.10.38-42. *c* Mat.26.6,&c.; Mar.14.3,&c.; ch.11.2.

d 2 Ki.5.20-27; Ps.50.18. *e* ch.13.29.

---

this place that he made his triumphant entry into the city. See Notes on Mat. xxi. 1.

2-8. See this passage explained in the Notes on Mat. xxvi. 3-16.

2. *A supper.* At the house of Simon the leper, Mat. xxvi. 6. ¶ *Lazarus was,* &c. The names of Martha and Lazarus are mentioned because it was not in their own house, but in that of Simon. Lazarus is particularly mentioned, since it was so remarkable that one who had been once dead should be enjoying again the endearments of friendship. This shows, also, that his resurrection was no illusion—that he was *really* restored to the blessings of life and friendship. Calmet thinks that this was about two months after his resurrection, and it is the last that we hear of him. How long he lived is unknown, nor is it recorded that he made any communication about the world of spirits. It is remarkable that none who have been restored to life from the dead have made any communications respecting that world. See Lu. xvi. 31, and Notes on 2 Co. xii. 4.

4. *Which should betray him.* Greek, "who was to betray him"—that is, who *would* do it.

5. *Three hundred pence.* About forty dollars, or £8, 10*s*. ¶ *And given to the poor.* The *avails* or value of it given to the poor.

6. *Had the bag.* The word translated *bag* is compounded of two words, meaning "tongue," and "to keep or preserve." It was used to denote the bag in which musicians used to keep the *tongues* or reeds of their pipes when travelling. Hence it came to mean any bag or purse in which travellers put their money or their most precious articles. The disciples appear to have had such a bag or purse in common, in which they put whatever money they had, and which was designed especially for the poor, Lu. viii. 3; Mat. xxviii. 55; Ac. ii. 44. The keeping of this, it seems, was intrusted to Judas; and it is remarkable that the only one among them who appears to have been naturally avaricious should have received this appointment. It shows us that every man is tried according to his native propensity. This is the object of trial—to bring out man's native character; and every man will find *opportunity* to do evil according to his native disposition, if he is inclined to it. ¶ *And bare,* &c. The word translated *bare* means literally to *carry* as a burden. Then it means to *carry away,* as in Jn. xx. 15: "If thou hast *borne* him hence." Hence it means to carry away *as a thief does,* and this is evidently its meaning here. It has this sense often in classic writers. Judas was a *thief,* and *stole* what was put into the bag. The money he desired to be intrusted to him, that he might secretly enrich himself. It is clear, however, that the disciples did not at this time *know* that this was his character, or they would have remonstrated against him. They learned it afterward. We may learn here, 1st. That it is not a new thing for members of the church to be covetous. Judas was so before them. 2d. That *such* members will be those who complain of the *great waste* in spreading the gospel. 3d. That this deadly, mean, and grovelling passion will work all evil in a church. It brought down the curse of God on the children of Israel in the case of Achan (Jos. vii.), and it betrayed our Lord to death. It

7 Then said Jesus, Let her alone; against the day of my burying hath she kept this.

8 For[f] the poor always ye have with you, but [g]me ye have not always.

9 Much people of the Jews therefore knew that he was there; and they came not for Jesus' sake only, but that they might see Lazarus also, whom he had raised from the dead.

10 But the chief priests consulted that they might [h]put Lazarus also to death;

11 Because[i] that by reason of him many of the Jews went away and believed on Jesus.

12 On[k] the next day, much people that were come to the feast, when they heard that Jesus was coming to Jerusalem,

13 Took branches of palm-trees, and went forth to meet him, and cried, [l]Hosanna! Blessed *is* the King of Israel, that cometh in the name of the Lord!

14 And Jesus, when he had found a young ass, sat thereon; as it is written,

15 Fear[m] not, daughter of Sion. Behold, thy King cometh, sitting on an ass's colt.

16 These [n]things understood not his disciples at the first; but [o]when Jesus was glorified, then [p]remembered they that these things were written of him, and *that* they had done these things unto him.

17 The people, therefore, that was with him when he called Lazarus out of his grave, and raised him from the dead, bare record.

18 For[q] this cause the people also met him, for that they heard that he had done this miracle.

19 The Pharisees therefore said among themselves, [r]Perceive ye how ye prevail nothing? behold, the world is gone after him.

20 And there were [s]certain

f De.15.11; Mat.26.11; Mar.14.7.
g Ca.5.6; ch.8.21; ver.35; ch.13.33; 16.5-7.
h Lu.16.31. i ch.11.45; ver.18.
k Mat.21.8,&c.; Mar.11.8,&c.; Lu.19.36,&c.
l Ps.118.25,26.
m Zec.9.9. n Lu.18.34. o ch.7.39.
p ch.14.26. q ver.11.
r ch.11.47,48. s Ac.17.4; Ro.1.16.

---

has often since brought blighting on the church; and many a time it has *betrayed* the cause of Christ, and drowned men in destruction and perdition, 1 Ti. vi. 9.

10. *That they might put Lazarus also to death.* When men are determined not to believe the gospel, there is no end to the crimes to which they are driven. Lazarus was alive, and the evidence of his resurrection was so clear that they could not resist it. They could neither deny it, nor prevent its effect on the people. As it was determined to kill Jesus, so they consulted about the propriety of removing Lazarus first, that the number of his followers might be lessened, and that the death of Jesus might make less commotion. Unbelief stops at no crime. Lazarus was innocent; they could bring no charge against him; but they deliberately plotted *murder* rather than believe on the Lord Jesus Christ.

12–19. See this passage explained in the Notes on Mat. xxi. 1–16. Also Mar. xi. 1–11; Lu. xix. 29–44.

16. *Was glorified.* Was raised from the dead, and had ascended to heaven.

17. *Bare record.* Testified that he had raised him, and, as was natural, spread the report through the city. This excited much attention, and the people came out in multitudes to meet one who had power to work such miracles.

19. *Prevail nothing.* All your efforts are ineffectual to stop the progress of his opinions, and to prevent the people from believing on him. ¶ *The world.* As we should say, "Everybody—all the city has gone out." The fact that he met with such success induced them to hasten their design of putting him to death, ch. xi. 53.

20. *Certain Greeks.* In the original, "some Hellenists"—the name commonly given to the Greeks. The same name was commonly used by the Jews to denote *all* the pagan nations, because most of those whom they knew spoke the Greek language, Jn. vii. 34; Ro. i. 16; ii. 9, 10; iii. 9. "Jews and Greeks." The Syriac translates this place, "Some

Greeks among [t]them that came up
to worship at the feast:
21 The same came therefore [u]to
Philip, which *was* of Bethsaida of
Galilee, and desired him, saying,
Sir, we would see Jesus.
22 Philip cometh and telleth
Andrew; and again Andrew and
Philip tell Jesus.
23 And Jesus answered them,
saying, [v]The hour is come that the
Son of man should be glorified.
24 Verily, verily, I say unto you,
Except a corn of wheat [w]fall into

t 1 Ki.8.41,42. *u* ch.1.44. *v* ch.13.32; 17.1. *w* 1 Co.15.36.

of the Gentiles." There are three opinions in regard to these persons: 1st. That they were *Jews* who spoke the Greek language, and dwelt in some of the Greek cities. It is known that Jews were scattered in Asia Minor, Greece, Macedonia, Egypt, &c., in all which places they had synagogues. See Notes on ch. vii. 35. 2d. That they were *proselytes* from the Greeks. 3d. That they were still Gentiles and idolaters, who came to bring offerings to Jehovah to be deposited in the temple. Lightfoot has shown that the surrounding pagans were accustomed not only to send presents, sacrifices, and offerings to the temple, but that they also frequently attended the great feasts of the Jews. Hence the outer court of the temple was called *the court of the Gentiles.* Which of these opinions is the correct one cannot be determined.

21. *Bethsaida of Galilee.* See Notes on ch. i. 44. ¶ *Would see Jesus.* It is probable that the word *see*, here, implies also a desire to converse with him, or to hear his doctrine about the nature of his kingdom. They had seen or heard of his triumphal entry into Jerusalem, and, either by curiosity or a desire to be instructed, they came and interceded with his disciples that they might be permitted to see him. In this there was nothing wrong. Christ made the *curiosity* of Zaccheus the means of his conversion, Lu. xix. 1-9. If we wish to find the Saviour, we must seek for him and take the proper means.

22. *Telleth Andrew.* Why he did not at once tell Jesus is not known. Possibly he was doubtful whether Jesus would wish to converse with *Gentiles*, and chose to consult with Andrew about it. ¶ *Tell Jesus.* Whether the Greeks were with them cannot be determined. From the following discourse it would seem probable that they were, or at least that Jesus admitted them to his presence and delivered the discourse to them.

23. *The hour is come.* The *time* is come. The word *hour* commonly means a definite part or a division of a day; but it also is used to denote a brief period, and a *fixed, definite, determined* time. It is used in this sense here. The appointed, fixed time is come—that is, is so near at hand that it may be said *to be come.* ¶ *The Son of man.* This is the favourite title which Jesus gives to himself, denoting his union with man, and the interest he felt in his welfare. The title is used here rather than "The Son of God," because as a *man* he had been humble, poor, and despised; but the time had come when, as a man, he was to receive the appropriate honours of the Messiah. ¶ *Be glorified.* Be honoured in an appropriate way—that is, by the testimony which God would give to him at his death, by his resurrection, and by his ascension to glory. See ch. vii. 39.

24. *Verily, verily.* An expression denoting the great importance of what he was about to say. We cannot but admire the wisdom by which he introduces the subject of his death. They had seen his triumph. They supposed that he was about to establish his kingdom. He told them that the time *had* come in which he was to be glorified, but not in the manner in which *they* expected. It was to be by his death. But as they would not at once see how this could be, as it would appear to dash their hopes, he takes occasion to illustrate it by a beautiful comparison. All the beauty and richness of the *harvest* results from the fact that the grain had *died.* If it had not died it would never have germinated or produced the glory of the yellow harvest. So with him. By this he still keeps before them the truth that he was to be glorified, but he delicately and beautifully introduces the idea still that he *must die.* ¶ *A corn.* A grain. ¶ *Of wheat.* Any kind of grain—wheat, barley, &c. The word includes all grain of this kind. ¶ *Into the ground.* Be buried in the earth, so as to be accessible by the proper moisture. ¶ *And*

the ground and die, it abideth alone; but if it die, it bringeth forth much fruit.

25 He[x] that loveth his life shall lose it; and he that hateth his life in this world shall keep it unto life eternal.

26 If[y] any man serve me, let him follow me; and [z]where I am, there shall also my servant be: [a]if any man serve me, him will *my* Father honour.

27 Now[b] is my soul troubled; and what shall I say? Father, save

x Mat.10.39; 16.25; Mar.8.35; Lu.9.24; 17.33.

y Lu.6.46; ch.14.15; 1 Jn.5.3.
z ch.14.3; 17.24; 1 Th.4.17. a 1 Sa.2.30; Pr.27.18.
b Mat.26.38,39; Lu.12.50; ch.13.21.

---

die. The whole *body* or substance of the grain, except the germ, dies in the earth or is decomposed, and this decomposed substance constitutes the first nourishment of the tender germ—a nutriment wonderfully adapted to it, and fitted to nourish it until it becomes vigorous enough to derive its support entirely from the ground. In this God has shown his wisdom and goodness. No one thing could be more *evidently* fitted for another than this provision made in the grain itself for the future wants of the tender germ. ¶ *Abideth alone.* Produces no fruit. It remains without producing the rich and beautiful harvest. So Jesus intimates that it was *only* by his death that he would be glorified in the salvation of men, and in the honours and rewards of heaven, He. ii. 9: "We see Jesus, who was made a little lower than the angels *for the suffering of death*, crowned with glory and honour." Phi. ii. 8, 9: "He humbled himself, and became obedient unto death, even the death of the cross; *wherefore* God also hath highly exalted him," &c. He. xii. 2: "Who, *for the joy* that was set before him, endured the cross, despising the shame, and is set down at the right hand of the throne of God." See also Ep. i. 20–23.

25. *He that loveth his life*, &c. This was a favourite principle, a sort of *axiom* with the Lord Jesus, which he applied to himself as well as to his followers. See Notes on Mat. x. 39; Lu. ix. 24.

26. *Serve me.* Will be my disciple, or will be a Christian. Perhaps this was said to inform the Greeks (ver. 20) of the nature of his religion. ¶ *Let him follow me.* Let him imitate me; do what I do, bear what I bear, and love what I love. He is discoursing here particularly of his own sufferings and death, and this passage has reference, therefore, to calamity and persecution. "You see me triumph—you see me enter Jerusalem, and you supposed that my kingdom was to be set up without opposition or calamity; but it is not. I am to die; and if *you* will serve me, you must follow me even in these scenes of calamity; be willing to endure trial and to bear shame, looking for future reward." ¶ *Where I am.* See ch. xiv. 3; xvii. 24. That is, he shall be in heaven, where the Son of God then *was* in his divine nature, and where he *would* be as the glorified Messiah. See Notes on Jn. iii. 13. The natural and obvious meaning of the expression "I am" implies that he was then in heaven. The design of this verse is to comfort them in the midst of persecution and trial. They were to *follow* him to any calamity; but, as *he* was to be glorified as the result of his sufferings, so *they* also were to look for their reward in the kingdom of heaven, Re. iii. 21: "To him that *overcometh* will I grant to sit with me in my throne."

27. *Now is my soul troubled.* The mention of his death brought before him its approaching horrors, its pains, its darkness, its unparalleled woes. Jesus was full of acute sensibility, and his human nature shrunk from the scenes through which he was to pass. See Luke xxiii. 41–44. ¶ *What shall I say?* This is an expression denoting intense anxiety and perplexity. *As if* it were a subject of debate whether he *could* bear those sufferings; or whether the work of man's redemption should be abandoned, and he should call upon God to save him. Blessed be his name that he was willing to endure these sorrows, and did not forsake man when he was *so near* being redeemed! On the decision of that moment—the fixed and unwavering purpose of the Son of God—depended man's salvation. If Jesus had forsaken his purpose then, all would have been lost. ¶ *Father, save me.* This ought undoubtedly to have been read as a question—"Shall I say, Father, save me?" Shall I apply to God to rescue me? or shall I go forward to bear these trials? As it is in our translation, it represents him as

me from this hour; [c]but for this cause came I unto this hour.

28 Father, glorify thy name. Then came there [d]a voice from heaven, *saying*, I have both glorified *it*, and will glorify *it* again.

29 The people, therefore, that stood by and heard *it*, said that it thundered; others said, An angel spake to him.

30 Jesus answered and said, This voice came not because of me, [e]but for your sakes.

31 Now is the judgment of this

c ch.18.37. d Mat.3.17. e ch.11.42.

---

actually offering the prayer, and then checking himself. The Greek will bear either interpretation. The whole verse is full of deep feeling and anxiety. Comp. Mat. xxvi. 38; Lu. xii. 50. ¶ *This hour*. These *calamities*. The word *hour*, here, doubtless has reference to his approaching sufferings—the appointed *hour* for him to suffer. Shall I ask my Father to save me from this *hour* —that is, from these approaching sufferings? That it *might* have been done, see Mat. xxvi. 53. ¶ *But for this cause*. That is, to suffer and die. As this was the *design* of his coming—as he did it deliberately—as the salvation of the world depended on it, he felt that it would not be proper to pray to be delivered from it. He came to suffer, and he submitted to it. See Lu. xxiii. 42.

28. *Glorify thy name*. The meaning of this expression in this connection is this: "I am willing to bear any trials; I will not shrink from any sufferings. Let thy name be honoured. Let thy character, wisdom, goodness, and plans of mercy be manifested and promoted, whatever sufferings it may cost me." Thus Jesus showed us that *God's glory* is to be the great end of our conduct, and that we are to seek that, whatever sufferings it may cost us. ¶ *I have both glorified* it. The word *it* is not here in the original, but it is not improperly supplied by the translators. There can be no doubt that when God says here that he *had* glorified his name, he refers to what had been done by Christ, and that this was to be understood as an *attestation* that he attended him and approved his work. See ver. 30. He *had* honoured his name, or had glorified *him*, by the pure instructions which he had given to man through him; by the power displayed in his miracles; by proclaiming his mercy through him; by appointing him to be the Messiah, &c. ¶ *Will glorify* it *again*. By the death, the resurrection, and ascension of his Son, and by extending the blessings of the gospel among all nations. It was thus that he sustained his Son in view of approaching trials; and we may learn, 1st. That God will minister grace to us in the prospect of suffering. 2d. That the fact that God will be honoured by our afflictions should make us willing to bear them. 3d. That whatever was done by Christ tended to honour the name of God. This was what he had in view. He lived and suffered, not for himself, but to glorify God in the salvation of men.

29. *The people*. A part of the people. ¶ *It thundered*. The unexpected sound of the voice would confound and amaze them; and though there is no reason to doubt that the words were spoken distinctly (Mat. iii. 17), yet some of the people, either from amazement or envy, would suppose that this was a mere natural phenomenon. ¶ *An angel spake*. It was the opinion of many of the Jews that God did not speak to men except by the ministry of angels, He. ii. 2: "The word spoken *by angels;*" Ga. iii. 19: "It was ordained *by angels* in the hand of a mediator."

30. *Came not because of me*. Not to strengthen or confirm me; not that *I* had any doubts about my course, or any apprehension that God would *not* approve me and glorify his name. ¶ *For your sakes*. To give you a striking and indubitable proof that I am the Messiah; that you may remember it when I am departed, and be *yourselves* comforted, supported, and saved.

31. *Now is the judgment of this world*. Greek, "crisis." This expression, doubtless, has reference to his approaching death, and whatever he means by *judgment* here relates to something that was to be accomplished *by* that death. It cannot mean that then was to be the time in which the world was to be finally judged, for he says that he did not come then to judge the world (ch. xii. 47; viii. 15), and he has clearly declared that there shall be a *future* day when he will judge all mankind. The meaning of it may be thus expressed:

world; now shall [f]the prince of this world be cast out.
32 And I, if I be [g]lifted up from the earth, [h]will draw all *men* unto me.

[f] Lu.10.18; ch.16.11; Ac.26.18; Ep.2.2. [g] ch.8.28. [h] Ro.5.18.

33 This he said, [i]signifying what death he should die.
34 The people answered him, [k]We have heard [l]out of the law that Christ abideth for ever; and

[i] ch.18.32. [k] Ps.89.36,37; 110.4; Is.9.7. [l] Ro.5.18; Ps.72.17-19.

"Now is approaching the decisive scene, the eventful period—*the crisis*—when it shall be determined who shall rule this world. There has been a long conflict between the powers of light and darkness — between God and the devil. Satan has so effectually ruled that he may be said to be the prince of this world; but my approaching death will destroy his kingdom, will break down his power, and will be the means of setting up the kingdom of God over man." The death of Christ was to be the most grand and effectual of all means that could be used to establish the authority of the law and the government of God, Ro. viii. 3, 4. This it did by showing the regard which God had for his law; by showing his hatred of sin, and presenting the strongest motives to induce man to leave the service of Satan; by securing the influences of the Holy Spirit, and by his putting forth his own direct power in the cause of virtue and of God. The death of Jesus was the determining cause, the grand crisis, the concentration of all that God had ever done, or ever will do, to break down the kingdom of Satan, and set up his power over man. Thus was fulfilled the prediction (Ge. iii. 15), "I will put enmity between thee and the woman, and between thy seed and her seed; it shall bruise thy head, and thou shalt bruise his heel." ¶ *Now shall the prince of this world.* Satan, or the devil, ch. xiv. 30; xvi. 11. He is also called the *god of this world*, 2 Co. iv. 4; Ep. vi. 12: "The rulers of the darkness of this world"—that is, the rulers of this *dark world*—a well-known Hebraism. He is also called "the prince of the power of the air, the spirit that now worketh in the children of disobedience," Ep. ii. 2. All these names are given him from the influence or power which he has over the men of this world, because the great mass of men have been under his control and subject to his will. ¶ *Be cast out.* His kingdom shall be destroyed; his empire shall come to an end. It does not mean that his reign over all men would entirely cease then, but that then would be the *crisis*, the grand conflict in which *he* would be vanquished, and from that time his kingdom begin to decline, until it would finally cease, and then be free altogether from his dominion. See Lu. x. 18; Col. i. 18–20; Ac. xxvi. 18; 1 Co. xv. 25, 26; Re. xx. 14.

32. *Be lifted up.* See ch. iii. 14; viii. 28. ¶ *Will draw.* Ch. vi. 44. The same word is used in both places. ¶ *All* men. I will incline all kinds of men; or will make the way open by the cross, so that all men may come. I will provide a way which shall present a strong motive or inducement—the strongest that *can* be presented—to all men to come to me.

34. *We have heard out of the law.* Out of the Old Testament; or rather we have been so taught by those who have interpreted the law to us. ¶ *That Christ.* That *the* Messiah. ¶ *Abideth for ever.* Will *remain* for ever, or will live for ever. The doctrine of many of them certainly was that the Messiah would not die; that he would reign as a prince for ever over the people. This opinion was founded on such passages of Scripture as these: Ps. cx. 4, "Thou art a priest for ever;" Da. ii. 44; viii. 13, 14. In the interpretation of these passages they had overlooked such places as Is. liii.; nor did they understand how the fact that he would reign for ever could be reconciled with the idea of his death. To us, who understand that his reign does not refer to a *temporal*, an *earthly* kingdom, it is easy. ¶ *How sayest thou*, &c. *We* have understood by the title "the Son of man" the same as the Messiah, and that he is to reign for ever. How can he be put to death? ¶ *Who is this Son of man?* "The Son of man *we* understand to be the Messiah spoken of by Daniel, who is to reign for ever. To *him*, therefore, you cannot refer when you say that he must be lifted up, or must die. Who is it—what *other Son of man* is referred to but the Messiah?" Either ignorantly or wilfully, they supposed he

how sayest thou, The Son of man must be lifted up? who is this Son of man?

35 Then Jesus said unto them, Yet a little while is [m]the light with[n] you. Walk while ye have the light, lest darkness come upon you; [o]for he that walketh in darkness knoweth not whither he goeth.

36 While ye have light believe in the light, that ye may be [p]the children of light. These things spake Jesus, and departed, and did hide himself from them.

37 But, though he had done so many miracles before them, yet they believed not on him;

38 That the saying of Esaias the prophet might be fulfilled which he spake, [q]Lord, who hath believed

m ch.8.12. n Je.13.16. o ch.11.10. p Ep.5.8. q Is.53.1.

---

referred to some one else than the Messiah.

35. *Yet a little while is the light with you.* Jesus did not reply directly to their question. He saw that they were offended by the mention of his death, and he endeavoured to arrive at the same thing *indirectly.* He tells them, therefore, that the light would be with them a little while, and that they ought to improve the opportunity while they had it to listen to his instructions, to inquire with candour, and thus to forsake their false notions respecting the Messiah. ¶ *The light.* Ch. i. 4. It is probable that they understood this as denoting the Messiah. See ch. viii. 12: "I am the light of the world;" ch. ix. 4. ¶ *Walk,* &c. Ch. xi. 9. Whatever you have to do, do it while you enjoy this light. Make good use of your privileges before they are removed. That is, while the Messiah is with you, avail yourselves of his instructions and learn the way to life. ¶ *Lest darkness.* Lest God should take away all your mercies, remove all light and instruction from you, and leave you to ignorance, blindness, and woe. This was true that darkness and calamity were to come upon the Jewish people when the Messiah was removed; and it is also true that God leaves a sinner to darkness and misery when he has long rejected the gospel. ¶ *For he,* &c. See ch. xi. 10.

36. *While ye have light.* This implied two things—1st. That *he* was the light, or was the Messiah. 2d. That he was soon to be taken away by death. In this manner he answered their question —not *directly,* but in a way to convey the truth to their minds, and at the same time to administer to them a useful admonition. Jesus never aroused the prejudices of men unnecessarily, yet he never shrank from declaring to them the truth *in some way,* however unpalatable it might be. ¶ *Believe in the light.* That is, in the Messiah, who is the light of the world. ¶ *That ye may be the children,* &c. That ye may be the friends and followers of the Messiah. See Notes on Mat. i. 1. Comp. Jn. viii. 12; Ep. v. 8: "Now are ye light in the Lord; walk as children of light." ¶ *Did hide himself from them.* Ch. viii. 59. He went out to Bethany, where he commonly passed the night, Lu. xxi. 37.

37. *So many miracles.* This does not refer to any miracles wrought on this occasion, but to all his miracles wrought in view of the nation, in healing the sick, opening the eyes of the blind, raising the dead, &c. John here gives the *summary* or the result of all his works. Though Jesus had given the most undeniable proof of his being the Messiah, yet the nation did not believe on him. ¶ *Before them.* Before the Jewish nation. Not in the presence of the people whom he was then addressing, but before the Jewish people. ¶ *They believed not.* The Jewish nation did not believe *as a nation,* but rejected him.

38. *The saying.* The *word* of Isaiah, or that which Isaiah predicted. This occurs in Is. liii. 1. ¶ *Might be fulfilled.* That the same effect should occur which occurred in the time of Isaiah. This does not mean that the Pharisees rejected Christ *in order* that the prophecy of Isaiah should be fulfilled, but that *by* their rejection of him the same thing had occurred which took place in the time of Isaiah. *His* message was despised by the nation, and he himself put to death. And it was also true—by the same causes, by the same nation—that the same gospel message was rejected by the Jews in the time of Christ. The same language of the prophet would express *both* events, and no doubt it was

our report? and to whom hath the arm of the Lord been revealed?
39 Therefore they could not believe, because that Esaias said again,
40 He[r] hath blinded their eyes,

r Is.6.9,10.

intended by the Holy Spirit to mark both events. In this way it was completely fulfilled. See Notes on Is. liii. 1. ¶ *Our report.* Literally, by *report* is meant "what is heard." Our speech, our message. That is, few or none have received the message. The form of the question is an emphatic way of saying that it was rejected. ¶ *The arm of the Lord.* The *arm* is a symbol of power, as it is the instrument by which we execute our purposes. It is put for the power of God, Is. li. 9; lii. 10. Thus he is said to have brought out the children of Israel from Egypt with *a high arm*—that is, with great power. It hence means God's power in defending his people, in overcoming his enemies, and in saving the soul. In this place it clearly denotes the power displayed by the miracles of Christ. ¶ *Revealed.* Made known, seen, understood. Though the power of God was *displayed*, yet the people did not see and understand it.

39. *They could not believe.* See Mark vi. 5: "He could there do no mighty works," &c. The works *can* and *could* are often used in the Bible to denote the existence of such obstacles as to make a result certain, or as affirming that while one thing exists another thing cannot follow. Thus, Jn. v. 44: "How *can* ye believe which receive honour one of another." That is, while this propensity to seek for honour exists, it will effectually prevent your believing. Thus (Ge. xxxvii. 4) it is said of the brethren of Joseph that they "*could* not speak peaceably unto him." That is, while their hatred continued so strong, the other result would follow. See also Mat. xii. 34; Ro. viii. 7; Jn. vi. 60; Am. iii. 3. In this case it means that there was some obstacle or difficulty that made it certain that while it existed they would not believe. What that was is stated in the next verse; and while that blindness of mind and that hardness of heart existed, it was impossible that they should believe, for the two things were incompatible. But this determines nothing about their power of *removing that blindness*, or of yielding their heart to the gospel. It simply affirms that while one exists the other cannot follow. Chrysostom and Augustine understand this of a *moral* *inability*, and not of any *natural* want of power. "They could not, because they would not" (Chrysostom *in loco*). So on Je. xiii. 23, "Can the Ethiopian change his skin," &c., he says, "he does not say it is impossible for a wicked man to do well, but, BECAUSE *they will not, therefore they cannot.*" Augustine says on this place: "If I be asked why they *could* not believe, I answer without hesitation, because they *would* not: because God foresaw their *evil will*, and he annouuced it beforehand by the prophet." ¶ *Said again*, Is. vi. 9, 10.

40. *He hath blinded their eyes.* The expression in Isaiah is, "Go, make the heart of this people fat, and shut their eyes." That is, go and proclaim truth to them—truth that will *result* in blinding their eyes. Go and proclaim the law and the will of God, and the *effect will be*, owing to the hardness of their heart, that their eyes will be blinded and their hearts hardened. As God knew that this would be the result—as it was to be the effect of the message, his commanding Isaiah to go and proclaim it was the same *in effect*, or *in the result*, as if he had commanded him to blind their eyes and harden their hearts. It is this *effect* or *result* to which the evangelist refers in this place. He states that God did it—that is, he did it in the manner mentioned in Isaiah, for we are limited to that in our interpretation of the passage. In that case it is clear that the mode specified is not a *direct* agency on the part of God in blinding the mind—which we cannot reconcile with any just notions of the divine character—but *in suffering the truth to produce a regular effect on sinful minds, without putting forth any positive supernatural influence to prevent it.* The effect of truth on such minds is to irritate, to enrage, and to harden, unless counteracted by the grace of God. See Ro. vii. 8, 9, 11; 2 Co. ii. 15, 16. And as God *knew* this, and, knowing it, still sent the message, and suffered it to produce the *regular* effect, the evangelist says "*he* hath blinded their minds," thus retaining the *substance* of the passage in Isaiah without quoting the precise language; but in proclaiming the *truth* there was nothing *wrong*

and hardened their heart; that they should not see with *their* eyes, nor understand with *their* heart, and be converted, and I should heal them.

41 These things said Esaias [s]when he saw his glory, and spake of him.

42 Nevertheless, among the chief rulers also many believed on him; but [t]because of the Pharisees they did not confess *him*, lest they should be put out of the synagogue;

43 For[u] they loved the praise of men more than the praise of God.

44 Jesus cried and said, [v]He that

s Is.6.1.

t ch.9.22. u ch.5.44; Ro.2.29. v Mar.9.37; 1 Pe.1.21.

---

on the part of God or of Isaiah, nor is there any indication that God was unwilling that *they* should believe and be saved. ¶ *That they should not see*, &c. This does not mean that it was the *design* of God that they should not be converted, but that it was the *effect* of their rejecting the message. See Notes on Mat. xiii. 14, 15.

41. *When he saw his glory*, Is. vi. 1–10. Isaiah saw the LORD (in Hebrew, JEHOVAH) sitting on a throne and surrounded with the seraphim. This is perhaps the only instance in the Bible in which Jehovah is said to have been seen by man, and *for* this the Jews affirm that Isaiah was put to death. God had said (Ex. xxxiii. 20), "No man shall see me and live;" and as Isaiah affirmed that he had seen Jehovah, the Jews, for that and other reasons, put him to death by sawing him asunder. See Introduction to Isaiah, § 2. In the prophecy Isaiah is said expressly to have seen JEHOVAH (ver. 1); and in ver. 5, "Mine eyes have seen the King JEHOVAH of hosts." By his *glory* is meant the manifestation of him—the *shechinah*, or visible cloud that was a representation of God, and that rested over the mercy-seat. This was regarded as equivalent to seeing God, and John here expressly applies this to the Lord Jesus Christ; for he is not affirming that the people did not believe *in God*, but is assigning the reason why they believed not on Jesus Christ as the Messiah. The whole discourse has respect to the Lord Jesus, and the natural construction of the passage requires us to refer it to him. John affirms that it was the glory *of the Messiah* that Isaiah saw, and yet Isaiah affirms that it was JEHOVAH; and from this the inference is irresistible that John regarded Jesus as the Jehovah whom Isaiah saw. The name Jehovah is never, in the Scriptures, applied to a man, or an angel, or to any creature. It is the peculiar, incommunicable name of God. So great was the reverence of the Jews for that name that they would not even *pronounce* it. This passage is therefore conclusive proof that Christ is equal with the Father. ¶ *Spake of him.* Of the Messiah. The connection requires this interpretation.

42. *The chief rulers.* Members of the Sanhedrim—Nicodemus, Joseph, and others like them. ¶ *Because of the Pharisees.* The Pharisees were a majority of the council. ¶ *Put out of the synagogue.* Excommunicated. See Notes on ch. ix. 22.

43. *The praise of men.* The approbation of men. It does not appear that they had a living, active faith, but that they were convinced in their understanding that he was the Messiah. They had that kind of faith which is so common among men—a speculative acknowledgment that religion is true, but an acknowledgment which leads to no self-denial, which shrinks from the active duties of piety, and fears man more than God. True faith is active. It overcomes the fear of man; it prompts to self-denying duties, He. xi. Nevertheless, it was no unimportant proof that Jesus was the Messiah, that *any part* of the great council of the Jews were even speculatively convinced of it: and it shows that the evidence could not have been slight when it overcame their prejudices and pride, and constrained them to admit that the lowly and poor man of Nazareth was the long-expected Messiah of their nation. ¶ *Did not confess him.* Did not openly avow their belief that he was the Messiah. Two of them, however, did afterward evince their attachment to him. These were Joseph and Nicodemus, ch. xix. 38, 39. That Joseph was one of them appears from Mar. xv. 43; Lu. xxiii. 50, 51.

44. *Jesus cried and said.* John does not say *where* or *when* this was; it is probable, however, that it was a continuation of the discourse recorded in ver. 30–36. Jesus saw their unbelief,

believeth on me, believeth not on me, but on him that sent me.

45 And he that seeth me, seeth him that sent me.

46 I[w] am come a light into the world, that whosoever believeth on me should not abide in darkness.

47 And if any man hear my words and believe not, I judge him not; [x]for I came not to judge the world, but to save the world.

48 He that rejecteth me, and [y]receiveth not my words, hath one that judgeth him: the word that I have spoken, the same shall judge him in the last day.

49 For I have not spoken of myself; but the Father which sent me, he gave me a commandment, what I should say, and what I should speak.

50 And I know that [z]his com-

w ch.1.5; 3.19. *x* ch.3.17.

y De.18.19; Lu.9.26. *z* 1 Jn.3.23.

and proceeded to state the consequence of believing on him, and of rejecting him and his message. ¶ *Believeth not on me.* That is, not on me *alone*, or his faith does not *terminate* on me. Comp. Mat. x. 20; Mar. ix. 37. It *involves*, also, belief in him that sent me. Jesus uniformly represents the union between himself and God as so intimate that there could not be faith in *him* unless there was also faith in God. *He* did the *same* works (ch. v. 17, 20, 36; x. 25, 37), and taught the very doctrine which God had commissioned him to do, ch. viii. 38; v. 30, 20-23.

45. *Seeth me*, &c. This verse is a strong confirmation of his equality with God. In no other way can it be true that he who saw Jesus saw him that sent him, unless he were the same in essence. Of no *man* could it be affirmed that he who saw him saw God. To say this of Paul or Isaiah would have been blasphemy. And yet Jesus uses this language familiarly and constantly. It shows that he had a consciousness that he was divine, and that it was the *natural* and proper way of speaking when speaking of himself. Comp. ch. v. 17.

46. *A light into the world.* Ch. viii. 12; i. 9; iii. 19. ¶ *Walk in darkness.* In gross and dangerous errors. Darkness is put for error as well as for sin, Jn. iii. 19; 1 Jn. i. 5. It is also used to denote the state when the *comforts* of religion are withdrawn from the soul, Is. viii. 22; Joel ii. 2; Is. lix. 9; Jn. viii. 12.

47. *I judge him not*, &c. Ch. viii. 15. It was not his *present* purpose to condemn men. He would come to *condemn* the guilty at a future time. At present he came to save them. Hence he did not now even pronounce decisively on the condition of those who rejected him, but still gave them an opportunity to be saved.

48. *He that rejecteth me.* Lu. x. 16. The word *reject* means to *despise*, or to refuse to receive him. ¶ *Hath one.* That is, he needs not my voice to condemn him. He will carry his own condemnation with him, even should I be silent. His own conscience will condemn him. The words which I have spoken will be remembered and will condemn him, if there were nothing farther. From this we learn, 1st. That a guilty conscience needs no accuser. 2d. That the words of Christ, and the messages of mercy which the sinner has rejected, will be remembered by him. 3d. That this will be the source of his condemnation. This will make him miserable, and there will be no possibility of his being happy. 4th. That the conscience of the sinner will *concur* with the sentence of Christ in the great day, and that he will go to eternity *self-condemned.* It is this which will make the pains of hell so intolerable to the sinner. 5th. The word that Christ has spoken, the doctrines of his gospel, and the messages of mercy, will be that by which the sinner will be judged in the last day. Every man will be judged by that message, and the sinner will be punished according to the frequency and clearness with which the rejected message has been presented to his mind, Mat. xii. 41.

49. *Of myself.* Ch. vii. 16-18.

50. *Is life everlasting.* Is the *cause* or *source* of everlasting life. He that *obeys* the commandment of God shall obtain everlasting life; and this is his commandment, that we believe in the name of his only-begotten Son, 1 Jn. iii. 22. We see here the reason of the earnestness and fidelity of the Lord Jesus. It was because he saw that *eternal life* depended on the faithful preaching of the message of God. He therefore pro-

mandment is life everlasting: whatsoever I speak, therefore, even as the Father said unto me, so I speak.

CHAPTER XIII.

NOW[a] before the feast of the passover, when Jesus knew that [b]his hour was come that he should depart out of this world unto the Father, [c]having loved his own which were in the world, he loved them unto the end.

2 And supper being ended, [d]the devil having now put into the heart of Judas Iscariot, Simon's *son*, to betray him,

3 Jesus [e]knowing that the Fa-

a Mat.26.2,&c. b ch.17.1,11. c Je.31.3; Ep.5.2; 1 Jn.4.19; Re.1.5. d Lu.22.3,53; ch.6.70. e Mat.28.18; He.2.8.

---

claimed it in the face of all opposition, contempt, and persecution. And we see also, 1st. That every minister of religion should have a deep and abiding conviction that he delivers a message that is to be connected with the eternal welfare of his hearers. And, 2d. Under the influence of this belief, he should fearlessly deliver his message in the face of bonds, poverty, contempt, persecution, and death.

It may not be improper to remark here that this is the *close* of the public preaching of Christ. The rest of his ministry was employed in the private instruction of his apostles, and in preparing them for his approaching death. It is such a close as all his ministers should desire to make—a solemn, deliberate, firm exhibition of the truth of God, under a belief that on it was depending the eternal salvation of his hearers, and uttering without fear the solemn message of the Most High to a lost world.

CHAPTER XIII.

1. *The feast of the passover.* See Notes on Mat. xxvi. 2, 17. ¶ *His hour was come.* The hour appointed in the purpose of God for him to die, ch. xii. 27. ¶ *Having loved his own.* Having given to them decisive and constant proofs of his love. This was done by his calling them to follow him; by patiently teaching them; by bearing with their errors and weaknesses; and by making them the heralds of his truth and the heirs of eternal life. ¶ *He loved them unto the end.* That is, he *continued* the proofs of his love until he was taken away from them by death. Instances of that love John proceeds immediately to record in his washing their feet and in the institution of the Supper. We may remark that Jesus is the same yesterday, to-day, and for ever. He does not change; he always loves the same traits of character; nor does he *withdraw* his love from the soul. If his people walk in darkness and wander from him, the fault is *theirs*, not *his*. His is the character of a friend that never leaves or forsakes us; a friend that sticketh closer than a brother. Ps. xxxvii. 28: "The Lord—forsaketh not his saints." Is. xlix. 14–17; Pr. xviii. 24.

2. *Supper being ended.* This translation expresses too much. The original means *while they were at supper;* and that this is the meaning is clear from the fact that we find them still eating after this. The Arabic and Persic translations give it this meaning. The Latin Vulgate renders it like the English. ¶ *The devil.* The leader or prince of evil spirits. ¶ *Having now put it into the heart.* Literally, having *cast it* into the heart. Comp. Ep. vi. 16: "The fiery darts of the wicked." See Ac. v. 3; Lu. xxii. 3. The meaning of this passage is that Satan inclined the mind of Judas to do this, or he tempted him to betray his Master. We know not precisely how this was done, but we know that it was by means of his *avarice.* Satan *could* tempt no one unless there was some inclination of the mind, some natural or depraved propensity that he could make use of. He presents objects in alluring forms fitted to that propensity, and under the influence of a strong or a corrupt inclination the soul yields to sin. In the case of Judas it was the love of money; and it was necessary to present to him only the possibility of obtaining money, and it *found* him ready for any crime.

3. *Jesus knowing,* &c. With the full understanding of his dignity and elevation of character, he yet condescended to wash their feet. The evangelist introduces his washing their feet by saying that he was fully conscious of his elevation above them, as being intrusted with all things, and this made his humi-

ther had given all things into his
hands, and that [f]he was come
from God, and went to God;
4 He riseth from supper, and laid
aside his garments, and took a
towel and girded himself.
5 After that he poureth water
into a basin, and began to wash
the disciples' feet, and to wipe
them with the towel wherewith he
was girded.
6 Then cometh he to Simon
Peter; and [1]Peter said unto him,
Lord, [g]dost thou wash my feet?
7 Jesus answered and said unto
him, What I do thou knowest not
now; but thou shalt know hereafter.

f ch.17.11. 1 *he.* g Mat.3.14.

liation the more striking and remarkable. Had he been a mere human teacher or a prophet, it would have been remarkable; but when we remember the dignity of his nature, it shows how low he would stoop to teach and save his people. ¶ *Had given all things,* &c. See Notes on Mat. xxviii. 18. ¶ *Was come from God.* See Notes on ch. viii. 42. ¶ *Went to God.* Was about to return to heaven. See ch. vi. 61, 62.

4. *He riseth from supper.* Evidently while they were eating. See ver. 2. ¶ *Laid aside his garments.* His outer garment. See Notes on Mat. v. 40. This was his *mantle* or robe, which is said to have been without seam. It was customary to lay this aside when they worked or ran, or in the heat of summer. ¶ *Took a towel and girded himself.* This was the manner of a servant or slave. See Notes on Lu. xvii. 8.

5. *Began to wash,* &c. It was uniformly the office of a servant to wash the feet of guests, 1 Sa. xxv. 41. It became a matter of necessity where they travelled without shoes, and where they reclined on couches at meals. It should be remembered here that the disciples were not *sitting* at the table, as we do, but were lying with their feet extended from the table, so that Jesus could easily have access to them. See Notes on Mat. xxiii. 6.

6. *Dost thou wash my feet?* Every word here is emphatic. Dost *thou*—the Son of God, the Messiah—perform the humble *office of a servant*—toward *me*, a sinner? This was an expression of Peter's humility, of his reverence for Jesus, and also a refusal to allow him to do it. It is *possible,* though not certain from the text, that he came to Simon Peter first.

7. *Thou knowest not now.* Though he saw the action of Jesus, yet he did not fully understand the *design* of it. It was a symbolical action, inculcating a lesson of humility, and intended to teach it to them in such a manner that it would be impossible for them ever to forget it. Had he simply *commanded* them to be humble, it would have been far less forcible and impressive than when they saw him actually performing the office of a servant. ¶ *Shalt know hereafter.* Jesus at that time partially explained it (ver. 14, 15); but he was teaching them by this expressive act a lesson which they would continue to learn all their lives. Every day they would see more and more the necessity of humility and of kindness to each other, and would see that *they* were the servants of Christ and of the church, and ought not to aspire to honours and offices, but to be willing to perform the humblest service to benefit the world. And we may remark here that God often does things which we do not fully understand now, but which we may hereafter. He often afflicts us; he disappoints us; he frustrates our plans. Why it is we do not know now, but we yet shall learn that it was for our good, and designed to teach us some important lesson of humility and piety. So he will, in heaven, scatter all doubts, remove all difficulties, and show us the reason of the whole of his mysterious dealings in his leading us in the way to our future rest. We ought also, in view of this, to submit ourselves to him; to hush every murmur, and to believe that he does all things well. It is one evidence of piety when we are willing to receive affliction at the hand of God, the *reason* of which we cannot see, content with the belief that we *may* see it hereafter; or, even if we never do, still having so much confidence in God as to believe that WHAT HE DOES IS RIGHT.

8. *Thou shalt never wash my feet.* This was a decided and firm expression of his reverence for his Master, and yet it was improper. Jesus had just declared that it had a meaning, and that he

8 Peter saith unto him, Thou shalt never wash my feet. Jesus answered him, [h]If I wash thee not, thou hast no part with me.

9 Simon Peter saith unto him, Lord, not my feet only, but also *my* hands and *my* head.

10 Jesus saith to him, He that is

h 1 Co.6.11; Ep.5.26; Tit.3.5.

---

ought to submit to it. We should yield to all the plain and positive requirements of God, even if we cannot *now* see how obedience would promote his glory. ¶ *If I wash thee not.* This had *immediate* reference to the act of washing his feet; and it denotes that if Peter had not so much confidence in him as to believe that an act which he performed was proper, though he could not see its propriety—if he was not willing to submit *his* will to that of Christ and implicitly obey him, he had no evidence of piety. As Christ, however, was accustomed to pass from temporal and sensible objects to those which were spiritual, and to draw instruction from whatever was before him, some have supposed that he here took occasion to state to Peter that if his soul was not made pure by him he could not be his follower. Washing is often thus put as an emblem of moral purification, 1 Co. vi. 11; Tit. iii. 5, 6. This is the meaning, also, of baptism. If this was the sense in which Jesus used these words, it denotes that unless Christ should purify Peter, he could have no evidence that he was his disciple. "Unless by my doctrine and spirit I shall purify you, and remove your *pride* (Mat. xxvi. 33), your want of constant watchfulness (ver. 40), your anger (ver. 51), your timidity and fear (ver. 70, 74), you can have no part in me" (Grotius). ¶ *Hast no part with me.* Nothing *in common* with me. No evidence of possessing my spirit, of being interested in my work, and no participation in my glory.

9. *Not my feet only*, &c. Peter, with characteristic readiness and ardour, saw now that everything depended on this. His whole salvation, the entire question of his attachment to his Master, was involved. If to refuse to have his feet washed was to be regarded as evidence that he had no part with Jesus, he was not only *willing*, but *desirous* that it should be done; not only anxious that his *feet* should be cleansed, but his hands and his head—that is, that he should be cleansed *entirely, thoroughly.* Perhaps he saw the spiritual meaning of the Saviour, and expressed his ardent wish that his whole soul might be made pure by the work of Christ. A true Christian is desirous of being cleansed from all sin. He has no reserve. He wishes not merely that *one* evil propensity should be removed, but all; *that every thought should be brought into captivity to the obedience of Christ* (2 Co. x. 5); and *that his whole body, soul, and spirit should be sanctified wholly and be preserved blameless unto the coming of the Lord Jesus Christ*, 1 Th. v. 23. His intellect, his will, his affections, his fancy, memory, judgment, he desires should be *all* brought under the influence of the gospel, and every power of the body and mind be consecrated unto God.

10. *He that is washed.* This is a difficult passage, and interpreters have been divided about its meaning. Some have supposed that it was customary to *bathe* before eating the paschal supper, and that the apostles did it; Jesus having said, "he that hath bathed his body is clean except in regard to his *feet*—to the dirt contracted in returning from the bath, and that there was need *only* that the feet should be washed in order to prepare them properly to receive the supper." They suppose, also, that the *lesson* which Jesus meant to teach was that they were really pure (ch. xv. 3); that they were qualified to partake of the ordinances of religion, and needed only to be purified from *occasional* blemishes and impurities (Grotius). Others say that there is not evidence that the Jews *bathed* before partaking of the paschal supper, but that reference is made to the custom of washing their *hands* and their *face.* It is known that this was practised. See Notes on Mat. xv. 2; Mar. vii. 3, 4. Peter had requested him to wash his hands and his head. Jesus told him that as that had been done, it was unnecessary to repeat it; but to wash the feet was an act of hospitality, the office of a servant, and that all that was needed now was for him to show this condescension and humility. Probably reference is had here to *internal purity*, as Jesus was fond of drawing illustrations from every quarter to teach them spiritual doctrine; as if he had said, "You are clean by my word and ministry (ch. xv. 3); you are my followers, and are prepared for the

washed needeth not save to wash
his feet, but is clean every whit;
and ye are clean, but not all.
11 For[i] he knew who should betray him; therefore said he, Ye are
not all clean.
12 So after he had washed their
feet, and had taken his garments,
and was set down again, he said
unto them, Know ye what I have
done to you?
13 Ye[k] call me Master and Lord;
and ye say well, for *so* I am.
14 If I, then, *your* Lord and
Master, have washed your feet, ye
also ought to wash one another's
feet.
15 For[l] I have given you an example, that ye should do as I have
done to you.
16 Verily, verily, I say unto you,
The servant is not greater than his
lord; neither he that is sent greater than he that sent him.
17 If[m] ye know these things,
happy are ye if ye do them.
18 I speak not of you all; I know
whom I have chosen; but that the

i ch.6.64. *k* Mat.23.8-10; Phi.2.11. *l* 1 Pe.2.21. *m* Ja.1.25.

scene before you. But one thing remains. And as, when we come to this rite, having washed, there remains no need of washing except to wash the feet, so there is now nothing remaining but for *me* to show you an example that you will always remember, and that shall *complete* my public instructions to you." ¶ *Is clean.* This word may apply to the *body* or the *soul.* ¶ *Every whit.* Altogether, wholly. ¶ *Ye are clean.* Here the word has doubtless reference to the mind and heart. ¶ *But not all.* You are not all my true followers, and fitted for the ordinance before us.

11. *Who should betray him.* Greek, "He knew him who was about to betray him."

12. *Know ye what*, &c. Do you know the *meaning* or *design* of what I have done unto you?

13. *Ye call me Master.* Teacher. ¶ *And Lord.* This word is applied to one who *rules*, and is often given to God as being the *Proprietor* and *Ruler* of all things. It is given to Christ many hundred times in the New Testament. ¶ *Ye say well*, &c. Mat. xxiii. 8, 10. ¶ So *I am.* That is, he was their *Teacher* and Instructor, and he was their Sovereign and King.

14, 15. *Ye also ought to wash*, &c. Some have understood this *literally as instituting a religious rite* which we ought to observe; but this was evidently not the design; for, 1st. There is no evidence that Jesus intended it as a *religious* observance, like the Lord's Supper or the ordinance of baptism. 2d. It was not observed by the apostles or the primitive Christians as a religious rite. 3d. It was a rite of hospitality among the Jews, a common, well-known thing, and performed by servants. 4th. It is the manifest design of Jesus here to inculcate a lesson of humility; to teach them by his example that they ought to condescend to the most humble offices for the benefit of others. They ought not to be proud, and vain, and unwilling to occupy a low place, but to regard themselves as the servants of each other, and as willing to befriend each other in every way. And especially as they were to be founders of the church, and to be greatly honoured, he took this occasion of warning them against the dangers of ambition, and of teaching them, by an example that they *could not forget*, the duty of humility.

16, 17. *The servant is not*, &c. This was universally true, and this they were to remember always, that *they* were to manifest the same spirit that he did, and that they were to expect the same treatment from the world. See Notes on Mat. x. 24, 25.

18. *I speak not of you all.* That is, in addressing you as *clean*, I do not mean to say that you *all* possess this character. ¶ *I know whom I have chosen.* He here means evidently to say that he had not chosen them all, implying that Judas had not been chosen. As, however, this word is applied to Judas in one place (Jn. vi. 70), "Have not I *chosen* you twelve, and one of you is a devil?" it must have a different meaning here from that which it has there. *There* it evidently refers to the *apostleship.* Jesus *had* chosen him to be an *apostle*, and had treated him as such. *Here* it refers to purity *of heart*, and Jesus implies that, though Judas had been chosen to the office of apostleship,

scripture may be fulfilled, [n]He that
eateth bread with me hath lifted
up his heel against me.
19 Now[2] I [o]tell you before it
come, that when it is come to pass
ye may believe that I am *he*.
20 Verily, verily, I say unto you,
[p]He that receiveth whomsoever I
send, receiveth me; and he that
receiveth me, receiveth him that
sent me.
21 When[q] Jesus had thus said,

n Ps.41.9. 2 or, *From henceforth*. *o* ch.14.29; 16.4. *p* Mat.10.40. *q* Mat.26.21; Mar.14.18; Lu.22.21.

yet he had not been chosen to purity of heart and life. The remaining eleven *had* been, and would be saved. It was not, however, the fault of Jesus that Judas was not saved, for he was admitted to the same teaching, the same familiarity, and the same office; but his execrable love of gold gained the ascendency, and rendered vain all the means used for his conversion. ¶ *But that the scripture*, &c. These things have occurred in order that the prophecies may receive their completion. It does not mean that Judas was *compelled* to this course in order that the Scripture might be fulfilled, but that this was foretold, and that *by this* the prophecy *did* receive a completion. ¶ *The scripture.* This is written in Ps. xli. 9. It is commonly understood of Ahithophel, and of the enemies of David who had been admitted to his friendship, and who had now proved ungrateful to him. ¶ *May be fulfilled.* See Notes on Mat. i. 22. It is difficult to tell whether this prophecy had a primary reference to Judas, or whether it be meant that it received a more complete fulfilment in his case than in the time of David. The cases were similar; the same words would describe both events, for there was an exhibition of similar ingratitude and baseness in both cases, so that the same words would fitly describe both events. ¶ *He that eateth bread with me.* To eat with one was a proof of friendship. See 2 Sa. ix. 11; Mat. ix. 11; Ge. xliii. 32. This means that Judas had been admitted to all the privileges of friendship, and had partaken of the usual evidences of affection. It was this which greatly aggravated his offence. It was base ingratitude as well as murder. ¶ *Hath lifted up his heel. Suidas* says that this figure is taken from those who are running in a race, when one attempts to trip the other up and make him fall. It was a base and ungrateful return for kindness to which the Lord Jesus referred, and it means that he who had been admitted to the intimacies of friendship had ungratefully and maliciously injured him. Some suppose the expression means to lay *snares* for one; others, to kick or injure a man after he is cast down (Calvin on Ps. xli. 9). It is clear that it denotes great injury, and injury aggravated by the fact of professed friendship. It was not merely the common people, the open enemies, the Jewish nation that did it, but one who had received all the usual proofs of kindness. It was this which greatly aggravated our Saviour's sufferings.

19. *Now I tell you before it come*, &c. They would see by that that he had a knowledge of the heart and the power of foretelling future events, and must therefore have been sent by God. This does not imply that they had no faith *before* this, but that their faith would be increased and strengthened by it.

20. *He that receiveth*, &c. This sentiment is found in the instructions which Jesus gave to his disciples in Mat. x. 40. Why he repeats it at this time cannot now be known. It is certain that it is not closely connected with the subject of his conversation. Perhaps, however, it was to show how intimately united he, his Father, his apostles, and all who received them were. They who received *them* received *him*, and they who received *him* received *God*. So he who betrayed *him*, betrayed, for the same reason, *God*. Hence Judas, who was about to betray *him*, was also about to betray the cause of religion in the world, and to betray God and his cause. Everything pertaining to religion is connected together. A man cannot do dishonour to one of the institutions of religion without injuring *all;* he cannot dishonour its ministers or the Saviour without dishonouring God. And this shows that one prominent ground of the Saviour's solicitude was that his Father might be honoured, and one source of his deep grief at the treason of Judas was that it would bring injury upon the whole cause of religion in the world.

21. *Troubled in spirit.* See ch. xii. 27. The reason of his trouble here was that Judas, a professed friend, was about to

he was troubled in spirit, and testified, and said, Verily, verily, I say unto you that one of you shall betray me.
22 Then the disciples looked one on another, doubting of whom he spake.
23 Now there was leaning on Jesus' bosom [r]one of his disciples, whom Jesus loved.
24 Simon Peter therefore beckoned to him that he should ask who it should be of whom he spake.
25 He then, lying on Jesus' breast, saith unto him, Lord, who is it?
26 Jesus answered, He it is to whom I shall give a [3]sop when I have dipped *it*. And when he had dipped the sop, he gave *it* to Judas Iscariot, *the son* of Simon.
27 And after the sop, [s]Satan en-

r ch.20.2; 21.7,20.

3 or, *morsel*. s Lu.22.3.

betray him. He doubtless foresaw the deep and dreadful sorrows of his approaching death, and was also deeply affected with the ingratitude and wickedness of a professed friend. Jesus was *man* as well as *God*, and he felt like other men. His human nature shrank from suffering, and his tender sensibilities were affected not less deeply than would be those of other men by baseness and treason. ¶ *Testified.* He bore witness to the truth; openly declared what he had before intimated—that one of them would betray him.

22. *Doubting of whom*, &c. The word translated *doubting* denotes that kind of anxiety which a man feels when he is in perplexity, and knows not what to say or do. We should say they were *at a loss*. See Notes on Mat. xxvi. 22.

23. *Leaning on Jesus' bosom.* This does not mean that he was at that time *actually* lying on his bosom, but that he occupied a situation *next* to him at the table, so that his head naturally fell back on his bosom when he spoke to him. See Notes on Mat. xxiii. 6. ¶ *Whom Jesus loved.* This was doubtless John himself. The evangelists are not accustomed to mention their own *names* when any mark of favour or any good deed is recorded. They did not seek publicity or notoriety. In this case the appellation is more tender and honourable than any mere *name*. John was admitted to peculiar friendship, perhaps, because the natural disposition of our Saviour was more nearly *like* the amiableness and mildness of John than any of the other disciples (Robert Hall). The highest honour that can be conferred on any man is to say that Jesus *loved him*. Yet this is an honour which *all may* possess, but which none *can* inherit without his spirit and without loving him. It is an honour which cannot be won by wealth or learning, by beauty or accomplishments, by rank or earthly honours, but only by the possession of a meek and quiet spirit, which is in the sight of God of great price, 1 Pe. iii. 4; comp. Ro. viii. 9.

25. *He then lying on Jesus' breast.* This is a different word from the one rendered (ver. 23) *leaning*. It means *falling back* or *reclining* on the bosom of Jesus. When Peter spake, John *laid his head back* on the bosom of Jesus, so that he could speak to him privately without being heard by others.

26. *Jesus answered.* That is, he answered *John*. It does not appear that either Judas or the other apostles heard him. ¶ *Shall give a sop.* The word translated *sop* means a *morsel*, a piece of bread, or anything else eaten—as much as we are accustomed to take at a mouthful. Jesus was about to *dip it* in the sauce which was used at the Passover. The word *dip*, in the original, is that from which is derived the word *baptize*. It means here that Jesus would dip it into the sauce as we do a piece of bread. It is probable that it was not an unusual thing for the master of a feast to help others in this way, as it does not appear to have attracted the attention of the others as at all remarkable. It was an indication to *John* who the betrayer was, and a hint which *Judas* also probably understood.

27. *After the sop.* After he had taken and probably eaten it. By this Judas saw that Jesus knew his design, and that he could not conceal his plan. He saw, also, that the other disciples would be acquainted with it; and, aroused by sudden anger, or with the apprehension that he should lose his reward, or that Jesus might escape, he resolved on executing his plan at once. ¶ *Satan entered into him.* The devil had *before*

tered into him. Then said Jesus
unto him, That thou doest, do
quickly.
28 Now no man at the table
knew for what intent he spake
this unto him.
29 For some *of them* thought,
because [t]Judas had the bag, that
Jesus had said unto him, Buy
those things that we have need of

t ch.12.6.

against the feast; or that he should
give something to the poor.
30 He then, having received the
sop, went immediately out; and it
was night.
31 Therefore, when he was gone
out, Jesus said, [u]Now is the Son
of man glorified, and [v]God is glorified in him.
32 If God be glorified in him,

u ch.12.23; 17.1-6. v ch.14.13; 1 Pe.4.11.

---

this put it into his heart to betray Jesus (ver. 2), but he now excited him to a more decided purpose. See Lu. xxii. 3; also Ac. v. 3: "Why hath Satan filled thine heart," &c. ¶ *What thou doest, do quickly.* This showed to Judas that Jesus was acquainted with his design. He did not *command* him to betray him, but he left him to his own purpose. He had used means enough to reclaim him and lead him to a holy life, and now he brought him to a decision. He gave him to understand that he was acquainted with his plan, and submitted it to the *conscience* of Judas to do quickly what he would do. If he relented, he called on him to do it at once. If he could still pursue his wicked plan, could go forward when he was conscious that the Saviour knew his design, he was to do it at once. God adopts all means to bring men to a decision. He calls upon them to act decisively, firmly, immediately. He does not allow them the privilege to *deliberate* about wicked deeds, but calls on them to act at once, and to show whether they will obey or disobey him; whether they will serve him, or whether they will betray his cause. He knows *all* their plans, as Jesus did that of Judas, and he calls on men to act under the full conviction that *he* knows all their soul. Sin thus is a vast evil. When men can sin knowing that God sees it all, it shows that the heart is *fully* set in them to do evil, and that there is nothing that *will* restrain them.

28, 29. *No man at the table knew.* This shows that Jesus had signified to *John* only who it was that should betray him. ¶ *The bag.* The travelling-bag in which they put their common property. See Notes on ch. xii. 6. ¶ *Have need of against the feast.* The feast of the Passover. This feast continued seven days, and they supposed that Jesus had directed him to make preparation for their wants on those days.

30. *It was night.* It was in the evening, or early part of the night. What is recorded in the following chapters took place the same night.

31. *Now is the Son of man glorified.* The last deed is done that was necessary to secure the death of the Son of man, the glory that shall result to him from that death, the wonderful success of the gospel, the exaltation of the Messiah, and the public and striking attestation of God to him in the view of the universe. See Notes on ch. xii. 32.

32. *If God be glorified in him.* If God be honoured by him. If the life and death of the Messiah be such as to lead to the honour of God, such as shall manifest its perfections, and show his goodness, truth, and justice, then he will *show* that he thus approves his work. ¶ *God shall also glorify him.* He will honour the Messiah. He will not suffer him to go without a proper attestation of his acceptance, and of the honour that God puts on him. Jesus here confidently anticipated that the Father *would* show that he was pleased with what he had done. He did it in the miracles that attended his death, in his resurrection, ascension, exaltation, and in the success of the gospel. We may remark that God *will always*, in the proper time and way, *manifest* his approbation of those who live so as to promote the honour of his name. ¶ *In himself.* Or *by* himself; by a direct and public expression of his approbation. Not by the ministry of *angels* or by any other *subordinate* attestation, but by an expression that shall be *direct* from him. This was done by his *direct* interposition in his resurrection and ascension to heaven. ¶ *Shall straightway.* Immediately, or without *delay.* This refers to the fact that the time when God

God shall also glorify him in himself, and shall straightway glorify him.

33 Little children, yet a little while I am with you. Ye shall seek me; and, [w]as I said unto the Jews, Whither I go ye cannot come; so now I say to you.

34 A[x] new commandment I give unto you, that ye love one

w ch.7.34; 8.21.
x Le.19.18; ch.15.12,17; Ep.5.2; 1 Th.4.9; Ja.2.8; 1 Pe.1.22; 1 Jn.2.7,8; 3.11,23; 4.20,21.

---

would put this honour on him was at hand. His death, resurrection, and ascension were near.

33. *Little children.* An expression of great tenderness, denoting his deep interest in their welfare. As he was about to leave them, he endeavours to mitigate their grief by the most tender expressions of attachment, showing that he felt for them the deep interest in their welfare which a parent feels for his children. The word *children* is often given to Christians as implying—1st. That God is their Father, and that they sustain toward him that endearing relation, Ro. viii. 14, 15. 2d. As denoting their need of teaching and guidance, as children need the aid and counsel of a father. See the corresponding term *babes* used in 1 Co. iii. 1; 1 Pe. ii. 2. 3d. It is used, as it is here, as an expression of *tenderness* and affection. See Ga. iv. 19; 1 Jn. ii. 1, 12, 28; iii. 7, 18; iv. 4; v. 21. ¶ *Yet a little while I am with you.* He did not conceal the fact that he was soon to leave them. There is something exceedingly tender in this address. It shows that he loved them to the end; that as their friend and guide, *as a man*, he felt deeply at the thoughts of parting from them, and leaving them to a cold and unfeeling world. A parting scene at death is always one of tenderness; and it is well when, like this, there is the presence of the Saviour to break the agony of the parting pang, and to console us with the words of his grace. ¶ *As I said unto the Jews.* See ch. vii. 34. ¶ *So now I say to you.* That is, they could not follow him *then*, ver. 36; ch. xiv. 2. He was about to die and return to God, and for a time they must be willing to be separated from him. But he consoled them (ver. 36) with the assurance that the separation would be only temporary, and that they should afterward follow him.

34. *A new commandment.* This command he gave them as he was about to leave them, to be a *badge* of discipleship, by which they might be known as his friends and followers, and by which they might be *distinguished* from all others. It is called *new*, not because there was no command before which required men to love their fellow-men, for one great precept of the law was that they should love their neighbour as themselves (Le. xix. 18); but it was *new* because it had never before been made that by which any class or body of men had been *known* and *distinguished.* The *Jew* was known by his external rites, by his peculiarity of dress, &c.; the philosopher by some other mark of distinction; the military man by another, &c. In none of these cases had love *for each other* been the distinguishing and peculiar badge by which they were known. But in the case of Christians they were *not* to be known by distinctions of wealth, or learning, or fame; they were not to aspire to earthly honours; they were not to adopt any peculiar style of dress or *badge*, but they were to be distinguished by tender and constant attachment to each other. This was to surmount all distinction of country, of colour, of rank, of office, of sect. Here they were to feel that they were on a level, that they had common wants, were redeemed by the same sacred blood, and were going to the same heaven. They were to befriend each other in trials; be careful of each other's feelings and reputation; deny themselves to promote each other's welfare. See 1 Jn. iii. 23; 1 Th. iv. 9; 1 Pe. i. 22; 2 Th. i. 3; Ga. vi. 2; 2 Pe. i. 7. In all these places the command of Jesus is repeated or referred to, and it shows that the first disciples considered this indeed as the peculiar law of Christ. This command or law was, moreover, *new* in regard to the *extent* to which this love was to be carried; for he immediately adds, "*As I have loved you, that ye also love one another.*" His love for them was strong, continued, unremitting, and he was now about to show his love for them in death. Ch. xv. 13: "Greater love hath no man than this, that a man lay down his life for his friends." So in 1 Jn. iii. 16 it is said that "we ought also to lay down our lives for the brethren." This

another; as I have loved you, that
ye also love one another.
35 By this shall all *men* know
that ye are my disciples, if ye have
love one to another.
36 Simon Peter said unto him,
Lord, whither goest thou? Jesus
answered him, Whither I go thou
canst not follow me now; [y]but
thou shalt follow me afterward.
37 Peter said unto him, Lord,
why cannot I follow thee now?
[z]I will lay down my life for thy
sake.
38 Jesus answered him, Wilt
thou lay down thy life for my
sake? Verily, verily, I say unto
thee, The cock shall not crow till
thou hast denied me thrice.

CHAPTER XIV.

LET[a] not your heart be troubled;
ye believe in God, [b]believe
also in me.

y ch.21.18; 2 Pe.1.14.

z Mat.26.33,&c.; Mar.14.29,&c.; Lu.22.33,&c.
a Is.43.1,2; ver.27; 2 Th.2.2.
b Is.12.2,3; Ep.1.12,13; 1 Pe.1.21.

was a *new* expression of love; and it showed the strength of attachment which *we* ought to have for Christians, and how ready we should be to endure hardships, to encounter dangers, and to practise self-denial, to benefit those for whom the Son of God laid down his life.

35. *By this shall all* men, &c. That is, your love for each other shall be so decisive evidence that you are like the Saviour, that all men shall see and know it. It shall be the thing by which you shall be known among all men. You shall not be known by peculiar rites or habits; not by a peculiar form of dress or manner of speech; not by peculiar austerities and unusual customs, like the Pharisees, the Essenes, or the scribes, but by deep, genuine, and tender affection. And it is well known it was this which eminently distinguished the first Christians, and was the subject of remark by the surrounding pagans. "See," said the heathen, "see how they love one another! They are ready to lay down their lives for each other." Alas! how changed is the spirit of the Christian world since then! Perhaps, of all the commands of Jesus, the observance of this is that which is least apparent to a surrounding world. It is not so much that they are divided into different sects, for this *may be* consistent with love for each other; but it is the want of deep-felt, genuine love toward Christians even of our own denomination; the absence of genuine self-denial; the pride of rank and wealth; and the fact that professed Christians are often known by *anything* else rather than by true attachment to those who bear the same Christian name and image. The true Christian loves religion wherever it is found—equally in a prince or in a slave, in the mansion of wealth or in the cottage of poverty, on the throne or in the hut of want. He overlooks the distinction of sect, of colour, and of nations; and wherever he finds a man who bears the Christian *name* and *manifests the Christian spirit*, he loves him. And this, more and more as the millennium draws near, will be the peculiar badge of the professed children of God. Christians will love their own denominations *less* than they love the spirit and temper of *the Christian*, wherever it may be found.

CHAPTER XIV.

1. *Let not your heart be troubled.* The disciples had been greatly distressed at what Jesus had said about leaving them. Comp. ch. xvi. 6, 22. Perhaps they had indicated their distress to him in some manner by their countenance or their expressions, and he proceeds now to administer to them such consolations as their circumstances made proper. The discourse in *this* chapter was delivered, doubtless, while they were sitting at the table partaking of the Supper (see ver. 31); that in the two following chapters, and the prayer in the 17th chapter, were while they were on their way to the *Mount of Olives.* There is nowhere to be found a discourse so beautiful, so tender, so full of weighty thoughts, and so adapted to produce comfort, as that which occurs in these three chapters of John. It is the *consolatory* part of our religion, where Christ brings to bear on the mind full of anxiety, and perplexity, and care, the tender and inimitably beautiful truths of his gospel — truths fitted to allay every fear, silence every murmur, and give every needed consolation to

2 In my Father's house are many mansions: if *it were* not *so* I would have told you. I[c] go to prepare a place for you.

c He.6.20; 9.8,24; Re.21.2.

3 And if I go and prepare a place for you, [d]I will come again, and receive you unto myself; that [e]where I am, *there* ye may be also.

d He.9.28. e ch.12.26; 17.24; 1 Th.4.17.

the soul. In the case of the disciples there *was* much to *trouble* them. They were about to part with their beloved, tender friend. They were to be left alone to meet persecutions and trials. They were without wealth, without friends, without honours. And it is not improbable that they felt that *his death* would demolish all their schemes, for they had not yet fully learned the doctrine that the Messiah must suffer and die, Lu. xxiv. 21. ¶ *Ye believe in God.* This may be read either in the indicative mood or the imperative. Probably it should be read in the imperative—"Believe on God, and believe on me." If there were no other reason for it, this is sufficient, that there was no more evidence that they *did* believe in God than that they believed in Jesus. All the ancient versions except the Latin read it thus. The Saviour told them that their consolation was to be found at this time in confidence in God and in him; and he intimated what he had so often told them and the Jews, that there was an *indissoluble union* between him and the Father. This union he takes occasion to explain to them more fully, ver. 7-12. ¶ *Believe in.* Put confidence in, rely on for support and consolation.

2, 3. *In my Father's house.* Most interpreters understand this of heaven, as the peculiar dwelling-place or *palace* of God; but it *may* include the *universe*, as the abode of the omnipresent God. ¶ *Are many mansions.* The word rendered *mansions* means either the *act* of dwelling in any place (ver. 23, "we will make our *abode* with him"), or it means *the place* where one dwells. It is taken from the verb *to remain*, and signifies the place where one dwells or remains. It is applied by the Greek writers to the *tents* or temporary habitations which soldiers pitch in their marches. It denotes a dwelling of less *permanency* than the word *house.* It is commonly understood as affirming that in heaven there is *ample room* to receive all who will come; that therefore the disciples might be sure that they would not be excluded. Some have understood it as affirming that there will be different *grades* in the joys of heaven; that some of the mansions of the saints will be nearer to God than others, agreeably to 1 Co. xv. 40, 41. But perhaps this passage may have a meaning which has not occurred to interpreters. Jesus was consoling his disciples, who were affected with grief at the idea of his separation. To comfort them he addresses them in this language: "The universe is the dwelling-place of my Father. All is his *house.* Whether on earth or in heaven, we are still in his habitation. In that vast abode of God there are many mansions. The earth is one of them, heaven is another. Whether here or there, we are still in the house, in one of the mansions of our Father, in one of the *apartments* of his vast abode. This we ought continually to feel, and to rejoice that we are permitted to occupy *any part* of his dwelling-place. Nor does it differ much whether we are in *this* mansion or another. It should not be a matter of grief when we are called to pass from one part of this vast habitation of God to another. I am indeed about to leave you, but I am going only to another part of the vast dwelling-place of God. I shall still be in the same universal habitation with you; still in the house of the same God; and am going for an important purpose—to fit up another abode for your eternal dwelling." If this be the meaning, then there is in the discourse true consolation. We see that the *death* of a Christian is not to be dreaded, nor is it an event over which we should immoderately weep. It is but removing from *one apartment* of God's universal dwelling-place to another—one where we shall still be in his house, and still feel the same interest in all that pertains to his kingdom. And especially the removal of the Saviour from the earth was an event over which Christians should rejoice, for he is still in the house of God, and still preparing mansions of rest for his people. ¶ *If* it were *not* so, &c. "I have concealed from you no truth. You have been cherishing this hope of a future abode with God. Had it been ill founded I would have told you plainly, as I have told you

4 And whither I go ye know,
and the way ye know.
5 Thomas saith unto him, Lord,
we know not whither thou goest,
and how can we know the way?
6 Jesus saith unto him, I am

---

other things. Had any of you been deceived, as Judas was, I would have made it known to you, as I did to him." ¶ *I go to prepare a place for you.* By his *going* is meant his death and ascent to heaven. The figure here is taken from one who is on a journey, who goes before his companions to provide a place to lodge in, and to make the necessary preparations for their entertainment. It evidently means that he, by the work he was yet to perform in heaven, would *secure* their admission there, and obtain for them the blessings of eternal life. That work would consist mainly in his *intercession*, He. x. 12, 13, 19-22; vii. 25-27; iv. 14, 16. ¶ *That where I am.* This language could be used by no one who was not *then* in the place of which he was speaking, and it is just such language as one would naturally use who was both God and man —in reference to his human nature, speaking of his *going* to his Father; and in reference to his divine nature, speaking as if he was *then* with God. ¶ *Ye may be also.* This was language eminently fitted to comfort them. Though about to leave them, yet he would not *always* be absent. He would come again at the day of judgment and gather all his friends to himself, and they should be ever with him, He. ix. 28. So shall *all* Christians be with him. And so, when we part with a beloved Christian friend by death, we may feel assured that the separation will not be *eternal*. We shall meet again, and dwell in a place where there shall be no more separation and no more tears.

4. *Whither I go ye know.* He had so often told them that he was to die, and rise, and ascend to heaven, that they could not but understand it, Mat. xvi. 21; Lu. ix. 22; xviii. 31, 32. ¶ *The way ye know.* That is, the way that leads to the dwelling-place to which he was going. The way which they were to tread was to obey his precepts, imitate his example, and follow him, ver. 6.

5. *We know not whither thou goest.* Though Jesus had so often told them of his approaching death and resurrection, yet it seems they did not understand him, nor did they fully comprehend him until after his resurrection. See Lu. xxiv. 21. They entertained the common notions of a *temporal kingdom;* they supposed still that he was to be an earthly prince and leader, and they did not comprehend the reason why he should die. Thomas confessed his ignorance, and the Saviour again patiently explained his meaning. All this shows the difficulty of believing when the mind is full of prejudice and of contrary opinions. Had Thomas *laid aside* his previous opinions—had he been willing to receive the truth as Jesus plainly spoke it, there would have been no difficulty. Faith would have been an easy and natural exercise of the mind. And so with the sinner. If he were *willing* to receive the plain and unequivocal doctrines of the Bible, there would be no difficulty; but his mind is full of opposite opinions and plans, occupied with errors and vanities, and these are the reasons, and the only reasons, why he is not a Christian. Yet who would say that, after the plain instructions of Jesus, Thomas *might not* have understood him? And who will dare to say that any sinner *may not* lay aside his prejudices and improper views, and receive the plain and simple teaching of the Bible?

6. *I am the way.* See Is. xxxv. 8. By this is meant, doubtless, that they and all others were to have access to God only by obeying the instructions, imitating the example, and depending on the merits of the Lord Jesus Christ. He was the *leader* in the road, the guide to the wandering, the teacher of the ignorant, and the example to all. See ch. vi. 68: "Thou hast the words of eternal life;" 1 Pe. ii. 21: "Christ—suffered for us, leaving us an example that ye should follow his steps;" He. ix. 8, 9. ¶ *The truth.* The source of truth, or he who originates and communicates truth for the salvation of men. Truth is a representation of things as they are. The life, the purity, and the teaching of Jesus Christ was the most complete and perfect representation of the things of the eternal world that has been or can be presented to man. The ceremonies of the Jews were shadows; the life of Jesus was the truth. The opinions of men are fancy, but the doctrines of Jesus were nothing more than a representation of *facts* as they

the[f] way, and [g]the truth, and the[h] life, [i]no man cometh unto the Father but by me.

7 If ye had known me, ye should have known my Father also; and from henceforth ye know him and have seen him.

8 Philip saith unto him, Lord, show us the Father, and it sufficeth us.

9 Jesus saith unto him, Have I been so long with you, and yet hast thou not known me, Philip? [k]he that hath seen me hath seen

f Is.35.8,9; ch.10.9; He.10.19,20. g ch.1.17; 15.1. h ch.1.4; 11.25. i Ac.4.12.

k Col.1.15.

exist in the government of God. It is implied in this, also, that Jesus was the fountain of all truth; that by *his* inspiration the prophets spoke, and that by him all truth is communicated to men. See Notes on ch. i. 17. ¶ *The life.* See ch. xi. 25, and Notes on ch. i. 4. ¶ *No man cometh to the Father but by me.* To come to the Father is to obtain his favour, to have access to his throne by prayer, and finally to enter his kingdom. No man can obtain any of these things except by the merits of the Lord Jesus Christ. By coming *by him* is meant coming in his name and depending on his merits. We are ignorant, and he alone can guide us. We are sinful, and it is only by his merits that we can be pardoned. We are blind, and he only can enlighten us. God has appointed him as the Mediator, and has ordained that all blessings shall descend to this world through him. Hence he has put the world under his control; has given the affairs of men into his hand, and has appointed him to dispense whatever may be necessary for our peace, pardon, and salvation, Ac. iv. 12; v. 31.

7. *If ye had known me.* By this Jesus does not intend to say that they were not truly his disciples, but that they had not a *full* and *accurate* knowledge of his character and designs. They still retained, to a large extent, the Jewish notions respecting a temporal Messiah, and did not fully understand that he was to die and be raised from the dead. ¶ *Ye should have known my Father also.* You would have known the *counsels* and *designs* of my Father respecting my death and resurrection. If you had been divested of your Jewish prejudices about the Messiah, if you had understood that it was proper for me to die, you would also have understood the purposes and plans of God in my death; and, *knowing that,* you would have seen that it was wise and best. We see here that a correct knowledge of the character and work of Christ is the same as a correct knowledge of the counsels and plans of God; and we see, also, that the reasons why we have not such a knowledge are our previous prejudices and erroneous views. ¶ *From henceforth.* From this time. From my death and resurrection you shall understand the plans and counsels of God. ¶ *Ye know him.* You shall have just views of his plans and designs. ¶ *Have seen him.* That is, they had seen Jesus Christ, his *image,* and the *brightness of his glory* (He. i. 3), which was *the same* as having seen the Father, ver. 9.

8. *Lord, show us the Father.* Philip here referred to some outward and visible manifestation of God. God had manifested himself in various ways to the prophets and saints of old, and Philip affirmed that if some such manifestation should be made to them they would be satisfied. It was right to desire evidence that Jesus was the Messiah, but such evidence *had been* afforded abundantly in the miracles and teaching of Jesus, and that *should* have sufficed them.

9. *So long time.* For more than three years Jesus had been with them. He had raised the dead, cast out devils, healed the sick, done those things which no one could have done who had not come from God. In that time they had had full opportunity to learn his character and his mission from God. Nor was it needful, after so many proofs of his divine mission, that God should *visibly manifest* himself to them in order that they might be convinced that he came from him. ¶ *He that hath seen me.* He that has seen my works, heard my doctrines, and understood my character. He that has given *proper attention* to the proofs that I have afforded that I came from God. ¶ *Hath seen the Father.* The word *Father* in these passages seems to be used with reference to the divine nature, or to God represented *as a Father*, and not particularly to the distinction in the Trinity of Father and Son. The idea is that God, *as* God, or

the Father; and how sayest thou, *then*, Show us the Father?

10 Believest thou not that I am in the Father, and the Father in me? The words that I speak unto you I speak not of myself; but the Father that dwelleth in me, he doeth the works.

11 Believe me that I *am* in the Father, and the Father in me; or else believe me for the very works' sake.

12 Verily, verily, I say unto you, [l] He that believeth on me, the works that I do shall he do also; and greater *works* than these shall he do, because I go unto my Father.

l Mat.21.21.

as a Father, had been manifested in the incarnation, the works, and the teachings of Christ, so that they who had seen and heard him might be said to have had a real view of God. When Jesus says, "hath *seen* the Father," this cannot refer to the *essence* or *substance* of God, for he is invisible, and in that respect no man has seen God at any time. All that is meant when it is said that *God is seen*, is that some *manifestation* of him has been made, or some such *exhibition* as that we may learn his *character*, his *will*, and his *plans*. In this case it cannot mean that he that had seen Jesus with the bodily eyes had *in the same sense* seen God; but he that had been a witness of his miracles and of his transfiguration—that had heard his doctrines and studied his character—had had full evidence of his divine mission, and of the *will and purpose* of the Father in sending him. The knowledge of the Son was itself, of course, the knowledge of the Father. There was such an intimate *union* in their nature and design that he who understood the one understood also the other. See Notes on Mat. xi. 27; also Lu. x. 22; Jn. i. 18.

10. *I am in the Father*. See Notes on ch. x. 38. ¶ *The words that I speak*, &c. See Notes on ch. vii. 16, 17. ¶ *The Father that dwelleth in me*. Literally, "The Father *remaining* in me." This denotes most *intimate union*, so that the works which Jesus did might be said to be done by the Father. It implies a more intimate union than can subsist between a mere *man* and *God*. Had Jesus been a mere *man*, like the prophets, he would have said, "The Father who *sent* or *commissioned* me doeth the works;" but here there is reference, doubtless, to that mysterious and peculiar union which subsists between the Father and the Son. ¶ *He doeth the works*. The miracles which had been wrought by Jesus. The Father could be said to do them on account of the intimate union between him and the Son. See ch. v. 17, 19, 36; x. 30.

11. *Believe me*, &c. Believe my declarations that I am in the Father, &c. There were two grounds on which they might believe; one was his *own testimony*, the other was *his works*. ¶ *Or else*. If credit is not given to my *words*, let there be to my miracles. ¶ *For the very works' sake*. On account of the works; or, be convinced by the miracles themselves. Either his own testimony was sufficient to convince them, or the many miracles which he had wrought in healing the sick, raising the dead, &c.

12. *He that believeth on me*. This promise had doubtless peculiar reference to the apostles themselves. They were full of grief at his departure, and Jesus, in order to console them, directed them to the great honour which was to be conferred on them, and to the assurance that God would not leave them, but would attend them in their ministry with the demonstrations of his mighty power. It cannot be understood of *all* his followers, for the circumstances of the promise do not require us to understand it thus, and it has not been a matter of fact that *all* Christians have possessed power to do greater works than the Lord Jesus. It is a general promise that greater works than he performed should be done by his followers, without specifying that *all* his followers would be instrumental in doing them. ¶ *The works that I do*. The miracles of healing the sick, raising the dead, &c. This was done by the apostles in many instances. See Ac. v. 15; xix. 12; xiii. 11; v. 1–10. ¶ *Greater* works *than these shall he do*. Interpreters have been at a loss in what way to understand this. The most probable meaning of the passage is the following: The word "greater" cannot refer to the miracles themselves, for the works of the apostles did not exceed

13 And[m] whatsoever ye shall ask in my name, that will I do, that the Father may be glorified in the Son.

14 If ye shall ask any thing in my name, I will do *it*.

15 If[n] ye love me, keep my commandments.

16 And I will pray the Father, and he shall give you [o]another Comforter, that he may abide with you for ever;

m 1 Jn.5.14. *n* ch.15.10,14; ver.21,23; 1 Jn.5.3. *o* ch.15.26.

---

those of Jesus in *power*. No higher exertion of power was put forth, or could be, than raising the dead. But, though not greater *in themselves considered*, yet they were greater *in their effects*. They made a deeper impression on mankind. They were attended with more extensive results. They were the means of the conversion of more sinners. The works of Jesus were confined to Judea. They were seen by few. The works of the apostles were witnessed by many nations, and the effect of their miracles and preaching was that thousands from among the Jews and Gentiles were converted to the Christian faith. The word *greater* here is used, therefore, not to denote the *absolute exertion of power*, but the *effect* which the miracles would have on mankind. The word "works" here probably denotes not merely *miracles*, but *all things that the apostles did* that made an impression on mankind, including their travels, their labours, their doctrine, &c. ¶ *Because I go unto my Father*. He would there intercede for them, and especially by his going to the Father the Holy Spirit would be sent down to attend them in their ministry, ver. 26, 28; xvi. 7–14. See Mat. xxviii. 18. By his going to the Father is particularly denoted his exaltation to heaven, and his being placed as head over all things to his church, Ep. i. 20–23; Phi. ii. 9–11. By his being exalted there the Holy Spirit was given (ch. xvi. 7), and by his power thus put forth the Gentiles were brought to hear and obey the gospel.

13. *Whatsoever ye shall ask*. This promise referred particularly to the apostles in their work of spreading the gospel; it is, however, true of all Christians, if what they ask is in *faith*, and according to the will of God, Ja. i. 6; 1 Jn. v. 14. ¶ *In my name*. This is equivalent to saying *on my account*, or *for my sake*. If a man who has money in a bank authorizes us to draw it, we are said to do it in his name. If a son authorizes us to apply to his father for aid because we are his friends, we do it in the name of the son, and the favour will be bestowed on us from the regard which the parent has to his son, and through him to all his friends. So we are permitted to apply to God in the name of his Son Jesus Christ, because God is in him well pleased (Mat. iii. 17), and because we are the friends of his Son he answers our requests. Though *we* are undeserving, yet he loves us on account of his Son, and because he sees in us his image. No privilege is greater than that of approaching God in the name of his Son; no blessings of salvation can be conferred on any who do not come in his name. ¶ *That will I do*. Being exalted, he will be possessed of all power in heaven and earth (Mat. xxviii. 18), and he therefore could fulfil all their desires. ¶ *That the Father may be glorified in the Son*. See Notes on ch. xiii. 31.

15. *If ye love me*. Do not show your love by grief at my departure merely, or by profession, but by obedience. ¶ *Keep my commandments*. This is the only proper evidence of love to Jesus, for mere profession is no proof of love; but that love for him which leads us to do all his will, to love each other, to deny ourselves, to take up our cross, and to follow him through evil report and through good report, is true attachment. The evidence which we have that a child loves its parents is when that child is willing, without hesitation, gainsaying, or murmuring, to do *all* that the parent requires him to do. So the disciples of Christ are required to show that they are attached to him supremely by yielding to all his requirements, and by patiently doing his will in the face of ridicule and opposition, 1 Jn. v. 2, 3.

16. *I will pray the Father*. This refers to his intercession after his death and ascension to heaven, for this prayer was to be connected with their keeping his commandments. In what *way* he makes *intercession* in heaven for his people we do not know. The *fact*, however, is

17 *Even* the Spirit of truth; whom[p] the world cannot receive, because it seeth him not, neither knoweth him; but ye know him,

p 1 Co.2.14.

clearly made known, Ro. viii. 34; He. iv. 14, 15; vii. 25. It is as the result of his intercession in heaven that we obtain all our blessings, and it is through him that our prayers are to be presented and made efficacious before God. ¶ *Another Comforter.* Jesus had been to them a counsellor, a guide, a friend, while he was with them. He had instructed them, had borne with their prejudices and ignorance, and had administered consolation to them in the times of despondency. But he was about to leave them now to go alone into an unfriendly world. The *other* Comforter was to be given as a compensation for his absence, or to perform the offices toward them which *he* would have done if he had remained personally with them. And from this we may learn, in part, what is the office of the Spirit. *It is to furnish to all Christians the instruction and consolation which would be given by the personal presence of Jesus*, ch. xvi. 14. To the apostles it was particularly to inspire them with the knowledge of all truth, ch. xiv. 26; xv. 26. Besides this, he came to convince men of sin. See Notes on ch. xvi. 8–11. It was proper that such an agent should be sent into the world—1st. Because it was a part of the plan that Jesus should ascend to heaven after his death. 2d. Unless some heavenly agent should be sent to carry forward the work of salvation, man would reject it and perish. 3d. Jesus could not be personally and bodily present in all places with the vast multitudes who should believe on him. The Holy Spirit is omnipresent, and can reach them all. See Notes on ch. xvi. 7. 4th. It was manifestly a part of the plan of redemption that each of the persons of the Trinity should perform his appropriate work—the Father in sending his Son, the Son in making atonement and interceding, and the Spirit in applying the work to the hearts of men.

The word translated *Comforter* is used in the New Testament five times. In four instances it is applied to the Holy Spirit—Jn. xiv. 16, 26; xv. 26; xvi. 7. In the other instance it is applied to the Lord Jesus—1 Jn. ii. 1: "We have an *advocate* (Paraclete—Comforter) with the Father, Jesus Christ the righteous." It is used, therefore, only by John. The verb from which it is taken has many significations. Its proper meaning is to *call one* to us (Ac. xxvii. 20); then to call one *to aid us*, as an advocate in a court; then to exhort or entreat, to pray or implore, as an advocate does, and to comfort or console, by suggesting *reasons* or *arguments* for consolation. The word "comforter" is frequently used by Greek writers to denote *an advocate* in a court; one who intercedes; a monitor, a teacher, an assistant, a helper. It is somewhat difficult, therefore, to fix the precise meaning of the word. It may be translated either advocate, monitor, teacher, or helper. What the office of the Holy Spirit in this respect is, is to be learned from what we are elsewhere told he does. We learn particularly from the accounts that our Saviour gives of his work that that office was, 1st. To comfort the disciples; to be with them in his absence and to supply his place; and this is properly expressed by the word *Comforter.* 2d. To *teach them*, or remind them of truth; and this might be expressed by the word *monitor* or *teacher*, ver. 26; xv. 26, 27. 3d. To *aid* them in their work; to advocate their cause, or to assist them in advocating the cause of religion in the world, and in bringing sinners to repentance; and this may be expressed by the word *advocate*, ch. xvi. 7–13. It was also by the Spirit that they were enabled to stand before kings and magistrates, and boldly to speak in the name of Jesus, Mat. x. 20. These seem to comprise all the meanings of the word in the New Testament, but no *single* word in our language expresses fully the sense of the original. ¶ *That he may abide with you for ever.* Not that he should remain with you for a few years, as I have done, and then leave you, but be with you in all places to the close of your life. He shall be your constant guide and attendant.

17. *The Spirit of truth.* He is thus called here because he would teach them the truth, or would guide them into all truth, ch. xvi. 13. He would keep them from all error, and teach them the truth, which, either by writing or preaching, they were to communicate to others. ¶ *The world.* The term *world* is often used to denote all who are entirely under

for he dwelleth with you, [q]and shall be in you.

18 I will not leave you [1]comfortless; [r]I will come to you.

19 Yet a little while, and the world seeth me no more; but ye see me: [s]because I live, ye shall live also.

q Ro.8.9; 1 Jn.2.27. 1 or, *orphans*. r ver.3,28.

s He.7.25.

the influence of the things of this world—pride, ambition, and pleasure; all who are not Christians, and especially all who are addicted to gross vices and pursuits, 1 Co. i. 21; xi. 32; Jn. xii. 31; 2 Co. iv. 4. ¶ *Cannot receive.* Cannot admit as a teacher or comforter, or cannot receive in his offices of enlightening and purifying. The reason why they *could not* do this is immediately added. ¶ *Because it seeth him not.* The men of the world are under the influence of the senses. They walk by *sight*, and not by *faith.* Hence what they cannot perceive by their senses, what does not gratify their sight, or taste, or feeling, makes no impression on them. As they cannot *see* the operations of the Spirit (Jn. iii. 8), they judge that all that is said of his influence is delusive, and hence they cannot receive him. They have an erroneous mode of judging of what is for the welfare of man. ¶ *Neither knoweth him.* To *know*, in the Scriptures, often means more than the act of the mind in simply *understanding* a thing. It denotes *every* act or *emotion* of the mind that is requisite in receiving the proper *impression* of a truth. Hence it often includes the idea of *approbation*, of *love*, of *cordial feeling*, Ps. i. 6; xxxvii. 18; cxxxviii. 6; Na. i. 7; 2 Ti. ii. 19. In this place it means the approbation of the heart; and as the people of the world do not *approve* of or *desire* the aid of the Spirit, so it is said they cannot receive him. They have no love for him, and they reject him. Men often consider his work in the conversion of sinners and in revivals as delusion. They love the world so much that they cannot understand his work or embrace him. ¶ *He dwelleth in you.* The Spirit dwells in Christians by his sacred influences. There is no personal union, no physical indwelling, for God is essentially present in one place as much as in another; but he works in us repentance, peace, joy, meekness, &c. He teaches us, guides us, and comforts us. See Notes on Ga. v. 22–24. Thus he is said to *dwell in us* when we are made pure, peaceable, holy, humble; when we become *like him*, and cherish his sacred influences. The word "dwelleth" means to *remain* with them. Jesus was to be taken away, but the Spirit would remain. It is also implied that they would *know* his presence, and have assurance that they were under his guidance. This was true of the apostles as *inspired men*, and it is true of all Christians that by ascertaining that they have the *graces of the Spirit*—joy, peace, long-suffering, &c.—they *know* that they are the children of God, 1 Jn. iii. 24; v. 10.

18. *Comfortless.* Greek, *orphans.* Jesus here addresses them as children, ch. xiii. 33. He says that he would show them the kindness of a *parent*, and, though he was going away, he would provide for their future welfare. And even while *he* was absent, yet they would sustain to him *still* the relation of children. Though he was to die, yet he would live again; though absent in body, yet he would be present with them by his Spirit; though he was to go away to heaven, yet he would return again to them. See ver. 3.

19. *A little while.* This was the day before his death. ¶ *Seeth me no more.* No more until the day of judgment. The men of the world would not see him *visibly*, and they had not the eye of faith to discern him. ¶ *But ye see me.* Ye shall continue to see me by faith, even when the world cannot. You will continue to see me by the eye of faith as still your gracious Saviour and Friend. ¶ *Because I live.* Though the Saviour was about to die, yet was he also about to be raised from the dead. He was to *continue* to live, and though absent from them, yet he would feel the same interest in their welfare as when he was with them on earth. This expression does not refer *particularly* to his *resurrection*, but his *continuing to live.* He had a nature which could not die. As Mediator also he would be raised and continue to live; and he would have both power and inclination to give them also life, to defend them, and bring them with him. ¶ *Ye shall live also.* This doubtless refers to their future life. And we learn from this, 1st. That the life of the Christian depends on that of Christ. They are united; and if they

20 At that day ye shall know that I *am* in my Father, and ye in me, and I in you.

21 He[t] that hath my commandments, and keepeth them, he it is that loveth me; and he that loveth me shall be loved of my Father; and I will love him, and will manifest myself to him.

22 Judas[u] saith unto him, (not Iscariot,) Lord, how is it that thou wilt manifest thyself unto us, and not unto the world?

23 Jesus answered and said unto him, If a man love me he will keep my words; and my Father will love him, [v]and we will come unto him, and make our abode with him.

t ver.15,23. *u* Lu.6.16. *v* 1 Jn.2.24; Re.3.20.

---

were separated, the Christian could neither enjoy spiritual life here nor eternal joy hereafter. 2d. The fact that Jesus lives is a pledge that all who believe in him shall be saved. He has power over all our spiritual foes, and he can deliver us from the hands of our enemies, and from all temptations and trials.

20. *At that day.* In the time when my life shall be fully manifested to you, and you shall receive the assurance that I live. This refers to the time *after* his resurrection, and to the manifestations which in various ways he would make that he was alive. ¶ *That I* am *in my Father*, &c. That we are most intimately and indissolubly united. See Notes on ch. x. 38. ¶ *Ye in me.* That there is a union between us which can never be severed. See Notes on ch. xv. 1–7.

21. *He that hath*, &c. This intimate union is farther manifested by these facts: 1st. That true love to Jesus will produce obedience. See ver. 15. 2d. That those who love *him* will be loved of the *Father*, showing that there is a union between the Father and the Son. 3d. That Jesus also will love them, evincing still the same union. Religion is love. The love of one holy being or object is the love of all. The kingdom of God is one. His people, though called by different names, are one. They are united to each other and to God, and the bond which unites the whole kingdom in one is love. ¶ *Will manifest myself to him.* To *manifest* is to show, to make appear, to place before the eyes so that an object may be seen. This means that Jesus would so *show* himself to his followers that they should *see* and *know* that he was their Saviour. In what way this is done, see ver. 23.

22. *Judas saith unto him.* This was the same as Lebbeus or Thaddeus. See Mat. x. 3. He was the brother of James, and the author of the Epistle of Jude. ¶ *How is it*, &c. Probably Judas thought that he spake *only* of his resurrection, and he did not readily see how it could be that he could show himself to them, and not be seen also by others.

23. *Will keep my words.* See ver. 15. ¶ *We will come to him.* We will come to him with the manifestation of pardon, peace of conscience, and joy in the Holy Ghost. It means that God will manifest himself to the soul as a Father and Friend; that Jesus will manifest himself as a Saviour; that is, that there will be shed abroad in the heart just views and proper feelings toward God and Christ. The Christian will rejoice in the perfections of God and of Christ, and will delight to contemplate the glories of a present Saviour. The condition of a sinner is represented as one who has gone astray from God, and from whom God has withdrawn, Ps. lviii. 3; Pr. xxviii. 10; Eze. xiv. 11. He is *alienated* from God, Ep. ii. 12; Is. i. 4; Ep. iv. 18; Col. i. 21. Religion is represented as God returning to the soul, and manifesting himself as reconciled through Jesus Christ, 2 Cor. v. 18; Col. i. 21. ¶ *Make our abode.* This is a figurative expression implying that God and Christ would *manifest* themselves in no *temporary* way, but that it would be the privilege of Christians to enjoy their presence continually. They would take up their residence in the heart as their dwelling-place, as a temple fit for their abode. See 1 Cor. iii. 16: "Ye are the temple of God;" vi. 19: "Your body is the temple of the Holy Ghost;" 2 Co. vi. 16: "Ye are the temple of the living God." This does not mean that there is any *personal union* between Christians and God—that there is any peculiar indwelling of the *essence* of God in us—for God is essentially present in all places in the same way; but it is a figurative mode of speaking, denoting that the Christian is under the influence of

24 He that loveth me not, keepeth
not my sayings; and the word
which ye hear is not mine, but
the Father's which sent me.
25 These things have I spoken
unto you, being *yet* present with
you.
26 But[w] the Comforter, *which is*
the Holy Ghost, whom the Father
will send in my name, [x]he shall
teach you all things, and bring all
things to your remembrance, whatsoever I have said unto you.
27 Peace[y] I leave with you, my
peace I give unto you: not as the
world giveth, give I unto you.

w ver.16.

x ch.16.13; 1 Jn.2.20,27. y Ep.2.14-17; Phi.4.7.

God; that he rejoices in his presence, and that he has the views, the feelings, the joys which God produces in a redeemed soul, and with which he is pleased.

24. *The word which ye hear is not mine.* See Notes on ch. v. 19; vii. 16.

25. *Have I spoken.* For your consolation and guidance. But, though he had said so many things to console them, yet *the Spirit* would be given also as their Comforter and Guide.

26. *Will send in my name.* On my account. To perfect my work. To execute it as I would in applying it to the hearts of men. See ver. 13. ¶ *Shall teach you all things.* All things which it was needful for them to understand in the apostolic office, and particularly those things which they were not prepared then to hear or could not then understand. See ch. xvi. 12. Comp. Notes on Mat. x. 19, 20. This was a full promise that they would be inspired, and that in organizing the church, and in recording the truths necessary for its edification, they would be under the infallible guidance of the Holy Ghost. ¶ *Bring all things to your remembrance.* This probably refers to two things: 1st. He would seasonably remind them of the sayings of Jesus, which they might otherwise have forgotten. In the organization of the church, and in composing the sacred history, he would preside over their *memories*, and recall such truths and doctrines as were necessary either for their comfort or the edification of his people. Amid the multitude of things which Jesus spake during a ministry of more than three years, it was to be expected that many things which he had uttered, that would be important for the edification of the church, would be forgotten. We see, hence, the nature of their inspiration. The Holy Spirit made use of their *memories*, and doubtless of all their natural faculties. He so presided *over* their memories as to recall what they had forgotten, and *then* it was recorded as a thing which they distinctly remembered, in the same way as we remember a thing which would have been forgotten had not some friend recalled it to our recollection. 2d. The Holy Spirit would teach them the *meaning* of those things which the Saviour had spoken. Thus they did not understand that he ought to be put to death till after his resurrection, though he had repeatedly told them of it, Lu. xxiv. 21, 25, 26. So they did not till then understand that the gospel was to be preached to the Gentiles, though this was also declared before. Comp. Mat. iv. 15, 16; xii. 21, with Ac. x. 44–48.

27. *Peace I leave with you.* This was a common form of benediction among the Jews. See Notes on Mat. x. 13. It is the invocation of the blessings of peace and happiness. In this place it was, however, much more than a mere *form* or an empty wish. It came from Him who had power to make peace and to confer it on all, Ep. ii. 15. It refers here particularly to the consolations which he gave to his disciples in view of his approaching death. He had exhorted them not to be troubled (ver. 1), and he had stated *reasons* why they should not be. He explained to them why he was about to leave them; he promised them that he would return; he assured them that the Holy Ghost would come to comfort, teach, and guide them. By all these truths and promises he provided for their peace in the time of his approaching departure. But the expression refers also, doubtless, to the *peace* which is given to all who love the Saviour. They are by nature enmity against God, Ro. viii. 7. Their minds are like the troubled sea, which cannot rest, whose waters cast up mire and dirt, Is. lvii. 20. They were at war with conscience, with the law and perfections of God, and with all the truths of religion. Their state after conversion is described as a state *of peace*. They are *reconciled* to God;

Let not your heart be troubled,
neither let it be afraid.
28 Ye have heard how I said
unto you, I go away, and come
again unto you. If ye loved me,
ye would rejoice, because I said,
[z]I go unto the Father; [a]for my
Father is greater than I.
29 And now I have told you
before it come to pass, that when it
is come to pass ye might believe.
30 Hereafter I will not talk much

z ver.12. a 1 Co.15.27,28.

---

they acquiesce in all his claims; and they have a joy which the world knows not in the word, the promises, the law, and the perfections of God, in the plan of salvation, and in the hopes of eternal life. See Ro. i. 7; v. 1; viii. 6; xiv. 7; Ga. v. 22; Ep. ii. 17; vi. 15; Phi. iv. 7; Col. iii. 15. ¶ *My peace.* Such as I only can impart. The peculiar peace which my religion is fitted to impart. ¶ *Not as the world.* 1st. Not as the objects which men commonly pursue—pleasure, fame, wealth. They leave care, anxiety, remorse. They do not meet the desires of the immortal mind, and they are incapable of affording that peace which the soul needs. 2d. Not as the men of the world give. They salute you with empty and flattering words, but their professed friendship is often feigned and has no sincerity. You cannot be sure that they are sincere, but I am. 3d. Not as systems of philosophy and false religion give. They profess to give peace, but it is not real. It does not still the voice of conscience; it does not take away sin; it does not reconcile the soul to God. 4th. My peace is such as meets all the wants of the soul, silences the alarms of conscience, is fixed and sure amid all external changes, and will abide in the hour of death and for ever. How desirable, in a world of anxiety and care, to possess this peace! and how should all who have it not, seek that which the world can neither give nor take away! ¶ *Neither let it be afraid.* Of any pain, persecutions, or trials. You have a Friend who will never leave you; a peace that shall always attend you. See ver. 1.

28. *Ye have heard*, &c. Ver. 2, 3. ¶ *If ye loved me.* The expression is not to be construed as if they had then no love to him, for they evidently had; but they had also low views of him as the Messiah; they had many Jewish prejudices, and they were slow to believe his plain and positive declarations. This is the slight and tender reproof of a friend, meaning manifestly if you had *proper* love for me; if you had the *highest* views of my character and work; if you would lay aside your Jewish prejudices, and put *entire, implicit* confidence in what I say. ¶ *Ye would rejoice.* Instead of grieving, you would rejoice in the completion of the plan which requires me to return to heaven, that greater blessings may descend on you by the influences of the Holy Spirit. ¶ *Unto the Father.* To heaven; to the immediate presence of God, from whom all the blessings of redemption are to descend. ¶ *For my Father is greater than I.* The object of Jesus here is not to compare his *nature* with that of the Father, but his *condition.* Ye would rejoice that I am to leave this state of suffering and humiliation, and resume that glory which I had with the Father before the world was. You ought to rejoice at my exaltation to bliss and glory with the Father (Professor Stuart). The object of this expression is to *console* the disciples in view of his absence. This he does by saying that *if* he goes away, the Holy Spirit will descend, and great success will attend the preaching of the gospel, ch. xvi. 7–10. In the plan of salvation the Father is represented as *giving* the Son, the Holy Spirit, and the various blessings of the gospel. As the *Appointer*, the *Giver*, the *Originator*, he may be represented as in office superior to the Son and the Holy Spirit. The discourse has no reference, manifestly, to the *nature* of Christ, and cannot therefore be adduced to prove that he is not divine. Its whole connection demands that we interpret it as relating solely to the imparting of the blessings connected with redemption, in which the Son is represented all along as having been *sent* or *given*, and in this respect as sustaining a relation subordinate to the Father.

29. *Before it come to pass.* Before my death, resurrection, and ascension. ¶ *Ye might believe.* You might be confirmed or strengthened in faith by the evidence which I gave that I came from God—the power of foretelling future events.

30. *Will not talk much.* The time of

with you; for the [b]prince of this world cometh, and [c]hath nothing in me.

31 But that the world may know that I love the Father; and as[d] the Father gave me commandment, even so I do. Arise, let us go hence.

b ch.16.11; Ep.2.2. c 2 Co.5.21; He.4.15; 1 Jn.3.5. d Ps.40.8; Phi.2.8.

CHAPTER XV.

I AM the [a]true vine, and my Father is the [b]husbandman.

a Is.4.2. b Ca.8.12.

my death draws nigh. It occurred the next day. ¶ *The prince of this world.* See Notes on ch. xii. 31. ¶ *Cometh.* Satan is represented as approaching him to try him in his sufferings, and it is commonly supposed that no small part of the pain endured in the garden of Gethsemane was from some dreadful conflict with the great enemy of man. See Lu. xxii. 53: "This is your hour *and the power of darkness.*" Comp. Lu. iv. 13. ¶ *Hath nothing in me.* There is in me no principle or feeling that accords with his, and nothing, therefore, by which he can prevail. Temptation has only power because there are some principles in us which accord with the designs of the tempter, and which may be *excited* by presenting corresponding objects till our virtue be overcome. Where there is no such propensity, temptation has no power. As the principles of Jesus were wholly on the side of virtue, the meaning here may be that, though he had the natural appetites of man, his virtue was so supreme that Satan "had nothing in him" which could constitute any danger that he would be led into sin, and that there was no fear of the result of the conflict before him.

31. *That the world may know that I love the Father.* That it might not be alleged that his virtue had not been subjected to *trial.* It *was* subjected. He was tempted in all points like as we are, yet without sin, He. iv. 15. He passed through the severest forms of temptation, that it might be seen and known that his holiness was proof to *all* trial, and that human nature *might be* so pure as to resist *all* forms of temptation. This *will* be the case with all the saints in heaven, and it *was* the case with Jesus on earth. ¶ *Even so I do.* In all things he obeyed; and he showed that, in the face of calamities, persecutions, and temptations, he was still disposed to obey his Father. This he did that the world might know that he loved the Father. So should we bear trials and resist temptation; and so, through persecution and calamity, should we show that we are actuated by the love of God. *Arise, let us go hence.* It has been commonly supposed that Jesus and the apostles now rose from the paschal supper and went to the Mount of Olives, and that the remainder of the discourse in ch. xv., xvi., together with the prayer in ch. xvii., was delivered while on the way to the garden of Gethsemane; but some have supposed that they merely rose from the table, and that the discourse was finished before they left the room. The former is the more correct opinion. It was now probably toward midnight, and the moon was at the full, and the scene was one, therefore, of great interest and tenderness. Jesus, with a little band, was himself about to die, and he went forth in the stillness of the night, counselling his little company in regard to their duties and dangers, and invoking the protection and blessing of God his Father to attend, to sanctify, and guide them in the arduous labours, the toils, and the persecutions they were yet to endure, ch. xvii.

CHAPTER XV.

1. *I am the true vine.* Some have supposed that this discourse was delivered in the room where the Lord's Supper was instituted, and that, as they had made use of *wine,* Jesus took occasion from that to say that he was the true vine, and to intimate that his blood was the real wine that was to give strength to the soul. Others have supposed that it was delivered in the temple, the entrance to which was adorned with a golden vine (Josephus), and that Jesus took occasion thence to say that he was the *true* vine; but it is most probable that it was spoken while they were going from the paschal supper to the Mount of Olives. Whether it was suggested by the sight of *vines* by the way, or by the wine of which they had just partaken, cannot now be determined. The comparison was frequent among the Jews, for Palestine abounded in

2 Every[c] branch in me that beareth not fruit he taketh away; and every *branch* [d]that beareth fruit, he purgeth it, that it may bring forth more fruit.

3 Now[e] ye are clean through

c Mat.15.13. d He.12.15; Re.3.19. e ch.17.17; Ep.5.26; 1 Pe.1.22.

vineyards, and the illustration was very striking. Thus the Jewish people are compared to a vine which God had planted, Is. v. 1–7; Ps. lxxx. 8–16; Joel i. 7; Je. ii. 21; Eze. xix. 10. When Jesus says he was the *true* vine, perhaps allusion is had to Je. ii. 21. The word *true*, here, is used in the sense of *real*, *genuine*. He really and truly gives what is emblematically represented by a vine. The point of the comparison or the meaning of the figure is this: A *vine* yields proper juice and nourishment to all the branches, whether these are large or small. All the nourishment of each branch and tendril passes through the main stalk, or the vine, that springs from the earth. So Jesus is the source of all real strength and grace to his disciples. He is their leader and teacher, and imparts to them, as they need, grace and strength to bear the fruits of holiness. ¶ *And my Father is the husbandman.* The word *vine-dresser* more properly expresses the sense of the original word than *husbandman*. It means one who has the care of a vineyard; whose office it is to nurture, trim, and defend the vine, and who of course feels a deep interest in its growth and welfare. See Notes on Mat. xxi. 33. The figure means that God gave, or appointed his Son *to be*, the source of blessings to man; that all grace descends *through* him; and that God takes care of all the branches of this vine—that is, of all who are by faith united to the Lord Jesus Christ. In Jesus and all his church he feels the deepest interest, and it is an object of great solicitude that his church *should* receive these blessings and bear much fruit.

2. *Every branch in me.* Every one that is a true follower of me, that is united to me by faith, and that truly derives grace and strength from me, as the branch does from the vine. The word *branch* includes all the boughs, and the smallest tendrils that shoot out from the parent stalk. Jesus here says that he sustains the same relation to his disciples that a parent stalk does to the branches; but this does not denote any *physical* or incomprehensible union. It is a union formed by *believing* on him; resulting from our feeling our dependence on him and our need of him; from embracing him as our Saviour, Redeemer, and Friend. We become united to him in all our interests, and have common feelings, common desires, and a common destiny with him. We seek the same objects, are willing to encounter the same trials, contempt, persecution, and want, and are desirous that *his* God shall be ours, and his eternal abode ours. It is a union of friendship, of love, and of dependence; a union of weakness with strength; of imperfection with perfection; of a dying nature with a living Saviour; of a lost sinner with an unchanging Friend and Redeemer. It is the most tender and interesting of all relations, but not more mysterious or more *physical* than the union of parent and child, of husband and wife (Ep. v. 23), or friend and friend. ¶ *That beareth not fruit.* As the vine-dresser will remove all branches that are dead or that bear no fruit, so will God take from his church all professed Christians who give no evidence by their lives that they are truly united to the Lord Jesus. He here refers to such cases as that of Judas, the apostatizing disciples, and all false and merely *nominal Christians* (Dr. Adam Clarke). ¶ *He taketh away.* The vine-dresser cuts it off. God removes such in various ways: 1st. By the discipline of the church. 2d. By suffering them to fall into temptation. 3d. By persecution and tribulation, by the deceitfulness of riches, and by the cares of the world (Mat. xiii. 21, 22); by suffering the man to be placed in such circumstances as Judas, Achan, and Ananias were—such as to show what *they were*, to bring their characters *fairly out*, and to let it be *seen* that they had no true love to God. 4th. By death, for God has power thus at any moment to remove unprofitable branches from the church. ¶ *Every* branch *that beareth fruit.* That is, all true Christians, for all such bear fruit. To *bear fruit* is to show by our lives that we are under the influence of the religion of Christ, and that that religion produces in us its appropriate effects, Ga. v. 22, 23. Notes on Mat. vii. 16–20. It is also to live so as to be useful to others. As a vineyard is worthless un-

the word which I have spoken unto you.

4 Abide[f] in me, and I in you. As[g] the branch cannot bear fruit of itself except it abide in the vine, no more can ye, except ye abide in me.

5 I am the vine, ye *are* the branches: he that abideth in me, and I in him, the same bringeth

f 1 Jn.2.6. *g* Ho.14.8; Ga.2.20; Phi.1.11.

less it bears fruit that may promote the happiness or subsistence of man, so the Christian principle would be worthless unless Christians should live so that others may be made holy and happy by their example and labours, and so that the *world* may be brought to the cross of the Saviour. ¶ *He purgeth it.* Or rather he *prunes* it, or cleanses it by pruning. There is a use of words here — a *paronomasia* — in the original which cannot be retained in the translation. It may be imperfectly seen by retaining the Greek words — "Every branch in me that beareth not fruit he *taketh away* (*airei*); every branch that beareth fruit, he purgeth it (*kathairei*); now ye *are clean* (*katharoi*)," &c. The same Greek word in different forms is still retained. God purifies all true Christians so that they may be more useful. He takes away that which hindered their usefulness; teaches them; quickens them; revives them; makes them more pure in motive and in life. This he does by the regular influences of his Spirit in sanctifying them, purifying their motives, teaching them the beauty of holiness, and inducing them to devote themselves more to him. He does it by taking away what opposes their usefulness, however much they may be attached to it, or however painful to part with it; as a vine-dresser will often feel himself compelled to lop off a branch that is large, apparently thrifty, and handsome, but which bears no fruit, and which *shades* or injures those which do. So God often takes away the *property* of his people, their children, or other idols. He removes the objects which bind their affections, and which render them inactive. He takes away the things around man, as he did the valued gourds of Jonah (Jonah iv. 5–11), so that he may feel his dependence, and live more to the honour of God, and bring forth more proof of humble and active piety.

3. *Now ye are clean.* Still keeping up the figure (*katharoi*). It does not mean that they were *perfect*, but that they had been under a process of *purifying* by his instructions all the time he had been with them. He had removed their erroneous notions of the Messiah; he had gradually reclaimed them from their fond and foolish views respecting earthly honours; he had taught them to be willing to forsake all things; and he had so trained and disciplined them that immediately after his death they would be ready to go and bear fruit among all nations to the honour of his name. In addition to this, *Judas* had been removed from their number, and they were now *all* true followers of the Saviour. See Notes on ch. xiii. 10. ¶ *Through the word.* By means of the *teachings* of Jesus while he had been with them.

4. *Abide in me.* Remain united to me by a living faith. Live a life of dependence on me, and obey my doctrines, imitate my example, and constantly exercise faith in me. ¶ *And I in you.* That is, if you remain attached to me, I will remain with you, and will teach, guide, and comfort you. This he proceeds to illustrate by a reference to the vine. If the branch should be cut off an instant, it would die and be fruitless. As long as it is in the vine, *from the nature of the case*, the parent stock imparts its juices, and furnishes a constant circulation of sap adapted to the growth and fruitfulness of the branch. So our piety, if we should be separate from Christ, or if we cease to feel our union to him and dependence on him, withers and droops. While we are united to him by a living faith, *from the nature of the case*, strength flows from him to us, and we receive help as we need. Piety then, manifested in good works, in love, and self-denial, is as natural, as easy, as unconstrained, and as lovely as the vine covered with fruitful branches is at once useful and enticing.

5. *I am the vine*, ver. 1. ¶ *Without me ye can do nothing.* The expression "without me" denotes the same as *separate from me.* As the branches, if separated from the parent stock, could produce no fruit, but would immediately wither and die, so Christians, if separate from Christ, could do nothing. The expression is one, therefore, strongly implying dependence. The Son of God

forth much fruit; for [1]without me ye can do nothing.

6 If[h] a man abide not in me, he is cast forth as a branch, and is withered; and men gather them, and cast *them* into the fire, and they are burned.

7 If ye abide in me, and my words abide in you, [i]ye shall ask what ye will, and it shall be done unto you.

8 Herein is my Father glorified, that ye bear much fruit; so shall ye be my disciples.

1 or, *severed from me.* *h* Mat.3.10; 7.19. *i* ch.16.23.

---

was the original source of life, Jn. i. 4. He also, by his work as Mediator, gives life to the world (Jn. vi. 33), and it is by the same grace and agency that it is continued in the Christian. We see hence, 1st. That to him is due all the praise for all the good works the Christian performs. 2d. That they will perform good works just in proportion as they feel their dependence on him and look to him. And 3d. That the reason why others fail of being holy is because they are unwilling to look to him, and seek grace and strength from him who alone is able to give it.

6. *If a man abide not in me*. See ver. 4. If a man is not truly united to him by faith, and does not live with a continual sense of his dependence on him. This doubtless refers to those who are professors of religion, but who have never known anything of true and real connection with him. ¶ *Is cast forth*. See Notes on ver. 2. Also Mat. viii. 12; xxii. 13. ¶ *Is withered.* Is dried up. A branch cut off withers. So of a soul unconnected with Christ, however fair it may have appeared, and however flourishing when a profession of religion was first made, yet when it is tried, and it is seen that there was no true grace, everything withers and dies. The zeal languishes, the professed love is gone, prayer is neglected, the sanctuary is forsaken, and the soul becomes like a withered branch reserved for the fire of the last great day. See a beautiful illustration of this in Eze. xv. ¶ *Men gather them.* The word *men* is not in the original, and should not have been in the translation. The Greek is "they gather them," a form of expression denoting simply *they are gathered*, without specifying by whom it is done. From Mat. xiii. 40–42, it seems that it will be done by the angels. The expression means, as the withered and useless branches of trees are gathered for fuel, so shall it be with all hypocrites and false professors of religion. ¶ *Are burned.* See Mat. xiii. 42.

7. *My words.* My doctrine; my commandments. ¶ *Abide in you.* Not only are *remembered*, but are suffered to remain in you as a living principle, to regulate your affections and life. ¶ *Ye shall ask*, &c. See ch. xiv. 13. This promise had particular reference to the apostles. It is applicable to other Christians only so far as they are in circumstances similar to the apostles, and only so far as they possess their spirit. We learn from it that it is only when we keep the commandments of Christ—only when we live by faith in him, and his words are suffered to control our conduct and affections, that our prayers will be heard. Were we *perfect* in all things, he would always hear us, and we should be kept from making an improper petition; but just so far as men regard iniquity in their heart, the Lord will not hear them, Ps. lxvi. 18.

8. *Herein.* In this—to wit, in your bearing much fruit. ¶ *Glorified.* Honoured. ¶ *Bear much fruit.* Are fruitful in good works; are faithful, zealous, humble, devoted, always abounding in the work of the Lord. This honours God, 1st. Because it shows the excellence of his law which requires it. 2d. Because it shows the power of his gospel, and of that grace which can overcome the evil propensities of the heart and *produce* it. 3d. Because the Christian is restored to the divine image, and it shows how excellent is the character after which they are formed. They imitate God, and the world sees that the whole tendency of the divine administration and character is to make man holy; to produce in us that which is lovely, and true, and honest, and of good report. Comp. Mat. vii. 20; Phi. iv. 8. ¶ *So.* That is, in doing this. ¶ *Shall ye be my disciples.* This is a true test of character. It is not by profession, but it is by a holy life, that the character is tried. This is a test which it is easy to apply, and one which decides the case. It is worthy of re-

9 As the Father hath loved me, so have I loved you: continue ye in my love.
10 If[k] ye keep my commandments, ye shall abide in my love; even as I have kept my Father's commandments, and abide in his love.
11 These things have I spoken unto you, that my joy might re-

k ch.14.21,23.

mark that the Saviour says that those who bear MUCH *fruit* are they who are his disciples. The design and tendency of his religion is to excite men to do *much* good, and to call forth *all* their strength, and time, and talents in the work for which the Saviour laid down his life. Nor should anyone take comfort in the belief that he is a Christian who does not aim to do *much* good, and who does not devote to God *all* that he has in an honest effort to glorify his name, and to benefit a dying world. The apostles obeyed this command of the Saviour, and went forth preaching the gospel everywhere, and aiming to bring all men to the knowledge of the truth; and it is this spirit only, manifested in a proper manner, which can constitute any certain evidence of piety.

9. *As the Father hath loved me.* The love of the Father toward his only-begotten Son is the highest affection of which we can conceive. Comp. Mat. iii. 17; xvii. 5. It is the love of God toward his coequal Son, who is like him in all things, who always pleased him, and who was willing to endure the greatest sacrifices and toils to accomplish his purpose of mercy. Yet this love is adduced to illustrate the tender affection which the Lord Jesus has for all his friends. ¶ *So have I loved you.* Not to the same degree, for this was impossible, but with the same *kind* of love—deep, tender, unchanging; love prompting to self-denials, toils, and sacrifices to secure their welfare. ¶ *Continue ye.* The reason which he gives for their doing this is the *strength* of the love which he had shown for them. His love was so great for them that he was about to lay down his life. This constitutes a strong reason why *we* should continue in his love. 1st. Because the love which he shows for us is unchanging. 2d. It is the love of our best friend—love whose strength was expressed by toils, and groans, and blood. 3d. As he is unchanging in the character and strength of his affection, so should *we* be. Thus only can we properly express our gratitude; thus only show that we are his true friends. 4th. Our happiness here and for ever depends altogether on our *continuing* in the love of Christ. We have no source of permanent joy but in that love. ¶ *In my love.* In love to me. Thus it is expressed in the Greek in the next verse. The connection also demands that we understand it of *our* love to him, and not of *his* love to us. The latter cannot be the subject of a command; the former may. See also Lu. xi. 42; 1 Jn. ii. 5; Jude 21.

10. See ch. xiv. 23, 24.

11. *These things.* The discourse in this and the previous chapter. This discourse was designed to comfort them by the promise of the Holy Spirit and of eternal life, and to direct them in the discharge of their duty. ¶ *My joy.* This expression probably denotes the happiness which Jesus had, and would continue to have, by their obedience, love, and fidelity. Their obedience was to him a source of joy. It was that which he sought and for which he had laboured. He now clearly taught them the path of duty, and encouraged them to persevere, notwithstanding he was about to leave them. If they obeyed him, it would continue to him to be a source of joy. Christ rejoices in the obedience of all his friends; and, though his happiness is not dependent on them, yet their fidelity is an object which he desires and in which he finds delight. The same sentiment is expressed in ch. xvii. 13. ¶ *Your joy might be full.* That you might be delivered from your despondency and grief at my departure; that you might see the reason why I leave you, be comforted by the Holy Spirit, and be sustained in the arduous trials of your ministry. See 1 Jn. i. 4; 2 Jn. 12. This promise of the Saviour was abundantly fulfilled. The apostles with great frequency speak of the fulness of their joy—joy produced in just the manner promised by the Saviour—by the presence of the Holy Spirit. And it showed his great love, that he promised such joy; his infinite knowledge, that, in the midst of their many trials and persecutions, he knew that

main in you, and *that* [l]your joy might be full.

12 This[m] is my commandment, That ye love one another, as I have loved you.

13 Greater[n] love hath no man than this, that a man lay down his life for his friends.

14 Ye[o] are my friends if ye do whatsoever I command you.

15 Henceforth I call you not servants, for the servant knoweth not what his lord doeth; but I have called you [p]friends, for all things that I have heard of my Father I have made known unto you.

16 Ye[q] have not chosen me, but I have chosen you, and [r]ordained you, that ye should go and bring

l ch.16.24; 17.13. *m* ch.13.34. *n* Ro.5.7,8. *o* ver.10. *p* Ja.2.23. *q* 1 Jn.4.10,19. *r* Ep.2.10.

they would possess it; and the glorious power and loveliness of his gospel, that it could impart such joy amid so many tribulations. See instances of this joy in Ac. xiii. 52; Ro. xiv. 17; 2 Co. ii. 3; Ga. v. 22; 1 Th. i. 6; ii. 19, 20; iii. 9; 1 Pe. i. 8; Ro. v. 11; 2 Co. vii. 4.

12. *This is my commandment.* The peculiar law of Christianity, called hence the *new* commandment. See Notes on ch. xiii. 34. ¶ *As I have loved you.* That is, with the same tender affection, willing to endure trials, to practise self-denials, and, if need be, to lay down your lives for each other, 1 Jn. iii. 16.

13. *Greater love hath,* &c. No higher expression of love could be given. Life is the most valuable object we possess; and when a man is willing to lay that down for his friends or his country, it shows the utmost extent of love. Even this love for friends has been rarely witnessed. A *very few* cases—like that of Damon and Pythias—have occurred where a man was willing to save the life of his friend by giving his own. It greatly enhances the love of Christ, that while the instances of those who have been willing to die for *friends* have been so rare, *he* was willing to die for enemies--bitter foes, who rejected his reign, persecuted him, reviled him, scorned him, and sought his life, 1 Jn. iv. 10; Ro. v. 6, 10. It also shows us the extent of his love that he gave himself up, not to *common* sufferings, but to the most bitter, painful, and protracted sorrows, not for himself, not for friends, but for a thoughtless and unbelieving world.

"O Lamb of God, was ever *pain*,
Was ever LOVE like thine!"

15. *I call you not servants.* This had been the *common* title by which he addressed them (Mat. x. 24, 25; Jn. xii. 26; xiii. 13); but he *had* also before this, on one occasion, called them friends (Lu. xii. 4), and on one occasion after this he called them servants, Jn. xv. 20. He here means that the *ordinary* title by which he would henceforth address them would be that of friends. ¶ *The servant knoweth not,* &c. He receives the command of his master without knowing the reason why this or that thing is ordered. It is one of the conditions of slavery not to be let into the counsels and plans of the master. It is the privilege of friendship to be made acquainted with the plans, wishes, and wants of the friend. This instance of friendship Jesus had given them by making them acquainted with the reasons why he was about to leave them, and with his secret wishes in regard to them. As he had given them this *proof* of friendship, it was proper that he should not withhold from them the *title* of friends. ¶ *His lord.* His master. ¶ *I have called you friends.* I have given you the name of friends. He does not mean that the usual appellation which he had given them had been than of friends, but that such was the title which he had now given them. ¶ *For all things,* &c. The reason why he *called* them friends was that he had now treated them *as* friends. He had opened to them his mind; made known his plans; acquainted them with the design of his coming, his death, his resurrection, and ascension; and, having thus given them the clearest *proof* of friendship, it was proper that he should give them the *name.* ¶ *That I have heard,* &c. Jesus frequently represents himself as commissioned or sent by God to accomplish an important work, and as being instructed by him in regard to the nature of that work. See Notes on Jn. v. 30. By what he had *heard of the Father,* he doubtless refers to the *design* of God in his coming and his death. This he had made known to them.

forth fruit, and *that* your fruit should remain; that [s]whatsoever ye shall ask of the Father in my name, he may give it you.

s ver.7; ch.14.13.

16. *Ye have not chosen me.* The word here translated *chosen* is that from which is derived the word *elect*, and means the same thing. It is frequently thus translated, Mar. xiii. 20; Mat. xxiv. 22, 24, 31; Col. iii. 12. It refers here, doubtless, to his choosing or electing them to be apostles. He says that it was not because *they* had chosen *him* to be their teacher and guide, but because *he* had designated them to be his apostles. See Jn. vi. 70; also Mat. iv. 18–22. He thus shows them that his love for them was pure and disinterested; that it commenced when they had no affection for him; that it was not a matter of obligation on his part, and that therefore it placed them under more tender and sacred obligations to be entirely devoted to his service. The same may be said of all who are endowed with talents of any kind, or raised to any office in the church or the state. It is not that they have originated these talents, or laid God under obligation. What they have they owe to his sovereign goodness, and they are bound to devote all to his service. Equally true is this of all Christians. It was not that by nature they were more *inclined* than others to seek God, or that they had any native goodness to recommend them to him, but it was because he graciously inclined them by his Holy Spirit to seek him; because, in the language of the Episcopal and Methodist articles of religion, "The grace of Christ PREVENTED them;" that is, *went before them*, *commenced* the work of their personal salvation, and thus God in sovereign mercy chose them as his own. Whatever Christians, then, possess, they owe to God, and by the most tender and sacred ties they are bound to be his followers. ¶ *I have chosen you.* To be apostles. Yet all whom he now addressed were true disciples. Judas had left them; and when Jesus says he had chosen them *to bear fruit*, it may mean, also, that he had "chosen them to salvation, through sanctification of the Spirit and belief of the truth," 2 Th. ii. 13. ¶ *Ordained you.* Literally, I have *placed you*, appointed you, set you apart. It does not mean that he had done this by any formal public act of the imposition of hands, as we now use the word, but that he had *designated* or appointed them to this work, Lu. vi. 13–16; Mat. x. 2–5. ¶ *Bring forth fruit.* That you should be rich in good works; faithful and successful in spreading my gospel. This was the great business to which they were set apart, and this they faithfully accomplished. It may be added that this is the great end for which Christians are chosen. It is not to be idle, or useless, or simply to seek enjoyment. It is to do good, and to spread as far as possible the rich temporal and spiritual blessings which the gospel is fitted to confer on mankind. ¶ *Your fruit should remain.* This probably means, 1st. That the effect of their labours would be *permanent* on mankind. Their efforts were not to be like those of false teachers, the result of whose labours soon vanish away (Ac. v. 38, 39), but their gospel was to spread—was to take a deep and permanent hold on men, and was ultimately to fill the world, Mat. xvi. 18. The Saviour knew this, and never was a prediction more cheering for man or more certain in its fulfilment. 2d. There is included, also, in this declaration the idea that their labours were to be *unremitted.* They were sent forth to be diligent in their work, and untiring in their efforts to spread the gospel, until the day of their death. Thus their fruit, the continued *product* or *growth* of religion in their souls, was to *remain*, or to be continually produced, until God should call them from their work. The Christian, and especially the Christian minister, is devoted to the Saviour for life. He is to toil without intermission, and without being weary of his work, till God shall call him home. The Saviour never called a disciple to serve him merely for a part of his life, nor to feel himself at liberty to relax his endeavours, nor to suppose himself to be a Christian when his religion produced no fruit. He that enlists under the banners of the Son of God does it for life. He that *expects* or *desires* to grow weary and cease to serve him, has never yet put on the Christian armour, or known anything of the grace of God. See Lu. ix. 62. ¶ *That whosoever*, &c. See ver. 7.

18. *If the world hate you.* The friendship of the world they were not to ex-

17 These[t] things I command you, that ye love one another.

18 If[u] the world hate you, ye know that it hated me before *it hated* you.

19 If ye were of the world, the world would love his own; but because ye are not of the world, but I have chosen you out of the world, [v]therefore the world hateth you.

20 Remember[w] the word that I said unto you, The servant is not greater than his lord. If they have persecuted me, they will also persecute you; [x]if they have kept my saying, they will keep yours also.

21 But[y] all these things will they do unto you for my name's sake, because they know not him that sent me.

22 If[z] I had not come and spoken unto them, they had not

t ver.12. *u* 1 Jn.3.13. *v* ch.17.14. *w* Mat.10.24; Lu.6.40; ch.13.16. *x* Eze.3.7. *y* Mat.10.22; 24.9; ch.16.3. *z* ch.9.41.

pect, but they were not to be deterred from their work by its hatred. They had seen the example of Jesus. No opposition of the proud, the wealthy, the learned, or the men of power, no persecution or gibes, had deterred him from his work. Remembering this, and having his example steadily in the eye, they were to labour *not less* because wicked men should oppose and deride them. It is enough for the disciple to be as his Master, and the servant as his Lord, Mat. x. 25.

19. *If ye were of the world.* If you were actuated by the principles of the world. If, like them, you were vain, earthly, sensual, given to pleasure, wealth, ambition, they would not oppose you. ¶ *Because ye are not of the world.* Because you are influenced by different principles from men of the world. You are actuated by the love of God and holiness; they by the love of sin. ¶ *I have chosen you out of the world.* I have, by choosing you to be my followers, separated you from their society, and placed you under the government of my holy laws. ¶ *Therefore,* &c. A Christian may esteem it as one evidence of his piety that he is hated by wicked men. Often most decided evidence is given that a man is the friend of God by the opposition excited against him by the profane, by Sabbath-breakers, and by the dissolute, 1 Jn. iii. 13; Jn. vii. 7.

20. *Remember the word that I said,* &c. At their first appointment to the apostolic office. See Mat. x. 24, 25.

21. *My name's sake.* On my account. Because you are my followers and possess my spirit. See Notes on ch. xiv. 13. ¶ *Because they know not him that sent me.* They will not believe that God has sent me. They do not so understand his character, his justice, or his law, as to see that it was fit that he should send his Son to die. They are so opposed to it, so filled with pride and opposition to a plan of salvation that is so humbling to men, as to be resolved *not* to believe it, and thus they persecute me, and will also you.

22. *And spoken unto them.* Declared unto them the will of God, and made known his requirements. Jesus had not less certainly shown by his own *arguments* that he was the Messiah than by his miracles. By *both* these kinds of proof their guilt was to be measured. See ver. 26. No small part of the gospel of John consists of arguments used by the Saviour to convince the Jews that he came from God. He here says if he had not used these arguments, and proved to them his divine mission, they had not had sin. ¶ *Had not had sin.* This is evidently to be understood of the particular sin of persecuting and rejecting him. Of this he was speaking; and though, if he had not come, they would have been guilty of many other sins, yet of this, their great crowning sin, they would not have been guilty. We may understand this, then, as teaching, 1st. That they would not have been guilty of this *kind of sin.* They would not have been chargeable with rejecting the signal grace of God if Jesus had not come and made an offer of mercy to them. 2d. They would not have been guilty of the same *degree of sin.* The rejection of the Messiah was the crowning act of rebellion which brought down the vengeance of God, and led on their peculiar national calamities. By way of eminence, therefore, this might be called *the sin*—the peculiar sin of their age and nation. Comp. Mat. xxiii. 34–39; xxvii. 25. And this shows us, what

had sin; [a]but now they have no cloak[2] for their sin.

23 He that hateth me, hateth my Father also.

24 If I had not done among them the [b]works which none other man did, they had not had sin; but now have they both seen and hated both me and my Father.

25 But *this cometh to pass*, that the word might be fulfilled that is written in their law, [c]They hated me without a cause.

26 But when the [d]Comforter is come, whom I will send unto you from the Father, *even* the Spirit of truth, which proceedeth from the Father, [e]he shall testify of me;

a Ja.4.17. 2 or, *excuse*. *b* ch.7.31. *c* Ps.35.19; 69.4. *d* ch.14.17. *e* 1 Jn.5.6.

is so often taught in the Scriptures, that our guilt will be in proportion to the light that we possess and the mercies that we reject, Mat. xi. 20–24; Lu. xii. 47, 48. If it was such a crime to reject the Saviour *then*, it is a crime now; and if the rejection of the Son of God brought such calamities on the Jewish nation, the same rejection will involve the sinner now in woe, and vengeance, and despair. ¶ *No cloak.* No covering, no excuse. The proof has been so clear that they cannot plead ignorance; it has been so often presented that they cannot allege that they had no opportunity of knowing it. It is still so with all sinners.

23. *He that hateth me*, &c. To show them that this was no slight crime, he reminds them that a rejection of himself is also a rejection of God. Such is the *union* between them, that no one can hate the one without also hating the other. See ch. v. 19, 20; xiv. 7, 9.

24. *The works which none other man did.* The miracles of Jesus surpassed those of Moses and the prophets—1st. In their number. He healed great multitudes, and no small part of his life was occupied in doing good by miraculous power. 2d. In their nature. They involved a greater exertion of power. He healed *all* forms of disease. He showed that his power was superior to all kinds of pain. He raised Lazarus after he had been four days dead. He probably refers also to the fact that he had performed miracles of a different *kind* from all the prophets. 3d. He did all this by his *own power;* Moses and the prophets by the invoked power of God. Jesus spake and it was done, showing that he had power of himself to do more than all the ancient prophets had done. It may be added that his miracles were done in a short time. They were constant, rapid, continued, in all places. Wherever he was, he showed that he had this power, and in the short space of three years and a half it is probable that he wrought *more* miracles than are recorded of Moses and Elijah, and all the prophets put together.

25. *In their law*, Ps. xxxv. 19. All the Old Testament was sometimes called *the law.* The meaning here is that the same thing happened to him which did to the psalmist. The same words which David used respecting his enemies would express, also, the conduct of the Jews and their treatment of the Messiah. In both cases it was without cause. Jesus had broken no law, he had done no injury to his country or to any individual. It is still true that sinners hate him in the same way. He injures no one, but, amid all their hatred, he seeks their welfare; and, while they reject him in a manner for which they *can give no reason in the day of judgment*, he still follows them with mercies and entreats them to return to him. Who has ever had any reason to *hate* the Lord Jesus? What injury has he ever done to any one of the human race? What evil has he ever said or thought of any one of them? What cause or reason had the Jews for putting him to death? What reason has the sinner for hating him now? What reason for neglecting him? No one can give a reason for it that will satisfy his own conscience, none that has the least show of plausibility. Yet no being on earth has ever been more hated, despised, or neglected, and in every instance it has been "without a cause." Reader, do *you* hate him? If so, I ask you WHY? Wherein has he injured you? or why should you think or speak reproachfully of the benevolent and pure Redeemer?

27. *Ye also shall bear witness.* You shall be witnesses to the world to urge on them the evidences that the Lord Jesus is the Messiah. ¶ *Have been with me.* They had for more than three years seen his works, and were therefore qualified to bear witness of his character and

27 And[f] ye also shall bear witness, because [g]ye have been with me from the beginning.

CHAPTER XVI.

THESE things have I spoken unto you, that ye should not be offended.

2 They shall put you out of the synagogues; yea, the time cometh, that [a]whosoever killeth you will think that he doeth God service.

3 And[b] these things will they do unto you, because [c]they have not known the Father, nor me.

4 But these things have I told you, that, when the time shall come, ye may remember that I

f Lu.24.48; Ac.2.32; 4.20,33; 2 Pe.1.16. g 1 Jn.1.2.

a Ac.26.9-11. b ch.15.21. c 1 Co.2.8; 1 Ti.1.13.

doctrines. ¶ *From the beginning.* From his entrance on the public work of the ministry, Mat. iv. 17–22. Comp. Ac i. 21, 22.

CHAPTER XVI.

1. *These things.* The things spoken in the two previous chapters, promising them divine aid and directing them in the path of duty. ¶ *Be offended.* For the meaning of the word *offend*, see Notes on Mat. v. 29. It means here the same as to *stumble* or *fall*—that is, to apostatize. He proceeds immediately to tell them, what he had often apprised them of, that they would be subject to great persecutions and trials. He was also himself about to be removed by death. They were to go into an unfriendly world. All these things were in themselves greatly fitted to shake their faith, and to expose them to the danger of apostasy. Comp. Lu. xxiv. 21. If they had not been apprised of this, if they had not known *why* Jesus was about to die, and if they had not been encouraged with the promised aid of the Holy Ghost, they would have sunk under these trials, and forsaken him and his cause. And we may learn hence, 1st. That if Christians were left to themselves they would fall away and perish. 2d. That God affords means and helps *beforehand* to keep them in the path of duty. 3d. That the instructions of the Bible and the help of the Holy Spirit are all granted to keep them from apostasy. 4th. That Jesus beforehand *secured* the fidelity and made certain the continuance in faith of his apostles, seeing all their dangers and knowing all their enemies. And, in like manner, we should be persuaded that "he is able to keep that which we commit to him against that day," 2 Ti. i. 12.

2. *Out of the synagogues.* See Notes on ch. ix. 22. They would *excommunicate* them from their religious assemblies. This was often done. Comp. Ac. vi. 13, 14; ix. 23, 24; xvii. 5; xxi. 27–31. ¶ *Whosoever killeth you.* This refers principally to the Jews. It is also true of the Gentiles, that in their persecution of Christians they supposed they were rendering acceptable service to their gods. ¶ *God service.* The Jews who persecuted the apostles regarded them as blasphemers, and as seeking to overthrow the temple service, and the system of religion which God had established. Thus they supposed they were rendering service to God in putting them to death, Ac. vi. 13, 14; xxi. 28–31. Sinners, especially hypocrites, often cloak enormous crimes under the pretence of great zeal for religion. Men often suppose, or profess to suppose, that they are rendering God service when they persecute others; and, under the pretence of great zeal for truth and purity, evince all possible bigotry, pride, malice, and uncharitableness. The people of God have suffered most from those who have been *conscientious persecutors;* and some of the most malignant foes which true Christians have ever had have been *in* the church, and have been professed ministers of the gospel, persecuting them under pretence of great zeal for the cause of purity and religion. It is no evidence of piety that a man is full of zeal against those whom he supposes to be heretics; and it is one of the best proofs that a man knows nothing of the religion of Jesus when he is eminent for self-conceit in his own views of orthodoxy, and firmly fixed in the opinion that all who differ from him and his sect *must* of course be wrong.

3. See ch. xv. 21.

4. *These things.* These things which are about to happen, ver. 1, 2. He had foretold them that they would take place. ¶ *Ye may remember*, &c. By calling to mind that he had foretold these things they would perceive that

told you of them. And these
things I said not unto you at the
beginning, because I was with you.
5 But now I go my way to him
that sent me; and none of you
asketh me, Whither goest thou?
6 But because I have said these
things unto you, [d]sorrow hath filled
your heart.
7 Nevertheless I tell you the
truth; It is expedient for you that
I go away; for if I go not away,

d ver.21.

he was omniscient, and would remember, also, the consolations which he had afforded them and the instructions which he had given them. Had these calamities come upon them without their having been foretold, their faith might have failed; they might have been tempted to suppose that Jesus was not aware of them, and of course that he was not the Messiah. God does not suffer his people to fall into trials without giving them sufficient warning, and without giving all the grace that is needful to bear them. ¶ *At the beginning.* In the early part of the ministry of Jesus. The expression *these things* here refers, probably, to *all* the topics contained in these chapters. He had, in the early part of his ministry, forewarned them of calamities and persecutions (Mat. x. 16; v. 10–12; ix. 15), but he had not so fully acquainted them with the nature, and design, and sources of their trials; he had not so fully apprised them of the fact, the circumstances, and the object of his death and of his ascension to heaven; he had not revealed to them so clearly that the Holy Spirit would descend, and sanctify, and guide them; and especially he had not, in one continued discourse, *grouped* all these things together, and placed their sorrows and consolations so fully before their minds. All these are included, it is supposed, in the expression "these things." ¶ *Because I was with you.* This is the reason which he gives why he had not *at first* made known to them clearly the certainty of their calamities and their joys; and it implies, 1st. That it was not needful to do it at once, as he was to be with them for more than three years, and could have abundant opportunity *gradually* to teach these things, and to prepare them for the more full announcement when he was about to leave them. 2d. That while he was with them he would go before them, and the weight of calamities would fall on *him*, and consequently they did not so much then need the presence and aid of the Holy Spirit as they would when he was gone. 3d. That his presence was to them what the presence of the Holy Spirit would be after his death, ver. 7. He could teach them all needful truth. He could console and guide them. Now that he was to leave them, he fully apprised them of what was before them, and of the descent of the Holy Spirit to do for them what *he* had done when with them.

5, 6. *Now I go my way.* Now I am about to die and leave you, and it is proper to announce all these things to you. ¶ *None of you asketh me*, &c. They gave themselves up to grief instead of inquiring why he was about to leave them. Had they made the inquiry, he was ready to answer them and to comfort them. When we are afflicted we should not yield ourselves to excessive grief. We should inquire *why* it is that God thus tries us; and we should never doubt that if we come to him, and spread out our sorrows before him, he will give us consolation.

7. *It is expedient for you*, &c. The reason why it was expedient for them that he should go away, he states to be, that in this way only would the Comforter be granted to them. Still, it may be asked why the presence of the Holy Spirit was more valuable to them than that of the Saviour himself? To this it may be answered, 1st. That by his departure, his death, and ascension—by having these great *facts* before their eyes—they would be led by the Holy Spirit to see more fully the design of his coming than they would by his presence. While he was with them, notwithstanding the plainest teaching, their minds were filled with prejudice and error. They still adhered to the expectation of a temporal kingdom, and were unwilling to believe that he was to die. When he should have actually left them they could no longer doubt on this subject, and would be *prepared* to understand why he came. And this was done. See the Acts of the Apostles everywhere. It is often needful that God should visit us with severe afflic-

the Comforter will not come unto you; but if I depart, I will send him unto you.

8 And when he is come, he will [1]reprove the world of sin, and of righteousness, and of judgment:

9 Of [e]sin, because they believe not on me;

1 or, *convince*, Ac.2.37. e Ro.3.20; 7.9.

tion before our pride will be humbled and we are willing to understand the plainest truths. 2d. While on the earth the Lord Jesus could be bodily present but in one place at one time. Yet, in order to secure the great design of saving men, it was needful that there should be some agent who could be in all places, who could attend all ministers, and who could, at the same time, apply the work of Christ to men in all parts of the earth. 3d. It was an evident arrangement in the great plan of redemption that each of the persons of the Trinity should perform a part. As it was not the work of the Spirit to make an atonement, so it was not the work of the Saviour to apply it. And until the Lord Jesus had performed this great work, the way was not open for the Holy Spirit to descend to perform his part of the great plan; yet, when the Saviour had completed *his* portion of the work and had left the earth, the Spirit would carry forward the same plan and apply it to men. 4th. It was to be expected that far more signal success would attend the preaching of the gospel when the atonement was actually made than before. It was the office of the Spirit to carry forward the work only when the Saviour had died and ascended; and this was actually the case. See Ac. ii. Hence it was expedient that the Lord Jesus should go away, that the Spirit might descend and apply the work to sinners. The departure of the Lord Jesus was to the apostles a source of deep affliction, but had they seen *the whole case* they would not have been thus afflicted. So God often takes away from us one blessing that he may bestow a greater. All affliction, if received in a proper manner, is of this description; and could the afflicted people of God always *see the whole case* as God sees it, they would think and feel, as *he* does, that it was *best* for them to be thus afflicted. ¶ *It is expedient.* It is *better* for you. ¶ *The Comforter.* See Notes on ch. xiv. 16.

8. *He will reprove.* The word translated *reprove* means commonly to demonstrate by argument, to prove, to persuade anyone to do a thing by presenting reasons. It hence means also to *convince* of anything, and particularly to *convince of crime.* This is its meaning here. He will *convince* or *convict* the world of sin. That is, he will so apply the truths of God to men's own minds as to *convince* them by fair and sufficient arguments that they are sinners, and cause them to *feel* this. This is the nature of conviction always. ¶ *The world.* Sinners. The men of the world. All men are by nature sinners, and the term *the world* may be applied to them all, Jn. i. 10; xii. 31; 1 Jn. v. 19.

9. *Of sin.* The first thing specified of which the world would be convinced is *sin.* Sin, in general, is any violation of a law of God, but the particular sin of which men are here said to be convinced is that of rejecting the Lord Jesus. This is placed *first*, and is deemed the sin of chief magnitude, as it is the principal one of which men are guilty. This was particularly true of the Jews who had rejected him and crucified him; and it was the great crime which, when brought home to their consciences by the preaching of the apostles, overwhelmed them with confusion, and filled their hearts with remorse. It was their rejection of the Son of God that was made the great truth that was instrumental of their conversion, Ac. ii. 22, 23, 37; iii. 13–15; iv.10, 26–28; comp. ver. 31–33. It is also true of other sinners. Sinners, when awakened, often feel that it has been the great crowning sin of their lives that they have rejected the tender mercy of God, and trampled on the blood of his Son; and that they have for months and years refused to submit to him, saying that they would not have him to reign over them. Thus is fulfilled what is spoken by Zechariah, xii. 10: "And they shall look upon me whom they have pierced, and mourn." Throughout the New Testament this is regarded as the sin that is pre-eminently offensive to God, and which, if unrepented of, will certainly lead to perdition, Mar. xvi. 16; Jn. iii. 36. Hence it is placed *first* in those sins of which the Spirit will convince men; and hence, if we have not yet been brought to see

10 Of [f]righteousness, because I go to my Father, and ye see me no more;

11 Of [g]judgment, because [h]the prince of this world is judged.

12 I have yet many things to say

f Is.42.21; Ro.1.17.

g Ac.17.31; Ro.2.2; Re.20.12,13. h ch.12.31.

our guilt in rejecting God's tender mercy through his Son, we are yet in the gall of bitterness and under the bond of iniquity.

10. *Of righteousness.* This seems clearly to refer to the righteousness or *innocence* of Jesus himself. He was now persecuted. He was soon to be arraigned on heavy charges, and condemned by the highest authority of the nation as guilty. Yet, though condemned, he says that the Holy Spirit would descend and *convince* the world that he was innocent. ¶ *Because I go to my Father.* That is, the amazing miracle of his resurrection and ascension to God would be a demonstration of his innocence that would satisfy the Jews and Gentiles. God would not raise up an impostor. If he had been truly *guilty*, as the Jews who condemned him pretended, God would not have set his seal to the imposture by raising him from the dead; but when he did raise him up and exalt him to his own right hand, he gave his attestation to his *innocence;* he showed that he approved his work, and gave evidence conclusive that Jesus was sent from God. To this proof of the *innocence* of Jesus the apostles often refer, Ac. ii. 22–24; xvii. 31; Ro. i. 4; 1 Co. xv. 14, &c.; 1 Ti. iii. 16. This same proof of the *innocence* or righteousness of the Saviour is as satisfactory now as it was then. One of the deepest feelings which an awakened sinner has, is his conviction of the righteousness of Jesus Christ. He sees that he is holy; that his own opposition to him has been unprovoked, unjust, and base; and it is this which so often overwhelms his soul with the conviction of his own unworthiness, and with earnest desires to obtain a better righteousness than his own. ¶ *And ye see me no more.* That is, he was to be taken away from them, and they would not see him till his return to judgment; yet this source of grief to *them* would be the means of establishing his religion and greatly blessing others.

11. *Of judgment.* That God is just, and will execute judgment. This is proved by what he immediately states. ¶ *The prince of this world.* Satan. See Notes on ch. xii. 31. The death of Christ was a judgment or a condemnation of Satan. In this struggle Jesus gained the victory and subdued the great enemy of man. This proves that God will execute judgment or justice on all his foes. If he vanquished his great enemy who had so long triumphed in this world, he will subdue all others in due time. All sinners in like manner may expect to be condemned. Of this great truth Jesus says the Holy Spirit will convince men. God showed himself to be *just* in subduing his great enemy. He showed that he was resolved to vanquish his foes, and that *all* his enemies in like manner must be subdued. This is deeply felt by the convicted sinner. He knows that he is guilty. He learns that God is just. He fears that he will condemn him, and trembles in the apprehension of approaching condemnation. From this state of alarm there is no refuge but to flee to Him who subdued the great enemy of man, and who is able to deliver him from the vengeance due to his sins. Convinced, then, of the righteousness of Jesus Christ, and of his ability and willingness to save him, he flees to his cross, and seeks in him a refuge from the coming storm of wrath.

In these verses we have a condensed and most striking view of the work of the Holy Spirit. These three things comprise the whole of his agency in the conversion of sinful men; and in the accomplishment of this work he still awakens, convinces, and renews. He attends the preaching of the gospel, and blesses the means of grace, and manifests his power in revivals of religion. He thus imparts to man the blessings purchased by the death of Jesus, carries forward and extends the same plan of mercy, and will yet apply it to all the kingdoms and tribes of men. Have *we* ever felt his power, and been brought by his influence to mourn over our sins, and seek the mercy of a dying Saviour?

12. *I have yet many things to say,* &c. There were many things pertaining to the work of the Spirit and the establishment of religion which might be said. Jesus had given them the outline; he had presented to them the great doctrines of the system, but he had not

unto you, but [i]ye cannot bear them
now.
13 Howbeit, when he, the Spirit
of truth, is come, [k]he will guide
you into all truth; for he shall not
speak of himself; but whatsoever
he shall hear, *that* shall he speak;
and [l]he will show you things to
come.
14 He shall glorify me; for he
shall receive of mine, and shall
show *it* unto you.
15 All things that the Father
hath are mine; therefore said I

i He.5.12. k ch.14.26. l Re.1.1,19.

gone into details. These were things which they could not then bear. They were still full of Jewish prejudices, and were not prepared for a full development of his plans. Probably he refers here to the great *changes* which were to take place in the Jewish system—the abolition of sacrifices and the priesthood, the change of the Sabbath, the rejection of the Jewish nation, &c. For these doctrines they were not prepared, but they would in due time be taught them by the Holy Spirit.

13. *The Spirit of truth.* So called because he would teach them all needful truth. ¶ *Will guide you into all truth.* That is, truth which pertained to the establishment of the Christian system, which they were not then prepared to hear. We may here remark that this is a full promise that they would be inspired and guided in founding the new church; and we may observe that the plan of the Saviour was replete with wisdom. Though they had been long with him, yet they were not prepared *then* to hear of the changes that were to occur; but his death would open their eyes, and the Holy Spirit, making use of the striking and impressive scenes of his death and ascension, would carry forward with vast rapidity their views of the nature of the Christian scheme. Perhaps in the few days that elapsed, of which we have a record in the first and second chapters of the Acts of the Apostles, they learned more of the true nature of the Christian plan than they would have done in months or years even under the teaching of Jesus himself. The more we study the plan of Christ, the more shall we admire the profound wisdom of the Christian scheme, and see that it was eminently fitted to the great design of its Founder—to introduce it in such a manner as to make on man the deepest impression of its wisdom and its truth. ¶ *Not speak of himself.* Not as *prompted* by himself. He shall declare what is communicated to him. See Notes on ch. vii. 18. ¶ *Whatsoever he shall hear.* What he shall receive of the Father and the Son; represented by *hearing*, because in this way instruction is commonly received. See Notes on ch. v. 30. ¶ *Things to come.* Probably this means *the meaning of things* which were to take place *after* the time when he was speaking to them—to wit, the design of his death, and the nature of the changes which were to take place in the Jewish nation. It is also true that the apostles were inspired by the Holy Spirit to predict future events which would take place in the church and the world. See Ac. xi. 28; xx. 29; xxi. 11; 1 Ti. iv. 1-3; 2 Ti. iii.; 2 Pe. i. 14; and the whole book of Revelation.

14. *Shall glorify me.* Shall honour me. The nature of his influence shall be such as to exalt my character and work in view of the mind. ¶ *Shall receive of mine.* Literally, "shall take of or from me." He shall receive his commission and instructions as an ambassador from me, to do my will and complete my work. ¶ *Shall show* it. Shall announce or communicate it to you. This is always the work of the Spirit. All serious impressions produced by him lead to the Lord Jesus (1 Co. xii. 3), and by this we may easily test our feelings. If we have been truly convicted of sin and renewed by the Holy Ghost, the tendency of all his influences has been to lead us to the Saviour; to show us our need of him; to reveal to us the loveliness of his character, and the fitness of his work to our wants; and to incline us to cast our eternal interests on his almighty arm, and commit all to his hands.

15. *All things*, &c. See Mat. xxviii. 18; xi. 27. No one could have said this who was not *equal* with the Father. The union was so intimate, though mysterious, that it might with propriety be said that whatever was done in relation to the Son, was also done in regard to the Father. See ch. xiv. 9.

16. *A little while* His death would

that he shall take of mine, and
shall show *it* unto you.
16 A little while, and ye shall not
see me; and again a little while,
and ye shall see me, because I go
to the Father.
17 Then said *some* of his disciples
among themselves, What is this
that he saith unto us, A little while,
and ye shall not see me; and again
a little while, and ye shall see me;
and, Because I go to the Father?
18 They said, therefore, What is
this that he saith, A little while?
We cannot tell what he saith.
19 Now[m] Jesus knew that they
were desirous to ask him, and said
unto them, Do ye inquire among
yourselves of that I said, [n]A little
while, and ye shall not see me;
and again a little while, and ye
shall see me?
20 Verily, verily, I say unto you,
That [o]ye shall weep and lament,
but the world shall rejoice; and
ye shall be sorrowful, but your sorrow shall be turned into joy.
21 A[p] woman when she is in
travail hath sorrow, because her
hour is come; but as soon as she
is delivered of the child, she remembereth no more the anguish,
for joy that a man is born into the
world.
22 And[q] ye now therefore have
sorrow; but [r]I will see you again,
and your heart shall rejoice, [s]and
your joy no man taketh from you.

m ch.2.24,25. *n* ver.16; ch.7.33; 13.33; 14.19. *o* Lu.24.17,21. *p* Is.26.17. *q* ver.6. *r* Lu.24.41,52; ch.20.20. *s* 1 Pe.1.8.

occur in a short time. It took place the next day. See ch. xiv. 19. ¶ *Ye shall not see me.* That is, he would be concealed from their view in the tomb. ¶ *And again a little while.* After three days he would rise again and appear to their view. ¶ *Because I go*, &c. Because it is a part of the plan that I should ascend to God, it is necessary that I should rise from the grave, and then you will see me, and have evidence that I am still your Friend. Comp. ch. vii. 33. Here are three important events foretold for the consolation of the disciples, yet they were stated in such a manner that, in *their* circumstances and with *their* prejudices, it appeared difficult to understand him.

20. *Ye shall weep*, &c. At my crucifixion, sufferings, and death. Comp. Lu. xxiii. 27. ¶ *The world.* Wicked men. The term *world* is frequently used in this sense. See ver. 8. It refers particularly, here, to the Jews who sought his death, and who would rejoice that their object was obtained. ¶ *Shall be turned into joy.* You will not only rejoice at my resurrection, but even my death, now the object of so much grief to you, will be to you a source of unspeakable joy. It will procure for you peace and pardon in this life, and eternal joy in the world to come. Thus their greatest apparent calamity would be to them, finally, the source of their highest comfort; and though *then* they could not see *how* it could be, yet if they had known *the whole case* they would have seen that they might rejoice. As it was, they were to be consoled by the assurance of the Saviour that it would be for their good. And thus, in our afflictions, if we could see the whole case, we should rejoice. As it is, when they appear dark and mysterious, we may trust in the promise of God that they will be for our welfare. We may also remark here that the apparent triumphs of the wicked, though they may produce grief at present in the minds of Christians, will be yet overruled for good. *Their* joy shall be turned into mourning, and the mourning of Christians into joy; and wicked men may be doing the very thing—as they were in the crucifixion of the Lord Jesus—that shall yet be made the means of promoting the glory of God and the good of his people, Ps. lxxvi. 10.

22. *I will see you again.* After my resurrection. ¶ *Your joy no man taketh from you.* You shall be so firmly persuaded that I have risen and that I am the Messiah, that neither the threats nor persecutions of men shall ever be able to shake your faith and produce doubt or unbelief, and thus take away your joy. This prediction was remarkably fulfilled. It is evident that after his ascension not one of the apostles ever *doubted* for a moment that he had risen from the dead. No persecution or trial was able to shake their faith;

23 And in that day ye shall ask
me nothing. Verily, verily, I say
unto you, Whatsoever ye shall ask
the Father in my name, he will
give *it* you.
24 Hitherto have ye asked nothing in my name: [t]ask, and ye
shall receive, [u]that your joy may
be full.
25 These things have I spoken
unto you in [2]proverbs; but the
time cometh when I shall no more
speak unto you in [2]proverbs, but
I shall show you plainly of the
Father.
26 At[v] that day ye shall ask in
my name; and I say not unto you
that I will pray the Father for you;

t Mat.7.7,8; Ja.4.2,3. *u* ch.15.11. 2 or, *parables*. *v* ver.23.

and thus, amid all their afflictions, they had an unshaken source of joy.

23. *In that day.* After my resurrection and ascension. ¶ *Ye shall ask me nothing.* The word rendered *ask* here may have two significations, one to ask by way of inquiry, the other to ask for assistance. Perhaps there is reference here to both these senses. While he was with them they had been accustomed to depend on him for the supply of their wants, and in a great degree to propose their trials to him, expecting his aid. See Mat. viii. 25; Jn. xi. 3. They were also dependent on his personal instructions to explain to them the mysteries of his religion, and to remove their perplexities on the subject of his doctrines. They had not sought to God through him *as the Mediator*, but they had directly applied to the Saviour himself. He now tells them that henceforward their requests were to be made to God in his name, and that *he*, by the influences of his Spirit, would make known to them what Jesus would himself do if bodily present. The emphasis in this verse is to be placed on the word "*me.*" Their requests were not to be made to *him*, but to the *Father*. ¶ *Whatsoever ye shall ask*, &c. See ch. xiv. 13.

24. *Hitherto.* During his ministry, and while he was with them. ¶ *Have ye asked*, &c. From the evangelists, as well as from this declaration, it seems that they had presented their requests for instruction and aid to Jesus himself. If they had prayed to God, it is probable that they had not done it in his name. This great truth—that we must approach God in the name of the Mediator—was reserved for the last that the Saviour was to communicate to them. It was to be presented at the close of his ministry. Then they were prepared in some degree to understand it; and then, amid trials, and wants, and a sense of their weakness and unworthiness, they would see its preciousness, and rejoice in the privilege of being thus permitted to draw near to God. Though he would be bodily absent, yet their blessings would still be given through the same unchanging Friend. ¶ *Ask*, &c. Now they had the assurance that they might approach God in his name; and, amid all their trials, they, as well as all Christians since, might draw near to God, knowing that he would hear and answer their prayers. ¶ *That your joy*, &c. See ch. xv. 11.

25. *In proverbs.* In a manner that appears obscure, enigmatical, and difficult to be understood. It is worthy of remark, that though his declarations in these chapters about his death and resurrection appear to *us* to be plain, yet to the apostles, filled with Jewish prejudices, and unwilling to believe that he was about to die, they would appear exceedingly obscure and perplexed. The plainest declarations to them on the subject would appear to be involved in mystery. ¶ *The time cometh.* This refers, doubtless, to the time *after* his ascension to heaven, when he would send the Holy Spirit to teach them the great truths of religion. It does not appear that he himself, after his resurrection, gave them any more clear or full instruction than he had done before. ¶ *I shall show you plainly.* As Jesus said that *he* would send the Holy Spirit (ver. 7), and as he came to carry forward the work of Christ, so it may be said that the teachings of the Holy Spirit were the teachings of Christ himself. ¶ *Of the Father. Concerning* the will and plan of the Father; particularly his plan in the establishment and spread of the Christian religion, and in organizing the church. See Ac. x.

26. *I say not unto you that I will pray*, &c. In ch. xiv. 16, Jesus says that he would pray the Father, and that he would send the Comforter. In ch. xvii. he offered a memorable prayer for them. In He. vii. 25, it is said that

27 For[w] the Father himself loveth you, because ye have loved me, and have believed that [x]I came out from God.

28 I came forth from the Father, and am come into the world; again, I leave the world and go to the Father.

29 His disciples said unto him, Lo, now speakest thou plainly, and speakest no [3]proverb.

30 Now are we sure that thou knowest all things, and needest not that any man should ask thee. By this we believe that thou camest forth from God.

31 Jesus answered them, Do ye now believe?

32 Behold,[y] the hour cometh, yea, is now come, that ye shall be scattered, every man to [4]his own, and shall leave me alone; and yet

w ch.14.21,23. *x* ver.30; ch.17.8. [3] or, *parable*. *y* Mat.26.31; Mar.14.27. [4] or, *his own home*.

Jesus ever liveth to make intercession for us; and it is constantly represented in the New Testament that it is by his intercession in heaven now that we obtain the blessings of pardon, peace, strength, and salvation. Comp. He. ix. 24. This declaration of Jesus, then, does not mean that he *would not* intercede for them, but that there was *no need* then of his mentioning it to them again. They knew that; and, in *addition* to that, he told them that God was ready and willing to confer on them all needful blessings.

27. See ch. xiv. 21, 23.

28. *I came forth from the Father.* I came sent by the Father. ¶ *And am come into the world.* See ch. iii. 19; vi. 14, 62; ix. 39.

29. *Now speakest thou plainly.* What he had said that perplexed them was that which is contained in ver. 16. Comp. ver. 17-19: "A little while and ye shall not see me," &c. This he had now explained by saying (ver. 28), "Again, I *leave the world*, and go to the Father." In this there was no ambiguity, and they expressed themselves satisfied with this explanation.

30. *Now are we sure that thou knowest,* &c. Their difficulty had been to understand what was the meaning of his declaration in ver. 16. About this they conversed among themselves, ver. 17-19. It is evident that they had not mentioned their difficulty to him, and that he had not even heard their conversation among themselves, ver. 19. When, therefore, by his answers to them (ver. 20-28), he showed that he clearly understood their doubts; and when he gave them an answer so satisfactory without their having *inquired* of him, it satisfied them that he knew the heart, and that he assuredly came from God. They were convinced that there was *no need that any man should ask him*, or propose his difficulties to him, since he knew them all and could answer them.

31. *Do ye now believe?* Do you truly and really believe? This question was evidently asked to put them on a full examination of their hearts. Though they supposed that they had unshaken faith—faith that would endure every trial, yet he told them that they were about to go through scenes that would test them, and where they would need all their confidence in God. When we feel strong in the faith we should examine ourselves. It may be that we are deceived; and it may be that God may even then be preparing trials for us that will shake our faith to its foundation. The Syriac and Arabic read this in the indicative as an affirmation—"Ye do now believe." The sense is not affected by this reading.

32. *The hour cometh.* To wit, on the next day, when he was crucified. ¶ *Ye shall be scattered.* See Mat. xxvi. 31. ¶ *Every man to his own.* That is, as in the margin, to his own home. You shall see me die, and suppose that my work is defeated, and return to your own dwellings. It is probable that the two disciples going to Emmaus were on their way to their dwellings, Lu. xxiv. After his death all the disciples retired into Galilee, and were engaged in their common employment of fishing, Jn. xxi. 1-14; Mat. xxviii. 7. ¶ *Leave me alone.* Leave me to die without human sympathy or compassion. See Notes on Mat. xxvi. 31, 56. ¶ *Because the Father is with me.* His Father was his friend. He had all along trusted in God. In the prospect of his sufferings he could still look to him for support. And though in his dying moments he suffered so much as to use the language, "Why hast thou forsaken me?" yet it

I[z] am not alone, because the Father is with me.

33 These things have I spoken unto you, that [a]in me ye might have peace. In[b] the world ye shall have tribulation; but be of good cheer; I have overcome the world.

z Is.50.7,9; ch.8.29. a ch.14.27; Ro.5.1; Ep.2.14. b ch.15.19-21; 2 Ti.3.12.

CHAPTER XVII.

THESE words spake Jesus, and lifted up his eyes to heaven, and said, Father, [a]the hour is come: glorify thy Son, that thy Son also may glorify thee;

2 As thou hast given him power

a ch.12.23; 13.32.

---

was language addressed to him still as *his* God—"*My* God, *my* God." Even then he had confidence in God—confidence so strong and unwavering that he could say, "Into *thy* hands I commend my spirit," Lu. xxiii. 46. In all these sufferings he had the assurance that God was his friend, that he was doing his will, that he was promoting his glory, and that he looked on him with approbation. It matters little who else forsakes us if God be with us in the hour of pain and of death; and though poor, forsaken, or despised, yet, if we have the consciousness of his presence and his favour, then we may fear no evil. His rod and his staff, they will comfort us. Without his favour then, death will be full of horrors, though we be surrounded by weeping relatives, and by all the honour, and splendour, and wealth which the world can bestow. The Christian can die saying, I am not alone, because the Father is with me. The sinner dies without a friend that can alleviate his sufferings—without one source of real joy.

33. *In me.* In my presence, and in the aid which I shall render you by the Holy Spirit. ¶ *In the world.* Among the men to whom you are going. You must expect to be persecuted, afflicted, tormented. ¶ *I have overcome the world.* He overcame the prince of this world by his death, Jn. xii. 31. He vanquished the great foe of man, and triumphed over all that would work our ruin. He brought down aid and strength from above by his death; and by procuring for us the friendship of God and the influence of the Spirit; by his own instructions and example; by revealing to us the glories of heaven, and opening our eyes to see the excellence of heavenly things, he has furnished us with the means of overcoming all our enemies, and of triumphing in all our temptations. See Notes on Jn. xiv. 19; also Ro. viii. 34-37; 1 Jn. iv. 4; v. 4; Re. xii. 11. Luther said of this verse "that it was worthy to be carried from Rome to Jerusalem upon one's knees." The world is a vanquished enemy; Satan is a humbled foe; and all that believers have to do is to put their trust in the Captain of their salvation, putting on the whole armour of God, assured that the victory is theirs, and that the church shall yet shine forth fair as the moon, clear as the sun, and terrible as an army with banners, Ca. vi. 10.

CHAPTER XVII.

1. *These words.* The words addressed to them in the preceding chapters. They were proceeding to the garden of Gethsemane. It adds much to the interest of this prayer that it was offered in the stillness of the night, in the open air, and in the peculiarly tender circumstances in which Jesus and his apostles were. It is the *longest* prayer recorded in the New Testament. It was offered on the most tender and solemn occasion that has ever occurred in our world, and it is perhaps the most sublime composition to be found anywhere. Jesus was about to die. Having expressed his love to his disciples, and made known to them his last desires, he now commends them to the protection and blessing of the God of grace. This prayer is moreover a specimen of the manner of his *intercession*, and evinces the interest which he felt in behalf of all who should become his followers in all ages of the world. ¶ *Lifted up his eyes.* This was the common attitude of prayer. Comp. Lu. xviii. 13. ¶ *The hour is come.* That is, the appointed *time* for his sufferings and death. Comp. Notes on ch. xii. 27. ¶ *Glorify thy Son.* *Honour* thy Son. See ch. xi. 4. Give to the world demonstration that I am thy Son. So sustain me, and so manifest thy power in my death, resurrection, and ascension, as to afford indubitable evidence that I am the Son of God. ¶ *That thy Son also may glorify thee.* This refers clearly to the manifestation of the hon-

over all flesh, [b]that he should give eternal life to as many as thou hast given him.

b ch.5.27; ver.24.

3 And [c]this is life eternal, that they might [d]know thee, [e]the only

c 1 Jn.5.11. d Je.9.23,24. e 1 Th.1.9.

our of God which would be made by the spread of the gospel among men, ver. 2. Jesus prayed that God would so honour him in his death that striking proof might be furnished that he was the Messiah, and men thus be brought to honour God. By his death the law, the truth, and the mercy of God were honoured. By the spread of his gospel and the conversion of sinners; by all that Christ will do, now that he is glorified, to spread his gospel, God will be honoured. The conversion of a single sinner honours God; a revival of religion is an eminent means of promoting his honour; and the spread of the gospel among all nations shall yet do more than all other things to promote the honour of God among men. Whatever honours the Saviour honours God. Just as he is exalted in view of the mind, so will God be honoured and obeyed.

2. *As thou hast given him power.* It was on the ground of this power given to Christ that the apostles were commanded to go and teach all nations. See Notes on Mat. xxviii. 18, 19. ¶ *All flesh.* All men, Mat. xxiv. 22; Lu. iii. 6. ¶ *That he should give eternal life.* See Notes on Jn. v. 24. ¶ *To as many as thou hast given him.* See Notes on Jn. x. 16; vi. 37. To all on whom the Father has purposed to bestow the blessings of redemption through his Son. God has a plan in all he does, extending to men as well as to other objects. One part of his plan was that the atonement of Christ should not be in vain. Hence he promised him that he should see of the travail of his soul and should be satisfied (Is. liii. 11); and hence the Saviour had the assurance that the Father had given him a portion of the human family, and would apply this great work to them. It is to be observed here that the Saviour in this prayer makes an important distinction between "all flesh" and those who were "given him." He has *power* over all. He can control, direct, restrain them. Wicked men are so far under his universal dominion, and so far restrained by his power, that they will not be *able* to prevent his bestowing redemption on those were given him—that is, all who will believe on him. Long ago, if they had been able, they would have banished religion from the world; but they are under the power of Christ, and it is his purpose that there shall be "a seed to serve him," and that "the gates of hell shall not prevail" against his church. Men who oppose the gospel should therefore feel that they *cannot* prevent the salvation of Christians, and should be alarmed lest they be found "fighting against God."

3. *This is life eternal.* This is *the source* of eternal life; or it is in this manner that it is to be obtained. The knowledge of God and of his Son Jesus Christ *is itself* a source of unspeakable and eternal joy. Comp. ch. xi. 25; vi. 63; xii. 50. ¶ *Might know thee.* The word *know* here, as in other places, expresses more than a mere speculative acquaintance with the character and perfections of God. *It includes all the impressions on the mind and life which a just view of God and of the Saviour is fitted to produce.* It includes, of course, love, reverence, obedience, honour, gratitude, supreme affection. To *know God as he is* is to know and regard him as a lawgiver, a sovereign, a parent, a friend. It is to yield the whole soul to him, and strive to obey his law. ¶ *The only true God.* The only God, in opposition to all false gods. What is said here is in opposition to idols, not to Jesus himself, who, in 1 Jn. v. 20, is called "the true God and eternal life." ¶ *And Jesus Christ.* To know Jesus Christ is to have a practical impression of him *as he is*—that is, to suffer his character and work to make their due impression on the heart and life. Simply to have *heard* that there is a Saviour is not to *know* it. To have been taught in childhood and trained up in the belief of it is not to know it. To know him is to have a just, practical view of him in all his perfections—as God and man; as a mediator; as a prophet, a priest, and a king. It is to feel our need of such a Saviour, to see that we are sinners, and to yield the whole soul to him, *knowing* that he is a Saviour fitted to our wants, and that in his hands our souls are safe. Comp. Ep. iii. 19; Tit. i. 16; Phi. iii. 10; 1 Jn. v. 20. In this

true God, and Jesus Christ, [f]whom
thou hast sent.
4 I[g] have glorified thee on the
earth; [h]I have finished the work
which thou gavest me to do.
5 And now, O Father, glorify
thou me with thine own self, [i]with
the glory which I had with thee
before the world was.
6 I[k] have manifested thy name
unto [l]the men which thou gavest
me out of the world: thine they

f ch.10.36. *g* ch.14.13. *h* ch.19.30; 2 Ti.4.7. *i* ch.1.1,2; Phi.2.6; He.1.3,10. *k* Ps.22.22; ver.26. *l* Ro.8.30; ver.2,9,11.

verse is contained the sum and essence of the Christian religion, as it is distinguished from all the schemes of idolatry and philosophy, and all the false plans on which men have sought to obtain eternal life. The Gentiles worshipped many gods; the Christian worships one—the living and the true God; the Jew, the Deist, the Mohammedan, the Socinian, profess to acknowledge one God, without any atoning sacrifice and Mediator; the true Christian approaches him through the great Mediator, equal with the Father, who for us became incarnate, and died that he might reconcile us to God.

4. *Have glorified thee.* In my instructions and life. See his discourses everywhere, the whole tendency of which is to put honour on God. ¶ *I have finished the work.* Comp. ch. xix. 30. When he says "I *have* finished," he probably means to include also his death. All the *preparations* for that death were made. He had preached to the Jews; he had given them full proof that he was the Messiah; he had collected his disciples; he had taught them the nature of his religion; he had given them his parting counsel, and there was nothing remaining to be done but to return to God. We see here that Jesus was careful that his great and important work should be done *before* his dying hour. He did not postpone it to be performed just as he was leaving the world. So completely had he done his work, that even *before* his death he could say, "*I have finished* the work." How happy would it be if men would imitate his example, and not leave their great work of life to be done on a dying bed! Christians should have their work accomplished, and when that hour approaches, have nothing to do but to die, and return to their Father in heaven.

5. *With thine own self.* In heaven, granting me a participation of the same honour which the Father has. He had just said that he *had* glorified God *on the earth;* he now prays that God would glorify him *in heaven.* ¶ *With the glory.* With the honour. This word also includes the notion of happiness, or everything which could render the condition blessed. ¶ *Before the world was.* There could not be a more distinct and clear declaration of the pre-existence of Christ than this. It means before the *creation* of the world; before there was any world. Of course, the speaker here must have existed then, and this is equivalent to saying that he existed from eternity. See Jn. i. 1, 2; vi. 62; iii. 13; xvi. 28. The glory which he had then was that which was proper to the Son of God, represented by the expression *being in the bosom of the Father* (Jn. i. 18), denoting intimacy, friendship, united felicity. The Son of God, by becoming incarnate, is represented as *humbling himself* (Greek, he "emptied himself"), Phi. ii. 8. He laid aside for a time the external aspect of honour, and consented to become despised, and to assume the form of a servant. He now prays that God would raise him up to the dignity and honour which he had before his incarnation. This is the state to which he is now exalted, with the *additional* honour of having made atonement for sin, and having opened the way to save a race of rebels from eternal death. The lowest condition on earth is frequently connected with the highest honours of heaven. Man looks on the outward appearance. God looks to him that is humble and of a contrite spirit.

6. *Have manifested thy name.* The word *name* here includes the attributes or character of God. Jesus had made known his character, his law, his will, his plan of mercy—or, in other words, he had revealed GOD to them. The word *name* is often used to designate the *person*, Jn. xv. 21; Mat. x. 22; Ro. ii. 24; 1 Ti. vi. 1. ¶ *Which thou gavest me.* God gave them to him in his purpose. He gave them by his providence. He so ordered affairs that they heard him preach and saw his miracles; and he gave them by disposing them to follow him when he called them. ¶ *Thine*

were, and thou gavest them me, and [m]they have kept thy word.

7 Now they have known that all things whatsoever thou hast given me are of thee.

8 For I have given unto them the[n] words which thou gavest me; and they have received *them*, and have known surely that I came out from thee, and they have believed that thou didst send me.

9 I pray for them: [o]I pray not for the world, but for them which thou hast given me; for they are thine.

10 And[p] all mine are thine, and thine are mine; and [q]I am glorified in them.

11 And now I am no more in the world, but these are in the world, and I come to thee. Holy Father, [r]keep through [s]thine own

m He.3.6. *n* ch.6.68; 14.10.

o 1 Jn.5.19. *p* ch.16.15. *q* Ga.1.24; 1 Pe.2.9. *r* 1 Pe.1.5; Jude 1,24. *s* Pr.18.10.

they were. All men are God's by creation and by preservation, and he has a right to do with them as seemeth good in his sight. These men he chose to designate to be the apostles of the Saviour; and he committed them to him to be taught, and then commissioned them to carry his gospel, though amid persecutions, to the ends of the world. God has a right to the services of all; and he has a right to appoint us to any labour, however humble, or hazardous, or wearisome, where we may promote his glory and honour his name.

7. *They have known.* They have been *taught* that and have believed it. ¶ *Hast given me.* This refers, doubtless, to the *doctrine* of Christ, ver. 8. They are assured that all my instructions are of God.

8. *The words.* The doctrines. Christ often represented himself as *instructed* and *sent* to teach certain great truths to men. Those he taught, and no others. See Notes on Jn. v. 30.

9, 10. *I pray for them.* In view of their dangers and trials, he sought the protection and blessing of God on them. His prayer was always answered. ¶ *Not for the world.* The term *world* here, as elsewhere, refers to wicked, rebellious, vicious men. The meaning of this expression here seems to be this: Jesus is praying for his disciples. As a *reason* why God should bless them, he says that they were not of the world; that they had been taken out of the world; that they belonged unto God. The petition was not offered for wicked, perverse, rebellious men, but for those who were the friends of God and were disposed to receive his favours. This passage, then, settles nothing about the question whether Christ prayed for sinners. He *then* prayed for his disciples, who were not those who hated him and disregarded his favours. He *afterward* extended the prayer for all who should become Christians, ver. 20. When on the cross he prayed for his crucifiers and murderers, Lu. xxiii. 34. ¶ *For they are thine.* This is urged as a *reason* why God should protect and guide them. His honour was concerned in keeping them; and we may always *fill our mouths with* such *arguments* when we come before God, and plead that his honour will be advanced by keeping *us* from evil, and granting us all needful grace. ¶ *I am glorified in them.* I am honoured by their preaching and lives. The sense of this passage is, "Those who are my disciples are thine. That which promotes my honour will also promote thine. I pray, therefore, that they may have needful grace to honour my gospel, and to proclaim it among men."

11. *I am no more in the world.* I have finished my work among men, and am about to leave the world. See ver. 4. ¶ *These are in the world.* They will be among wicked men and malignant foes. They will be subject to trials and persecutions. They will *need* the same protection which *I* could give them if I were with them. ¶ *Keep.* Preserve, defend, sustain them in trials, and save them from apostasy. ¶ *Through thine own name.* Our translators seem to have understood this expression as meaning "keep by thy power," but this probably is not its meaning. It is literally "keep *in* thy name." And if the term *name* be taken to denote God himself and his perfections (see Note on ver. 6), it means "keep in the knowledge of thyself. Preserve them in obedience to thee and to thy cause. Suffer them not to fall away from thee and to become apostates." ¶ *That they may be one.* That they may be united. ¶ *As we* are. This refers not to a union

name those whom thou hast given
me, that they may be one, as we *are*.
12 While I was with them in the
world, I kept them in thy name:
those that thou gavest me I have
kept; and none of them is lost but
the son of perdition; [t]that the
scripture might be fulfilled.
13 And now come I to thee; and
these things I speak in the world,
that they might have my joy fulfilled in themselves.
14 I have given them thy word;
and [u]the world hath hated them,
because they are not of the world,
even as I am not of the world.
15 I pray not that thou shouldest take them out of the world,
but [v]that thou shouldest keep them
from the evil.
16 They are not of the world,
even as I am not of the world.
17 Sanctify[w] them through thy
truth; [x]thy word is truth.

t Ps.109.8; Ac.1.20.

u ch.15.18,19. v Ga.1.4. w Ac.15.9; Ep.5.26; 2 Th.2.13. x Ps.119.151.

of *nature*, but of feeling, plan, purpose. Any other union between Christians is impossible; but a union *of affection* is what the Saviour sought, and this he desired might be so strong as to be an illustration of the unchanging love between the Father and the Son. See ver. 21-23.

12. *While I was with them in the world.* While I was engaged with them among other men--surrounded by the people and the temptations of the world. Jesus had now finished his work among the men of the world, and was performing his last offices with his disciples. ¶ *I kept them.* By my example, instructions, and miracles. I preserved them from apostasy. ¶ *In thy name.* In the knowledge and worship of thee. See ver. 6-11. ¶ *Those that thou gavest me*, &c. The word "gavest" is evidently used by the Saviour to denote not only to give to him to be his real followers, but also as apostles. It is here used, probably, in the sense of giving as apostles. God had so ordered it by his providence that they had been given to him to be his apostles and followers; but the terms "thou gavest me" do not of necessity prove that they were true believers. Of Judas Jesus knew that he was a deceiver and a devil, Jn. vi. 70: "Have not I *chosen* you twelve, and one of you is a devil?" Judas is there represented as having been *chosen* by the Saviour to the apostleship, and this is equivalent to saying that he was given to him for this work; yet at the same time he knew his character, and understood that he had never been renewed. ¶ *None of them.* None of those chosen to the apostolic office. ¶ *But the son of perdition.* See Notes on Mat. i. 1. The term *son* was given by the Hebrews to those who possessed the character described by the word or name following. Thus, sons of Belial—those who possessed his character; children of wisdom—those who were wise, Mat. xi. 19. Thus Judas is called a son of perdition because he had the character of a *destroyer.* He was a traitor and a murderer. And this shows that he who knew the heart regarded his character as that of a wicked man—one whose appropriate name was that of a son of perdition. ¶ *That the scripture*, &c. See Notes on ch. xiii. 18. Comp. Ps. xli. 9.

13. *My joy fulfilled*, &c. See Notes on ch. xv. 11. The expression "my joy" here probably refers to the joy of the apostles respecting the Saviour—the joy which would result from his resurrection, ascension, and intercession in heaven.

14. *I have given them*, &c. See ver. 8. ¶ *The world hath hated them*, &c. Ch. xv. 18-21.

15. *That thou shouldest take them out of the world.* Though they were going into trials and persecutions, yet Jesus did not pray that they might be removed soon from them. It was better that they should endure them, and thus spread abroad the knowledge of his name. It would be easy for God to remove his people at once to heaven, but it is better for them to remain, and show the power of religion in supporting the soul in the midst of trial, and to spread his gospel among men. ¶ *Shouldest keep them from the evil.* This may mean either from the evil one—that is, the devil, or from evil in general—that is, from apostasy, from sinking in temptation. Preserve them from that evil, or give them such grace that they may endure all trials and be sustained amid them. See Notes on Mat. vi. 13. It

18 As thou hast sent me into the world, even so have I also sent them into the world.
19 And[y] for their sakes I sanctify myself, that they also might be [1]sanctified through the truth.
20 Neither pray I for these alone,

y 1 Co.1.2,30.

1 or, *truly sanctified.*

matters little how long we are in this world if we are kept in this manner.

16. See ch. xv. 19.

17. *Sanctify them.* This word means to render pure, or to cleanse from sins, 1 Th. v. 23; 1 Co. vi. 11. Sanctification in the heart of a Christian is progressive. It consists in his becoming more like God and less attached to the world; in his getting the ascendency over evil thoughts, and passions, and impure desires; and in his becoming more and more weaned from earthly objects, and attached to those things which are unseen and eternal. The word also means to *consecrate*, to set apart to a holy office or purpose. See ver. 19; also Notes on ch. x. 36. When Jesus prayed here that God would *sanctify* them, he probably included both these ideas, that they might be made personally more holy, and might be truly consecrated to God as the ministers of his religion. Ministers of the gospel will be *really* devoted to the service of God just in proportion as they are personally pure. ¶ *Through thy truth.* Truth is a representation of things as they are. The Saviour prayed that through those just views of God and of themselves they might be made holy. To see things as they are is to see God to be infinitely lovely and pure; his commands to be reasonable and just; heaven to be holy and desirable; his service to be easy, and religion pleasant, and sin odious; to see that life is short, that death is near; that the pride, pomp, pleasures, wealth, and honours of this world are of little value, and that it is of infinite importance to be prepared to enter on the eternal state of being. He that sees all this, or *that looks on things as they are*, will desire to be holy. He will make it his great object to live near to God and to glorify his name. In the sanctification of the soul God makes use of *all truth*, or of everything fitted to make a representation of things as they are to the mind. His Word states that and no more; his Spirit and his providence do it. The earth and the heavens, the seasons, the sunshine and the rain, are all fitted to teach us his goodness and power, and lead us to him. His daily mercies tend to the same end, and afflictions have the same design. Our own sickness teaches us that we are soon to die. The death of a friend teaches us the instability of all earthly comforts, and the necessity of seeking better joys. All these things are fitted to make *just representations* to the mind, and thus to sanctify the soul. As the Christian is constantly amid these objects, so he should be constantly growing in grace, and daily and hourly gaining new and deeper impressions of the great truths of religion. ¶ *Thy word is truth.* All that thou hast *spoken*—that is, all that is contained in the Bible. All the commands and promises of God; his representations of his own character and that of man; his account of the mission and death of his Son; of the grave, the resurrection, judgment, and eternity, all tend to *represent things as they are*, and are thus fitted to sanctify the soul. We have here also the testimony of the Saviour that the revelation which God has given is true. *All* that God has spoken is true, and the Christian should rejoice and the sinner should tremble. See Ps. xix. 7-14.

19. *I sanctify myself.* I consecrate myself exclusively to the service of God. The word *sanctify* does not refer here to *personal* sanctification, for he had no sin, but to setting himself apart entirely to the work of redemption. ¶ *That they also*, &c. 1st. That they might have an *example* of the proper manner of labouring in the ministry, and might learn of me *how* to discharge its duties. Ministers will understand their work best when they most faithfully study the example of their great model, the Son of God. 2d. That they might be made pure by the *effect* of my sanctifying myself—that is, that they might be made pure by the shedding *of that blood which cleanses from all sin.* By this only can men be made holy; and it was because the Saviour *so* sanctified himself, or set himself to this work so unreservedly as to shed his own blood, that any soul can be made pure and fit for the kingdom of God.

20, 21. *Neither pray I for these alone*, &c. Not for the apostles only, but for all who shall be converted under the

but for them also which shall believe on me through their word;
21 That[z] they all may be one;
as thou, Father, *art* in me, and I
in thee, that they also may be one
in us; that the world may believe
that thou hast sent me.

z Ro.12.5.

22 And[a] the glory which thou
gavest me I have given them; that
they may be one, even as we are
one;
23 I in them, and thou in me,
that they may be made perfect in
one; and that the world may know

a 2 Co.3.18.

---

preaching of the gospel. They will all need similar grace and be exposed to similar trials. It is a matter of unspeakable joy that *each* Christian, however humble or unknown to men—however poor, unlearned, or despised, can reflect that he was remembered in prayer by *him whom God heareth always.* We value the prayers of pious friends. How much more should we value this petition of the Son of God! To that single prayer we who are Christians owe infinitely more real benefits than the world can ever bestow; and in the midst of any trials we may remember that the Son of God *prayed for us*, and that the prayer was assuredly heard, and will be answered in reference to all who truly believe. ¶ *All may be one.* May be united as brethren. Christians are all redeemed by the same blood, and are going to the same heaven. They have the same wants, the same enemies, the same joys. Though they are divided into different denominations, yet they will meet at last in the same abodes of glory. Hence they *should* feel that they belong to the same family, and are children of the same God and Father. There are no ties so tender as those which bind us in the gospel. There is no friendship so pure and enduring as that which results from having the same attachment to the Lord Jesus. Hence Christians, in the New Testament, are represented as being indissolubly united—parts of the same body, and members of the same family, Ac. iv. 32–35; 1 Co. xii. 4–31; Ep. ii. 20–22; Ro. xii. 5. On the ground of this union they are exhorted to love one another, to bear one another's burdens, and to study the things that make for peace, and things wherewith one may edify another, Ep. iv. 3; Ro. xii. 5–16. ¶ *As thou, Father,* art *in me.* See ch. xiv. 10. This does not affirm that the union between Christians should be *in all respects* like that between the Father and the Son, but only in the points in which they *are capable of being compared.* It is not the union of *nature* which is referred to, but the union of plan, of counsel, of purpose—seeking the same objects, and manifesting attachment to the same things, and a desire to promote the same ends. ¶ *That they also may be one in us.* To be *in* God and *in* Christ is to be *united to* God and Christ. The expression is common in the New Testament. The phrase here used denotes *a union among all Christians founded on and resulting from a union to the same God and Saviour.* ¶ *That the world may believe,* &c. That the world, so full of animosities and fightings, may see the power of Christian principle in overcoming the sources of contention and producing love, and may thus see that a religion that could produce this *must* be from heaven. See Notes on ch. xiii. 34. This was done. Such was the attachment of the early Christians to each other, that a heathen was constrained to say, "See how these Christians love one another!"

22. *And the glory,* &c. The *honour* which thou hast conferred on *me* by admitting me to *union* with thee, the same honour I have conferred on them by admitting them to *like union* with me. ¶ *May be one, even as we are one.* Not in *nature*, or in the mode of existence—for this was not the subject of discourse, and would be impossible—but in feeling, in principle, in purpose. Evincing, as the Father and the Son had always done, the same great aim and plan; not pursuing different interests, or counteracting each other's purposes, or forming parties, but seeking the same ends by the same means. This is the union between the Father and the Son. Always, in the creation, preservation, and redemption of the world, the Father and the Son have sought the same object, and this is to be the model on which Christians should act.

23. *May be made perfect in one.* That their union may be complete. That there may be no jars, discords, or contentions. A machine is perfect or com-

that thou hast sent me, and hast
loved them as thou hast loved me.
24 Father, I will that they also
whom thou hast given me [b]be with
me where I am, that they may behold my glory which thou hast
given me; for thou lovedst me before the foundation of the world.
25 O righteous Father, the world
hath not known thee; but I have
known thee, and these have known
that thou hast sent me.
26 And I have declared unto

b 1 Th.4.17.

---

plete when it has all its parts and is in good order—when there is no portion of it wanting. So the union of Christians, for which the Saviour prayed, would be complete or perfect if there were no controversies, no envyings, no contentions, and no heart-burnings and jealousies. It is worthy of remark here how entirely *the union of his people* occupied the mind of Jesus as he drew near to death. He saw the danger of strifes and contentions in the church. He knew the imperfections of even the best of men. He saw how prone they would be to passion and ambition; how ready to mistake love of sect or party for zeal for pure religion; how selfish and worldly men in the church might divide his followers, and produce unholy feeling and contention; and he saw, also, how much this would do to dishonour religion. Hence he took occasion, when he was about to die, to impress the importance of union on his disciples. By solemn admonition, and by most tender and affecting appeals to God in supplication, he showed *his* sense of the value of this union. He used the most sublime and impressive illustration; he adverted to the eternal union between the Father and himself; he reminded them of his love, and of the effect that their union would have on the world, to fix it more deeply in their hearts. The effect has shown the infinite wisdom of the Saviour. The contentions and strifes of Christians have shown his knowledge in foreseeing it. The effect of all this on religion has shown that *he* understood the value of union. Christians have contended long enough. It is time that they should hear the parting admonitions of their Redeemer, and go unitedly against their common foe. The world still lies in wickedness; and the friends of Jesus, bound by the cords of eternal love, should advance together against the common enemy, and spread the triumphs of the gospel around the globe. All that is needful now, under the blessing of God, to convince the world *that God sent the Lord Jesus, is that very union among all Christians for which he prayed;* and when that union of feeling, and purpose, and action shall take place, the task of sending the gospel to all nations will be soon accomplished, and the morning of the millennial glory will dawn upon the world.

24. *I will.* This expression, though it commonly denotes *command*, is here only expressive of *desire*. It is used in *prayer*, and it was not the custom of the Saviour to use language of *command* when addressing God. It is often used to express *strong* and *earnest* desire, or a pressing and importunate *wish*, such as we are exceedingly anxious should not be denied, Mar. vi. 25; x. 35; Mat. xii. 38; xv. 28. ¶ *Where I am.* In heaven. The Son of God was still in the bosom of the Father, Jn. i. 18. See Notes on Jn. vii. 34. Probably the expression here means where *I shall be.* ¶ *My glory.* My honour and dignity when exalted to the right hand of God. The word "behold" implies more than simply *seeing;* it means also to *participate*, to *enjoy*. See Notes on ch. iii. 3; Mat. v. 8. ¶ *Thou lovedst me*, &c. This is another of the numerous passages which prove that the Lord Jesus existed before the creation of the world. It is not possible to explain it on any other supposition.

25. *Hath not known thee.* See Notes on ver. 3.

26. *Thy name.* See Notes on ver. 6. ¶ *And will declare* it. After my resurrection, and by the influence of the Holy Spirit, Lu. xxiv. 45; Ac. i. 3. ¶ *I in them.* By my doctrines and the influences of my Spirit. That my religion may show its power, and produce its proper fruits in their minds, Ga. iv. 19.

The discourse in the xivth, xvth, and xvith chapters is the most tender and sublime that was ever pronounced in our world. No composition can be found anywhere so fitted to sustain the soul in trial or to support it in death. This

them thy name, and will declare *it;*
that the love wherewith thou hast
loved me may be in them, and I
in them.

CHAPTER XVIII.

WHEN Jesus had spoken these
words, he went forth with
his disciples over the brook [a]Ce-
dron, where was a garden, into the
which he entered, and his disciples.
2 And Judas also, which betrayed him, knew the place; for Jesus
ofttimes resorted thither with his
disciples.
3 Judas[b] then, having received
a band *of men* and officers from the
chief priests and Pharisees, cometh
thither with lanterns, and torches,
and weapons.
4 Jesus therefore, [c]knowing all
things that should come upon him,
went forth, and said unto them,
Whom seek ye?
5 They answered him, [d]Jesus of
Nazareth. Jesus saith unto them,

a 2 Sa.15.23.

b Mat.26.47,&c.; Mar.14.43,&c.; Lu.22.47,&c. c ch.10.17,18; Ac.2.28. d Mat.2.23; ch.19.19.

---

sublime and beautiful discourse is appropriately closed by a solemn and most affecting prayer—a prayer at once expressive of the profoundest reverence for God and the tenderest love for men—simple, grave, tender, sublime, and full of consolation. It is the model for our prayers, and with like reverence, faith, and love we should come before God. This prayer for the church will yet be fully answered; and he who loves the church and the world cannot but cast his eyes onward to that time when all believers shall be one; when contentions, bigotry, strife, and anger shall cease; and when, in perpetual union and love, Christians shall show forth the power and purity of that holy gospel with which the Saviour came to bless mankind. Soon may that happy day arise!

CHAPTER XVIII.

1. *The brook Cedron.* This was a small stream that flowed to the east of Jerusalem, through the valley of Jehoshaphat, and divided the city from the Mount of Olives. It was also called *Kidron* and *Kedron.* In summer it is almost dry. The word used here by the evangelist—χειμάῤῥου—denotes properly a water-stream (from χεῖμα, *shower* or *water*, and ῥέω, ῥόος, to *flow, flowing*), and the idea is that of a stream that was swollen by rain or by the melting of the snow (Passow, *Lex.*). This small rivulet runs along on the east of Jerusalem till it is joined by the water of the pool of Siloam, and the water that flows down on the west side of the city through the valley of Jehoshaphat, and then goes off in a south-east direction to the Dead Sea. (See the Map of the Environs of Jerusalem in vol. i.) Over this brook David passed when he fled from Absalom, 2 Sa. xv. 23. It is often mentioned in the Old Testament, 1 Ki. xv. 13; 2 Ch. xv. 16; xxx. 14; 2 Ki. xxiii. 6, 12. ¶ *Where was a garden.* On the west side of the Mount of Olives. This was called *Gethsemane.* See Notes on Mat. xxvi. 36. It is probable that this was the property of some wealthy man in Jerusalem—perhaps some friend of the Saviour. It was customary for the rich in great cities to have country-seats in the vicinity. This, it seems, was so accessible that Jesus was accustomed to visit it, and yet so retired as to be a suitable place for devotion.

2. *Jesus ofttimes resorted thither.* For what purpose he went there is not declared, but it is probable that it was for retirement and prayer. He had no home in the city, and he sought this place, away from the bustle and confusion of the capital, for private communion with God. Every Christian should have some place—be it a grove, a room, or a garden—where he may be alone and offer his devotions to God. We are not told much of the private habits of Jesus, but we are permitted to know so much of him as to be assured that he was accustomed to seek for a place of retirement, and during the great feasts of the Jews the Mount of Olives was the place which he chose, Lu. xxi. 37; Mat. xxi. 17; Jn. viii. 1.

3. *A band.* See Notes on Mat. xxvi. 47; xxvii. 27. John passes over the agony of Jesus in the garden, probably because it was so fully described by the other evangelists. ¶ *Lanterns,* &c. This was the time of the full moon, but it might have been cloudy, and their taking lights with them shows their determination to find him.

I am *he*. And Judas also, which betrayed him, stood with them.

6 As soon then as he had said unto them, I am *he*, [e]they went backward and fell to the ground.

7 Then asked he them again, Whom seek ye? And they said, Jesus of Nazareth.

8 Jesus answered, I have told you that I am *he*; [f]if, therefore, ye seek me, let these go their way;

9 That the saying might be fulfilled which he spake, [g]Of them which thou gavest me have I lost none.

10 Then[h] Simon Peter, having a sword, drew it, and smote the high-priest's servant, and cut off his right ear. The servant's name was Malchus.

11 Then said Jesus unto Peter, Put up thy sword into the sheath: [i]the cup which my Father hath given me, shall I not drink it?

12 Then the band, and the captain, and officers of the Jews took Jesus, and bound him,

13 And led him away to [k]Annas first; for he was father-in-law to Caiaphas, which was the high-priest that same year.[1]

14 Now Caiaphas was he which

e Ps.27.2; 40.14. f Is.53.6; Ep.5.25. g ch.17.12. h Mat.26.51; Mar.14.47; Lu.22.49,50.

i Mat.20.22; 26.39,42. k Lu.3.2.
1 *And Annas sent Christ bound unto Caiaphas, the high-priest*, ver.24.

---

6. *They went backward*, &c. The *cause* of their retiring in this manner is not mentioned. Various things might have produced it. The frank, open, and fearless *manner* in which Jesus addressed them may have convinced them of his innocence, and deterred them from prosecuting their wicked attempt. His disclosure of himself was sudden and unexpected; and while they perhaps anticipated that he would make an effort to escape, they were amazed at his open and bold profession. Their consciences reproved them for their crimes, and probably the firm, decided, and yet mild manner in which Jesus addressed them, the expression of his unequalled power in knowing how to find the way to the consciences of men, made them feel that they were in the presence of more than mortal man. There is no proof that there was here any miraculous power, any mere physical force, and to suppose that there was greatly detracts from the moral sublimity of the scene.

8. *Let these go their way*. These apostles. This shows his care and love even in the hour of danger. *He* expected to die. *They* were to carry the news of his death to the ends of the earth. Hence he, the faithful Captain of salvation, went foremost into trials; he, the Good Shepherd, secured the safety of the flock, and went before them into danger. By the *question* which he asked those who came out against him, he had secured the safety of his apostles. He was answered that they sought for *him*. He demanded that, agreeably to their declaration, they should take *him* only, and leave his followers at liberty. The wisdom, caution, and prudence of Jesus forsook him in no peril, however sudden, and in no circumstances, however difficult or trying.

9. *The saying*. Ch. xvii. 12. As he *had* kept them for more than three years, so he still sought their welfare, even when his death was near.

10, 11. See Notes on Mat. xxvi. 51, 52. ¶ *The servant's name was Malchus*. His name is mentioned by neither of the other evangelists, nor is it said by the other evangelists who was the disciple that gave the blow. It is probable that both Peter and the servant were alive when the other gospels were written.

12. See Mat. xxvi. 50.

13. *To Annas first*. Probably his house was nearest to them, and he had great authority and influence in the Jewish nation. He had been himself a long time high-priest; he had had five sons who had successively enjoyed the office of high-priest, and that office was now filled by his son-in-law. It was of importance, therefore, to obtain his sanction and counsel in their work of evil. ¶ *That same year*. Ch. xi. 49.

14. *Which gave counsel*, &c. Ch. xi. 49, 50. This is referred to here, probably, to show how little prospect there was that Jesus would have *justice* done him in the hands of a man who had already pronounced on the case.

15–18. See Notes on Mat. xxvi. 57,

gave[l] counsel to the Jews that it was expedient that one man should die for the people.

15 And[m] Simon Peter followed Jesus, and *so did* another disciple. That disciple was known unto the high-priest, and went in with Jesus into the palace of the high-priest.

16 But Peter stood at the door without. Then went out that other disciple, which was known unto the high-priest, and spake unto her that kept the door, and brought in Peter.

17 Then saith the damsel that kept the door unto Peter, Art not thou also *one* of this man's disciples? He saith, I am not.

18 And the servants and officers stood there, who had made a fire of coals, for it was cold; and they warmed themselves; and Peter stood with them and warmed himself.

19 The high-priest then asked Jesus of his disciples, and of his doctrine.

20 Jesus answered him, [n]I spake openly to the world: I ever taught in the synagogue, and in the temple, whither the Jews always resort; and [o]in secret have I said nothing.

21 Why askest thou me? Ask them which heard me what I have

l ch.11.49,50. *m* Mat.26.58,&c.; Mar.14.54; Lu.22.54.

n Lu.4.15; ch.7.14,26,28; 8.2. *o* Ac.26.26.

---

58. ¶ *Another disciple.* Not improbably John. Some critics, however, have supposed that this disciple was one who dwelt at Jerusalem, and who, not being a Galilean, could enter the palace without suspicion. John, however, mentions the circumstance of his being *known* to them, to show why it was that he was not questioned as Peter was. It is not probable that any danger resulted from its being known that he was a follower of Jesus, or that any harm was meditated on *them* for this. The questions asked *Peter* were not asked by those in authority, and his apprehensions which led to his denial were groundless.

19. *The high-priest then asked Jesus of his disciples.* To ascertain their *number* and *power*. The charge on which they wished to arraign him was that of sedition, or of rebellion against Cæsar. To make that plausible, it was necessary to show that he had made *so many* disciples as to form a strong and dangerous faction; but, as they had no direct proof of that, the high-priest insidiously and improperly attempted to draw the Saviour into a confession. Of this he was aware, and referred him to the proper source of evidence—his open, undisguised conduct before the world. ¶ *His doctrine.* His teaching. The sentiments that he inculcated. The object was doubtless to convict him of teaching sentiments that tended to subvert the Mosaic institutions, or that were treasonable against the Roman government. Either would have answered the design of the Jews, and they doubtless expected that he—an unarmed and despised Galilean, now completely in their power—would easily be drawn into confessions which art and malice could use to procure his condemnation.

20. *Openly to the world.* If his doctrine had tended to excite sedition and tumult, if he had aimed to overthrow the government, he would have trained his friends in secret; he would have retired from public view, and would have laid his plans in private. This is the case with all who attempt to subvert existing establishments. Instead of that, he had proclaimed his views to all. He had done it in every place of public concourse—in the synagogue and in the temple. He here speaks the language of one conscious of innocence and determined to insist on his rights. ¶ *Always resort.* Constantly assemble. They were required to assemble there three times in a year, and great multitudes were there constantly. ¶ *In secret,* &c. He had taught no private or concealed doctrine. He had taught nothing to his disciples which he had not himself taught in public and commanded them to do, Mat. x. 27; Lu. xii. 3.

21. *Why askest thou me? Ask them,* &c. Jesus here insisted on his *rights*, and reproves the high-priest for his unjust and illegal manner of extorting a confession from him. If he had done wrong, or taught erroneous and seditious doctrines, it was easy to prove it, and the course which he had a right to

said unto them; behold, they know what I said.

22 And when he had thus spoken, one of the officers which stood by [p]struck Jesus [2]with the palm of his hand, saying, Answerest thou the high-priest so?

23 Jesus answered him, If I have spoken evil, bear witness of the evil; [q]but if well, why smitest thou me?

24 Now[3] Annas had sent him bound unto Caiaphas the high-priest.

p Job 16.10; Je.20.2; Ac.23.2,3. q 1 Pe.2.19-23.
2 or, *with a rod.* 3 See ver.13.

25 And Simon Peter stood and warmed himself. They said, therefore, unto him, Art not thou also *one* of his disciples? He denied *it,* and said, I am not.

26 One of the servants of the high-priest, being *his* kinsman whose ear Peter cut off, saith, Did not I see thee in the garden with him?

27 Peter then denied again; [r]and immediately the cock crew.

28 Then[s] led they Jesus from Caiaphas unto [4]the hall of judg-

r Mat.26.74; Mar.14.72; Lu.22.60; ch.13.38.
s Mat.27.2,&c.; Mar.15.1,&c.; Lu.23.1,&c.
4 or, *Pilate's house.*

demand was that they should establish the charge by fair and incontrovertible evidence. We may here learn, 1st. That, though Jesus was willing to be reviled and persecuted, yet he also insisted that *justice* should be done him. 2d. He was conscious of innocence, and he had been so open in his conduct that he could appeal to the vast multitudes which had heard him as witnesses in his favour. 3d. It is proper for us, when persecuted and reviled, meekly but firmly to insist on our rights, and to demand that justice shall be done us. Laws are made to *protect* the innocent as well as to condemn the guilty. 4th. Christians, like their Saviour, should so live that they may confidently appeal to all who have known them as witnesses of the sincerity, purity, and rectitude of their lives, 1 Pe. iv. 13-16.

22. *One of the officers.* One of the *inferior* officers, or those who attended on the court. ¶ *With the palm of his hand.* This may mean, "Gave him a blow either with the open hand or with a rod"—the Greek does not determine which. In whatever way it was done, it was a violation of all law and justice. Jesus had showed no disrespect for the office of the high-priest, and if he had, *this* was not the proper way to punish it. The Syriac reads thus: "Smote the *cheek* of Jesus." The Vulgate and Arabic: "Gave him a blow."

23. *Spoken evil.* In my answer to the high-priest. If there was any disrespect to the office, and want of regard for the law which appointed him, then testify to the fact, and let punishment be inflicted according to the law; comp. Ex. xxii. 28. ¶ *But if well,* &c. While an accused person is on trial he is under the protection of the court, and has a right to *demand* that all *legal* measures shall be taken to secure his rights. On this right Jesus insisted, and thus showed that, though he had no disposition to take revenge, yet he claimed that, when arraigned, strict justice should be done. This shows that his precept that *when we are smitten on one cheek we should turn the other* (Mat. v. 39), is consistent with a firm demand that justice should be done us. That precept refers, besides, rather to *private* matters than to judicial proceedings. It does not demand that, when we are unjustly arraigned or assaulted, and when the law is in our favour, we should sacrifice our rights to the malignant accuser. Such a surrender would be injustice to the law and to the community, and be giving *legal* triumph to the wicked, and destroying the very *end* of all law. In private matters this effect would not follow, and we should there bear injuries without reviling or seeking for vengeance.

24. Comp. ver. 13 with Mat. xxvi. 57.

25, 26. See Notes on Mat. xxvi. 72-74.

28. See Mat. xxvii. 1, 2. ¶ *Hall of judgment.* The *prætorium*—the same word that in Mat. xxvii. 27, is translated *common hall.* See Notes on that place. It was the place where the Roman *prætor,* or governor, heard and decided cases brought before him. Jesus had been condemned by the Sanhedrim, and pronounced guilty of death (Mat. xxvi. 66); but they had not power to carry their sentence into execution (ver. 31), and they therefore sought that he

ment; and it was early; and they themselves went not into the judgment-hall, [t]lest they should be defiled, but that they might eat the passover.

29 Pilate then went out unto them, and said, What accusation bring ye against this man?

30 They answered and said unto him, If he were not a malefactor, we would not have delivered him up unto thee.

31 Then said Pilate unto them, Take ye him, and judge him according to your law. The Jews therefore said unto him, [u]It is

t Ac.10.28.

u Ge.49.10; Eze.21.27.

---

might be condemned and executed by Pilate. ¶ *Lest they should be defiled.* They considered the *touch* of a Gentile to be a defilement, and on this occasion, at least, seemed to regard it as a pollution to enter the *house* of a Gentile. They took care, therefore, to guard themselves against what they considered ceremonial pollution, while they were wholly unconcerned at the enormous crime of putting the innocent Saviour to death, and imbruing their hands in their Messiah's blood. Probably there is not anywhere to be found among men another such instance of petty regard to the mere ceremonies of the law and attempting to keep from pollution, at the same time that their hearts were filled with malice, and they were meditating the most enormous of all crimes. But it shows us how much more concerned men will be at the violation of the mere *forms* and *ceremonies* of religion than at real crime, and how they endeavour to keep their consciences at ease amid their deeds of wickedness by the observance of some of the outward ceremonies of religion—by mere sanctimoniousness. ¶ *That they might eat the passover.* See Notes on Mat. xxvi. 2, 17. This defilement, produced by contact with *a Gentile*, they considered as equivalent to that of the contact of a dead body (Le. xxii. 4–6; Nu. v. 2), and as disqualifying them to partake of the passover in a proper manner. The word translated *passover* means properly the paschal lamb which was slain and eaten on the observance of this feast. This rite Jesus had observed with his disciples the day before this. It has been supposed by many that he *anticipated* the usual time of observing it one day, and was crucified on the day on which the Jews observed it: but this opinion is improbable. The *very day* of keeping the ordinance was specified in the law of Moses, and it is not probable that the Saviour departed from the commandment. All the circumstances, also, lead us to suppose that he observed it at the usual time and manner, Mat. xxvi. 17, 19. The only passage which has led to a contrary opinion is this in John; but here the word *passover* does not, of necessity, mean the *paschal lamb.* It probably refers to the *feast* which followed the sacrifice of the lamb, and which continued seven days. Comp. Nu. xxviii. 16, 17. *The whole feast* was called the Passover, and they were unwilling to defile themselves, even though the paschal lamb had been killed, because it would disqualify them for participating in the remainder of the ceremonies (Lightfoot).

30. *If he were not a malefactor.* A violator of the law. If we had not *determined* that he was such, and was worthy of death, Mat. xxvi. 66. From this it appears that they did not deliver him up to be *tried*, but hoped that Pilate would *at once* give sentence that he should be executed according to their request. It is probable that in ordinary cases the Roman governor was not accustomed to make very strict inquiry into the justice of the sentence. The Jewish Sanhedrim tried causes and pronounced sentence, and the sentence was usually approved by the governor; but in this case Pilate, evidently contrary to their expectations, proceeded *himself* to rehear and retry the cause. He had doubtless heard of the miracles of Jesus. He seems to have been strongly prepossessed with the belief of his innocence. He knew that they had delivered him from mere envy (Mat. xxvii. 18), and hence he inquired of them the nature of the case, and the kind of charge which they expected to substantiate against him.

31. *Judge him,* &c. The Jews had not directly *informed* him that they *had* judged him and pronounced him worthy of death. Pilate therefore tells them to inquire into the case; to ascertain the proof of his guilt, and to decide on what

not lawful for us to put any man
to death:
32 That[v] the saying of Jesus
might be fulfilled which he spake,
signifying what death he should
die.
33 Then Pilate entered into the
judgment-hall again, and called
Jesus, and said unto him, Art
thou the King of the Jews?
34 Jesus answered him, Sayest
thou this thing of thyself, or did
others tell it thee of me?
35 Pilate answered, Am I a Jew?

v Mat.20.19; Lu.18.32,33.

the law of Moses pronounced. It has been doubted whether this gave them the power of putting him to death, or whether it was not rather a direction to them to inquire into the case, and inflict on him, if they judged him guilty, the mild punishment which they were yet at liberty to inflict on criminals. Probably the former is intended. As they had already determined that in their view this case demanded the punishment of death, so in their answer to Pilate they *implied* that they *had* pronounced on it, and that he ought to die. They still, therefore, *pressed* it on his attention, and refused to obey his injunction to judge him. ¶ *It is not lawful*, &c. The Jews were accustomed to put persons to death still in a popular tumult (Ac. vii. 59, 60), but they had not the power to do it in any case in a regular way of justice. When they first laid the plan of arresting the Saviour, they did it *to kill him* (Mat. xxvi. 4); but whether they intended to do this secretly, or in a tumult, or by the concurrence of the Roman governor, is uncertain. The Jews themselves say that the power of inflicting capital punishment was taken away about forty years before the destruction of the temple; but still it is probable that in the time of Christ they had the power of determining on capital cases in instances that pertained to religion (Josephus, *Antiq.*, b. xiv. ch. 10, § 2; comp. *Jewish Wars*, b. vi. ch. 2, § 4). In this case, however, it is supposed that their sentence was to be *confirmed* by the Roman governor. But it is admitted on all hands that they had *not* this power in the case of seditions, tumults, or treason against the Roman government. If they had this power in the case of blasphemy and irreligion, they did not dare to exert it here, because they were afraid of tumult among the people (Mat. xxvi. 5); hence they sought to bring in the authority of Pilate. To do this, they endeavoured to make it appear that it was a case of *sedition* and *treason*, and one which therefore *demanded* the interference of the Roman governor. Hence it was on *this charge* that they arraigned him, Lu. xxiii. 2. Thus a tumult might be avoided, and the *odium* of putting him to death they expected would fall, not on themselves, but on Pilate.

32. *That the saying of Jesus*, &c. To wit, that he would be delivered into the hands of the *Gentiles* and be *crucified*, Mat. xx. 19. Neither of these things would have happened if he had been put to death in the way that the Jews first contemplated, Mat. xxvi. 4. Though it should be admitted that they had the power, in *religious cases*, to do this, yet in such a case it would not have been done, as Jesus predicted, by the Gentiles; and even if it should be admitted that they had the right to take life, yet they had *not* the right to do it by *crucifixion*. This was particularly a Roman punishment. And thus it was ordered, in the providence of God, that the prediction of Jesus in both these respects was fulfilled.

33. *Art thou the King of the Jews?* This was *after* they had accused him of perverting the nation, and forbidding to give tribute to Cæsar, Lu. xxiii. 2, 3.

34. *Of thyself*. From any conviction of your own mind, or any apprehension of danger. During all the time in which you have been prætor, have you seen anything in me that has led you to apprehend sedition or danger to the Roman power? This evidently was intended to remind Pilate that nothing was proved against him, and to caution him against being influenced by the malicious accusations of others. Jesus demanded a just trial, and claimed that Pilate should not be influenced by any *reports* that he might have heard of him.

35. *Am I a Jew?* Am I likely to be influenced by Jewish prejudices and partialities? Am not I, being a Roman, likely to judge impartially, and to decide on the accusations without being biassed by the malignant charges of the accusers? ¶ *Thine own nation*, &c. In this Pilate denies that it was from any-

Thine [w]own nation and the chief priests have delivered thee unto me: what hast thou done?

36 Jesus [x]answered, [y]My kingdom is not of this world. If my kingdom were of this world, then would my servants fight, that I should not be delivered to the Jews; but now is my kingdom not from hence.

37 Pilate therefore said unto him, Art thou a king then? Jesus answered, Thou sayest that I am a king. To this end was I born, and for this cause came I into the world, that I should [z]bear witness unto the truth. Every[a] one that is of the truth heareth my voice.

38 Pilate saith unto him, What is truth? And when he had said this, he went out again unto the

w ch.19.11; Ac.3.13. *x* 1 Ti.6.13. *y* Ps.45.3,6; Is.9.6,7; Da.2.44; 7.14; Zec.9.9; Lu.12.14; ch.6.15; Ro.14.17; Col.1.13.

z Is.55.4; Re.1.5; 3.14. *a* ch.8.47; 1 Jn.4.6.

---

thing that *he* had observed that Jesus was arraigned. He admits that it was from the accusation of others; but then he tells the Saviour that the charge was one of moment, and worthy of the deepest attention. It had come from the *very nation* of Jesus, from his own countrymen, and from the highest authority among the people. As such it demanded consideration, and Pilate besought him to tell him *what he had done*—that is, what there had been in his conduct that had given occasion for this charge.

36. *My kingdom*, &c. The charge on which Jesus was arraigned was that of laying claim to the office of a king. He here substantially admits that he *did* claim to be a king, but not in the sense in which the Jews understood it. *They* charged him with attempting to set up an *earthly* kingdom, and of exciting sedition against Cæsar. In reply to this, Jesus says that *his kingdom is not of this world*—that is, it is not of the same nature as earthly kingdoms. It was not originated for the same purpose, or conducted on the same plan. He immediately adds a circumstance in which they differ. The kingdoms of the world are defended by arms; they maintain armies and engage in wars. If the kingdom of Jesus had been of *this* kind, he would have excited the multitudes that followed him to prepare for battle. He would have armed the hosts that attended him to Jerusalem. He would not have been alone and unarmed in the garden of Gethsemane. But though he *was* a king, yet his dominion was over the heart, subduing evil passions and corrupt desires, and bringing the soul to the love of peace and unity. ¶ *Not from hence.* That is, not from *this world.*

37. *Art thou a king then?* Dost thou *admit* the charge in any sense, or dost thou lay claim to a kingdom of any kind? ¶ *Thou sayest*, &c. This is a form of expression denoting *affirmation.* It is equivalent to *yes.* ¶ *That I am a king.* This does not mean simply that Pilate *affirmed* that he was a king; it does not appear that he had done this; but it means, "Thou affirmest the truth; thou declarest what is correct, *for* I am a king." I *am* a king in a certain sense, and do not deny it. ¶ *To this end*, &c. Comp. ch. iii. 11, 12, &c. Jesus does not here affirm that he was born to *reign*, or that this was the *design* of his coming; but it was to bear witness to and to exhibit *the truth.* By this he showed what was the *nature* of his kingdom. It was not to assert power; not to collect armies; not to subdue nations in battle. It was simply to present *truth* to men, and to exercise dominion only *by* the truth. Hence the only power put forth in restraining the wicked, in convincing the sinner, in converting the heart, in guiding and leading his people, and in sanctifying them, is that which is produced by applying *truth* to the mind. Men are not *forced* or *compelled* to be Christians. They are made to *see* that they are sinners, that God is merciful, that they need a Redeemer, and that the Lord Jesus is fitted to their case, and yield themselves then wholly to his reign. This is all the *power* ever used in the kingdom of Christ, and no men in his church have a right to use any other. Alas! how little have persecutors remembered this! And how often, under the pretence of great regard for the kingdom of Jesus, have bigots attempted by force and flames to make all men think as *they* do! We see here the importance which Jesus attached to *truth.* It was his *sole* business in coming into the world. He had no

Jews, and saith unto them, I find
in him no fault *at all.*
39 But ye have a custom, that I
should release unto you one at the
passover; will ye, therefore, that I
release unto you the King of the
Jews?
40 Then cried they all again,
saying, Not this man, but Barabbas.
Now Barabbas was a robber.

CHAPTER XIX.

THEN [a] Pilate therefore took
Jesus and [b]scourged *him.*
2 And the soldiers platted a
crown of thorns, and put *it* on his
head, and they put on him a purple
robe,
3 And said, Hail, King of the
Jews! and they smote him with
their hands.
4 Pilate therefore went forth
again, and saith unto them, Behold,
I bring him forth to you,
that ye may know that [c]I find no
fault in him.
5 Then came Jesus forth, wearing
the crown of thorns, and the

a Mat.27.26,&c.; Mar.15.15,&c. *b* Is.53.5. *c* ch.18.38; ver.6.

other end than to establish it. *We* therefore should value it, and seek for it as for hid treasures, Pr. xxiii. 23. ¶ *Every one*, &c. See ch. viii. 47.

38. *What is truth?* This question was probably asked in *contempt*, and hence Jesus did not answer it. Had the question been sincere, and had Pilate *really* sought it as Nicodemus had done (ch. iii.), Jesus would not have hesitated to explain to him the nature of his kingdom. They were now alone in the judgment-hall (ver. 33), and as soon as Pilate had asked the question, without waiting for an answer, he went out. It is evident that he was satisfied, from the answer of Jesus (ver. 36, 37), that he was not a king in the sense in which the Jews accused him; that he would not endanger the Roman government, and consequently that he was *innocent* of the charge alleged against him. He regarded him, clearly, as a *fanatic*—poor, ignorant, and deluded, but innocent and not dangerous. Hence he sought to release him; and hence, in *contempt*, he asked him this question, and immediately went out, not expecting an answer. This question had long agitated the world. It was the great subject of inquiry in all the schools of the Greeks. Different sects of philosophers had held different opinions, and Pilate now, in derision, asked him, whom *he* esteemed an ignorant fanatic, whether *he* could solve this long-agitated question. He *might* have had an answer. Had he patiently waited in sincerity, Jesus would have told him what it was. Thousands ask the question in the same way. They have a fixed contempt for the Bible; they deride the instructions of religion; they are unwilling to *investigate* and to wait at the gates of wisdom; and hence, like Pilate, they remain ignorant of the great Source of truth, and die in darkness and in error. *All might* find truth if they would seek it; none ever *will* find it if they do not apply for it to the great source of light—the God of truth, and seek it patiently in the way in which he has chosen to communicate it to mankind. How highly should we prize the Bible! And how patiently and prayerfully should we *search* the Scriptures, that we may not err and die for ever! See Notes on ch. xiv. 6. ¶ *I find in him no fault.* See Lu. xxiii. 4.

39, 40. See Notes on Mat. xxvii. 15–21.

CHAPTER XIX.

1–3. See Notes on Mat. xxvii. 26–30.

4. *Behold, I bring him forth*, &c. Pilate, after examining Jesus, had gone forth and *declared* to the Jews that he found no fault in him, ch. xviii. 38. At that time Jesus remained in the judgment-hall. The Jews were not satisfied with that, but demanded still that he should be put to death, ver. 39, 40. Pilate, disposed to gratify the Jews, returned to Jesus and ordered him to be scourged, as if preparatory to death, ch. xix. 1. The patience and meekness with which Jesus bore this seem to have convinced him still more that he was innocent, and he *again* went forth to *declare* his conviction of this; and, to do it more effectually, he said, "Behold, I bring him forth to you, that ye may know," &c.—that they might themselves *see*, and be satisfied, as he had been, of his innocence.

purple robe. And *Pilate* saith unto them, Behold the man!
6 When the chief priests, therefore, and officers saw him, they cried out, saying, Crucify *him*, crucify *him!* Pilate saith unto them, Take ye him, and crucify *him:* for I find no fault in him.
7 The Jews answered him, [d]We have a law, and by our law he ought to die, [e]because he made himself the Son of God.

d Le.24.16. *e* ch.5.18; 10.33.

All this shows his anxiety to release him, and also shows that the meekness, purity, and sincerity of Jesus had power to convince a Roman governor that he was not guilty. Thus the highest evidence was given that the charges were false, even when he was condemned to die.

5. *Behold the man!* It is probable that Pilate *pointed* to the Saviour, and his object evidently was to move them to compassion, and to convince them, by a sight of the Saviour himself, that he was innocent. Hence he brought him forth with the crown of thorns, and the purple robe, and with the marks of scourging. Amid all this Jesus was meek, patient, and calm, giving evident proofs of innocence. The conduct of Pilate was as if he had said, "See! The man whom you accuse is arrayed in a gorgeous robe, as if a king. He has been scourged and mocked. All this he has borne with patience. See! How calm and peaceful! Behold his countenance! How mild! His body scourged, his head pierced with thorns! Yet in all this he is meek and patient. This is the man that you accuse; and he is now brought forth, that you may *see* that he is not guilty."

6. *They cried out, saying, Crucify* him, &c. The view of the Saviour's meekness only exasperated them the more. They had *resolved* on his death; and as they saw Pilate disposed to acquit him, they redoubled their cries, and endeavoured to gain by tumult, and clamour, and terror, what they saw they could not obtain by justice. When men are *determined* on evil, they cannot be reasoned with. Every *argument* tends to defeat their plans, and they press on in iniquity with the more earnestness in proportion as sound reasons are urged to stay their course. Thus sinners go in the way of wickedness down to death. They make up in firmness of purpose what they lack in reason. They are more fixed in their plans in proportion as God faithfully warns them and their friends admonish them. ¶ *Take ye him,* &c. These are evidently the words of a man *weary* with their importunity and with the subject, and yet resolved not to sanction their conduct. It was not the act of a *judge* delivering him up according to the forms of the law, for they did not understand it so. It was equivalent to this: "*I* am satisfied of his innocence, and shall not pronounce the sentence of death. If *you* are bent on his ruin—if you are determined to put to death an innocent man—if *my* judgment does not satisfy you—take him and put him to death *on your own responsibility*, and take the consequences. It cannot be done with my consent, nor in the due form of law; and *if* done, it must be by *you*, without authority, and in the face of justice." See Mat. xxvii. 24.

7. *We have a law.* The law respecting blasphemy, Le. xxiv. 16; De. xiii. 1–5. They had arraigned Jesus on that charge before the Sanhedrim, and condemned him for it, Mat. xxvi. 63–65. But *this* was not the charge on which they had arraigned him before Pilate. They had accused him of *sedition*, Lu. xxiii. 2. On *this charge* they were now convinced that they could not get Pilate to condemn him. He declared him innocent. Still bent on his ruin, and resolved to gain their purpose, they now, contrary to their first intention, adduced the *original* accusation on which they had already pronounced him guilty. If they could not obtain his condemnation as *a rebel*, they now sought it as *a blasphemer*, and they appealed to Pilate to sanction what they believed was required in their law. Thus to Pilate himself it became more manifest that he was innocent, that they had attempted to *deceive* HIM, and that the charge on which they had arraigned him was a mere pretence to obtain *his* sanction to their wicked design. ¶ *Made himself.* Declared himself, or claimed to be. ¶ *The Son of God.* The law did not forbid this, but it forbade *blasphemy*, and they considered the assumption of this title as the same as blasphemy (Jn. x. 30, 33, 36), and therefore condemned him.

8 When Pilate therefore heard that saying, he was the more afraid;

9 And went again into the judgment-hall, and saith unto Jesus, Whence art thou? But [f] Jesus gave him no answer.

10 Then saith Pilate unto him, Speakest thou not unto me? knowest thou not that [g] I have power to crucify thee, and have power to release thee?

11 Jesus answered, [h] Thou couldest have no power *at all* against me

f Ps.38.13; Is.53.7; Mat.27.12,14; Phi.1.28. g Da.3.14,15. h Lu.22.53; ch.7.30.

8. *When Pilate therefore heard that saying.* That they had accused him of blasphemy. As this was not the charge on which they had arraigned him before his bar, he had not before heard it, and it now convinced him more of their malignity and wickedness. ¶ *He was the more afraid.* What was the ground of his *fear* is not declared by the evangelist. It was probably, however, the alarm of his *conscience*, and the fear of *vengeance* if he suffered such an act of injustice to be done as to put an innocent man to death. He was convinced of his innocence. He saw more and more clearly the design of the Jews; and it is not improbable that a *heathen*, who believed that the *gods* often manifested themselves to men, dreaded their vengeance if he suffered one who *claimed* to be divine, and who *might* be, to be put to death. It is clear that Pilate was convinced that Jesus was innocent; and in this state of agitation between the convictions of his own conscience, and the clamours of the Jews, and the fear of vengeance, and the certainty that he would do wrong if he gave him up, he was thrown into this state of alarm, and resolved again to question Jesus, that he might obtain satisfaction on the subjects that agitated his mind.

9. *Whence art thou?* See Notes on ch. vii. 27. Pilate knew that he was a Galilean, but this question was asked to ascertain whether he claimed to be the Son of God—whether a mere man, or whether divine. ¶ *Jesus gave him no answer.* Probably for the following reasons: 1st. He had already told him his design, and the nature of his kingdom, ch. xviii. 36, 37. 2d. He had said enough to satisfy him of his innocence. Of that Pilate was convinced. His duty was clear, and if he had had firmness to do it, he would not have asked this. Jesus, by his silence, therefore *rebuked* him for his want of firmness, and his unwillingness to do what his conscience told him was right. 3d. It is not probable that Pilate would have understood him if he had declared to him the truth about his origin, and about his being the Son of God. 4th. After what had been done—after he had satisfied Pilate of his innocence, and then had been beaten and mocked by his permission—he had no reason to expect justice at his hands, and therefore properly declined to make any farther defence. By this the prophecy (Is. liii. 7) was remarkably fulfilled.

10. *Speakest thou not*, &c. This is the expression of a man of pride. He was not accustomed to be met with silence like this. He endeavoured, therefore, to address the *fears* of Jesus, and to appal him with the declaration that his life was at his disposal, and that his safety depended on his favour. This arrogance called forth the reply of the Saviour, and he told him that he had *no* power except what was given him from above. Jesus was not, therefore, to be intimidated by any claim of *power* in Pilate. His life was not in his hands, and he could not stoop to ask the *favour* of a *man*.

11. *No power.* No such power as you claim. You have not *originated* the power which you have. You have just as much as is *given*, and your ability extends no farther. ¶ *Except it were given thee.* It has been conceded or granted to you. God has ordered your life, your circumstances, and the extent of your dominion. This was a reproof of a proud man in office, who was forgetful of the great Source of his authority, and who supposed that by his own talents or fortune he had risen to his present place. Alas! how many men *in office* forget that *God* gives them their rank, and vainly think that it is owing to their own talents or merits that they have risen to such an elevation. Men of office and talent, as well as others, should remember that *God* gives them what they have, and that they have no influence except as it is conceded to

except[i] it were given thee from
above; therefore [k]he that delivered
me unto thee hath [l]the greater sin.
12 And from thenceforth Pilate
sought to release him; but the Jews
cried out, saying, If thou let this
man go thou art not Cæsar's friend:
[m]whosoever maketh himself a king,
speaketh against Cæsar.
13 When[n] Pilate therefore heard
that saying, he brought Jesus forth,
and sat down in the judgment-seat,
in a place that is called the Pavement,
but in the Hebrew, Gabbatha.

i Ps.39.9. *k* Mar.14.44; ch.18.3. *l* He.6.4-8; Ja.4.17. *m* Lu.23.2; Ac.17.7. *n* Pr.29.25; Ac.4.19.

them from on high. ¶ *From above.* From God, or by his direction, and by the arrangements of his providence. Ro. xiii. 1: "There is no power but of God; the powers that be are ordained of God." The words "from above" often refer to *God* or to *heaven*, Ja. i. 17; iii. 15, 17; Jn. iii. 3 (in the Greek). The providence of God was remarkable in so ordering affairs that a man, flexible and yielding like Pilate, should be intrusted with power in Judea. Had it been a man firm and unyielding in his duty—one who could not be terrified or awed by the multitude—Jesus would *not* have been delivered to be crucified, Ac. ii. 23. God thus brings about his wise ends; and while Pilate was *free*, and *acted out his nature* without compulsion, yet the purposes of God, long before predicted, were fulfilled, and Jesus made an atonement for the sins of the world. Thus God overrules the wickedness and folly of men. He so orders affairs that the *true character* of men shall be *brought out*, and makes use of that character to advance his own great purposes. ¶ *Therefore.* On this account. "You are a magistrate. Your power, as such, is given you by God. You are not, indeed, guilty for *accusing* me, or malignantly arraigning me; but you have power *intrusted* to you over my life; and the Jews, who *knew* this, and who knew that the power of a magistrate was given to him by God, have the *greater sin* for seeking my condemnation before a tribunal *appointed by God*, and for endeavouring to obtain so solemn a sanction to their own malignant and wicked purposes. They have endeavoured to avail themselves of the civil power, the sacred appointment of God, and *on this account* their sin is greater." This does not mean that their sin was greater than that of Pilate, though that was true; but their sin was greater *on account* of the fact that they perseveringly and malignantly endeavoured to obtain the sanction of the magistrate to their wicked proceedings. Nor does it mean, because God had *purposed* his death (Ac. ii. 23), and given power to Pilate, that *therefore* their sin was greater, for *God's purpose* in the case made it neither more nor less. It did not change the *nature* of their free acts. This passage teaches no such doctrine, but that their sin was *aggravated* by malignantly endeavouring to obtain the sanction of a *magistrate* who was invested with authority *by God*, and who wielded the power that *God* gave him. By this Pilate *ought* to have been convinced, and *was* convinced, of their wickedness, and hence he sought more and more to release him. ¶ *He that delivered me.* The singular here is put for the plural, including Judas, the high-priests, and the Sanhedrim.

12. *Sought to release him.* He was more and more convinced of his innocence, and more unwilling to yield him to mere malice and envy in the face of justice. ¶ *But the Jews cried out*, &c. This moved Pilate to deliver Jesus into their hands. He feared that he would be accused of unfaithfulness to the interests of the Roman emperor if he did not condemn a man whom *his own nation* had accused of sedition. The Roman emperor then on the throne was exceedingly jealous and tyrannical, and the *fear* of losing his favour induced Pilate to deliver Jesus into their hands. ¶ *Cæsar's friend.* The friend of the Roman emperor. The name of the reigning emperor was Tiberius. After the time of Julius Cæsar all the emperors were called *Cæsar*, as all the kings of Egypt were called *Pharaoh*. This emperor was, during the latter part of his reign, the most cruel, jealous, and wicked that ever sat on the Roman throne.

13. *Judgment-seat.* The tribunal or place of pronouncing sentence. He came here to deliver him, in due form of law, into the hands of the Jews. ¶ *Pavement.* This was an area or room of the judgment-hall whose floor was made of small square stones of various

14 And[o] it was the preparation
of the passover, and about the sixth
hour; and he saith unto the Jews,
Behold your King!
15 But they cried out, Away
with *him*, away with *him;* crucify
him! Pilate saith unto them, Shall
I crucify your King? The chief
priests answered, [p]We have no king
but Cæsar.
16 Then[q] delivered he him, therefore, unto them to be crucified.
And they took Jesus, and led *him*
away.
17 And he, bearing his cross,
went[r] forth into a place called
the place of a skull, which is called
in the Hebrew, Golgotha;
18 Where they crucified him,
and two others with him, on either
side one, and Jesus in the midst.
19 And[s] Pilate wrote a title,
and put *it* on the cross. And the
writing was, JESUS OF NAZA-
RETH, THE KING OF THE
JEWS.
20 This title then read many
of the Jews; for the place where
Jesus was crucified was nigh to
the city; and it was written in
Hebrew, *and* Greek, *and* Latin.
21 Then said the chief priests of
the Jews to Pilate, Write not, The
King of the Jews; but that he
said, I am King of the Jews.
22 Pilate answered, What I have
written I have written.
23 Then the soldiers, when they
had crucified Jesus, took his garments, and made four parts, to
every soldier a part; and also *his*
coat: now the coat was without
seam, [1]woven[t] from the top
throughout.
24 They said, therefore, among
themselves, Let us not rend it,
but cast lots for it, whose it shall
be; that the scripture might be
fulfilled which saith, [u]They parted
my raiment among them, and for
my vesture they did cast lots.
These things, therefore, the soldiers did.

o Mat.27.62. *p* Ge.49.10.
q Mat.27.26,&c.; Mar.15.15,&c.; Lu.23.24,&c.
r Nu.15.36; He.13.12.
s Mat.27.37; Mar.15.26; Lu.23.38.

1 or, *wrought*. *t* Ex.39.22. *u* Ps.22.18.

colours. This was common in palaces and houses of wealth and splendour. See Notes on Mat. ix. 2. ¶ *Gabbatha*. This word is not elsewhere used. It comes from a word signifying to be *elevated*. The name given to the place by the Hebrews was conferred from its being the place of the *tribunal*, as an *elevated* place.

14. *The preparation of the passover*. See Notes on Mar. xv. 42. ¶ *The sixth hour*. Twelve o'clock. Mark says (ch. xv. 25) that it was the *third* hour. See the difficulty explained in the Notes on that place.

16–22. See Notes on Mat. xxvii. 32–37.

22. *What I have written*, &c. This declaration implied that he would make no change. He was impatient, and weary of their solicitations. He had yielded to them contrary to the convictions of his own conscience, and he now declared his purpose to yield no farther.

23. *His garments*. The plural here is used to denote the *outer garment*. It was made, commonly, so as to be easily thrown on or off, and when they laboured or walked it was girded about the loins. See Notes on Mat. v. 40. ¶ *Four parts*. It seems, from this, that there were *four* soldiers employed as his executioners. ¶ His *coat*. His under garment, called the *tunic*. ¶ *Was without seam*. Josephus (*Antiq.*, b. iii. ch. 8, § 4) says of the garment or coat of the high-priest that "this vesture was not composed of two pieces, nor was it sewed together upon the shoulders and the sides; but it was one long vestment, so woven as to have an aperture for the neck. It was also parted where the hands were to come out." It seems that the Lord Jesus, the great High-priest of his people, had also a coat made in a similar manner. Comp. Ex. xxxix. 22.

24. *Let us not rend it*. It would then have been useless. The *outer* garment, being composed of several parts—fringes, borders, &c. (De. xii. 12)—could be easily divided. ¶ *That the scripture*, &c. Ps. xxii. 18.

25 Now there stood by the cross of Jesus his mother, and his mother's sister, Mary the *wife* of [2]Cleophas, [v]and Mary Magdalene.
26 When Jesus therefore saw his mother, and [w]the disciple standing by whom he loved, he saith unto his mother, [x]Woman, behold thy son!
27 Then saith he to the disciple, Behold thy [y]mother! And from that hour that disciple took her unto [z]his own *home*.
28 After this, Jesus, knowing that all things were now accomplished, that the [a]scripture might be fulfilled, saith, I thirst.
29 Now there was set a vessel full of vinegar: and they filled a sponge with vinegar, and put *it* upon hyssop, and put *it* to his mouth.
30 When Jesus therefore had

2 or, *Clopas*. *v* Lu.24.18. *w* ch.13.23. *x* ch.2.4. *y* 1 Ti.5.2. *z* ch.16.32. *a* Ps.69.21.

26. *The disciple—whom he loved.* See ch. xiii. 23. ¶ *Woman.* This appellation certainly implied no disrespect. See Notes on ch. ii. 4. ¶ *Behold thy son!* This refers to *John*, not to Jesus himself. Behold, my beloved disciple shall be to you *a son*, and provide for you, and discharge toward you the duties of an affectionate child. Mary was poor. It would even seem that now she had no home. Jesus, in his dying moments, filled with tender regard for his mother, secured for her an adopted son, obtained for her a home, and consoled her grief by the prospect of attention from him who was the most beloved of all the apostles. What an example of filial attention! What a model to all children! And how lovely appears the dying Saviour, thus remembering his afflicted mother, and making *her* welfare one of his last cares on the cross, and even when making atonement for the sins of the world!

27. *Behold thy mother!* One who is to be to thee *as* a mother. The fact that she was the mother of Jesus would secure the kindness of John, and the fact that she was now intrusted to him demanded of him affectionate regard and tender care. ¶ *From that hour*, &c. John seems to have been in better circumstances than the other apostles. See ch. xviii. 16. Tradition says that she continued to live with him in Judea till the time of her death, which occurred about fifteen years after the death of Christ.

28–30. See Notes on Mat. xxvii. 46–50. ¶ *That the scripture might be fulfilled, saith, I thirst.* See Ps. lxix. 21. *Thirst* was one of the most distressing circumstances attending the crucifixion. The wounds were highly inflamed, and a raging fever was caused, usually, by the sufferings on the cross, and this was accompanied by insupportable thirst. See Notes on Mat. xxvii. 35. A Mameluke, or Turkish officer, was crucified, it is said in an Arabic manuscript recently translated, on the banks of the river Barada, under the castle of Damascus. He was nailed to the cross on Friday, and remained till Sunday noon, when he died. After giving an account of the crucifixion, the narrator proceeds: "I have heard this from one who witnessed it; and he thus remained till he died, patient and silent, without wailing, but looking around him to the right and the left, upon the people. But he begged for water, and none was given him; and the hearts of the people were melted with compassion for him, and with pity on one of God's creatures, who, yet a boy, was suffering under so grievous a trial. In the meantime the water was flowing around him, and he gazed upon it, and longed for one drop of it; and he complained of thirst all the first day, after which he was silent, for God gave him strength."—Wiseman's *Lectures*, p. 164, 165, ed. Andover.

30. *It is finished.* The sufferings and agonies in redeeming man are over. The work long contemplated, long promised, long expected by prophets and saints, is done. The toils in the ministry, the persecutions and mockeries, and the pangs of the garden and the cross, are ended, and man is redeemed. What a wonderful declaration was this! How full of consolation to man! And how should this dying declaration of the Saviour reach every heart and affect every soul!

31. *The preparation.* Ver. 14. ¶ *That the bodies*, &c. The law required that the bodies of those who were hung

received the vinegar, he said, [b]It is finished; and he bowed his head and [c]gave up the ghost.

31 The Jews, therefore, because it was [d]the preparation, that [e]the bodies should not remain upon the cross on the sabbath-day, ([f]for that sabbath-day was an high day,) besought Pilate that their legs might be broken, and *that* they might be taken away.

32 Then came the soldiers and brake the legs of the first, and of the other which was crucified with him.

33 But when they came to Jesus, and saw that he was dead already, they brake not his legs;

34 But one of the soldiers with a spear pierced his side, and forthwith came thereout [g]blood and [h]water.

b ch.17.4. *c* Is.53.10,12; He.2.14,15. *d* ver.42. *e* De.21.23. *f* Le.23.7,8.

g He.9.22,23; 1 Jn.5.6,8. *h* 1 Pe.3.21.

should not remain suspended during the night. See De. xxi. 22, 23. That law was made when the punishment by crucifixion was unknown, and when those who were suspended would almost immediately expire. In the punishment by crucifixion, life was lengthened out for four, five, or eight days. The Jews therefore requested that their death might be hastened, and that the land might not be polluted by their bodies remaining suspended on the Sabbath-day. ¶ *Was an high day.* It was, 1st. The Sabbath. 2d. It was the day on which the paschal feast properly commenced. It was called a *high day* because that year the feast of the Passover *commenced* on the Sabbath. Greek, "*Great day.*" ¶ *Their legs might be broken.* To hasten their death. The effect of this, while they were suspended on the cross, would be to increase their pain by the *act* of breaking them, and to deprive their body of the support which it received from the feet, and to throw the whole weight on the hands. By this increased torment their lives were soon ended. Lactantius says that this was commonly done by the Romans to persons who were crucified. The common period to which persons crucified would live was several days. To *compensate* for those *lingering* agonies, so that the full amount of suffering might be endured, they *increased* their sufferings by breaking their limbs, and thus hastening their death.

33. *Saw that he was dead.* Saw by the indications of death on his person, and perhaps by the testimony of the centurion, Mat. xxvii. 54. The death of Jesus was doubtless hastened by the intense agony of the garden, and the peculiar sufferings endured as an atonement for sin on the cross. Comp. Mat. xxvii. 46.

34. *One of the soldiers.* One of those appointed to watch the bodies till they were dead. This man appears to have doubted whether he was dead, and, in order to see whether he was not yet sensible, he pierced him with his spear. The Jews designed that his legs should be broken, but this was prevented by the providence of God; yet in another way more satisfactory proof was obtained of his death than would have been by the breaking of his legs. This was so ordered, no doubt, that there might be the *fullest proof* that he was truly dead; that it could not be pretended that he had swooned away and revived, and so, therefore, that there could not be the least doubt of his resurrection to life. ¶ *With a spear.* The common spear which soldiers used in war. There can be no doubt that such a stroke from the strong arm of a Roman soldier would have caused death, if he had not been already dead; and it was, doubtless, to furnish this conclusive proof that he was *actually dead*, and that an atonement had thus been made for mankind, that John mentions so particularly this fact. Let the following circumstances be remembered, showing that death *must* have ensued from such a wound: (1.) The Saviour was elevated but a little from the ground, so as to be easily reached by the spear of a soldier. (2.) The wound must have been *transversely upward*, so as to have penetrated into the body, as he could not have stood directly under him. (3.) It was probably made with a strong arm and with violence. (4.) The spear of the Roman soldier was a lance which tapered very gently to a point, and would penetrate easily. (5.) The wound was comparatively a *large* wound. It was so large *as to admit the hand* (Jn. xx. 27); but for a lance thus tapering to have

35 And[i] he that saw *it* bare
record, and his record is true; and
he knoweth that he saith true,
that ye might believe.
36 For these things were done
that the [k]scripture should be fulfilled, A bone of him shall not be
broken.
37 And again [l]another scripture saith, They shall look on him
whom they pierced.
38 And after this, Joseph of Ari-

i 1 Jn.1.1-3. k Ex.12.46; Nu.9.12; Ps.34.20. l Ps.22.16; Zec.12.10; Re.1.7.

made a wound so wide as to admit the hand, it must have been *at least* four or five inches in depth, and must have been such as to have made death certain. If it be remembered that this blow was *probably* in the left side, the conclusion is inevitable that death would have been the consequence of such a blow. To make out this fact was of special importance, probably, in the time of John, as the reality of the death of Jesus was denied by the Gnostics, many of whom maintained that he died *in appearance only*. ¶ *Pierced his side.* Which side is not mentioned, nor can it be certainly known. The common opinion is that it was the left side. Car. Frid. Gruner (*Commentatio Antiquaria Medica de Jesu Christi Morte*, p. 30–36) has attempted to show that it must have been the left side. See Wiseman's *Lectures*, p. 161, 162, and Kuinoel on Jn. xix. 34, where the arguments of Gruner are fully stated. It is clear that the spear pierced to the region of the heart. ¶ *And forthwith came*, &c. This was evidently a *natural* effect of thus piercing the side. Such a flowing of blood and water makes it probable that the spear reached the heart, and if Jesus had not before been dead, this would have closed his life. The heart is surrounded by a membrane called the *pericardium*. This membrane contains a serous matter or liquor resembling water, which prevents the surface of the heart from becoming dry by its continual motion (Webster). It was this which was pierced and from which the water flowed. The point of the spear also reached one of the ventricles of the heart, and the blood, yet warm, rushed forth, either mingled with or followed by the water of the pericardium, so as to *appear* to John to be blood and water flowing together. This was a natural effect, and would follow in any other case. Commentators have almost uniformly supposed that this was significant; as, for example, that the blood was an emblem of the eucharist, and the water of baptism, or that the blood denoted justification, and the water sanctification; but that this was the design there is not the slightest evidence. It was strictly a natural result, adduced by John to establish *one* fact on which the whole of Christianity turns —*that he was truly dead.* On this depends the doctrine of the atonement, of his resurrection, and all the prominent doctrines of religion. This fact it was of importance to prove, that it might not be pretended that he had only suffered a *syncope*, or had fainted. This John establishes. He shows that those who were sent to hasten his death *believed* that he had expired; that then a soldier inflicted a wound which *would* have terminated life if he had not been already dead; and that the infliction of this wound was followed by the fullest proof that he had truly expired. On this *fact* he dwells with the interest which became a subject of so much importance to the world, and thus laid the foundation for undoubted assurance that the Lord Jesus *died* for the sins of men.

35. *He that saw* it. John himself. He is accustomed to speak of himself in the third person. ¶ *His record is true.* His testimony is true. Such was the *known* character of this writer, such his sacred regard for truth, that he could appeal to that with full assurance that all would put confidence in him. He often appeals thus to the fact that his testimony was *known* to be true. It would be well if *all* Christians had such a character that their *word* would be assuredly believed.

36. *That the scripture should be fulfilled.* See Ex. xii. 46. John here regards the paschal lamb as an emblem of Christ; and as in the law it was commanded that a bone of that lamb should not be broken, so, in the providence of God, it was ordered that a bone of the Saviour should not be broken. The Scripture thus received a complete fulfilment respecting both the type and the antitype. Some have supposed, however, that John referred to Ps. xxxiv. 20.

mathea, being a disciple of Jesus, but secretly [m]for fear of the Jews, besought Pilate that he might take away the body of Jesus; and Pilate gave *him* leave. He came, therefore, and took the body of Jesus.

39 And there came also [n]Nicodemus, (which at the first came to Jesus by night,) and [o]brought a mixture of myrrh and aloes, about an hundred pound *weight*.

40 Then took they the body of Jesus, and [p]wound it in linen clothes with the spices, as the manner of the Jews is to bury.

41 Now in the place where he was crucified there was a garden, and in the garden a new sepulchre, wherein was never man yet laid.

42 There[q] laid they Jesus, therefore, [r]because of the Jews' preparation *day;* for the sepulchre was nigh at hand.

CHAPTER XX.

THE[a] first *day* of the week cometh Mary Magdalene early, when it was yet dark, unto the sepulchre, and seeth the stone taken away from the sepulchre.

2 Then she runneth, and cometh to Simon Peter, and to the other disciple [b]whom Jesus loved, and saith unto them, They have taken away the Lord out of the sepulchre, and we know not where they have laid him.

3 Peter[c] therefore went forth, and that other disciple, and came to the sepulchre.

4 So they ran both together; and the other disciple did [d]outrun Peter, and came first to the sepulchre.

5 And he, stooping down, *and looking in*, saw [e]the linen clothes lying; yet went he not in.

6 Then cometh Simon Peter following him, and went into the sepulchre, and seeth the linen clothes lie;

7 And the [f]napkin that was about his head, not lying with the linen clothes, but wrapped together in a place by itself.

8 Then went in also that other disciple which came first to the sepulchre, and he saw and believed.

9 For as yet they knew not [g]the scripture, that he must rise again from the dead.

10 Then the disciples went away again unto their own home.

11 But Mary stood without at the sepulchre, weeping; and as she wept she stooped down, *and* [h]*looked* into the sepulchre.

12 And seeth two angels in white, sitting, the one at the head and the

m ch.9.22; 12.42. *n* ch.3.1,2; 7.50. *o* 2 Ch.16.14. *p* Ac.5.6. *q* Is.53.9; 1 Co.15.4. *r* ver.31. *a* Mat.28.1,&c.; Mar.16.1,&c.; Lu.24.1,&c. *b* ch.13.23; 19.26; 21.7,24.

c Lu.24.12. *d* Lu.13.30. *e* ch.19.40. *f* ch.11.44. *g* Ps.16.10; Ac.2.25-31; 13.34,35. *h* Mar.16.5.

37. *Another scripture*, Zec. xii. 10. We must here be struck with the wonderful providence of God, that so *many* scriptures were fulfilled in his death. All these things happened without any such *design* on the part of the men engaged in these scenes; but whatever was done by Jew or Gentile tended to the fulfilment of prophecies long on record, and with which the Jews themselves ought to have been familiar. Little did they suppose, when delivering him to Pilate —when he was mocked—when they parted his garments—when they pierced him—that they were fulfilling ancient predictions. But in this way God had so ordered it that the firmest foundation should be laid for the belief that he was the true Messiah, and that the designs of wicked men should all be overruled to the fulfilment of the great plans which God had in sending his Son.

38-42. See Notes on Mat. xxvii. 57-61.

CHAPTER XX.

1-12. For an account of the resurrection of Christ, see Notes on Mat. xxviii.

9. *The scripture*. See Lu. xxiv. 26, 46. The sense or meaning of the various predictions that foretold his death, as, for example, Ps. ii. 7, comp. Ac. xiii. 33;

other at the feet, where the body
of Jesus had lain.

13 And they say unto her, Woman,
why weepest thou? She saith unto
them, Because they have taken away
my Lord, and I know not where
they have laid him.

14 And when she had thus said,
she turned herself back, and [i]saw
Jesus standing, and [k]knew not that
it was Jesus.

15 Jesus saith unto her, Woman,
why weepest thou? whom seekest
thou? She, supposing him to be
the gardener, saith unto him, Sir,
if thou have borne him hence, tell
me where thou hast laid him, [l]and
I will take him away.

16 Jesus saith unto her, [m]Mary.
She[n] turned herself, and saith unto
him, Rabboni; which is to say,
Master.

17 Jesus saith unto her, Touch
me not; for I am not yet ascended
to my Father; but go to [o]my
brethren, and say unto them, [p]I
ascend unto my Father and [q]your
Father, and *to* [r]my God and [s]your
God.

18 Mary[t] Magdalene came and

i Mat.28.9; Mar.16.9. *k* Lu.24.16,31; ch.21.4.

l Ca.3.2. *m* Is.43.1; ch.10.3. *n* Ca.3.4. *o* Ps.22.22; Ro.8.29; He.2.11. *p* ch.16.28. *q* Ro.8.14,15; 2 Co.6.18; Ga.3.26; 4.6,7. *r* Ep.1.17. *s* Ge.17.7,8; Ps.43.4,5; 48.14; Is.41.10; Je.31.33; Eze. 36.28; Zec.13.9; He.11.16; Re.21.3. *t* Mat.28.10.

Ps. xvi. 9, 10, comp. Ac. ii. 25–32; Ps. cx. 1, comp. Ac. ii. 34, 35.

13. *They have taken away.* That is, the disciples or friends of Jesus who had laid him there. Perhaps it was understood that the body was deposited there only to remain over the Sabbath, with an intention then of removing it to some other place of burial. Hence they hastened *early* in the morning to make preparation, and Mary supposed they had arrived before her and had taken him away.

14. *Knew not that it was Jesus.* She was not *expecting* to see him. It was yet also twilight, and she could not see distinctly.

16. *Jesus saith unto her, Mary.* This was spoken, doubtless, in a tone of voice that at once recalled him to her recollection. ¶ *Rabboni.* This is a Hebrew word denoting, literally, *my great master.* It was one of the titles given to Jewish teachers. This title was given under three forms: (*a*) *Rab*, or master—the lowest degree of honour. (*b*) *Rabbi*, my master—a title of higher dignity. (*c*) *Rabboni*, my great master—the most honourable of all. This title, among the Jews, was only given to seven persons, all persons of great eminence. As given by Mary to the Saviour, it was at once an expression of her joy, and an acknowledgment of him as her Lord and Master. It is not improbable that she, filled with joy, was about to cast herself at his feet.

17. *Touch me not,* &c. This passage has given rise to a variety of interpretations. Jesus required Thomas to touch him (ver. 27), and it has been difficult to ascertain why he forbade this now to Mary. The reason why he directed Thomas to do this was, that he doubted whether he had been restored to life. Mary did not doubt that. The reason why he forbade her to touch him now is to be sought in the circumstances of the case. Mary, filled with joy and gratitude, was about to prostrate herself at his feet, disposed to *remain* with him, and offer him there her homage as her risen Lord. This is probably included in the word *touch* in this place; and the language of Jesus may mean this: "Do not approach me *now* for this purpose. Do not *delay* here. Other opportunities will yet be afforded to see me. I have not yet ascended—that is, I am not *about* to ascend *immediately*, but shall remain yet on earth to afford opportunity to my disciples to enjoy my presence." From Mat. xxviii. 9, it appears that the women, when they met Jesus, *held him by the feet and worshipped him.* This species of adoration it was probably the intention of Mary to offer, and this, *at that time*, Jesus forbade, and directed her to go at once and give his disciples notice that he had risen. ¶ *My brethren.* See ch. xv. 15. ¶ *My Father and your Father,* &c. Nothing was better fitted to afford them consolation than this assurance that *his* God was *theirs*, and that, though he had been slain, they were still indissolubly united in attachment to the same Father and God.

19. *The same day at evening.* On the first day of the week, the day of the

bread, and giveth them, and fish
likewise.
14 This[g] is now the third time
that Jesus showed himself to his
disciples after that he was risen
from the dead.
15 So when they had dined,
Jesus saith to Simon Peter, Simon,
son of Jonas, lovest thou me [h]more
than these? He saith unto him,
Yea, Lord; thou knowest that I
love thee. He saith unto him,
[i]Feed my lambs.
16 He saith to him again the

g ch.20.19,26.

h Mat.26.33,35.
i Is.40.11; Je.3.15; Eze.34.2-10; Ac.20.28; 1 Pe.5.2,4.

---

for utility. He remained with them, was with them at their meal, conversed with them, and thus convinced them that he was the same Friend who had died.

14. *The third time.* See the "Harmony of the Accounts of the Resurrection of Jesus" at the end of Matthew.

15. *Lovest thou me more than these?* There is a slight ambiguity here in the original, as there is in our translation. The word *these* may be in the *neuter* gender, and refer to these *things*—his boat, his fishing utensils, and his employments; or it may be in the masculine, and refer to the apostles. In the former sense it would mean, "Lovest thou me more than thou lovest these objects? Art thou now willing, from love to me, to forsake all these, and go and preach my gospel to the nations of the earth?" In the other sense, which is probably the true sense, it would mean, "Lovest thou me more than these other apostles love me?" In this question Jesus refers to the profession of superior attachment to him which Peter had made before his death (Mat. xxvi. 33): "Though all men shall be offended because of thee, yet will I never be offended." Comp. Jn. xiii. 37. Jesus here slightly reproves him for that confident assertion, reminds him of his sad and painful denial, and now puts this direct and pointed question to him to know what was the *present* state of his feelings. After all that Peter had had to humble him, the Saviour inquired of him what had been the *effect* on his mind, and whether it had tended to prepare him for the arduous toils in which he was about to engage. This question we should all put to ourselves. It is a matter of much importance that we should ourselves know what is the effect of the dealings of divine Providence on our hearts, and what is our *present* state of feeling toward the Lord Jesus Christ. ¶ *Thou knowest that I love thee.* Peter now made no pretensions to love superior to his brethren. His sad denial had convinced him of the folly of that claim; but still he could appeal to the Searcher of the heart, and say that he *knew* that he loved him. Here is the expression of a humbled soul—a soul made sensible of its weakness and need of strength, yet with evidence of true attachment to the Saviour. It is not the most confident pretensions that constitute the highest proof of love to Christ; and the happiest and best state of feeling is when we can with humility, yet with confidence, look to the Lord Jesus and say, "Thou *knowest* that I love thee." ¶ *Feed my lambs.* The word *here* rendered *feed* means the care afforded by furnishing *nutriment* for the flock. In the next verse there is a change in the Greek, and the word rendered *feed* denotes rather the *care, guidance,* and *protection* which a shepherd extends to his flock. By the use of both these words, it is supposed that our Saviour intended that a shepherd was both to offer the proper food for his flock and to govern it; or, as we express it, to exercise the office of a pastor. The expression is taken from the office of a *shepherd,* with which the office of a minister of the gospel is frequently compared. It means, as a good shepherd provides for the wants of his flock, so the pastor in the church is to furnish food for the soul, or so to exhibit truth that the faith of believers may be strengthened and their hope confirmed. ¶ *My lambs.* The church is often compared to a flock. See ch. x. 1–16. Here the expression *my lambs* undoubtedly refers to the *tender* and the *young* in the Christian church; to those who are young in years and in Christian experience. The Lord Jesus saw, what has been confirmed in the experience of the church, that the success of the gospel among men depended on the care which the ministry would extend to those in early life. It is in obedience to this command that Sunday-schools have been established, and no means of fulfilling this command

therefore, and now they were not
able to draw it for the multitude
of fishes.
7 Therefore that disciple whom
Jesus loved saith unto Peter, It
is the Lord. Now when Simon
Peter heard that it was the Lord,
he girt *his* fisher's coat *unto him*,
(for he was naked,) and did cast
himself into the sea.
8 And the other disciples came
in a little ship, (for they were not
far from land, but as it were two
hundred cubits,) dragging the net
with fishes.
9 As soon, then, as they were
come to land, they saw a fire of
coals there, and fish laid thereon,
and bread.
10 Jesus saith unto them, Bring
of the fish which ye have now
caught.
11 Simon Peter went up, and
drew the net to land full of great
fishes, an hundred and fifty and
three; and, for all there were so
many, yet was not the net broken.
12 Jesus saith unto them, Come
and dine. And none of the disciples durst ask him, Who art thou?
knowing that it was the Lord.
13 Jesus[f] then cometh, and taketh

f Ac.10.41.

eaten with bread. It was used by the Greeks especially to denote *fish* (Schleusner).

6. *On the right side.* Why the *right* side is mentioned is not known. Grotius supposes that it was the side nearest the shore, where there was *less* probability of taking fish. It does not appear that they yet recognized the Lord Jesus, but from some cause they had sufficient confidence in him to make another trial. Perhaps they judged that he was one skilled in that employment, and knew where there was the greatest probability of success.

7. *Therefore that disciple whom Jesus loved.* John, ch. xiii. 23. ¶ *It is the Lord.* He was convinced, perhaps, by the apparent miracle, and by looking more attentively on the person of one who had been the means of such unexpected and remarkable success. ¶ His *fisher's coat.* His upper or outer garment or tunic, in distinction from the inner garment or tunic which was worn next the skin. In the case of Peter it may have been made of coarse materials such as fishermen commonly wore, or such as Peter usually wore when he was engaged in this employment. Such garments are common with men of this occupation. This outer garment he probably had laid aside. ¶ *He was naked.* He was *undressed*, with nothing on but the under garment or tunic. The word does not require us to suppose a greater degree of nakedness than this. See Notes on Mar. xiv. 51; also 1 Sa. xix. 24. ¶ *Did cast himself into the sea.* With characteristic ardour, desirous of meeting again his Lord, and showing his affection for him.

8. *Two hundred cubits.* About 350 feet, or a little more than 20 rods.

9. *They saw a fire*, &c. We have no knowledge whence this was produced—whether it was, as Grotius supposes, by a miracle, or whether it was a place occupied by other fishermen, where *they* also might cook the fish which they had caught. As no miracle is mentioned, however, there is no reason for supposing that any existed in the case.

11. *An hundred and fifty and three.* The number is mentioned because it seems to have been a very unusual draught, and it was particularly gratifying and striking to them after they had spent the whole night and had caught *nothing.* This convinced them that it was no other than the same Saviour who had so often worked wonders before them that was now with them.

12. *Come* and *dine.* The word in the original means the meal which is taken in the *morning*, or breakfast.

13. *Jesus then cometh, and taketh bread*, &c. It is not said that Jesus himself *ate* with them, but he gave them food. The design of this interview seems to have been to convince them that he had truly risen from the dead. Hence he performed a miracle *before* they suspected that it was he, that there might be no room to say that they had ascribed to him the power of the miracle through friendship and collusion with him. The miracle was such as to satisfy them of its truth, and was, in accordance with all his works, not for mere display, but

told the disciples that she had seen the Lord, and *that* he had spoken these things unto her.

19 Then[u] the same day at evening, being the first *day* of the week, when the doors were shut where the disciples were assembled for fear of the Jews, came Jesus, and stood in the midst, and saith unto them, Peace *be* unto you.

20 And when he had so said, he showed unto them *his* hands and his side. Then[v] were the disciples glad when they saw the Lord.

21 Then said Jesus to them again, [w]Peace *be* unto you: as *my* Father hath sent me, even [x]so send I you.

22 And when he had said this, he breathed on *them*, and saith unto them, [y]Receive ye the Holy Ghost.

u Mar.16.14; Lu.24.36; 1 Co.15.5.
v ch.16.22. w ch.14.27. x Mat.28.19; ch.17.18; 2 Ti.2.2; He.3.1. y Ac.2.4,38.

resurrection of Christ. ¶ *When the doors were shut.* This does not mean that the doors were *fastened*, though that might have been the case, but only that they were closed. Jesus had been taken from them, and it was natural that they should apprehend that the Jews would next attempt to wreak their vengeance on his followers. Hence they met in the evening, and with closed doors, lest the Jews should bring against them the same charge of sedition that they had against the Lord Jesus. It is not certainly said what was the *object* of their assembling, but it is not unreasonable to suppose that it was to talk over the events which had just occurred, to deliberate about their condition, and to engage in acts of worship. Their minds were doubtless much agitated. They had seen their Master taken away and put to death; but a part of their number also had affirmed that they had seen him alive. In this state of things they naturally came together in a time and place of safety. It was not uncommon for the early Christians to hold their meetings for worship in the *night.* In times of persecution they were forbidden to assemble during the day, and hence they were compelled to meet in the night. Pliny the younger, writing to Trajan, the Roman emperor, and giving an account of Christians, says that "they were wont to meet together on a stated day before it was light, and sing among themselves alternately a hymn to Christ as God." True Christians will love to meet together for worship. Nothing will prevent this; and one of the evidences of piety is a desire to assemble to hear the Word of God, and to offer to him prayer and praise. It is worthy of remark that this is the first assembly that was convened for worship on the Lord's day, and in that assembly Jesus was present. Since that time, the day has been observed in the church as the Christian Sabbath, particularly to commemorate the resurrection of Christ. ¶ *Came Jesus,* &c. There is no evidence that he came into their assembly in any *miraculous* manner. For anything that appears to the contrary, Jesus entered in the usual way and manner, though *his* sudden appearance alarmed them. ¶ *Peace* be *unto you.* The *sudden* manner of his appearance, and the fact that most of them had not before seen him since his resurrection, tended to alarm them. Hence he addressed them in the usual form of salutation to allay their fears, and to assure them that it was their *own* Saviour and Friend.

20. *He showed unto them* his *hands,* &c. In this manner he gave them indubitable proofs of his identity. He showed them that he was the *same* Being who had suffered; that he had truly risen from the dead, and had come forth with the same body. That body had not yet put on its glorified form. It was necessary *first* to establish the proof of his resurrection, and that could be done *only* by his appearing *as he was* when he died.

21. *As* my *Father hath sent me.* As God sent me to preach, to be persecuted, and to suffer; to make known his will, and to offer pardon to men, so I send you. This is the design and the extent of the commission of the ministers of the Lord Jesus. He is their model; and they will be successful only as they *study* HIS *character* and imitate his example. This commission he proceeds to confirm by endowing them all with the gift of the Holy Ghost.

22. *He breathed on* them. It was customary for the prophets to use some significant act to *represent* the nature of their message. See Je. xiii., xviii., &c. In this case the act of *breathing*

23 Whose[z] soever sins ye remit,
they are remitted unto them; *and*
whose soever *sins* ye retain, they
are retained.
24 But [a]Thomas, one of the
twelve, called Didymus, was not
with them when Jesus came.
25 The other disciples therefore
said unto him, We have seen the
Lord. But [b]he said unto them,
Except I shall see in his hands
the print of the nails, and put my
finger into the print of the nails,
and thrust my hand into his side,
I will not believe.
26 And after eight days, again

z Mat.16.19; 18.18. a ch.11.16. b Ps.78.11,32.

---

was used to represent the *nature* of the influence that would come upon them, and the *source* of that influence. When man was created, God *breathed* into him the breath of life, Ge. ii. 7. The word rendered *spirit* in the Scriptures denotes *wind, air, breath,* as well as Spirit. Hence the operations of the Holy Spirit are compared to the wind, Jn. iii. 8; Ac. ii. 2. ¶ *Receive ye the Holy Ghost.* His breathing on them was a certain sign or pledge that they would be endowed with the influences of the Holy Spirit. Comp. Ac. i. 4; ch. ii.

23. *Whose soever sins,* &c. See Notes on Mat. xvi. 19; xviii. 18. It is worthy of remark here that Jesus confers the same power on *all* the apostles. He gives to no one of them any peculiar authority. If *Peter,* as the Papists pretend, had been appointed to any peculiar authority, it is wonderful that the Saviour did not here hint at any such pre-eminence. This passage conclusively proves that they were invested with equal power in organizing and governing the church. The authority which he had given Peter to preach the gospel *first* to the Jews and the Gentiles, does not militate against this. See Notes on Mat. xvi. 18, 19. This authority given them was full proof that they were inspired. The meaning of the passage is not that *man* can forgive sins—that belongs only to God (Is. xliii. 23), but that they should be *inspired;* that in founding the church, and in declaring the will of God, they should be taught by the Holy Ghost to *declare on what terms, to what characters,* and *to what temper of mind* God would extend forgiveness of sins. It was not authority to *forgive individuals,* but to establish in all the churches the *terms* and *conditions* on which men might be pardoned, with a promise that God would *confirm* all that they taught; that all might have assurance of forgiveness who would comply with those terms; and that those who did not comply should not be forgiven, but that their sins should be retained. This commission is *as far as possible* from the authority which the Roman Catholic claims of remitting sin and of pronouncing pardon.

25. *Except I shall see,* &c. It is not known what was the ground of the incredulity of Thomas. It is probable, however, that it was, in part, at least, the effect of deep grief, and of that despondency which fills the mind when a long-cherished hope is taken away. In such a case it requires proof of uncommon clearness and strength to overcome the despondency, and to convince us that we *may* obtain the object of our desires. Thomas has been much blamed by expositors, but he asked only for proof that would be satisfactory in his circumstances. The testimony of *ten* disciples *should* have been indeed sufficient, but an opportunity was thus given to the Saviour to convince the last of them of the truth of his resurrection. This incident shows, what all the conduct of the apostles proves, that they had not *conspired* together to impose on the world. Even they were slow to believe, and one of them refused to rely even on the testimony of *ten* of his brethren. How unlike this to the conduct of men who *agree* to impose a story on mankind! Many are like Thomas. Many *now* are unwilling to believe because they do not *see* the Lord Jesus, and with just as little reason as Thomas had. The *testimony* of those eleven men—including Thomas—who saw him alive after he was crucified; who were willing to lay down their lives to attest that they had seen him alive; who had nothing to gain by imposture, and whose conduct was removed as far as possible from the appearance of imposture, should be regarded as ample proof of the fact that he rose from the dead.

26. *And after eight days again.* That is, on the return of the first day of the

his disciples were within, and
Thomas with them. *Then* came
Jesus, the doors being shut, and
stood in the midst, and said, [c]Peace
be unto you.
27 Then saith he to Thomas,
Reach hither thy finger, and behold my hands; and reach hither
thy [d]hand, and thrust *it* into my
side; and [e]be not faithless, but
believing.
28 And Thomas answered and
said unto him, [f]My Lord and my
God.
29 Jesus saith unto him, Thomas,
because thou hast seen me, thou
hast believed; [g]blessed *are* they
that have not seen, and *yet* have
believed.
30 And[h] many other signs truly
did Jesus in the presence of his
disciples, which are not written in
this book.
31 But[i] these are written that ye

c Is.26.12. d 1 Jn.1.1. e 1 Ti.1.14.
f Ps.118.28; ch.5.23; 1 Ti.3.16. g 1 Pe.1.8. h ch.21.25. i Lu.1.4.

---

week. From this it appears that they thus early set apart this day for assembling together, and Jesus countenanced it by appearing twice with them. It was *natural* that the apostles should observe this day, but not probable that they would do it without the sanction of the Lord Jesus. His repeated presence gave such a sanction, and the historical fact is indisputable that from this time this day was observed as the Christian Sabbath. See Ac. xx. 7; 1 Co. xvi. 2; Re. i. 10.

28. *My Lord and my God.* In this passage the name *God* is expressly given to Christ, in his own presence and by one of his own apostles. This declaration has been considered as a clear proof of the divinity of Christ, for the following reasons: 1st. There is no evidence that this was a mere expression, as some have supposed, of surprise or astonishment. 2d. The language was addressed to Jesus himself—"*Thomas—said* UNTO HIM." 3d. The Saviour did not *reprove* him or *check* him as using any improper language. If he had *not* been divine, it is impossible to reconcile it with his *honesty* that he did not rebuke the disciple. No *pious man* would have allowed such language to be addressed to him. Comp. Ac. xiv. 13-15; Re. xxii. 8, 9. 4th. The Saviour proceeds immediately to *commend* Thomas for believing; but what was the *evidence* of his believing? It was this declaration, and this only. If this was a mere exclamation of *surprise*, what proof was it that Thomas believed? Before this he doubted. Now he believed, and gave utterance to his belief, *that Jesus was his Lord and his God.* 5th. If this was *not* the meaning of Thomas, then his exclamation was a mere act of profaneness, and the Saviour would not have commended him for taking the name of the Lord his God in vain. The passage proves, therefore, that it is proper to apply to Christ the name *Lord* and GOD, and thus accords with what John affirmed in ch. i. 1, and which is established. throughout this gospel.

29. *Because thou hast seen me.* Because you have looked upon my body, and seen the proofs that I am the same Saviour that was crucified. Jesus here *approves* the faith of Thomas, but more highly commends the faith of those who should believe without having seen. ¶ *Blessed.* Happy, or worthy of the divine approbation. The word has here the force of the comparative degree, signifying that they would be in some respects *more* blessed than Thomas. They would evince higher faith. ¶ *That have not seen*, &c. Those who should be convinced by the testimony of the apostles, and by the influences of the Spirit. They would evince *stronger faith. All* faith is of things not seen; and God blesses those most who most implicitly rely on his word.

30. *Other signs.* Other miracles. Many were recorded by the other evangelists, and many which he performed were never recorded, ch. xxi. 25.

31. *These are written.* Those recorded in this *gospel.* ¶ *That ye might believe*, &c. This is a *clue* to the design which John had in view in writing this gospel. The whole *scope* or *end* of the book is to accomplish two objects: 1st. To prove that Jesus was the Messiah; and, 2d. That they who looked at the proof might be convinced and have eternal life. This design is kept in view throughout the book. The miracles, facts, arguments, instructions, and conversations of our Lord all tend to this. This

might believe that Jesus is the Christ, the Son of God; [k]and that, believing, ye might have life through his name.

CHAPTER XXI.

AFTER these things Jesus showed himself again to the disciples at the sea of Tiberias; and on this wise showed he *himself*.

2 There were together Simon Peter, and Thomas called Didymus, and [a]Nathanael of Cana in Galilee, and [b]the *sons* of Zebedee, and two other of his disciples.

k ch.3.15,16; 5.24; 10.10; 1 Pe.1.9. *a* ch.1.45. *b* Mat.4.21.

3 Simon Peter saith unto them, I go a fishing. They say unto him, We also go with thee. They went forth, and entered into a ship immediately; and that night they caught nothing.

4 But when the morning was now come, Jesus stood on the shore; but the disciples [c]knew not that it was Jesus.

5 Then[d] Jesus saith unto them, [1]Children, have ye any meat? They answered him, No.

6 And he said unto them, [e]Cast the net on the right side of the ship, and ye shall find. They cast,

c ch.20.14. *d* Lu.24.41. 1 or, *Sirs*. *e* Lu.5.4-7.

point had not been kept in view so directly by either of the other evangelists, and it was reserved for the last of the apostles to collect those arguments, and make out a connected demonstration *that Jesus was the Messiah*. If this design of John is kept steadily in view, it will throw much light on the book, and the argument is unanswerable, framed after the strictest rules of reasoning, infinitely beyond the skill of man, and having throughout the clearest evidence of demonstration.

CHAPTER XXI.

1. *The sea of Tiberias.* Called also the Sea of Galilee, being situated in Galilee. See Notes on Mat. iv. 18. In this place Jesus had promised to meet them, Mar. xiv. 28; xvi. 7; Mat. xxvi. 32; xxviii. 10. This interview of Jesus is but just mentioned by Matthew (ch. xxviii. 16), and is omitted by both Mark and Luke. This is the reason why John relates so particularly what occurred there. Galilee was a retired place where they would be free from danger, and was therefore a safe and convenient situation for Jesus to meet them, in order to give them his last instructions. ¶ *On this wise.* Thus. In this manner.

2. *There were together.* Probably residing in the same place. While they were waiting for the promise of the Holy Spirit, they still found it proper to be usefully employed. Their Master had been taken away by death, and the promised Spirit had not descended on them. In the interval—before the promised Spirit was poured upon them—they chose not to be idle, and therefore returned to their former employment. It is to be remarked, also, that they had no other means of support. While with Jesus, they were commonly supplied by the kindness of the people; but now, when the Saviour had died, they were cut off from this means of support, and returned to the honest labour of their early lives. Moreover, they had been directed by the Saviour to repair to a mountain in Galilee, where he would meet them, Mat. xxviii. 10. This was probably not far from the Sea of Galilee, so that, until he came to them, they would naturally be engaged in their old employment. Ministers of the gospel should be willing to labour, if necessary, for their own support, and should not esteem such labour dishonourable. God has made *employment* indispensable to man, and if the field of labour is not open in one way, they should seek it in another. If at any time the people withhold the supply of their wants, they should be able and willing to seek support in some other honest occupation.

3. *That night they caught nothing.* This was so ordered in the providence of God that the miracle which was wrought might appear more remarkable.

4. *Knew not that it was Jesus.* Probably it was yet twilight, and in the distance they could not distinctly recognize him.

5. *Children.* A term of affection and friendship, 1 Jn. ii. 18. ¶ *Any meat.* This word (Greek) means anything

second time, Simon, *son* of Jonas,
lovest thou me? He saith unto
him, Yea, Lord; thou knowest
that I love thee. He saith unto
him, [k]Feed my sheep.
17 He saith unto him the third
time, Simon, *son* of Jonas, lovest
thou me? Peter was [l]grieved
because he said unto him the third
time, Lovest thou me? and he said
unto him, Lord, [m]thou knowest all
things; thou knowest that I love
thee. Jesus saith unto him, Feed
my sheep.
18 Verily, verily, I say unto
thee, [n]When thou wast young,
thou girdedst thyself, and walkedst
whither thou wouldest; but when
thou shalt be old, thou shalt stretch
forth thy hands, and another [o]shall

k He.13.20; 1 Pe.2.25. *l* La.3.33. *m* ch.16.30. *n* ch.13.36; Ac.12.3,4. *o* Ac.21.11.

---

of the Saviour have been found so effectual as to extend patronage to those schools. It is not merely, therefore, the *privilege*, it is the solemn *duty* of ministers of the gospel to countenance and patronize those schools.

16. *Feed my sheep.* The word here rendered *feed*, as has been remarked, is different from the word in the previous verse. It has the sense of *governing, caring for, guiding, protecting*—the kind of faithful vigilance which a shepherd uses to guide his flock, and to make provision against their wants and dangers. It *may* be implied here that the care needed for the young in the church is to *instruct* them, and for those in advanced years *both* to instruct and govern them. ¶ *My sheep.* This term commonly denotes the church in general, without respect to age, ch. x.

17. *The third time.* It is probable that Jesus proposed this question three times because Peter had thrice denied him. Thus he tenderly admonished him of his fault and reminded him of his sin, while he solemnly charged him to be faithful and vigilant in the discharge of the duties of the pastoral office. The reason why the Saviour addressed *Peter* in this manner was doubtless because he had just denied him—had given a most melancholy instance of the instability and weakness of his faith, and of his liability to fall. As he had thus been prominent in forsaking him, he took this occasion to give to him a *special* charge, and to *secure* his future obedience. Hence he so administered the charge as to remind him of his fault; and he made him so prominent as to show the solicitude of the Saviour that henceforward he might not be left to dishonour his high calling. This same charge, in substance, he had on other occasions given to the apostles (Mat. xviii. 18), and there is not the slightest evidence here that Christ intended, as the Papists pretend, to give Peter any *peculiar* primacy or eminence in the church. The charge to Peter arose, manifestly, from his prominent and melancholy act in denying him, and was the kind and tender means used by a faithful Saviour to keep him from similar acts in the future dangers and trials of life. It is worthy of remark that the admonition was effectual. Henceforward Peter was one of the most firm and unwavering of all the apostles, and thus fully justified the appellation of *a rock*, which the Saviour by anticipation had given him. See Notes on Jn. i. 42.

18. *When thou wast young.* When in early life thou didst gird *thyself*, &c. The Jews, in walking or running, *girded* their outer garments around them, that they might not be impeded. See Notes on Mat. v. 38-41. ¶ *Thou girdedst.* The expression here denotes *freedom.* He did as he pleased—he girded himself or not—he went or remained, as he chose. Perhaps the expression refers rather *to that time* than to the previous period of Peter's life. "Thou being now young or in the vigour of life, hast just girded thyself and come freely to the shore." In either case the Saviour intimates that at the end of his life he would not be thus free. ¶ *When thou shalt be old.* Ancient writers say that Peter was put to death about thirty-four years after this. His precise age at that time is not known. ¶ *Thou shalt stretch forth thy hands.* When Peter was put to death, we are told that he requested that he might be crucified with his head downward, saying that he who had denied his Lord as he had done was not *worthy* to die as he did. This expression of Christ may intimate the *readiness* of Peter thus to die. Though he was not at liberty as when he was

gird thee, and carry *thee* whither
thou wouldest not.
19 This spake he, signifying by
what [p]death he should glorify God.
And when he had spoken this, he
saith unto him, [q]Follow me.
20 Then Peter, turning about,
seeth the disciple whom Jesus
loved following, which also leaned
on his breast at supper, and said,
Lord, which is he that betrayeth
thee?
21 Peter, seeing him, saith to
Jesus, Lord, and what *shall* this
man *do?*
22 Jesus saith unto him, If I

p 2 Pe.1.14.
q Nu.14.24; 1 Sa.12.20; Mat.19.28; ch.12.26.

---

young, though bound by others, yet he *freely* stretched out his hands on the cross, and was ready to give up his life. ¶ *Another shall gird thee.* Another shall *bind* thee. The limbs of persons crucified were often *bound* instead of being *nailed*, and even the *body* was sometimes girded to the cross. See Notes on Mat. xxvii. 35. ¶ *Carry* thee, &c. Shall *bear* thee, or shall *compel* thee to go to prison and to death. This is not said to intimate that Peter would be unwilling to suffer martyrdom, but it stands opposed to the freedom of his early life. Though willing when compelled to do it, yet he would not *seek it;* and though he would not needlessly expose himself to it, yet he would not shrink from it when it was the will of God.

19. *By what death*, &c. In these words two things are implied: 1st. That Peter would die a violent death; and, 2d. That his death would be such as to honour God. The ancients say that Peter was crucified at Rome, about thirty-four years after this, with his head downward. Clemens says that he was led to the crucifixion with his wife, and sustained her in her sufferings by exhorting her to remember the example of her Lord. He also adds that he died, not as the philosophers did, but with a firm hope of heaven, and patiently endured the pangs of the cross (*Strom.* vii.). This declaration of the Saviour was doubtless continually before the mind of Peter, and to the hour of his death he maintained the utmost constancy and fidelity in his cause, thus justifying the appellation which the Lord Jesus gave him—*a rock.*

20. *Which also leaned*, &c. See ch. xiii. 24, 25.

21. *What* shall *this man* do? This question probably means, "What death shall he die?" But it is impossible to ascertain certainly why Peter asked this question. John was a favourite disciple, and *perhaps* Peter suspected that he would have a happier lot, and not be put to death in this manner. Peter was *grieved* at the question of Jesus; he was probably deeply affected with the account of his own approaching sufferings; and, with *perhaps* a mixture of grief and *envy*, he asked what would be *his* lot. But it is *possible*, also, that it was from *kindness* to John—a deep solicitude about him, and a wish that he might not die in the same manner as one who had denied his Lord. Whatever the motive was, it was a curiosity which the Lord Jesus did not choose to gratify.

22. *That he tarry.* That he *live.* The same word is used to express life in Phi. i. 24, 25; 1 Co. xv. 6. ¶ *Till I come.* Some have supposed this to refer to the destruction of Jerusalem; others to the day of judgment; others to signify that he would not die a violent death; but the plain meaning is, "If I will that he should not *die at all*, it is nothing to thee." In this way the apostles evidently understood it, and hence raised a report that he would *not* die. It is remarkable that John *was* the last of the apostles; that he lived to nearly the close of the first century, and then died a peaceful death at Ephesus, being the only one, as is supposed, of the apostles who did not suffer martyrdom. The testimony of antiquity is clear on this point; and though there have been many idle *conjectures* about this passage and about the fate of John, yet no fact of history is better attested than that John died and was buried at Ephesus. ¶ *What* is that *to thee?* From this passage we learn, 1st. That our main business is to follow the Lord Jesus Christ. 2d. That there are many subjects of religion on which a vain and impertinent curiosity is exercised. All such curiosity Jesus here reproves. 3d. That Jesus will take care of *all* his true disciples, and that we should not be unduly solicitous about them. 4th. That we should go forward to whatever he calls

will that he tarry till [r] I come, what *is that* to thee? [s] Follow thou me.

23 Then went this saying abroad among the brethren, that that disciple should not die; yet Jesus said not unto him, He shall not die; but, If I will that he tarry till I come, what *is that* to thee?

24 This is the disciple which testifieth of these things, and wrote these things; [t] and we know that his testimony is true.

25 And [u] there are also many

r Mat.25.31; Re.1.7; 22.20. s ver.19. t ch.19.35; 3 Jn.12. u ch.20.30.

---

us—to persecution or death—not envying the lot of any other man, and anxious only to do the will of God.

23. *Then went this saying*, &c. This mistake arose very naturally—1st. From the *words* of Jesus, which might be easily misunderstood to mean that he should not die; and, 2d. It was probably confirmed when it was seen that John survived *all* the other apostles, had escaped all the dangers of persecution, and was leading a peaceful life at Ephesus. This mistake John deemed it proper to correct before he died, and has thus left on record what Jesus *said* and what he *meant*.

24. *This is the disciple*, &c. This *proves* that the beloved disciple was John. ¶ *We know*. That is, *it is known;* it is universally admitted. It was so decidedly his character that he always declared the truth, that it had become *known* and was unquestioned, so that *he himself* might appeal to the universal testimony in his behalf. In this case, therefore, we have the testimony of a man whose character for nearly *a century* was that of a man of truth—so much so that it had become, in a manner, proverbial, and was put beyond a doubt. It is impossible to believe that such a man would sit down deliberately to *impose* on mankind, or to write a book which was false; and if not, then *this* book is true, and that is the same as saying that Christianity is a religion from heaven.

25. *Many other things*. Many miracles, ch. xx. 30. Many discourses delivered, &c. ¶ *I suppose*, &c. This is evidently the figure of speech called a *hyperbole*. It is a mode of speech where the *words* express more or less than is *literally* true. It is common among all writers; and as the sacred writers, in recording a revelation to men, used human language, it was proper that they should express themselves as men ordinarily do if they wished to be understood. This figure of speech is commonly the effect of *surprise*, or having the mind *full* of some object, and not having words to express the ideas: at the same time, the words convey no *falsehood*. The statement is to be taken *as it would be understood* among the persons to whom it is addressed; and as no one *supposes* that the author means to be understood *literally*, so there is no deception in the case, and consequently no impeachment of his veracity or inspiration. Thus, when Longinus said of a man that "he was the owner of a piece of ground not larger than a Lacedæmonian letter," no one understood him literally. He meant, evidently, a *very small* piece of land, and no one would be deceived. So Virgil says of a man, "he was so tall as to reach the stars," and means only that he was *very tall*. So when John says that the world could not contain the books that would be written if *all* the deeds and sayings of Jesus were recorded, he clearly intends nothing more than that *a great many* books would be required, or that it would be extremely difficult to record them all; intimating that his life was active, that his discourses were numerous, and that *he* had not *pretended* to give them all, but only such as would go to establish the main point for which he wrote—that he was the Messiah, ch. xx. 30, 31. The figure which John uses here is not uncommon in the Scriptures, Ge. xi. 4; xv. 5; Nu. xiii. 33; Da. iv. 20.

This gospel contains in itself the clearest proof of inspiration. It is the work of a fisherman of Galilee, without any proof that he had any unusual advantages. It is a connected, clear, and satisfactory *argument* to establish the great truth that Jesus was the Messiah. It was written many years after the ascension of Jesus. It contains the record of the Saviour's profoundest discourses, of his most convincing arguments with the Jews, and of his declarations respecting himself and God. It contains the purest and most elevated views of God to be found anywhere,

other things which Jesus did, the which, if they should be written every one, I suppose that even [v]the world itself could not contain the books that should be written. Amen.

v Am.7.10.

as far exceeding all the speculations of philosophers as the sun does the blaze of a taper. It is in the highest degree absurd to suppose that an unlettered fisherman could have *originated* this book. Anyone may be convinced of this by comparing it with what *would be* the production of a man in that rank of life now. But if John has preserved the record of what has occurred so many years before, then it shows that he was under the divine guidance, and is himself a proof, a full and standing proof, of the fulfilment of the promise which he has recorded—that the Holy Spirit would guide the apostles into all truth, Jn. xiv. 26. Of this book we may, in conclusion, apply the words spoken by John respecting his vision of the future events of the church: "Blessed is he that readeth and they that hear the words of this" book, "and keep those things which are written therein, for the time is at hand," Re. i. 3.

A CHRONOLOGICAL TABLE

OF THE

PRINCIPAL EVENTS OCCURRING IN JUDEA, AND THE CORRESPONDING EVENTS IN THE ROMAN EMPIRE,

FROM THE

CONQUEST OF JUDEA BY POMPEY TO THE DESTRUCTION OF JERUSALEM BY TITUS.

BEFORE CHRIST.

77–68. Alexandra Queen of the Jews. She leaves two sons, Hyrcanus and Aristobulus. Both claim the crown—Aristobulus seizing upon it by force, and Hyrcanus being placed on the throne by the Pharisees. In a battle between the two brothers Hyrcanus is overcome, and Aristobulus secures the crown.

70. Pompey and Crassus consuls in Rome.

66. Pompey conquers Mithridates and reduces Pontus.

65. In Syria the dynasty of the Seleucidæ ends with Antiochus XII., who is overcome by Pompey. Syria becomes a Roman province.

67–63. Aristobulus II. King of the Jews. He had been high-priest under the reign of his mother nine years. Was then king and high-priest. Was afterward priest nineteen years. Then ethnarch four years. Then Herod's captive and sport eight years. Hyrcanus, at the instigation of Antipater, the father of Herod the Great, seeks the aid of Aretas, the king of Arabia. Antipater, or Antipas, was an Idumean by birth, but had adopted the Jewish religion, and was governor of Idumea during the reign of Alexander Janneus and his widow Alexandra. Antipater joins the party of Hyrcanus. He and Hyrcanus flee to Aretas, king of Arabia. Aretas agrees to place him on the throne, and conducts him to Judea with an army of 50,000 men. Takes Jerusalem, and restores him to the throne. Aristobulus flees to the temple, and then appeals to Scaurus, the Roman general at Damascus, for aid. Scaurus writes to Aretas; threatens to declare him an enemy of the Roman people if he does not withdraw. He withdraws, and Aristobulus pursues him, and defeats him in a battle.

63. Pompey the Great, who had come to Damascus, commands the two brothers to appear before him. The two brothers appear before him, and urge their respective claims—Hyrcanus pleading his birth, Aristobulus the necessity of the case. Aristobulus, foreseeing that the decision would be against him, withdraws, and fortifies himself in Jerusalem. Aristobulus surrenders himself to Pompey, but his party shut the gates against the Romans, and Pompey puts Aristobulus in chains, and begins a siege. The city is taken by the Romans because the Jews would not fight on the Sabbath, and is brought under the Roman power, according to Calmet 59 years, according to Hales 63 years, and according to Jahn 63 years before Christ. Pompey confirms Hyrcanus in the high-priesthood.

63–55. Hyrcanus II. Prince and High-priest of the Jews. Judea a Roman Province.

60. The first Triumvirate—Pompey, Crassus, and Julius Cæsar.

58. Clodius procures the banishment of Cicero.

55. Cæsar invades Britain.

54. Alexander, son of Aristobulus, escapes from those who were carrying him to Rome, and returns to Judea and raises soldiers. Hyrcanus, not being able to defend himself, applies to Gabinius, the Roman general. Antipater, the father

of Herod the Great, joins the Roman army. Alexander is defeated. Gabinius confirms Hyrcanus in the high-priesthood, but changes the form of the government to an ARISTOCRACY. This continues until the year 44 B.C., when Cæsar comes to Judea and restores Hyrcanus to his former power.

53. Aristobulus escapes from Rome, and comes to Judea with his younger son, Antigonus. They are taken prisoners and sent to Rome.

54. Gabinius is removed from Judea. Crassus is made proconsul of Syria, and comes to Syria. He comes to Jerusalem, and robs the temple of 8000 talents of gold, equal to about £40,000,000. Makes war with the Parthians, and is put to death. Cassius Longinus succeeds him in the command of the army; brings the remainder of the army over the Euphrates, and takes about 30,000 Jewish captives.

53. Augustus, afterward the Roman emperor, is born.

48. Calpurnius Bibulus made governor of Syria.

48. About this time Ptolemy Auletes, king of Egypt, died.

46–44. Hyrcanus II. high-priest.

46. Civil war between Cæsar and Pompey.

45. Battle of Pharsalia, in Thessaly, where Pompey is defeated. Pompey flees to Egypt, and is beheaded.

45. ANTIPATER, THE FATHER OF HEROD THE GREAT, IS MADE GOVERNOR OF JUDEA. He is appointed to this office by Julius Cæsar. Cæsar confirms Hyrcanus in the high-priesthood, and gives him permission to build the walls of Jerusalem, which had been demolished by Pompey.

44. Hyrcanus sends to Rome a golden shield, and the Jews are, by a decree of the Senate, acknowledged as the allies of the Romans.

44. Antipater rebuilds the walls of Jerusalem. He makes his eldest son, Phazael, governor of Jerusalem, and HEROD, afterward Herod the Great, governor of Galilee.

44. Cæsar subdues all Egypt, and gives it into the hands of Cleopatra. Is again made dictator.

Herod attacks and subdues the robbers in Galilee.

Herod is summoned before the Sanhedrim on the charge of the exercise of arbitrary power. He appears before them in a purple robe, and attended by his life-guard, and defies them. He departs from Jerusalem, and goes to Sextus Cæsar at Damascus, and obtains the government of all Cœle-Syria.

43. The Roman calendar reformed by Julius Cæsar. This year was called the *Year of Confusion*, and consisted of 445 days.

41. Julius Cæsar restores to the Jews all that they had formerly possessed, and confirms them in the enjoyment of all their privileges.

Cæsar is put to death in the senate-house.

40. TRIUMVIRATE — Octavianus Cæsar (afterward Augustus), Antony, and Lepidus.

40. Jewish ambassadors appear at Rome to pray that their privileges may be confirmed. Their request is granted.

39. Malichus causes Antipater, the father of Herod, to be poisoned.

38. Herod causes Malichus to be killed to revenge the death of his father.

39. Battle of Philippi, in which Brutus and Cassius are defeated.

39. Herod and Phazael tetrarchs of Judea. They are accused by the Jews before Antony. More than a thousand Jews appear with these complaints. Antony regards it as rebellion, and causes many of them to be slain, and confirms the brothers as tetrarchs of the Jews.

Antigonus, son of Aristobulus, prevails on the Parthians to place him on the throne of Judea. The Parthians seize Hyrcanus and Phazael, and deliver them up to Antigonus.

Phazael beats out his own brains. Antigonus cuts off the ears of Hyrcanus and sends him beyond the Euphrates.

37. *Herod is forced to flee to Jerusalem, and thence to Rome, to implore the aid of*

Antony. He obtains the grant of the KINGDOM *of Judea from the Senate, and the governors of Syria are required to aid him in securing it.* He is conducted to the Capitol at Rome by Antony and Octavianus, and there crowned king with idolatrous sacrifices. He reigned thirty-seven years.

37. HEROD KING OF JUDEA. He was the second son of Antipater, an Idumean by birth, who had been governor of Judea.

37. Ventidius, a Roman, has command of the forces in the East. Appointed by Antony.

Herod returns to Judea, having been absent but three months. He raises an army. Hastens to relieve his family in the fortress of Massada, where they were besieged by Antigonus. Goes to Idumea, and takes possession of a strong fortress by the name of Ressa, and then returns and lays siege to Jerusalem. Unable to take the city, he is obliged to decamp. Marches to Galilee, and endeavours to clear the country of robbers.

36. Herod renews his attacks on the robbers. Is obliged to let down his soldiers in chests by ropes over the mouth of the caves, and to fight them there. Having subdued the robbers, he marches to Samaria against Antigonus, but is obliged to return to Galilee to quell the robbers.

The brother of Herod, Joseph, is surrounded and slain by the army of Antigonus near Jericho.

36. Antony leads an army against the Parthians. Commits the government of Syria to Sosius, and returns to Italy.

The Roman Triumvirate continues, and Antony has assigned to him the affairs of the East.

35. Herod marches against Jerusalem, and lays siege again to the city.

He is married to Mariamne, to whom he had been betrothed four years. She was the daughter of Alexander, the son of King Aristobulus, by Alexandra, the daughter of Hyrcanus II., and was thus granddaughter to both these brothers. Herod hoped by this marriage to reconcile the Jews to him, as the Asmonean family, from which she was descended, was in high favour with the Jews. She was a woman of uncommon beauty. Herod is joined by the Roman general, Sosius.

34. Jerusalem is taken by Herod, and Antigonus surrenders himself. He is treated with the greatest indignity. Is sent to Antioch, and beheaded by the command of Antony, and thus the reign of the Asmoneans, which had lasted 126 years, is ended, and HEROD IS CONFIRMED IN THE KINGDOM.

REIGN OF HEROD THE GREAT.

34. Herod condemns to death all the members of the Sanhedrim except Sameas and Pollio.

32. He appoints to the office of high-priest Ananel, of Babylon, a common priest, but a descendant of the ancient high-priests.

He invites Hyrcanus II. to come to Jerusalem from Seleucia, where he had been kindly entertained by the Oriental Jews. Hyrcanus comes to Jerusalem, where he is treated by Herod with great respect.

32. Herod, at the earnest solicitations of Alexandra and Mariamne, deprives Ananel of the high-priesthood, and confers it on Aristobulus, the brother of Mariamne, then only seventeen years old. Herod is displeased with the interference of Alexandra in this business, and she and her son Aristobulus attempt to escape to Cleopatra in Egypt. Aristobulus is drowned by order of Herod in a lake near Jericho on account of the affection shown for him by the people.

32. Antony comes into Syria, but goes then into Egypt, where he spends a whole year with Cleopatra. Lepidus and Octavianus come to an open rupture, and Lepidus retires as a private man, and the Roman power is left in the hands of Antony and Octavianus, afterward Augustus.

31. Herod is sent for by Antony to justify himself against the charge of having murdered Aristobulus. Gives his kingdom to the care of his uncle Joseph. Charges him, in case *he* is condemned, to put Mariamne to death, that she might not be possessed by Antony. Joseph informs her of the charge of Herod, and is imprisoned on his return.

30. Ananel high-priest the second time.

War between Augustus and Antony. Herod sides with Antony.

Antony gives to Cleopatra the most fertile part of Judea, but Herod agrees to pay her a yearly tribute of two hundred talents.

Cleopatra visits Herod at Jerusalem, and attempts in vain to entangle him in her snares.

Antony makes war on Armenia. Appoints Cæsario, son of Julius Cæsar by Cleopatra, king of Egypt. Makes his eldest son, Alexander, king of Armenia and Parthia.

27. Herod makes war with the Arabians at the command of Antony. Is defeated near Cana. A great earthquake in Judea.

27. The Battle of Actium, between Antony and Octavianus, which decides the destiny of the Roman world. Antony is defeated.

26. Antony and Cleopatra kill themselves.

26. Hyrcanus, then eighty years of age, attempts to escape, and Herod gladly embraces this opportunity to put him to death. Goes to Rome to pay court to Augustus and to conciliate his favour. Places Mariamne and her mother Alexandra in the castle of Alexandrium, with orders to the keepers to put them to death if he is slain. Confesses to Augustus all that he had done for Antony, and is confirmed in his kingdom.

25. Augustus visits Judea, and is magnificently entertained by Herod.

24. Mariamne becomes irreconcilably opposed to Herod. Herod becomes jealous. Orders the most faithful servant of Mariamne to be put to the torture. Accuses Mariamne of adultery before judges of his own selection. She is condemned, in accordance with the wishes of Herod, and immediately executed. Herod, filled with remorse, loses all self-command.

23. Herod puts to death the sons of Babas, at the instigation of his sister Salome, and thus cuts off the last remains of the Asmonean race. They were the descendants of Hyrcanus, and Herod now felt himself secure from any claimant to the throne.

21. Plague and famine in Judea. Herod lays the foundation of a palace on Mount Zion.

He marries Mariamne, the daughter of the priest Simon.

21. Augustus is made emperor. He was the nephew of Julius Cæsar.

19. Herod builds Cæsarea in Palestine, and fortifies Samaria. Sends to Rome his two sons, Alexander and Aristobulus, whom he had by the murdered Mariamne. Agrippa, the favourite of Augustus, is made Governor of the East.

18. Augustus visits Antioch, and, at the request of Herod, raises his brother Pheroras to the dignity of a tetrarch.

17. Agrippa comes into Asia. Herod visits him.

16. Herod, in order to conciliate the affection of the Jews, resolves on rebuilding the temple in a style of much greater magnificence than the former temple. Two years are spent in collecting materials. The old temple is taken down by degrees, as fast as its parts could be replaced by the new building. The main body of the edifice completed in nine years and a half, but the whole not completed until long after the death of Herod. (Notes on Jn. ii. 20.)

13. Herod goes to Rome. Takes his two sons with him on his return, and marries them, the one to a daughter of the king of Cappadocia and the other to a daughter of his sister Salome.

12. Agrippa visits the East, and is magnificently entertained by Herod at Jerusalem.

8. Herod goes to Rome, and accuses his two sons, Alexander and Aristobulus, of a design against his life. To this he is instigated principally by his brother Pheroras and his sister Salome, on account of their hatred of Mariamne.

7. Cæsarea, a city built in honour of Augustus, is dedicated with great pomp.

Herod is finally reconciled to his sons by the influence of Archelaus, king of

Cappadocia, whose daughter Alexander had married. He goes into Arabia, takes the fortress of Repta, and puts the garrison to the sword.

5. He breaks open the tomb of David, and takes out a large amount of treasures.

3. The suspicions of Herod are again excited against his two sons, Alexander and Aristobulus. They are arrested, tried, condemned, and sent to Samaria, where they are strangled by order of their father.

1. Pheroras, the brother of Herod, and Antipater, the son of Herod, form a conspiracy against his life. The plan is to poison him. Pheroras is taken sick and dies. Antipater at the time is in Rome. The whole plot is discovered by the widow of Pheroras, and Herod divorces his wife Mariamne, daughter of Simon, for being an accomplice, strikes the name of Antipater from his will, deposes Simon from the high-priesthood, and puts many persons to death. All this is kept secret from Antipater at Rome, and Herod sends for him to come home, with many expressions of his paternal love.

Augustus the Roman Emperor. The Temple of Janus shut as a sign of universal peace.

The birth of Christ four years before the common Christian era. That era began to be used about A.D. 526, being first employed by Dionysius, and is supposed to have been placed about four years too late. Some make the difference two, others three, four, five, and even eight years. He was born at the commencement of the last year of the reign of Herod, or at the close of the year preceding. Herod had been king thirty-seven years, Augustus emperor about sixteen.

Antipater returns from Rome. Is accused and convicted of a design to murder Herod, and is put to death by his order. The flight into Egypt, Mat. ii. 13–15. The murder of the innocents at Bethlehem, Mat. ii. 16.

Herod dies at Jericho five days after his son Antipater, in the seventieth year of his age, of a most loathsome and painful disease. He called around him the principal men of the nation, and charged his sister Salome and her husband to confine them in the Hippodrome, and to massacre them as soon as he had breathed his last, that the Jews might have some cause to mourn when he died.

By the will of Herod, Archelaus is appointed his successor in the kingdom, Herod Antipas made tetrarch of Perea and Galilee, and Philip tetrarch of Batanea, Gaulonitis, Trachonitis, and Paneas. To his sister Salome he gives Jamnia and some other places. As soon as Herod was dead, his sister Salome dismissed all the Jewish nobles who had been confined in the Hippodrome, and who had been ordered to be put to death.

AFTER CHRIST.

2–11. ARCHELAUS. Goes to Rome to obtain the confirmation of his title as king from Augustus. The decision of Augustus is delayed. Archelaus takes the high-priesthood from Joazer and gives it to Eleazar.

Great tumult in Judea. The nation in arms against the Roman power. The temple is attacked, but the Romans are repulsed.

Augustus confirms Archelaus in the kingdom, but with the title of *ethnarch* instead of *king*. Archelaus rebuilds Jericho. Is accused by the Jews and Samaritans of tyranny before Augustus, and is banished to Vienne, in Gaul, in the tenth year of his reign.

12–26. JUDEA A ROMAN PROVINCE. In the year 12 A.D. Augustus united Judea and Samaria to Syria, and appointed Publius Sulpitius Quirinus (*Cyrenius*, Lu. ii. 2) governor of the province. At the same time Coponius is made procurator of Judea.

14. The temple at Jerusalem is polluted by some Samaritans, who entered it by night and strewed there the bones of dead men.

17. Augustus dies at Rola, in Campania, in the seventy-sixth year of his age and the fifty-seventh year of his reign. He is succeeded by Tiberius, the son of his wife Julia.

18. Valerius Gratus made procurator of Judea by Tiberius. He deposes Ananus and makes Ismael high-priest. Afterward he gives the office to Eleazar, son of Ananus; then to Simeon, and at last to Joseph, called in the New Testament *Caiaphas.*

Herod Antipas builds the city of Tiberias.

26. PONTIUS PILATE MADE PROCURATOR OF JUDEA BY TIBERIUS.

He attempts to set up Roman colours and ensigns in Jerusalem, but is opposed by the Jews.

29. John the Baptist begins to preach.

30. Jesus is baptized by John.

Tiberius banishes all who professed the Jewish religion from Rome.

About this time hostilities existed between Herod Antipas and Aretas, king of Arabia. Herod Antipas had married a daughter of Aretas. On his way to Rome he saw and fell in love with Herodias, the wife of his brother, and agreed to marry her and put away the daughter of Aretas. She, hearing this, fled to her father, and the consequence was a war, in which Herod was defeated and his army dispersed.

30. John the Baptist declares this marriage unlawful, and is imprisoned by Herod.

31. John the Baptist in prison. Sends a deputation to Jesus to know if he was the Messiah.

32. Is slain by the order of Herod, at the instigation of Herodias.

33. Jesus is crucified on Friday, April 3. Supposed to have been at about three o'clock P.M.

34. Stephen put to death. Paul converted on his way to Damascus.

35. Agrippa the Younger, being involved in debt, resolves to go to Rome. Attaches himself to the party of Caius, and incurs the displeasure of Tiberius. This year died Philip, tetrarch of Trachonitis, &c., a son of Herod the Great. He was mild and equitable in his government, and had ruled thirty-seven years. The countries over which he had presided were at his death united to the province of Syria.

37. Tiberius dies a most profligate and abandoned man. He is succeeded by Caius Caligula.

37. Pilate is recalled by Caligula, and banished to Vienne, in Gaul, where he is said to have put an end to his own life.

38–45. AGRIPPA THE YOUNGER, KING OF THE JEWS. He was the son of Aristobulus and grandson of Mariamne. Shortly before the death of Herod the Great (his grandfather) he goes to Rome, squanders his property there, and is reduced to want. Goes to Idumea, and resolves to commit suicide. Persuaded to abandon his plan by his wife. Obtains the government from Tiberius. Is accused by his half-brother Aristobulus, and goes again to Rome. Is favourably received by Tiberius. Is accused, however, of having made a treasonable remark respecting Tiberius, and imprisoned till the death of that emperor. Is released by Caligula from prison, and made king of Gaulonitis, Batanea, and Trachonitis.

42. Herod Antipas, at the instigation of Agrippa, is banished to Lyons, and his tetrarchy given to King Agrippa.

Caligula orders Petronius to place his statue in the temple at Jerusalem. It is delayed at the instance of Agrippa.

42. Caligula is assassinated at Rome, and succeeded by Claudius.

42. Agrippa is raised by Claudius to the rank of consul; Samaria and Judea are given him, and thus he obtains the entire kingdom of Herod the Great.

42. Agrippa arrives at Jerusalem.

43. Deprives the high-priest Matthias of the priesthood, and bestows it on Elioneus.

Causes the Apostle James the Greater to be put to death (Ac. xii. 1), and imprisons Peter. Soon afterward dies at Cæsarea in great misery, Ac. xii. 21–23.

A famine at Rome.

45. Cuspius Fadus is sent into Judea as governor or procurator. He continues in the office two years.

A great famine in Judea.

Fadus demands that the vestments of the high-priest should be placed under Roman custody. Longinus comes to Jerusalem to enforce this order.

Claudius places Herod, the brother of the deceased Agrippa, over the temple and the treasury.

A celebrated false Messiah appears. He persuades the people to follow him to the Jordan. Promises to stop the river by a word, and to lead them over on dry ground. Is pursued by the Roman cavalry and beheaded.

A second famine in the reign of Claudius. This was in Palestine, Ac. xi. 28.

46. Fadus is recalled. Tiberius, an apostate Jew, is made governor of Judea in his place.

47. Claudius takes away the authority of Herod and gives it to Agrippa, the son of King Agrippa, who died at Cæsarea. *This* was the Agrippa before whom Paul afterward appeared, Ac. xxvi.

47. Tiberius is recalled, and Cumanus is made procurator of Judea. Violent disturbances in Judea.

53. Cumanus is recalled and expelled from Rome. Claudius appoints FELIX procurator of Judea. Felix was a freedman of Claudius. Claudius gives to Agrippa the tetrarchy which had formerly belonged to Philip—Gaulonitis, Batanea, and Trachonitis.

Claudius expels the Jews from Rome, because, in expectation of the Messiah, they are constantly exciting disturbances.

55. Claudius dies, being poisoned by the Empress Agrippina, the mother of Nero. Nero succeeds him. Nero soon put many persons to death, and, among others, his own mother.

56. Nero gives to Agrippa the cities Tiberias, Tarichæa, Abila, and Julias, and the districts belonging to them.

Felix captures a number of robbers and crucifies them.

The *Sicarii*, or robbers with short swords, appear and abound in Judea. Felix hires one of them to assassinate the high-priest Jonathan. Many false prophets appear in Judea.

58. Paul goes into Judea to carry contributions. Is seized in the temple at Jerusalem, and sent to Cæsarea. Ishmael made high-priest. Paul makes his defence before Felix (Ac. xxiv.) at Cæsarea. Is imprisoned two years.

60. PORCIUS FESTUS MADE GOVERNOR OF JUDEA. Felix is accused at Rome.

Paul appeals to the emperor. Makes his speech before Agrippa (Ac. xxvi.), and is put on shipboard to be sent to Rome. Is shipwrecked at Malta.

Festus finds the country overrun with robbers. A false Messiah is taken and slain. Agrippa at Jerusalem builds a high apartment in the palace of Herod, by which he can overlook all that is done in the temple. The Jews build a high wall on the west side of the temple to intercept his view. The case is submitted to Nero. Nero allows the wall to stand.

63. FESTUS DIES IN JUDEA, AND ALBINUS MADE HIS SUCCESSOR.

64. Martyrdom of James the Less at Jerusalem. According to Josephus, he was stoned.

64. Herod's temple at Jerusalem is completed, and about 18,000 workmen are discharged from employment, many of whom become robbers.

65. GESSIUS FLORUS MADE PROCURATOR OF JUDEA—a man *worse* than any of his predecessors. He was cruel, tyrannical, and insatiably avaricious.

Josephus says that at that time there were 3,000,000 Jews in Jerusalem.

Rome set on fire—probably by order of Nero. He charges it on the Christians, several of whom are put to death by being inclosed in pitch and set on fire, to illuminate the gardens of the emperor.

66. BEGINNING OF THE JEWISH WAR.

The probable year of the martyrdom of Paul and Peter at Rome.

An edict of the emperor is issued by which the Syrian and Greek inhabitants of Cæsarea are raised above the Jews. The dissatisfaction which this occasions is the first cause of the war. The Syrians and Greeks at Cæsarea sacrifice birds on the bottom of an earthen vessel, in order to irritate the Jews. A tumult is excited. Florus demands seventeen talents from the temple for the use of the emperor. The Jews are exasperated, and take possession of the lower city. They attack the castle of Antonia, and take it after two days.

The Christians in Jerusalem, seeing that a war is about to break out, retire to Pella, in the kingdom of Agrippa, beyond Jordan.

67. Vespasian is appointed by Nero to prosecute the Jewish war. Comes to Antioch, and forms a numerous army. Division in Jerusalem, and general revolt in Judea. Titus, the son of Vespasian, is sent to Alexandria to collect an army, and to proceed to Palestine in aid of his father. Vespasian subdues Galilee.

Josephus besieged in Jotapata. Jotapata taken, and Josephus surrenders to Vespasian.

The Zealots in Jerusalem seize the temple, and depose Theophilus from being high-priest, and put Phannias in his place. They send for the Idumeans to aid them.

68. Vespasian takes all the places of strength in Judea, around Jerusalem. Nero dies. Galba succeeds him.

69. Josephus set at liberty.

Eleazar, son of Simon, forms a third party, and makes himself master of the inner temple.

Galba dies. Otho declared emperor. Otho dies. Vitellius proclaimed emperor by the German legions. Vespasian proclaimed by the army in the East. Vespasian secures the throne.

70. Titus marches against Jerusalem to besiege it. Approaches it some days before the Passover.

The factions in Jerusalem at first unite against the Romans, but afterward divide again.

The Romans make a wall all around Jerusalem, to reduce it to famine.

July 17. The perpetual daily sacrifice ceases.

A Roman soldier sets the temple on fire, notwithstanding the orders of Titus to the contrary.

71. Titus demolishes the temple to its foundation, and also the city, reserving the towers of Hippicus, Phazael, and Mariamne.

Titus returns to Rome, to his father, Vespasian. A triumph decreed them, and the arch erected in Rome, which is still standing.

The Jewish war ended; Bassus sent into Judea as lieutenant, and Judea is subdued.

CHRONOLOGICAL ARRANGEMENT AND HARMONY OF THE FOUR GOSPELS.

[*From Dr. Townsend's Historical and Chronological Arrangement of the Old and New Testaments.*]

PERIOD I.—FROM THE BIRTH OF CHRIST TO THE TEMPTATION.

DATE.	EVENTS.	SCRIPTURES.
B.C.		
—	General Preface, - - - - - - -	Mar. i. 1; Lu. i. 1–4.
—	The Divinity, Humanity, and Office of Christ, -	Jn. i. 1–18.
6	Birth of John the Baptist, - - - - -	Lu. i. 5–25.
5	The Annunciation, - - - - - - -	Lu. i. 26–38.
...	Interview between Mary and Elizabeth, - -	Lu. i. 39–56.
...	Birth and Naming of John the Baptist, - -	Lu. i. 57, to end.
...	An Angel appears to Joseph, - - - -	Mat. i. 18-25.
...	Birth of Christ at Bethlehem, - - - -	Lu. ii. 1–7.
...	The Genealogies of Christ, - - - -	Mat. i. 1–17; Lu. iii. 23, to end.
...	The Angels appear to the Shepherds, - -	Lu. ii. 8–20.
...	The Circumcision, - - - - - - -	Lu. ii. 21.
...	The Purification. Presentation of Christ in the Temple, where he is acknowledged by Simeon and Anna, - - - - - - -	Lu. ii. 22–39.
...	The Offering of the Magi, - - - - - -	Mat. ii. 1–12.
...	The Flight into Egypt, - - - - - -	Mat. ii. 13–15.
...	Slaughter of the Children at Bethlehem, - -	Mat. ii. 16–18.
A.D.		
3	Joseph returns from Egypt, - - - -	Mat. ii. 19, to end; Lu. ii. 40.
7	History of Christ at the age of 12 years, - -	Lu. ii. 41, to end.
26	Commencement of the Ministry of John the Baptist, - - - - - - - -	Mat. iii. 1–12; Mar. i. 2–8; Lu. iii. 1–18.
...	The Baptism of Christ, - - - - -	Mat. iii. 13, to end; Mar. i. 9–11; Lu. iii. 21, 22, and part of 23.
...	The Temptation of Christ, - - - -	Mat. iv. 1–11; Mar. i. 12, 13; Lu. iv. 1–13.

PERIOD II.—FROM THE TEMPTATION OF CHRIST TO THE COMMENCEMENT OF HIS MORE PUBLIC MINISTRY AFTER THE IMPRISONMENT OF JOHN.

DATE.	EVENTS.	SCRIPTURES.
26	Further Testimony of John the Baptist, - -	Jn. i. 19–34.
...	Christ obtains his first Disciples from John, -	Jn. i. 35, to end.
27	Marriage at Cana, in Galilee, - - - - -	Jn. ii. 1–11.
...	Christ goes down to Capernaum, and continues there some short time, - - - - -	Jn. ii. 12.
...	The Buyers and Sellers driven from the Temple,	Jn. ii. 13, to end.
...	Conversation of Christ with Nicodemus, - -	Jn. iii. 1–21.
...	John's last Testimony to Christ, - - -	Jn. iii. 22, to end.
...	Imprisonment of John the Baptist, - -	Mat. xiv. 3–5; Mar. vi. 17–20; Lu. iii. 19, 20.

Period III.—From the Commencement of the more public Ministry of Christ to the Mission of the Twelve Apostles.

Date.	Events.	Scriptures.
A.D. 27	General Introduction to the History of Christ's more public ministry, - - - - -	Mat. iv. 12–17; Mar. i. 14, 15; Lu. iv. 14, 15.
...	Christ's Conversation with the Woman of Samaria,	Jn. iv. 1–42.
...	Second Miracle at Cana in Galilee, - - -	Jn. iv. 43, to end.
...	First public Preaching of Christ in the Synagogue at Nazareth, and his Danger there,	Lu. iv. 16–30.
...	Christ sojourns at Capernaum, - - - - -	Lu. iv. 31, 32.
...	The Miraculous Draught of Fishes, and the Calling of Andrew and Peter, James and John,	Mat. iv. 18–22; Mar. i. 16–20; Lu. v. 1–11.
...	The Demoniac healed at Capernaum, -	Mar. i. 21–28; Lu. iv. 33–37.
...	Peter's Mother-in-law cured of a Fever, -	Mat. viii. 14, 15; Mar. i. 29–31; Lu. iv. 38, 39.
...	Christ teaches, and performs Miracles and Cures throughout Galilee, - - -	Mat. iv. 23–25; viii. 16, 17; Mar. i. 32–39; Lu. iv. 40, to end.
...	Christ Cures a Leper, - - - - -	Mat. viii. 2–4; Mar. i. 40, to end; Lu. v. 12–16.
...	The Paralytic cured; and the Power of Christ to forgive Sins asserted, - - -	Mat. ix. 2–8; Mar. ii. 1–12; Lu. v. 17–26.
...	The Calling of Matthew, - - - - -	Mat. ix. 9; Mar. ii. 13, 14; Lu. v. 27, 28.
...	The Infirm Man healed at the Pool of Bethesda,	Jn. v. 1–15.
...	Christ vindicates the Miracle, and asserts the Dignity of his Office, - - - - -	Jn. v. 16, to end.
...	Christ defends his Disciples for plucking the Ears of Corn on the Sabbath-day, - -	Mat. xii. 1–8; Mar. ii. 23, to end; Lu. vi. 1–5.
...	Christ heals the Withered Hand, - -	Mat. xii. 9–14; Mar. iii. 1–6; Lu. vi. 6–11.
...	Christ is followed by great Multitudes, whose Diseases he heals, - - - - - -	Mat. xii. 15–21; Mar. iii. 7–12.
...	Preparation for the Sermon on the Mount—Election of the Twelve Apostles, - -	Mar. iii. 13–19; Lu. vi. 12–19.
...	The Sermon on the Mount, - - - -	Mat. v. 6, 7; and viii. 1; Lu. vi. 20, to end.
...	The Centurion's Servant healed, - -	Mat. viii. 5–13; Lu. vii. 1–10.
...	The Widow's Son at Nain is raised to Life, -	Lu. vii. 11–18.
...	Message from John, who was still in Prison, to Christ, - - - - - - - -	Mat. xi. 2–6; Lu. vii. 19–23.
...	Christ's Testimony concerning John, -	Mat. xi. 7–15; Lu. vii. 24–30.
...	Christ reproaches the Jews for their Impenitence and Insensibility, - - - - - -	Mat. xi. 16–24; Lu. vii. 31–35.
...	Christ invites all to come to him, - - -	Mat. xi. 25, to end.
...	Christ forgives the Sins of a female Penitent, at the House of a Pharisee, - - -	Lu. vii. 36, to end.
...	Christ preaches again throughout Galilee, -	Lu. viii. 1–3.
...	Christ cures a Demoniac—Conduct of the Scribes and Pharisees, - - - - - -	Mat. xii. 22–45; Mar. iii. 19–30; Lu. xi. 14–28.
...	Christ declares his faithful Disciples to be his real Kindred, - - - - - -	Mat. xii. 46, to end; Mar. iii. 31, to end; Lu. viii. 19–21.
...	Parable of the Sower, - - - - -	Mat. xiii. 1–9; Mar. iv. 1–9; Lu. viii. 4–8.

DATE.	EVENTS.	SCRIPTURES.
A.D.		
27	Reasons for Teaching by Parables, - -	Mat. xiii. 10–17; Mar. iv. 10–12; Lu. viii. 9, 10.
...	Explanation of the Parable of the Sower, -	Mat. xiii. 18–23; Mar. iv. 13–23; Lu. viii. part of ver. 9, and 11–17.
...	Christ directs his Hearers to practise what they hear, - - - - - - - -	Mar. iv. 24, 25; Lu. viii. 18.
...	Various Parables descriptive of Christ's kingdom,	Mat. xiii. 24–53; Mar. iv. 26–34.
...	Christ crosses the Sea of Galilee, and calms the Tempest, - - - - - - -	Mat. viii. 18–27; Mar. iv. 35, to end; Lu. viii. 22-25.
...	Christ heals the Gadarene Demoniac, -	Mat. viii. 28, to end; Mar. v. 1–20; Lu. viii. 26–40.
...	Christ dines with Matthew, - - - -	Mat. ix. 10–17; Mar. ii. 15–22; Lu. v. 29, to end.
...	Jairus' Daughter is healed, and the Infirm Woman, - - - - - - -	Mat. ix. 1, 18–26; Mar. v. 21, to end; Lu. viii. 40, to end.
...	Christ restores two Blind Men to sight, - -	Mat. ix. 27–31.
...	Christ casts out a Dumb Spirit, - - -	Mat. ix. 32–34.
...	Christ returns to Nazareth, and is again ill-treated there, - - - - - -	Mat. xiii. 54, to end; Mar. vi. 1–6.
28	Christ preaches again throughout Galilee, -	Mat. ix. 35, to end.

PERIOD IV.—FROM THE MISSION OF THE TWELVE APOSTLES TO THE MISSION OF THE SEVENTY.

DATE.	EVENTS.	SCRIPTURES.
28	Christ's Mission of the Twelve Apostles, -	Mat. x. and xi. 1; Mar. vi. 7–13; Lu. ix. 1–6.
...	Death of John the Baptist—Herod desires to see Christ, - - - - - - - - -	Mat. xiv. 1–12; Mar. vi. 14–29; Lu. ix. 7–9.
...	The Twelve return, and Jesus retires with them to the Desert of Bethsaida, - - - -	Mat. xiv. 13, 14; Mar. vi. 30–34; Lu. ix. 10, 11; Jn. vi. 1, 2.
...	Five thousand are fed miraculously, - -	Mat. xiv. 15–21; Mar. vi. 35–44; Lu. ix. 12–17; Jn. vi. 3–14.
...	Christ sends the Multitude away, and prays alone, - - - - - - - - - -	Mat. xiv. 22, 23; Mar. vi. 45, 46; Jn. vi. 15.
...	Christ walks on the Sea to his Disciples, who are overtaken with a Storm, - - -	Mat. xiv. 24–33; Mar. vi. 47–52; Jn. vi. 16–21.
...	Christ heals many People, - - - -	Mat. xiv. 34–36; Mar. vi. 53, to end.
...	Christ teaches in the Synagogue of Capernaum —His Conversation there, - - - -	Jn. vi. 22, to end; and vii. 1.
...	Christ converses with the Scribes and Pharisees on the subject of Jewish Traditions, -	Mat. xv. 1–20; Mar. vii. 1–23.
...	Christ heals the Daughter of the Canaanite, or Syro-Phœnician Woman, - - -	Mat. xv. 21–28; Mar. vii. 24–30.
...	Christ goes through Decapolis, healing and teaching, - - - - - - -	Mat. xv. 29–31; Mar. vii. 31, to end.
...	Four thousand Men are fed miraculously,	Mat. xv. 32, to end; Mar. viii. 1–10.
...	The Pharisees require other Signs—Christ charges them with hypocrisy, - -	Mat. xvi. 1–12; Mar. viii. 11–21.
...	Christ heals a blind Man at Bethsaida, - -	Mar. viii. 22–26.
...	Peter confesses Christ to be the Messiah, -	Mat. xvi. 13-20; Mar. viii. 27–30; Lu. ix. 18–21.

DATE.	EVENTS.	SCRIPTURES.
A. D. 28	Christ astonishes the Disciples by declaring the necessity of his Death and Resurrection,	Mat. xvi. 21, to end; Mar. viii. 31, to end, and ix. 1; Lu. ix. 22-27.
...	The Transfiguration of Christ, - - -	Mat. xvii. 1-13; Mar. ix. 2-13; Lu. ix. 28-36.
...	The Deaf and Dumb Spirit cast out, -	Mat. xvii. 14-21; Mar. ix. 14-29; Lu. ix. 37-42, and part of 43.
...	Christ again foretells his Death and Resurrection, - - - - - - - -	Mat. xvii. 22, 23; Mar. ix. 30-32, and part of 33; Lu. ix. 43-46.
...	Christ works a Miracle to pay the Half-shekel for the Temple Service, - - - -	Mat. xvii. 24, to end.
...	The Disciples contend for superiority, -	Mat. xviii. 1, to end; Mar. ix. part of 33, to end; Lu. ix. 47-50.

PERIOD V.—FROM THE MISSION OF THE SEVENTY DISCIPLES TO THE TRIUMPHAL ENTRY OF CHRIST INTO JERUSALEM, SIX DAYS BEFORE THE CRUCIFIXION.

DATE.	EVENTS.	SCRIPTURES.
28	The Mission of the Seventy Disciples, - -	Lu. x. 1-16.
...	Christ goes up to the Feast of Tabernacles,	Mat. xix. 1; Mar. x. 1; Jn. vii. 2-10.
...	Agitation of the Public Mind at Jerusalem concerning Christ, - - - - - -	Jn. vii. 11-52.
...	Conduct of Christ to the Adulteress and her Accusers, - - - - - - -	Jn. vii. 53; viii. 1-11.
...	Christ declares himself to be the Son of God, -	Jn. viii. 12-20.
...	Christ declares the Manner of his Death, - -	Jn. viii. 21, to end.
...	The Seventy return with joy, - - - -	Lu. x. 17-24.
...	Christ directs the Lawyer how he may attain Eternal Life, - - - - - - -	Lu. x. 25-28.
...	The Parable of the Good Samaritan, - -	Lu. x. 29-37.
...	Christ in the House of Martha, - - -	Lu. x. 38, to end.
...	Christ teaches his Disciples to pray, - - -	Lu. xi. 1-13.
...	Christ reproaches the Pharisees and Lawyers, -	Lu. xi. 37, to end.
...	Christ cautions his Disciples against Hypocrisy,	Lu. xii. 1-12.
...	Christ refuses to act as Judge, - - - -	Lu. xii. 13, 14.
...	Christ cautions the Multitude against Worldly-mindedness, - - - - - - -	Lu. xii. 15-34.
...	Christ exhorts to Watchfulness, Fidelity, and Repentance, - - - - - - -	Lu. xii. 35, to end xiii. 1-9.
...	Christ cures an Infirm Woman in the Synagogue,	Lu. xiii. 10-17.
...	Christ begins his journey towards Jerusalem, to be present at the Feast of the Dedication,	Lu. xiii. 22, 18-21.
...	Christ restores to sight a Blind Man, who is summoned before the Sanhedrim, - -	Jn. ix. 1-34.
...	Christ declares that he is the True Shepherd,	Jn. ix. 35, to end; x. 1-21.
...	Christ publicly asserts his Divinity, - - -	Jn. x. 22-38.
...	In consequence of the opposition of the Jews, Christ retires beyond Jordan, - -	Jn. x. 39, to end.
...	Christ, leaving the City, laments over Jerusalem,	Lu. xiii. 23, to end.
...	Christs dines with a Pharisee—Parable of the Great Supper, - - - - - -	Lu. xiv. 1-24.
...	Christ's Disciples must forsake the World, -	Lu. xiv. 25, to end.

DATE.	EVENTS.	SCRIPTURES.
A.D. 28	Parables of the Lost Sheep, and of the Lost Piece of Silver, - - - - - - -	Lu. xv. 1–10.
...	Parable of the Prodigal Son, - - - -	Lu. xv. 11, to end.
...	Parable of the Unjust Steward, - - -	Lu. xvi. 1–13.
...	Christ reproves the Pharisees, - - - -	Lu. xvi. 14–17.
...	Christ answers the Question concerning Divorce and Marriage, - - - - - -	Mat. xix. 3–12; Mar. x. 2–12; Lu. xvi. 18.
...	Christ receives and blesses little Children,	Mat. xix. 13–15; Mar. x. 13–17; Lu. xviii. 15–17.
...	Parable of the Rich Man and Lazarus, - -	Lu. xvi. 19, to end.
...	On Forgiveness of Injuries, - - - -	Lu. xvii. 1–10.
...	Christ journeys towards Jerusalem, - - -	Lu.ix.51,to end;xvii.11.
...	Christ heals ten Lepers, - - - - -	Lu. xvii. 12–19.
...	Christ declares the Lowliness of his Kingdom and the sudden Destruction of Jerusalem,	Lu. xvii. 20, to end.
...	Christ teacheth the true Nature of Prayer, -	Lu. xviii. 1–8.
...	Parable of the Publican and Pharisee, - -	Lu. xviii. 9–14.
...	From the Conduct of the young Ruler, Christ cautions his Disciples on the Dangers of Wealth,	Mat.xix.16–29; Mar. x. 17–30;Lu.xviii.18–30.
...	Parable of the Labourers in the Vineyard, -	Mat. xix. 30; xx. 1–16; Mar. x. 31.
...	Christ is informed of the Sickness of Lazarus, -	Jn. xi. 1–16.
29	Christ again predicts his Sufferings and Death,	Mat. xx. 17–19; Mar. x. 32–34; Lu.xviii.31–34.
...	Ambition of the Sons of Zebedee, - -	Mat. xx. 20–28; Mar. x. 35–45.
...	Two Blind Men healed at Jericho, - -	Mat. xx. 29, to end; Mar. x. 46, to end; Lu. xviii. 35, to end.
...	Conversion of Zaccheus, and the Parable of the Pounds, - - - - - - -	Lu. xix. 1–28.
...	The Resurrection of Lazarus, - - - -	Jn. xi. 17–46.
...	The Sanhedrim assemble to deliberate concerning the Resurrection of Lazarus, - -	Jn. xi. 47, 48.
...	Caiaphas prophesies, - - - - - - -	Jn. xi. 49–52.
...	The Sanhedrim resolves to put Christ to death,	Jn. xi. 53.
...	Christ retires to Ephraim, or Ephrata, - -	Jn. xi. 54.
...	State of the Public Mind at Jerusalem, immediately preceding the last Passover, at which Christ attended, - - - - - -	Jn. xi. 55, to end.
...	Christ comes to Bethany, where he is anointed by Mary, - - - - - - -	Mat. xxvi. 6–13; Mar. xiv. 3–9; Jn. xii. 1–11.
...	Christ prepares to enter Jerusalem, - -	Mat. xxi. 1–7; Mar. xi. 1–7; Lu. xix. 29–40; Jn. xii. 12–18.

PERIOD VI.—FROM CHRIST'S TRIUMPHANT ENTRY INTO JERUSALEM, TO HIS APPREHENSION—SUNDAY, THE FIFTH DAY BEFORE THE LAST PASSOVER.

DATE.	EVENTS.	SCRIPTURES.
29	The people meet Christ with Hosannahs. Christ approaches Jerusalem, - - - -	Mat. xxi. 8, 9; Mar. xi. 8–10; Lu. xix. 36–40; Jn. xii. 19.
...	Christ's Lamentation over Jerusalem, and the Prophecy of its Destruction, - - -	Lu. xix. 41–44.
...	Christ, on entering the City, casts the Buyers and Sellers out of the Temple, - -	Mat. xxi. 10–13; Mar. xi. part of ver. 11; Lu. xix. 45, 46.

Date.	Events.	Scriptures.
A.D. 29	Christ heals the Sick in the Temple, and reproves the Chief Priests, - - - - - - -	Mat. xxi. 14–16.
...	Some Greeks at Jerusalem desire to see Christ. The Bath Col [Voice from Heaven] is heard,	Jn. xii. 20–43.
...	Christ declares the Object of his Mission, - -	Jn. xii. 44, to end.
...	Christ leaves Jerusalem in the Evening, and goes to Bethany, - - - - - - -	Mat. xxi. 17; Mar. xi. part of ver. 11.
...	Monday—Fourth Day before the Passover. Christ, entering Jerusalem, again curses the barren Fig-tree, - - - - - - -	Mat. xxi. 18, 19; Mar. xi. 12–14.
...	Christ again casts the Buyers and Sellers out of the Temple, - - - - - - - -	Mar. xi. 15–17.
...	The Scribes and Chief Priests seek to destroy Jesus, - - - - - - - - -	Mar. xi. 18; Lu. xix. 47, 48.
...	Christ retires in the Evening from the City, -	Mar. xi. 19.
...	Tuesday—Third Day before the Passover. The Fig-tree is now withered, - - - -	Mat. xxi. 20–22; Mar. xi. 20–26.
...	Christ answers the Chief Priests who inquire concerning the Authority by which he acted. Parables of the Vineyard and Marriage Feast,	Mat. xxi. 23, to end; xxii. 1–14; Mar. xi. 27, to end; xii. 1–12; Lu. xix. 1–19.
...	Christ replies to the Herodians, - -	Mat. xxii. 15–22; Mar. xii. 13–17; Lu. xx. 20–26.
...	Christ replies to the Sadducees, - -	Mat. xxii. 23–33; Mar. xii. 18–27; Lu. xx. 27–40.
...	Christ replies to the Pharisees, - - -	Mat. xxii. 34–40; Mar. xii. 28–35.
...	Christ inquires of the Pharisees concerning the Messiah, - - - - - - -	Mat. xxii. 41, to end; Mar. xii. 35–37; Lu. xx. 41–44.
...	Christ severely reproves the Pharisees, -	Mat. xxiii. 1, to end; Mar. xii. 38–40; Lu. xx. 45, to end.
...	Christ applauds the Liberality of the poor Widow, - - - - - - - - - -	Mar. xii. 41, to end; Lu. xxi. 1–4.
...	Christ foretells the Destruction of Jerusalem, the End of the Jewish Dispensation, and of the World, - - - - - - -	Mat. xxiv. 1–35; Mar. xiii. 1–31; Lu. xxi. 5–33.
...	Christ compares the Suddenness of his Second Advent to the Coming of the Deluge, -	Mat. xxiv. 36, to end; Mar. xiii. 32, to end; Lu. xxi. 34–36.
...	The Parable of the Wise and Foolish Virgins, - - - - - - - - -	Mat. xxv. 1–13.
...	The Parable of the Servants and the Talents, -	Mat. xxv. 14–30.
...	Christ declares the Proceedings at the Day of Judgment, - - - - - - - -	Mat. xxv. 31, to end.
...	Christ retires from the City to the Mount of Olives, - - - - - - - - -	Lu. xxi. 37, 38.
...	Wednesday—Second Day before the Crucifixion. Christ foretells his approaching Death, -	Mat. xxvi. 1, 2; Mar. xiv. part of ver. 1.
...	The Rulers consult how they may take Christ,	Mat. xxvi. 3–5; Mar. xiv. part of ver. 1, ver. 2; Lu. xxii. 1, 2.
...	Judas agrees with the Chief Priests to betray Christ, - - - - - - - -	Mat. xxvi. 14–16; Mar. xiv. 10, 11; Lu. xxii. 3–6.

DATE.	EVENTS.	SCRIPTURES.
A.D. 29	Thursday — The day before the Crucifixion. Christ directs two of his Disciples to prepare the Passover, - - - - - - -	Mat. xxvi. 17–19; Mar. xiv. 12–16; Lu. xxii. 7–13.
...	Christ partakes of the last Passover, -	Mat. xxvi. 20; Mar. xiv. 17; Lu. xxii. 14–18; Jn. xiii. 1.
...	Christ again reproves the Ambition of his Disciples, - - - - - - - - -	Lu. xxii. 24–27; Jn. xiii. 2–16.
...	Christ, sitting at the Passover, and continuing the Conversation, speaks of his Betrayer,	Mat. xxvi. 21–25; Mar. xiv. 18–21; Lu. xxii. 21–23; Jn. xiii. 17–30.
...	Judas goes out to betray Christ, who predicts Peter's Denial of him, and the Danger of the rest of the Apostles, - - - - -	Lu. xxii. 28–38; Jn. xiii. 31, to end.
...	Christ institutes the Eucharist, - -	Mat. xxvi. 26–29; Mar. xiv. 22–25; Lu. xxii. 19, 20.
...	Christ exhorts the Apostles, and consoles them on his approaching Death, - - - -	Jn. xiv.
...	Christ goes with his Disciples to the Mount of Olives, - - - - - - - - -	Mat. xxvi. 30; Mar. xiv. 26; Lu. xxii. 39.
...	Christ declares himself to be the True Vine, -	Jn. xv. 1–8.
...	Christ exhorts his Apostles to mutual Love, and to prepare for Persecution, - - - -	Jn. xv. 9, to end; xvi. 1–4.
...	Christ promises the Gifts of the Holy Spirit, -	Jn. xvi. 5, to end.
...	Christ intercedes for all his Followers, - -	Jn. xvii.
...	Christ again predicts Peter's Denial of him,	Mat. xxvi. 31–35; Mar. xiv. 27–31.
...	Christ goes into the Garden of Gethsemane—His agony there, - - - - - -	Mat. xxvi. 36–46; Mar. xiv. 32–42; Lu. xxii. 40–46; Jn. xviii. 1, 2.
...	Christ is betrayed and apprehended. The Resistance of Peter, - - - - - - -	Mat. xxvi. 47–56; Mar. xiv. 43–50; Lu. xxii. 47–53; Jn. xviii. 3–11.

PERIOD VII.—FROM THE APPREHENSION OF CHRIST TO THE CRUCIFIXION.

DATE.	EVENTS.	SCRIPTURES.
29	Christ is taken to Annas, and to the Palace of Caiaphas, - - - - - - -	Mat. xxvi. 57; Mar. xiv. 51–53; Lu. xxii. 54; Jn. xviii. 12–14.
...	Peter and John follow their Master, -	Mat. xxvi. 58; Mar. xiv. 54; Lu. xxii. 55; Jn. xviii. 15, 16.
...	Christ is first examined and condemned in the House of the High Priest, - - -	Mat. xxvi. 59–66; Mar. xiv. 55–64; Jn. xviii. 19–24.
...	Twelve at Night. Christ is struck and insulted by the Soldiers, - - - - - -	Mat. xxvi. 67, 68; Mar. xiv. 65; Lu. xxii. 63–65.
...	Peter's First Denial of Christ, at the fire, in the Hall of the High Priest's Palace, . -	Mat. xxvi. 69, 70; Mar. xiv. 66–68; Lu. xxii. 56, 57; Jn. xviii. 17, 18, 25–27.
...	After Midnight. Peter's Second Denial of Christ, at the Porch of the Palace of the High Priest, - - - - - - -	Mat. xxvi. 71, 72; Mar. xiv. 69, part of 70; Lu. xxii. 58.

Date.	Events.	Scriptures.
A.D. 29	Friday, the day of the Crucifixion—Time, about three in the Morning. Peter's Third Denial of Christ, in the Room where Christ was waiting among the Soldiers till the Dawn of Day,	Mat. xxvi. 73, to end; Mar. xiv. part of 70, to end; Lu. xxii. 59-61.
...	Christ is taken before the Sanhedrim, and condemned, - - - - - - -	Mat. xxvii. 1; Mar. xv. part of 1; Lu. xxii. 66, to end.
...	Judas declares the Innocence of Christ, - -	Mat. xxvii. 3-10.
...	Christ is accused before Pilate, and is by him also declared to be innocent, - - -	Mat. xxvii. 2, 11-14; Mar. xv. 1-5; Lu. xxiii. 1-4; Jn. xviii. 28-38.
...	Christ is sent by Pilate to Herod, - - -	Lu. xxiii. 5-12.
...	Christ is brought back again to Pilate, who again declares him innocent, and endeavours to persuade the people to ask for his release, -	Mat. xxvii. 15-20; Mar. xv. 6-11; Lu. xxiii. 13-19; Jn. xviii. 39.
...	Pilate three times endeavours again to release Christ, - - - - - - - -	Mat. xxvii. 21-23; Mar. xv. 12-14; Lu. xxiii. 20-23; Jn. xviii. 40.
...	The Jews imprecate the punishment of Christ's Death upon themselves, - - -	Mat. xxvii. 24, 25.
...	Pilate releases Barabbas, and delivers Christ to be Crucified, - - - - - -	Mat. xxvii. 26-30; Mar. xv. 15-19; Lu. xxiii. 24, 25; Jn. xix. 1-16.
...	Christ is led away from the Judgment-hall of Pilate to Mount Calvary, - - -	Mat. xxvii. 31, 32; Mar. xv. 20, 21; Lu. xxiii. 26-32; Jn. xix. part of 16, and 17.
...	Christ arrives at Mount Calvary, and is Crucified, - - - - - - - -	Mat. xxvii. 33, 34, 37, 38; Mar. xv. 22, 23, 26-28; Lu. xxiii. 33-38; Jn. xix. 18-22.
...	Christ prays for his Murderers, - - -	Lu. xxiii. part of 34.
...	The Soldiers divide and cast Lots for the Raiment of Christ, - - - - -	Mat. xxvii. 35, 36; Mar. xv. 24, 25; Lu. xxiii. part of 34; Jn. xix. 23, 24.
...	Christ is reviled, when on the Cross, by the Chief Priests, the Rulers, the Soldiers, the Passengers, and the Malefactors, -	Mat. xxvii. 39-44; Mar. xv. 29-32; Lu. xxiii. 35-37.
...	Christ, when Dying as a Man, asserts his Divinity, in his Answer to the Penitent Thief,	Lu. xxiii. 39-43.
...	Christ commends his Mother to the care of John,	Jn. xix. 25-27.
...	The Death of Christ and its attendant circumstances, - - - - - - - -	Mat. xxvii. 45-51, 54-56; Mar. xv. 33-41; Lu. xxiii. 44-49; Jn. xix. 28-37.

Period VIII.—From the Death of Christ till his Ascension into Heaven.

Date.	Events.	Scriptures.
29	Joseph of Arimathea and Nicodemus bury the Body of Christ, - - - - - -	Mat. xxvii. 57-60; Mar. xv. 42-46; Lu. xxiii. 50-54; Jn. xix. 38, to end.
...	Mary Magdalene, and the other Mary, and the Women from Galilee, observe where the body of Christ was laid, - - - - -	Mar. xv. 47; Lu. xxiii. 55.
...	The Women from Galilee hasten to return Home before the Sabbath began, to prepare Spices,	Lu. xxiii. 56.
...	Mary Magdalene and the other Mary continue to sit opposite the Sepulchre till it is too late to prepare their Spices, - - - -	Mat. xxvii. 61.

DATE.	EVENTS.	SCRIPTURES.
A.D. 29	The Sabbath being ended, the Chief Priests prepare a Guard of Soldiers to watch the Sepulchre,	Mat. xxvii. 62, to end.
...	The Sabbath being over, Mary Magdalene, the other Mary, and Salomé, purchase their Spices to anoint the Body of Christ, - - -	Mar. xvi. 1.
...	The Morning of Easter-day. Mary Magdalene, the other Mary, and Salomé, leave their homes very early to go to the Sepulchre, -	Mat. xxviii. 1; Mar. xvi. part of 2; Jn. xx. part of 1.
...	After they had left their Homes, and before their arrival at the Sepulchre, Christ rises from the Dead, - - - - - - -	Mat. xxviii. 2–4.
...	The Bodies of many come out of their Graves, and go to Jerusalem, - - - - - -	Mat. xxvii. part of 52, and 53.
...	Mary Magdalene, the other Mary, and Salomé, arrive at the Sepulchre, and find the Stone rolled away, - - - - - - -	Mar. xvi. part of 2, and 3, 4; Jn. xx. part of 1.
...	Mary Magdalene leaves the other Mary and Salomé to tell Peter, - - - - -	Jn. xx. 2.
...	Salomé and the other Mary, during the absence of Mary Magdalene, enter the porch of the Sepulchre, and see one Angel, who commands them to inform the Disciples that Jesus was risen, - - - - - - - - -	Mat. xxviii. 5–7; Mar. xvi. 5–7.
...	Salomé and the other Mary leave the Sepulchre,	Mat. xxviii. 8; Mar. xvi. 8.
...	Peter and John, as soon as they hear the report of Mary Magdalene, hasten to the Sepulchre, which they inspect, and immediately depart,	Jn. xx. 3–10.
...	Mary Magdalene, having followed Peter and John, remains at the Sepulchre after their departure, - - - - - - -	Jn. xx. part of 11.
...	Mary Magdalene looks into the Tomb, and sees two Angels, - - - - - - -	Jn. xx. part of 11, 12, 13, and part of 14.
...	Christ first appears to Mary Magdalene, and commands her to inform the Disciples that he has risen, - - - - - - -	Mar. xvi. 9; Jn. xx. part of 14, and 15–17.
...	Mary Magdalene, when going to inform the Disciples that Christ had risen, meets again with Salomé and the other Mary. Christ appears to the three Women, - -	Mat. xxviii. 9, 10; Jn. xx. 18.
...	The Soldiers, who had fled from the Sepulchre, report to the High Priests the Resurrection of Christ, - - - - - - -	Mat. xxviii. 11–15.
...	The Second Party of Women, from Galilee, who had bought their Spices on the evening previous to the Sabbath, having had a longer way to come to the Sepulchre, arrive after the departure of the others, and find the Stone rolled away, - - - - - - -	Lu. xxiv. 1–3.
...	Two Angels appear also to the Second Party of Women, from Galilee, assuring them that Christ was risen, and reminding them of his foretelling this fact, - - - - -	Lu. xxiv. 4–9.
...	Mary Magdalene unites her Testimony to that of the Galilean Women, - - - -	Mar. xvi. 10; Lu. xxiv. 10.
...	The Apostles are still incredulous, - - -	Mar. xvi. 11; Lu. xxiv. 11.
...	Peter goes again to the Sepulchre, - - -	Lu. xxiv. part of 12.
...	Peter, who had probably seen Christ, departs from the Sepulchre, - - - -	Lu. xxiv. part of 12.

DATE.	EVENTS.	SCRIPTURES.
A.D. 29	Christ appears to Cleopas and another disciple, going to Emmaus, - - - - - -	Mar. xvi. 12; Lu. xxiv. 13–32.
...	Cleopas and his Companion return to Jerusalem, and assure the Apostles that Christ had certainly risen, - - - - - -	Mar. xvi. 13; Lu. xxiv. 33–35.
...	Christ appears to the assembled Apostles, Thomas only being absent, convinces them of the Identity of his Resurrection Body, and blesses them, - - - - - -	Lu. xxiv. 36–43; Jn. xx. 19-23.
...	Thomas is still incredulous, - - - - -	Jn. xx. 24, 25.
...	Christ appears to the Eleven, Thomas being present, - - - - - - -	Mar. xvi. 14; Jn. xx. 26–29.
...	Christ appears to a large number of his Disciples on a Mountain in Galilee, - -	Mat. xxviii. 16, 17, and part of 18.
...	Christ appears again at the Sea of Tiberias—His Conversation with St. Peter, - -	Jn. xxi. 1–24.
...	Christ appears to his Apostles at Jerusalem, and commissions them to convert the World,	Lu. xxiv. 44–49; Ac. i. 4, 5.
...	Christ leads out his Apostles to Bethany, within sight of Jerusalem, gives them their final commission, blesses them, and ascends visibly into Heaven; from whence he will come to judge the living and the dead, - -	Mat. xxviii. part of 18–20; Mar. xvi. 15, to end; Lu. xxiv. 50, to end; Ac. i. 6–12.
...	St. John's Conclusion to the Gospel History of Jesus Christ, - - - - - -	Jn. xx. 30, 31, and xxi. 25.

SCRIPTURE WEIGHTS, MEASURES, AND MONEY.

I.—Scriptural Measures of Length, reduced to English Measure.

								Feet.	Inches.
A Digit,								,0	0·912
4	A Palm,							0	3·648
12	3	A Span,						0	10·944
24	6	3	A Cubit,					1	9·888
96	24	6	2	A Fathom,				7	3·552
144	36	12	6	1·5	Ezekiel's Reed,			10	11·328
192	48	16	8	2	1·3	An Arabian Pole,		14	7·104
1920	480	160	80	20	13·3	10	A *Schœnus*, or Measuring Line,	145	11·04

II.—The Long Scripture Measures.

						Miles.	Paces.	Feet.
A Cubit,						0	0	1·824
400	A Stadium, or Furlong,					0	145	4·6
2000	5	A Sabbath Day's Journey,				0	729	3
4000	10	2	An Eastern Mile,			1	403	1
12000	30	6	3	A Parasang,		4	153	3
96000	240	48	24	8	A Day's Journey,	33	172	4

III.—Jewish Money reduced to our Standard.

					£	s.	d.
A Gerah,					0	0	1·2687
10	A Bekah,				0	1	1·6875
20	2	A Shekel,			0	2	3·375
1200	120	50	A Maneh, or Mina,		5	14	0·75
60000	6000	3000	60	A Talent of silver,	342	3	9
A gold Shekel was worth					1	16	6
A Talent of gold was worth					5475	0	0

IV.—Roman Money, mentioned in the New Testament, reduced to our Standard.

A Mite, about three-eighths of a farthing.
A Farthing, about three-fourths of a farthing.
A Penny or Denarius, sevenpence three farthings.
A Pound or Mina, three pounds two shillings and sixpence.

INDEX

TO THE NOTES ON THE GOSPELS BY

LUKE AND JOHN.